# Juvenile Justice SOURCEBOOK

EDITED BY Albert R. Roberts

# Juvenile Justice
# SOURCEBOOK

## Past, Present, and Future

OXFORD
UNIVERSITY PRESS

2004

# OXFORD

UNIVERSITY PRESS

Oxford   New York
Auckland  Bangkok  Buenos Aires  Cape Town  Chennai
Dar es Salaam  Delhi  Hong Kong  Istanbul  Karachi  Kolkata
Kuala Lumpur  Madrid  Melbourne  Mexico City  Mumbai  Nairobi
São Paulo  Shanghai  Taipei  Tokyo  Toronto

Published by Oxford University Press, Inc.
198 Madison Avenue, New York, New York 10016

www.oup.com

Oxford is a registered trademark of Oxford University Press

Library of Congress Cataloging-in-Publication Data
Juvenile justice sourcebook : past, present, and future / edited by
Albert R. Roberts.
       p. cm.
Includes bibliographical references and index.
   ISBN 0-19-516755-4
   1. Juvenile justice, Administration of—United States.   2. Juvenile courts—United States.   I. Roberts,
Albert R.   II. Title.
   HV9104.J868 2004
   364.36'0973—dc23      2003016989

9 8 7 6 5 4 3 2 1

Printed in the United States of America
on acid-free paper

This book is dedicated in loving memory of my parents, Harry and Evelyn Roberts, whose love, support, faith, and encouragement during my turbulent adolescent years still serve as an inspiration to me.

To the loving memory of my older brother William C. Roberts whose brotherly love, energy, competitiveness, and educational and work achievements in civil and public health engineering have served as a source of strength and inspiration to me.

# Foreword

The *Juvenile Justice Sourcebook* is remarkable for the breadth and depth that Dr. Albert Roberts and his esteemed author team bring to the topic. It truly is a "sourcebook" that will be beneficial to both academicians and practitioners. Roberts has compiled an excellent resource that addresses current and future trends. It is a "must read" for those interested in the topic of juvenile justice. *Juvenile Justice Sourcebook* is extraordinarily readable, original, informative, and comprehensive. As the title implies, this book provides an in-depth discussion of the critical issues and basic controversies in the field of juvenile justice and the problems encountered by the persons trying to unravel the causes, processes, intervention programs, and outcomes for juvenile offenders.

The twenty-one original chapters in this book are organized into five sections. Each chapter includes real-life case illustrations, extensive reviews of the latest research, and detailed descriptions of the specific objectives and intervention strategies utilized by the most innovative programs. Roberts and his contributing authors examine important critical issues and suggest alternative solutions and legal remedies.

Starting in chapter 1, Roberts refers to the emergence of evidence-based practices and "treatments that work" as promising. He is being somewhat modest as what Roberts calls "promising" represents, from my perspective, the major strengths and assets of all future juvenile offender rehabilitation programs. The 10 model juvenile offender treatment programs documented in Roberts's national survey bode extremely well for the development and rapid expansion of evidence-based programs during the current decade.

There has been a shift in emphasis toward practice-based research and outcome studies documenting the most effective juvenile and adult offender treatment programs. For example, the Campbell Collaboration, a group of evidence-based researchers, met in Washington, D.C., in February 2004. Over three hundred participants from all over the world met for 3 days to discuss the latest findings from systematic reviews of evidence-based policies and practices in criminal justice and social welfare. Evidence-based practice has been defined as the conscientious, explicit, and careful utilization of the best available evidence in professional decision making. More specifically, it is the use of scientifically validated assessment, intervention, and evaluation procedures with specific client groups (e.g., mentally ill juvenile offenders, adult schizophrenics). In a sophisticated and step-by-step approach, Roberts and his author team examine a wide spectrum of theories and evidence-based program developments. Each contributor emphasizes the importance of careful assessment, treatment planning, and evaluation research in juvenile justice. This approach uses critical thinking and empirically based evidence in order to determine which program or intervention strategy is likely to achieve the intended outcome.

Often by the time a juvenile is adjudicated a delinquent, he/she has already experienced undiagnosed learning disabilities, school failures, suspensions, and expulsions; domestic violence; substance abuse or alcoholism; and/or psychological problems requiring mental health treatment. The emotional and family abuse problems may be the most apparent. In addition, most juveniles usually do not get caught or arrested after their first few petty offenses—vandalism, shoplifting, underage drinking, and/or possession of illegal drugs. Even when they get caught and are arrested, charges for first-time offenders are usually dropped, dismissed, or they receive a suspended sentence. As a result, juvenile offenders with the most serious and multiple problems are the ones who are officially processed through the juvenile court. Therefore, this volume aptly focuses on identifying and effectively intervening with juvenile offenders with multiple and complex problems.

Roberts and his team of expert contributors are to be congratulated for identifying the obstacles to reforming the juvenile justice system, synthesizing and describing the latest information on evidence-based juvenile rehabilitation programs, and systematically examining the ten most effective juvenile offender treatment programs that should be replicated nationwide. System change is often difficult and slow moving. However, with the realistic policies and programs highlighted in this book, it will be a lot easier to advocate to our legislators for new and expanded policy initiatives and program expansions that are effective in rehabilitating juvenile offenders so they become productive and law abiding citizens. This outstanding and essential book should be required reading for all prosecutors, defense attorneys, probation officers, youth counselors, addictions treatment staff, judges, juvenile offender treatment specialists, police supervisors, correctional administrators, guardians ad litem, and undergraduate and graduate students in criminal justice.

Laura J. Moriarty, Ph.D., Professor of Criminal Justice
First Vice-President, Academy of Criminal Justice Sciences (ACJS)
Virginia Commonwealth University, Richmond, Virginia

# Preface

Like many individuals—informed citizens, legislators, attorneys, police officers, judges, librarians, and juvenile justice professionals—I have been fascinated, frustrated, and challenged by the agencies and institutions that constitute the juvenile justice system. My journey started early when at age 16, I had a minor brush with the law, which left a lasting impression. While driving in New York City, I was arrested and placed in an adult detention facility for several hours for speeding and driving with a junior license (i.e., the bearer of a junior license was prohibited from driving within New York City limits until completing a driver education course and being 17 years of age). I was driving my older brother's car, but the police stopped me because my brother's car was allegedly the same make and color of someone else's car that had been stolen. Fortunately, my father hired an excellent attorney to defend me and I was given a suspended sentence.

The impetus for this book grows out of my research projects, program evaluations of juvenile offender treatment programs, and teaching of juvenile justice and juvenile delinquency over the past 30 years. The decision to write and edit this book was based on my belief that an up-to-date text was needed by upper-division undergraduate and graduate students majoring in criminology and criminal justice that addressed juvenile justice trends, critical issues, policies, programs, and research. This volume should also prove useful to practitioners and administrators both as a desktop reference and as a resource for updating their knowledge about the most effective interventions and practices with juvenile offenders. Early in my career, after being awarded my Master's degree in Sociology and Criminology, and before obtaining my doctorate and embarking on my teaching career, I had worked for the Maryland Department of Correctional Services as a Management and Research Analyst. Then, during the second half of the 1970s, I had completed a national study of instructional technology in youth and adult correctional institutions throughout the United States under a Law Enforcement Assistance Administration (L.E.A.A.) federal grant to the American Correctional Association. As principal investigator of this research project, I had the opportunity to visit and evaluate prison schools in Arkansas, Connecticut, Florida, Maryland, Massachusetts, New Jersey, New York, and Texas. Prior to the national survey I was a consultant to the U.S. Office of Education Teacher Corps in Corrections

Projects, and Research for Better Schools (Philadelphia) correctional education evaluation project throughout the Garden State School District in New Jersey.

In 1978, I completed my doctoral dissertation at the University of Maryland School of Social Work and Community Planning on juvenile status offenders and adolescent runaways in crisis. The dissertation was published in 1981 as *Runaways and Non-runaways in an American Suburb*. My research in Indiana's and Ohio's juvenile correctional institutions during the late 1980s, and in New Jersey's juvenile correctional facilities in the 1990s renewed my interest in helping juvenile offenders get a fresh start through evidence-based academic and vocational education, and crisis intervention and substance abuse counseling programs. These efforts led to the recent completion of my national survey on the 10 most effective juvenile offender treatment programs and the summary of my findings are included in chapter 21 of this book.

This book has nine special features:

1. It provides a comprehensive discussion of the critical issues, controversies, public policies, and intervention strategies and programs of the juvenile justice system.
2. It features up-to-date and poignant case studies to illustrate and profile juvenile drug dealers, murderers, burglars, mentally ill offenders, auto thieves, violent gang members, runaways, and youths growing up in violent homes.
3. It presents the latest information on prevalence trends, and juvenile justice processing and decision-making from arrest and intake, to prosecution, adjudication, and case disposition.
4. It presents the latest research evidence indicating that putting juvenile offenders into adult jails and secure juvenile institutions leads many juveniles into committing more serious and violent crimes upon release.
5. It presents the latest longitudinal research evidence on the 10 model programs most likely to reduce recidivism.
6. It presents the latest descriptive information on the types, functions, and legal responsibilities of the various juvenile justice agencies and institutions.
7. It provides a complete discussion on the landmark U.S. Supreme Court cases on the legal rights of juveniles, including death penalty cases of the past and predictions for the year 2,020.
8. It provides an extensive discussion of the strengths and limitations of institutions, residential treatment centers, group homes, probation, family counseling, structured wilderness programs, vocational training programs; and conflict resolution programs in schools, skill-based programs in juvenile detention, group therapy with mentally ill and substance

abusing juveniles; and restitution, electronic monitoring, and victim-offender mediation programs in probation settings.

**9.** It includes a detailed glossary of key terms and definitions.

The field of juvenile justice is too complex in its subsystems—police, juvenile court and probation, detention, corrections, substance abuse treatment, and other community treatment centers—for any one person to be an expert in all facets of it. Therefore, to supplement my ten chapters, I invited 23 prominent juvenile justice specialists, each with extensive knowledge and expertise in a specific area of juvenile justice, to write or co-author original chapters for this book. These chapters thoroughly document and summarize the most current developments and emerging trends in the care, treatment, and rehabilitation of juvenile offenders.

Several million reported and unreported delinquent acts take place each year. According to the U.S. Department of Justice and the U.S. Bureau of Justice Statistics, juvenile delinquency, acting-out and conduct disorders, illegal drugs, guns, and youth violence pervade American society. The *Juvenile Justice Sourcebook* is the first comprehensive volume devoted exclusively to examining the scope of the delinquency problem, screening and risk assessment, police and juvenile court processing, and evidence-based institutional and community-based treatment and rehabilitation of juvenile offenders. The overriding objective of this sourcebook is to trace the tremendous progress made in the last decade toward resolving juvenile justice issues, dilemmas, and controversies, while providing a future vision for the juvenile justice field. The chapters, authored by preeminent expert practitioners and researchers, explore topics ranging from innovative counseling and multisystemic programs, to restorative justice, and from rehabilitation programs such as wilderness programs, family treatment, and substance abuse treatment, to restitution and aftercare.

This volume, grounded in history, program evaluations, and extensive research, presents the latest evidence-based policies, programs, and innovative treatment alternatives. Examining the entire juvenile justice system, including juvenile law, policies, practices, and research, the *Juvenile Justice Sourcebook* will prove invaluable to all juvenile justice practitioners, policy analysts, researchers, and undergraduate and graduate students.

In an earlier book, *Juvenile Justice: Policies, Programs, and Services*, published in 1989, I expressed hope that 5 to 10 years into the future, there would be a proliferation of humanistic juvenile offender treatment and prevention programs. The future has arrived and it is 2004. Although progress has been slow and legislation has been incremental, the most promising aspect of the twenty-first century is evidence-based practice. For the first time, the national survey findings reported in the Epilogue to this book documents the 10 most effective juvenile offender treatment programs on the basis of longitudinal research. It is my hope that legislators, administrators, and federal and state funding sources will build on the research included in this book and only replicate programs where there is clear and convincing evidence that recidivism rates of program completers is considerably reduced. I am grateful to Elizabeth Plionis, Kenneth Yeager, Colleen O'Brien, Beverely J. Roberts, and Oscar Trapp for technical assistance and suggestions with the tables and figures in chapter 1 and the Epilogue.

Albert R. Roberts, Ph.D.
Piscataway, New Jersey
March 2004

# Contents

# Contributors

## About the Editor

Albert R. Roberts, Ph.D., is Professor of Criminal Justice and Director of Faculty Development, Interdisciplinary Criminal Justice Programs, Faculty of Arts and Sciences, at Rutgers, the State University of New Jersey, Livingston College Campus (Piscataway), and a Fellow at Rutgers College on the New Brunswick Campus. He also directs the Certificate Program in Criminal Justice Policies and Practices at Rutgers University. Dr. Roberts is the founding Editor-in-Chief of the quarterly journal *Brief Treatment and Crisis Intervention* and has authored, co-authored, or edited over 170 scholarly publications including 25 books. Recent books include *Critical Issues in Crime and Justice*, 2d edition, the *Crisis Intervention Handbook: Assessment, Treatment and Research,* 2d edition (Oxford, 2000), the *Handbook of Domestic Violence Intervention Strategies* (Oxford, 2002), the award-winning *Social Workers' Desk Reference* (Oxford, 2002), and the *Evidence-Based Practice Manual: Research and Outcome Measures in Health and Human Services* (Oxford, 2004). For more information on Dr. Roberts's research and publications, see his website at www.crisisinterventionnetwork .com.

Gordon Bazemore, Ph.D.
Professor of Criminal Justice
Department of Public Administration
Florida Atlantic University
Ft. Lauderdale and Boca Raton, FL

Meda Chesney-Lind, Ph.D.
Professor
Department of Women Studies
University of Hawaii
Honolulu, HA

Richard Dembo, Ph.D.
Professor
Department of Criminology
University of South Florida
Tampa, FL

Maurice Elias, Ph.D.
Professor
Department of Psychology
Rutgers University
Livingston College Campus
Piscataway, NJ

William J. Flynn, M.A.
Lt. and Training Director
New Brunswick Police Department
and Adjunct Lecturer
Rutgers University
New Brunswick, NJ

Kenneth C. Haas, Ph.D.
Professor of Criminology and
Criminal Justice
Department of Sociology, Criminal
Justice and Social Work
University of Delaware
Newark, DE

Kathleen M. Heide, Ph.D.
Professor of Criminology and
Interim Dean, College of Arts and
Sciences
University of South Florida
Tampa, FL

Lisa Hunter, Ph.D.
Assistant Professor
Department of Psychology
Yale University
New Haven, CT

Sherry Jackson, Ph.D.
Assistant Professor
School of Criminology and Criminal
Justice
The Florida State University
Tallahassee, FL

Gordon MacNeil, Ph.D.
Associate Professor
School of Social Work
University of Alabama
Tuscaloosa, AL

Brian McDonough, M.A.
Captain
Jersey City Police Department
Jersey City, NJ

C. Aaron McNeece, Ph.D.
Walter Hudson Professor of Social
Work Research
School of Social Work
The Florida State University
Tallahassee, FL

Scott K. Okamoto, Ph.D.
Assistant Professor of Social Work
Arizona State University East
Phoenix, AZ

Carrie J. Petrucci, Ph.D.
Assistant Professor
Department of Social Work
California State University at Long
Beach
Long Beach, CA

Lisa Rapp-Palicchi, Ph.D.
Associate Professor
School of Social Work
University of South Florida
Tampa, FL

Albert R. Roberts, Ph.D.
Professor and Director of Faculty
Development
Administration of Justice and
Interdisciplinary Criminal Justice
Programs
Rutgers University
Livingston College Campus
Piscataway, NJ

David W. Roush, Ph.D.
Director and Associate Professor
National Center for the Study of
Juvenile Detention
School of Criminal Justice
Michigan State University
East Lansing, MI

H. Ted Rubin, J.D., M.S.W.
Consultant on Juvenile Justice and
the Law
Former Juvenile Court Judge
Denver, CO

James Schmeidler, Ph.D.
Associate Research Professor
Department of Community Medicine
Mt. Sinai Hospital and Medical
Center
New York, NY

David W. Springer, Ph.D.
Associate Dean of Academic Affairs
and Associate Professor
School of Social Work
University of Texas
Austin, TX

Mark Umbreit, Ph.D.
Professor and Director
Center for Restorative Justice and
Victim-Offender Mediation
School of Social Work
University of Minnesota
Minneapolis, MI

Wansley Walters, Ph.D.
Research Associate
Child Mental Health Institute and
Department of Criminology
University of South Florida
Tampa, FL

Kenneth R. Yeager, Ph.D.
Director of Quality Assurance and
Administrative Director, Outpatient
Clinics
Department of Psychiatry
Ohio State University Medical
Center
Columbus, OH

# Juvenile Justice SOURCEBOOK

# I

# Trends, Policies, Critical Issues, and Controversies

# An Overview of Juvenile Justice and Juvenile Delinquency

## Cases, Definitions, Trends, and Intervention Strategies

Albert R. Roberts

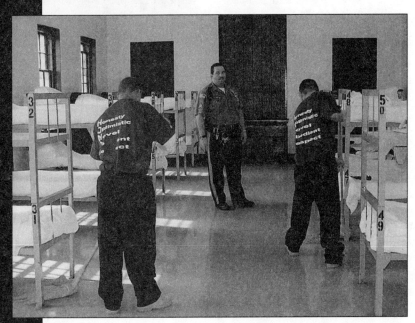

**N.J. Training School
for Boys, Honor Unit**

everal million juveniles commit delinquent acts each year. Violent and property crimes committed by juveniles are one of the major social and public health problems in American society. Newspapers and other media saturate us with graphic depictions of individual youths and gangs committing violence in the schools, in the streets, in parking lots, and in the home. The reality is that although almost 2.4 million juvenile arrests were reported by the FBI and the Office of Juvenile Justice and Delinquency Prevention (OJJDP) in 2000 (Snyder, 2002), the approximate number of juvenile delinquent acts could be between 13 and 15 million annually because many crimes committed by juveniles go unreported or undetected, or no arrest is made. Nevertheless, almost all types of juvenile violent and property crimes have been declining each year since the mid-1990s. Most legislators, agency administrators, practitioners, and students are unaware of the latest model juvenile offender treatment and prevention programs and of the growing research evidence of their success in sharply reducing recidivism. Therefore, a major emphasis of this book is to present the latest information on prevalence trends and on policies and programs that are effective in reducing juvenile delinquency and juvenile status offenses.

This chapter provides an orientation to the critical issues, trends, policies, programs, and intervention strategies of the juvenile justice system. It discusses the types, functions, and legal responsibilities of the various juvenile justice agencies and institutions. This overview chapter lays the foundation and groundwork for the study of juvenile delinquency and the juvenile justice process by providing case illustrations of the different types of delinquency and status offense cases, delineating the legal definitions of *juvenile status offenses* and *juvenile delinquency*, examining the 9 steps in the juvenile justice caseflow process and showing the scope of the problem in terms of official and unofficial delinquency statistics.

## ■ Case Illustrations

■ *A 15-year-old male runaway is before the juvenile court judge for possession of a concealed, unloaded .38-caliber handgun. The juvenile probation officer who conducted the predispositional investigation recommends detention for the youth on the handgun charge. The public defender states that the 3 days the youth has already spent in detention have had a profound effect on him and requests leniency. The judge rules that the youth and his parents must attend 12 sessions of family counseling provided through the probation department and that the stepfather, who works as a security guard, must keep his revolver in a lockbox so that the boy is not able to take it again.*

■ *A 16-year-old female named Suzie fought with another girl when it was learned that Suzie had become pregnant by the other girl's boyfriend. During the argument, Suzie cut the other girl with a broken bottle. The juvenile court judge suspends commitment to the state girl's training school and places her in a group home for adolescent girls for 1 year.*

■ *A 15-year-old male broke into the home of an elderly woman to search for cash and valuables. The woman returned home to find the youth ransacking her house; in a fit of rage, he brutally assaulted and raped her. The judge rules that the boy, although only 15 years old, is to be tried as an adult. Found guilty by a jury, he is sentenced to 6–10 years of incarceration.*

■ *Candace, a 14-year-old female, stole a car and has repeatedly run away from the group home where she was placed because her mother could not handle her at home. Candace's mother has two jobs; the girl has never met her biological father. Candace was suspended from school three times in the past year for possession of marijuana and twice for possession of designer drugs. Her case record reflects that she was sexually abused by her mother's boyfriend. The judge adjudicates Candace to the girl's training school until she reaches age 16.*

In general, youths can be charged with two types of wrongdoing: juvenile delinquency offenses, which are criminal acts (e.g., auto theft, forcible rape, breaking and entering) for which they would be held accountable if they were adults, and status offenses (e.g., truancy, incorrigibility, and running away from home), which are illegal only for juveniles. Violent juvenile crimes receive the most media attention and serve to intensify the fear and outrage of concerned citizens. This fear and outrage, in turn, frequently influence prosecutors, juvenile court judges, and correctional administrators to subject more juvenile offenders to harsher penalties. Far more prevalent than violent crimes are juveniles who commit status offenses or nonviolent property crimes, as in the following examples:

■ *A 13-year-old boy was brought to the county juvenile detention center after his mother complained that he was on drugs and was uncontrollable. The social worker's investigation for the court revealed that the mother had been released from the state hospital 3 months earlier. She had a history of psychotic episodes. The judge ruled that the boy should live with the aunt and uncle with whom he lived while his mother was confined in the state hospital, and receive 90 days of substance abuse counseling.*

■ *A 16-year-old male whose mother was an alcoholic had been reared in a home in which he was neglected and there was no discipline or limit setting. He had a history of 12 arrests for petty theft and shoplifting starting at the age of 11. Following the most recent arrest, he was sent to a rehabilitation-oriented juvenile training school that provided group therapy 6 days a week, a behavior modification program, and vocational training. The youth was learning to be an auto mechanic and proudly demonstrated his knowledge of automobile repair.*

Students and practitioners working in juvenile justice agencies, on either a volunteer or paid basis, sometimes encounter the discretionary, deficient, flawed, and often overcrowded system of juvenile justice. At other times, students and practitioners encounter caring and compassionate juvenile justice volunteers and practitioners. Although the goal of justice-oriented agencies is to protect society and to humanely care for and rehabilitate our deviant children and youth, in actuality the juvenile justice system sometimes labels, stigmatizes, mistakenly punishes, and reinforces delinquent patterns of behavior. In a number of jurisdictions, the controlling, biased, and punitive orientation of some juvenile justice officials has led to a revolving-door system in which we find an overrepresentation of children and youth from African American, low-income, neglectful, and/or abusive homes. For example, in 2000 a disproportionate number of juvenile arrests involved minorities. After converting the total reported arrest numbers into arrest rates per 100,000 juveniles in each racial group, the violent crime arrest rate for African American juveniles (555) was almost 4 times the arrest rate for American Indian juveniles (151) and White juveniles (146) and 7 times the arrest rate for Asian American juveniles (75). With regard to property crime arrest statistics, the arrest rate for African American juveniles (1,885) was more than two thirds higher than the rate for American Indian juveniles (1,149) and almost double the arrest rate for White juveniles (958). In some states, juveniles who are members of minority races are more likely to be incarcerated than White juvenile offenders. For example, in Georgia, New Jersey, and Virginia, research that controlled for adjudication offense and previous delinquency record indicated that African American juveniles charged with serious crimes were more likely to be adjudicated delinquent and receive longer terms of incarceration than White juveniles (Brooks & Jeon, 2001; New Jersey Juvenile Justice Commission, 2000; Williams & Cohen, 1993). See chapter 11 for a discussion of racial and ethnic disparities in juvenile court processing and chapter 13 for documentation and a discussion of the overrepresentation of African American juvenile death penalty cases in Texas.

This chapter examines three primary areas related to learning about the juvenile justice system: definitions of juvenile delinquency and status offenses, the stages in the juvenile justice process, and the scope and extent of juvenile delinquency. The following 19 chapters focus on the full range of punishment-oriented policies and programs, rehabilitation-oriented policies and programs, correlates of juvenile offenses, and research and outcome studies on the most effective juvenile offender treatment programs.

## ■ Defining Juvenile Justice

What is the juvenile justice system? It is the agencies and institutions whose primary responsibility is handling juvenile offenders. These agencies and their programs concern themselves with delinquent youths and with those children and youths labeled incorrigible, truant, or runaway. Juvenile justice focuses on the needs of the more than 2 million youths who are taken into custody, diverted into special programs or processed through the juvenile court and adjudicated, and placed on probation, referred to a community-based day treatment program, or placed in a group home or a secure facility.

The history of juvenile justice has involved the development of policies, programs, and agencies for dealing with youths involved in legal violations. As we examine the juvenile justice system, we focus on the interrelated, yet different, functions of several agencies and programs: the police, pretrial diversion projects, the juvenile court, children's shelters and detention facilities, juvenile correctional facilities, group homes, wilderness programs, family counseling programs, restitution programs, and aftercare programs.

What has been done during the past 100 years to provide juvenile offenders with equal opportunities for justice? Which policies and program alternatives are currently prevalent within the juvenile justice subsystems (police, courts, and juvenile corrections)? What are the latest trends in processing and treating juvenile offenders? What does the future hold? This book explores the answers to these questions. The next section of this chapter focuses on the legal and behavioral definitions of juvenile delinquency and status offenses.

## ■ Defining Juvenile Delinquency

*Juvenile delinquency* is a broad, generic term that includes many diverse forms of antisocial behavior by a minor. In general, most state criminal codes define juvenile delinquency as behavior that is in violation of the criminal code and committed by a youth who has not reached adult age. The specific acts by the juvenile that constitute delinquent behavior vary from state to state. A definition that is broad in scope and commonly used was developed by the U.S. Children's Bureau (1967):

> Juvenile delinquency cases are those referred to courts for acts defined in the statutes of the State as the violation of a state law or municipal ordinance by children or youth of juvenile court age, or for conduct so seriously antisocial as to interfere with the rights of others or to menace the welfare of the delinquent himself or of the community.

Other agencies define as delinquent those juveniles who have been arrested or contacted by the police, even though many of these individuals are merely reprimanded or sent home when their parents pick them up. Less than half of the juveniles handled by the police are referred to the juvenile court. These are the children and youths the Children's Bureau would classify as delinquents.

The legal definitions of what constitutes juvenile delinquency appear in state juvenile codes and statutes and vary somewhat from state to state. Generally, a criminal law definition of juvenile delinquency holds that any person, usually under 18 years of age, who commits an illegal act is considered a delinquent when he or she is officially processed through juvenile or family court. A juvenile does not become a delinquent until he or she is officially labeled as such by the specialized judicial agency (e.g., the juvenile court). For example, Ohio defines a *delinquent child* as a child:

a) Who violates any law of this State, the United States or any ordinance or regulation of a political subdivision of the state, which would be a crime if committed by an adult. . . .

b) Who violates any lawful order of the court. . . . (Chapter 2151.02. *Page's Ohio Revised Code Annotated*, 1994).

A Montana statute specifies that a delinquent youth is one who has either committed a crime or who has violated the terms of his or her probation, while the Mississippi statute defines a *delinquent child* broadly as a youth (10 years of age or older) "who is habitually disobedient, whose associations are injurious to the welfare of other children" (Binder, Geis, & Bruce, 1988, p. 6). Therefore, a youth who could be defined as a "delinquent" under the Mississippi statute in many situations would not be so considered under the Ohio or Montana codes.

It is important to carefully note the difference between a "delinquent" and a delinquent act. The specific act is the behavior that has violated the state criminal code, and the term *delinquent* is the official label frequently assigned to a youth who deviates from the accepted community norms. A juvenile who commits an illegal act is not immediately or automatically defined as a delinquent. Assaulting another youth or breaking a school window does not automatically make one a delinquent. Isolated single incidents usually are tolerated by the community or neighborhood. For the most part, society-at-large reserves judgment until after a number or series of legally defined delinquent acts are committed. Police officers and prosecutors handle juveniles differently depending on age and the nature, severity, and frequency of the juvenile's acts. See chapter 9 for a detailed discussion of police work with juveniles. Prosecutorial and judicial discretion with juvenile offenders and their beliefs about punishment versus rehabilitation explain why two different youths are usually handled differently by the juvenile court, even if they commit the same offense. See chapter 11 for a detailed discussion of juvenile court and prosecutorial discretion and processing decisions.

There are two primary types of juvenile delinquency. As discussed above, the first are the criminal offenses: those acts considered illegal whether committed by an adult or a juvenile. Such illegal acts include aggravated assault, arson, homicide, rape, burglary, larceny, auto theft, and drug-related crimes. These types of serious offenses are the primary concern of juvenile corrections officials. According to the national and local statutes on juvenile criminality, burglary and larceny are the most frequently committed offenses. The brutal crimes of homicide and forcible rape are only a small percentage of the total number of crimes committed by juveniles.

The second major type of juvenile delinquency is known as status offenses: misbehavior that would not be considered a crime if engaged in by an adult. Examples of status offenses are truancy, incorrigibility, curfew violations, and running away from home. Approximately half of the states include status offenses in their definition of juvenile delinquency offenses. Other states have passed separate legislation that distinguishes juveniles who have committed criminal acts from those who have committed status offenses. In those states, status offenders are viewed as individuals "in need of supervision" and are designated as CHINS, CINS, MINS, PINS, or JINS. The first letter of the acronym varies, based on whether the initial word is *children*, *minors*, *persons*, or *juveniles*, but the rest of the phrase is always the same: in need of supervision.

## Juvenile Justice Processing and Case Flow

The juvenile justice process usually involves the formal agencies and procedures developed to handle those children and youths suspected or accused of violating their state's juvenile code. The juvenile justice agencies are police and sheriff's department's youth or juvenile aid divisions, juvenile and family courts, and community-based and institutional juvenile correctional facilities. There are nine stages in delinquency case processing through the juvenile justice system:

- ☐ Initial contact by law enforcement agencies
- ☐ Law enforcement informal handling, diversion, arrest, and/or referral to the juvenile court
- ☐ Court intake via the juvenile probation intake unit or the prosecutor's office
- ☐ Preadjudication juvenile detention
- ☐ Prosecutors file a delinquency petition in juvenile court or waive to adult criminal court
- ☐ Investigation or predisposition report prepared by a probation officer
- ☐ Juvenile court judge's adjudicatory decision and sanctions
- ☐ Participation and completion of mandated juvenile offender treatment program
- ☐ Juvenile aftercare plan

Because of discretion exercised by police and judicial officers, there is some variation from one city or county to the next in the processing of juvenile cases. Therefore, while there is a sequential series of critical decision points in case processing, there is also some variation in how, when, and which types of decisions are made. In general, alleged juvenile offenders have their first encounter with the juvenile justice system through police officers or sheriff's deputies.

## Initial Contact and Handling by the Police

Law enforcement officers frequently divert juvenile delinquents and status offenders out of the juvenile justice system. However, in many instances an officer has sufficient evidence to arrest a juvenile and immediately bring the suspect to the police precinct or department. An *arrest* is defined as taking an individual into custody for purposes of interviewing or charging an individual with a delinquency offense. Upon arresting the youth, a decision is made based on whether there is sufficient evidence to either send the juvenile to probation intake and detention or to divert the case out of the system into alternative educational or recreational programs. In most cases, the police juvenile officer makes this decision, after discussions with the victim, the juvenile, and the parent or guardian and after carefully determining the nature and extent of the youth's previous contacts with the police and juvenile courts. Federal regulations clearly discourage detaining juveniles in adult county or city jails and lockups. If a police officer believes that it is necessary to detain a youth in secure custody for a short period in order to allow a parent to pick up a youth or to arrange transport to the county juvenile detention facility, then federal regulations require that the youth be detained for a maximum of 6 hours and in a restricted area where no adult detainees can be observed or heard from.

### Juvenile Court Intake and Preadjudication Juvenile Detention

The overwhelming majority of juvenile court referrals come from police sending the juvenile to the county or city probation intake unit. The remaining referrals usually come from parents, victims, and school personnel. In general, juvenile court intake units are staffed by the juvenile probation department or the prosecutor's office. At this decision point, the probation intake officer must decide whether to dismiss the case, handle the juvenile informally, or request formal adjudication by the juvenile court. Before making this decision, the intake officer is required to examine the type and seriousness of the alleged offense and to make a determination of whether there is clear and convincing evidence to prove the allegation. If there are no clear legal merits, such as eyewitnesses, then the case is dismissed. If there is sufficient evidence, then the intake probation officer makes a determination as to whether official juvenile court processing is appropriate.

Approximately half of all juvenile cases referred by intake officers are handled informally. The overwhelming majority of these cases are dismissed. In the other informally handled cases, the youth voluntarily signs a written agreement outlining specific conditions for an informal disposition for a specified time period. Typical conditions often include victim restitution, drug education and intensive counseling, school attendance, or a curfew. In many jurisdictions, a youth may be offered an informal disposition only after verbalizing remorse for the crime. Compliance with the agreement is frequently monitored by a probation officer and sometimes referred to as "informal probation." At the end of the specified period and as long as the youth successfully complies with the written agreement, the case is dismissed. If the youth fails to comply with the written agreement, then the probation officer may refer the case for formal prosecution. If that is the case, then the juvenile is mandated to an adjudicatory hearing.

### Preadjudication Juvenile Detention

A youth may be held in a secure juvenile detention facility during the processing of his or her case if the intake officer believes detention is needed to protect the community or the child. When a youth is accused of having committed a serious crime, the police usually bring him or her to the juvenile detention facility. Most juvenile detention facilities have an intake unit where detention intake or juvenile probation officers review the facts of the case and the juvenile's background and home situation and then make the decision as to whether the juvenile should be detained, pending a hearing by a judge. In all states, a detention hearing should be held within a time period defined by statute, generally within 24 hours on a weekday or within 72 hours if the youth is referred on the weekend. At the detention hearing, a court-appointed referee or judge reviews the case and then determines if continued detention is necessary. Detention sometimes extends after the adjudicatory and dispositional hearings. Unfortunately, as a result of overcrowded state-operated juvenile facilities, short-term detention can continue beyond formal adjudication until a bed opens up at the state juvenile correctional or drug treatment facility.

### Prosecutors File a Case in Either Juvenile or Criminal Court

In many states, prosecutors are mandated by the criminal code to file certain (generally serious violent) juvenile cases in the adult criminal court. These are violent cases in which the state legislature has decided the youth should be waived to criminal court and be handled as a criminal offender. In a growing number of states, the legislature has allowed the prosecutor the sole discretion of filing a defined list of serious cases in either juvenile court or adult criminal court. In these states, the prosecutor selects the court that will hear the case. If the case is handled by a juvenile court judge, then two types of formal petitions may be filed: delinquency or waiver to adult court. A delinquency petition formally describes the allegations and requests the juvenile court to *adjudicate* (or judge) the juvenile a delinquent, making the juvenile offender a ward of the court. This legal language is different from that applied in the criminal court system, where an offender is *convicted and sentenced*. With regard to delinquency petitions, an adjudicatory judicial hearing is scheduled. At the adjudicatory hearing (trial), the juvenile is represented by counsel, and witnesses are called to present the facts of the case. In most adjudicatory hearings, the judge (rather than a jury) determines whether the juvenile committed the offense(s).

### Investigation or Predisposition Report Prepared by a Probation Officer

Between the decision to process the case through the juvenile court and the disposition hearing, the probation staff prepares a predisposition report. If the juvenile is adjudicated a delinquent by the judge, then a disposition plan is developed. A disposition can be defined as a decision to administer punitive sanctions as a result of a delinquency adjudication. The probation officer preparing this plan for the judge may order psychological testing and forensic evaluations, diagnostic tests, or a short period of confinement in a diagnostic and classification facility. At the disposition hearing, specific treatment and program recommendations are presented to the judge. The prosecutor and the youth's parent or the youth may also prepare and present dispositional recommendations. After reviewing all of the options, the juvenile court judge orders a disposition in the case.

There are three main types of juvenile dispositions: *nominal*, *conditional*, and *custodial* options. *Nominal* dispositions are frequently utilized with nonviolent first offenders and include reprimands or warnings that the juvenile will be incarcerated for a long time if he or she returns to the court for a new offense. *Conditional* dispositions often require juvenile offenders to comply with certain conditions of probation, such as participating in 2 months of addictions treatment including 6 days a week of intensive group therapy, psychosocial assessment and individual clinical treatment twice a week, completion of a vocational evaluation and placement program, or full restitution to victims and the juvenile court, which are monitored by the probation officer. *Custodial* dispositions limit juveniles' freedom of movement by placing them in nonsecure custody foster homes, community-based temporary confinement, secure custody, or secure confinement, including home detention with electronic monitoring devices, group homes, forestry camps, structured wilderness programs, schools, and secure juvenile institutions. (See Figure 1.1.)

### The Juvenile Court Judge's Decision and Sanctions

Juvenile court judges have the responsibility of ordering sanctions on adjudicated delinquents that can result in a turning point for juvenile lawbreakers. Participation in short-term residential or community treatment programs can break the cycle of habitual delinquency and criminality. On the other hand, being sent to a state training school for 2 years or longer can further corrupt a young delinquent and eventually lead to a life of habitual crime and long periods of incarceration. Regular probation, intensive probation supervision, and probation-monitored restitution are the preferred sanctions of many juvenile court judges. However, about one third of these delinquents are committed to residential treatment programs. These commitments may be for a specific short term of 3 or 4 months or for an indeterminate time period. The juvenile residential facility may be publicly or privately operated and may have a secure lockup and institutional environment or an open setting with extensive educational and recreational facilities. In a large number of states, after the judge commits a youth to the state department of juvenile services or corrections, the department then determines in which facility the juvenile will be placed and the date the juvenile will be released. In other cases, the judge controls the placement and length of stay. In either situation, review hearings on a monthly basis are important in order to assess the progress of the juvenile.

A probation sanction may include individual drug counseling, daily participation in AA or NA meetings, weekend confinement in the local detention

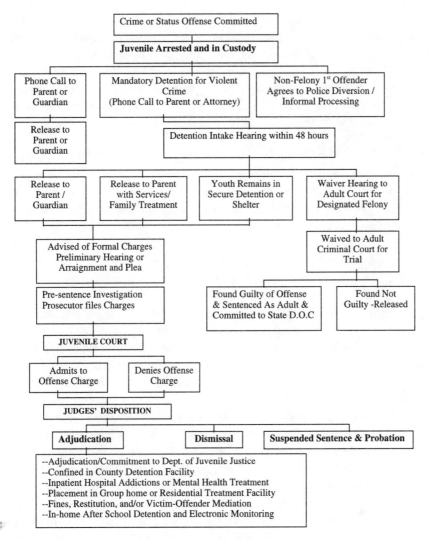

**Figure 1.1    Juvenile Justice System Flowchart**

center, and community service or victim restitution. The term and conditions of probation are usually very specific. In some cases, however, the length of the probation order is open ended and determined by the probation officer, based on the progress of the probationer. After the probation officer reports to the court that all conditions have been successfully met, the judge terminates the case.

### Juvenile Aftercare Plan

Upon release from a state training school, also known as a juvenile correctional institution, the juvenile may be ordered to a period of intensive aftercare or parole. During this period, the juvenile may be monitored or under the supervision of the juvenile court or the corrections department. Aftercare programs should include a continuum of services and scheduled activities, such as after-school recreational and creative arts programs, alternative dispute resolution programs, mentoring and tutoring programs, career development and vocational training programs, religious group meetings, family counseling, volunteer work with the homeless and disabled, and neighborhood crime prevention projects. The juvenile who does not adhere to the conditions of aftercare may be remanded to the same juvenile correctional facility or to another facility.

### The Processing of Status Offense Cases Differs From That of Delinquency Cases

As discussed earlier in this chapter, a delinquency offense is an act committed by a minor for which an adult could be prosecuted in criminal court. However status offenses are behaviors that are violations of the state juvenile code only for children and youths of minor status, for example, running away from home, chronic truancy, ungovernability, staying out all night without permission, and underage drinking. In a number of ways, the law enforcement and court processing of status offense cases parallels that of delinquency cases.

However, not all states consider all of these behaviors to be law violations. Most states view these behaviors as indications that the youth is in need of closer supervision and respond to the behavior through the provision of social and family services. This different perspective of status offenses often results in their being handled more like dependency than delinquency cases. Status offenders are just as likely to enter the juvenile justice system through a child welfare agency as through law enforcement.

The landmark Juvenile Justice and Delinquency Prevention Act of 1974 strongly discouraged holding status offenders in secure juvenile correctional facilities, either for detention or placement. This important legislation and policy mandate is called *deinstitutionalization of status offenders*. An exception to this deinstitutionalization policy takes place when the juvenile status offender violates a valid court order, such as a probation order that requires the adjudicated status offender to reside in a group home for 30 days or one that requires attendance at school 5 days a week and an 8 P.M. curfew. The status offender who violates the court order or group home placement may then be confined in a secure detention or correctional facility.

### Juvenile Court Referrals and Case Dispositions

The overwhelming number (83%) of juvenile delinquency cases processed by the juvenile courts during 1999 were referred by police and sheriff's departments. The remaining referrals to juvenile courts came from probation departments as a result of probation violations, followed by referrals from school personnel and parents. Juvenile delinquency cases that are referred to a county or city juvenile court are usually screened by a probation or juvenile intake department (either located within or attached to the court, or outside the court). The intake unit or department decides whether to dismiss the case because of a lack of sufficient legal cause or to resolve the matter through a

formal petition or informally through referral to a social service or family counseling agency, substance abuse treatment program, or restitution. In 1999, 57%
of all juvenile delinquency cases that were disposed of by the juvenile courts
were handled formally while 43% were handled informally (see Figure 1.2).
Among nonpetitioned delinquency cases, 39% were dismissed at the intake or
precourt level, frequently for a lack of legal justification. However, in the remaining 61% of cases, the troubled youths voluntarily accepted informal sanctions, such as referral to a social service or counseling agency, informal probation or restricted curfews, payment of fines, community service, or voluntary
monetary restitution.

When the intake department makes a decision that a case needs to be
formally processed within the juvenile court, a petition is filed and the case is
then placed on the juvenile court's calendar (or docket) for an adjudicatory
hearing and judicial disposition. The probation or juvenile detention intake
officer may recommend that a case be removed from juvenile court and waived
to adult criminal court. In these relatively few serious cases, a petition is often
filed in the juvenile court to formally request a transfer or waiver hearing, at
which time the juvenile court judge or referee is asked to waive or set aside
jurisdiction over the juvenile case.

For example, during 1999, 66% (382 out of 575) of all the formally processed delinquency cases (adjudicated, nonadjudicated, or waived) in the
United States had an outcome of the youth being adjudicated a juvenile delinquent. In approximately 33% of these alleged delinquency cases, the youths
were not adjudicated, and the remaining 1% of formally processed cases were
judicially waived to criminal court (see Figure 1.2).

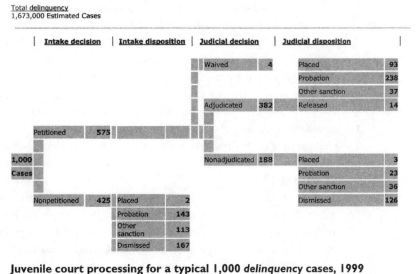

**Figure 1.2**   **Juvenile court processing for a typical 1,000 *delinquency* cases, 1999**

Data Source: National Juvenile Court Data Archive. National Center for Juvenile Justice. Pittsburgh, PA. May, 2002

It is the juvenile court judge's responsibility at the disposition hearing to determine the most reasonable and appropriate sanction, as a result of carefully reviewing a predisposition psychosocial and delinquency history report prepared by the county or city probation department. The full range of adjudication options available to a typical juvenile court includes commitment to a juvenile institution or a residential drug treatment facility, placement in a group home or foster care, traditional or intensive probation supervision, court-monitored home-based electronic monitoring, referral to an outside community agency, prevocational program, psychosocial day treatment, or a community mental health program, a fine, community service in a local hospital, nursing home, or public works program, or restitution.

During 1999, clearly the most common sanction for adjudicated youth was formal probation, the result of 62% of formally adjudicated cases, compared with the 24% of adjudicated youths who were placed in a residential facility.

With regard to juvenile court dispositional hearings, judges usually do their best to determine appropriate and effective sanctions for delinquent youth in order to break the cycle of juvenile delinquency recidivism. In a growing number of delinquency dispositions, the juvenile court imposes a combination of sanctions, such as probation for 1 year with the first 3 months spent in a residential drug treatment facility or commitment to a group home for 6 months, with the stipulation that the adjudicated youth attend an alternative school 5 days a week and 2 hours of group therapy every night. Other sanctions include commitment to a juvenile correctional institution's maximum security MICA unit (mentally ill and chemically dependent juvenile offenders), probation, and/or electronically monitored home detention.

As depicted in Figure 1.3, the number and percentage of delinquency adjudications resulting in residential placements increased by approximately 24% from 1990 to 1999. In 1999, adjudicated delinquent youths were court ordered to residential placement in 155,200 delinquency cases. The number of adjudicated delinquency cases resulting in formal probation increased approximately 80% from 1990 to 1999. In 1999, 62% (about 400,000) of all adjudicated delinquency cases led to formal juvenile probation. Furthermore, in 1999, other court-ordered sanctions, including community service, day treatment, and restitution, were imposed in 62,500 (10%) of the adjudicated delinquency cases. In a very small number of cases (4%), although the youth was adjudicated delinquent, the case was dismissed or the youth was otherwise released (see Figure 1.3).

According to the U.S. Department of Justice data, probation is the most common form of sanction given by the juvenile court. Since 1989, with more than 1 million juvenile court cases per year, the number of juvenile offenders formally placed on probation has increased from almost half to more than three fifths (62%) of the total sanctions given. Noteworthy is the total number and percentage increase in the juvenile probation sector, an increase of more than 50%, from 225,000 to slightly more than 400,000 juvenile probation

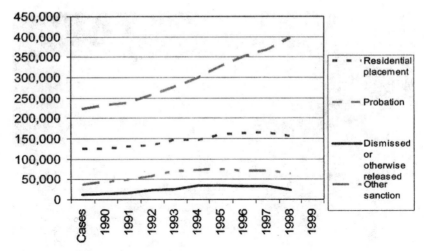

**Figure 1.3    Delinquency Case Dispositions**

Source: Stahl, A., Finnegan, T., & Kang, W. (2002). Easy access to juvenile court statistics: 1990–1999 [data analysis and presentation package]. Pittsburgh, PA: National Center for Juvenile Justice [producer]. Washington, DC: Office of Juvenile Justice and Delinquency Prevention. Washington, DC: U.S. Government Printing Office.

cases during the 10-year period from 1989 to 1999. This is a vast increase when compared with other possible juvenile court sanctions, which saw increases of about 5% to 20% since 1990. The other two forms of sanctions show very slight increases, if any at all. The number of cases waived to the adult criminal courts seemed to stay at the same relative level, with small increases throughout the entire period.

With the increase in the number of overall juvenile court cases from 1989 to 1999, increases in the number of sanctions given out by the court should be expected. But the trend we are beginning to witness is that juvenile court judges seem to be adjudicating some form of probation (e.g., intensive probation supervision, probation-monitored restitution and community service, or traditional probation) as a preferred form of sanction. This is evidenced by the percentage increase compared with the overall rise in all forms of sanctions.

# ■ Juvenile Court Jurisdiction and Upper Age Limits

According to Figure 1.4, during the last four decades of the 20th century, the number of juvenile court cases increased significantly from only 405,000 cases in 1961 to 1.75 million by the year 2000 (Puzzanchera et al., 2001; Snyder, 2002). More specifically, juvenile court cases rapidly increased from 405,000 in 1961 to 1.25 million in 1977, with a small decline to 1.1 million in 1984 and 1985 and then a gradual year-by-year increase to 1.83 million cases by 1996. By 1975, the number of juvenile court cases had more than doubled at 1,051,000 since the 1961 statistics. The all-time peak of 1,828,800 occurred in 1996. Since the peak in 1996, there has been a decline in juvenile court cases for the following 3 years, as illustrated in Figure 1.4.

All 50 states and the District of Columbia have legal statutes that define an upper age limit for juvenile court jurisdictions. But states differ on the age at which a juvenile's wrongdoing is handled as a criminal (adult) offense rather than a juvenile offense. The oldest age at which an offender is still treated as a juvenile ranges from 15 to 18. In the overwhelming majority of states and the District of Columbia, an individual is under the jurisdiction of the juvenile court until the age of 18 (see Figure 1.5). However, youths in the states of Connecticut, New York, and North Carolina who violate their state's criminal code when they are age 16 (or older) are within the jurisdiction of the criminal court (Hamparian et al., 1982; Torbet & Szymanski, 1998).

In contrast to this practice of specifying maximum ages for juvenile court jurisdiction, only a few states designate a specific minimum age in their juvenile code. Most state juvenile and criminal codes implicitly follow the English common-law position that a child under the age of 7 is incapable of criminal intent. Therefore, a child below the age of 7 who commits a crime is not held morally or criminally responsible for that act.

An increasing number of state legislatures have determined that juvenile offenders accused of brutal crimes should be processed by criminal courts rather than juvenile courts. Many states have authorized a waiver of jurisdiction that automatically gives the adult criminal courts jurisdiction over certain vi-

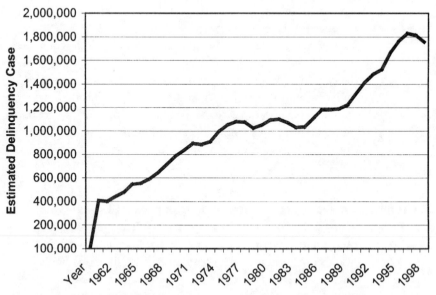

**Figure 1.4**     **Juvenile Court Cases 1960–1998**

Source: Adapted from Puzzanchera, C., Stahl, A., Finnegan, T., Snyder, H., Poole, R., & Tierney, N. (2001). *Juvenile court statistics, 1998.* Washington, DC: Office of Juvenile Justice and Delinquency Prevention, U.S. Government Printing Office.

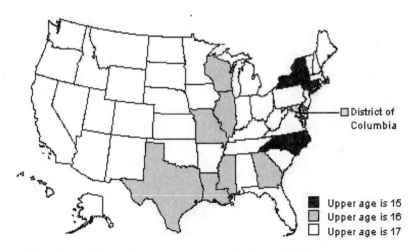

**Figure 1.5**   **Upper Age of Original Juvenile Court Jurisdiction, 1997**
Source: Sickmund, M. Upper age of original juvenile court jurisdiction, 1997. Adapted from
Torbet, P., & Szymanski, L. *State legislative responses to violent juvenile crime: 1996–97 update.*

olent juveniles. For example, in 1978, New York State passed legislation creating a classification of juvenile offenses called "designated felonies." Under
this state law, 14- and 15-year-olds charged with committing murder, kidnap-
ping, arson, manslaughter, rape, or assault were tried in designated felony
courts. If the accused offenders were found guilty of the charges, they could
be imprisoned for up to 5 years (Prescott, 1982, p. 1). This is an increase over
the typical sentence for a juvenile offender, which averages 12 months. Chapters 10 and 12 provide further information on the criminal courts' handling
of and intervention with repeat violent juvenile offenders.

### Handling Juvenile Status Offenders

There has been considerable debate over the appropriate way to handle status
offenders. The major issue is whether the juvenile court should retain authority
over them. Those in favor of the court's continuing authority believe that a
youth's habitual misbehavior will eventually lead to more serious delinquent
acts; therefore, it is wise for the court to retain its jurisdiction over the status
offender. An opposing view (often advanced by deviance theorists with a societal reaction or labeling-theory perspective) holds that status offenders who
are defined as delinquents may actually become delinquents as the result of a
self-fulfilling prophecy, leading to secondary deviance (Becker, 1963; Lemert,
1971; Schur, 1973).

Another belief held by a number of social workers is that the needs of
status offenders can be better met within the community social service and
child welfare service systems (Boisvert & Wells, 1980; Roberts, 1987; Springer,
2001). For example, Roberts's (1987) research documented the need for the
full range of social services, including 24-hour telephone hotlines, short-term

runaway shelters, family treatment programs, education and treatment services for abusive parents, and vocational training and placement services.

At issue is the type of treatment status offenders should receive. Should they be sentenced to a secure juvenile facility or referred to a community social service agency for counseling? For many years, it was common for juvenile status offenders to be sentenced to juvenile training schools, where they were confined in the same institution with youths convicted of serious crimes. The practice of sending status offenders to juvenile correctional institutions has become much less common in recent years because of the deinstitutionalization of status offenders. However, in certain circumstances a minor who has committed no crime can still be sent to a juvenile training school. For example, a youth with a history of chronic runaway behavior is placed in a group home by the court. If the juvenile then runs away from that facility, the court views that act as a delinquency offense, and the youth is usually sent to a secure juvenile institution.

Probation officers often believe that although most status offenders do not pose a danger to others, they do frequently exhibit destructive behavior patterns such as drug abuse, alcohol abuse, or suicide ideation. They often come from dysfunctional, conflict-ridden families where physical, sexual, or emotional abuse is prevalent. Thus the social work perspective urges that a continuum of services be provided for status offenders and their families through a social service agency, a family service agency, or a juvenile court–based program. Available services should include family counseling, individual and group counseling, addiction treatment, alternative education programs, and vocational evaluation, education, and training.

For an in-depth analysis of the nature and types of social service and counseling programs to which status offenders are referred, see chapters 8, 14, and 15 on the emergence, proliferation, and characteristics of contemporary juvenile diversion and community-based programs.

## ■ Model Juvenile Offender Intervention Programs

The controversial issue of what works, what does not work, and which programs are most promising in rehabilitating juvenile and adult offenders and in preventing further criminality has received considerable attention during the past decade. There has been a gradual increase in the number of program evaluations and outcome studies measuring the effectiveness of different types of juvenile offender interventions. The most promising programs and those worthy of replication in other jurisdictions have demonstrated effectiveness in terms of sharply reduced recidivism 12 months after program completion, compared with much higher recidivism for matched controls in traditional institutional programs. As a result of my national survey of juvenile offender treatment programs, I identified 10 model programs, including the Eckerd Foundation Structured Wilderness Education Programs in Florida, the Associated Marine Institutes in eight states, the Gulf Coast Trades Center in Texas, Milwaukee Wraparound Services, and the Earn-It juvenile restitution program in New Hampshire. These model programs and the longitudinal follow-up data demonstrating effectiveness in reducing recidivism are discussed in the final chapter in this book.

In a congressionally mandated study funded by the National Institute of Justice, Lawrence Sherman and associates (1998) at the University of Maryland found that the bulk of the $3 billion allocated each year by the federal government to state and local agencies to prevent crime was spent on operations and staffing. In addition, it bodes well for the future of juvenile justice reforms and evaluation research that the University of Maryland team of criminologists documented that only a very small part of the federal grants were used for program evaluations and research. In this vein, Sherman and associates (1998) aptly recommended that Congress require a statutory plan for utilizing scientific methods and rigorous methodology in conducting research and rating the program effectiveness of all federally funded crime prevention programs.

I highly recommend that juvenile justice officials and administrators give priority to hiring consultants at independent research institutes and university-based researchers to plan and conduct quasi-experimental outcome studies to determine the efficacy and effectiveness of juvenile offender treatment and prevention programs. Each outcome study should include several recidivism measures, such as the number and severity of rearrests, the number and severity of readjudications, technical parole violations, frequency of new detentions, and confinement in state institutions. In addition, all studies should measure positive social adjustments and changes in math and reading levels by documenting attendance in academic or vocational programs, hours worked in the community, attitude and self-esteem measures, scores on psychological assessment scales, and a battery of neurological tests.

Once the most effective intervention programs are identified, they should be replicated in selected jurisdictions throughout the country with standardized, built-in evaluation components. A good start would be implementation of all model and promising programs in at least 6 of the 12 federal regions of the United States. The two most important components of any rigorous outcome study are an experimental or quasi-experimental research design and longitudinal follow-up periods. In other words, juveniles in the model program should be compared with a matched comparison group or control group based on random assignment whenever possible. Finally, systematic follow-up data should be collected at 3, 6, 12, 24, and 36 months after treatment completion.

## Official and Unofficial Statistics

Juvenile delinquency trends and estimates of the scope of the delinquency problem come from both official statistics and unofficial self-report studies. The four major sources of data on delinquency and victimization are:

Table 1.1    Program Comparison of 8 Evidence-Based Model Juvenile Rehabilitation Programs Based on National Survey

| Program | Location | Program Goals | Treatment | Duration | Population | Outcome | Sample Size |
|---|---|---|---|---|---|---|---|
| Associated Marine Institutes (AMI) | 7 states and the Cayman Islands | • Vocational Training<br>• Improve Academic Level<br>• Emphasizing Core Values | • Involvement in Marine Research Projects, such as aquatics, diving, oceanography, seamanship, marine biology<br>• Education | Ongoing | Adjudicated Youth, 14–18 yrs of age<br>Average of 8-12 offenses before coming to AMI | • 28.5% new adjud.-Recidivism Rate (1 year after release); most common offenses—car theft & Burglary | • 2741<br>• 54% of the 782 youths that recidivated did so within 4 months |
| AMI's Last Chance Ranch; also Known as Florida Environmental Institute | Florida Everglades | • Behavior Management<br>• To Improve Academic Level | • Behavior Modification Program Based on a Point System<br>• Educat; 22 juv.at a time<br>• Physical Labor on the Ranch<br>• Involvement in Environmental Projects | Minimum 1 Year (Ongoing) | Adjudicated Youth with Felony Offenses | • 15.8% Recidivism Rate (after 12 months) as defined as new adjudication. Most common offenses—car theft & Burglary | • 57 |
| Bethesda Day Treatment Center | West Milton, Pa | • Positive Socialization | • Alternative Education<br>• Drug Counseling<br>• Family Systems Counseling<br>• Short-Term Foster Care (Community Based) | 55+ hours a week (Ongoing) | Adjudicated, Non-adjudicated, Avg. Intake Age: 14.1 (10–17 yrs), "High-Risk" status offenders referred for truancy, incorrigibility, running away from home, or theft. IQ: 82% Below Avg. | • 10.4% Recidivism Rate within the first 12 months post discharge-new status offense | • NA |
| Earn-It | Keene, NH | • Restitution<br>• Low Cost Operation | • Employment for Restitution (Community Based) Court ordered monthly restitution; arranging work placement & community service | Ongoing | Adjudicated, Avg. Age 15.3 (12–18 yrs), "Low-Risk" Youth, Below Grade Level | • 5 to 14% Recidivism Rate after 12 mo.; Only 5% reoffense rate in all of 2000.<br>• 72% Program Completion | • 105 |

| Program | Location | Goals | Services | Duration | Population | Outcomes | Number |
|---|---|---|---|---|---|---|---|
| Eckerd Wilderness Educational System | 18 Facilities (7 States) | | • Group Activities • Education • Therapy • Community Service | 1 Year (Ongoing) | Adjudicated, Non-adjudicated Avg. Intake Age: 14.5 (11–17 yrs) Below Grade Level | • 1.3-Year Grade Level Increase • 26.7% Recidivism Rate ; after 21 months | • 820 eligible • 418 graduates |
| Eckerd Wilderness Educational System (NC) | North Carolina | • Improve Academic level, Vocational and Social Skills | • Group Activities • Education • Therapy • Community Service | 1 Year (Ongoing) | Adjudicated, Non-adjudicated Avg. Intake Age: 14.4 (11–17 yr) Avg. IQ: 91.2 | • 19.1%-new adjudication; Recidivism Rate (12 months) | • 406 |
| Gulf Coast Trades Center (TYC) | New Waverly, Texas | • Occupational Training, 9 trades • Academic Skills Training | • Work Placement • Location Monitoring (Community Based) Intensive aftercare and job placement | 6–9 Months | Adjudicated, 13–17 yrs. Of age; 65% of program graduates find employment in their chosen trade | • 15.7% Recidivism Rate,-12 month (Re-incarceration) | 249 in 2000 311 in 2001 262 in 2002 |
| Wraparound Milwaukee | Milwaukee, WI | • Address Mental Health, Substance Abuse, Emotional and Behavioral Need • Provide Support in a Non-Residential Setting | • Community Based Care Ongoing • Family Services • Ongoing Evaluations • Team Driven Servicing for the Child and Family • Strengths based treatment approach | Ongoing | Children and adolescents who have a serious emotional, behavioral or mental health disturbance that must have persisted for 6 months and who are at an immediate risk of residential treatment, or juvenile correctional placement. | • 15% Property Offenses, 5% Assault, 3% Weapons 2% Sex Offenses, 6% for Drug Offenses—One yr. Recidivism Rates | • 490 (based on program participants referred by probation) |

1 **Official police statistics**, such as the FBI Uniform Crime Report, which is published annually by the FBI. These data are based on crimes cleared by arrest and are limited because they do not indicate the total number of juveniles adjudicated for the offense for which they were arrested and detained.

   To improve the accuracy of FBI crime statistics, the new National Incident Based Reporting System (NIBRS) was implemented in 23 states to collect data on offenses reported to or observed by law enforcement officers. The NIBRS has individual incident records for the 8 index crimes and 38 other offenses (Bureau of Justice Statistics, 2000).

2 **Official statewide and national juvenile court statistics** and trend data are collected by the National Center for Juvenile Justice and the OJJDP on delinquency, child neglect, and dependency cases processed through juvenile and family courts nationwide.

3 **Self-report studies**, such as the National Youth Survey, involve asking youths whether they have engaged in one or more delinquent behaviors in the past year (e.g., damaging or destroying school property, making obscene phone calls, running away from home).

4 **Victimization studies**, like the National Crime Victimization Survey (NCVS), involve interviews every 6 months with a large sample of individuals and household heads in order to estimate the frequency of crimes, the characteristics of self-reported crime victims, and the likelihood of victimization.

## Official Statistics

According to the latest OJJDP report (Snyder, 2002), in the year 2000 police agencies throughout the United States made almost 2.4 million arrests of youths under the age of 18. As documented by the FBI, children and youths accounted for about 17% of all arrests and an estimated 16% of all arrests for violent crimes in 2000. While juvenile crime is a prevalent social and public health problem, the violent crime index offenses—murder, forcible rape, robbery, and aggravated assault—peaked in 1994 and have declined each year for 6 consecutive years. The most promising development is that the juvenile murder arrest rate has fallen to its lowest level since the mid-1960s. In 2000, there were 1,200 juvenile arrests for murder and almost 1,600 murder victims under the age of 18 at the time of their murder. The peak year for juveniles being murdered was 1993, with nearly 2,900 juvenile murder victims. The number of juvenile and adult murders combined also peaked in 1993 with 24,526 reported murders in the United States, in comparison with 15,517 murders reported to police agencies in the year 2000 (Snyder, 2002). Murder is a crime that is almost always reported. Therefore, the FBI statistics on murder are definitely the most accurate and valid in light of the limitations on the reporting of other offenses.

Since 1972, the U.S. Children's Bureau has issued periodic estimates on the number of juvenile delinquents in the United States. Their figures, based on reports from a sampling of juvenile courts across the country, show a significant increase in the number of crimes committed by juveniles. In 1930, they estimated that there were 200,000 delinquents; in 1950, the figure climbed to 435,000 (Robinson, 1960). In 1966, more than 1 million individuals under the age of 18 were arrested. Alfred Blumstein (1967) estimated that 27% of all male juveniles would probably be arrested before reaching age 18.

During the 1960s and 1970s, the federal Office of Youth Development reported a significant increase in juvenile court cases. This surge markedly exceeded the growth of the population of children in the 10 to 17 age group. Between 1960 and 1970 the number of delinquency cases more than doubled, climbing from 510,000 to 1,052,000, while the child population increased by only 29%, from 25.4 million to 32.6 million (Youth Development and Delinquency Prevention Administration, 1973).

As a result of the growth of the U.S. population of children and youths and the larger law enforcement agencies, police made approximately 2.4 million arrests of youths under the age of 18 in the year 2000 (Snyder, 2002). Historically, in 1984 the total number of arrests for youths under age 18 had exceeded 2 million (2,062,448). The juvenile most likely to be arrested (regardless of the type of offense) was over 15 years of age by almost 3 to 1 (1,537,688 to 524,760). Table 1.2 lists the most frequent offense categories for older juveniles between the ages of 15 and 18.

We now turn our attention to the eight major index crimes. As shown in Table 1.3, the vast majority of juvenile arrests are for property offenses rather than violent crimes. Property crimes include burglary, larceny, theft, motor vehicle theft, and arson. Violent crimes include murder, forcible rape, robbery, and aggravated assault.

As documented in Table 1.3, juvenile crime increases dramatically with age. In comparing the crime rate for juveniles under 15 with those age 15 to 17, arrests for property crimes more than doubled while arrests for violent crimes more than tripled. Although the majority of the crimes were property

**Table 1.2**   **Most Frequent Offenses by Older Juveniles, 1984**

| Offense Charged | Number of Juveniles Arrested |
| --- | --- |
| Larceny/theft | 338,785 |
| Burglary | 127,708 |
| Runaway | 114,275 |
| Liquor law violations | 101,904 |
| Vandalism | 87,135 |
| Disorderly conduct | 73,552 |
| Curfew and loitering law violations | 67,243 |
| Drug abuse violations | 67,211 |
| Motor vehicle theft | 33,838 |

Source: U.S. Department of Justice. (1985). *Crime in the United States: Uniform crime reports, 1984*. Washington, DC: U.S. Government Printing Office.

**Table 1.3**     **Total Arrests of Juveniles for Property and Violent Crime, 1984**

| Offense Charged | Number of Juveniles Arrested | | | |
| --- | --- | --- | --- | --- |
| | Under 15 | 15–17 | 18–20 | All Ages |
| Property crimes | 218,894 | 506,575 | 743,801 | 1,469,270 |
| Violent crimes | 18,791 | 64,344 | 122,543 | 205,678 |
| Crime index total | 237,685 | 570,919 | 866,344 | 1,674,948 |

Source: U.S. Department of Justice. (1984). *Sourcebook of criminal justice statistics.* Washington, DC: U.S. Government Printing Office.

related, there is a noticeable trend toward violent crime as juveniles become older. In the under-15 population, property crimes were 92% of total crimes while violent crimes were 8%. Violent crime increased by 3 percentage points for the 15- to 17-year-olds and another 3 points for the 18- to 20-year-olds, whose crimes were 14% violent. These data on juvenile arrests represent only the tip of the iceberg. They do not include status offenses, nor do they reflect the number of juvenile lawbreakers who were not apprehended or who committed offenses that were never reported to the police.

Table 1.4 provides a useful perspective on person offenses cases handled by the juvenile courts. Between 1989 and 1998, the number of cases handled increased by 88%. However, the biggest increase took place between 1989 and 1994. The period between 1994 and 1998 saw an increase of only 12%, minimal compared with the overall span. Although the total number of juvenile court cases seemed to continually increase over this 10-year period, over the last 5 years of the chart (1994–1998), the number of juvenile court cases for violent crimes decreased. This 22% drop is indicative of a decrease in violent crimes committed by juveniles. It shows a promising trend with regard to juvenile violent crimes handled by the juvenile courts. It seems to show that in recent years there has been a decrease among juveniles committing the most violent crimes, while the rates of the lesser violent offenses such as simple assault (e.g., slapping or punching, with no severe injuries) and sex offenses, except forcible rape and prostitution, showed a slight increase.

Table 1.5 clearly indicates that juvenile arrests for violent and property crimes peaked in 1994 and have been declining each year since then. During any given period of time, the crime rate may well shift. Sometimes this shift results in a decrease, a gradual increase, or a cyclical up-and-down pattern. Over the 20-year period between 1980 and 2000, the juvenile crime rate shows a cyclical pattern.

The first half of the 1980s, mainly the period from 1980 to 1984, saw a gradual decline in the overall crime rate for juveniles. This decline was due to the decrease in both property and violent crimes. However, beginning in the mid-1980s through the mid-1990s, the number of crimes began to shift. Both violent and property crimes increased. The peak for juvenile property crimes was reached in 1991, and the peak for juvenile crimes of violence was 1993 and 1994. Gradually, by the end of 2000, the overall juvenile crime rate once again

**Table 1.4**  **Persons Offenses Cases Handled by U.S. Juvenile Courts, 1989–1998**

| Cases Disposed | 1989 | 1994 | 1996 | Percentage Change 1989–98 | 1994–98 |
|---|---|---|---|---|---|
| Total persons offenses[a] | 214,300 | 360,900 | 403,600 | 88 | 12 |
| Violent crime index | 77,300 | 131,700 | 102,600 | 33 | −22 |
| Criminal homicide | 1,900 | 3,100 | 2,000 | 6 | −36 |
| Forcible rape | 4,800 | 6,600 | 6,000 | 26 | −9 |
| Robbery | 22,900 | 38,300 | 29,600 | 29 | −23 |
| Aggravated assault | 47,800 | 83,700 | 65,100 | 36 | −22 |
| Simple assault | 115,000 | 197,800 | 262,400 | 128 | 33 |
| Case rate[b] | 8.5 | 13.0 | 13.9 | 64 | 7 |
| Total persons offenses[a] | 3.1 | 4.7 | 3.5 | 15 | −26 |
| Criminal homicide | 0.1 | 0.1 | 0.1 | −8 | −39 |
| Forcible rape | 0.2 | 0.2 | 0.2 | 10 | −13 |
| Robbery | 0.9 | 1.4 | 1.0 | 12 | −26 |
| Aggravated assault | 1.9 | 3.0 | 2.2 | 18 | −26 |
| Simple assault | 4.5 | 7.1 | 9.0 | 98 | 27 |

Note: Percent changes are calculated using rounded numbers.

[a]Total includes other persons offenses categories not listed.

[b]Per 1,000 youth age 10 through the upper age of juvenile court jurisdiction.

Source: U.S. Department of Justice, OJJDP, Office of Justice Programs. (2001). *Fact sheet: Delinquency cases in juvenile court.* Washington, DC: Author.

shifted back to close to its level in 1980. In large part, this was due to a major decrease in the number of both violent and property crimes, especially in the period between 1995 and 2000. This statistical trend bodes well for the future because not only did the violent crime rate fall back to its 1980 annual rate but also there was a considerable decrease in the total number of property crimes.

According to Table 1.6, drug cases in the juvenile court have remained virtually steady. Two of the three demographic variables, gender and age, saw practically no change at all from 1989 to 1998. The only significant change occurred on the race demographic variable. Between 1989 and 1998, there was a slow, steady increase in the number of juvenile cases committed by Whites. This increase from 58% to 68% had an obvious effect on the Black group variable, which decreased from 40% to 29% over the 10-year span.

While the official statistics may be appropriate in examining the extent of the labeling process, law enforcement and juvenile court statistics do not give the full picture of the extent and volume of delinquent behavior. In other words, official statistics provide only a limited index of the total volume of delinquency. Because not all delinquent behavior is detected (and, therefore, cannot be officially recorded), the acts that are officially recorded should be combined with unofficial national surveys in order to obtain a more representative sample of all delinquent acts.

**Table 1.5**  **Juvenile (ages 10–17) Arrest Rates for 1980–1999 (per 100,000)**

| Year | Violent Crime | Property Crime | All Crimes |
|------|---------------|----------------|------------|
| 1980 | 334.09 | 2562.16 | 7414.28 |
| 1981 | 322.64 | 2442.85 | 7384.78 |
| 1982 | 314.48 | 2373.32 | 7344.97 |
| 1983 | 295.98 | 2244.41 | 6750.79 |
| 1984 | 297.46 | 2220.73 | 6765.81 |
| 1985 | 302.97 | 2370.74 | 7245.20 |
| 1986 | 316.70 | 2427.07 | 7505.04 |
| 1987 | 310.55 | 2451.39 | 7527.47 |
| 1988 | 326.48 | 2418.73 | 7599.86 |
| 1989 | 381.56 | 2433.80 | 7730.89 |
| 1990 | 428.48 | 2563.65 | 8032.85 |
| 1991 | 461.06 | 2611.51 | 8381.43 |
| 1992 | 482.14 | 2522.62 | 8239.23 |
| 1993 | 504.48 | 2431.01 | 8437.49 |
| 1994 | 526.64 | 2545.56 | 9274.63 |
| 1995 | 517.74 | 2445.62 | 9312.64 |
| 1996 | 460.27 | 2381.78 | 9477.16 |
| 1997 | 442.46 | 2265.12 | 9441.76 |
| 1998 | 369.64 | 1959.62 | 8567.91 |
| 1999 | 339.14 | 1750.75 | 7928.68 |

Note: Rates are arrests of persons ages 10–17 per 100,000 persons in the resident population. The violent crime index includes the offenses of murder and nonnegligent manslaughter, forcible rape, robbery, and aggravated assault. The property crime index includes burglary, larceny-theft, motor vehicle theft, and arson.

Source: Adapted from Snyder, H. (2000). *Juvenile arrests 1999.* Washington, DC: Office of Juvenile Justice and Delinquency Prevention.

## Unofficial Methods of Measuring Delinquency

Researchers have been quite persistent in their attempts to identify juvenile delinquents and to measure juvenile delinquency. The primary sources of data have been self-reports, victimization surveys, and observational studies in gang hangouts and schools. The major limitation of these methods relates to the representativeness of the individuals reported as delinquent.

### Self-Report Delinquency Studies

Self-report questionnaires were first introduced as a method of measuring delinquency by Short and Nye (1958). Several other prominent sociologists and criminologists used the self-report approach: Empey and Erickson (1966); Gold (1966, 1970); Hindelang, Hirschi, and Weis (1981); and Hirschi (1969). Some self-report studies focus on measuring the proportion of youths who have engaged in delinquent acts, asking such questions as "Have you ever stolen something?" or "Have you stolen something since you were 9 years old?"

**Table 1.6    Drug Cases in Juvenile Court: 1989, 1994, and 1998**

|  | 1989 (%) | 1994 (%) | 1998 (%) |
|---|---|---|---|
| Male | 86 | 86 | 84 |
| Female | 14 | 14 | 16 |
| *Age (years) at time of referral* | | | |
| 14 and younger | 18 | 20 | 19 |
| 15 | 22 | 23 | 21 |
| 16 | 30 | 30 | 31 |
| 17 and older | 30 | 28 | 29 |
| *Race ethnicity* | | | |
| White | 58 | 61 | 68 |
| Black | 40 | 37 | 29 |
| Other | 2 | 2 | 3 |

Source: U.S. Department of Justice, Office of Justice Programs. (2001). *Fact sheet: Drug Offenses Juvenile Court, 1989–1998*. Washington, DC: Author.

These types of studies gather data on the extent of participation in specific delinquent behaviors. Other self-report delinquency studies make inquiries about the frequency of individual involvement in delinquent behaviors over a specific period, such as within the past year or two. Studies having time bounds of 4 or more years have only limited usefulness because of memory decay and filtering of recall.

Most self-report surveys indicate that the number of youths who break the law is much greater than official statistics report. These surveys reveal that the most common juvenile offenses are truancy, alcohol abuse, shoplifting, use of false identification, fighting, marijuana use, and damaging the property of others (Farrington, 1973; Hindelang, 1973).

Some of the more striking findings of self-report studies relate to the extent of delinquency and status offenses. According to estimates of the President's Commission on Law Enforcement and Administration of Justice (1967), self-report studies indicate that the overwhelming majority of all juveniles commit delinquent and criminal acts for which they could have been adjudicated.

Erickson and Empey (1963) studied self-reported delinquency behavior among high school boys aged 15 to 17 in Provo, Utah. Using a list of 22 criminal and delinquent offenses to question the youths about their illegal activities, the researchers found that 90% of minor offenses (such as traffic violations, curfew violations, minor thefts, liquor law violations, and destroying property) went undetected. They compared the self-reported delinquency of boys who were officially nondelinquent with a group of official delinquents—those who had been processed by the court only once, those on probation, and those who were incarcerated. The results were surprising: The nondelinquents admitted to an average of almost 158 delinquent or status offense acts per youth. However, official delinquents' self-reports greatly exceeded the reports of nondelinquents: Youths with a one-time court appearance had an average of 185 delinquent acts, repeat offenders who had been on probation had an average of 855 delinquent acts, and incarcerated delinquents had an average of 1,272 delinquent acts. In sharp contrast, Williams and Gold (1972) found that "Eighty-eight percent of the teenagers in the sample confessed to committing at least one chargeable offense in the three years prior to their interview" (p. 213).

The "dark figure of crime"—the unreported delinquent acts—are difficult to determine. Self-report studies indicated that the dark or unknown figure may be more than 9 times greater than the official estimate, given that about 9 of every 10 juvenile law violations are either undetected or not officially acted upon. The overwhelming majority of juveniles have broken the law, even though their offenses are usually minor. Yet, there is a small group of chronic, violent offenders; these are the youths who habitually violate the law and, as a result, are more likely to be apprehended and formally adjudicated.

Empey (1982) offers an analogy comparing juvenile offenders to fish caught in a net in an ocean:

> The chances are small that most fish will be caught. And even when some are caught, they manage to escape or are released because they are too small. But because a few fish are much more active than others, and because they are bigger, they are caught more than once. Each time this occurs, moreover, the chances that they will escape or be thrown back decrease. At the very end, therefore, they form a very select group whose behavior clearly separates them from most of the fish still in the ocean. (p. 113)

The most important and enlightening developments in research on hidden delinquency came from the national youth surveys. Beginning in 1967, the National Institute of Mental Health (NIMH) implemented the first national survey of a representative sample of adolescents, focusing on their attitudes and behaviors, including delinquent behavior. In 1972, the national youth survey (NAYS) was repeated; in 1976, the National Institute of Juvenile Justice and Delinquency Prevention became the cosponsor of what developed into an annual survey of self-reported delinquent behavior, based on a national probability panel of teenage youths from 11 to 17 years of age (Weis, 1983).

These longitudinal, national surveys were based on a carefully drawn sample ($N = 1,725$) of adolescents from throughout the United States who were asked to report on their delinquent behavior for 5 consecutive years.

The major survey findings indicated that the overwhelming majority of American youths (11 to 17 years old) in the sample admitted that they had committed one or more juvenile offenses. In agreement with other self-report studies, the NAYS has found that the majority of youths had committed minor offenses, especially as they grew older. Notably, less than 6% of the youths in the survey (Elliot, 1983) admitted having committed one of the more serious index offenses that are listed in the FBI Uniform Crime Reports. The trends in self-reported delinquency reveal that youths in the 1980s seemed to be no more delinquent than youths in the early 1970s.

The survey found that those youths living with both natural parents reported lower delinquency rates than juveniles who came from single-parent or reconstituted families. It also found that youths who stayed in school reported less involvement in delinquency than those who dropped out. In addition, school dropouts admitted they had participated in crimes such as felony assault and theft, hard drug use, disorderly conduct, and general delinquency to a much greater extent than the in-school youths. In contrast, the higher percentages of in-school youth indicated they had participated in minor assaults, vandalism, and school delinquency (Thornberry, Moore, & Christenson, 1985). Finally, the 1978–1980 national youth surveys asked about attendance at religious services. Those youths who reported regular attendance at religious services also reported less involvement in virtually all types of delinquent behaviors.

### Trends on Illegal Drug Use and Juvenile Crime

The National Household Survey on Drug Abuse (NHSDA) collects self-report data from a representative sample of almost 69,000 youths 12 to 17 years of age in all 50 states on current use of illegal drugs (Substance Abuse and Mental Health Services Administration, 2002). Highlights of the report indicate that 10.8% of youths in the 12 to 17 age group abused drugs in 2001, compared with 9.7% for the 12 months of 2000. There was a dramatic rise in the number of persons indicating that they had used Ecstasy (MDMA) in 2001 from the estimates in 2000; there were 8.1 million persons who tried it in 2001 compared with 6.5 million in 2000. The abuse of OxyContin for nonmedical reasons increased more than 400% from 221,000 in 1999 to 957,000 in 2001. In addition, approximately 10.1 million individuals in the 12 to 20 age group used alcohol during 2001; almost 6.8 million were binge drinkers, and more than 2 million (6%) were chronic drinkers.

The abuse of crack, cocaine, marijuana, and alcohol escalated in the 1980s and resulted in a large number of juveniles being arrested and adjudicated for the sale and distribution of narcotics, as well as liquor law violations. Then in the second half of the 1990s, adjudications of juveniles for drug-related offenses declined. Now in the early 21st century we are witnessing abuse of methamphetamines, ice, crystal, speed, OxyContin, and Ecstasy. Heavy drug use can destroy the brain functioning and lives of adolescent and young adult addicts. Specifically, heavy use of cocaine or methamphetamines often leads to hallucinations, delusions, psychotic episodes, suicide attempts, and juvenile violence. Possession, sale, manufacture, and distribution of illegal substances are criminal offenses. In addition, adolescent drug users frequently commit burglaries, thefts, and robberies and prostitute themselves to support their drug cravings. For a detailed discussion of the juvenile drug abuse trends and the connection between youth substance abuse and crime, see chapter 3.

The most comprehensive compendium of official and unofficial criminal justice statistics is the *Sourcebook of Criminal Justice Statistics*, published each year by the Hindelang Criminal Justice Research Center at the State University of New York at Albany (Maguire & Pastore, 2001, 2002). This huge volume includes FBI Uniform Crime Reports, Bureau of Justice Statistics reports and bulletins, OJJDP reports, NCVS tables, and large-scale national surveys of high school students on unreported crimes, such as the Pride school confidential questionnaire (see Table 1.7).

**Table 1.7**  **Students Reporting Problem Behaviors by Grade Level of Respondent, 1999–2000**

|  | Never (%) | Seldom (%) | Sometimes (%) | Often (%) | A lot (%) |
|---|---|---|---|---|---|
| Have you been in trouble with the police? | 77.6 | 13.2 | 5.4 | 1.9 | 2.0 |
| Grades 6 to 8 | 81.0 | 10.7 | 4.7 | 1.7 | 1.8 |
| Grades 9 to 12 | 73.9 | 15.8 | 6.1 | 2.0 | 2.2 |
| 12th grade | 72.5 | 17.5 | 6.3 | 1.7 | 2.1 |
| Do you take part in gang activities? | 90.8 | 4.1 | 2.3 | 1.0 | 1.7 |
| Grades 6 to 8 | 90.8 | 4.2 | 2.4 | 1.0 | 1.5 |
| Grades 9 to 12 | 90.7 | 4.0 | 2.3 | 1.0 | 1.9 |
| 12th grade | 92.0 | 3.2 | 2.0 | 0.8 | 2.0 |
| Do you use drugs at home? | 89.9 | 3.9 | 2.9 | 1.5 | 1.8 |
| Grades 6 to 8 | 94.3 | 2.4 | 1.6 | 0.7 | 1.0 |
| Grades 9 to 12 | 85.1 | 5.6 | 4.4 | 2.3 | 2.7 |
| 12th grade | 82.9 | 6.4 | 4.8 | 2.6 | 3.3 |
| Have you threatened to harm a teacher? | 93.4 | 3.8 | 1.5 | 0.5 | 0.9 |
| Grades 6 to 8 | 94.3 | 3.3 | 1.3 | 0.4 | 0.7 |
| Grades 9 to 12 | 92.4 | 4.3 | 1.6 | 0.6 | 1.1 |
| 12th grade | 92.7 | 4.0 | 1.5 | 0.5 | 1.3 |

Note: These data are from a survey of 6th- through 12th-grade students conducted between September 1999 and June 2000 by PRIDE Surveys. Participating schools are sent the PRIDE questionnaire with explicit instructions for administering the anonymous, self-report survey. Schools that administer the PRIDE questionnaire do so voluntarily or in compliance with a school district or state request. For the 1999–2000 academic year, survey results are based on students from 24 states. To prevent any one state from having a disproportionate influence on the summary results, random samples of students were drawn from those states where disproportionately large numbers of students were surveyed. Therefore, no state comprises more than 10% of the sample. The results presented are based on a sample consisting of 114,318 students drawn

Note: Percents may not add to 100 because of rounding.

Green, KY: PRIDE Surveys, 2000 (mimeographed), p. 66, Table 6.15; p. 67; p. 69, Table 6.24; p. 70, Tables 6.25 and 6.26. Table adapted by *Sourcebook* staff. Reprinted by permission. *Sourcebook of criminal justice statistics*. (2000). Washington, DC: U.S. Government Printing Office.

*Victimization Surveys*

Victimization studies have been completed in a large number of cities through-out the United States. These studies have been conducted as joint efforts by the U.S. Bureau of Justice Statistics and the Bureau of the Census. The best known victimization survey is the NCVS, a massive, annual, house-to-house survey of a random sample of 60,000 households and 136,000 individuals (Flanagan & McCloud, 1983). The NCVS provides annual estimates of the total number of crimes committed by both adult and juvenile offenders. The six types of crime measured are rape, robbery, assault, household burglary, personal and household larceny, and motor vehicle theft. Based on the survey data, it has been estimated that 40 million serious crimes occur each year in the United States. The NCVS estimate is 4 times greater than that reported in the FBI Uniform Crime Reports. These data indicate that underreporting is far more pervasive than was generally recognized before the completion of the national victimization surveys (Roberts, 1998).

This survey also provided estimates of the juvenile offense rates for a limited number of crimes: rape, robbery, assault, and personal larceny. His-torically, Laub's (1983) analysis indicated that the rates of delinquency for the years 1973 to 1981 remained relatively stable. In addition, there has been very little change in the types of persons who are victimized by juveniles. For the most part, juvenile perpetrators victimized other youths, rather than adults; males were the victims twice as frequently as females. Figure 1.6 graphically shows some of the changes in victimization rates in recent years.

Figure 1.6 shows the percent of victimization committed by juveniles from 1973 to 1997. Over the 25-year period, robbery was the most common vic-timization committed by juveniles. From 1973 to 1987, there was a slow de-

**Figure 1.6     Percent of Victimization Committed by Juveniles**

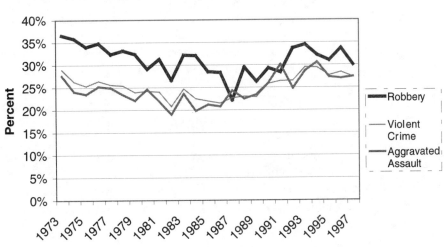

crease in the percentage of robbery. However, this trend was short-lived, as the percentage slowly and inconsistently increased once again. Although the robbery percentage increased, the rate in 1999 was still lower than the initial 1973 rate.

Violent crime and aggravated assault saw trends similar to the robbery percentage. Both of these variables saw slow and choppy declines in their rates, only to see them once again return to their original starting level. This graph shows how the victimizations committed by juveniles, although sometimes fluctuating, overall stay fairly consistent, with robbery offenses the most likely to fluctuate, and aggravated assault and violent crime staying fairly equal in their percentage rates.

The findings related to the extent of violence among juvenile offenders were that (a) there was very little change in the use of guns, knives, and other weapons during the 9-year period; (b) only 27% of the juvenile crimes involved weapons use, contradicting the view that most juvenile offenders use a deadly weapon; and (c) the number of victims who required hospitalization in the aftermath of a delinquent act seemed to remain stable over the 9-year period.

Recent longitudinal research (Loeber, Kalb, & Huizinga, 2001) based on 4,000 participants who were interviewed for a decade in Rochester, New York; Denver, Colorado; and Pittsburgh, Pennsylvania indicated that a sizable proportion of male and female youths reported being crime victims. For example, in Pittsburgh, approximately 11% of males between 16.5 and 18.5 years of age sustained serious injuries when they were assaulted or robbed. In Denver, approximately 20% of males and 10% of females indicated that they had been victims of crime between the ages of 13 and 17. At both sites, African American males were considerably more likely to be victims. The overwhelming majority of the juvenile crime victims in the two research sites exhibited the following victimization risk factors: involved in gang or group fights, carrying a weapon, selling drugs, committing a serious assault, and frequently associating and interacting with delinquent peers. In addition, 50% of males who were violent juvenile offenders were also violently victimized, compared with only 10% of their nondelinquent peers. The implication is that being a victim of a violent crime at a young age may lead to becoming an offender, particularly retaliatory acts of violence in schools against cliques and gangs (Loeber, Kalb, & Huizinga, 2001). Finally, more data are critically needed concerning juvenile victims who are not participating in high-risk behaviors but who visit or live in areas where gangs congregate, so that safety precautions and protocols can be developed for this vulnerable group of youths.

Although juvenile delinquency and victimization rates seem to have stabilized during the current decade, millions of adolescents continue to become involved in juvenile delinquency each year, and it continues to be a complex and difficult social problem with no easy solutions.

## Summary

Every youth who violates the law is not labeled a juvenile delinquent. Many either escape detection entirely or, when apprehended by the local police, receive a strict lecture or warning and then are taken home. Most authorities do not consider law-breaking youths to be juvenile delinquents unless they are officially processed through the juvenile court and adjudicated a delinquent.

Youths can be referred to the juvenile court for three types of offenses:

☐ Delinquency offenses: illegal acts that are considered crimes whether committed by an adult or a juvenile (e.g., aggravated assault, arson, burglary, drug-related offenses, theft, and rape)

☐ Status offenses: deviant acts or misbehavior that, if engaged in by an adult, would not be considered crimes (e.g., truancy, incorrigibility, and running away from home)

☐ Dependency cases: a documented pattern of child neglect, physical abuse, or sexual abuse and identification of a minor needing foster care or other residential placement outside the home

For status offenders, many states have separate legislation that views these juveniles as individuals "in need of supervision." An array of crisis intervention services, runaway shelters, youth service bureaus, addiction treatment programs, day treatment programs, and family counseling programs have been developed to serve these youths (Roberts, 1998; Springer, 2001).

This chapter laid the groundwork for an examination of the field of juvenile justice. This was done by presenting legalistic, sociological, and criminological information that focuses on the nature of the juvenile justice system and its subsystems, the definition of the terms *juvenile delinquency* and *status offenses*, and juvenile justice processing, including referrals by police and schools to juvenile court, intake decisions and dispositions, juvenile court judges' decisions and dispositions, and official and unofficial trends and statistics on the extent of juvenile delinquency in the United States.

As defined in this chapter, *delinquency* refers to a juvenile who has been apprehended for any activity that is a violation of a state juvenile code. The juvenile justice system is concerned with caring for, controlling, and rehabilitating these juvenile law violators. A number of the chapters in this book examine the policies, agencies, programs, treatment alternatives, and services that have been developed to control and rehabilitate juvenile offenders. Emphasis is placed on examining the juvenile offender treatment programs that have reduced recidivism based on consistent longitudinal research.

███████ **Discussion Questions**

**1** Define *juvenile delinquency*.

**2** Compare and contrast the terms *juvenile delinquency offenses* and *status offenses*.

**3** Divide the class into two groups for a debate. Ask one group to adopt and defend a conservative perspective and the other group to adopt and defend a progressive perspective on the following issues:

☐ Should state legislatures authorize a waiver of jurisdiction to process juvenile offenders in adult criminal court who have been accused of brutal crimes and are over the age of 14?

☐ Should the juvenile court retain jurisdiction over habitual status offenders, or should they be diverted to a continuum of community social services?

**4** Using official juvenile court statistics, discuss the recent trends in juvenile delinquency.

**5** According to H. Snyder's recent report, identify and discuss what happened to the juvenile arrest rates between 1994 and 2000.

**6** List and describe the functions of the juvenile and criminal justice agencies in your county or city that have primary responsibility for handling juvenile status offenders and juvenile delinquents.

███████ **References**

Becker, H. S. (1963). *Outsiders: Studies in the sociology of deviance.* New York: Free Press.

Blumstein, A. (1967). Systems analysis and the criminal justice system. *Annals of the American Academy of Political and Social Science,* Vol. 474.

Boisvert, M. J., & Wells, R. (1980). Toward a rational policy on status offenders. *Social Work, 25,* 230–234.

Brooks, R. W., & Jeon, S. H. (2001). Race, income and perceptions of the U.S. court system. *Behavioral Sciences and the Law, 19,* 249–264.

Bureau of Justice Statistics. (2000). *Effects of NIBRS on crime statistics: BJS special report.* Washington, DC: U.S. Government Printing Office.

Empey, L. T. (1982). *American delinquency: Its meaning and construction.* Chicago: Dorsey.

Empey, L. T., & Erickson, M. L. (1966). Hidden delinquency and social status. *Social Forces, 44,* 546–554.

Erickson, M. L., & Empey, L. T. (1963). Court records, undetected delinquency, and decision making. *Journal of Criminal Law, Criminology, and Police Science, 54,* 456–469.

Farrington, D. P. (1973). Self-reports of deviant behavior. Predictive and stable? *Journal of Criminal Law and Criminology, 44,* 99–111.

Flanagan, T. J., & McCloud, M. (1983). *Sourcebook of criminal justice statistics, 1982.* Washington, DC: U.S. Department of Justice.

Gold, M. (1966). Undetected delinquent behavior. *Journal of Research in Crime and Delinquency, 3,* 27–46.

Gold, M. (1970). *Delinquent behavior in an American city.* Belmont, CA: Brooks/Cole.

Gold, M., & Reimer, D. J. (1974). Changing patterns of delinquent behavior among Americans 13–16 years old: 1967–1972. *National survey of youth,* Report No. 1. Ann Arbor: Institute for Social Research, University of Michigan.

Hamparian, D., et al. (1982) *Major issues in juvenile justice information and training, youth in adult courts: Between two worlds.* Washington, DC: U.S. Department of Justice.

Hindelang, M. J. (1973). Causes of delinquency: A partial replication and extension. *Social Problems, 20*(4), 471–487.

Hindelang, M. J., Hirschi, T., & Weiss, J. (1981). *Measuring delinquency.* Beverly Hills, CA: Sage.

Hirschi, T. (1969). *Causes of delinquency.* Berkeley: University of California Press.

Huizinga, D., & Elliot, D. S. (1984). *Self-reported measures of delinquency and crime: Methodological issues and comparative findings.* Boulder, CO: Behavioral Research Institute.

Laub, J. H. (1983). *Juvenile criminal behavior in the United States: An analysis of an offender and victim characteristics.* Albany, NY: The Michael J. Hindelang Criminal Justice Research Center, State University of New York at Albany.

Lemert, E. M. (1971). *Instead of court: Division in juvenile justice.* Chevy Chase, MD: National Institute of Mental Health, Center for the Studies of Crime and Delinquency.

Loeber, R., Kalb, L., & Huizinga, D. (2001). *Juvenile delinquency and serious injury victimization* (Juvenile Justice Bulletin, NCJ No. 188676). Washington, DC: Office of Juvenile Justice and Delinquency Prevention.

Maguire, K., & Pastore, A. L. (Eds.). (2001). *Sourcebook of criminal justice statistics: 2000.* Albany, NY: The Hindelang Criminal Justice Research Center, State University of New York at Albany (Funded by the Bureau of Justice Statistics of the U.S. Department of Justice. Washington, DC: U.S. Government Printing Office).

Maguire, K., & Pastore, A. L. (Eds.). (2002). *Sourcebook of criminal justice statistics: 2001.* Albany, NY: The Hindelang Criminal Justice Research Center, State University of New York at Albany (Funded by the Bureau of Justice Statistics of the U.S. Department of Justice. Washington, DC: U.S. Government Printing Office).

Prescott, P. S. (1981). *The child savers.* New York: Alfred A. Knopf.

President's Commission on Law Enforcement and Administration of Justice. (1967). *Task force report: Juvenile delinquency and youth crime.* Washington, DC: U.S. Government Printing Office.

Puzzanchera, C., Stahl, A., Finnegin, T., Snyder, H., Poole, R., & Tierney, N. (2001). *Juvenile court statistics, 1998.* Washington, DC: Office of Juvenile Justice and Delinquency Prevention, U.S. Government Printing Office.

Puzzanchera, C., Stahl, A., Finnegan, T., Snyder, H., Poole, R., & Tierney, N. (2001). *Juvenile court statistics, 1998.* Washington, DC: Office of Juvenile Justice and Delinquency Prevention, U.S. Government Printing Office.

Roberts, A. R. (1987). *Runaways and nonrunaways.* Chicago: Dorsey.

Roberts, A. R. (1998). *Juvenile justice: Policies, programs and services.* Chicago: Nelson-Hall.

Robinson, S. M. (1960). *Juvenile delinquency: Its nature and control.* New York: Holt, Rinehart & Winston.

Schur, E. (1973). *Radical nonintervention: Rethinking the delinquency problem.* Englewood Cliffs, NJ: Prentice-Hall.

Sherman, L., et al. (1998). *What works, what doesn't work, and what is promising.* Washington, DC: National Institute of Justice, U.S. Government Printing Office.

Short, J. F. Jr., & Nye, F. I. (1958). Extent of unrecorded delinquency, tentative conclusions. *Journal of Criminal Law, 49,* 296–302.

Snyder, H. N. (2000). *Juvenile arrests 1999.* Washington, DC: Office of Juvenile Justice and Delinquency Prevention, Office of Justice Programs.

Snyder, H. N. (2002). *Juvenile arrests 2000.* Washington, DC: Office of Juvenile Justice and Delinquency Prevention, Office of Justice Programs.

Springer, D. W. (2001). Runaway adolescents: Today's Huckleberry Finn crisis. *Brief Treatment and Crisis Intervention, 1*(2), 131–152.

Stahl, A., Finnegan, T., & Kang, W. (2002). *Easy access to juvenile court statistics: 1990–1999* [Data analysis and presentation package]. Pittsburgh, PA: National Center for Juvenile Justice.

Substance Abuse and Mental Health Services Administration. (2002). *The national household survey on drug abuse: Preliminary findings 2002.* Rockville, MD: SAMSHA, Office of Applied Studies.

Thornberry, T. P., Moore, M., & Christenson, R. L. (1985). The effect of dropping out of high school on subsequent criminal behavior. *Criminology, 23,* 3–18.

U.S. Children's Bureau. (1967). *Juvenile court statistics, 1966* (Statistical Series 90). Washington, DC: U.S. Government Printing Office.

U.S. Children's Bureau. (1973). *Juvenile court statistics, 1972.* Washington, DC: U.S. Government Printing Office.

U.S. Department of Justice. (1983). *Crime in the United States, 1982: Uniform crime reports.* Washington, DC: U.S. Government Printing Office.

U.S. Department of Justice. (1984). *Sourcebook of criminal justice statistics.* Washington, DC: U.S. Government Printing Office.

U.S. Department of Justice. (1985). *Crime in the United States, 1984: Uniform crime reports.* Washington, DC: U.S. Government Printing Office.

U.S. Department of Justice. (2001). *Sourcebook on criminal justice statistics 2000.* Washington, DC: U.S. Government Printing Office.

U.S. Department of Justice, Federal Bureau of Investigation. (1976). *Crime in the United States, 1975: Uniform crime reports.* Washington, DC: U.S. Government Printing Office.

U.S. Department of Justice, National Criminal Justice Information and Statistics Service. (1974) *Children in custody: A report on the juvenile detention and correctional facility census of 1971.* Washington, DC: U.S. Government Printing Office.

Weis, J. G. (1983). Crime statistics: Reporting systems and methods. In *Encyclopedia of crime and justice* (Vol. 1). New York: Free Press.

Williams, J. R., & Gold, M. (1972). From delinquent behavior to official delinquency. *Social Problems, 20,* 209–229.

Williams, K., & Cohen, M. I. (1993). *Determinants of disproportionate representation of minority juveniles in secure settings: Final report.* Fairfax, VA: Fairfax Juvenile and Domestic Relations District Court.

Youth, Development and Delinquency Prevention Administration. (1973). *The challenge of youth service bureaus.* Washington, DC: U.S. Government Printing Office.

# 2 Juvenile Justice Policy

## Current Trends and 21st-Century Issues

C. Aaron McNeece and Sherry Jackson

On October 29, 1997, 11-year-old Nathaniel Abraham and a White playmate were firing a .22-caliber rifle at trees. An 18-year-old Black youth, Ronnie Greene Jr., was hit by a bullet and died. In November of 1997, Nathaniel Abraham, a Black child with an IQ of 75, was prosecuted as an adult for a crime he had committed at the age of 11 years. He became the youngest child to be tried as an adult in the 20th century (Merlo, 2000). At the trial Nathaniel was so small that his legs couldn't reach the floor as he sat in the courtroom. Unaware of the seriousness of the charges, he kept asking, "When can I go home?" (Porter, 2002). An expert marksman testified that the chances of anyone being able to hit a target at that distance with a rifle without a stock, as in this case, were nearly impossible. A forensics expert's report stated that the trajectory of the bullet that killed Ronnie Greene Jr. could not have come directly from the spot where Nathaniel was standing. Evidence that members of a local gang were firing a .22-caliber weapon at the same time and in the same area where Ronnie Greene was killed was never presented to the jury. Although the presiding judge called the law under which he was charged "fundamentally flawed," Nathaniel Abraham was tried and convicted in adult criminal court and will be incarcerated until he is 21 years of age and then released, whether he is rehabilitated or not (Goodman, 2001). Nathaniel Abraham was not so much the victim of our "justice" system as the victim of a continuing trend of retribution and punishment for juvenile offenders, a trend that has been reinforced by a number of high-profile, widely publicized juvenile crimes.

On April 20, 1999, Eric Harris and Dylan Klebold arrived at Columbine High School in Littleton, Colorado. Harris spoke to one student, warning him to leave the school. Shortly thereafter, Harris and Klebold unloaded an arsenal of weapons, wounded 20 people, and killed 15 others—including themselves (CNN, 2003). Seven highly publicized school shootings have occurred since the fall of 1997, including the terrible tragedy at Columbine High. At the same time, statistics from state and federal agencies show clearly that juvenile violent crime is decreasing (Snyder, 1999). Yet punitiveness toward juvenile offenders is clearly becoming harsher. According to Woolard, Fondacaro, and Slobogin (2001), "The common wisdom in juvenile justice policy is that rehabilitation, if not dead, is in serious decline . . . the public appetite for retribution and punishment is growing" (p. 13).

Between 1992 and 1997, 45 states modified state laws and juvenile procedures in order to make their juvenile justice systems more punitive (Snyder & Sickmund, 1999). Texas recently modified its sentencing structure to provide a continuum that bridges the juvenile and adult systems. Sentences that begin in the juvenile system may be completed in the adult system (Mears, 2000). Louisiana passed a law that requires juveniles who reach age 17 while incarcerated in a juvenile facility to be automatically transferred to an adult institution (Ellis & Sowers, 2001). California voters overwhelmingly endorsed

Proposition 21, which allows a 14-year-old juvenile to be tried as an adult without judicial authorization (Nieves, 2000).

In the following discussion of trends in juvenile offenses and case dispositions, bear in mind that we are dealing only with estimates that are based on officially reported offenses. The official cases are those that proceed beyond police encounters with juveniles. In cities such as Tallahassee, where police estimate they spend 90% of their time dealing with juvenile crime, there is a tendency to ignore misdemeanors and concentrate on the more serious felony offenses, such as the murder of a tourist. When there are inadequate personnel and resources to deal with serious juvenile felony offenses, juvenile misdemeanors are ignored. The majority of police encounters with juveniles and the overwhelming bulk of juvenile crimes are never recorded in any official statistics. In most cases, only the juvenile who has established a history of relatively serious delinquent behavior will be referred to the court.

## ◼ Major Policy Shifts

Three major shifts in federal juvenile policy have occurred since the 1960s (Ohlin, 1983). Community organization models were used in the early 1960s by federal policy makers to foster local responsibility for juvenile misbehavior. Unfortunately, these programs were generally not successful. The second shift in policy came from a number of presidential commissions studying the problems of crime and violence. In 1967 the first of these commissions recommended dramatic policy innovations such as the decriminalization of status offenses, the diversion of juvenile offenders from official court processing, and the deinstitutionalization of juvenile offenders. The Juvenile Justice and Delinquency Prevention Act (JJDPA) of 1974 was the culmination of this policy shift (McNeece, 1980). Although the bill was opposed by both the Nixon and Ford administrations, it passed in the House of Representatives by a vote of 329 to 20, and it received only one negative vote in the Senate. The intent of this bill was to deinstitutionalize status offenders, provide additional funds to communities to improve delinquency prevention programs, establish new mechanisms for dealing with runaway youths, and remove juveniles from adult jails and lockup facilities (Bartol & Bartol, 1989).

A third major change in juvenile justice policy began in the mid-1970s with a federal shift toward a "law and order" philosophy. Although basically preventive in its approach, the result of the JJDPA legislation soon became more controlling. The act was amended in 1977, partly as a response to alleged increases in school violence and vandalism, to allow more flexibility in the deinstitutionalization process. Throughout the late 1970s, an "iron-fisted" punitive approach to nonstatus offenders emerged (Hellum, 1979), and a growing fear of crime pushed the juvenile justice system toward more repressive action (Ohlin, 1983).

The Reagan administration targeted serious or repetitive juvenile offenders for special attention in 1981, once more shifting the system in the direction of control. In 1984 the National Advisory Committee for Juvenile Justice and Delinquency Prevention recommended that grants to states for the continued deinstitutionalization of status offenders not be renewed. The Reagan administration believed that for too long the juvenile justice system had been overly concerned with the protection of juvenile offenders at the expense of society and its victims (Bartol & Bartol, 1989). This new "get tough" approach was evident in the Comprehensive Crime Control Act of 1984.

Since 1992, most states have adopted tougher laws regarding the prosecution of serious, violent, and chronic juvenile offenders. Such laws lower the age at which a juvenile can be transferred to adult court, expand the list of crimes for which a juvenile can be transferred, and make the process for transferring the juvenile easier (Mears, 2000; Office of Juvenile Justice and Delinquency Prevention [OJJDP], 1996; Snyder & Sickmund, 1999).

## ■ Diversion and Deinstitutionalization Programs

The enthusiastic application of "diversion" programs actually has resulted in the creation of a new semilegal, semiwelfare bureaucracy, which has broadened the effective social control mechanisms of the juvenile justice system without paying much attention to the legal rights of children (Blomberg, 1983; Empey & Stafford, 1991). Although many juvenile offenses have been decriminalized and separate dispositional alternatives for status offenders have been created, it is difficult to say that children are being treated much differently now than they were before, apart from changes in the labels they now wear. Approximately half of all the juveniles in institutions prior to the passage of the Juvenile Justice and Delinquency Prevention Act of 1974 were status offenders. The implementation of this act resulted in a relatively small reduction in public institutional populations (McNeece, 1980). The number of status offenders in private institutions increased substantially between 1979 and 1989, roughly equivalent to the drop in the number of status offenders in public institutions (OJJDP, 1991). The bottom line is that there has been little or no change in the number of juvenile status offenders in custody, despite two decades of "reform." A 1985 review (U.S. Dept. of Justice, OJJDP) of more than 70 empirical studies of status-offender deinstitutionalization in 19 states concluded that "the failure of implementation has occurred both for diversion and deinstitutionalization" at both the local and state levels (p. 2). Even more disturbing was the finding that even where it had "succeeded," deinstitutionalizing status offenders seemed to make little or no difference in the ultimate outcomes for juveniles. Compared with status offenders who were *not* deinstitutionalized, 57.14% of the deinstitutionalized youths experienced no change in their recidivism rates, and equal numbers (21.43% each) experienced higher and lower recidivism rates (U.S. Dept. of Justice, OJJDP, 1985, p. 7).

Most states have at least one loophole that allows the continued incarceration of status offenders; the 1980 amendments to the Juvenile Justice Act permit juveniles who have run away from valid court placements to be charged with contempt of court, a delinquent act (U.S. Dept. of Justice, OJJDP, 1985), which may result in the offender being reclassified as a juvenile delinquent. Official statistics show that the number of juveniles held in public institutions did decrease between 1971 and 1977 (Bureau of Justice Statistics, 1981), but there was a corresponding increase in private correctional facilities, residential treatment programs, and psychiatric units of hospitals to serve juvenile offenders. Although confinement to traditional long-term public facilities did decline somewhat, the use of private facilities offset those declines (Lerman, 1980). Between 1974 and 1983, the total number of status offenders held in secure facilities increased from 79,017 to 80,097 (U.S. Dept. of Justice, OJJDP, 1985, p. 13). A subsequent report by OJJDP (U.S. Dept. of Justice, 1991), *Juveniles Taken into Custody*, indicates that the trend has continued, with declines in the number of status offenders in public facilities offset by increases in the number of such youths in private facilities (p. 6).

## ■ Jail Removal Programs

In 1973 Dr. Rosemary Sarri, one of the nation's foremost experts on juvenile justice, testified to the Senate Subcommittee to Investigate Juvenile Delinquency that:

> An accurate portrait of the extent of juvenile jailing in the United States does not exist. Furthermore, it is difficult to develop one because of the lack of reliable and comparable information from the cities, counties, states and federal government. (U.S. Congress, Senate, 1973)

In the winter of 1973, Senator Birch Bayh, chair of the subcommittee, introduced the Juvenile Justice and Delinquency Prevention Act of 1973, which contained a strong provision on jailing juveniles. Juveniles "shall not be detained or confined in any institutions in which adult persons convicted of a crime or awaiting trial on criminal charges are incarcerated" (U.S. Congress, Senate, 1974). However, the bill that eventually passed was considerably weakened. A compromise allowed juveniles to be confined in jails so long as they were kept separate from adult prisoners.

In 1980 President Carter signed the reauthorization of the Juvenile Justice and Delinquency Prevention Act into law. This revised act contained a historic amendment mandating the removal of juveniles from adult jails. Only those juveniles who are tried as adults for criminal felonies are allowed to be detained or incarcerated in adult jails. The OJJDP focused attention on rural jails, which were often the only place police could detain juveniles. The degree of success varied considerably from state to state. In Colorado the number of juveniles admitted to adult jails decreased from 6,117 in 1980 to 1,522 in 1984 (Schwartz, 1992). On the other hand, New York and Florida reported a 400% increase in jailed juveniles between 1978 and 1983. New York and Florida accounted for an astounding 36% of all juveniles in jail on June 30, 1983 (U.S. Dept. of Justice, OJJDP, 1985). Alaska, one of the more successful states, reduced the detention of status offenders in adult jails by 78% between 1987 and 1988.

However, the Office of Juvenile Justice and Delinquency Prevention (1991) reported that the percentage of jail inmates who were juveniles rose from 1.3% in 1983 to 1.5% in 1989. By June 30, 1992, an estimated 0.63% of jail inmates were juveniles (U.S. Dept. of Justice, Bureau of Justice Statistics [BJS], 1993), a dramatic decrease in just 3 years. In 1990 the National Coalition of State Juvenile Justice Advisory Groups concluded that the jail removal program had been generally successful (OJJDP, 1991). The latest available BJS data indicate an average daily juvenile population of 2,527 in adult jails (U.S. Dept. of Justice, BJS, 1993). However, "the proportion of juveniles who were housed in adult jails in accordance with [the 1980 amendment] is not available" (p. 10). The OJJDP annual report for the year 2000 indicates that only 11 states were in full compliance with the jail and lockup removal program, but 38 others had only minor exceptions to full compliance.

Perhaps the most important impact of this legislation is that states that are out of compliance with its juvenile jail removal mandates can be sued.

## ■ "New Age" Juvenile Justice: Mediation, Restorative Justice, Acupuncture, Boot Camps, Drug Treatment, and Privatization

Diversion and deinstitutionalization, whether they have worked or not, are old news. Dozens of new approaches to the problems of juvenile delinquency have been introduced to the juvenile justice system within the past few years. The oldest of these "new" ideas is probably mediation, which has been around since the development of community dispute resolution centers in the 1950s (Ray, 1992). Mediation seems to have had a rebirth within the past decade, and recent evaluations indicate that outcomes are just as desirable as more costly alternatives (Umbreit, Coates, & Kalanj, 1994). In some cases, juveniles are mandated by the court to participate in a mediation program involving the victim(s). In other cases victims and juvenile offenders are offered an option of mediation as an alternative to formal court processing. Juveniles participating in a mediation program were more likely to pay restitution and less likely to recidivate than those offenders in other programs (Umbreit & Coates, 1993).

Restorative justice is closely linked with mediation. It emphasizes three goals: (a) identifying the obligation created by the juvenile's offense and en-suring that he or she is held responsible for it (accountability), (b) returning the offender to the community competent to interact in a successful prosocial manner (competence), and (c) ensuring that the community is not further injured by the juvenile's future delinquent behavior (public safety) (Ellis & Sowers, 2001).

Boot camps experienced a decade of political popularity as a promising new treatment option, with millions of dollars set aside for such programs in the Violent Crime Control Act of 1994. Boot camps all follow much the same regimen. Offenders rise early for drill, rigorous exercise, and obstacle courses. Their routine is characterized by harsh, summary discipline, a rigid dress code, and frequent inspections. Almost all require some drug treatment, education, and psychological counseling (Marlette, 1991). Despite the early enthusiasm for boot camps, recent research indicates that they are no more effective than the more traditional institutional approaches (Zhang, 2001).

Many studies have indicated that many of the factors associated with de-linquency also are predictive of drug use among adolescents (Hawkins, Cata-lano, & Miller, 1992). This suggests, of course, that drug abuse intervention and treatment programs are sorely needed in the juvenile justice system. Un-fortunately, local governments frequently lack the resources to effectively treat juveniles with substance abuse problems. In many cases juvenile justice per-sonnel do not even have the assessment tools needed to determine the severity of drug use among clients they serve (Stone, 1990). Among those programs most often recommended for drug-involved juvenile offenders are (a) social skills training, (b) family therapy, (c) case management, and (d) posttreatment supports such as self-help groups, relapse prevention, and aftercare (Jenson, 1998).

Acupuncture is one of the more recent and more controversial treatment options for drug-involved juvenile offenders. The theory is that acupuncture, generally in the ear, stimulates the production of a beta-endorphin that reduces the client's craving for drugs. It is much more likely to be used with adults or "youthful offenders" than with juveniles, and there is little evidence of its ef-fectiveness with either juveniles or adults (Springer, McNeece, & Arnold, 2003).

An increasing trend in the justice system, for both juveniles and adults, is the privatization of services. We now have "rent-a-cops" employed by private corporations and homeowners' associations, "rent-a-judges" used in some types of civil disputes and mediation procedures, offenders housed in privately owned jails and prisons, and treatment services for offenders, purchased from private corporations (Bowman, Hakim, & Seidenstat, 1992). Some fear that public accountability for justice system programs may suffer through privati-zation. Others fear the danger of sacrificing rehabilitation and treatment goals to the overriding concerns of cost efficiency within a completely privatized system (McNeece, 1995). Private for-profit companies currently operate secure juvenile facilities in 23 states and the District of Columbia (Building Blocks for Youth, 2003). It does appear that privatization has contributed to the problem of lack of coordination in services for juvenile offenders (Ellis & Sowers, 2001).

## ■ Delinquency Prevention Programs

The 1992 amendments to the Juvenile Justice and Delinquency Prevention Act of 1974 (P.L. 93-415) also expanded the funding for delinquency prevention programs. By 1996, more than 230 local governments were awarded grants for "community prevention." Common goals for all of these communities included community mobilization, assessment and planning, initiation of prevention efforts, and institutionalization and monitoring of prevention programs (OJJDP, 1996). Whether this represents a paradigm shift in the overall get-tough, law enforcement–oriented delinquency policy remains to be seen. Although generally discredited by recent research, the nation's D.A.R.E. (Drug Abuse Resistance Education) programs seem to remain very popular with schools, law enforcement, and parents. However, recent criticisms have led to an overhaul of the D.A.R.E. curriculum, and many school districts are looking for alternatives (McNeece & DiNitto, 2003).

## ■ "Just Desserts" in Juvenile Justice

Certain policy reforms have spilled over into the juvenile justice system from the adult criminal justice system. More than a decade ago, the state of Washington adopted a determinate sentencing policy for juvenile offenders. Under the policy, juvenile offenders are sentenced to a specific term of incarceration related to the severity of the offense. The attempt is to "make the punishment fit the crime" (Sertill, 1980). This concept obviously is not congruent with the rehabilitative ideal so prevalent in our juvenile justice system, but reformers believe it will be more equitable and just. Unfortunately, other states have followed suit (Ellis & Sowers, 2001; Mears, 2000; Merlo, 2000).

Such changes may also reflect a general sense of frustration and powerlessness in dealing with juvenile offenders. Even worse, they may also indicate a shift in the public mood to favoring punishment rather than rehabilitation. Evidence of this shift is reflected in the policy changes mentioned earlier, with 45 states making changes in their statutes to make it easier to place juveniles in the adult criminal justice system (Merlo, 2000). Further evidence of this mood is found in trends in case dispositions for juvenile offenders throughout the nation. The proportion of juvenile cases processed formally increased from 49.8% in 1990 to 57.8% 2000 (see Table 2.4). The proportion of cases resulting in an adjudication (found "delinquent") increased from 30.0% in 1990 to 38.3% in 2000 (see Table 2.3). While the proportion of waivers to adult court dropped slightly (see Table 2.6), the overall number of children placed in the adult criminal justice system grew geometrically because of new laws allowing prosecutors to file charges directly in criminal court. One organization (Building Blocks for Youth [BBY], 2003) estimates that 85% of the decisions to prosecute juveniles as adults are made by prosecutors, not judges. In addition, 82% of youths charged in adult court were minority youths. According to Amnesty International (1998), as many as 200,000 youths under age 18 are processed in adult criminal court annually. Of those, 180,000 are from 13 states that set the upper age of juvenile jurisdiction at 15 or 16 years, and the great majority of the others are from states that allow prosecutorial discretion in charging children as adults. At every stage of processing, minority youths are overrepresented and treated more harshly than other youths (BBY, 2003; Krisberg, 1992; Snyder & Sickmund, 1999), especially those accused of drug-related offenses (see Table 2.8). Obviously, the nation is in no mood to tolerate juvenile crime or to provide a great deal of new funding for treatment or rehabilitation programs. Indeed, punishment seems to be increasingly more severe.

## ■ Due Process

Beginning in the 1960s, "the legal foundations of the juvenile justice system began to unravel completely" (Butts & Mears, 2001, p. 173). Since the beginning of the juvenile court movement at the turn of the century, disparities in the legal rights accorded to children and adults have been tolerated. The less rigorous standards applied to juveniles were justified as being in the child's best interest. Children were also believed to have substantially different constitutional rights than adults. Beginning in the mid-1960s, however, a number of Supreme Court decisions strengthened some of the rights of children. *Kent* (1966) extended limited due process guarantees to juveniles. *In re Gault* (1967) provided juveniles with the right to notice of the charges, the right to counsel, the privilege against self-incrimination, and the right to confront and examine witnesses. *In re Winship* (1970) applied the "reasonable doubt" standard to juvenile cases.

Nevertheless, in *McKeiver v. Pennsylvania* (1970), the Supreme Court maintained some different standards for juveniles in rejecting the argument that children were entitled to a jury trial. Proof that the *parens patriae* concept was still alive came in the *Schall v. Martin* (1984) decision, when the court said that "juveniles, unlike adults, are always in some form of custody." Thus, while children still do not have exactly the same constitutional guarantees as adults, the legal system has moved in that direction. Juveniles accused of criminal offenses may not be treated as arbitrarily or capriciously as they were in the first half of the last century.

A unanimous decision in *Oklahoma Publishing Co. v. District Court in and for Oklahoma City* (1977) allowed the press to use the name and picture of a minor in a juvenile court proceeding in circumstances where members of the press were present during the court proceeding and no objection to their presence was made. The pretrial use of detention for juveniles presenting a serious risk of committing other offenses was upheld by the Supreme Court in *Schall v. Martin,* a New York case (1984).

In 1989 the Supreme Court held in *Stanford v. Kentucky* that the imposition of capital punishment on individuals for murders committed at the age of 16 or 17 years does not constitute cruel and unusual punishment in violation of the Eighth Amendment. In 1992 the Supreme Court held in *Reno v. Flores* that releasing alien juveniles who were detained pending deportation hearings only to parents, guardians, or other close relatives was not a violation of Fifth Amendment rights.

Beginning in the mid-1970s, several states adopted legislation that mandated minimal or determinate sentences for juveniles. Today a majority of the states use explicitly punitive juvenile sentencing strategies. At least 17 states have recently revised their purpose clause or mission statements for juvenile courts to emphasize public safety, punishment, and offender accountability (Torbet & Szymanski, 1998). This has virtually eliminated the differences between juvenile and adult sentencing in those states. It is difficult to believe that the imposition of a mandatory minimum sentence given on the basis of the offense has anything to do with the child's "real needs" or "best interests." The fact that "the purposes of the juvenile process have become more punitive, its procedures formalistic, adversarial and public, and the consequences of conviction much more harsh" was acknowledged in *In re Javier A.* (1984).

We have corrected a serious deficiency in the juvenile justice system by requiring closer attention to matters of procedural rights, but it will take much more than a mere declaration of those rights by appellate courts before much real change can be expected. For example, ensuring that accused juveniles are provided legal counsel will not per se make any significant difference in case outcomes. Several studies have shown that there is no substantial difference in adjudication or disposition decisions when attorneys are assigned to represent juveniles (Burriss & Kempf-Leonard, 2002). In fact, some studies show that juveniles who are represented by legal counsel are more likely to receive harsher depositions (McNeece, 1976; Stapleton & Teitlebaum, 1972). The problem is the prevailing attitude concerning procedural rights that still exists in the juvenile justice system. Many attorneys who represent juvenile clients remain convinced that because the juvenile court is really an institution for providing treatment to their clients, they should not aggressively pursue the protection of the legal rights of such clients. After all, the court is still presumed to act "in the best interests of the child."

On the other hand, other attorneys (Feld, 2003) believe that *Gault* precipitated a revolution in the juvenile court system that has unintentionally sidetracked its original progressive and rehabilitative ideals and "transformed the juvenile court into a scaled-down, second-class criminal court for young offenders" (p. 16).

In recent years, reforms at the state level have been suggested in at least three different areas. Several states have lowered the age at which youths may be tried as adult offenders for serious offenses, and other states have made it much easier to waive juveniles of any age to adult courts. Some have called for the abolition of the juvenile court altogether, arguing that the U.S. Supreme Court has made the juvenile and adult systems so similar that having separate systems no longer makes sense (Schichor, 1983). Other people have suggested that we abandon therapy or rehabilitation in favor of protecting the public by punishing and confining dangerous young offenders. Unfortunately, this has become a politically popular position.

One could reasonably assume that the courts might respond to the current conservative backlash regarding juvenile offenders by taking somewhat more punitive actions in processing at least a portion of these clients. We will be looking for those trends in the data described in the following pages.

## ■ Funding for Juvenile Justice

Another useful way to analyze policy changes in juvenile justice is to examine the changes in funding patterns, because financial support of programs is one of the keys to successful implementation. If decision makers are serious about changes in policy, those changes will be reflected in budgets. A major change in funding programs in the area of juvenile justice occurred with the passage of the Law Enforcement Assistance Act (LEAA) in 1965 (P.L. 89-197) and the Omnibus Crime Control and Safe Streets Act of 1968 (P.L. 90-351). Together, these two laws provide money and the administrative apparatus for new grants to state and local agencies for law enforcement and related programs. In 1974, the Office of Juvenile Justice and Delinquency Prevention was created within LEAA to coordinate efforts to control delinquency (P.L. 93-415). For the fiscal years 1975 through 1977, 89,125 JJDP formula grants to state and local agencies were approved (U.S. Dept. of Justice, OJJDP, 1979). In 1977, $47,625,000 was available through OJJDP for delinquency control and prevention programs.

Budget authority for OJJDP was scheduled to increase to $100 million in 1981 and $135 million in 1982 under the proposed Carter budget (Executive Office of the President, Office of Management and Budget [OMB], 1981b). The actual expenditure for juvenile justice formula grants in 1980 was $68 million (Executive Office of the President, OMB, 1981b).

Meanwhile, disenchantment of Congress with LEAA resulted in an order to dismantle the agency well before the end of the Carter administration. While the actual expenditure for all LEAA programs in 1980 was $444,781,000, the executive budget request for 1982 was only $159,691,000. The few remaining

LEAA grants ended in 1982 (Executive Office of the President, OMB, 1981a), and funds that would have been allocated as grants through OJJDP were converted to block grants to the states (Executive Office of the President, OMB, 1981c). Until the recent passage of the Violent Crime Control Act of 1994, few new federal funds were directed specifically at delinquency prevention or delinquency programs. With the election of a new, more conservative Congress then, it remains to be seen how large a share of the approved funds will actually be allocated to juvenile programs.

Many of the original advocates of the federal cost-sharing approach to crime and delinquency programs now believe that a serious mistake was made in allowing billions of dollars to be spent on criminal and juvenile programs. Some even believe that not only was this money wasted but also it might have made matters worse. Wilson (1975) believes that these billions of dollars did not add much to our knowledge about which approaches and programs were most effective, and that rather than testing our theories about rehabilitation and prevention we were merely "funding our fears."

For better or for worse, it appears that the federal largesse in juvenile corrections has ended. As one example, the base budget for OJJDP in FY 2002 was $297,379,000, but the president's budget request for FY 2003 asked for only $249,320,000, a decrease of 16% (OJJDP, 2003). A large part of this decrease comes from the elimination of the Juvenile Incentive Block Grant Program (OMB, 2003). States and localities will continue to bear the bulk of the financial burden for institutional programs and other postadjudication dispositions, cities and counties will finance most law enforcement programs, and courts and probation staff will be supported by both state and local revenues. Because federal money was largely responsible for the development of delinquency prevention, there is a real possibility that states and communities may return to their previous pattern of funding only the more "traditional" juvenile programs—that is, institutions and probation.

## Official Statistics

Since 1929, the primary source of information on activities of the nation's juvenile courts has been the series *Juvenile Court Statistics*. The first report described cases handled by 42 courts during 1927. This was (and still is) a voluntary reporting system, and few courts maintained and reported case-level data on juvenile clients. By 1937, case-level reporting was dropped for dependency cases, and a few years later the decision was made to switch the reporting system for both dependency and delinquency cases to aggregate counts only.

In 1957 the Children's Bureau initiated a new data collection program that enabled the production of national estimates of juvenile court actions through a stratified probability sample of more than 500 courts. Although this early effort was aborted, the National Center for Juvenile Justice (NCJJ) was awarded a grant by the Office of Juvenile Justice and Delinquency Prevention in 1975.

**Table 2.1**     **National Estimates of Referrals to Juvenile Court (in Thousands)**

| 1990 | 1991 | 1992 | 1993 | 1994 | 1995 | 1996 | 1997 | 1998 | 1999 | 2000 |
|------|------|------|------|------|------|------|------|------|------|------|
| 1,317 | 1,413 | 1,483 | 1,522 | 1,666 | 1,766 | 1,802 | 1,816 | 1,746 | 1,671 | 1,658 |

By this time many more corts were keeping authomated records on juvenile cases to meet their own needs, so that estimating national trends became somewhat easier. Table 2.1 summarizes estimates of the delinquency cases disposed by juvenile courts in the United States for the years 1990 to 2000. These estimates are based on (a) minimum samples of at least a half million individual case records from more than 1,000 communities with jurisdiction over about half of the nation's youth population at risk and (b) a sample of compatible court-level aggregate statistics on more than 100,000 additional delinquency cases from other states. Estimates based on these data are further described in the reports *Juvenile Court Statistics* for each of the years 1990 through 2000, which are published by the U.S. Department of Justice.

The official statistics indicate that more than 1.5 million juvenile arrests are made each year (FBI, 2000), but only about half of those arrested are referred to juvenile court. The others are not charged, or the charges against them are dropped. Another 250,000 juveniles are referred to court without an arrest, by parents, schools, human service agencies, and others. Of the total number of cases referred to juvenile court (approximately 1,657,533 in 2000), about half subsequently involve a delinquency hearing. Of those youths, three fourths will be adjudicated as "delinquent" and either placed on probation, made to pay fines or restitution, ordered to undergo counseling, or placed in an institution (NCJJ, 2003).

The number of juvenile offenders processed by the courts has declined in recent years after several years of moderate growth (Table 2.1). We must keep in mind, however, that while the total number of juvenile cases processed increased nearly 26% between 1990 and 2000, the population of youths under 18 increased nearly 14% (U.S. Dept. of Commerce, 1992, 2002), so much of the overall increase in referrals is explained by the increase in the child population. However, referrals have been decreasing since 1997. Whether that trend will continue remains to be seen.

The greatest increase in juvenile referrals was among those 17 years of age, with an increase of 36% between 1990 and 2000. However, referrals for 17-year-olds also peaked in 1997 and declined by 5% by 1999. Referrals of 17-year-olds were up again slightly in 2000.

## Offense

The distribution of offenses in four broad categories from 1990 through 2000 is provided in Table 2.2. These offense categories are defined as:

**Table 2.2**     **National Estimates of Juvenile Delinquency Cases: Offenses, 1990–2000**

|  | Person | Property | Drugs | Public Order | Total |
|---|---|---|---|---|---|
| 1990 | 249,542 | 772,797 | 71,049 | 223,625 | 1,317,013 |
|  | 19% | 59% | 5% | 17% | 100% |
| 1991 | 278,120 | 848,876 | 65,410 | 221,016 | 1,413,422 |
|  | 20% | 60% | 5% | 16% | 100% |
| 1992 | 308,657 | 862,632 | 72,632 | 238,589 | 1,482,510 |
|  | 21% | 58% | 5% | 16% | 100% |
| 1993 | 326,110 | 833,568 | 92,185 | 269,932 | 1,521,795 |
|  | 21% | 55% | 6% | 18% | 100% |
| 1994 | 360,704 | 867,923 | 131,194 | 306,482 | 1,666,303 |
|  | 22% | 52% | 8% | 18% | 100% |
| 1995 | 387,027 | 887,386 | 165,390 | 325,817 | 1,765,620 |
|  | 22% | 50% | 9% | 18% | 100% |
| 1996 | 382,367 | 877,475 | 184,497 | 358,063 | 1,802,402 |
|  | 21% | 49% | 10% | 20% | 100% |
| 1997 | 390,595 | 849,142 | 193,628 | 382,362 | 1,815,727 |
|  | 22% | 47% | 11% | 21% | 100% |
| 1998 | 392,475 | 780,466 | 193,657 | 379,805 | 1,746,403 |
|  | 22% | 45% | 11% | 22% | 100% |
| 1999 | 386,094 | 704,738 | 191,137 | 388,610 | 1,670,579 |
|  | 23% | 42% | 11% | 23% | 100% |
| 2000 | 378,604 | 678,683 | 198,526 | 401,720 | 1,657,533 |
|  | 23% | 41% | 12% | 24% | 100% |
| % change since 1990 | 51.7% | −12.2% | 179.4% | 79.6% | 25.9% |

*Crimes Against Persons*—This category includes criminal homicide, forcible rape, robbery, aggravated assault, simple assault, and other person offenses.

*Crimes Against Property*—This category includes burglary, larceny, motor vehicle theft, arson, vandalism, stolen property offenses, trespassing, and other property offenses.

*Drug Law Violations*—Unlawful sale, purchase, distribution, manufacture, cultivation, transport, possession, or use of a controlled or prohibited substance or drug, or drug paraphernalia, or attempt to commit these acts. Sniffing of glue, paint, gasoline, or other inhalants is also included; hence, the term is broader than the Uniform Crime Report category of drug abuse violations.

*Offenses Against Public Order*—This category includes weapons offenses, nonviolent sex offenses, liquor law violations (not status), disorderly conduct, obstruction of justice, and other offenses against public order.

# ■ Recent Trends

The overall increase of 25.9% between 1990 and 2000 masks some important changes in specific offense categories. Property offenses peaked in 1995 and person offenses in 1998, while drug and public order offenses continued to grow.

Juvenile property crimes, the largest category of juvenile crimes, dropped 12% since 1990, but during the same period, person offenses increased nearly 52%, public order offenses increased nearly 80%, and drug offenses increased by 179%. Encouragingly, however, these trends have slowed or reversed since 1997, when juvenile offending was at its peak. Between 1997 and 2000, total juvenile offenses declined nearly 9%, led by a 20% drop in property crimes. Person crimes dropped 3% during that same period, while drug offenses rose 2.5% and public order offenses rose 5%. However, this trend would need to continue for many years to return to 1990 levels of juvenile offending.

While the proportion of drug crimes attributed to Nonwhite juveniles rose 51% between 1990 and 2000, drug offenses among White youths rose 287%. Similarly, person offenses rose 66% among White youths but only 32% among Nonwhites. Although the vast majority of all juvenile delinquency referrals are male (75% in 2000), female referrals have increased more quickly than male referrals in all categories. In the case of property offenses, female referrals rose while male referrals declined.

Between 1990 and 2000, person offenses increased almost 107% among female juveniles but only 38% among their male counterparts. The media and policy makers have taken note of the increase in female youths entering the juvenile justice system, particularly the increase in female referrals for violent offenses. Although the image of violent, gang-involved girls makes for dramatic news headlines and has even been blamed by some on women's increasing equality in the family and the workplace, recent research tells a different story. Histories of physical and sexual abuse appear to be the rule rather than the exception among female offenders, and what little research has been done with female delinquents suggests that much of their offending may be a direct or indirect result of abuse. In fact, some researchers have pointed out that female juveniles are often charged with domestic violence for incidents in which an adult caregiver is actually the aggressor and the juvenile defends herself from an attack (McNeece, Jackson, & Winokur, 2003). Although states and jurisdictions have increased their capacity to incarcerate female juveniles (Florida recently opened a maximum-risk juvenile prison for girls), insufficient attention is generally paid to the underlying problems that drive girls into delinquency.

## Detention

Detention refers to the placement of a youth in a restrictive facility between referral to court intake and case disposition. Table 2.3 provides the national estimates for detention decisions between 1990 and 2000.

The *number* of juveniles detained increased between 1990 and 2000. However, the *percentage* of juvenile offenders detained has decreased from 23% in 1990 to 19.5% in 2000. A decrease in the percentage of youths detained was observed for males and females as well as for both White and Nonwhite youths. One reason for the decrease in detention may be that youths who might otherwise have been detained are being processed in the adult system.

From 1989 to 1998, the increase in number of detained females (56%) was greater than for males (20%) because of the large increase in the number of female delinquency cases involving person offenses (157%). During the same time, the number of White juveniles detained grew more (33%) than for African American juveniles (15%), also because of the higher increase of person

**Table 2.3**     **National Estimates of Juvenile Delinquency Cases: Detention Decisions, 1990–2000**

| | Detained | Not Detained | Total |
|---|---|---|---|
| 1990 | 302,795 | 1,014,218 | 1,317,013 |
| | 23.0% | 77.0% | 100.0% |
| 1991 | 292,831 | 1,120,591 | 1,413,422 |
| | 20.7% | 79.3% | 100.0% |
| 1992 | 297,551 | 1,184,959 | 1,482,510 |
| | 20.1% | 79.9% | 100.0% |
| 1993 | 289,775 | 1,232,020 | 1,521,795 |
| | 19.0% | 81.0% | 100.0% |
| 1994 | 316,102 | 1,350,201 | 1,666,303 |
| | 19.0% | 81.0% | 100.0% |
| 1995 | 295,390 | 1,470,230 | 1,765,620 |
| | 16.7% | 83.3% | 100.0% |
| 1996 | 299,662 | 1,502,740 | 1,802,402 |
| | 16.6% | 83.4% | 100.0% |
| 1997 | 328,328 | 1,487,399 | 1,815,727 |
| | 18.1% | 81.9% | 100.0% |
| 1998 | 331,743 | 1,414,660 | 1,746,403 |
| | 19.0% | 81.0% | 100.0% |
| 1999 | 335,373 | 1,335,206 | 1,670,579 |
| | 20.1% | 79.9% | 100.0% |
| 2000 | 322,628 | 1,334,905 | 1,657,533 |
| | 19.5% | 80.5% | 100.0% |
| % change since 1990 | 6.5% | 31.6% | 25.9% |

and drug offenses for White youths. It may be due in part to the much higher proportion of African American youths being processed in the adult system (OJJDP, 2002).

## Manner of Handling

The manner of handling is a general classification of case processing within the court system. Petitioned (formally handled) cases are those that appear on the official court calendar in response to the filing of a petition or other legal instrument requesting the court to adjudicate the youth a delinquent, status offender, or dependent child or to waive the youth to criminal court for processing as an adult. Nonpetitioned (informally handled) cases are those cases in which duly authorized court personnel screen for adjustment prior to the filing of a formal petition. Such personnel can include judges, referees, probation officers, other officers of the court, and an agency statutorily designated to conduct petition screening for the juvenile court.

The percentage of cases that were petitioned (Table 2.4) increased from

**Table 2.4**  **National Estimates of Juvenile Delinquency Cases: Manner of Handling, 1990–2000**

|  | Formal | Informal | Total |
|---|---|---|---|
| 1990 | 655,570 | 661,443 | 1,317,013 |
|  | 49.8% | 50.2% | 100.0% |
| 1991 | 705,454 | 707,968 | 1,413,422 |
|  | 49.9% | 50.1% | 100.0% |
| 1992 | 745,283 | 737,227 | 1,482,510 |
|  | 50.3% | 49.7% | 100.0% |
| 1993 | 797,312 | 724,483 | 1,521,795 |
|  | 52.4% | 47.6% | 100.0% |
| 1994 | 883,320 | 782,983 | 1,666,303 |
|  | 53.0% | 47.0% | 100.0% |
| 1995 | 951,855 | 813,765 | 1,765,620 |
|  | 53.9% | 46.1% | 100.0% |
| 1996 | 1,001,626 | 800,776 | 1,802,402 |
|  | 55.6% | 44.4% | 100.0% |
| 1997 | 1,019,998 | 795,729 | 1,815,727 |
|  | 56.2% | 43.8% | 100.0% |
| 1998 | 1,000,082 | 746,321 | 1,746,403 |
|  | 57.3% | 42.7% | 100.0% |
| 1999 | 959,711 | 710,868 | 1,670,579 |
|  | 57.4% | 42.6% | 100.0% |
| 2000 | 957,875 | 699,658 | 1,657,533 |
|  | 57.8% | 42.2% | 100.0% |
| % change since 1990 | 46.1% | 5.8% | 25.9% |

49.8% to 57.8% between 1990 and 2000. As overall delinquency cases increased 25.8%, formally petitioned cases increased 46%. The number of male youths formally petitioned increased 35%, while the number of female youths petitioned increased 107%. The number of White youths formally petitioned increased 58%, while the number of Nonwhite youths petitioned increased 28%. Earlier studies had indicated that juvenile courts did not handle alcohol and drug cases with a formal petition as often as they did other delinquency cases but that drug cases (47%) were more likely than alcohol cases (38%) to be formally petitioned (National Institute of Justice, 1989). Unfortunately, current national data do not allow distinctions to be made between drug and alcohol offenses, only between drug and public order offenses (OJJDP, 2002).

## ■ Adjudication Decisions

A juvenile who is adjudicated is judicially determined (judged) to be a delinquent or status offender. Table 2.5 provides the national estimates of both adjudicated and nonadjudicated juvenile cases from 1990 to 2000.

Adjudicated cases grew faster (60.6%) than the overall growth rate (25.8%). The growth rate in female adjudications (132.8%) was much greater than the growth rate in male adjudications (49.1%), and the growth rate in adjudications of White youths (71.5%) was greater than the growth rate among Nonwhite youths (42.8%).

### Dispositions

Dispositions are categorized here as the most severe action taken or treatment plan decided upon or initiated in a particular case. Case dispositions are coded into the following categories:

*Waived*—Cases that are waived or transferred to a criminal court as the result of a waiver or transfer hearing.

*Placement*—Cases in which youths are placed out of the home in a residential facility housing delinquents or status offenders or are otherwise removed from their homes.

*Probation*—Cases in which youths are placed on informal/voluntary or formal court-ordered probation or supervision.

*Dismissed*—Cases that are dismissed (including those warned, counseled, and released) with no further disposition anticipated.

*Other*—A variety of miscellaneous dispositions not included in the other categories. This category includes such dispositions as fines, restitution, community service, and referrals outside the court for services with minimal or no further court involvement anticipated.

**Table 2.5**  **National Estimates of Juvenile Delinquency Cases: Adjudication Decisions, 1990–2000**

|  | Adjudicated | Not Adjudicated | Total |
|---|---|---|---|
| 1990 | 394,927 | 922,086 | 1,317,013 |
|  | 30.0% | 70.0% | 100.0% |
| 1991 | 414,547 | 998,875 | 1,413,422 |
|  | 29.3% | 70.7% | 100.0% |
| 1992 | 432,792 | 1,049,718 | 1,482,510 |
|  | 29.2% | 70.8% | 100.0% |
| 1993 | 473,129 | 1,048,666 | 1,521,795 |
|  | 31.1% | 68.9% | 100.0% |
| 1994 | 517,058 | 1,149,245 | 1,666,303 |
|  | 31.0% | 69.0% | 100.0% |
| 1995 | 552,248 | 1,213,372 | 1,765,620 |
|  | 31.3% | 68.7% | 100.0% |
| 1996 | 591,434 | 1,210,968 | 1,802,402 |
|  | 32.8% | 67.2% | 100.0% |
| 1997 | 617,717 | 1,198,010 | 1,815,727 |
|  | 34.0% | 66.0% | 100.0% |
| 1998 | 632,475 | 1,113,928 | 1,746,403 |
|  | 36.2% | 63.8% | 100.0% |
| 1999 | 637,632 | 1,032,947 | 1,670,579 |
|  | 38.2% | 61.8% | 100.0% |
| 2000 | 634,497 | 1,023,036 | 1,657,533 |
|  | 38.3% | 61.7% | 100.0% |
| % change since 1990 | 60.7% | 10.9% | 25.9% |

One category of dispositions merits particular note. Juvenile waivers to adult court, which rose for years and then peaked in 1994, dropped 29.3% since 1990, and dropped 51.4% since 1994, the peak year for this waiver to adult court. The decline was most dramatic among Nonwhite youths, dropping 41.3%, compared with a 14.6% drop among White youths. White males experienced a 16% drop in waivers compared with a 43.4% drop among Nonwhite males.

In Florida, one of the states that has led the nation in juvenile waivers to adult court, the number of waivers fell 58.4% between fiscal year 1996–1997 and fiscal year 2000–2001. The drop was between 50% to 60% for both sexes and for both White and Nonwhite youths.

Nationally, although the overall number of juvenile waivers dropped between 1990 and 2000 (Table 2.6), for females, waivers rose 17.6% compared with a 31.4% drop for males. However, female waivers have declined 26.2% from the peak year, 1994. The rise in female waivers was much more pronounced among Nonwhite girls, for whom waivers increased 39.3%, compared with an increase of just 6.5% for White girls between 1990 and 2000. However,

**Table 2.6**     **National Estimates of Juvenile Delinquency Cases: Dispositions, 1990–2000**

|  | Waived | Placed | Probation | Released | Other | Total |
|---|---|---|---|---|---|---|
| 1990 | 8,298 | 131,261 | 469,645 | 501,774 | 206,035 | 1,317,013 |
|  | 0.6% | 10.0% | 35.7% | 38.1% | 15.6% | 100.0% |
| 1991 | 10,699 | 132,344 | 506,908 | 519,000 | 244,471 | 1,413,422 |
|  | 0.8% | 9.4% | 35.9% | 36.7% | 17.3% | 100.0% |
| 1992 | 10,224 | 138,450 | 531,532 | 535,465 | 266,839 | 1,482,510 |
|  | 0.7% | 9.3% | 35.9% | 36.1% | 18.0% | 100.0% |
| 1993 | 11,226 | 144,954 | 517,054 | 580,651 | 267,910 | 1,521,795 |
|  | 0.7% | 9.5% | 34.0% | 38.2% | 17.6% | 100.0% |
| 1994 | 12,067 | 159,964 | 563,205 | 634,182 | 296,885 | 1,666,303 |
|  | 0.7% | 9.6% | 33.8% | 38.1% | 17.8% | 100.0% |
| 1995 | 10,442 | 161,233 | 616,432 | 670,574 | 306,939 | 1,765,620 |
|  | 0.6% | 9.1% | 34.9% | 38.0% | 17.4% | 100.0% |
| 1996 | 10,825 | 165,149 | 653,728 | 624,037 | 348,663 | 1,802,402 |
|  | 0.6% | 9.2% | 36.3% | 34.6% | 19.3% | 100.0% |
| 1997 | 9,133 | 168,139 | 683,712 | 601,097 | 353,646 | 1,815,727 |
|  | 0.5% | 9.3% | 37.7% | 33.1% | 19.5% | 100.0% |
| 1998 | 8,173 | 166,508 | 676,577 | 562,223 | 332,922 | 1,746,403 |
|  | 0.5% | 9.5% | 38.7% | 32.2% | 19.1% | 100.0% |
| 1999 | 7,516 | 163,006 | 675,506 | 512,461 | 312,090 | 1,670,579 |
|  | 0.4% | 9.8% | 40.4% | 30.7% | 18.7% | 100.0% |
| 2000 | 5,864 | 159,994 | 679,449 | 494,935 | 317,291 | 1,657,533 |
|  | 0.4% | 9.7% | 41.0% | 29.9% | 19.1% | 100.0% |
| % change since 1990 | −29.3% | 21.9% | 44.7% | −1.4% | 54.0% | 25.9% |

waiver rates have fallen for all females since the peak year for waivers, 1994. In 2000, females represented 408 of the 5,864 youths transferred to adult court, or 6.9% of the total.

While waivers to adult court fell between 1990 and 2000, out-of-home placements rose 21.9%. The rise in out-of-home placements did not quite keep pace with the overall rise of 25.8% in juvenile offending. Females experienced a dramatic rise of 61.1% for out-of-home placements, compared with a rise of 16.7% for males. Out-of-home placements of White youths rose 32.4%, compared with a relatively small increase of 6.9% for Nonwhite youths. The number of youths placed on probation outpaced the rise in juvenile offending, with a 44.7% rise between 1990 and 2000.

## ◼ Disturbing Trends in Offenses and Case Processing

On the surface, it appears that racial disparities are becoming more equitable in case processing decisions in the juvenile justice system in recent years. The rate of increase in formal handling has been more than twice as high for White as for minority youths, the rates of increase in detention and adjudication have been much greater for White than for minority youths, out-of-home placements for White youths grew at almost 5 times the rate for minority youths, and waivers to adult court declined 3 times as much for minority than White youths. Waivers of minority youths have declined consistently for every category of offense since the mid-1990s. Overall, waivers of minority youths are down 41% between 1990 and 2000 (Table 2.7).

So are things really getting better for minority youths? Hardly! The new era of punitiveness has been tough on all youths—but particularly African Americans. Things only look better for minorities in the justice system because so many of them are being processed as adults. True, waivers to juvenile court have fallen, but most juveniles don't get into the adult system through a waiver.

Earlier we discussed the get-tough legislation passed in 45 states between 1992 and 1997 (Snyder & Sickmund, 1999). The effect of that legislation was to increase prosecutorial discretion in trying juveniles as adults, lower the statutory age for referral to the adult court, and broaden the categories of offenses that go to adult court. True, judges aren't waiving kids as often today. But only 15% of those decisions to waive to adult court are made by judges; 85% are made by prosecutors or legislative bodies, and 82% of kids processed as adults are minority youths (BBY, 2003). The result is that 200,000 children per year are processed in the adult criminal justice system (Amnesty International, 1998).

Neither are minority youths being treated more gently in the juvenile system. To further illustrate the risk of more severe handling experienced by Nonwhite youths, we have compared dispositions for White and Nonwhite

**Table 2.7** **National Estimates of Juvenile Delinquency Cases: Nonwhite Males Waived to Adult Court by Offense, 1990–2000**

| Count | Person | Property | Drugs | Public Order | Total |
|---|---|---|---|---|---|
| 1990 | 1,766 | 1,397 | 1,010 | 395 | 4,568 |
| 1991 | 2,091 | 1,676 | 1,545 | 403 | 5,715 |
| 1992 | 2,325 | 1,617 | 976 | 494 | 5,412 |
| 1993 | 2,891 | 1,687 | 929 | 532 | 6,039 |
| 1994 | 2,992 | 1,553 | 942 | 456 | 5,943 |
| 1995 | 2,816 | 1,303 | 906 | 396 | 5,421 |
| 1996 | 2,430 | 1,371 | 922 | 352 | 5,075 |
| 1997 | 2,016 | 1,148 | 806 | 362 | 4,332 |
| 1998 | 1,502 | 1,017 | 855 | 306 | 3,680 |
| 1999 | 1,266 | 1,044 | 764 | 381 | 3,455 |
| 2000 | 1,075 | 786 | 546 | 274 | 2,681 |
| % change since 1990 | −39% | −44% | −46% | −31% | −41% |

**Table 2.8** **National Estimates of Juvenile Delinquency Cases: 2000 Disposition by Race for 17-Year-Old Males Charged With Drug Offenses**

| Count | Waived | Placed | Probation | Released | Other | Total |
|---|---|---|---|---|---|---|
| White | 172 | 2,465 | 13,841 | 8,691 | 8,020 | 33,189 |
| | 0.5% | 7.4% | 41.7% | 26.2% | 24.2% | 100.0% |
| Nonwhite | 275 | 1,979 | 4,194 | 3,583 | 1,868 | 11,899 |
| | 2.3% | 16.6% | 35.2% | 30.1% | 15.7% | 100.0% |
| Total | 447 | 4,444 | 18,035 | 12,274 | 9,888 | 45,088 |

17-year-old male drug offenders in Table 2.8. The Nonwhite juveniles in this group are much more likely to be waived or placed, while White juveniles tend to have their charges dismissed or to be placed on probation more often. The bottom line is that we seem to have decided that minority youths, especially those who are older and commit drug offenses, are not amenable to treatment in the juvenile system. We treat them as adults. We have come full cycle, as if the juvenile court movement of a century ago had never taken place.

## ■ Females in Juvenile Justice

Approximately one quarter of juveniles who are arrested are female. Girls typically commit less serious offenses than their male counterparts, and the majority of female juvenile offending continues to consist of status offenses and relatively minor delinquency (OJJDP, 1998). However, in recent years, girls have entered the juvenile justice system in increasing numbers and for increasingly serious offenses. In fact, since 1985, the number of female youths charged with person offenses rose 188%, compared with an 89.3% increase for males for the same time period.

The statistics on girls' offending, and particularly their serious offending, appear alarming. However, there is debate regarding the factors underlying these increases. Some research suggests that female juveniles are treated more harshly than their male counterparts (OJJDP, 1998). For example, a report published by the Florida Department of Juvenile Justice (2001) notes that girls committed to secure placement for their first commitment have less serious offense histories than boys given the same sanctions. Another study reported that girls are more likely to be placed in detention and are detained for less serious offenses than boys (OJJDP, 1998).

Media accounts, particularly in the mid-1990s, often suggested a link between women's increasing economic opportunities and the rise in female delinquency. However, research with delinquent girls tells a very different story—namely, that delinquent girls generally have backgrounds of victimization. Many researchers have noted that girls who become involved in juvenile justice systems generally have been sexually or physically abused, and their offending is often related to the abuse. Chesney-Lind (1997) describes the "criminalization of girls' survival strategies," whereby abused girls run away from home and are arrested for running away or for engaging in crime to survive on the streets. There is also evidence that a good portion of the increase in official statistics on girls' violent offending is being driven by girls who are abuse victims who are charged with domestic violence when they attempt to defend themselves or strike back during a violent episode. Critics have noted that programming and treatment tactics developed for boys are generically applied to delinquent girls, resulting in a juvenile justice system that fails to address the gender-specific issues associated with their offending (OJJDP, 1998).

The U.S. Congress acknowledged the apparent rise in female juvenile offending and the different issues underlying their delinquency. When the JJDP Act was reauthorized in 1992, it included grant funding to assist states in "developing and adopting policies to prohibit gender bias in placement and treatment and establishing programs to ensure that female youths have access to the full range of health and mental health services, treatment for physical or sexual assault and abuse, self-defense instruction, education in parenting in general and other training and vocational services" (Title 42, Chapter 72, Subchapter II, Part E, Sec. 5667c). A number of states have received research funding under this provision of the JJDP Act. However, there is much evidence that harsher sanctions, as well as treatment more appropriate for boys, persist in the processing and rehabilitation of female offenders.

## ■ Recommendations

Obviously, more research is needed on female delinquency and the treatment of female delinquents. We have responded to the rapid increase in female delinquency by treating female delinquents more or less as males. More research is needed on the effectiveness of all delinquency programs. Until we know what is effective, we should try to maximize the degree of care we provide to juveniles and minimize the harm done to them. Let's put a moratorium on additional punitive legislation.

Two decades ago, I suggested in an article on juvenile justice policy that until we know how to provide effective treatment for juvenile offenders, we should concentrate on making the juvenile justice system as equitable, just, and humane as possible (McNeece, 1983). While we have not addressed the issue of humaneness in this chapter, it is obvious that we still have problems in achieving equity, and it is doubtful that justice is being done. We should take action immediately to address the differential processing of minority and nonminority juvenile offenders. Even if a disproportionate number of older, Black youths are involved in felony drug cases, rather than continuing to commit them to adult prisons, we should take whatever action is necessary to prevent these tragedies from occurring in the first place. Unfortunately, as the current budget indicates, prevention programs are not as popular as punishment.

To allow the present situation to continue is no more justifiable than allowing a disproportionate number of minority adults to be sentenced to death. Until our legal system seriously addresses the issue of equal justice for both juveniles and adults, we are likely to remain a nation divided.

## Conclusion

There is a terrible irony in the fact that juvenile violent crime has been decreasing, while state legislatures have been making the juvenile justice system more punitive and adultlike. Part of the explanation undoubtedly lies in the media coverage of events like the tragedy at Columbine (Merlo, 2000). Media coverage and politics have interacted to the detriment of juveniles. Justice as a symbolic value is easily dispensed by political leaders. It is cost-free and very popular (Merlo & Benekos, 2000). I apologize for not painting a more optimistic picture of the juvenile justice system and juvenile justice policy. In 2003, 5 years after the second edition of this book, we still find ourselves in a get-tough period of juvenile justice. Recent legislation indicates that our political leaders are in no mood to spend more money looking for effective and humane solutions to the problems associated with juvenile crime. In this era of boot camps, minimum mandatory sentences, "three strikes and you're out" policies, and the contracting of services to the lowest bidders, juvenile justice system policy may experience little improvement until the next national election.

## Discussion Questions

1   What are the three major shifts in federal juvenile policy since the 1960s?

2   How would you describe the impact of juvenile diversion programs?

3   How successful has the deinstitutionalization movement been regarding juvenile offenders?

4   In what way(s) are minority youths treated differently in the justice system?

5   What impact has the provision of "due process" to juveniles had on the juvenile justice system?

6   Discuss federal financial support for juvenile justice programs.

7   What are the ways that children are processed into the adult criminal justice system?

8   Discuss the trends in case processing decisions in juvenile courts.

# References

Amnesty International. (1998, November). *Betraying the young*. Amnesty International. Retrieved from *http://web.amnesty.org* on June 12, 2003.

Bartol, C., & Bartol, A. (1989). *Juvenile delinquency: A systems approach*. Englewood Cliffs, NJ: Prentice-Hall.

Blomberg, T. (1983). Diversion's disparate results and unresolved questions: An evaluation perspective. *Journal of Research in Crime and Delinquency, 20*, 24–38.

Bowman, G. W., Hakim, S., & Seidenstat, P. (1992). *Privatizing the United States justice system: Police, adjudication, and correction services from the private sector*. Jefferson, NC: McFarland.

Building Blocks for Youth. (2003). *Transfer to adult court/Trying kids as adults*. Retrieved February 4, 2003, from *www.buildingblocksforyouth.org/issues/transfer/facts_transfer.html*

Burruss, G., & Kempf-Leonard, K. (2002). Questionable advantage of defense counsel in juvenile court. *Justice Quarterly, 19*, 37–68.

Butts, J. A., & Mears, D. P. (2001). Reviving juvenile justice in a get-tough era. *Youth and Society, 33*(2), 169–198.

Chesney-Lind, M. (1997). *The female offender: Girls, women, and crime*. Thousand Oaks, CA: Sage.

CNN (Cable News Network). (2003). *Jefferson County Sheriff's Department*. Retrieved February 13, 2003, from *http://www.cnn.com/SPECIALS/2000/columbine.cd/frameset.exclude.html*

Ellis, R. A., & Sowers, K. M. (2001). *Juvenile justice practice: A cross-disciplinary approach to intervention*. Pacific Grove, CA: Brooks/Cole.

Empey, L. T., & Stafford, M. C. (1991). *American delinquency: Its meaning and construction*(3d ed.). Belmont, CA: Wadsworth.

Executive Office of the President, Office of Management and Budget. (1981a). *Budget of the United States government, fiscal year 1982*. Washington, DC: U.S. Government Printing Office.

Executive Office of the President, Office of Management and Budget. (1981b). *Budget of the United States government, fiscal year 1982, appendix*. Washington, DC: U.S. Government Printing Office.

Executive Office of the President, Office of Management and Budget. (1981c). *Budget of the United States government, fiscal year 1982, budget revisions: Additional details on budget savings*. Washington, DC: U.S. Government Printing Office.

Federal Bureau of Investigation. (2000). Crime in the United States—2000. Washington, D.C.: U.S. Government Printing Office.

Feld, B. C. (2003). *Juvenile justice administration*. St. Paul, MN: Thomson/West.

Florida Department of Juvenile Justice. (2001). *2001 outcome evaluation*. Tallahassee, FL: Author.

Goodman, D. (2001). Abraham sentenced to juvenile facility. Retrieved February 13, 2002, from *http://abcnews.go.com/sections/us/DailyNews/abraham000113.html*

Hawkins, J., Catalano, R., & Miller, J. (1992). Risk and protective factors for alcohol and other drug problems in adolescence and early adulthood: Implications for substance abuse prevention. *Psychological Bulletin, 112*(1), 64–105.

Hellum, F. (1979). Juvenile justice: The second revolution. *Crime and Delinquency, 25*, 299–317.

Jenson, J. (1998). Juvenile delinquency and drug abuse: Implications for social work practice in the justice system. In C. McNeece & A. Roberts (Eds.), *Policy and practice in the justice system*. Chicago: Nelson-Hall.

Krisberg, B. (1992). *Juvenile justice: Improving the quality of care*. Washington, DC: National Council on Crime and Delinquency.

Lerman, P. (1980). Trends and issues in the deinstitutionalization of youths in trouble. *Crime and Delinquency, 26,* 281–298.

Marlette, M. (1991). Boot camp prisons thrive. *Corrections Compendium,* 16, 6–8, 10.

McNeece, C. A. (1976). *Juvenile courts in the community environment.* Unpublished doctoral dissertation, University of Michigan.

McNeece, C. A. (1980). "Justice" in the juvenile court: Some suggestions for reform. *Journal of Humanics,* May, 77–97.

McNeece C. A. (1983). Juvenile justice policy. In A. Roberts (Ed.), *Social work in justice settings.* Springfield, IL: Charles C. Thomas.

McNeece, C. A. (1995). Adult corrections. *Encyclopedia of social work.* Washington, DC: National Association of Social Workers.

McNeece, C. A., & DiNitto, D. (2003). *Chemical dependency: A systems approach* (3rd ed.). Needham Heights, MA: Allyn & Bacon.

McNeece, C. A., Jackson, S., & Winokur, K. (2003). *The impact of gender on domestic violence charges against juveniles.* Paper presented at the annual meeting of the Society for Social Work and Research, Washington, DC.

Mears, D. P. (2000). Assessing the effectiveness of juvenile justice reforms: A closer look at the criteria and the impacts on diverse stakeholders. *Law and Policy,* 22, 175–202.

Merlo, A. V. (2000). Juvenile justice at the crossroads: Presidential address to the Academy Of Criminal Justice Sciences. *Justice Quarterly,* 17(4), 639–661.

Merlo, A. V., & Benekos, P. J. (2000). *What's wrong with the criminal justice system: Ideology, politics, and the media.* Cincinnati, OH: Anderson.

National Center for Juvenile Justice. (2003). National juvenile court data archive. Retrieved from *http://www.ojjdp.ncjns.org* on September 23, 2003.

National Institute of Justice. (1989). Juvenile courts vary greatly in how they handle drug and alcohol cases. In *OJJDP update on statistics.* Washington, DC: U.S. Government Printing Office.

Nieves, E. (2000, March 9). California proposal toughens penalties for young criminals. *New York Times,* p. A23.

Office of Juvenile Justice and Delinquency Prevention, U.S. Dept. of Justice. (1991). *Juveniles taken into custody: Fiscal year 1990 report.* Washington, DC: U.S. Government Printing Office.

Office of Juvenile Justice and Delinquency Prevention, U.S. Dept. of Justice. (1996). *1996 report to Congress, Title V, Incentive grants for local delinquency prevention programs.* Washington, DC: U.S. Government Printing Office.

Office of Juvenile Justice and Delinquency Prevention, U.S. Dept. of Justice. (1998). *Guiding principles for promising female programming: An inventory of best practices.* Washington, DC: U.S. Government Printing Office.

Office of Juvenile Justice and Delinquency Prevention, U.S. Dept. of Justice. (2002, January). *Detention in delinquency cases, 1989–1999* (OJJDP Fact Sheet No. 01). Washington, D.C.: U.S. Government Printing Office.

Office of Juvenile Justice and Delinquency Prevention, U.S. Dept. of Justice. (2003). *Easy access to juvenile court statistics.* Retrieved February 8, 2003, from http://ojjdp.ncjrs.org/ojstatbb/njcda/

Office of Management and Budget. (2003). *President's budget request, FY 2003.* Executive Office of the President. Washington, D.C.: U.S. Government Printing Office

Ohlin, L. (1983). Interview with Lloyd E. Ohlin, June 22, 1979. In J. Laub (Ed.), *Criminology in the making: An oral history.* Boston: Northeastern University Press.

Porter, L. (2002). *Michigan judge rejects early release for Nathaniel Abraham.* Retrieved February 13, 2003, from *http://www.wsws.org/articles/2002/sep2002/abra-s10.shtml*

Ray, L. (1992). Privatization of justice. In *Privatizing the United States justice system: Police, adjudication, and correction services from the private sector?.* Jefferson, NC: McFarland.

Schichor, D. (1983). Historical and current trends in American juvenile justice. *Juvenile and Family Court Journal, 34,* 61–75.

Schwartz, I. M. (1992). *Juvenile justice and public policy: Toward a national agenda.* New York: Macmillan.

Sertill, M. S. (1980). Washington's new juvenile code. *Corrections Magazine, 7,* 36–41.

Snyder, H. N. (1999, December). Juvenile arrests 1998. *Juvenile Justice Bulletin,* pp. 1–11.

Snyder, H. N., & Sickmund, M. (1999). Juvenile offenders and victims: 1999 national report. Washington, DC: Office of Juvenile Justice and Delinquency Prevention.

Springer, D. W., McNeece, C. A., & Arnold, E. M. (2003). *Substance abuse treatment for criminal and juvenile offenders: An evidence-based approach.* Washington, DC: American Psychological Association.

Stapleton, V., & Teitlebaum, L. (1972). *In defense of youth.* New York: Russell Sage.

Stone, K. (1990). Determining the primacy of substance abuse disorders among juvenile offenders. *Alcoholism Treatment Quarterly, 7*(2), 81–93.

Torbet, P., & Szymanski, L. (1998). *State legislative responses to violent juvenile crime: 1996–1997 update.* Washington, DC: Office of Juvenile Justice and Delinquency Prevention.

Umbreit, M. S., & Coates, R. B. (1993). Cross-site analysis of victim-offender mediation in four states. *Crime and Delinquency, 39,* 565–585.

Umbreit, M. S., Coates, R. B., & Kalanj, B. (1994). *Victim meets offender: The impact of restorative justice and mediation.* Monsey, NY: Willow Tree Press.

U.S. Congress, Senate. (1973). Hearings before the Senate subcommittee on juvenile delinquency on S.B. 821. Washington, DC: U.S. Government Printing Office.

U.S. Congress, Senate. (1974). Juvenile Justice and Delinquency Prevention Act. S.B. 821 (P.L. 93-415). Washington, DC: U.S. Government Printing Office.

U.S. Dept. of Commerce. (1992). *1990 census of population, general population characteristics, United States.* Washington, DC: U.S. Government Printing Office.

U.S. Dept. of Commerce. (2002). *2000 census of the population of the United States.* Washington, DC: U.S. Government Printing Office.

U.S. Dept. of Justice, Bureau of Justice Statistics. (1981). *Sourcebook of criminal justice statistics.* Washington, DC: U.S. Government Printing Office.

U.S. Dept. of Justice, Bureau of Justice Statistics. (1993). *Sourcebook of criminal justice statistics, 1992.* Washington, DC: U.S. Government Printing Office.

U.S. Dept. of Justice, Office of Juvenile Justice and Delinquency Prevention. (1979). *Second analysis and evaluation, federal juvenile delinquency programs,* Vol. 1. Washington, DC: U.S. Government Printing Office.

U.S. Dept. of Justice, Office of Juvenile Justice and Delinquency Prevention. (1980). *A national assessment of case disposition and classification in the juvenile justice system: Inconsistent labeling: Vol. 11. Results of a literature search.* Washington, DC: U.S. Government Printing Office.

U.S. Dept. of Justice, Office of Juvenile Justice and Delinquency Prevention. (1985). *Reports of the national juvenile justice assessment centers: The impact of deinstitutionalization on recidivism and secure confinement of status offenders.* Washington, DC: U.S. Government Printing Office.

U.S. Dept. of Justice, Office of Juvenile Justice and Delinquency Prevention. (1991). *Juveniles taken into custody: Fiscal year 1990 report.* Washington, DC: U.S. Government Printing Office.

Wilson, James Q. (1975). *Thinking about crime.* New York: Basic Books.

Woolard, J. L., Fondacaro, M. R., & Slobogin, C. (2001). Informing juvenile justice policy: Directions for behavioral research. *Law and Human Behavior, 25*(1), 13–24.

Zhang, S. X. (2001). *Evaluation of the Los Angeles County juvenile drug treatment boot camp: Executive summary* (NCJ Report 187678). Washington, DC: U.S. Government Printing Office.

## Cases

*In re Gault*, 387 U.S. 1 (1967).
*In re JavierA.*, 159 Cal., App. 3d 913, 206 Cal Rptr. 386 (1984).
*In re Winship*, 397 U.S. 358 (1970).
*Kent v. U.S.*, 383 U.S. 541, (1966).
*McKeiver v. Pennsylvannia, 403 U.S. 528 (1970)*
*Oklahoma Publishing Co. v. District Court in and for Oklahoma City*, 430 U.S. 308 (1977).
*Schall v. Martin*, 467 U.S. 253 (1984).
*Stanford v. Kentucky*, 492 U.S. 361 (1989).
*Reno v. Flores*, 507 U.S., 113 S. Ct., 123 L.Ed.2dl (1992).

# 3

# Lessons Learned From the Storm of Violence and Inner-City Crime of the 1990s

## The Relationship Between Juvenile Crime Trends and Drug Addiction

Albert R. Roberts and Kenneth R. Yeager

Jonathon M. is 16 years old and has been adjudicated by the juvenile court 7 times in the past 3 years, including the following:

First charges: possession of a weapon (fourth-degree crime) 2 months before his 14th birthday; he pled guilty and was given 1-year deferred disposition contingent on his attending school and having a 9 P.M. curfew.

Almost 2 years later, he was charged with possession of drug paraphernalia, drug possession, and consumption of alcohol by a minor. He was given 1 year of probation and required to attend school, maintain a part-time job, and submit to random urinalysis, a 9 P.M. curfew, no contact with codefendants, and a $40 a month fine.

One month later, he was charged with possession of an alcoholic beverage by a minor; he pled guilty, and his original 1-year probation term was extended by 1 month on the same conditions, but he was given 30 days to find a part-time job.

Seven months later, at age 16, Jonathon was charged with burglary, theft, criminal mischief, possession of drug paraphernalia, and possession of burglary tools. He pled guilty to burglary, theft, and possession of drug paraphernalia, and the other two charges were dismissed. Jonathon received an adjudication to 2 years of probation and ordered to attend and complete a 90-day Daytop Village drug treatment program, remain drug free and attend Narcotics Anonymous (NA) meetings twice a week, have his driving privileges suspended for 6 months, get As and Bs in all school subjects, and have his grades mailed to the juvenile court by the school.

Approximately 5 weeks later, he was charged with escape while being transported by bus from the Daytop Village residential drug program to the probation office for family counseling.

The latest charge was violation of probation and escaping from the bus that was transporting him to juvenile probation and court offices. The probation officer and judge agreed to give Jonathon one final chance because he seemed remorseful and admitted that he was cheeking his medication, Zyprexa, depakote, Zoloft, and albuterol, which were supposed to help with his delusions, impulsivity and emotional problems. The probation officer told Jonathon and his parents that if there is one more violation of probation, he will be incarcerated for a period of 6 months to 1 year. Jonathon was classified by the child study team as ED and a multiply disabled client who has a short attention span, low reading ability, and attention-deficit/hyperactivity disorder (ADHD). The client stated he practices the Catholic religion, believes in a Higher Power, and hopes this will facilitate his recovery. He has one younger brother, age 14, and he resides with both his parents. Unfortunately, both his mother and younger brother have neurofibromatosis, and his father is legally blind and has obsessive-compulsive disorder. His mother works in a local supermarket, and his father is disabled and does not work. Jonathan first used marijuana at the age of 13, and by age 14 he was experimenting with cocaine and Ecstasy. At age 15, heroin became his drug of choice; he started by snorting it for several months and then began shooting it.

Upon his return to the Daytop drug treatment center, he admitted that heroin was consuming him, and he gave specific dates during a 3-month period when he was "shooting up." He has cooperated in the program for the past 60 days and recently told the social worker that he was aware that he had been injecting "poison" into his body. He indicated that his former girlfriend never took drugs and had tried to help him. He wants to get back together with his old girlfriend and return to living with his parents. He still gets cravings for heroin, as well as nicotine, but indicates that he would like to change and go back to school to finish high school. His latest adjudication resulted in a suspended sentence and 3 years of probation.

## Case Autopsy

Jonathon's road to recovery was difficult. He reported that the Ultram given to assist with his outpatient detoxification was of minimal assistance. Jonathon indicated that many days he was "dope sick" and would have rather stayed in bed. However, he remembered what his counselor had said, that doing nothing is the quickest way to stick a needle in his arm again. Jonathon's most difficult day came when the girlfriend he hoped would help with his recovery said she didn't want to live her life with a "junkie." Jonathon indicated he then felt there was no reason to stay clean. During the same period, he was given an assignment by his counselor to list the right and wrong ways he was treating his disease. Jonathon indicated that living his life for himself became extremely clear and that the prospect of stealing to support his dope craving was no way to live his life. At the same time, Jonathan began an atypical antipsychotic medication. Although he felt somewhat groggy at first, he admits that over time he began to see that this medication was helping. His grades began to improve gradually, and he was able to focus and concentrate for possibly the first time in his life.

Jonathon became active briefly in NA but transitioned to Alcoholics Anonymous (AA), stating that the "war stories" in NA were killing him. Jonathon indicates he experienced remarkable cravings for 6 months. He knew remaining around persons talking dope stories would eventually lead to a hit, so Jonathan sought out a new support group. His counselor suggested a noon AA meeting. It was in this AA group that Jonathon found a Vietnam vet who had a history of heroin use while in country. Jonathon and his new friend and sponsor became very close. They worked through all of the 12 steps, just like the AA program suggests. There was an immediate bond between Jonathon and his sponsor, Hank. Jonathon began to hang with his new friend and talk about Harley Davidson motorcycles. Since their initial meeting, Jonathon has attained full-time employment and has tentatively enrolled in school for the autumn term. He has solidified not only his program of recovery but also his spiritual beliefs, despite Hank's agnostic perspective on life. Perhaps the most telling activity in recovery was when Jonathon's sponsor hooked him up with what to most people looked like a pile of junk, but to Jonathon, the rusted and beat-up old Harley was the most beautiful restoration project he had ever seen. Jonathon indicates he is now staying clean out of the benefits, not as he had done previously, living his life in fear and craving. Jonathon indicates that there are still tough times, but his life is certainly better than it was a year ago.

On his 1-year anniversary, Jonathon shared. He shared his frustration at times with his lack of progress and his disappointment with the false hope and promise of his medications. He shared his sadness, loss, and realization that often those who are addicted hurt the people they love the most, by rejecting their offers to help. He acknowledged that those who are addicted understand what they want only after they have lost those they love. Jonathan shared that despite his mental illness and his addiction, and in spite of himself, his life will continue and that, most important, he is responsible for making the most of his life with the tools given to him by people he only recently met but who have treated and understood him as if they were family.

## ■ Case 2

Stacy is a 15-year-old Latina girl currently being held at the county youth correctional facility. Her family history indicates that her father is incarcerated in a maximum-security prison and that Stacy was beaten by her alcoholic mother's boyfriends periodically from ages 10 to 12. She also stated that her mother and her mother's boyfriend sexually abused her at age 12. Her mother admitted that she punched and slapped Stacy on numerous occasions because of her own alcoholism and explosive anger.

At 13 years of age, Stacy was admitted for inpatient adolescent treatment after exhibiting suicidal ideation and running away from a group home. Stacy has a 2-year history of out-of-home placements as a result of abusing drugs, sexually promiscuous behavior, pregnancy and childbirth (baby girl at age 14), self-mutilation (cutting her arms, leg piercing, and piercing her nipples), and cursing out the school principal (which led to school suspension). One month after her 15th birthday, she used a box cutter to savagely cut a former girlfriend because she saw her making out with her boyfriend. When she arrived at the assistant principal's office, she slashed the assistant principal and was subsequently arrested. Stacy told the arresting officer that she had to cut the assistant principal's face because she does not like people who wear suits and ties. She kicked out the window in the police car while being transported and had to be taken to the emergency room, where she received 16 stitches for her injuries.

Every time Stacy goes home to her mother's house, she goes back to abusing drugs and alcohol, cutting school, getting into fights, breaking curfew, and spending several nights away from home without notifying anyone. Her probation officer recently learned that Stacy is part of a gang.

Stacy's probation officer indicates that she is an adolescent experiencing a series of crises, is on a destructive path, and has no family support system. Her mother was recently diagnosed HIV-positive, and her father is expected to be in the state penitentiary for another 5 to 8 years.

The probation officer recommends placement in a residential treatment facility for 2 years, with intensive substance abuse, anger management, and mental health counseling.

## Case Autopsy

As one might expect, Stacy's transition into a residential treatment program was not smooth. Her oppositional defiant stance led to several remarkable conflicts between Stacy, peers, and staff of the facility. Within days of admission, Stacy attempted suicide with 38 cuts to her arms and legs, combined with ingesting 30 acetaminophen tablets. Stacy was transported to the local hospital, where gastric lavage was performed. Once stabilized, Stacy was transferred to the inpatient psychiatric facility. Within 24 hours, Stacy found herself in four-point restraints after hitting one of the staff and breaking his nose. Following this act of violence, the unit crisis team responded. Six men were required to secure and transport Stacy into the restraint room.

While in restraints, Stacy met her social worker, Amy, who proceeded to discuss Stacy's history and to develop an ongoing plan for care. Amy very carefully explored the history of Stacy's abuse and tragic upbringing. Near the end of the session, Amy, seeking to establish rapport with Stacy, stated: "You're sitting on top of a lot of anger, hurt and frustration. . . . What steps do you think we can take to begin to deal with this anger?"

Stacy responded:

> It really doesn't matter. . . . I know I'm always going to have pain. My life is all about pain and I'm the person who can deal with all the ass-holes out there like you who think you can fix people. Well, I'm not broke, and if I wasn't in these leather handcuffs, I'd just kick your ass and be done with you!

Amy suggested to Stacy that her attempts to push her away would not work. She made this statement come true by visiting with Stacy for 10 minutes every hour of her shift while Stacy was in restraints. Slowly, Stacy became less argumentative during her time with Amy, and by the end of the day Stacy had contracted to not lash out toward staff. She had been placed on medications

(Haldol and Ativan) at the time of restraint. These were discontinued, and Stacy was placed on an atypical antipsychotic medication.

Utilizing the strengths perspective, Amy began to explore with Stacy the skills she had to address her situation. Stacy was able to identify she was a fighter and agreed with Amy that she should fight to make things right in her life. Building on this simple premise, Amy and Stacy began working together to identify major life problems. Stacy was clearly victimized through years of abuse and was responding to both the physical and emotional pain experienced. Issues such as anger, frustration, hurt, and loss were all explored. Amy and Stacy worked closely to explore and begin dealing with Stacy's volatile feelings and emotions. Within 2 weeks, Stacy's self-inflicted injuries had healed to the extent that she was able to begin utilizing the hospital gym as a physical release for her anger and frustration. Stacy's day was balanced with proper nutrition, group therapy, individual sessions, medication management group, medications, music and art therapy, and support groups.

Within the third week of the hospitalization, Amy and Stacy began to address plans for her return to the residential treatment facility. The plan included two transitional visits to the day treatment group, followed by debriefing sessions to address any issues that presented. Finally, Stacy was discharged back to the residential treatment program. Within the discharge conference, Stacy agreed to give this facility a chance, something she acknowledged she had not done in the past. Stacy acknowledged that she had much to live for and that she and Amy had constructed a plan to work toward, with vocational training, parenting courses potentially leading to the return of her daughter, ongoing medication management, therapy, and support group attendance.

The transition to the residential treatment program was not without incident. Over the next 2 years Stacy was rehospitalized on three occasions, each following an act of violence toward herself or others. Eventually, Stacy was able to enter the transitional teen program and to successfully establish independent living. Stacy and Amy always returned to the action plan established on the initial admission, with the agreement that the plan wasn't the problem: Compliance with the agreed-upon goals had been lacking, and reconnection with Stacy's plan would eventually lead to the stated goals.

This chapter examines delinquency trends and rates and discusses the fact that the prediction of storms of juvenile violence and the surge of violent youth predators in the second half of the 1990s never happened. In sharp contrast, chapter 1's review of the juvenile delinquency and juvenile court statistics for the past two decades reveals a decline in violent crimes among juveniles every year, starting in 1996. This chapter focuses on the inescapable link between juvenile criminal activities and drug and alcohol use and abuse. Understanding the nature and trends in juvenile drug offenses helps explain the surge in juvenile arrests and adjudications for drug-related crimes (e.g., curfew violations, weapons charges, possession of illegal and controlled substances, simple assault) through 2000 and the decline since 1996 in non-drug-related juvenile offenses, such as burglary, criminal homicide, forcible rape, aggravated assault, and robbery. Although some offenders are not addicted to drugs or alcohol, statistics indicate a positive correlation between alcohol and drug abuse and crime. In addition, this chapter will examine several prominent contributing factors to juvenile crime, including but not limited to learning disability, fetal alcohol syndrome, inner city characteristics, and family and peer influences that appear to work in concert to exacerbate criminal activities under certain circumstances. In closing, this chapter will discuss potential predictive models for examining the linkage between criminal activities and drug use, as well as appropriate treatment approaches.

## ■ Overview

According to the National Household Survey on Drug Abuse, a representative sample of 68,929 youths ages 12 to 17, 10.8% reported current use of illicit drugs in 2001. This is an increase from the 9.7% rate reported in 2000. Among this age group in 2001, the percent using illegal drugs was higher for boys (14.4%) than for girls (10.2%) (Substance Abuse and Mental Health Services Administration [SAMHSA], 2002).

Within the representative sample of 68,929, the 30-day prevalence rate of using any illicit drug is the highest among 12th graders (25.7%), second in 10th graders (22.7%), and lowest among 8th graders (11.7%). By the eighth grade, 50.5% of youth reported having tried alcohol, and 23.4% reported drinking to the point of intoxication. But what about other drugs? As high as 10.2% of the population of eighth-graders reported use of amphetamine compounds, and when all illicit drugs were considered, 14.8% of eighth graders have tried some illicit substance other than cannabis.

To calculate the consequences of drug use, the Drug Abuse Warning Network measures the number of persons seeking emergency department (ED) treatment for drug-related emergencies. From 1999 to 2001, the number of drug-related ED episodes increased from 17.1% of patients age 12 to 17 to 19% nationally (from 52,685 to 61,695). Within this population of 61,695, 16,516 indicated cannabis use, 3,509 reported cocaine use, 1,253 were accounted for by methamphetamine use, and 843 were related to heroin (SAMHSA, 2002).

In addressing the complicated issue of juvenile drug abuse, assessment and treatment approaches vary widely across the United States. The number of adolescents age 12 to 17 admitted to treatment facilities increased by approximately 20% between 1994 (109,055 admissions) and 1999 (131,294 admissions). Within this population group, cannabis accounted for 60% of all

**Table 3.1**

| Most Serious Offenses | Estimated # of Arrests | Percent Change 1990–1999 |
|---|---|---|
| Total | 2,468,800 | −8% |
| Crime Index Total | 645,400 | −10% |
| Violent Crime Index | 103,900 | −8% |
| Murder and nonnegligent manslaughter | 1,400 | −31% |
| Forcible rape | 5,000 | −9% |
| Robbery | 28,000 | −14% |
| Aggravated assault | 69,600 | −5% |
| Robbery Crime Index | 541,500 | −11% |
| Burglary | 101,000 | −15% |
| Larceny-theft | 380,500 | −10% |
| Motor Vehicle Theft | 50,800 | −5% |
| Arson | 9,200 | 1% |

admissions for youth in 1999, 51% of all adolescent admissions involved the use of both alcohol and cannabis, and 71% of adolescent admissions (76% of cannabis abuse admissions) were male (SAMHSA, 2001).

According to the Drug Abuse Monitoring Program, the number of juvenile court cases involving drug offenses more than doubled between 1993 and 1998. During 1998, U.S. juvenile courts handled an estimated 192,500 delinquency cases in which a drug offense was the most serious charge (U.S. Department of Justice, 2001). According to the FBI's Uniform Crime Reports 2001 data, there were 139,024 persons under the age of 18 arrested for drug violations.

In 1999, arrests of persons under the age of 18 accumulated to a remarkable 2,468,800 arrests. The crime index accounted for 645,400 arrests. Within this population, the violent crime index included 103,900 arrests, and the robbery crime index indicated 541,500 arrests. In all areas with the exception of arson, there was a decrease in the crime index. The logical assumption is that violent crime in the United States is decreasing. However, this may not be the case. It is possible that as a result of well-defined criminal systems, drug-related crimes have simply stabilized. This concept is examined in greater detail later in this chapter.

## ■ The Drug-Crime Relationship

Drugs and crime are related in many ways. However, the simplest and most straightforward relationship is that it's a crime to use, process, manufacture, and/or distribute drugs of abuse—specifically, cocaine, heroin, cannabis, and amphetamine compounds, to name a few. There are also secondary relationship correlates between crime and drugs. These are best represented by the behaviors demonstrated by those on drugs. Frequently, the effects of alcohol or other mood-altering drugs include repression of cognitive thought processes, leading to increased violent behavior, stealing, driving under the influence, domestic violence, and drug trafficking (Brownstein, Crimmins, & Spunt, 2000).

There have been numerous studies linking drug use and crime (e.g., Brownstein et al., 2000; Carpenter, Glassner, Johnson, & Loughlin, 1988; De la Rosa & Soriano, 1992; Dembro et al., 1987, 1990; Greenbaum, 1994; Kingery, Pruitt, & Hurley, 1992; Lattimore, Trudeau, Riley, Leiter, & Edwards, 1997; Milgram, 1993; Roth, 1994; Spunt, Goldstein, Brownstein, Fendrich, & Langley, 1995). In addition, numerous studies have been funded to answer fundamental questions regarding the relationship between drugs and crime. Recent studies have attempted to answer specific queries surrounding what are believed to be common correlates between drug and alcohol use and crime. Summaries of these recent studies are presented next.

## Do Arrestees Frequently Test Positive for Recent Drug Use?

The Bureau of Justice Statistics (BJS) completed an assessment of drug use by 570,000 inmates of the nation's prisons. At this time, 51% (290,700) reported using mood-altering substances at the time of their arrest. More than 360,000 prisoners (about a third in state prisons and about a quarter of federal prisoners) said they had participated in drug or alcohol treatment or other substance abuse programs since admission.

Taking into consideration gender, female arrestees tested positive in varying degrees based on location, with the lowest percentage population demonstrating a 33.3% prevalence (188,100 persons) with a positive drug test and the highest prevalence in New York City, with 82.1% testing positive. The arrest charge was given consideration. Within the male population, drug possession or sales demonstrated the greatest likelihood for testing positive upon arrest. For the female population, charges against prisoners most frequently testing positive for drug use upon arrest were prostitution and drug possession or sales. Similar prevalence for positive drug testing was found for stolen vehicles, robbery, and burglary. Furthermore, there was a remarkable correlation to polysubstance abuse; of the individuals testing positive for opiates, three fourths also tested positive for another mood-altering substance (National Institute of Justice, 1999; U.S. Department of Justice, 1999).

Within this study, juvenile offenders were also tested. Findings indicate similarities between adult and juvenile populations, as most were charged with drug possession or selling/distributing charges. Juveniles were less likely to test positive for drugs of abuse, but for those who did test positive, cannabis was the certainly drug of choice. In general, 50% of the juvenile population tested

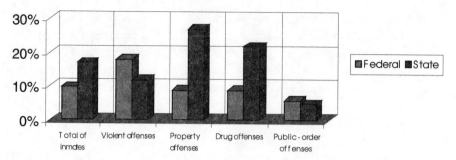

**Figure 3.1    Committed offense to obtain money to buy drugs**

positive for a mood-altering substance. Of those arrested, those who were in school were less likely to test positive for drugs than those who were not in school (U.S. Department of Justice, 1999).

### Do Drug Offenders Commit Offenses to Support Their Drug Habits?

According to a 1997 survey conducted jointly between federal (7,933 age 24 or younger) and state (209,343 age 24 or younger) prison inmate populations, an estimated 17% of state prisoners and 10% of federal prisoners reported they committed the crime they were arrested for to obtain money to buy drugs. Of those committing robbery, 27% of both state and federal prisoners reported committing crimes to obtain money for buying drugs (Figure 3.1; U.S. Department of Justice, 1999).

### How Many Incarcerated Offenders Were Under the Influence of Drugs When They Committed Their Offenses?

In 1997 the Bureau of the Census surveyed sentenced federal and state inmates as to whether they were under the influence of drugs at the time they committed the offense that resulted in their incarceration. Answers varied across both drug and crime categories and are shown in detail in Figure 3.2. To

**Figure 3.2    Percent of Crimes Committed While Under the Influence of Mood-altering Substances**

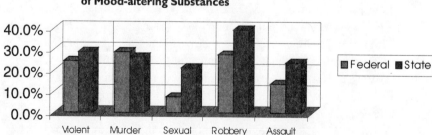

summarize, the study found that drug offenders and those committing robbery most frequently reported being under the influence of a drug at the time of their crime. This reporting trend was prevalent within the state prison system. Within the federal prison population, inmates were less likely to report an influence of drugs on their offenses, with the notable exception of murder and weapons offenses (U.S. Department of Justice, 1998).

## Does Drug Abuse Generate Violent Crime?

The drug trade has been characterized as extremely violent; however, questions arise regarding the correlation between crime and drug trafficking. Secondary data analysis conducted by the Drug Policy Information Clearinghouse staff from the FBI's (1999) *Crime in the United States: Uniform Crime Reports, 1991–1998*, indicate that trafficking in illicit drugs tends to be associated with violent crimes. Yet there are important differentiations to be made between trafficking and drug abuse or dependence. Studies indicate that the relationship between drugs and violence is tied specifically to drug trafficking with the strongest correlative factors being:

☐ Competition for drug markets and customers
☐ Disputes and rip-offs among individuals involved in the illegal drug market
☐ The tendency toward drug violence among individuals who participate in the drug trade

Within this context, consideration must be given to the locations in which street drug markets proliferate (Brownstein, 2000). Typically these areas are economically and socially disadvantaged. Within such environments, attempts to impact drug trade and violence through social controls and legal intervention tend to be ineffective (Brownstein, 1996). Additionally, there are reported increases in the utilization of lethal weapons. Nevertheless, crime statistics indicate that despite the proliferation of illegal weapons, the actual percentage of identified drug-related homicides has dropped consistently from 1991 at 6.2% to 1998 at 4.8% (U.S. Department of Justice, 2000).

## Are There Limitations to the Understanding of the Drug–Crime Relationship?

Despite the correlations presented and the growing body of evidence pointing to an interrelationship between drugs and crime, this relationship should be interpreted cautiously. The interrelationships between drugs and crime are extremely difficult to quantify. There are several critical contributing factors within this complex interaction, making the inclusion of all contributing factors nearly impossible to calculate. Factors contributing to difficulty in measuring the interaction are:

□ Personal factors
□ Situational factors
□ Cultural factors
□ Economic factors

Furthermore, even when drugs are identified as a contributing factor, it is only one factor among many (Brownstein, 2000; Crimmins, Brownstein, Spunt, & Ryder, 1998; De la Rosa & Soriano, 1992).

There are also questions around the definition of "drug-related," which varies from study to study. Some studies interpret the presence of drugs as having a causal relevance. Others may interpret the relationship via narrower criteria, such as positive drug testing, as presented previously. However, while drug urinalysis provides a quantifiable measure, some drugs such as cocaine or hallucinogens may not be detected because of an extremely short half-life or the cutoff level or specificity of each test administered. Thus only drug tests within hours of arrest, combined with those that screen to minute levels for all substances of abuse, are considered accurate. Still other reports rely heavily on prisoner self-report. Problems exist with this method because reports by offenders pertinent to their drug use may be skewed toward exaggeration or minimization of the impact of drugs on the offense (Brunelle, Brochu, & Cousineau, 2000).

Despite these limitations, evidence indicates that persons engaging in drug trafficking and those who use drugs are more likely to commit crimes, that arrestees are frequently found to be under the influence at the time they commit their offenses, and that drugs tend to generate violent responses. Caution should be exercised, as these assumptions are based on what can best be described as problematic evidence. As a result, indicating with any quantitative certainty the exact impact of drugs on crime is not currently possible (Brownstein, 2000; Brunelle, Brochu, & Cousineau, 2000; Crimmins, Brownstein, Spunt, & Ryder, 1998).

## ■ Ability to Predict National Crime Trends

The business of predicting national crime trends presents challenges similar to those faced by the National Weather Service in predicting the presence of severe weather. Although the ability to identify particular trends contributing to the possible emergence of a severe storm is well documented, the ability to pinpoint the precise date and time of a severe storm remains elusive, to say the least. The same is true in the prediction of juvenile delinquency and violent crime trends.

In 1995 John J. Dilulio Jr., then professor of politics and public affairs at Princeton University, noted the nationwide presence of an enormous number of children under the age of 10 and suggested that this population of approximately 40 million children would be the largest cohort of adolescents in a generation. Dilulio further characterized this population as fatherless, godless, and jobless (Dilulio, 1985, p. 18). Within the same time frame, Louis J. Freeh, director of the Federal Bureau of Investigation, commented on the "ominous increase in juvenile crime, coupled with population trends, portend future crime and violence at nearly unprecedented levels" (cited in Butterfield, 1995, p. 18). Dilulio further stated that violent crime is concentrated in decaying and impoverished urban areas that have high rates of unemployment and drug abuse. Large numbers of victims and perpetrators are relatively illiterate, jobless, and drug dependent (Roberts, 1998).

In retrospect, the basis of this form of prediction is somewhat clearer. Frequently, it is said that those who do not know history are condemned to repeat it. This is also true for the examination of patterns pertaining to drug use. Given what is known about drugs throughout the history of America and the tendency for cocaine and heroin (opiates) to wax and wane in popularity, the potential for an explosive combination was right in 1995. Beginning in the mid-1970s, cocaine began to reemerge as a drug of choice. At this time there was no remarkable growth of cocaine among the average population, secondary to the expense. It quickly became recognized as the drug of choice for the very few very wealthy who could afford to buy this high-class stimulant. Few experienced any problems with this drug because the primary method of ingestion was intranasal and in relatively low doses. Many indicated that cocaine was not addictive (Yeager, 2000). Specifically, Ashley (1975) reported that cocaine was neither addictive nor a dangerous drug (p. 186). Ashley ignored the history of cocaine as an addictive drug.

Unknowingly, Ashley was headed down the same path traveled by a young physician working in Vienna more than a century ago. This physician was searching for a new and effective drug for the treatment of numerous physical ailments, as well as an effective treatment for depression. That young physician was none other than Sigmund Freud, who was first recognized for his writings "On coca," in which he championed the effectiveness of cocaine in treating numerous illnesses from indigestion to syphilis.

In a similar course to that of Ashley, Freud unknowingly triggered the first major emergence of cocaine use. Freud's initial study of cocaine was conducted on a friend, Ernst von-Fleischl, whom Freud was treating for, among other issues, morphine addiction. While von-Fleischl initially appeared to be responding well to the treatments, his tolerance for cocaine grew rapidly. Unaware of the neurophysiological implications of rapidly increasing the dose, von-Fleischl began to experience the characteristic overdose symptoms associated with cocaine. Von-Fleischl's condition rapidly deteriorated, as he began experiencing paranoid delusions and formication syndrome ("coke bugs"), best described as tactile hallucinations of bugs crawling under one's skin (Byck, 1974; Maisto, Galizio, & Connors, 1999; Yeager, 1999).

Freud later denounced his earlier work, indicating the dangers of cocaine;

however, the damage had already been done. The same is true for the work of Ashley in the United States as for Freud in Europe. The desire to view cocaine as a recreational drug became the springboard to an expanding appetite for cocaine in the United States (Byck, 1974; Maisto, Galizio, & Conners, 1999).

So how, then, do Freud and Ashley tie into Dilulio's prediction of a coming storm of criminal violence from youthful superpredators? Ashley's comments set the stage for an acceptance of cocaine among many. Although there had been noted cases of remarkable cocaine addiction, most notably Dallas Cowboys linebacker Hollywood Henderson, who in 1978 acknowledged his cocaine addiction of $1,000 a day, cocaine addiction appeared to be the exception rather than the rule. As the popularity of cocaine grew, so did the availability of less expensive cocaine, leading many to take the drug in higher doses. At the same time, patterns of use were changing. Although the initial use of cocaine was typically intranasal, trends toward intravenous use of cocaine emerged. In the late 1970s and early 1980s, cocaine use began to take on a new form, freebasing (Maisto et al., 1999).

Cocaine is a remarkably versatile drug. In its white powder form, cocaine is made from combining a paste of coca leaves and hydrochloric acid solution to form a salt known as cocaine hydrochloride. The salt base of cocaine leads to the versatility of this drug. Because cocaine is water-soluble, it can be taken intranasally and absorbed through the mucous membranes of the nose. In addition, being water-soluble, cocaine can also be taken intravenously, a method that provides more intense cocaine highs but is accompanied with greater risks for characteristic cocaine overdose and cocaine-induced hallucinations and delusions. However, the most rapid absorption of cocaine is accomplished by smoking the drug (Allen, 1987).

When smoked, cocaine is absorbed completely and rapidly, and the result is nearly immediate euphoria. This euphoric state is short-lived, but it is extremely reinforcing. Many acknowledge the severe cocaine crash but quickly add, "The next high is worth it." While freebasing provided a remarkable high, there were problems with this method, which involved mixing cocaine powder with ether, a remarkably flammable substance. Again, a popular figure became the victim of cocaine, when comedian Richard Pryor was severely burned while freebasing cocaine (Siegel, 1985).

The true explosion of cocaine and the criminal activities associated with it did not occur until the mid-1980s, when a cheap and effective method of freeing cocaine from its sodium base was developed. The process safely separated cocaine from its base by dissolving the cocaine salt in an alkaline solution, and common baking soda became the alkaline of choice. When the water in this solution is boiled off, the resulting residue is a hard substance similar to small stones and frequently referred to as "rock." Crack cocaine melts when a flame is applied; the vapors are inhaled, providing a rapid, concentrated flow of cocaine to the brain. Although the high is extremely intense, it is extremely short in duration. When the high wears off, the cocaine addict is faced with two alternatives: dealing with the crash or buying and using more cocaine. By the late 1980s, the National Institute of Drug Abuse reported that cocaine had become an American epidemic, with millions of Americans having tried crack cocaine (Caldwell, Croft, & Server, 1980; Garwin, 1991).

> [Cocaine use] was all about getting away at first, then it was all about getting the drug. Being a mother of three and the grandmother of seven I spent all my time taking care of others. I said this high was for me. Oh, I got away, I got away from the church, my family, my job, and my freedom. I got so far away I was doing things that I would never do. In the end I got so far away I didn't even know who I was. Before that night I smoked that joint with the crack in it, I didn't even drink on a regular basis. It took a total of eight months for me to lose everything, end up bankrupt, busted and sick.

As the cocaine trade began to expand, so did the prevalence of criminal activities surrounding the use of this drug, a trend many were watching at the time Dilulio made his prediction. The indicators were clear. Most notable was the emergence of well-organized gangs such as the Bloods and Crips. Within this emergence of gang activity, juvenile gang membership began to grow and thrive. Young adults were used as dealers and as "mules," a term for those moving cocaine from location to location.

During the 1980s and 1990s, some researchers studying the drugs–violence connection shifted their focus from violence as an individual phenomenon to a violence within the community phenomenon (Blumstein, 1995; Brownstein, 1996; Jacobs, 1999). In time, the importance of placing more emphasis on the relationship between the drug trade, the establishment of drug markets, and violence emerged as a remarkable area of study in understanding the drug–crime connection and possibly explaining why Dilulio's prediction did not evolve to the degree predicted. Recent research indicates the initial increase in violent crime within large U.S. cities from the early to mid 1990s was largely the result of the introduction and expansion of the crack cocaine trade. However, in the late 1990s through 2000, there has been a documented decrease in crime. Brownstein, Crimmins, and Spunt (2000) indicate that this decrease in crime is not actually a reduction in crime but rather a stabilization of the crack cocaine markets.

Brownstein, Crimmins, and Spunt (2000) suggest a framework to conceptualize violence and drug-related crime based on two specific drug markets. First is a drug market that is well established and organized; within this market, authority lines have been established, boundaries have been clearly defined, and there are clearly established and organized processes associated with drug trafficking (Dembo, Hughes, Jackson, & Mieczkowski, 1993; Jacobs, 1999). The second drug market encompasses those that are newly emerging, with unclear lines of authority and territory. In such an environment, there is greater competition for the market, which is less stable, thus translating into potential for greater violence (Dembo et al., 1993; Jacobs, 1999). Certain patterns have developed that are consistent with the two models regarding drug markets and juvenile crime. Key indicators, including but not limited to aggravated assault, weapons charges, robbery charges, and curfew and loitering violations, appear to demonstrate trends across years that are consistent with the drug market conceptualizations outlined by Brownstein et al. (2000). The tables in Figure 3.3 are utilized to document what appears to be a correlation between the

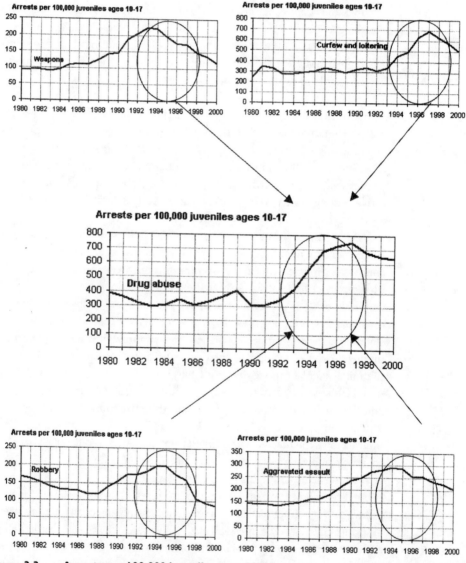

**Figure 3.3**     **Arrests per 100,000 juveniles ages 10–17**

Adapted from: Snyder, H. (2002). Juvenile Arrests 2000. Washington, D.C. Office of Juvenile Justice and Delinquency Prevention.

increases in drug abuse that coincide with the emergence of crack cocaine to increases in violent crimes—specifically, weapons charges, curfew and loitering, aggravated assault, and robbery—within the same time period. One may question the significance of curfew violations, but this factor is important, as most violent crimes were committed after curfew hours. It is additionally indicative of a stepwise progression away from established societal norms for behavior (Brownstein, 2000).

Clearly, cocaine is not the only contributing factor to juvenile delinquency trends. Although stabilization has been noted across the area of violent crimes, the trend line for drug abuse has remained significantly above the initial 1980 data. What, then, are the current drugs of choice among the young adult population of the United States? Since the mid-1990s, two drug classifications have emerged as leading drugs of choice among the young adult population: club or designer drugs and opiate substances.

## ■ Overview of Designer Drugs

Designer and club drugs are the latest rave among the young adult population. The term *designer drugs* stems from these substances being modified versions of FDA-controlled substances. The end result is a group of drugs that because of the redesign oftentimes are not technically illegal. The process is one of staying one step ahead of the Drug Enforcement Administration and other law enforcement agencies (Glennon, 1996; Kirsh, 1986). Typically, designer drugs are developed clandestinely in illegal labs. Recently, the trend has been toward combining various substances to heighten the sexual effects of the drug combinations. Recent toxicology results have demonstrated some very interesting combinations, including one test that was positive for the following combination, despite the client indicating taking only one tablet: a "new designer combination" including methylenedioxymethamphetamine (MDMA), sildenafil citrate (Viagra), and diazepam (Valium).

Methylenedioxymethamphetamine (MDMA) is also known as Ecstasy, XTC, X, Adam, Clarity, and Lover's speed. It was developed in the late nineteenth century as a weight loss medication but was not used secondary to the remarkable side effects of the drug. MDMA was utilized briefly in the 1970s by psychiatrists to assist "their patients to emote." Although this was successful, the side effects were simply too great for psychiatric practice (Kosten & Price, 1992; Grob, Bravo, Walsh, & Liester, 1992). Side effects of this drug can include malignant hyperthermia, leading to muscle breakdown, and kidney and cardiovascular system failure. The end result can be heart attacks, strokes, and most commonly seizures. MDMA is considered highly neurotoxic, and prolonged use can result in long-lasting and possibly permanent damage to the neurons that regulate the release of serotonin (McMann & Ricaurte, 1995; McCann, Ridenour, Shaham, & Ricaurte, 1993). Common adverse side effects include but are not limited to sweating, rapid and irregular heartbeats, fatigue, muscle aches, involuntary muscle contractions, and insomnia. Drug-induced psychosis has been reported with the use of this drug by people with a family history of psychiatric illness (Concar, 1997; Johnson, Letter, Merchant, Hanson, & Gibb, 1988).

Because of the psychosexual effects of the combination designer drugs, they are quickly becoming the favorite of today's youths. Initially, the club drugs were popularized at "raves," large parties with many engaging in the use of this drug. That is not to say that all who attend raves are using this substance, for many raves are about music and interactions without the use of mood-altering substances. Increasingly, the use of club drugs, as with any substances, is migrating to small, personalized groups. This drug class is continuing to grow in popularity among the high school and college population (Concar, 1997).

Methamphetamine is frequently referred to as speed, ice, meth, crystal-meth, and glass, among other names. This drug is available in various forms and can be smoked, snorted, orally ingested, or injected. Methamphetamine has maintained a consistent popularity, with approximately 9.4 million Americans having tried this drug. Methamphetamine stimulates an excess of dopamine, which creates a remarkable feeling of euphoria during the high state, which can last for several hours when taken orally. When smoked or injected, the high is much shorter in duration but extremely intense. There is a crash following the use of this drug that is similar to the crash associated with crack cocaine (Concar, 1997). Methamphetamine use is associated with serious health consequences, including potential cardiac and neurological damage (Davis, Hatoum, & Walters, 1987; Grinspoon & Bakalar, 1979; Kirsch, 1986). More common side effects include memory loss, agitation, aggression, violence, and at times psychotic behavior (Davis, Hatoum, & Walters, 1987; Grinspoon & Bakalar, 1979; Kirsch, 1986).

Ketamine, sometimes called Special K, K, Vitamin K, and Cat, is an injectable anesthetic mostly used by veterinarians. Ketamine is very similar in effect to phencyclidine (PCP) and is known for dreamlike hallucinations. Its greatest danger is of the individual's getting hurt as a result of using this drug because the individual is essentially anesthetized. Severe side effects that can occur at high doses include delirium, amnesia, impaired motor function, high blood pressure, depression, and potentially fatal respiratory problems. Ketamine is most frequently produced as either a liquid or powder. In its liquid form, it can be injected intramuscularly (mostly done on the East and West Coast) or dropped into the eye. The powder form can be snorted or smoked with cannabis or tobacco (National Institute on Drug Abuse, 2001).

## ■ Inhalants

Within the juvenile drug group, one particular drug of abuse cannot be over-looked, the use of inhalants. This drug group covers a wide variety of products, a large number of which can be found in the home. These include but are not limited to adhesives, aerosols, solvents, and food products such as vegetable oil spray and whipped cream. This group includes gases, most specifically nitrous oxide found in "head shops" in the form of Whippets (Bruckner & Peterson, 1977; National Institute of Drug Abuse, 2001; Rosenberg & Sharp, 1992).

Inhalants are quickly absorbed into the bloodstream and distributed throughout the brain and body, affecting the central and peripheral nervous systems. Some effects can be long term. Chronic use has demonstrated struc-tural brain changes. Early teens and young adults are the largest growing pop-ulation using inhalants, which are freely available at home, and many have limited access to other drugs or the means to purchase these drugs (Garriott, 1992; Rosenberg & Sharp, 1992; Zacny et al., 1996). The interaction with crime is limited primarily to shoplifting to obtain inhalants, as the majority of these substances are not illegal and are readily available in any grocery store for under $5.

## ■ Overview of Opiates

In the previous wave of heroin and opiate dependence in the late 1960s, the thought of needle use served as a powerful deterrent to many would-be heroin users. Today that simply is not the case, as the heroin on the street now is much more refined, providing the opportunity to snort or smoke it. The changes in processing heroin have made the drug more popular with people under the age of 18. This was further fueled by the popularity of the "grunge" or Seattle Sound groups of the mid to late 1990s, such as Kurt Cobain of Nirvana. This increased popularity has also been driven by the irrational belief that snorting or smoking heroin will be less likely to cause addiction (Maisto, Galizio, & Connors, 1999).

Pulse Check, an agency monitoring trends of drug use across the United States, indicates that heroin is beginning to replace cocaine in most major cities as the most frequently used illicit drug. As of November 2001, heroin was most frequently used illicit drug, and additionally, 10 cities consider heroin the second most commonly used illicit drug in their communities. The survey cities span the country and include Baltimore, Philadelphia, Portland (Oregon), El Paso, Chicago, and Denver (Office of Drug Control Policy, 2001).

Recent estimates are that more than 2.4 million people have used heroin at some point in their lives, with 87% of the use population under the age of 26. Additional information indicates that severe medical consequences sec-ondary to heroin abuse are expanding. The Drug Abuse Warning Network notes that heroin-related emergency room visits have doubled since 1998. Within the past year, OxyContin, the pharmaceutical opiate oxycodone, has emerged as a popular opiate across the United States. However, this drug is cost prohibitive, as the opiate-dependent individual's tolerance quickly exceeds financial ability to maintain the dependence (Office of Drug Control Policy, 2001; SAMHSA, 2001).

Currently, heroin prices appear to be relatively stable. The most commonly reported heroin street sales unit is 0.1 gram, with prices ranging from $10 to $120, depending of the type and purity of the drug. The most common type of heroin across the nation is reported to be South American White. Heroin is sold in various forms: in capsules, known on the street as pills, for approximate $10; by the gram from $150 to $300; and by the "eight ball" or ⅛ ounce for $400 to $600, depending on purity (Office of National Drug Control Policy, 2001).

Medical consequences of chronic heroin abuse include scarred and collapsed veins, bacterial infections of blood vessels and heart valves, abscesses, and other soft-tissue infections. There are also remarkable correlations to kidney and liver disease. Related complications include lung disease such as pneumonia and tuberculosis. There is a high correlation with the onset of infectious diseases; within the IV heroin population, these most commonly include HIV-AIDS and hepatitis B and C (Holmberg, 1996; SAMHSA, 2000).

Persons using heroin report short-term effects of what can be characterized as a "rush" or surge of a generally pleasing warm sensation, followed by clouded mental functioning. At times there is nausea and vomiting; however, most frequently extreme fatigue and relaxation occurs. Many users report an emergence of energy following the use of heroin, but as use progresses, the feeling of well-being stems from the realization that the pain of pending withdrawal will be going away (Luce, 1972).

Physical dependence on heroin and other opiate substances develops quickly, and withdrawal may occur within a few hours after the last use of the drug. Characteristic withdrawal symptoms include restlessness, insomnia, diarrhea, vomiting, cold flashes, and muscle and bone pain. Withdrawal symptoms typically last from 5 to 7 days; however, long-term or protracted withdrawal symptoms can last for months after the last opiate use (National Institute of Drug Abuse Infofax, 2001).

## ◼ Cannabis Overview

Cannabis is possibly the most widely used illicit drug among the youths of the United States. There have been remarkable debates regarding the addiction potential for this substance, as demonstrated by a quick Internet search using the key word *marijuana*. Several thousand Internet pages will be available to you, attempting to sway your decision one way or another.

Among the youths who have reported using drugs, approximately 60% report use of cannabis. Most feel this drug is not addictive. To add complications, a growing number of cannabis users are between the ages of 12 and 17, with the number of eighth-graders who have tried cannabis in the last decade doubling (National Household Survey on Drug Abuse, 2001).

Studies indicate that long-term use of cannabis leads to changes within the brain structure similar to those created by cocaine. In fact, cannabis follows the same neuropathway as cocaine; however, the impact is not nearly as severe. Research indicates that heavy cannabis use impairs the ability to concentrate and to retain information. Additionally, cannabis use can exacerbate psychiatric conditions such as anxiety, panic attacks, and depression in persons with these disorders. Anxiety and depression with suicide ideation have been demonstrated in conjunction with cannabis use (Brookoff, 1994).

The most noted health effects are respiratory complications similar to those caused by smoking tobacco, including persistent cough and phlegm, frequent chest colds, increased risk for lung infection, tissue damage, and increased risk for cancer (Brookoff, 1994).

In recent studies completed by SAMHSA, adolescents between the ages of 12 and 17 who use cannabis weekly are nearly 4 times more likely to engage in violence than those who do not and are more likely to engage in destruction of property, stealing, and physical violence against others. Cannabis was noted in 1999 as the most frequently used drug among both male and female juvenile detainees (SAMHSA, 1999).

## ■ Additional Contributing Factors

Within the complex interactions that comprise delinquency and youth violence, it is acknowledged that chronic offenders have multiple risk factors. These can include deficits in family, school, peers, and neighborhood environment. It is also believed that clusters of cumulative factors interact to create a complex web of contributing factors to long-term behavioral outcomes.

Factors of abuse and maltreatment can range from emotional abuse to physical and sexual abuse. There is remarkable evidence demonstrating that children who are mistreated are at greater risk for early onset of violent delinquency and other remarkable problem behaviors. Cicchetti and Toth (1995) and Paschall and Hubbard (1998) indicate that problematic behaviors include substance abuse, poor academic performance, mental health issues, and teen pregnancy, in addition to delinquent behaviors involving legal intervention. Child abuse is a national epidemic with numbers approaching 1 million reported cases of child abuse and neglect nationwide. Of this group, 85% involve abuse and neglect by parents. Fifty-two percent of maltreated children suffered neglect, 24% physical abuse, 12% sexual abuse, and 6% emotional abuse. Many suffered more than one form of abuse (Knutson, 1995; Preski & Shelton,

2001; Sedlak & Broadhurst, 1996). Thornberry (1994) found a greater risk for violent behavior in children who were victims of child abuse at an early age. In addition, when neglect occurred, these children were more likely to begin offending earlier in life, making a connection between abuse and delinquent behavior.

Community risk factors that have been identified include availability of drugs and guns within the environment. Given community norms that favor drug use, firearm use, and crime, prevalence of delinquency at a younger age has been demonstrated. Economic deprivation and health problems have also shown positive correlates to development of delinquency (U.S. Department of Justice, 2000).

Family factors contributing to problem behaviors include paternal criminal behavior, maternal mental illness, negative parental attitudes, and poor family management issues, and witnessing or experiencing multiple acts of violence in the home leads to children who are twice as likely to commit violent acts (Fingerhut, Kleinman, Godfrey, & Rosenberg, 1991; Rutter, Cox, Tuppling, Berger, & Yule, 1975; Shelton, 2000).

Individual characteristics associated with delinquency include dropping out of school, drug use, early sexual activity, early independence from family, gun use, and early parenthood (Thornberry, 1994).

Preski and Shelton (2001) asked, "Which individual, family and community characteristics predict greater criminality in an juvenile delinquent population?" Within their work, 10 independent variables were examined: exposure to community violence, mother's mental illness, mother's involvement with child, father's substance abuse, parent's significant other's criminal history, parent's significant other's substance abuse, sibling's criminal history, sibling's substance abuse, sibling's physical illness, and the youth's substance abuse. The study included 1,704 less serious crimes and 170 serious crimes. Findings indicate those exposed to community violence or having a mother with mental illness were 4 times more likely to commit serious crimes. Those who abused mood-altering substances or whose fathers abused mood-altering substances were at 3 times greater risk to commit serious crimes (Figure 3.4).

Therefore, treatment approaches should focus on those risk factors believed to accentuate potential for juvenile delinquency and violence. Initial assessments should be designed to incorporate known predictive and risk factors including:

## ■ History Interview

☐ Exposure to violence throughout life
☐ Presence and history of family mental illness (specifically, mother's mental illness)

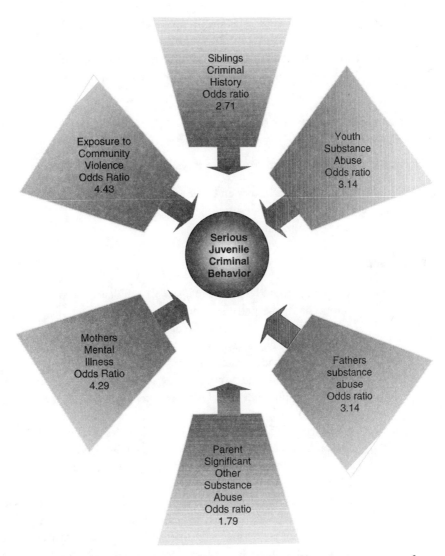

**Figure 3.4**   **Odds of committing serious juvenile criminal behavior given presence of stated independent variable**

Adapted from Preski & Shelton, 2001.

☐   Family history of substance abuse (specifically, father's history of addiction)

☐   Youth history or presence of comorbid mental illness and substance abuse

☐   Youth history of substance abuse, including progression into substance abuse

☐   Significant other and peer group history of substance abuse

☐   Sibling criminal activities

☐   Peer group criminal activities

- ☐ Parent–youth relationship (presence or absence of conflict and aggression in home)
- ☐ Presence of diagnosed learning disability, attention-deficit disorder diagnosis; school performance and achievement scores

## ■ Effective Treatment Interventions

### Physical and Psychological to Rule Out Physiological Basis for Behavior

- ☐ Complete history and physical examination
- ☐ Psychological testing
- ☐ Neuropsychological testing

### Program Design

Programs should be multidimensional, multilevel approaches to fully address the needs of the juvenile offender, including educational factors and needs associated with substance abuse or dependence. Development and implementation of specialized psychoeducational programming to address knowledge defects in individualized need areas is a must.

Programs should provide inmate staff models to foster and further develop mentoring and modeling of socially accepted behavior. Interactive learning is the key to moving juvenile offenders into realistic situations where skills are challenged and enhanced through hands-on experiential learning versus media-driven overstimulation. When possible, development of positive peer environments is key in the rehabilitation process. All too often, practitioners believe life-changing decisions are the work of a facilitated group or individual session. This simply is not the case. The most important decision comes long after the counseling staff has gone home for the evening and one patient asks another, "Are you going to do this stuff?" and the other patient indicates the importance of making positive changes. That is the essence of rehabilitation and hence the importance of developing a supportive peer environment.

Finally is the importance of skill development. For success to be sustained, people need not only education in how to treat their substance dependence but also lifelong skills. The primary focus should be:

Academic
    Needs assessment
    Study skills
    Awareness of most effective learning processes
Prevocational
    Skill group
    Testing for best fit
    Assessment of learning need

Vocational education
    Basic skills
    Learning environment
    On-the-job placement
    Specialized skill training
Technology (computer)
    Word processing
    Internet
    Spreadsheet
    Database development
    Networking
    Presentation
Interviewing skills
    Introduction
    Interaction
    Follow-up
Job placement assistance

Once initial phases are completed, juveniles will require step-down services. Following the initial inpatient treatment or incarceration, focus should be on completion of day treatment programming, 5 to 7 days per week and 8 to 10 hours per day with wraparound support, for the transition back into the social environment. The next step should be transition to intensive outpatient programming, 3 times per week 3 hours per day, for a period of 6 to 10 weeks, depending on the severity of the case. Then outpatient group and individual counseling should be provided, based on individualized need.

Before moving on, there are some specific truisms that should be addressed. These truisms are based in the lore of criminology but are actually myths.

## ■ Delinquency Myth versus Reality

Given the work noted in this chapter, the ability to predict delinquency or violent behavior in early childhood will not be based on the presence of a diagnosis of conduct disorder, or that is associated with behavioral discontrol as children. Rather, the stronger predictive factors are the child's adult and peer relationships, specifically, those experienced within the environment and the home environment (Satcher, 2001).

A second common myth is that African American and Hispanic youths are more likely to commit violent crimes. The reality is that in controlled studies, based on confidential interviews, there is little difference in prevalence rates for serious violent behavior among racial groups (Satcher, 2001).

The third myth is the belief that getting tough with juvenile offenders by trying them in adult courts reduces the likelihood that they will commit more crimes. The reality is that youths transferred to adult criminal court are significantly more likely to reoffend than youths who remain in the juvenile justice system (Satcher, 2001).

The final myth is that violence within school systems has increased dramatically in the last 5 years. The reality is that with the exception of a few high-profile cases, schools are relatively safe when compared with the homes and neighborhoods in which youths live, with the number of school homicides decreasing consistently throughout the 1990s. In addition, fewer students are bringing guns to school (Satcher, 2001).

## ◾ Delinquency and Biological Factors

In recent years, there have been shifts in trends of drugs abused by pregnant women. According to the Centers for Disease Control and Prevention (CDC) and the National Center on Birth Defects and Developmental Disabilities, the rate of alcohol abuse during pregnancy has declined; however, rates of binge drinking (five or more drinks per setting) and frequent drinking (seven or more drinks per week) did not decline, either during pregnancy or among nonpregnant women of childbearing age (Weber, Floyd, Riley, & Snider, 2002). The CDC indicates that 1 in 30 women are drinking at levels that could produce children with fetal alcohol syndrome (FAS). It is estimated that 1 in 8 women continue to drink during pregnancy. The estimated impact of this is that 130,000 pregnant women per year in the United States are drinking alcohol at levels shown to increase the risk of having a baby with FAS or other alcohol-related conditions (Weber, Floyd, Riley, & Snider, 2002).

Recently, O'Malley and Nanson (2002) identified clinical implications of a link between fetal alcohol spectrum disorder (FASD) and attention-deficit/ hyperactivity disorder (ADHD). One of the implications of this research is that ADHD within this population is of earlier onset and the inattention subtype, with potentially high correlative factors for comorbid developmental, psychiatric, and medical conditions. Furthermore, this population may be presenting with differential response to standard psychopharmacologic approaches, including the common use of psychostimulants for the treatment of ADHD. Within this study, developmental disorders considered to potentially increase the risk of comorbidity were working memory problems and mixed receptive-expressive language disorder with deficits in social cognition. Identified potential psychiatric comorbid disorders include anxiety, mood, conduct, or explosive disorders (Waldie & Spreen, 2001).

Taking this information in conjunction with the work of Malmgren, Abbott, and Hawkins (1999) that links learning disability and juvenile delinquent behaviors, there is an indication that this special population is at no greater risk for delinquency. In their study, Malmgren, Abbott, and Hawkins (1999) collected data over a 7-year period while completing their longitudinal prospective study design. Findings indicate that 9.9% of the 515 students studied self-reported data on delinquent activities. However, an analysis utilizing seven separate analyses that used different measures of delinquency as criterion variables, controlling for demographic variables of age, ethnicity, and socioeconomic status, indicated no accounting for a significant portion of unique variance in delinquency variables. However, research conducted by Waldie and Spreen (2001) indicated that certain personality characteristics, such as impulsivity and poor judgment, discriminate between persisting and nonpersisting delinquency in youth with learning disabilities.

In the mid-1980s, the term *crack baby* emerged to describe children born to women who had smoked crack cocaine while pregnant. From the onset, this label led to strong reactions from legal, child protective, and medical professionals. The name implied that these children would suffer severe and irreparable physical, emotional, and intellectual damage. However, recent research has challenged this myth. Debrah Frank (2002) searched studies on prenatal cocaine exposure conducted between 1984 and 2000. Samples were prospectively recruited, and examiners of the children were masked as to their cocaine exposure status. In addition, the cocaine-exposed cohort did not include a large portion of children also exposed in utero to other substances such as opiates, amphetamines, or phencyclidine. Nor were their mothers infected with HIV. Researchers focused on physical growth, cognitive assessment, language skills, motor skills and behavior, attention, affect, and neurophysiology.

Within the area of cognitive skills, one of nine studies indicated that children of mothers who used cocaine, alcohol, and cannabis demonstrated mean scores lower than controls. However, these scores were identical to those whose mothers used alcohol and cannabis without cocaine. Additional studies found no differences between infants whose mothers had used cocaine and whose mothers had used alcohol and/or marijuana. Numerous studies conducted to determine impact on learning and cognitive development demonstrated that prenatal cocaine exposure had no effect of IQ. There was no significant correlation between prenatal cocaine exposure and receptive or expressive language scores on standardized measures. In the area of motor skills, no study found a conclusive cocaine effect on motor development. There was a single study indicating delayed muscle development prior to 7 months; however, questions remain as to whether prenatal tobacco use was the major predictor (Harvard Mental Health Letter, 2001). Finally, the area of behavior, attention, affect, and neurophysiology indicated differences in affective expression between prenatal exposed and unexposed infants. These studies found that cocaine-exposed children showed less arousal, interest, joy, or sadness during learning tasks. The authors noted that prenatal cocaine exposure independent of exposure to alcohol has not been found to be associated with behavioral disturbances; however, this issue is to be further examined in future research (Frank, Augustyn, & Knight, 2001).

# References

Allen, D. E. (1987). *History of cocaine: The cocaine crisis*. New York: Plenum.

Ashley, R. (1975). *Cocaine: Its history, uses and effects*. New York: Warner.

Blumstein, A. (1995, August). Violence by young people: Why the deadly nexus? In *National Institute of Justice Journal*. Washington, DC: U.S. Department of Justice.

Brookoff, D. (1994). Marijuana facts. *New England Journal of Medicine, 331*, 518–522.

Brownstein, H. H. (1996). *The rise and fall of a violent crime wave: Crack cocaine and the social construction of a crime problem*. Guilderland, NY: Harrow and Heston.

Brownstein, H. H. (2000). *The social reality of violence and violent crime*. Boston: Allyn & Bacon.

Brownstein, H. H., Crimmins, S., & Spunt, B. J. (2000). A conceptual framework for operationalizing the relationship between violence and drug market stability. *Contemporary Drug Problems, 27*, 867–890.

Brownstein, H. H., Spunt, B. J., Crimmins, S., & Langley, S. (1995). Women who kill in drug market situations. *Justice Quarterly, 12*, 473–498.

Bruckner, J. V., & Peterson, R. G. (1977). Review of aliphatic and aromatic hydrocarbons. In C. W. Sharp & M. L. Brem (Eds.), *Review of inhalants: Euphoria to dysfunction* (research monograph 15, 124–163). Washington, DC: National Institute on Drug Abuse.

Butterfield, Fox. (1999). "Parents in prison: A special report; as inmate population grows, so does a focus on children." The New York Times, April 7: A1.

Byck, R. (Ed.). (1974). *Cocaine papers by Sigmund Freud*. New York: Stonehill.

Caldwell, J., Croft, J. E., & Server, P. S. (1980). Tolerance to the amphetamines: An examination of possible mechanisms. In J. Caldwell & S. J. Mule (Eds.), *Amphetamines and related stimulants: Chemical, biological, clinical and sociological aspects* (pp. 341–346). Boca Raton, FL: CRC.

Carpenter, C., Glassner, B., Johnson, B. D., & Loughlin, J. (1988). *Kids, drugs and crime*. Lexington, MA: Lexington.

Cicchetti, D., & Toth, S. (1995). A developmental psychology perspective on child abuse. *Journal of the Academy of Child and Adolescent Psychiatry, 34*(5), 541–562.

Cicchett, D., & Toth, S. (1995). Developmental psychopathology and disorders of affect. In D. Cicchetti and D. Cohen (eds.). *Developmental psycholpathology, Volume 2: Risk, disorder, and adaptation* (pp. 369–420). New York: John Wiley & Sons.

Concar, D. (1997). After the rave, the ecstasy hangover. *New Scientist, 54*, 4.

Crimmins, S. M., Brownstein, H. H., Sprunt, B. J., & Ryder J. A. (1998). *Learning about violence and drugs among adolescents (LAVIDA): A final report to the National Institute on Drug Abuse*. Rockville, MD.

Davis, W. M., Hatoum, H. T., & Walters, I. W. (1987). Toxicity of MDA 3,4, methylenedioxy-amphetamine considered for relevance to hazards of MDMA (ecstasy) abuse. *Alcohol and Drug Research, 7*, 123–134.

De la Rosa, M., & Soriano, F. I. (1992). Understanding criminal activity and use of alcohol and cocaine derivatives by multi-ethnic gang members. In R. Cervantes (Ed.), *Substance abuse and gang violence*. Newbury Park, CA: Sage.

Dembo, R., Hughes, P., Jackson, L., & Mieczkowski, T. (1993). Crack cocaine dealing by adolescents in two public housing projects: A pilot study. *Human Organization, 52*, 89–96.

Dembo, R., Washburn, M., Wish, E. D., Yeung, H., Getreu, A., Berry, E., et al. (1987). Heavy marijuana use and crime among youths entering a juvenile detention center. *Journal of Psychoactive Drugs, 19*, 47–56.

Dembo, R., Williams, L., Wothke, W., Schmeidler, J., Getreu, A., Berry, E., et al. (1990). The relationship between cocaine use, drug sales and other delinquency among a cohort of high risk youths over time. In M. de la Rosa, E. Y. Lambert, & B. Gropper (Eds.), *Drugs and violence causes correlations and consequences* (NIDA research monograph No. 103). Rockville, MD: National Institute of Drug Abuse.

Federal Bureau of Investigation. (1999). *Crime in the United States: Uniform crime reports, 1998*. October 1999.

Fingerhut, L., Kleinman, J., Godfrey, E., & Rosenberg, H. (1991). Firearm mortality among children, youth and young adults 1–34 years of age: Trends and current status: United States, 1979–1988. *Monthly Vital Statistics Report, 39* (Suppl. 11), 1–15.

Frank, D. A. (2001). Researchers debunk stigma of crack babies. *Brown University Digest of Addiction Theory & Application, 20*(6), 1–2.

Frank, D. A., Augustyn, M., Grant-Knight, W., Pell, T., & Zuckerman, B. (2001). Growth, development, and behavior in early childhood following prenatal cocaine exposure: A systematic review. *Journal of the American Medical Association, 285* (12), 1613–1625.

Garriott, J. C. (1992). Death among inhalant abusers. In C. W. Sharp, E. Beauvais, & R. Spence (Eds.), *Inhalant abuse: A volatile research agenda* (research monograph 129, 181–191). Rockville, MD: National Institute on Drug Abuse.

Garwin, F. H. (1991). Cocaine addiction: Psychological and neurophysiology. *Science, 251*, 1580–1586.

Glennon, R. A. (1996). Classical hallucinogens. In C. R. Shuster & M. J. Kuhar (Eds.), *Pharmacology aspects of drug dependence: Toward an integrated neurobehavioral approach* (pp. 343–369). Berlin: Springer-Verlag.

Greenbaum, S. (1994). Drugs, delinquency, and other data. In *Juvenile justice* (Vol. 2, pp. 2–8). Washington, DC: Office of Juvenile Justice and Delinquency Prevention.

Grinspoon, L., & Bakalar, J. B. (1979). *Psychedelic reflections*. New York: Human Sciences Press.

Holmberg, S. D. (1996). The estimated prevalence and incidence of HIV in 96 large U.S. metropolitan areas. *American Journal of Public Health, 86*, 642–654.

Jacobs, B. (1999) *Dealing crack: The social world of street corner selling*. Boston: Northeastern University Press.

Johnson, M., Letter, A. A., Merchant, K., Hanson, G. R., & Gibb, J. W. (1988). Effects of 3,4, methyleneddioxyamphetamine dismers on central serotonergic, dopaminergic and nigral neurotensis systems in the rat. *Journal of Pharamacology and Experimental Therapeutics, 244*, 997–982.

Kingery, P. M., Pruitt, B. E., & Hurley, R. S. (1992) Violence and illegal drug use among adolescents: Evidence from the U.S. National Adolescent Student Health survey. *International Journal of the Addictions, 27*, 1445–1464.

Kirsch, M. M. (1986). *Designer drugs*. Minneapolis, MN: CompCare.

Knutson, J. F. (1995). Psychological characteristics of maltreated children. *Annual Review of Psychology, 46*, 401–431.

Kosten, T. R., & Price, L. H. (1992). Phenomenology and sequelae of 3,4, methylenedioxymethamphetamine use. *Journal of Nervous and Mental Disease, 180*, 353–354.

Lattimore, P. K., Trudeau, J., Riley, K. J., Leiter, J., & Edwards, S. (1997). *Homicide in eight U.S. cities: Trends context, and policy implications* (November NCJ, 167262). Washington, DC: National Institute of Justice.

Lester, M. B., Grob, C. S., Bravo, G. L., & Waslh, R. N. (1992). Phenomenology and sequelae of 3,4, methylenedioxymethamphetamine use. *Journal of Nervous and Mental Disease, 180*, 345–352.

Luce, J. (1972). End of the road: A case study. In D. E. Smith & G. R. Gay (Eds.), *It's so good, don't even try it once* (pp. 143–147). Englewood Cliffs, NJ: Prentice Hall.

Maisto, S. A., Galizio, M., & Connors, G. J. (1999). *Drug use and abuse* (3rd ed., pp. 117–140). Fort Worth, TX: Harcourt Brace.

Malmgren, K., Abbott, D., & Hawkins, J. D. (1999). LD and delinquency: Rethinking the link. *Journal of Learning Disabilities, 52*(3), 194–200.

McCann, U. D., & Ricaurte, G. A., (1995). On the neurotoxicity of MDMA and related amphetamine derivatives. *Journal of Clinical Psychopharamacology, 15,* 295–296.

McCann, U. D., Ridenour, A., Shaham, Y., & Ricaurte, G. A. (1993). Evidence for serotonin neurotoxicity in recreational MDMA users: A controlled study. *Abstracts of the Society for Neuroscience Annual Meeting, 19,* 1169.

Milgram, G. G. (1993). Adolescents, alcohol and aggression. *Journal of Studies on Alcohol, 11* (Suppl.), 53–61.

NIDA Infofax. (2001). http://www.nida.nih.gove/infofax/infofaxindex.html

National Institute of Justice. (1999). *1988 ADAM: Annual report on drug use among adult and juvenile arrestees* (NCJ-175656).

Office of National Drug Control Policy. (2001). *Pulse check: Trends in drug abuse.* Washington, DC: Author.

Preski, S., & Shelton, D. (2001). The role of contextual, child and parent factors in predicting criminal outcomes in adolescence. *Issues in Mental Health Nursing, 22,* 197–205.

Roberts, A. R. (1998). *Juvenile justice: Policies, programs and services* (2nd ed.). Chicago: Nelson-Hall.

Rosenberg, N. L., & Sharp, C. W. (1992). Solvent toxicity: A neurological focus. In C. W. Sharp, E. Beauvais, & R. Spence (Eds.), *Inhalant abuse: A volatile research agenda* (research monograph 129, pp. 117–171). Rockville, MD: National Institute on Drug Abuse.

Roth, J. A. (1994). *Psychoactive substances and violence* (National Institute of Justice Research in Brief). Washington, DC: U.S. Department of Justice.

Rutter, M., Cox, A., Tuppling, C., Berger, M., & Yuel, W. (1975). Attainment and adjustment in two geographical areas: The prevalence of psychiatric disorder. *British Journal of Psychiatry, 126,* 495–509.

Satcher, D. (2001). Surgeon General: Youth violence epidemic not over. *Brown University Child & Adolescent Behavior Letter, 17*(3), 1–5.

Sedlak, A. J., & Broadhurst, D. D. (1996). Third national incidence study of child abuse and neglect. Washington, DC: U.S. Department of Health and Human Services.

Shelton, D. (2000). Health status of young offenders and their families. *Journal of Nursing Scholarship, 32*(2), 173–178.

Siegel, R. K. (1985). New patterns of cocaine use: Changing doses and routes. In N. J. Kozel & E. H. Adams (Eds.), *Cocaine use in America: Epidemiological and clinical perspectives* (NIDA research monograph 61, pp. 204–220). Department of Health and Human Services Publication No. (ADM) 90-1414.

Spiess, M., & Fallow, D. (2000, March). *Drug related crime* (Drug Policy Information Clearinghouse fact sheet). Washington, DC: Office of National Drug Control Policy, Executive Office of the President.

Spunt, B. J., Goldstein, P. J., Brownstein, H. H., Fendrich, M., & Langley, S. (1994). Alcohol and homicide: Interviews with prison inmates. *Journal of Drug Issues, 24,* 143–163.

Substance Abuse and Mental Health Services Administration. (2001). *The National Household Survey on Drug Abuse: Main findings 2001.* Washington, DC: Author, Office of Applied Studies.

Substance Abuse and Mental Health Services Administration. (2002). *Results from the 2001 National Household Survey on Drug Abuse: Volume 1. Summary of National Findings.* (Office of Applied Studies, NHSDA Series H-17, DHHS Publication No. SMA 02-3758.) Rockville, MD.

Substance Abuse Mental Health Services Administration. (2003). Alcohol and Drug Services

Study: The National Substance Abuse Treatment Systems: Facilities, Clients, Services, and Staffing. Office of Applied Studies. Rockville, MD.

Substance Abuse and Mental Health Services Administration. (2002). *The National Household Survey on Drug Abuse: Preliminary findings 2002.* Washington, DC: Author, Office of Applied Studies.Taylor, B. G., Fitzgerald, N., Hunt, D., Reardon, J. A., & Brownstein, H. (2001). ADAM Preliminary 2000 Findings on Drug Use and Drug Markets—Adult Male Arrestees Research Report National Institute of Justice.

Thornberry, T. (1994). *Violent families and youth violence* (fact sheet 21). Washington, DC: U.S. Department of Justice, Office of Juvenile Justice and Delinquency Prevention.

U.S. Department of Health and Human Services, National Institute of Health. *The University of Michigan monitoring the future, 2001, data from in-school surveys on 8th, 10th, and 12th grade students.* Washington, DC: Author.

U.S. Department of Justice, Bureau of Justice Statistics. (1998). *Alcohol and crime* (NCJ-168632). Washington, DC: Author.

U.S. Department of Justice, Bureau of Justice Statistics. (1999). *Mental health and treatment of inmates and probationers* (NCJ-74463). Washington, DC: Author.

U.S. Department of Justice, Bureau of Justice Statistics. (2000). *Profile of state prisoners under age 18, 1985–97* (NCJ-176989). Washington, DC: Author.

Waldie, K., & Spreen, O. (2001). The relationship between learning disabilities and persisting delinquency. *Journal of Learning Disabilities, 26*(6), 417–423.

Weber, M. K., Floyd, R. L., Riley, E. P., & Snider D. E. (2002). Defining the national agenda for fetal alcohol syndrome and other prenatal alcohol-related effects. *National Task Force on Fetal Alcohol Syndrome and Fetal Alcohol Effect, 51* (RR-14), 9–19.

Yeager, K. R. (2000). The role of intermittent crisis intervention in early recovery from cocaine addiction. *Journal of Crisis Intervention and Time Limited Treatment, 5*(3) 302–310.

Zacny, J. P., Lichtor, J. L., Coalson, D. W., Alessi, R., Goldsher, G., Young, C. J., et al. (1996). Examining the subjective, psychomotor and reinforcing effects of nitrous oxide in healthy volunteers: A dose response analysis. *Behavioral Pharmacology, 7,* 194–199.

# 4   School Violence

## Prevalence, Policies, and Prevention

Lisa Hunter, Gordon MacNeil, and Maurice Elias

This chapter examines the problem of school violence by defining the problem, discussing its prevalence, addressing its prevention, and reviewing the efficacy of existing programs designed to combat it.

Incidents of violence occur every day in schools across the United States. Although controversy exists over whether school violence is on the rise and more prevalent than it has been in the past, it is generally agreed that school and youth violence is a serious problem that must be addressed by policy makers, legislators, juvenile justice officials, and educational administrators.

There are two broad approaches to school violence: preventive and reactive. Preventive approaches try to teach skills and alter the school environment in ways that will decrease the likelihood of violent events occurring. Reactive approaches attempt to respond to violence once it has occurred. Preventive approaches offer much more promise as a strategy of reducing school violence. Reactive approaches to school violence tend to rely on tough disciplinary action and punishment. While this "zero tolerance" stance has tended to remove individuals from the school environment, relying on punitive measures has not generally resulted in lower rates of violence in school settings.

Jonesboro, Arkansas; Littleton, Colorado; El Cajon, California—uttering these names in the context of school violence evokes images of carnage and death. These are the images that have galvanized the media and brought attention to the potential for assaults and homicides in schools in our own communities. And yet, the horrendous acts of violence that happened in these towns are not the everyday incidents that typify school violence; they do not reflect the pervasive victimization that is present in virtually every public school in our nation. Bullying, psychological intimidation, verbal abuse, isolated punches and grabs and taunts, and fistfights are the forms of violence that pervade our schools (MacNeil & Stewart, 2000). Experts have commented on the futility of trying to profile children likely to exhibit behaviors similar to the assailants at Columbine High School; there simply isn't a single typology (Poland & McCormick, 1999; Will & Neufeld, 2002).

The heightened awareness of terrorism in our country should not skew our efforts to address school violence. The major threat of school violence is the pernicious everyday violence that has existed for more than a half century. Children are safer in schools than they are outside of schools (Bowen, Bowen, Richman, & Woolley, 2002), and yet much of the media's attention centers on *school* violence. Even in the face of reductions in the number of violent events in schools nationwide (see Bowen et al., 2002; Brooks, Schiraldi, & Ziedenberg, 2000; Kaufman et al., 2000), the problem of school violence remains central in our society's attempts to address social ills. This attention is warranted. These attempts to create and maintain safe learning environments for tomorrow's productive citizenry are necessary. We have far to go in order to establish schools that satisfy the promise of secure and safe harbors in which children can develop and grow.

## ■ The Prevalence of School Violence: Scope of the Problem

☐ Crime in schools continues to decline. There were 59 violent victimizations per 1,000 students in 1993 and 26 per 1,000 students in 2000 (a 46% decline).

☐ Despite this decline, students ages 12 through 18 were victims of about 700,000 violent crimes and 1.2 million crimes of theft at school in the year 2000.

☐ In 1993, 10% of all students said they were victims of crime at school (violent and property crimes), and 6% did so in 2001. Much of this decline can be attributed to lower rates of theft.

☐ Between the years 1993 and 2001, there were no reported differences in the rates of students reporting being threatened or injured with a weapon on school property.

☐ In 2000, students were more than twice as likely to be victims of serious violent crime away from school as at school. In 2000, students aged 12 through 18 were victims of about 1.9 million total crimes of violence or theft at school. In that same year, students in this age range were victims of about 128,000 serious violent crimes at school (i.e., rape, sexual assault, robbery, and aggravated assault). There were also 47 school-associated violent deaths in the United States between July 1, 1998, and June 30, 1999, including 38 homicides, 33 of which involved school-age children.

☐ The prevalence of other problem behavior at school has increased. For example, in 2001, 8% of students reported that they had been bullied at school in the last 6 months, up from 5% in 1999 (DeVoe et al., 2002).

These statistics (from DeVoe et al., the Bureau of Justice Statistics, 2002) suggest that although the mass media promotes the idea that school violence is rampant, violence-related behaviors in U.S. schools have declined in recent years. Most other researchers, using different sources of data, reach similar conclusions (see Astor, Pitmer, Benbenishty, & Meyer, 2002; Brener, Simon, Krug, & Lowry, 1999; MacNeil & Stewart, 2000). Despite this reduction, school violence remains a significant problem in our culture (Hamburg, 1998; Mercy & Rosenberg, 1998; U. S. Office of Juvenile Justice and Delinquency Prevention, 1999). As Astor and his colleagues suggest, perhaps the issue isn't whether the numerical indicators of school violence are changing but rather whether the political and philosophical understanding of the issue is changing (Astor et al., 2002). In other words, reductions of the number of incidents may not be sufficient if we as a society are becoming more sensitive to the issue and set stricter limits of acceptable behavior. The determination that a problem is a "big" problem is a political issue rather than an empirical one.

### Methods of Assessing School Violence

Measurement issues make it difficult to compare results of multiple studies, and it is difficult to know how pervasive the problem of school violence is because our indicators are limited and poorly operationalized (Small & Tetrick, 2001). Assessing the scope of school violence is typically done through three methods, each of which is subject to bias: self-report surveys, victimization surveys, and opinion surveys (Furlong & Morrison, 1994). Self-report surveys ask school officials to indicate how often specific acts of violence occur at their school. Victimization surveys ask students how often they have been the victim of a violent act. Opinion surveys ask community members their perceptions and opinions about school violence.

Each of these methods is likely to report different statistics of school violence. Opinion surveys are the least accurate indicators because they are based on individuals' perception of—as opposed to their actual experience with—school violence and are therefore subject to bias based on these perceptions. Self-report and victimization surveys may report different levels of school violence because school officials are not necessarily aware of all the acts of violence that occur in a school.

Arrest rate statistics are also used to determine rates of crime. However, these statistics tend to exaggerate the problem of youth violence because they represent the number of juveniles arrested for a violent crime, not the number of violent crimes committed by juveniles. Juveniles tend to commit violent crimes in groups. Thus, arrest statistics overstate levels of juvenile violence and contribute to the public's perception of a "crisis" of youth violence (Jones & Krisberg, 1994). Further, statistics reported by Hyman, Weller, Shanock, and Britton (1995) and Jones and Krisberg (1995) indicate that school crime has not significantly increased since 1977.

## ■ Defining the Problem: What Is School Violence?

The *Shorter Oxford English Dictionary* defines *violence* as the "exercise of physical force so as to cause injury or damage to a person, property, etc." (Trumble, Brown, Bailey, & Siefring, 2002, p. 3540). Schools have traditionally defined *violence* according to this dictionary definition. Thus, acts of assault, theft, and vandalism within the school are all examples of school violence. Until the 1990s, the federal government's definition included only rape, robbery, and simple and aggravated assaults (Bastian & Taylor, 1992), although in fairness this more restrictive definition was intended to provide a narrow focus for research studies (Alexander & Curtis, 1998).

However, the term *school violence* is commonly thought to encompass an array of behaviors, ranging from verbal taunts to bombing persons in a school building. These behaviors have in common that they are overt, aggressive acts that result in physical or psychological pain, injury, or death (Fredrick, Middleton, & Butler, 1995).

Some researchers believe the traditional definition of *violence* is too narrow and does not fully capture the pervasiveness of this problem within the schools. According to Batsche and Knoff (1994), "Violence should be defined more broadly to include any conditions or acts that create a climate in which individual students and teachers feel fear or intimidation in addition to being the victims of assault, theft, or vandalism" (p. 165). Morrison, Furlong, and Morrison (1994) suggest *violence* should be defined as physical and nonphysical harm toward others. This definition is similar to the definition proposed by Batsche and Knoff (1994) and emphasizes that violence has subjective and objective elements. Similarly, Astor (1998) suggests a definition in which the behavior includes intention or a perceived intention to cause harm. Astor promotes this definition because it includes milder forms of aggression common in elementary schools. He contends tolerance for milder forms of aggression in lower grades fosters more severe aggressive acts in later grades.

Expanding the traditional definition of *violence* to include subjective elements has important implications for schools. A broad definition of *school violence* emphasizes the importance of making schools safe, not just violence free (Morrison et al., 1994). The concept of safety incorporates the subjective and objective elements of a broad definition of violence. Safe schools are schools in which students and staff are not victims of physical assault and feel secure and peaceful (MacNeil & Stewart, 2000).

Additional issues need to be considered in the discussion of the meaning of *school violence*. For instance, violence includes behaviors that aggress against property as well as persons. Thus, school vandalism can be seen as a form of school violence. Perhaps a more important issue relates to the boundaries of the meaning of *school*. Laws relating to in loco parentis suggest that the school serves as surrogate parents from the moment children leave their homes for school until they return home. Thus, *school violence* would include violent acts well beyond the physical plant of the school. However, most of the literature relating to this issue limits the scope of the concern to behaviors evidenced on the grounds of the school itself.

It should not be surprising that school administrators are less likely to adopt broad definitions of *school violence*, despite their advantages. Physical acts of violence are much easier for school officials to document; they demand attention by virtue of their visibility and tendency to provoke outrage. Nonphysical acts of violence involving feelings of intimidation or fear are difficult to document and less likely to be reported. These differences between physical and nonphysical acts of violence contribute to the tendency of schools to focus exclusively on the former. Additionally, the indicators typically used to demonstrate that a school district has satisfied the requirements for federal funds from the Safe and Drug-Free Schools and Community Act (see Simons-Rudolph et al., 2003) and the Persistently Dangerous School and Unsafe School options of the No Child Left Behind Act of 2001 (Title IX, sec. 9532) emphasize physical acts of violence. The latter is particularly important, as it states:

> The federal No Child Left Behind Act of 2001, at Title IX, Section 9532, entitled "Unsafe School Choice Option," requires each state receiving funds under the Act to establish and implement a statewide policy requiring that a student attending a persistently dangerous public elementary school or secondary school, as determined by the state in consultation with a representative sample of local educational agencies, or who becomes a victim of a violent criminal offense, as determined by State law, while in or on the grounds of a public elementary school or secondary school that the student attends, be allowed to attend a safe public elementary school or secondary school within the local educational agency, including a public charter school. (The No Child Left Behind Act of 2001)

It is clear that the onus is on school administrators to demonstrate that they are providing safe environments in which students can learn, or those students can take their business elsewhere.

For our discussion, we ascribe to the operational definition that school violence is any intentional verbal or physical act producing pain in the recipient of that act while the recipient is under the supervision of the school.

What can one conclude from prevalence rates and discussions of definition that seem to cloud rather than clarify our understanding of school violence? Perhaps that there is a notable problem with school violence in our country, but that it is no worse than conditions outside our schools—and it seems to be somewhat better than the general environment, in fact. However, the problem of school violence is not fully understood by the numeric markers of violent acts or even those violent acts that are "caught." *Violence* also connotes verbal and physical acts that inflict psychological harm on the recipient, and these are not so easily counted. So long as the school provides refuge to those who inflict harm on others rather than safety to all, we have a problem with school violence.

Schools—especially public schools—are the single institution that must strive to eliminate inequities based on race, ethnicity, creed, or social status. Indeed, for learning to take place efficiently and effectively, schools and their surroundings must be places of safety, with minimal distractions from class disruptions, disciplinary incidents, and acts of verbal and physical aggression and intimidation. School and youth violence is a serious problem that must be addressed with determination by policy makers, legislators, key educational and juvenile justice officials and administrators, and all others concerned with living in a society that allows individuals a chance to grow to their fullest potential in a secure environment. Although it is important to keep the problem of violence in the schools in perspective, it is necessary and appropriate to view the problem systemically and to have a low tolerance for it in any and all contexts.

## ■ What Can Be Done About School Violence?

As of July 1, 1998, all public schools receiving funds through the Safe and Drug-Free Schools and Communities Act (SDFSCA) were required to assure that they are meeting the principles of effectiveness developed to ensure that schools implement science-based drug and violence prevention programs. These principles mandate that schools will (a) base their drug and violence prevention programs on needs assessment data, (b) develop measurable program goals and objectives, (c) implement programs with research evidence of effectiveness, and (d) periodically evaluate programs relative to their goals and objectives (U.S. Department of Education, 1998). Most schools are not adept at using evidence-based approaches to address problems they encounter. Historically, they have relied on data provided by developers of the programs they have purchased to establish the worthiness of the programs. In short, SDFSCA requires schools to meet a new standard of accountability. Fortunately, concerted efforts are being made to address this need (see Astor et al., 2002; Mytton, 2002). In 2000, for instance, 34 family-strengthening programs identified in a publication of recommended, research-based practices were endorsed by two federal agencies: the Office of Juvenile Justice and Delinquency Prevention and the Center for Substance Abuse Prevention. Three years of rigorous reviews by groups of national experts identified the 34 family-based prevention approaches (McDonald, 2002). Although these are family based, many are, in fact, collaborations with schools. Despite problems in the adoption of evidence-based programs due to a number of biases (see McDonald, 2002), the programs included in this list have been scrutinized to a far greater extent than most of the programs adopted on the basis of their "face appeal." One of the programs in this list is described in this chapter.

There are two broad approaches to school violence: reactive and preventive. Reactive approaches attempt to respond to violence after it has occurred. Preventive approaches try to teach skills and alter the school environment in ways that will decrease the likelihood of a violent event occurring.

## ■ Prevention Approaches

Most of the literature related to intervening in school violence focuses on prevention efforts. Prevention is easier, cheaper, and more effective than actually curing the results of violence once it has been perpetrated (Rich, 1992). These approaches can be as simple as installing metal detectors or involve more complicated interventions such as social skills training, conflict resolution training, and organizational changes. Preventive approaches are based on the belief that identifiable risk factors are associated with violence. Interventions that address these risk factors are likely to reduce violence. Many components of school violence prevention models can serve as points of departure for postoccurrence interventions with the perpetrators. Our focus in this chapter will be on what can be done from a school-based perspective.

A number of reviews and meta-analyses of prevention programs have been presented in the literature (see Astor et al., 2002; Catalano, Arthur, Hawkins, Berglund, & Olson, 1998; Dryfoos, 1990; Durlak, 1995; Gottfredson, 1997, 2001; Samples & Aber, 1998; Wilson, Gottfredson, & Najaka, 2001). Each of them points to the positive outcomes resulting from preventing rather than remediating violent behavior. However, many popular school-based prevention programs have not been subjected to rigorous examination, and thus their adoption should be tempered by the need for additional study (Wilson et al., 2001). Specifically, question should be raised about evaluations that use multiple baselines over time rather than control or comparison groups. Given the large declines in national rates of school violence, designs using multiple baselines during recent years may be reflecting national trends rather than the effectiveness of the specific program (Astor et al., 2002).

In their meta-analysis of prevention programs, Wilson et al. found that prevention programs are effective in reducing conduct problems. However, the average effect size for measures of delinquency was small. This may be due to extensive heterogeneity in the various programs, differences in evaluation methods employed, and types of populations served by the programs (Wilson et al., 2001). More rigorous studies produced higher effect sizes. Prevention programs targeted both general school populations and high-risk groups. These authors concluded that prevention strategies are particularly effective with the higher risk populations.

Wilson and his colleagues observed a large range of effect sizes across methodological categories, but none of the prevention programs produced truly large effect sizes. Self-control or social competency promotion using cognitive-behavioral and behavioral instructional methods produced consistently positive outcomes, whereas social work, counseling other than cognitive-behavioral, and other therapeutic interventions produced consistently negative effects with regard to reducing behaviors associated with conduct disorders. However, Astor and his colleagues conclude that a psychological or behavioral focus that is geared toward individual children (or their families) who are acting out has been ineffective in reducing school violence (Astor et al., 2002). Environmentally focused interventions also produced large effect sizes for positive outcomes related to reducing delinquency (Wilson et al., 2001). Wilson and colleagues conclude that many of the existing prevention curricula can be improved by including new instructional methodologies rather than by replacing the content of their programs. The cognitive-behavioral and behavioral modeling methods faring better in evaluations involved repeated exposure to new behaviors with rehearsal and feedback or cues to elicit the desired behaviors, as well as identification of specific behavioral goals and use of positive or negative reinforcement. Researchers have favored these methods because of the ease with which they can produce measurable outcomes.

It is clear that no single school-based strategy to prevent school violence, implemented in isolation, will have a large effect (Astor et al., 2002; Mytton, 2002; Wilson et al., 2001). However, there is disagreement as to whether school administrators are currently using interventions focusing on only one or two variables (see Astor et al., 2002) or whether schools tend to offer many different types of prevention programs simultaneously (see Wilson et al., 2001). It would appear that school-based prevention, in practice, is a *mix* of many different activities that schools implement. Wilson and his colleagues conclude that this suggests that the question "Which program works?" is not as pertinent as questions such as "Which combinations or sequences of strategies work best?' " and "How can schools effectively design comprehensive packages of prevention strategies and implement them in a high quality fashion?" (p. 269). We know little about the potential additive and multiplicative effect of combinations of distinct programs, but mandates by the federal government such as SDFSCA are prompting efforts to produce answers to these questions.

## Promising Violence Prevention Programs for Youths

### Changes to the Physical Plant

Several changes can be made to the physical layout of a school to prevent violence. For example, limiting access to school grounds, limiting places for loitering, patrolling bathrooms, placing lockers where supervision is possible, and installing parabolic or convex mirrors in stairwells or video surveillance equipment are all ways of improving school safety and reducing violence in schools (Morrison et al., 1994; Nilsson, 2002; Stephens, 1994).

The installation of metal detectors has become a very popular response to school violence, particularly after the Columbine High School event. The availability of firearms has had "the single most important impact on youth violence in general and juvenile homicide specifically" during the past 10 years (Jones & Krisberg, 1994, p. 15). Thus, preventing youths from bringing firearms into the school through the use of metal detectors is viewed as a justifiable violence prevention strategy.

There is evidence to suggest that metal detectors act as a deterrent (Mawson, Lapsley, & Hoffman, 2002). However, some studies indicate that the presence of a metal detector has no effect on the number of threats or physical fights reported (Ginsberg & Loffredo, 1993). Toby (2002) argues that this strategy does not address the root problem of violence in the community, where most violent acts occur for school-age children (Kaufman et al., 2001). Toby (2002) suggests that:

I Lethal school violence is comparatively rare in most school systems and does not justify the cost involved in setting up a system that may prevent such rare events.

**2** Schools are architecturally unsuited to perimeter defense. Most schools have too many doors and windows through which a student in the school can admit others with weapons.

**3** It is extremely inconvenient to keep out of schools everything that can be turned into lethal weapons because (a) school shops and classrooms use tools that are in effect weapons and (b) quite ordinary objects like nail files and cutlery can be utilized as weapons.

Violence prevention programs that focus solely on making changes to the physical plant of the school are unlikely to have a significant impact on the overall rates of school violence. These programs are important but do not change the underlying causes of school violence. Rather, they focus on increasing the likelihood of catching students who are about to or have acted violently. Efforts that emphasize law enforcement strategies as a means to prevent school violence tend to promote "us versus them" attitudes among students and authorities, while efforts that rely on all members of the school community collectively in producing a safer environment tend to promote a joint ownership of the outcomes (Furlong & Morrison, 2000). To effectively reduce school violence, students need to learn to act nonviolently not just because they will be punished if they do but because violence is an inappropriate and ultimately ineffective solution to problems (Pelton, 2002).

### Antibullying Programs

Antibullying programs have been employed internationally for decades and provide a model for school violence prevention programs, particularly as bullying is often seen as an early indicator of violent behavior toward others (see Astor et al., 2002; MacNeil, 2002; MacNeil & Stewart, 2000). A number of specific models have emerged, but most share the following elements:

**1** The planning stage includes as many stakeholders as possible.

**2** The workgroup develops an antibullying, antiviolence philosophy to which all constituents agree.

**3** The philosophy is translated into a policy to which all constituents agree.

**4** The policy provides clear definitions of behavioral expectations that identify and define the culture of the school.

**5** Programs are developed to introduce and promote the ongoing maintenance of the policy. These should target the silent majority of students, asking them to stand up to bullies, get adult help, and reach out in friendship to peers who are excluded. The goals of this component are to build peer pressure against bullying, to stop copycat bullying, and to increase support for victims.

**6** Performing to the behavioral expectations is rewarded by an ongoing recognition system.

**7** Misbehavior results in corrections. Problem behaviors aren't ignored or rewarded. Consequences are predictable, inevitable, immediate, and escalating, and they are based on uniform expectations for all. Inconsistent enforcement makes the problem worse.

8 Information concerning student behavior is collected and analyzed in an ongoing manner (Horner & Sugai, 2000; Olweus, Limber, & Mihalic, 1999; Rigby, 1996; Sullivan, 2000; Tattum & Herbert, 1993).

How adults in positions of authority respond to reports of victimization has an impact on future reports from students. If adult responses do not solve violence problems, students feel unsupported or betrayed by these adults and are vulnerable to more victimization. In essence, the victim is violated twice—once by a bully and once by the system that is supposed to protect them (see MacNeil, 2002; MacNeil & Stewart, 2000; Rigby, 1996).

Noteworthy—and consistent with all antibullying prevention programs—is the concept that the school environment is a synergistic reflection of the energy that all members of the school give it. That is, the school is a reflection of the people there; if everyone knows what is expected and what the consequences of their behavior will be, they can create a positive and safe environment where they can focus on learning and growing rather than on discipline and punishment. Only through the consistent application of standardized policies is this accomplished (Olweus et al., 1999; Rigby, 1996).

The model identified here provides a plan for schoolwide intervention, to which classroom-based components and individual-based components can be added. These latter two intervention components should provide discipline and counseling for the perpetrator and support for the victim (Olweus, 1993; Olweus et al., 1999). Discipline and therapy are interrelated, but they are separate issues and should not be performed by the same people (Hazler, 1996). Three tasks are necessary in an intervention program: recognition of the problem, enforcement of school policies, and counseling. Everyone in the school should perform the recognition task. Minor transgressions can be handled by teachers, but most problems are best resolved when the different tasks are performed by separate people, as role confusion and distrust result when a single person is charged with multiple tasks (Hazler, 1996).

## Early Childhood Education

Astor and his colleagues (2002) comment that high-quality early childhood education can provide a measure of school violence prevention. Several early comprehensive intervention programs have had favorable impacts on the prevention of delinquency and violence (see "Studies Tout Early Intervention," 2003). These programs include the Perry Preschool Project, the Houston Parent–Child Development Center, and the Syracuse Family Development Research Project. These programs have been thoroughly described elsewhere (see Zigler, Taussig, & Black, 1992), and we review only the Perry Preschool Project here.

The Perry Preschool Project was designed for low-income, Black children between the ages of 3 and 4 considered at risk for below-average intellectual functioning and eventual school failure (Zigler et al., 1992). Children attended preschools where they received high-quality cognitively oriented early childhood education for 1 to 2 academic years. Parents of these children attended monthly small group meetings for support and the exchange of ideas. Home visits by preschool teachers were also part of the program.

Results of a longitudinal study comparing students who were part of the project with those who were in the control group until age 19 indicated that children who were part of the project had better attitudes toward school, better grades and standardized test scores, and fewer arrests or charges for delinquent behavior (Schweinhart, Barnes, & Weikart, 1993; Zigler et al., 1992).

The longitudinal results of programs like the Perry Preschool Project offer strong support for the efficacy of early comprehensive interventions as a method of preventing delinquency and violence. These programs follow the social development approach toward prevention, which seeks to reduce identified risk factors by enhancing known protective factors (Hawkins, Catalano, & Brewer, 1994).

### Targeting Interpersonal Skill Difficulties

There is a growing realization that problems of violence are linked to an array of interpersonal skill difficulties and, correspondingly, a paucity of alternative prosocial behaviors (Pepler & Slaby, 1994). These critical areas have been summarized as incorporating self-control, group participation and social awareness skills, and critical thinking skills for thinking through everyday problems and decisions, as well as for managing difficult choices under stress. Some children are likely to benefit from prescriptive models of intervention that focus on training youths to be competent in interpersonal interactions. Goldstein's Prepare Curriculum is an example of this model (Goldstein, 1989).

The Prepare Curriculum includes components that provide social skills training (skillstreaming), anger control training, moral reasoning training, problem-solving training, empathy training, situational perception training, cooperation training, recruiting supportive models, and understanding and using group process modules (Goldstein, 1989). The first three modules serve as the core for the program. Youths are taught appropriate social skills through a social skills training program. Through a role-playing and performance-feedback process, youths master the skills. They are taught to control their anger by identifying their personal physiological and psychological triggers and by developing new ways to respond to those triggers. The moral reasoning element is taught by introducing a series of moral dilemmas in group sessions, with youths discussing possible responses to the dilemmas. Others have suggested that this kind of curriculum needs to be complemented by education that stresses acknowledging actions and restitution as consequences for the misbehavior (Olweus, 1993; Olweus et al., 1999).

## Conflict Resolution and Mediation

Although some programs employ peer mediators, increasingly, schoolwide approaches teach conflict resolution and mediation skills to all students. These approaches emphasize communication, anger management, and perspective-taking skills and are usually taught as a curriculum unit with a prescribed number of lessons. According to Webster (1993), conflict resolution programs are unlikely to reduce violence among youths because classroom-based curricula have generally failed to produce lasting behavior changes among youths unless these curricula were coupled with other supporting interventions, and also because the assumptions regarding conflict resolution programs and violence are questionable. For example, one premise of these programs is that the desire to be healthy and safe will motivate students to reduce and avoid violence. This premise is false for many inner-city youths who believe that being tough and willing to fight, carrying a gun, and shooting a gun are necessary for survival and a symbol of status among peers (Webster, 1993). Conflict resolution programs also may not have an impact on violence because conflict resolution skills are not always the appropriate response to violence. "If someone is beating, shooting, or burning another person, the degree of violence is beyond sitting down and working out a peaceful solution" (Prutzman, 1994, p. 75). Nonetheless, programs such as Peace Builders are becoming increasingly popular. Peace Builders is a schoolwide violence prevention program that incorporates strategies to change the school environment by promoting positive behavior and enhancing social competence based on the following five principles: (a) Praise people, (b) avoid put-downs, (c) seek wise people as advisers and friends, (d) notice and correct any hurts you cause, and (e) right wrongs (Flaxman, Schwartz, Weiler, & Lahey, 1998). Rather than being curriculum-based, Peace Builders promotes itself as being a "lifestyle." However, much of the program material is, in fact, expected to be infused into the current academic curriculum.

The Peace Builders program targets bullying and aggression. In this sense it is a focused organizational approach; it uses the organization of the school to address only one or two specific behaviors of concern. Other programs may be more general in their "targeting." These can be referred to, respectively, as focused and general organizational change programs.

## Academic-Related and Classroom-Management Prevention Strategies

Research has shown that schools organized in certain ways experience lower levels of violence and vandalism than other schools. The following conditions have been identified as factors that are conducive to low rates of violence (see Hawkins & Lam, 1987):

1 Students perceive their courses to be relevant.
2 Students perceive that they have some control over what happens to them at school.

3 Students perceive school discipline policies as firm, fair, clear, and consistently enforced.

4 Students see that there is a rational reward structure in the school that recognizes students for their achievements.

5 There is strong and effective school governance, with a consistent structure of order and strong principal leadership.

6 Ways are found to decrease the impersonality of the school and increase the amount of continuing contact between students and teachers.

Hawkins and Lam (1987) sought to prevent violence and delinquency in seventh-grade Seattle students through school-focused interventions that had an impact on these areas. The central area targeted for change was classroom instruction.

Proactive classroom management, interactive teaching, and cooperative learning were the three techniques used to alter methods of classroom instruction. Proactive classroom management instructs teachers how to give clear and explicit instruction for student behavior and to recognize and reward attempts to cooperate (Hawkins & Lam, 1987). Interactive teaching focuses on the mastery of clearly specified learning objectives and grades students in reference to their mastery and improvement rather than in comparison with other students. In cooperative learning, students work together in heterogeneous groups to master curriculum material.

Teachers in the three middle schools in the study were randomly assigned to experimental or control classrooms. Results indicated that students in experimental classrooms after 1 year of the project were more likely to engage in learning activities and less likely to be off task, spent more time on homework, and developed greater educational aspirations. In addition, students in experimental classrooms were less likely to be suspended or expelled from school. These results suggest that instructional changes have benefits on students prone to delinquency and violence. Related programs summarized by Slavin, Karweit, and Wasik (1992, 1992–93) have shown promise in modifying instructional conditions that can lead to school alienation and dropping out.

## Second-Generation Social Decision-Making Strategies

The family of programs referred to as second-generation social decision making, social problem solving, and interpersonal cognitive problem solving are organizational because they are implemented by teachers and parents (Elias & Clabby, 1992). Their principles become part of school and home routines. Thus, teachers and parents are instructed to use social decision making and problem solving in a wide variety of situations; most critically, by so doing, they find themselves in new, positive relationships with their children, relationships that serve to bolster children's mental health and prepare them for social and academic success (Clabby & Elias, 1986; Elias, 1993).

Elias and Clabby's (1992) Social Decision Making program has been designed to incorporate many skills implicit in the ability to form bicultural identities and multicultural sensitivity, as well as to curb tendencies toward verbal and physical violence, to act counter to media and other messages and models, and, prosocially, to act in a positive, constructive, and competent manner toward others in individual and group situations, regardless of ethnic, racial, or cultural background, gender, or age (Brendtro, Brokenleg, Van Bockern, & Blue Bird, 1991; Cortes, 1990; Phinney, 1989).

There are three curriculum components, or phases, of the program:

1 Self-control skills. These skills are necessary for accurate processing of social information, for delay of behavior long enough to engage in thoughtful accessing of one's social decision-making abilities, and for being able to approach others in a way that avoids provoking their anger or annoyance.

2 Social awareness and group participation skills. These skills underlie the exercise of social responsibility and positive interactions in groups.

3 Social decision-making and problem-solving skills. This is a set of skills that combine to form a strategy to guide one in thoughtful decision making in the face of choices or problematic situations, particularly when one is under stress.

The major documented effects of the program (Elias & Clabby, 1992) are that involved children were more sensitive to others' feelings, had improved means–ends thinking skills, had higher self-esteem, showed more positive prosocial behavior, handled the difficult transition to middle school more effectively, and displayed lower than expected levels of antisocial, self-destructive, and socially disordered behavior, even when followed up into high school.

### Comprehensive Organizational Change Focus

Brendtro and Long (1995) believe that prevailing approaches to violence prevention must incorporate attention to four sets of risk factors: fragile or broken social bonds; stress and conflict in school, home, and neighborhood; a culture of violence that includes such incongruous images as schools that use corporal punishment of students and religious leaders who sanction violence against those who do not share their beliefs; and cognitive impairments resulting from learning disabilities, alcohol and other drug use, fetal alcohol and drug use, and poor nutrition.

There are two examples of comprehensive programs that serve to illustrate the operation and potential of this approach. Project CARE is an organizational program that was utilized by a Baltimore City public school as part of an effort to reduce school disorder. The project was developed by using Program Development Evaluation (PDE), an organizational method developed by Gottfredson (1984). PDE is based on the following assumptions:

1 Projects guided by explicit theories that can be translated into action will be most effective.

**2** Projects will be implemented with the most enthusiasm, be strongest, and contribute most to knowledge of school improvement if the theories on which the projects are based are regarded as sensible by project implementers and are in accord with evidence from previous research and evaluation.

**3** Effective implementation of an intervention or innovation is more likely if blueprints for the intervention are available and if the implementation is guided by data about the extent to which project activities are in accord with the blueprint.

**4** Effective adoption of an innovation is more likely when explicit plans for adoption are available and when these plans are likely to overcome obstacles to organizational change.

**5** Projects will become more effective in the presence of "evaluation pressure." Evaluation pressure takes many forms, such as pressure to focus on theory and to heed relevant information from previous research and evaluation and from current data about program strength, fidelity, and effectiveness.

**6** Organizations that internalize these principles will be more effective than those that simply comply with them. (Gottfredson, 1984, pp. 1101–1102)

Project CARE had eight main components. Two of these components were classroom management techniques and classroom instructional approaches. The two classroom management techniques used were assertive discipline and reality therapy. Assertive discipline focused on teaching teachers how to set limits and specify consequences for students, provide uniform follow-through, and reinforce appropriate behavior with warmth, support, and rewards (Gottfredson, 1987). Reality therapy attempts to persuade students to make a commitment to change their behavior.

Student team learning was used as a classroom instructional approach to change the classroom climate from social to academic and to encourage student motivation and mastery of academic material. Additional components of Project CARE included a school discipline and review and revision component, parent volunteer program, community support program, an intervention that informed parents about classroom behavior, extracurricular activities, and a career exploration intervention (Gottfredson, 1987).

The efficacy of Project CARE was evaluated over a 3-year period. Organizational health, rebellious behavior among students, and students' attitudes and experiences were assessed. The impact Project CARE had on rebellious behavior is particularly relevant to this chapter's focus on school violence. Virtually all indices of delinquency and conduct favored the experimental schools over matched comparison schools. The largest differences were in serious delinquency and school suspensions. Social bonding data suggested that alienation decreased significantly in the experimental schools, while attachment for school increased significantly for experimental middle schools and decreased significantly in the matched controls. Finally, school safety increased to a higher degree in experimental schools than in controls (Gottfredson, 1986).

Other findings from the study were not as strong. Most noteworthy was the relative lack of impact on at-risk youths. Taken together, these results suggest that the potential of organizational approaches may well depend on the specific interventions used as part of the various components. This strategy suggests that school violence will not be effectively ameliorated until the level of expertise in school-based prevention is both increased and respected.

## Risk Factors as Targets of Prevention Efforts

A number of interventions are based on the premise that identified risk and protective factors in the child's character and environment (specifically in the child's family) can serve as the focus of interventions. There are several known risk factors for the development of violent behavior (see Kazdin, 1995; Mac-Neil, 2002). Many of these factors can be identified early in a child's life. Buka and Earls (1993) identified several child and family characteristics as early determinants of delinquency and violence. Several factors have been identified that contribute to participation in aggression and violent behavior (Bowen et al., 2002; Dryfoos, 1998; Kazdin, 1995; Williams, Ayers, & Arthur, 1997).

One set of these risk factors encompasses an adolescent's environment and includes such variables as family income level, the local availability of drugs and alcohol, and the degree of neighborhood crime and disorganization. A second group of risk factors includes biological and psychosocial characteristics such as an adolescent's degree of impulse control, the age at which a child first engages in illegal behavior, the child's family history regarding alcoholism, and the degree to which an adolescent is subject to genetic disorders. Research with genetics and other biological factors continues to produce promising results despite the current lack of concrete findings.

Another set of related risk factors concerns the social world of the adolescent, including interpersonal relationships. These factors include a lack of adequate parental supervision, inconsistent or overly harsh disciplinary practices, higher rates of drug and alcohol use by peers and family members, lack of interest in school on the part of the youth and/or the youth's parents, and an adolescent's poor academic performance.

Research indicates that families of delinquent adolescents can be distinguished from other families on the basis of five characteristics (Dryfoos, 1998; Kazdin, 1995; Williams et al., 1997; Tolan & Mitchell, 1990). Families of delinquents have long-standing and high-frequency parental conflict. In these families, there is a lack of differentiation between parental and child influences over family decisions. A lack of positive affect in family interactions and a tendency for aggressive communications are also characteristic of families of delinquents. Finally, when these families do communicate, communication time is dominated by one or two members.

These characteristics of families of delinquents have guided the development of family therapy with delinquents. A range of techniques can be used with these families, including behavioral contracting, communication skills training, and behavioral management training (Tolan, Cromwell, & Brasswell, 1986). Research generally shows that improvement in family functioning leads to reduced delinquency (see Kazdin, 1995; Rigby, 1996).

Most of the family approaches that have been evaluated are examples of secondary prevention methods. These approaches seek to prevent delinquency from recurring. Family therapy also has a role in primary prevention of delinquency and violence. Teaching families how to communicate effectively, monitor their children, and discipline fairly may prevent delinquency and violence from ever occurring. There are several types of primary prevention for families, however, such as routine prenatal and perinatal care to reduce the chances of early complications. Health education for mothers and immunization programs for infants are also associated with lowering risks for the development of violence. A variety of home and family interventions such as parent training, social support for mothers, and programs designed to enhance parent–child interaction are associated with lowering some of the family risk factors for the development of violence.

The multiple child and family risk factors for delinquency and violence suggest that "there is no single shot preventive agent to keep a child from developing into a violent and aggressive adolescent" (Buka & Earls, 1993, p. 58). According to Hawkins et al. (1994), behavior problems, aggression, stealing, lying, and dishonesty are the strongest individual-level predictors of violence in adolescence. Prevention programs targeting risk factors should use multiple strategies to reduce the multiple risk factors associated with the development of violence. Early comprehensive interventions for violence seek to address the risk factors of violence from "conception to age six" (Hawkins et al., 1994).

One prevention program that is based on identified risk factors for delinquency is the Families and Schools Together (FAST) program, which applies community organizing principles, group work practices, and child and family therapy strategies in multifamily groups to enhance protective factors for children and reduce delinquency, drug abuse, and school failure (McDonald, 2002). The criteria for inclusion are based on identified family risk factors, and the program seeks to provide services to families before delinquent behaviors are manifested (McDonald, 2002). The process includes creating a collaborative team, outreach to stressed and isolated families, 8 multifamily weekly group meetings run by the team, and 22 monthly multifamily groups run by FAST parent graduates (McDonald & Frey, 1999; McDonald & Sayger, 1998).

The multifamily meetings are limited to eight families. Rather than lectures, the families engage in structured, enjoyable, interactive activities, and with repetitions, the families build stronger relationships over the course of 8 weeks. Activities stress development of communication skills, conflict resolution skills, and bonding among family members (particularly through one-on-one activities within the sessions). Additionally, each week parents meet in dyads for 15 minutes for "buddy" relationships. This peer mentoring has been well received by participants, and outcome measures suggest that it is an effective mechanism for increasing parenting skills (McDonald & Frey, 1999; McDonald & Sayger, 1998). Programs such as FAST address the need for integration between schools and other institutions—churches, social service agencies, law enforcement and judicial systems, and families themselves—in addressing school violence in a preventive fashion.

## ■ Reactive Approaches

The recent public frenzy over school violence has influenced the type of approach that is taken toward school violence. Many concerned parents, educators, and politicians advocate "get tough" and "zero tolerance" policies for youths responsible for school violence (see Astor et al., 2002; Bowen et al., 2002; Morrison et al., 1994, for examples). Catch phrases like *get tough* and *zero tolerance* translate into reactive and punitive disciplinary actions. Federal, local, and state police reflect this punitive approach to violence prevention (Elliott, Hamburg, & Williams, 1998). The Crime Control Act of 1990 (including Title XVII, the Gun Free School Zones Act) prohibits the possession or discharge of firearms on or within 1,000 feet of private, parochial, or public school grounds. Persons convicted of transgressing this law receive heavy prison sentences or fines. Students who commit violent crimes in schools are suspended, expelled, and/or sent to jail, as the case merits. Advocates of reactive approaches believe that tough disciplinary action against the perpetrators of violent school crimes will dissuade others from committing such crimes. However, few evaluations have been made on the most common interventions used in schools, such as expulsion, suspension, and referral to special education and detention, and those that have been produced show little or no positive effect on violence reduction (Astor, 2002; Elliott et al., 1998). To the contrary, the evidence indicates that incarcerating large numbers of young people for prolonged periods is ineffective and counterproductive (Fagan, 1996; Sherman et al., 1997; Wilson, 1994). Given the fact that the United States has the highest crime rate among all Western democracies even though it is the most punitive nation, reactive approaches to school violence are unlikely to have a significant impact (Hyman et al., 1995). Students who commit violent school crimes must face some consequences, but relying exclusively on punishment will not reduce school violence.

As Mawson et al. (2002) suggest, "Far from deterring, inhibiting, or preventing violence, punishment is the most powerful stimulant to violence yet discovered. Sixty years of research on child rearing has shown that the more severely children are punished, the more violent they become both as children and adults" (p. 247).

## Conclusion

Prevention of violence will result only from comprehensive efforts across the full range of societal institutions. This approach has been entitled Comprehensive Social Competence and Health Education (C-SCAHE) (Weissberg & Elias, 1993). It highlights the synergy that results from having a focus on enhancing students' health and social competence through coordinated intervention strategies at both the person/small group and organizational/environmental levels. As such, C-SCAHE requires developmentally appropriate, planned, sequential, and coordinated policies, practices, and infrastructures, incorporating peers, parents, the full array of school resources, and community members.

Prevention of school violence and crisis intervention after occurrences will always be needed. School district administrators, principals, and social service agency administrators are advised to plan and develop both prevention and postoccurrence crisis management plans in order to create safe schools and address the issue of school violence and potentially volatile school situations (MacNeil & Stewart, 2000).

While the evidence to date is far from conclusive, there are some guidelines for those concerned with violence prevention that can be drawn based on available knowledge. Organizational approaches that employ as their program components the most proven of current techniques, as outlined earlier, are likely to have the most lasting impact on violence. These approaches, however, must be supplemented by early and continuing intervention into the parenting process, thereby providing not only assistance to parents and children during a critical developmental period but also a forum for socialization of parents with regard to their expected involvement in the education of their children throughout their school careers. Concomitantly, the school violence prevention programs must embrace parental involvement and seek to maximize this in a genuine manner, something that has not yet been an integral part of comprehensive school-based interventions.

Finally, efforts must be understood as being dynamic and therefore subject to constant monitoring and refinement along the lines of what Elias and Clabby (1992) describe as an ongoing action research cycle of program monitoring, evaluation, feedback, and modification. For this to occur, educational administrators must be prepared to be on-site action researchers, ready to work in a spirit of continuous improvement to ensure that the youths under their charge are being provided with the conditions needed for their comprehensive social and academic competence and engagement in school and community life. This is a minimal job description for a community or society that is concerned about the well-being of its children and the future of its citizenry and social institutions, as well as committed to the dramatic reduction of interpersonal violence and victimization.

## References

Alexander, R., & Curtis, C. (1995). A critical review of strategies to reduce school violence. *Social Work in Education, 17*(2), 73–82.

Astor, R. A. (1998). School violence: A blueprint for elementary school interventions. In E. M Freeman, C. G. Franklin, R. Fong, G. L. Shaffer, & E. M. Timberlake (Eds.), *Multisystem skills and interventions in school social work practice* (pp. 281–295). Washington, DC: National Association of Social Workers Press.

Astor, R. A., Pitmer, R. O., Benbenishty, R., & Meyer, H. (2002). Public concern and focus on school violence. In L. Rapp-Paglicci, A. Roberts, & J. Woodarski (Eds.), *Handbook of violence* (pp. 262–302). New York: Wiley.

Bastian, L. D., & Taylor, B. M. (1991). *School crime: A national crime victimization survey report* (U.S. Department of Justice, Bureau of Justice Statistics, NCJ-131645). Rockville, MD: U.S. Department of Justice.

Batsche, G. M., & Knoff, H. M. (1994). Bullies and their victims: Understanding a pervasive problem in the schools. *School Psychology Review, 23*(2), 165–174.

Bowen, G. L., Bowen, N. K., Richman, J. M., & Woolley, M. E. (2002). Reducing school violence: A social capacity framework. In L. Rapp-Paglicci, A. Roberts, & J. Woodarski (Eds.), *Handbook of violence* (pp. 303–325). New York: Wiley.

Brendtro, L., Brokenleg, M., Van Bockern, S., & Blue Bird, G. (1991). The circle of courage. *Beyond Behavior 2*(1), 5–12.

Brendtro, L., & Long, N. (1995). Breaking the cycle of violence. *Educational Leadership, 52*(5), 52–56.

Brener, N. D., Simon, T. R., Krug, E. G., & Lowry, R. (1999). Recent trends in violence-related behaviors among high school students in the United States. *Journal of the American Medical Association, 282*(5), 440–446.

Brooks, K., Schiraldi, V., & Ziedenberg, J. (2000). *School house hype: Two years later*. Washington, DC: Justice Policy Institute; Covington, KY: Children's Law Center.

Buka, S., & Earls, F. (1993). Early determinants of delinquency and violence. *Health Affairs, 12*(4), 46–79.

Bureau of Alcohol, Tobacco, and Firearms. (1998). *Crime gun analysis branch CGAB shots*. Falling Waters, WV: Author.

Catalano, R. F., Arthur, M. W., Hawkins, J. D., Berglund, L., & Olson, J. J. (1998). Comprehensive community and school-based interventions to prevent antisocial behavior. In R. Loeber & D. P. Farrington (Eds.), *Serious and violent juvenile offenders: Risk factors and successful interventions* (pp. 248–283). Thousand Oaks, CA: Sage.

Clabby, J. F., & Elias, M. J. (1986). *Teach your child decision making*. New York: Doubleday. (Out of print; now distributed by Psychological Enterprises Inc., 160 Hanover Avenue, Suite 103, Cedar Knolls, NJ 07927)

Cortes, C. (1990). A curricular basis for multicultural education. *Doubts and Uncertainties, 4*, 1–5.

DeVoe, J. F., Peter, K., Kaufman, P., Ruddy, S. A., Miller, A. K., Planty, M., et al. (2002). *Indicators of school crime and safety: 2002*. Washington, DC: U.S. Departments of Education and Justice and Bureau of Justice Statistics, NCES 2003-009/NCJ 196753.

Dryfoos, J. G. (1990). *Adolescents at risk: Prevalence and prevention.* New York: Oxford University Press.

Dryfoos, J. (1998). Safe passage: Making it through adolescence in a risky society. New York: Oxford University Press.

Durlak, J. A. (1995). School-based prevention programs for children and adolescents. Thousand Oaks, CA: Sage.

Elias, M. J. (Ed.). (1993). *Social decision making and life skills development.* Gaithersburg, MD: Aspen.

Elias, M. J., & Clabby, J. F. (1992). *Building social problem solving skills: Guidelines from a school-based program.* San Francisco, CA: Jossey-Bass.

Elliott, D. S., Hamburg, B. A., & Williams, K. R. (Eds.). (1998). *Violence in American schools: A new perspective.* New York: Cambridge University Press.

Fagan, J. (1996). Comparative advantage of juvenile vs. criminal sanctions on recidivism among adolescent felony offenders. *Law Policy, 18,* 77–113.

Fingerhut, L. A., Cox, C. S. (1998). *Comparative analysis of injury mortality: Advance data.* Hyattsville, MD: National Center for Health Statistics.

Flaxman, E., Schwartz, W., Weiler, J., & Lahey, M. (1998). Trends and issues in urban education, 1998. Retrieved January 20, 1999, from http://eric-web.tc.columbia.edu/mono/ti20 .pdf

Fredrick, A. D., Middleton, E. J., & Butler, D. (1995). Identification of various levels of school violence. In R. Duhon-Sells (Ed.), *Dealing with youth violence: What schools and communities need to know* (pp. 26–31). Bloomington, IN: National Educational Service.

Furlong, M. J., & Morrison, O. M. (1994). School violence and safety in perspective. *School Psychology Review, 23*(2), 139–150.

Ginsberg, C., & Loifredo, L. (1993). Violence-related attitudes and behaviors of high school students—New York City, 1992. *Journal of School Health, 63*(10), 438–440.

Goldstein, A. P. (1989). *The prepare curriculum.* Champaign, IL: Research Press.

Gottfredson, D. C. (1986). An empirical test of school-based environmental and individual interventions to reduce the risk of delinquent behavior. *Criminology, 24,* 705–731.

Gottfredson, D. C. (1987). An evaluation of an organization development approach to reducing school disorder. *Evaluation Review, 11*(6), 739–763.

Gottfredson, D. C. (1997). School-based crime prevention. In L. W. Sherman, D. C. Gottfredson, D. MacKenzie, J. Eck, P. Reuter, & S. Bushway (Eds.), *Preventing crime: What works, what doesn't, what's promising: A report to the United States Congress* (pp. 5.1–5.71). Washington, DC: U.S. Department of Justice, Office of Justice Programs.

Gottfredson, D. C. (2001). *Schools and delinquency.* New York: Cambridge University Press.

Gottfredson, O. D. (1984). A theory-ridden approach to program evaluation: A method for stimulating researcher-implementer collaboration. *American Psychologist, 39,* 1101–1112.

Hamburg, M. A. (1998). Youth violence is a public health concern. In D.S. Elliott, B. A. Hamburg, & K. R. Williams (Eds.), *Violence in American schools: A new perspective.* New York: Cambridge University Press.

Hawkins, J. D., Catalano, R. F., & Brewer, D. D. (1994). *Preventing serious, violent, and chronic delinquency and crime: Effective strategies from conception to age six.* Seattle, WA: Developmental Research and Programs.

Hawkins, J. D., & Lam., T. (1987). Teacher practices, social development, and delinquency. In J. D. Burchard & S. N. Burchard (Eds.), *Prevention of delinquent behavior* (pp. 241–274). Newbury Park, CA: Sage.

Hazler, R. J. (1996). *Breaking the cycle of violence: Interventions for bullying and victimization.* Washington, DC: Accelerated Development.

Horner, R. H., & Sugai, G. (2000). School-wide behavior support. *Journal of Positive Behavior Interventions, 2*(4), 231.

Hyman, I. A., Weller, E., Shanock, A., & Britton, O. (1995). Schools as a safe haven: The politics of punitiveness and its effect on educators. *Educational Week, 14*(23), 48.

Jones, M. A., & Krisberg, B. (1994). *Juvenile crime, youth violence and public policy.* San Francisco: National Council on Crime and Delinquency.

Kachur, S. P., Stennies, G. M., Powell, K. E., Modzeleski, W., Stephens, R., Murphy, R., Krusnow, N., Sleet, D., & Lowrey, R. (1996). School-associated violent deaths in the United States, 1992–1994. *Journal of the American Medical Association, 275,* 1729–1733.

Kaufman, P., Xianglei, C., Choy, S. P., Ruddy, S. A., Miller, A. K., Fleury, J. K., et al. (2001). *Indicators of school crime and safety, 2001.* Washington, DC: U.S. Government Printing Office.

Kazdin. A. E. (1995). *Conduct disorders in childhood and adolescence* (2nd ed.). Thousand Oaks, CA: Sage.

MacNeil, G. (2002). School bullying: An overview. In L. Rapp-Paglicci, A. R. Roberts, & John Wodarski (Eds.), *Handbook of violence* (pp. 247–261). New York: Wiley.

MacNeil, G., & Stewart, C. (2000). Crisis intervention with school violence problems and volatile situations. In A. R. Roberts (Ed.), *Crisis intervention handbook: Assessment, treatment and research* (2nd ed., pp. 229–248). New York: Oxford University Press.

Maguire, K., & Pastore, A. L. (Eds.). (1996). *Sourcebook of criminal justice statistics, 1995.* Washington, DC: U.S. Department of Justice, Bureau of Justice Statistics.

Mawson, A. R., Lapsley, P. M., & Hoffman, A. M. (2002). Preventing lethal violence in schools: The case for entry-based weapons screening. *Journal of Health Politics, Policy and Law, 27*(2), 243–260.

McDonald, L. (2002). Evidence-based family strengthening strategies to reduce delinquency: FAST—families and schools together. In A. R. Roberts & G. Greene (Eds.), *Social workers' desk reference.* New York: Oxford University Press.

McDonald, L., & Frey, H. (1999). Families and schools together: Building relationships. In *Juvenile Justice Bulletin* (pp. 1–20), NCJ No. 17423. Washington, DC.

McDonald, L., & Sayger, T. (1998). Impact of a family and school based prevention program on protective factors for high risk youth: Issues in evaluation. *Drugs and Society, 12,* 61–86.

Mercy, J. A., & Rosenberg, M. L. (1998). Preventing firearm violence in and around schools. In D. S. Elliott, B. A. Hamburg, & K. R. Williams (Eds.), *Violence in American schools: A new perspective.* New York: Cambridge University Press.

Morrison, O. M., Furlong, M. J., & Morrison, R. L. (1994). School violence to school safety: Reframing the issue for school psychologists. *School Psychology Review, 23*(2), 236–256.

Mytton, J. A. (2002). Schoolbased violence prevention programs: Systematic review of secondary prevention trials. *Archives of Pediatric and Adolescent Medicine, 156,* 752–762.

Nilsson, F. (2002, July). The groundwork for safety: Schools can build high-tech security and surveillance systems via networked security. *American School and University,* pp. 26–29.

The No Child Left Behind Act of 2001, Pub. L. No. 197-110, 115 Stat. 1425 (2002).

Olweus, D. (1993). *Bullying at school: What we know and what we can do.* London: Blackwell.

Olweus, D., Limber, S., & Mihalic, S. F. (1999). *Blueprints for violence prevention, book nine: Bullying prevention program.* Boulder, CO: Center for the Study and Prevention of Violence.

Pelton, M. H. (2002). Fixing a culture of school violence. *Principal Leadership, 3,* 81–82.

Pepler, D. J., & Slaby, R. (1994). Theoretical and developmental perspectives on youth and violence. In L. Eron, J. Gentry, & P. Schlegel (Eds.), *Reason to hope: A psychosocial perspective on violence and youth* (pp. 27–58). Washington, DC: American Psychological Association.

Phinney, J. (1989). Stages of ethnic identity development in minority group adolescents. *Journal of Early Adolescence, 9*(1–2), 34–49.

Poland, S., & McCormick, J. (1999). *Coping with crisis: Lessons learned.* Longmont, CO: Sopris West.

Prutzman, P. (1994). Bias-related incidents, hate crimes, and conflict resolution. *Education and Urban Society, 27*(1), 71–81.

Rich, J. (1992). Predicting and controlling school violence. *Contemporary Education, 64*(1), 35–39.

Rigby, K. (1996). *Bullying in schools: And what to do about it.* Melbourne, Victoria, Australia: ACER.

Samples, F., & Aber, L. (1998). Evaluation of school-based violence prevention programs. In D. S. Elliott, B. A. Hamburg, & K. R. Williams (Eds.), *Violence in American schools* (pp. 217–252). New York: Cambridge University Press.

Schweinhart, L., Barnes, H., & Weikart, D. (1993). Significant benefits: The high/scope Perry preschool study through age 27. *Monographs of the High/Scope Education Research Foundation* (No. 10). Ypsilanti, MI: High/Scope Press.

Sherman, L. D., Gottfredson, D., MacKenzie, J., Eck, D., Reuter, P., & Bushway, S. (Eds.). (1997). *Preventing crime: What works, what doesn't, what's promising.* U.S. Department of Justice Research Report NCJ 165366. Washington, DC: U.S. Department of Justice.

Sickmund, M., Snyder, H. N., & Poe-Yamagata, E. (1997). *Juvenile offenders and victims: 1997 update on violence.* Washington, DC: U.S. Office of Juvenile Justice and Delinquency Prevention, U.S. Department of Justice.

Simons-Rudolph, A. P., Ennett, S. T., Ringwalt, C. L., Rohrbach, L. A., Vincus, A. A., & Johnson, R. E. (2003). The principles of effectiveness: Early awareness and plans for implementation in a national sample of public schools and their districts. *Journal of School Health, 73*(5), 181–185.

Slavin, R. E., Karweit, N. L., & Wasik, B. A. (1992–93). Preventing early school failure: What works? *Educational Leadership, 50*(4), 10–18.

Small, M., & Tetrick, K. D. (2001). School violence: An overview. *Juvenile Justice, 8*(1), 3–12.

Stephens, R. D. (1994). Planning for safer and better schools: School violence prevention and intervention strategies. *School Psychology Review, 23*(2), 204–215.

Studies tout early intervention in preventing youth violence. (2003). *Brown University Child and Adolescent Behavior Letter,* 6–7.

Sullivan, K. (2000). *The anti-bullying handbook.* Oxford: Oxford University Press.

Tatum, D., & Herbert, G. (1993). *Countering bullying: Initiatives by schools and local authorities.* Stoke-on-Trent, England: Trentham Books.

Toby, J. (2002). Is a weapons-screening strategy for public schools good public policy? *Journal of Health Politics, Policy and Law, 27*(2), 261–265.

Tolan, P. H., Cromwell, R. E., & Brasswell, M. (1986). Family therapy with delinquents: A critical review of the literature. *Family Process, 25*(4), 619–649.

Tolan, P. H., & Mitchell, M. E. (1990). Families and the therapy of antisocial and delinquent behavior. *Journal of Psychotherapy and the Family, 6*(¾), 29–49.

Trumble, W. R., Brown, L., Bailey, C., & Siefring, J. (Eds.). (2002). *Shorter Oxford English dictionary* (5th ed.). New York: Oxford University Press.

U.S. Department of Education. Safe and Drug-Free Schools Programs: Notice of Final Principles of Effectiveness, 63 Fed. Reg. 29,902-29,906 (1998).

U.S. Office of Juvenile Justice and Delinquency Prevention. (1999). Report to Congress on juvenile violence research. Washington, DC: Author.

Webster, D. W. (1993). The unconvincing case for school-based conflict resolution programs for adolescents. *Health Affairs, 12*(4), 126–141.

Weissberg, R. P., & Elias, M. J. (1993). Enhancing young people's social competence and health behavior: An important challenge for educators, scientists, policymakers, and funders. *Applied and Preventive Psychology, 2,* 179–190.

Will, J. D., & Neufeld, P. J. (2002). Keep bullying from growing into greater violence. *Principal Leadership, 3,* 51–54.

Williams, Ayers, & Arthur (1997). Risk and protective factors in the development of delinquency and conduct disorder. In M. W. Fraser (Ed.), *Risk and resilience in childhood: An ecological perspective* (pp. 140–170). Washington, DC: NASW Press.

Wilson, D. B., Gottfredson, D. C., & Najaka, S. S. (2001). School-based prevention of problem behaviors: A meta-analysis. *Journal of Quantitative Criminology, 17*(3), 247–272.

Wilson, J. Q. (1994, March,). Just take away the guns. *New York Times Magazine, 20,* 46–47.

Zigler, E., Taussig, C., & Black, K. (1992). Early childhood intervention: A promising preventative for juvenile delinquency. *American Psychologist, 47*(8), 997–1006.

# Historical Perspective

# 5 Treating Juveniles in Institutional and Open Settings

Albert R. Roberts

Carole Roberts '88

This chapter reviews the history of institutional treatment for juveniles. It traces the point of departure to the early colonial practice of magistrates ordering parents to take their rowdy and out-of-control youths home for a whipping. The chapter then examines the American colonists' practice of incarcerating juveniles with adult offenders, as well as the completely separate facilities developed for juveniles in the 1800s. Also presented are the deplorable conditions in juvenile detention facilities, with recommendations for change. The final section of this chapter focuses on the opening of forestry camps and junior probation camps during the 1930s, 1940s, and early 1950s.

## ■ Historical Roots of Institutional Treatment

In England, the early institutions served as a catchall for all "needy" children, with no distinctions for background or behavior. For example, the purpose of Christ's Hospital, which opened in London in 1552, was to house orphaned, destitute, and delinquent children (Mennel, 1973).

Later, differentiations as to who would receive which service were made on the basis of the degree of stigma involved. One such distinction was legitimacy at birth: "Different programs were organized for children born out of wedlock and for those born in wedlock but orphaned" (Kahn, 1953, pp. 3–4).

During Elizabethan times, public officials utilized a system of apprenticeships to exert social control over roguish juveniles. These apprenticeships, however, were vastly different from those that prepared youths to be master craftsmen. Destitute or delinquent boys were assigned to serve as laborers in generalized tasks such as farmers' helpers, while girls were put to work as domestics. According to Dunlop and Denman (1912), the purpose of the Elizabethan apprenticeship laws "was not for the education of boys in arts but for charity to keep them and relieve them from turning to roguery and idleness so a man's house was, as it were, a hospital in that case, rather than a shop of trade."

It was common practice in both England and the American colonies for the head of the house to discipline all the young people who lived in his house. Punishment for juvenile delinquent acts was generally carried out in the home rather than in public institutions. For example, in Massachusetts, children brought before the magistrates because of delinquent acts were often sent to their own homes for a court-observed whipping. Another British method continued by the colonists was indenturing poor and delinquent children. It has been said that the most likely candidates to be transported to the colonies were the youths whose parents had encouraged them to pick pockets and commit other crimes.

However, by 1700 it was generally acknowledged that the system of apprenticeships often failed to teach or control the rowdy youths. It was not uncommon for apprentices to desert their apprenticeships (Mennel, 1973). When it became apparent that apprenticeships were not serving the intended purpose for delinquent youths, the American colonists turned to the alternative of incarcerating youths in prisons that had been created for adult offenders. By the mid-1700s, it was common for juvenile and adult offenders to be locked up together.

During the 1700s, a change took place in the meaning society ascribed to the term *juvenile delinquency*. It ceased to mean "a form of misbehavior common to all children" and became instead a euphemism for the crimes and conditions of poor children. Rising distrust of the ability of poor families to raise their own children fused with dissatisfaction with the operation of the law as it affected delinquent children (Mennel, 1973, p. xxvi). Thus, when the 1800s began, the label of juvenile delinquent was already being applied mainly to children in the lower socioeconomic classes. The children unfortunate enough to be apprehended were imprisoned with hardened adult offenders in dirty, rat-infested cells with very little in the way of recreation, education, or rehabilitative treatment.

The movement to establish separate institutions for juvenile offenders began in New York City in 1819, when the Society for the Prevention of Pauperism reported on the horrendous conditions at Bellevue Prison. They focused on the plight of young children confined there with adult offenders. This report and the subsequent study by the society pointed to the correlation between crime and delinquency, and poverty and parental neglect. In 1823, the society reorganized and became known as the Society for the Reformation of Juvenile Delinquents (New Jersey Juvenile Delinquency Commission, 1939).

The first prison for juveniles that was completely separate from an adult prison was called the House of Refuge. It opened in New York on January 21, 1825. Similar juvenile institutions opened in 1826 and 1828 in Boston and Philadelphia, respectively (Peirce, 1969). Between 1845 and 1854, several other large cities established houses of refuge for juvenile offenders (New Jersey Juvenile Delinquency Commission, 1939; Platt, 1969).

These first houses of refuge were built to counteract the poverty, vice, and neglectful families that were breeding grounds for delinquency. Based on a family model, these child-saving institutions were viewed as parent surrogates and as society's superparents. The houses of refuge were supposed to provide a home for unruly and troubled children, where they would be reformed, educated, and disciplined. Children were put in such places for protection from the temptations of immoral, unfit, and neglectful families and vice-ridden, disorganized communities. Houses of refuge were built as secure facilities. Some were surrounded by brick walls, and their interiors were designed to confine inmates securely while instilling order, respect for authority, and strict and steady discipline.

The buildings were usually four stories high, with two long hallways running along either side of a row of cells. The rooms, following one after another, were all five by eight feet wide, seven feet high, window-less, with an iron-lattice slab for a door and flues for ventilation near the ceiling. Each group of eleven cells could be locked or unlocked simulta-neously with one master key; every aperture within an inmate's reach was guarded by iron sashes; every exit door from the asylum was made of iron. . . . On the fourth floor were ten special punishment cells. In keeping with the external design, all inmates wore uniforms of coarse and solid-colored material. No sooner did they enter the institution than they were stripped, washed, their hair cut to a standard length, and put into common dress. (Rothman, 1971, p. 226)

The basic schedule and daily routine at each institution were very similar; order, discipline, and moral teachings were emphasized. The youths were awakened by a bell at sunrise. Fifteen minutes later, the second bell sounded to signal the guards to unlock the cells. The youths marched in formation to the washroom, paraded outside for inspection, marched to chapel for prayer, attended school for 1 hour, and went to breakfast when the 7 o'clock bells rang. From 7:30 A.M. until 5 P.M., the boys worked in the shops, making brass nails or cane seats, while the girls mended clothes, did laundry, cooked, and cleaned. They did receive 1 hour from noon to 1 P.M. for lunch. After work at 5 P.M., they were allowed half an hour for washing and eating. Following this was two and a half hours of evening classes; then came evening prayers, a march back to their cells, and lock-in.

Silence was maintained at all times. Any youth who caused trouble or broke the rules was punished. The milder forms of punishment included either placing offenders on a bread-and-water diet or depriving them of meals altogether. More severe punishments included bread-and-water rations combined with solitary confinement, corporal punishment in the form of whippings with a cat-o'-nine-tails, or manacling with a ball and chain (Roth-man, 1971).

The basic sentence for juveniles was indeterminate. In other words, the superintendents determined how long the youths would be confined. In the majority of cases, confinement was under 2 years; only a few remained for over 4 years (Rothman, 1971). The average stay at the New York House of Refuge was 16 months, at Philadelphia 12 months, and at Cincinnati 14 months. The overwhelming majority of youths who had adhered to the insti-tutions' rules were apprenticed to semiskilled artisans or placed in the homes of farmers. Juvenile offenders who did not show signs of improvement and were judged as untrustworthy were exiled out of the country on extended whaling voyages. The managers of the refuges were therefore able to get rid of the most recalcitrant inmates.

As a result of the depression of 1857, these institutions had become overcrowded by the beginning of the Civil War in 1861. Finding employment for the youths was also a common problem. These poor conditions did not change through the war years. The most serious criticism of the juvenile institutions came from reformers who felt that the refuges and reformatories were just like prisons for adults. Charles Loring Brace, the leading reformer and director of the New York Children's Aid Society, asserted that because of rigid punishments, strict schedules, and the military regimentation of the refuge, youths were not reformed. The longer the youth is in a refuge, "the less likely he is to do well in outside life" (Brace, 1872, pp. 224–225).

Brace contributed to the myth that institutions for children should be located in rural areas of the country. The child savers were against the evils of urban corruption—the dirty city with its taverns, gambling halls, and gangs. They asserted that placement in homes, farms, and institutions in rural areas would cleanse and reform children from the vice, evil associations, and bad habits of the city. Administrators and philanthropists at the National Conference of Charities and Correction supported and defended Brace's position. These prominent reformers included Enoch C. Wines (secretary of the New York Prison Association and president of the First International Penal Congress, held in London in 1872), Theodore Dwight (the first dean of Columbia Law School), Zebulon Brockway (superintendent of Elmira Reformatory in upstate New York), and Frank Sanborn (secretary of the Massachusetts State Board of Charities) (Platt, 1969).

The late 1800s witnessed the flourishing of the reformatory movement. Enoch Wines is credited with being one of the 19th century's foremost American authorities on reformatories for children. In 1872 he became the first president of the International Penal Congress. The underlying philosophy behind the reformatory movement was that proper training in a residential environment could offset the early experiences of poverty, poor family life, and corruption. The goal was to prepare the youth for the future by removing him from his adverse living conditions and placing him "in the midst of wholesome material and moral surroundings," the reformatory. Wines expressed great faith in the rehabilitative power of these institutions:

> The spirit of our reformatories is that of hope and effort, while listless indifference or despair too often reigns in our prisons. The sentences of young offenders are wisely regulated for their amendment; they are not absurdly shortened as if they signified only so much endurance of vindictive suffering. The whole machinery of the establishment is set in the reformatories for the good training of the child, while in prisons it is too often allowed to chafe and wear upon the moral nature and chill the best aspirations of the adult convict. America has little reason to be proud of her prisons; but she can justly take pride in her juvenile reformatories, from the very beginning of their work fifty years ago until now. (Wines, 1880, pp. 80–81)

The philosophy and goals of reformatories emphasized the values of sobriety, thrift, industry, prudence, and ambition. Juveniles were to receive only an elementary education so that they could direct the majority of their time and energy to industrial and agricultural training. Inmates were to be "protected" from idleness and laziness by means of military drill, physical exercise, and continual supervision. In addition to the aforementioned goals, which seem quite rigid and harsh, there were some philosophies that in theory sounded good: Juvenile offenders were to be segregated from the corrupting influences of adult offenders; the atmosphere in a reformatory was supposed to be one of love and guidance combined with firmness; indeterminate sentences were preferred over fixed determinate sentences to encourage youths to participate actively in their own reform (Elmore, 1884, pp. 84–91). Although some of those goals appeared to be reasonable and workable, it was not long before theoretical and abstract philosophies were changed into a system very different from what had been hoped for.

The situation at Elmira Reformatory in New York illustrates the harsh reality of reformatories in the 1800s. Although thought to be a model reformatory, it suffered from serious overcrowding. In the late 1890s, Elmira contained 500 cells, which were jammed with as many as 1,500 juveniles. Max Grunhut (1948), an outspoken penal reformer, stated: "What had begun as a bold experiment lost the inspiring impulse of its first promoters and became routine work and mass treatment."

To make matters worse, influential Elmira physician Hamilton Wey (1888) held the view, popular in some circles in those days, that juvenile offenders as a group were physically different from nondelinquent youths. He insisted that the youthful criminal was usually "undersized, his weight being disproportionate to his height, with a tendency to flat-footedness. He is coarse in fiber and heavy in his movements, lacking anatomical symmetry and beauty. The head is markedly asymmetrical . . . characteristic of a degenerative physiognomy" (p. 191). As treatment for these deficiencies, Wey recommended strenuous physical training and military drills (1888, pp. 181–193; Platt, 1969, pp. 23–24).

Homer Folks, a consistent critic of the American reformatory system, stated in 1891 that in many cases a reformatory could not serve as a substitute for parental affection. He went on to suggest that reformatories could even have the effect of encouraging parents to evade moral and financial obligations to their children. Folks's theories were a forerunner of the sociological theories on the stigma of labeling. He spoke of the "inherent evil" of the reformatory system and its effect of leaving an "enduring stigma" on its inmates. He criticized the system also because it did not prepare the youths for reintegration into society. He warned of the danger of confining youths in a reformatory environment and then, without adequate preparation, releasing them to resume their place on the outside. When the juvenile is released, said Folks, he is "thrown into the midst of temptation, doubly powerful because of novelty.

Just at this moment the strict discipline must be withdrawn. The routine of life by which he has been carried along is removed" (p. 138).

Anthony Platt (1969) points to the fact that not only were juvenile offenders removed from their homes when they were placed in residential institutions but also they were put into institutions in rural country settings, usually many miles from family and friends. The underlying philosophy was that the city was a "corrupting influence" on the youths. To help them become "reformed," it was necessary to remove them to the country, where they could be "reunited with nature and wholesomeness" (p. 65). Thus no effort was made to help the inmates adjust to the ways of life in the city—the environment from which they had come and in all probability the environment to which they would return.

It should be noted that Homer Folks was one of the more outspoken critics of the reformatory movement. While some others shared his beliefs, they comprised a small minority. The overwhelming majority of penologists during the late 1800s praised the reformatory for both its principles and its practices.

## ◼ Institutionalized Treatment in the Twentieth Century

In the 1930s, a new wave of concern for the treatment of juvenile offenders swept the country. Because of the serious financial plight wrought by the Great Depression, considerable numbers of juveniles resorted to truancy from school to find odd jobs, or to stealing to help their families. Many of the youths who were arrested for various delinquent acts were unable to meet the stiff bail that was imposed.

Robert Bremner (1974) cited a 1934 report from Massachusetts that documents the fact that in that year 547 juveniles were sent to jail for temporary detention. In some instances, the detention resulted from the inability to furnish a high bail, ordinarily $2,500 and running as high as $6,000 (especially excessive by 1934 financial standards). To quote from the report: "The sole object of bail . . . being to insure the appearance of the child in court when wanted, these facts compel serious consideration of other means of securing that end. If the care of the child to his own home is not feasible, the provision of specially supervised foster homes is positively indicated" (p. 1008).

In addition to concerns about excessive bail, serious questions about the legal rights of juveniles were being raised. Three important issues evolved regarding treatment of juvenile offenders: (a) Were some juveniles (especially poor Blacks) being given unusually stiff sentences? (b) Were some youths being denied basic legal rights that were granted to adult offenders? (c) Were juvenile offenders incarcerated in deplorable institutions? How could those conditions be ameliorated?

In July 1937, the *New York Times* contained a report that awakened many people to the realities of juvenile incarceration. It involved the case of the

Scottsboro boys, four Black youths convicted of rape in 1931 and sentenced to the electric chair. At the time of the rape, the accused juveniles (Eugene Williams, Roy Wright, Olen Montgomery, and Willie Roberson) were all under 16 years of age. They were held in jail for 6 and a half years before being set free. According to the *New York Times*, the day after the rape occurred a doctor had examined Willie Roberson, age 12. The physician stated that Willie was "sick, suffering with a severe venereal disease, and that in his condition it would have been very painful for him to have committed that crime, and that he would not have had any inclination to commit it." With regard to another of the juveniles, Olen Montgomery (age 13), the paper reported: "He was practically blind and has also told a plausible story, which has been unshaken all through the litigation, which put him some distance from the commission of the crime. The State is without proof other than the prosecutrix as to his being in the gondola car, and we feel that it is a case of mistaken identity" (Bremner, 1974, p. 1006). The newspaper report continued with the district attorney's decision to free the boys after more than 6 years in prison: "Counsel for the state think that in view of the fact they have been in jail for six-and-half years the ends of justice would be met at this time by releasing these . . . juveniles, on condition that they leave the state, never to return" (p. 1007).

In the 1930s and 1940s, Roy Casey, an inspector for the Federal Bureau of Prisons, was concerned about the treatment children received while in jail awaiting a trial, hearing, or investigation. Based on visits that he made to most of the county jails in approximately half of the states, he made a number of observations and recommendations. He urged that "vindictiveness" on the part of police officers and prosecuting attorneys be abated. Casey (1943) estimated that there were "tens of thousands" of children in U.S. jails and lockups:

> The unfitness of the vast majority of city and county jails for the incarceration of adults should be well known. . . . If then these jails are unfit for adults from every standard held by modern penology, what can be said of them as places to confine first offenders, and girls and boys of the lower teen ages? Simply this, that society is committing a crime not only against these children but also against itself in permitting this deplorable situation to continue. (p. 175)

Casey (1943) provides vivid case examples from his inspections of the jails. On the day of his inspection at one institution (Casey declined to give its name), it held 20 children, all of them 17 years old and younger.

> Among them was a sixteen-year-old boy who had been given two sentences of one year each to run consecutively for the offense of larceny. Another boy was in the same cell block awaiting transfer to the state penitentiary. He was only fifteen years of age and his commitment papers indicated that he had once been an inmate in the state institution for the feebleminded. His offense was burglary and larceny without

deadly weapons, yet he was being sent to a penitentiary notoriously known . . . for the desperate and hardened criminals and perverts among its inmates, and the child's three sentences read one to ten years, one to twenty-five years, and one year to life. (p. 176)

In describing the lack of segregation between juveniles and adults, Casey (1943) called for the development of detention centers for juveniles completely separate from jails for adults. He described the conditions in a jail located in the capital city of a northern state:

> The jail held four children somewhere within the dark and filthy cells of its vermin-infested cell blocks, along with criminals, vags, sex perverts, and the insane. The officials spoke of how they were handicapped by not having segregation quarters for juveniles, but it did not appear that they were greatly concerned over the matter and had considered it only a minor thing to have to put fifteen, sixteen, and seventeen-year-old boys with hardened criminals. . . . They laughingly recited the details of how sodomy was practiced on one of the fat boys and the discomfort he experienced from lacerations. (pp. 178–179)

As further indication of the horrendous problem that existed in the 1930s and 1940s, Negley Teeters and John Reinemann cited statistics pointing to the magnitude of the problem of children in prison. The report of the Wickersham Commission in 1931 stated that 54.8% of the prisoner population at that time was under the age of 21 when committed. Teeters and Reinemann reported that in 1946 approximately 166 public facilities served juvenile offenders. Of these, 115 were state and national institutions and 51 were under county and municipal auspices. The authors estimated that more than 30,000 juveniles were imprisoned (Teeters & Reinemann, 1950, pp. 448, 514).

Sherwood Norman reported to the 1946 National Conference of Social Work that the National Probation Association had undertaken a study of the best detention facilities in the United States for the purpose of developing principles and standards. The study covered 68 facilities in 22 states throughout the country. In 1944 they studied 29 communities and found a total of 2,382 children. However, since in many places no records were kept, that figure is actually just a low estimate. Norman (1947) commented on the routine practices that were uncovered in the study and needed to be changed.

> We found that some courts detained routinely every child on whom a petition was filed, and the petitions were filed recklessly. In most courts children who should never have been detained were thus penalized for the simple reason that the juvenile court offices were closed for the day or for the week-end and there was no court representative available to take the responsibility for releasing them to their homes. This practice is almost universal. . . . We found no uniformity in the administration of detention homes. Two thirds of the homes were overcrowded. Some-

times two and three times as many children were held as could be normally provided for by the quarters.

. . . There was a tendency in almost every community to concentrate on one type of detention care to the detriment of the children who needed other types of care. For instance, detention homes geared to the care of dependent and neglected children failed to provide security for the older delinquent group who were relegated to the jail. Other homes were operated as though all the children detained therein were young criminals. Nowhere did we find really adequate provision for the sixteen and seventeen-year-old delinquent youngster, although juvenile court jurisdiction in over half of our states now includes this group. (pp. 399–400)

A key point made by Norman (1947) in his presentation at the conference was that some of the detention homes studied were characterized by the same conditions that had been recognized as contributing to delinquency in the community: the lack of concerned, warm relationships between the youths and adult workers; the presence of youths who had committed very serious crimes and from whom more sophisticated delinquent behavior could be learned; the scarcity of an adequate recreation program; the nonexistence of a meaningful educational program; and the lack of professional social work services. According to Norman's findings, institutionalization for juveniles was almost totally devoid of meaningful rehabilitation. In fact, the institutions were harmful to the youths because incarceration necessitated uprooting youths from family and community and taking away the rights of freedom of choice. Results of the study belied the claim that these institutions were in any way beneficial.

Norman (1947) also presented a composite picture of the atmosphere and standards at the majority of detention homes. To provide a vivid picture of the situation encountered by thousands of juveniles, he presented scenarios in which he is receiving a guided tour of a detention center. He is the narrator, and the "tour guide" is a composite of many administrators encountered on his visits:

"And we are really proud of the food we serve these children. It costs the county only thirty-five cents a day for each child." You remember that this was the minimum standard set for children's institutions in 1941 and that there has been considerable increase in food costs since then. From the window you see a small courtyard where boys are milling about with a ball. "Can't they have baseball bats?" you ask. "Oh, no!" is the reply, "the space isn't large enough, and anyway a bat in the hands of these delinquent boys would be too dangerous for our staff."

Twenty-five girls are lounging about in a sparsely furnished recreation room, playing cards, looking at comic books, or just sitting or looking wistfully out of the window. "Couldn't this room have a shuffleboard game painted on the floor, a victrola, or perhaps a crafts corner?" Your guide is horrified at the danger of putting shuffleboard sticks in the hands of delinquents and tips you off that most of the matrons would quit if they had that sort of thing with which to contend. You hear from more than one of your own workers, "There's no point in giving them more things to do, they just break up anything you give them." . . .

In returning to the office you pass the delinquent boys coming up from the yard in silence and marching in line with arms folded. "Why is this necessary?" you ask. "Because if they are allowed to talk they become too noisy, and if their arms are not folded they are always pushing each other. One person can handle twenty-five or thirty of these boys very smoothly by just sticking to these time-tested rules."

To your growing list of frustrations you add the building, which is so ill adapted to any kind of meaningful life for children that regimentation is almost inevitable. Nothing can be done about the way the home is used by social agencies because of the loopholes in the juvenile court law and the difficulty of securing interagency cooperation. You cannot secure psychological and casework services because the clinic has its hands full with routine diagnosis for the court. . . . You eat your heart out, seeing so many eager boys and girls with real potentialities thrust toward the prisons. (pp. 401–403)

Norman offered his opinion as to why these deplorable conditions existed. He believed that administrators in detention homes were unsure as to what components were needed in a rehabilitation-oriented facility. Norman said that blame should not necessarily be placed on the superintendents of the institutions. Many superintendents were sincerely trying to provide adequate detention facilities but were hindered by limited budgets, untrained staff, and, above all, narrow concepts.

However, the picture Norman presented was not totally bleak. At least five juvenile courts had devised satisfactory controls for detention intake. Professional casework services were provided at several facilities, and on a few occasions a child guidance clinic was used to provide in-service training. There were occasional facilities in which the adult–youth relationship seemed to be more a camper–counselor arrangement than a prisoner–guard one. In these facilities, children were helped to use the program as a creative outlet for their tensions and anxieties.

On the basis of his findings, Norman (1947, p. 408) made recommendations for improving the system of detention for juveniles. He urged:

I Revamping of the whole detention concept. Priorities were reorganized, safe physical care and custody (which had yet to be achieved many places) would not be the only concerns. The goal of meeting the emotional needs of populations served was vitally important.

**2** Strengthening the court intake process so that children who did not need to be detained could be kept out of detention.

**3** Strengthening community services, with the following goals: keep children out of court, shorten the length of stay by making available improved institutional and foster home placements, and upgrade the level of detention home administrators.

Finally, he urged that social workers and the courts work together to improve the quality of services.

Norman (1958) estimated that approximately half of all the children and youths (age 7 to 17) who were brought before the court were held in some type of detention facility or jail. About 100,000 youths were detained in county jails and police lockups prior to adjudication, while another 100,000 were confined in juvenile detention centers, detention homes, or basement cells. Many of these facilities were substandard, with poor heating and ventilation, and devoid of any educational programs or medical care.

By the late 1960s, the conditions in short-term detention facilities had improved to some degree, although a number of jurisdictions continued to "warehouse" juvenile offenders throughout the decade. During the first half of the 1960s, in accord with the National Council on Crime and Delinquency's (NCCD) guidelines for detention home design, more than 100 specially designed detention centers were built, primarily in urban areas, to replace old county jails and makeshift facilities. Many modern facilities included specialized group units for 8 to 15 juveniles. A number of the new facilities also had individual rooms for each detainee, with attractive, yet sturdy, metal furnishings. These new facilities were staffed increasingly by professionally trained employees and provided group work and group counseling, casework services, school programs, and recreational programs.

In the mid-1960s, the total number of juveniles confined to detention homes and jails was above 409,000. The length of detention ranged from 1 day to 68 days, with the average being 18 days (President's Commission on Law Enforcement and Administration of Justice, 1967).

An NCCD national survey of conditions in detention facilities documented the lack of constructive educational, therapeutic, and recreational programs, such as:

☐ 28% of the detention facilities did not have any provisions for regular medical care of detainees.
☐ 58% did not have any casework or counseling services.
☐ 53% did not have even one full-time or part-time visiting teacher to provide educational services.
☐ 52% had no recreational program. (President's Commission, 1967, pp. 120–121)

For an in-depth analysis of detention trends, policies, and practices of the 1970s and 1980s, see chapter 8.

Although treatment of juvenile offenders has improved considerably since the end of World War II, there have been numerous instances of atrocities perpetrated against juveniles being held in detention facilities and training schools. As an illustration, two reports from 1971 are cited here.

The first case is of Nathan Smith Jr., a 15-year-old Black youth. He was an inmate of the Mississippi County Penal Farm, where he drowned in the strong current of a deep drainage ditch. Before being sent to the penal farm, he had been convicted in his hometown of Osceola, Arkansas, of petty larceny for allegedly stealing several inexpensive items from a local store. At the trial, Nathan Smith, not represented by counsel, was sentenced to 6 months at the penal farm. An account of his death was provided by a prisoner who had been an eyewitness:

> "The captain dropped his can of tobacco into the water and told the kid to go down and get it." The witness said the youth was reluctant because the stream was swollen by recent heavy rain and the current was extremely swift. The guard drew his pistol, the prisoner's account contends, and forced the youngster into the water. After the can of tobacco was retrieved, the guard ordered the boy to stay in the water and shove large timbers away from the bank and into the current. "Somehow the kid got caught in the timber and that was the last we saw of him." . . . (Bremner, 1974, pp. 1015–1016)

In the second case, 85 Black high school students were arrested and put in the county jail in Warrenton, North Carolina, on December 2, 1970, following 2 days of disturbances at a local high school. Although the students were held in jail for only a short time, they reported receiving "harsh and brutal" treatment. With the rising number of student demonstrations in the late 1960s and early 1970s, mass arrests leading to brief periods in jail were not uncommon. The students' account of their treatment in jail was reported in a 1971 issue of *New South*:

> The thirty-eight girls arrested told of being herded together in cells and given no food or water. They were insulted by white guards, refused bathroom facilities. Those in need of sanitary supplies said they were not only denied such supplies but that their requests were responded to with suggestive and obscene language. They were denied the right to make a telephone call. (Tornquist, 1971, p. 63)

However, these students were relatively lucky. They were allowed out on bail after only 1 day in jail.

## ■ Treating Juvenile Offenders in Open Settings

The deleterious effects of incarcerating a youthful offender in a prison atmosphere were discussed in the previous section. However, many policy makers, while recognizing the weaknesses of institutional treatment, were unaware of viable alternatives for dealing with juveniles who had committed delinquent acts. One extreme approach would be to send the youth back to his community without providing any treatment services whatsoever; at the other extreme would be putting the youth in a prison or reformatory where rehabilitative and educational services were sorely lacking. Rehabilitation-minded policy makers recognized that neither extreme was sound, and gradually there emerged the concept of forestry camps, a hoped-for middle ground between two unworkable alternatives that would be suitable for certain types of youths.

The first known camp of its type was established in 1932. The concept was developed by Judge Samuel R. Blake, Kenyon Scudder, and Karl Holton to meet the needs of transient boys; implementation was carried out by the Los Angeles County Probation Department. In 1935, the California legislature passed a bill providing for forestry camps to be set up for juvenile offenders, who would be sent there by the juvenile courts. These camps were to be run by the county (Kogon, 1958). According to Weber (1960), the early camps for juvenile delinquents were generally modeled after the Civilian Conservation Corps camps that were operating between 1933 and 1943. The goal of those camps was to provide a treatment program that included conservation of natural resources in addition to employment and vocational training.

Forestry camps were utilized because they were an open setting with no gates, bars, guns, or isolation facilities. In short, it was not a prison atmosphere. However, boys with a long history of delinquent behavior were not referred, nor were boys with "deep-seated emotional problems requiring psychotherapy." Boys had to be of average intelligence to benefit from the school program, which was an integral part of the forestry camp. Youths with physical handicaps had to be excluded. Boys were usually given an indeterminate stay but generally stayed an average of 6 to 9 months (Kogon, 1958, p. 36).

Two basic types of camps developed in the late 1940s and early 1950s: senior forestry camps and junior probation camps. A senior forestry camp was for youths between the ages of 16 and 18. Emphasis was on work such as nursery, reforestation, various maintenance and construction activities, brush clearance, and fire suppression (Kamm, Hunt, & Fleming, 1968). Most camps had their own nursery, where, under the guidance of a forestry horticulturist, youths were shown how to gather and bed seeds in the mountainous areas. These were taken care of until they could be planted in burned-out areas (Kogon, 1958). According to Kamm et al., the senior forestry camps also focused on counseling and group activity programs. The night school classes consisted of regular public school subjects geared to the individuals' needs (remedial education was often needed). In the junior camps, for boys between the ages of 13 and 15, the emphasis was mainly on education. The youths attended a minimum of 4 hours of classes each day. There was also an active athletic program and some counseling. Each day the youths participated in 2-hour work sessions very similar to the work the senior boys were doing.

During World War II, the forestry camps added to their program training in the fundamentals of military life and drill (provided by the army). A number of boys who received this training went directly from the camp into military service, where they served their country well (Bremner, 1974).

Kogon (1958) states that by the 1950s probation camps in California had evolved into an integral part of the probation process. A youth was sent to the camp by the juvenile court and assigned to a probation officer. The relationship between youth and probation officer continued during the stay in the camp and then for approximately 6 months after the juvenile returned to his own home. In Kogon's opinion, delinquent youths who were sent to these camps learned how to relate constructively to peers and staff. As an example of the good work done by these boys, Kogon stated that in 1957 youths in California forestry camps responded to 848 fire calls, where they rendered invaluable assistance to the professional firefighters.

Another type of camping experience for juvenile delinquents developed in Dallas, Texas. The impetus for the program came from a group of people who had formed the Salesmanship Club in Dallas in 1921. The emphasis on children in trouble began in 1946 under the leadership of Campbell Lough-miller. The core of this program has been a year-round rugged camp in northeastern Texas. Boys sleep outdoors winter and summer in canvas shelters that they have built. The camp is under the supervision of social workers, who deal mainly with the parents of these boys. There is also an eight-bed halfway house for youths whose home situations are so destructive that they cannot go home (James, 1969).

At the Texas camp, the boys are divided by age into four groups of 10. Each group is guided by two sensitive, rugged college graduates. Activities include mountain climbing, canoeing, fishing, hiking, and learning to survive in the wilderness. A type of group therapy is practiced—dealing with individual or group problems whenever they develop. Boys can remain in the program up to 2 years. Juveniles are referred from a number of sources, including the courts, welfare department, schools, and mental health officials. This program claims a good rate of returning boys to public schools, though no follow-up has been provided.

Kogon (1958) and Kamm et al. (1968) have reported that the forestry camps are a valuable placement for youthful offenders, offering distinct advantages over the traditional prison environment. However, Weber (1960) has stated his concern that the camps did not provide consistent or complete treatment programs. He raised questions about the counseling, which is a stated component of the treatment approach:

> The counseling techniques . . . frequently fail to meet the basic problems at the root of the delinquency and are usually restricted to surface problems that arise in a boy's adjustment to the camp. . . . In practice, the camps are often characterized by diverse aims and methods. On the one

hand, they emphasize conservation work and education; on the other hand, they try to be an institution of treatment. (p. 447)

While I agree with Weber that the counseling component at many of the camps was probably not highly developed, I take issue with his criticism of the camp model and believe the camp atmosphere was certainly preferable to the confining prison environment. It would seem that the potential for meaningful rehabilitation is present in a forestry camp with the addition of a more structured outdoor experience, as well as a group work and aftercare component.

## Summary

Early apprenticeship systems and institutional facilities were developed in response to the perceived problem of having a large number of individuals identified as either neglected, abandoned, destitute, or idle or causing embarrassment or pain to community members through delinquent acts. Initially, public officials developed a system of apprenticeships to exert social control over needy and troubled youths. When it became apparent that the juveniles were being exploited and many were deserting their apprenticeships, the practice of incarcerating law-breaking youths in adult prisons became widely used.

Several leading reformers and societies became aware of the plight of young children incarcerated in horrendous, unsanitary, and corrupting facilities, such as New York's Bellevue Prison. Reformers (including Enoch C. Wines, Frank Sanborn, and Homer Folks) and advocacy groups such as the Society for the Reformation of Juvenile Delinquents studied the problem, prepared reports, and advocated with legislators to change the system. Norman's national study of the horrendous conditions in 68 detention facilities provided a detailed description of the problems that existed in the 1930s and 1940s, the administrative reasons for the deplorable conditions, and recommendations for improving the detention system.

The final section of the chapter describes the emergence of forestry camps and junior probation camps during the 1940s and 1950s.

## Discussion Questions

1   Identify the purpose and nature of apprenticeships for roguish juveniles during Elizabethan times.

2   Discuss the major contribution of the Society for the Reformation of Juvenile Delinquents during the first half of the 1800s.

3   What was the purpose of the early houses of refuge?

4   Describe the schedule and daily routine at the houses of refuge.

**5** Identify the philosophy and goals of Elmira and other reformatories.

**6** What was Homer Folks's specific criticism about the American reformatory system?

**7** Based on the survey of 68 detention facilities throughout the United States, what were Sherwood Norman's (National Probation Association) three recommendations?

**8** Discuss the major strength as well as the major weakness of the forestry camps and probation camps of the 1930s and 1940s.

## References

Brace, C. L. (1872/1973). *The dangerous classes of New York and twenty years work among them.* New York: NASW Classic Series.

Bremner, R. H. (Ed.). (1974). *Children and youth in America: A documentary history,* Vol. 3, pts. 5–7. Cambridge, MA: Harvard University Press.

Casey, R. (1943). Children in jail. In M. Bell (Ed.), *Delinquency and the community in wartime: Yearbook of the National Probation Association* (pp. 175–179). New York: National Probation Association.

Dunlop, J. O., & Denman, R. D. (1912). *English apprenticeship and child labour: A history.* New York: Macmillan.

Elmore, A. E. (1884). Report of the Committee on Reformatories and Houses of Refuge. In *Proceedings of the national conference of charities and correction, 1946* (pp. 84–91). New York: Columbia University Press.

Folks, H. (1891). The care of delinquent children. In *Proceedings of the national conference of charities and correction, 1946.* New York: Columbia University Press.

Grunhut, M. (1948). *Penal reform.* Oxford: Clarendon.

James, H. (1969). *Children in trouble, a national scandal.* New York: David McKay.

Kahn, A. J. (1953). *A court for children: A study of the New York City Children's Court.* New York: Columbia University Press.

Kamm, E. R., Hunt, D., & Fleming, J. A. (1968). *Juvenile law and procedure in California.* Beverly Hills, CA: Glencoe Press.

Kogon, B. (1958). Probation camps. *Federal Probation, 22*(3), 35–36.

Mennel, R. M. (1973). *Thorns and thistles: Juvenile delinquents in the United States, 1825–1940.* Hanover, NH: University Press of New England.

New Jersey Juvenile Delinquency Commission. (1939). *Justice and the child in New Jersey.* Trenton: Author.

Norman, S. (1947). Detention facilities for children. In *Proceedings of the National Conference of Social Work, 1946* (pp. 399–400). New York: Columbia University Press.

Norman, S. (1958). *Standards and guides for the detention of children and youth.* New York: National Probation and Parole Association.

Peirce, B. K. (1969). *A half century with juvenile delinquents: The New York House of Refuge and its times.* Montclair, NJ: Patterson Smith.

Platt, M. (1969). *The child savers.* Chicago: University of Chicago Press.

President's Commission on Law Enforcement and Administration of Justice. (1967). *Task force report: Corrections.* Washington, DC: U.S. Government Printing Office.

Rothman, D. J. (1971). *The discovery of the asylum.* Boston: Little, Brown.

Teeters, N. K. & Reinemann, J. O. (1950). *The challenge of delinquency*. New York: Prentice-Hall.

Tornquist, E. (1971, Summer). Juvenile corrections in North Carolina. *New South 26*, 63–68.

Weber, G. H. (1960). *Camps for delinquent boys: A guide to planning*. Children's Bureau Publication No. 385. Washington, DC: U.S. Government Printing Office.

Wey, H. (1888). A plea for physical training of youthful criminals. In *Proceedings of the annual conference of the National Prison Association* (pp. 181–193). Boston: National Prison Association.

Wines, E. C. (1880). *The state of prisons and of child saving institutions in the civilized world*. Cambridge, MA: Harvard University Press.

# 6

# Community Strategies With Juvenile Offenders

Albert R. Roberts

This chapter shows how community organization approaches to delinquency prevention were developed out of an ecological model and Cloward and Ohlin's (1960) opportunity theory. Also presented are the objectives and accomplishments of several of the most widely known examples of a coordinated community program aimed at both reduction and prevention of juvenile delinquency: the Chicago Area Project, New York City's Mobilization for Youth (MFY), and Boston's Midcity Project. The last section of this chapter examines the modern-day version of a coordinating council—the youth service bureau. The reader will learn about the five basic goals, the sources of funding, the organizational structure and staffing patterns, and the youth development and delinquency prevention activities and services common to youth service bureaus.

The overriding purpose of the early community organizational strategies was to combine community groups and agencies in an umbrella type of community service approach to delinquency prevention. McMillen (1947), in outlining the role of community organization in social work, identified the following needs:

1 To strengthen intergroup cooperation for the full attainment of welfare objectives
2 To make the public aware of community resources
3 To assist in effective case-finding and referral practices

Based on the writings of McMillen (1947) and Beam (1937), three levels of participation in early community organization can be delineated: At the first level, agencies concentrated their efforts primarily on community organization activities, generally in areas of social work specialization such as child labor, tuberculosis, or delinquency (e.g., the community coordinating council). In this type of community agency, any direct assistance to clients represents a secondary function of the agency. The second level of participation included agencies that concentrated their efforts primarily on organizational concerns, directing their efforts more globally to encompass many areas of social welfare. Councils of social agencies, welfare federations, community chests, and neighborhood youth councils are examples of this type of agency. The third level is comprised of agencies that provided direct service to clients as their primary function, with community organization activities being of secondary importance. Most voluntary and governmental social agencies were of this type.

The field of delinquency prevention has involved various community organization strategies, ranging from neighborhood-run councils to social workers doing outreach with urban gangs. Five of the best-known projects and approaches of the past 80 years geared to delinquency prevention are:

☐ Community coordinating councils
☐ Chicago Area Project
☐ Boston's Midcity Project

- New York's Mobilization for Youth project
- Youth service bureaus

## ■ Community Coordinating Councils

The coordinating council movement was a significant step in the treatment and prevention of juvenile delinquency. Its roots can be traced to the founding of several national organizations in the early 1900s: the National Probation Association in 1907, the Family Welfare Association in 1911, the Big Brother and Big Sister Federation in 1917, and the Child Welfare League of America in 1920. The major focus of these organizations was on improvement of standards of community service and development of national policies.

The community coordinating council movement to combat juvenile delinquency began in Berkeley, California, in 1919. The original objectives of the Berkeley Coordinating Council were to conduct research and professional conferences, as well as to work with problem children. This council contained three committees: "the adjustment committee, the character building committee, and the environment committee" (Pursuit, Gerletti, Brown, & Ward, 1972, p. 42). During the 1930s, coordinating councils proliferated rapidly with the expansion of the Los Angeles Coordinating Councils for the Prevention of Delinquency (Beam, 1937; Scudder, 1946). They continued to grow during the 1940s, when their efforts to combat delinquency were publicly acclaimed by people such as Kenyon Scudder (warden at the California Institution for Men, located in Chino). Speaking at the attorney general's conference on crime in December 1944, Scudder made the following remarks:

> The conference recognizes that criminal careers usually originate in the early years of neglected childhood, and the most fundamental and hopeful measures of crime prevention are those directed toward discovering the underlying factors in the delinquency of children and strengthening and coordinating the resources of the home, the school, and the community. . . . It commends the progress that has been made in certain states and localities in drawing together through such agencies as coordinating councils all available local forces to combat unwholesome influences upon youth. It urges state and national leadership through appropriate governmental and voluntary organizations, in fostering the development of these coordinating agencies, the provision of constructive educational, vocational, and recreational opportunities for youth, and provision of competent, skilled service to children in need of guidance and correction.

The success of these councils was based on their ability to enlist the cooperation and coordinated efforts of community facilities. Councils that functioned most effectively not only stimulated and utilized the skills of local residents but also had access to a planning board or a broader coordinated community organization that supplied personnel, funds, and planners.

Social historians have noted that the coordinating council movement played an active role in delinquency prevention efforts during the 1930s. Beam's (1937) survey (sponsored by the National Probation Association) indicated the widespread adoption of these community efforts. He reported that more than 250 coordinating councils were operating in 163 cities and towns in 20 states during 1935 and 1936.

## ■ Chicago Area Project

One of the most widely known examples of a coordinated program aimed at the reduction of juvenile delinquency was the Chicago Area Project, initiated by the Institute for Juvenile Research and the Behavioral Research Fund in 1929. Clifford R. Shaw was the founder and director of the project, which consisted of a series of studies from 1929 to 1933, as well as a legendary experiment in delinquency prevention at the local level that lasted until 1962. The studies conducted by Shaw and McKay (1972) concentrated on two areas: (a) the epidemiology of delinquency in different areas of Chicago and (b) the acquisition of delinquent beliefs and behavior from delinquent subcultures. Shaw and McKay found that a disproportionately large number of juvenile delinquents came from certain areas of Chicago. The high-rate sectors were termed *delinquency* areas (Kobrin, 1959).

Shaw and his associates found that people who lived in the delinquency areas were primarily immigrants who had lived a rural lifestyle before coming to the United States. "As a group they occupied the least desirable status in the economic, political and social hierarchies of the metropolitan society" (Kobrin, 1959, p. 21). The studies indicated that in Chicago and other cities, the areas located within the central business district and adjacent to industrial and manufacturing plants had had disproportionately high rates of delinquency for many decades.

This ecological phenomenon began at the beginning of the 20th century. As urban areas grew and commercial and industrial facilities expanded, large numbers of people moved to the suburbs, out of the less desirable and overcrowded areas. Researchers concluded that those areas, which had high rates of delinquency, were lacking in social stability, normative consensus, and social cohesion. In the high-delinquency area, various forms of lawlessness had been passed from one generation to the next. Such cultural transmission of delinquency was demonstrated through in-depth case histories of individual delinquents (Shaw, 1930, 1931).

The basic assumptions and objectives of the Chicago Area Project were summarized as follows:

The Chicago Project operates on the assumption that much of the delinquency of slum areas is to be attributed to lack of neighborhood cohesiveness and to the consequent lack of concern on the part of many residents about the welfare of children. The project strives to counteract
this situation through encouraging local self-help enterprises through
which a sense of neighborliness and mutual responsibility *will* develop.
It *is* expected that delinquency *will* decline as youngsters become better
integrated into community life and thereby influenced by the values of
conventional society rather than those of the underworld. (Witmer &
Tufts, 1954, p. 11)

The major finding of the Chicago Area Project was that in most instances
delinquent behavior was attributable to the simple process of social learning
as a result of the breakdown of "the machinery of spontaneous social control."
Kobrin described this breakdown:

The breakdown is precipitated by the cataclysmic pace of social change
to which migrants from a peasant or rural background are subjected
when they enter the city. In its more specific aspects, delinquency was
seen as adaptive behavior on the part of the male child of rural migrants
acting as members of adolescent peer groups in their efforts to find their
way to meaningful and respected adult roles essentially unaided by the
older generation and under the influence of criminal models for whom
the inner city areas furnish a haven. (Kobrin, 1959, p. 23)

Other findings of the project were:

1 Youth welfare organizations could be developed among residents of high-
   delinquency areas, thus justifying Shaw's assumption that the high-
   delinquency sectors had the capacity to contribute to the solution of the
   problems.
2 Existing programs in the local recreation and character-building agencies were not adequate for modifying the behavior of the boys involved
   in delinquent acts. "In all probability, the Chicago Area Project was the
   first organized program in the United States to use workers to establish
   direct and personal contact with the 'unreached' boys" (Kobrin, 1959,
   p. 28).
3 Disorganization was not so severe as to be devoid of individuals to serve
   as positive role models. A major effort of the project was directed toward finding an effective method whereby social workers, police, and
   teachers could work effectively with these juveniles.
4 The project was a pioneer in exploring the ways in which an urban bureaucracy (schools, police officers, probation departments, training
   schools, etc.) attempted to control and correct delinquent youths.

After Shaw and McKay conducted their early research and documentation of ecological causations of delinquency in Chicago's slum neighborhoods, community committees were developed in six parts of the city: Hegewisch, Russell Square, South Side, Near North Side, Near West Side, and Near Northwest Side (Kobrin, 1959; Schlossman & Sedlak, 1983). Neighborhood centers were formed that reached over 7,500 children and youth in these areas.

The core of this self-help community crime prevention effort was the neighborhood center, a recreational facility or educational center staffed by community residents. More than 20 different projects were initiated, including discussion groups, counseling services, hobby groups, adult education programs, summer camps, and recreation activities (Schlossman & Sedlak, 1983; Shaw & McKay, 1972; Sorrentino, 1983).

Neighborhood committees were organized with the assistance of a staff member from the Chicago Area Project, who served primarily as an adviser (for example, to mobilize resources if the committee requested such assistance). Professional field workers functioned as consultants and community organizers, offering guidance but avoiding the tendency to manipulate or control the local leaders. To a great extent, these community organizational efforts used the natural leaders from within each neighborhood to plan, staff, and manage project activities. It was the responsibility of the neighborhood committee to make all policy decisions and to select the director, who was required to be a neighborhood resident.

Besides developing community resources and activities for youths, committees made efforts to prevent further delinquency by regular contact with local police youth officers, probation officers, and parole officers. In five of the area projects, community groups worked intensively with young parolees, local residents often assisting the parolees in obtaining jobs and returning to school. It was not uncommon for successful parolees to join the local community committees and eventually be elected as officers of the committees.

Efforts similar to those initiated in Chicago were developed in such other cities as Cleveland, Detroit, Philadelphia, and Richmond. In downstate Illinois, approximately 100 self-governing citizens' groups were established.

## ■ Boston's Midcity Project (1954–1957)

In the 1950s, other delinquency control programs somewhat similar to the Chicago Area Project were initiated. One of the best known was the Midcity Project, which was developed in 1954 in one of Boston's lower-class districts. This social action demonstration project, utilizing a "total community" philosophy, focused on improving three of the societal units that seemed to be an important influence in the genesis and perpetuation of delinquency: the gang, the community, and the family (Miller, 1962).

The project's primary emphasis was its work with gangs. Professional social workers known as "detached street workers" reached out to approximately 400 youths who were members of 21 gangs. The staff met with the groups three to four times a week, visiting with the gang members for 5 to 6 hours at a time. Contact was maintained for a period ranging from 10 to 34 months.

The approach used by project staff differed from earlier programs in three ways: First, all staff were professional social workers; second, each staff member (with one exception) worked primarily with one group over an extended period of time; third, workers were able to consult regularly with psychiatric specialists.

The community component of the project had two major goals: (a) helping to establish and strengthen area citizens' groups so that they could act on their own to combat problems such as juvenile delinquency and (b) forging a cooperative approach among local professional organizations having contact with juveniles (e.g., schools, courts, settlement houses, and psychiatric and medical clinics).

The family component of the Midcity Project was geared toward treating "chronic problem" families. Project staff identified families having a long-term history of receiving public welfare services and provided them with intensive, psychiatrically oriented casework services (Miller, 1962; Miller, Baum, & McNeil, 1968).

As part of a thorough evaluation of the Midcity Project, researchers analyzed the following 14 behavior categories: theft, assault, drinking, sex, mating, work, education, religion, and involvement with the courts, police, corrections, social welfare, family, and other gangs. Of these 14 areas, only one category—school-oriented behavior—showed a statistically significant decrease in inappropriate behavior. The researchers also concluded that there was no significant reduction in the frequency of illegal activity as a result of the project. A slight decrease was found in the total sample, but it was attributable to minor offenses and reduced illegal activity by the girls in the sample. In contrast, major offenses by boys actually increased in frequency during the project, while "major offenses by younger boys increased most of all" (Miller, 1962, p. 180).

## ■ Mobilization for Youth

In 1961, one of the most ambitious efforts to prevent and control juvenile delinquency was developed. This demonstration project—New York's Mobilization for Youth (MFY)—became the prototype for many federally funded delinquency prevention programs developed in other cities during the Kennedy and Johnson administrations. Originally funded under a grant from the National Institute of Mental Health (NIMH), in 1962 it received an action grant from President Kennedy's Committee on Juvenile Delinquency and Youth Crime.

The target area chosen for the MFY demonstration project was Manhattan's Lower East Side, the longtime port of entry into the United States for new immigrant groups. This location was chosen by the pioneering area settlement houses: the Grand Street, Henry Street, and University settlement houses.

In the early 1960s, the Lower East Side was characterized by the typical problems of overcrowded lower-class slum neighborhoods, with high rates of unemployment, juvenile delinquency, school failure, drug addiction, petty crime, and families receiving public assistance. In response to the alarmingly high incidence of juvenile delinquency and gang welfare on the Lower East Side, Helen Hall (director of the Henry Street Settlement House) and sociologist Richard Cloward (of Columbia University's School of Social Work) developed the plan for Mobilization for Youth, with Cloward becoming its first director.

Cloward and Ohlin's (1960) opportunity theory postulated that delinquent subcultures emerge because lower-class youths strive to achieve legitimate goals—primarily the acquisition of money—and are unsuccessful because legitimate avenues for success are blocked. They stated: "It is our view that pressures toward the formation of delinquent subcultures originate in marked discrepancies between culturally induced aspirations among lower-class youth and the possibilities of achieving them by legitimate means" (p. 105).

Opportunity theory asserts that there is a major disparity between the aspirations of lower-class youth and the legitimate opportunities available to them. Lower-class youths internalize a set of conventional values and goals. Despite very limited access to legitimate avenues for achieving these goals, they are unable to lower their aspirations. Blaming others rather than themselves for their limited access to the opportunity structure, many of these alienated youths join delinquent subcultures.

Thus according to this theory, the organization of a neighborhood resulted in the formation of both legitimate and illegitimate opportunity structures to which youths in the community were differentially exposed. To maximize the long-term impact of antidelinquency programs, it was therefore important to modify the opportunity structures, as well as the delinquent subcultures they spawned.

Alfred Kahn (1967) acclaimed the MFY effort because it resulted in the development of "indigenous social organizations" and was more "attuned to complex urban political processes" (p. 495). The program sought to reduce delinquency by orienting the youths toward social change; it emphasized education, work, and social organization, including the use of social casework. MFY sought to convince youths that there were viable, law-abiding ways to participate in community life.

Mobilization for Youth included 30 separate "action" programs in the four major areas of work, education, community organization, and group service. As previously mentioned, one of the underlying themes of MFY was that urban lower-class adolescents must be given genuine opportunities to act in nondelinquent ways to prevent them from participating in delinquent acts.

An important aspect of the program was related to job training and placement. An urban Youth Service Corps was developed that hired several hundred unemployed neighborhood youths to work in a variety of activities, including conservation. The Youth Service Corps focused on fostering the types of attitudes and behaviors (e.g., following orders, reporting to work on time) necessary to succeed in the world of work and on strengthening the participants' job skills. A youth jobs center was created to locate permanent jobs for those who successfully completed the training program.

Many educational programs were initiated, such as the "homework helper" program, in which bright, low-income high school students were hired to tutor children in elementary school. By August 1964, more than 1,000 Lower East Side children had been taught to read. MFY also established a laboratory school in which effective ways to teach lower-class children were demonstrated.

In the area of community involvement, much effort was devoted to strengthening an already established organization, the Lower East Side Neighborhood Association. MFY staff also sought to develop social organizations among neighborhood residents who had not been affiliated with any community group. "Problem" families living in the target area received social services from neighborhood service centers, which were developed in four locations.

The group service aspect of the project included services for delinquent youths who had joined a gang, as well as a delinquency prevention program aimed at children. For youths 8 to 12 years of age, MFY developed a character-building organization similar to the Boy Scouts and Girl Scouts. This organization, known as the Adventure Corps, was designed to reach delinquency-prone youths. It provided exciting recreational and educational activities for young people as an alternative to gang membership. Squad leaders and their assistants were neighborhood residents who were paid a stipend (Task Force on Juvenile Delinquency, 1967).

Cloward and Ohlin's writings had a significant impact on delinquency prevention policy. They urged those interested in alleviating delinquency to take action to reorganize slum neighborhoods:

> The major effort of those who wish to eliminate delinquency should be directed to the reorganization of slum communities. Slum neighborhoods appear . . . to be undergoing progressive disintegration. The old structures, which provided social control and avenues of social ascent, are breaking down. Legitimate but functional substitutes for these traditional structures must be developed if we are to stem the trend toward violence and retreatism among adolescents in urban slums. (1960, p. 211)

In the early 1960s, this approach to delinquency prevention became the major strategy for the new federal delinquency initiatives endorsed by the President's Committee on Juvenile Delinquency and Youth Crime (Knapp, 1971; Maris & Rein, 1967; Moynihan, 1970; Schlesinger, 1977). The work of President Kennedy's committees led to the funding of 16 urban planning grants and 5 major delinquency prevention projects following the model developed by New York City's Mobilization for Youth project. It became the prototype project for many of the federally funded "war on poverty" programs developed during the 1960s.

## ■ Youth Service Bureaus

The modern-day version of a coordinating council is a youth service bureau (YSB). Developed to provide and coordinate programs and services for both delinquent and nondelinquent youths, these youth service bureaus have five basic goals:

1 Divert juveniles from the juvenile justice system.
2 Fill gaps in service by advocating for and developing services for youths and their families.
3 Provide case coordination and program coordinating.
4 Provide modification of systems of youth services.
5 Involve youth in the decision-making process.

In 1967, President Johnson's Commission on Law Enforcement and Administration of Justice provided a strong impetus for the establishment of youth service bureaus. Its major recommendation for preventing delinquency called for the development of such bureaus throughout the nation. It envisioned them as model coordinating units for the delivery of communitywide services to youth.

The commission urged communities to set up central coordinating units to serve status offenders, delinquents, and nondelinquents referred by the police, juvenile courts, probation departments, and schools. Many of these bureaus were federally funded through the Law Enforcement Assistance Administration (LEAA), the Youth Development and Delinquency Prevention Administration (YDDPA) of the Department of Health, Education, and Welfare, and the Model Cities Program of the Department of Housing and Urban Development (HUD). Only a small percentage of referrals came from the police; youths generally learned about the program from a parent, friend, or schoolmate.

The commission's recommendation appeared in its 1967 report, *The Challenge of Crime in a Free Society*. The report described the concept and focus for youth service bureaus:

Communities should establish neighborhood youth service agencies—
Youth Service Bureaus—located if possible in comprehensive neighborhood community centers and receiving juveniles (delinquent and nondelinquent) referred by the police, the juvenile court, parents, schools
and other sources. These agencies would act as central coordinators of
all community services for young people and would also provide services lacking in the community or neighborhood, especially ones designed for less seriously delinquent juveniles. (President's Commission,
1967, p. 83)

However, the commission did not identify the specific process for establishing
and operating these bureaus. In recognition of the need to prepare program
development guidelines, the YDDPA held a series of meetings that resulted in
the 1971 publication of a booklet, *Youth Service Bureaus and Delinquency Prevention*, containing suggestions and guidelines for implementing and coordinating services in a youth service bureau.

The National Council on Crime and Delinquency also developed operational guidelines for youth service bureaus. It began by defining the YSB as a:

Noncoercive independent public agency established to divert children
and youth from the justice system by: (1) mobilizing community resources to solve youth problems; (2) strengthening existing youth resources and developing new ones; and (3) promoting positive programs
to remedy delinquency-breeding conditions. (Norman, 1972, p. 8)

By 1971, 4 years after the strong endorsement of the President's Commission
on Law Enforcement and Administration of Justice and with the aid of federal
funding, 262 youth service bureaus had been developed (YDDP, 1973). Studies
on YSBs were conducted by such researchers as John Martin, William Underwood, and Elaine Duxbury. In 1972, Martin and his associates conducted a
national study of 195 youth service bureaus (YDDPA, 1973). Their findings
provide an overview of the organizational structure and function of youth
service bureaus in the early 1970s.

The staffing patterns of these bureaus ranged from 1 full-time person
assisted by a few volunteers to large staffs of 10 or more employees. Typically,
programs were staffed by 5 to 6 full-time workers and anywhere from 1 to 50
volunteers. The majority of program directors (63.8%) indicated that diverting
youths from the juvenile justice system was their primary objective. Other
directors described their primary activities as delinquency prevention or youth
development projects such as recreation programs, tutoring, group counseling,
drug treatment, family counseling, and job referral.

Two thirds of the 195 programs were located in urban or Model City
neighborhoods. These areas were primarily lower socioeconomic class and
were characterized by high rates of unemployment and crime and limited
resources for youths.

The target population was youths in the 14 to 17 age group. The survey found that program participants were on average 15½ years old. Approximately 60% of the participants were male, and the average project served 350 youths each year. Referrals came from several sources, including the police, school, parents, and self-referrals, but no single source appeared to be dominant.

Information on funding was provided by 188 of the programs. Eighty-two percent of the programs indicated that their primary funding source was a federal grant. The most frequent source of federal funding was the LEAA, through the state criminal justice planning agencies; of the 155 programs receiving federal funds, 135 had an LEAA grant. The other federal agencies that provided funding were YDDPA, Model Cities, and the U.S. Department of Labor (Youth Development, 1973). The average annual budget of youth service bureaus ranged from $50,000 to $75,000. In order to obtain a federal grant, a program was required to have in-kind matching funds, which usually came from either a local or state agency (e.g., the state's division of youth services).

In Underwood's (1972) nationwide study of 400 cases from 28 youth service bureaus, he found that approximately 13% of the referrals were from law enforcement agencies, while the most frequent referral sources (30%) were self-referrals, friends, or family. The second most frequent referral source was the schools (21%). Duxbury's (1972) study of California's nine pilot community youth service bureaus indicated a slightly higher percentage of referrals from law enforcement (21%). In that study, only 13% of referrals came from the schools, while an additional 11% came from county probation agencies. Duxbury indicated that 47.7%, or 2,069 new cases, were individuals referred by themselves or by parents, friends, or neighbors. These studies reveal that youth service bureaus were underutilized by criminal justice agencies and that the largest proportion of youth voluntarily sought the assistance of YSBs.

In contrast to this pattern of referrals, a number of communities established programs in neighborhood storefronts or offices close to local police departments. In addition, in several communities police juvenile offices were assigned full time (on a rotating basis) to counsel youths and their families at local youth service bureaus. Such efforts were matched by YSB social workers who participated in police ride-along programs. Predictably, youth service bureaus that made an effort to work closely with the police received a large percentage of their referrals from the police department.

The success of YSBs was often directly related to their location and accessibility to the population they were intended to serve. For example, many bureaus remained open at night and on weekends to serve juveniles in their community. Youth service bureaus located near high schools, near police departments, or in a downtown area frequented by youths were more likely to have a greater number of referrals.

By the late 1970s, LEAA had shifted its priority to funding law enforcement and rehabilitation programs rather than prevention projects. LEAA had intended its YSB grants to be limited to seed money (usually for 2 or 3 years), with the understanding that county or city governments or private agencies would gradually assume full fiscal responsibility. In some cases, when the federal grant ended, the local agency did provide full funding for the youth service bureau under its auspices. However, by 1982, as a direct result of the demise of LEAA and other cutbacks in federal funding for juvenile justice, a number of these model youth services bureaus (those that were not supported by full funding from another source) were phased out because of a lack of funds.

## Conclusion

Juvenile delinquency is a social problem that requires comprehensive casework and service delivery to children and youths before they became serious and chronic offenders. Integral to the development of comprehensive services is the expansion of neighborhood-based delinquency prevention programs.

Delinquency prevention strategies should involve neighborhood residents and professional social workers (as was evident in the past). Prevention efforts should also provide individual and family counseling, job training and placement, substance abuse treatment, and school remediation programs.

## Discussion Questions

**1** Discuss the basic assumptions and objectives of the Chicago Area Project.

**2** List the three approaches used by the staff of Boston's Midcity Project that differed from earlier delinquency control and prevention programs.

**3** New York's Mobilization for Youth (MFY) demonstration project was based on Cloward and Ohlin's opportunity theory. Discuss the postulates of opportunity theory.

**4** List and describe the purposes of three specific MFY action programs.

**5** List the five basic goals of youth service bureaus.

**6** What three federal agencies provided major funding to local youth service bureaus?

**7** The success of youth service bureaus was often attributed to their location and accessibility to the population they were intended to serve. Discuss two examples of ways in which the location and operating hours of a youth service bureau improved participation by local youths.

# References

Beam, S. (1937). Community coordination for prevention of delinquency. In *National Probation Association yearbook* (pp. 89–90, 113–115). Boston: National Probation Association.

Cloward, R., & Ohlin, L. (1960). *Delinquency and opportunity: A theory of delinquent gangs.*
New York: Free Press.

Duxbury, E. (1972). *Youth service bureaus in California.* Progress Report No. 3, State of California. Sacramento, CA: Department of the Youth Authority.

Kahn, A. J. (1967). From delinquency treatment to community development. In P. F. Lazars-
feld, W. H. Sewell, & H. L. Wilensky (Eds.), *The uses of sociology* (pp. 477–505). New
York: Basic Books.

Knapp, J. (1971). *Scouting the war on poverty: Social reform politics in the Kennedy administration.*
Lexington, MA: Lexington Books.

Kobrin, S. (1959). The Chicago Area Project: A 25-year assessment. *Annals of the American
Academy of Political and Social Science, 322,* 20–29.

Maris, P., & Rein, M. (1967). *Dilemmas of social reform: Poverty and community action in the
United States.* New York: Atherton.

McMillen, W. (1947). Community organization in social work. In *Social Work Yearbook*
(pp. 110–117). Washington, DC: National Association of Social Workers.

Miller, W. B. (1962). The impact of a "total community" delinquency control project. *Social
Problems, 10,* 168–191.

Miller, W. B., Baum, R. C., & McNeil, R. (1968). Delinquency prevention and organizational
relations. In S. Wheeler (Ed.), *Controlling delinquents* (pp. 1–100). New York: Wiley.

Moynihan, D. P. (1970). *Maximum feasible misunderstanding: Community action in the war on
poverty.* New York: Free Press.

Norman, S. (1972). *The youth service bureau: A key to delinquency prevention.* Paramus, NJ:
National Council on Crime and Delinquency.

President's Commission on Law Enforcement and Administration of Justice. (1967). *The challenge of crime in a free society.* Washington, DC: U.S. Government Printing Office.

Pursuit, D. G., Gerletti, J. D., Brown, R. M., & Ward, S. M. (1972). *Police programs for preventing
crime and delinquency.* Springfield, IL: Charles C. Thomas.

Schlesinger, A. M., Jr. (1977). *A thousand days.* Boston: Houghton Mifflin.

Schlossman, S., & Sedlak, M. (1983). The Chicago Area Project revisited. *Crime and Delinquency, 29,* 398–462.

Scudder, K. J. (1946). The coordinating council at work. In *National Probation Association yearbook* (pp. 67–77). Boston: National Probation Association.

Shaw, C. R. (1930). *The jack-roller.* Chicago: University of Chicago Press.

Shaw, C. R. (1931). *The natural history of a delinquent career.* Chicago: University of Chicago
Press.

Shaw, C. R., & McKay, H. D. (1972). *Juvenile delinquency and urban areas* (rev. ed.). Chicago:
University of Chicago Press.

Sorrentino, A. (1983). Community programs. In S. H. Kadish (Ed.), *Encyclopedia of crime and
justice* (pp. 358–361). New York: Free Press.

Task Force on Juvenile Delinquency, President's Commission on Law Enforcement and Administration of Justice. (1967). *Task force report: Juvenile delinquency and youth crime.*
Washington, DC: U.S. Government Printing Office.

Underwood, W. (1972). *The national study of youth service bureaus.* Washington, DC: U.S.
Dept. of Health, Education, and Welfare, Youth Development and Delinquency Prevention Administration.

Witmer, H. L., & Tufts, E. (1954). *The effectiveness of delinquency prevention programs.* U.S.

Children's Bureau Publication No. 350. Washington, DC: U.S. Department of Health, Education, and Welfare.

Youth Development and Delinquency Prevention Administration. (1973). *The challenge of youth service bureaus.* Publication No. SRS 73-26024. Washington, DC: U.S. Government Printing Office.

# 7 The Emergence of the Juvenile Court and Probation Services

Albert R. Roberts

This chapter highlights some of the developmental trends, problems, and accomplishments of the juvenile court and begins with a discussion of the impetus for the first juvenile court in America, established in 1899 in Cook County, Illinois. The chapter proceeds with a summary of the early surveys on the effectiveness of the juvenile court and documentation of several critical problems, such as lack of suitable facilities for placement of juveniles, lack of financial support for hiring and in-service training of caseworkers and probation officers, the heavy burden and numerous cases placed on juvenile court judges, and the lack of a uniform policy among juvenile courts. Also discussed are the use of volunteers to the court, the child guidance clinics' connection with the courts, and due process safeguards to protect the rights of juveniles. The chapter concludes by citing the progress made in the past decade toward more equitable and humane treatment of juveniles.

## ■ Establishment of the Juvenile Court

According to H. Warren Dunham, a precedent for the establishment of the juvenile court system in the United States came from the English courts, specifically from the 1772 case of *Eyre v. Shaftsbury*. From this case evolved the principle of *parens patriae*, enabling the court to act in lieu of the parents who were found to be unwilling or unable to give their child appropriate guidance. This paved the way for the juvenile court in the United States to assume jurisdiction for dependent and neglected children (Dunham, 1958).

There has been some confusion between the terms *parens patriae* and *in loco parentis*. The former refers to the responsibility of government to serve the welfare of the child, not (as the latter might suggest) to replace the parents. According to Schlossman (1983, p. 962), "*parens patriae* had sanctioned the right of the Crown to interrupt or supplant natural family relations whenever a child's welfare was threatened." Although initially it was applied only in cases of property disputes regarding well-to-do juveniles, in later years the doctrine was interpreted more broadly. By the 19th century, all of the states had affirmed their right to serve as guardian for children in accordance with the states' "legal inheritance" from England.

The English common-law foundation for the juvenile court is from civil rather than criminal law. Great Britain's common-law doctrine is based on the idea of chancery or equity. "The essential idea of chancery is welfare or balancing of interest. It stands for flexibility, guardianship and protection rather than rigidity and punishment" (Lou, 1927, p. 2). The founders of the first juvenile court in America had intended the juvenile court to be as much a place to educate errant children and negligent parents as an institution that handed down sanctions.

When the term *parens patriae* is used in modern times, it generally refers to the state's legal obligation and right to protect the young, the dependent or neglected child, and the incompetent child. However, as stated by Supreme Court Justice Abe Fortas in the Court's decision on the Gault case: "its meaning is murky and its historical credentials are of dubious relevance to juvenile delinquency proceedings" (*In re Gault*, 1967).

The doctrine of *parens patriae* was used in order to free the juvenile court judge to accept social and psychological evaluations and provide informal proceedings, thus departing from due process of law. It also justified the court's right to save children who had committed noncriminal offenses, such as disobeying parents, truancy, and associating with immoral and criminal persons.

Historically, the state of Massachusetts has been an innovator of various movements to improve the type of treatment juvenile offenders receive. However, it was in New York City in 1825 that the first House of Refuge for children was opened. Boston established a similar project a year later. By 1860, 16 similar institutions had been opened throughout the country. The impetus for building juvenile institutions came from the sound belief that youths who had violated a law should not be confined with adult criminals in prisons. Even though this belief had evolved in the early 1800s, a juvenile court for the purpose of separating and individualizing juveniles' cases was not established until 1899 (Dunham, 1958).

In Massachusetts in 1869, the first definite action was taken on behalf of a juvenile's rights in court. In that year a law was passed requiring the governor to assign a "visiting agent" to work for the best interest of the juvenile who was in trouble with the law. The visiting agent had to be informed before any youth under the age of 16 could be committed to jail or any other type of institution. The visiting agent was present at the hearing and made recommendations to the judge with regard to the child's welfare (Sullenger, 1936). As of 1870, Massachusetts law required that juvenile offenders under the age of 16 have their cases heard "separate from the general and ordinary criminal business" (Kamm, Hunt, & Fleming, 1968, p. 3). Although this concept was a forerunner of the juvenile court, the law did not actually establish a separate juvenile court system.

The first juvenile court law in the United States was enacted by the Illinois state legislature on April 21, 1899.[1] It was a culmination of a series of concerted efforts by a number of renowned social work professionals, lawyers, and other humanitarians. At the time of the law's enactment, establishment of the juvenile court was seen as a milestone in the developmental process of American justice. Grace Abbott, in *The Child and the State*, described the efforts that paved the way for the first juvenile court:

> Lucy L. Flower, Julia C. Lathrop, and Jane Addams were the moving spirits in formulating the new and basically different conception of the treatment of juvenile delinquents which it represented. They first became interested in the more than five hundred children in the Chicago House of Correction, and under their leadership the Chicago Woman's

Club induced the Board of Education to establish a "school" for the boys in this institution. But this obviously did not meet the need, and they began a more fundamental attack on the problem. . . . A committee was appointed by the Illinois State Conference of Charities at its meeting in 1898. [They] urged that the conference undertake to get a law drafted. The problem was to find how to make a fundamental change in criminal law and criminal procedure which would be upheld by the courts as constitutional. In co-operation with a committee of the Chicago Bar Association, a bill was finally worked out and agreed upon by the interested groups. (Abbott, Abbott, & Breckinridge, 1938, pp. 330–331)

Julia Lathrop had been appointed by Illinois governor John Altgeld to the Board of State Commissioners of Public Charities. In this role she inspected all of the state's county jails and poorhouses; her attention was focused on the treatment of juveniles. She expressed her concern in an 1898 report:

There are at the present moment in the State of Illinois, especially in the City of Chicago, thousands of children in need of active intervention for their preservation from physical, mental and moral destruction. Such intervention is demanded, not only by sympathetic consideration for their well-being, but also in the name of the commonwealth, for the preservation of the State. If the child is the material out of which men and women are made, the neglected child is the material out of which paupers and criminals are made. (Mennel, 1973, p. 129)

In addition to Julia Lathrop, others helped to arouse public concern over the treatment of juveniles. For example, an encounter was reported between a Chicago police officer and a 4-year-old child who was caught stealing cakes. The policeman, finally deciding to let the child go, yelled, "If you git into my hands again I'll cut your ears off close ter yer head, and I'll sew yer mouth up so's yer can't eat no cakes. . . . Now git. Yer little bastard, and ter hell wid you" (Mennel, 1973, p. 129). Apparently such treatment of children was not uncommon in those days.

The law passed by the Illinois legislature (with widespread support from the Chicago Bar Association and philanthropic reformers) gave the juvenile court the power to send delinquent youths to appropriate institutions. But "the preference was . . . to place them on probation either in their own or foster homes." The court was also empowered to appoint as probation officers "one or more persons of good character" (Mennel, 1973, p. 130). Thus, when the juvenile court system first developed, there was more emphasis on community-based treatment of juvenile offenders and less interest in sending youths to institutions.

The major features and components of the juvenile court were as follows:

1 An emphasis on informal procedures at every stage of court intake, adjudication, and disposition.
2 A separate, sanitary detention center where doctors, social workers, and other staff would systematically observe and study the child's personality and motivation. This evaluation would form part of the prehearing investigation.
3 Passage of enabling legislation that would have encouraged judges to fine and sentence adults to jail when they were negligent or had contributed to the delinquency of a minor.
4 Probation, the most important component of the new courts. The primary goal of the juvenile court was the rehabilitation of children and youths in their own homes.

Rothman's (1980) analysis of aggregate data from the 1920s and 1930s indicates that the most frequently pronounced disposition from the juvenile court was probation surveillance.

## ▇ Positive and Negative Reactions to the Juvenile Court

In the early 1900s, widespread support for the new juvenile court system led to the establishment of many other juvenile courts modeled after the original one in Chicago. Progressive reformers, concerned with the treatment of juveniles, regarded the development of juvenile courts as a significant achievement. As stated in the previous section, Grace Abbott (who later served as chief of the U.S. Children's Bureau) and Jane Addams were among the many social work professionals who endorsed the juvenile court system. Addams (1935, p. 137), talking about the climate soon after establishment of the first juvenile court, stated:

> There was almost a change in mores when the juvenile court was established. The child was brought before the judge with no one to prosecute him and none to defend him—the judge and all concerned were merely trying to find out what could be done on his behalf. The element of conflict was absolutely eliminated and with it all notions of punishment as such.

Frederic Howe (1913, p. 133) exclaimed that because of the juvenile court, "the budding crop of crime of the next decade will be largely diminished, at great savings to life and character, as well as to the purse of the community." Judges, too, were supportive of the establishment of the juvenile courts. The willingness of many judges to utilize the new system can be seen in part from an endorsement made by Judge Edward Lindsey in 1914 after he and Judge Edward F. Waite had investigated the status of delinquent youth. He believed that every child had the right to a fair hearing of the type established by the juvenile court system: "No child should be restrained simply because he has been accused of crime, whether he is guilty or not" (Lindsey, 1914, p. 145).

The broad-based support for the juvenile court in the early 1900s led some reformers to advocate the creation of a family court to treat the adult(s) responsible for the child's behavior. Flexner and Baldwin (1912, p. vii) urged that such a court could be more effective in reaching the family. They believed that the delinquent youth was just "a factor in the larger and more complicated problem." By 1923, all the states, with the exception of Connecticut and Wyoming,[2] had passed legislation defining a juvenile delinquent and establishing a special court for juveniles[3] (Dunham, 1958, p. 372).

Not all of the reactions to the juvenile court system were positive. Some, in the minority at first, questioned the thoroughness of the planning that preceded the establishment of the new system. In the opinion of Lemert (1971, pp. 5–6):

> The establishment of the first juvenile courts reveals them to have been less a carefully planned innovation than the climax of a nineteenth century reform movement to rescue children from the depravity and immorality of lower class urban environments. The envisioned ideal that delinquent children would thereafter be defined and treated as "neglected" proved false; in practice, the reverse often was true, that is, dependent and neglected children fell under the pall of delinquency and in many cases were subjected to the same kinds of sanctions.

A case study of the Milwaukee County juvenile court in the early 1900s reveals that while this court did attain the structure and components recommended by the founders, it failed to meet the progressive practices that the founders had expected. In 1901, the court opened with a makeshift detention center (acquired from a local charitable society), a contributory delinquency law, and a probation staff; unfortunately, probation officers were assigned to an average of 200 cases at a time when 60 cases was viewed as a high caseload. Within a few years, a new detention facility was built to provide a safe place for the confinement of juveniles, but the staff rarely provided the judge with individualized reports on the juvenile prior to adjudication. Finally, the contributory delinquency statute was rarely used against abusive parents or other community members who coaxed children into criminal conduct. The judge and probation officers in Milwaukee relied mainly on fear, threats, and short-term detention to coerce children into cooperating (Schlossman, 1977). In contrast to the situation in Milwaukee, other jurisdictions, such as Judge Lindsey's court in Denver, were known for being compassionate and having a highly efficient probation service.

During the early years of the 20th century, at approximately the same time that juvenile courts were emerging throughout the country, the number of delinquent acts rose. Dunham (1958) attributes this to a combination of rapid industrialization and an influx of immigrants that led to rapid, unprecedented growth of the cities. European immigrants faced their own problems in trying to overcome cultural and language barriers and to support their families. Dunham suggested that the children of these families were caught in the upheaval of this new way of life, divided between European peasant values and the different values inherent in the American way of life, and responded to the confusion by committing acts which were labeled "delinquent." Many of their parents were unable to comprehend or cope with these situations. This situation fostered the need for the emerging family court to take on additional functions—for example, aiding immigrant families in the adjustment process, serving to acquaint families with American customs and values, and protecting the child from serious problems in the home (p. 373).

One of the first surveys of the effectiveness of the juvenile court system was completed in 1927. Examining Pennsylvania's juvenile court system for the U.S. Children's Bureau, Judge Charles W. Hoffman was appalled to discover many youths languishing in detention homes and county jails despite state laws that specifically forbade imprisonment of juveniles. The judge raised two significant questions: "What has the advanced legal status accomplished? Is it not clear that the juvenile courts are not functioning?" (U.S. Children's Bureau, 1922, p. 146). Hoffman's survey was the forerunner of numerous statements about the efficacy of the juvenile courts. Feelings were strong both for and against the competence and fairness of this system for treating the ever-rising numbers of juvenile offenders.

Over the years, the factors that adversely affected the functioning of the juvenile courts have been examined. Criticism has centered on the lack of suitable facilities for placement of juveniles, the heavy burden placed on juvenile court judges, the lack of a uniform policy among juvenile courts, and the lack of financial support for hiring and in-service training of caseworkers and probation personnel.

Writing in the 1940s, Kahn (1953) pointed to the "perplexing and urgent problem" of finding suitable long-term placement for juvenile offenders. He was concerned because the juvenile courts faced the dilemma of effecting a suitable placement for adjudicated delinquents without having the direct power to remedy the severe problems that existed in the juvenile institutions. Kahn's study reviewed the case records of 152 juveniles on probation. The records showed that attempts at placement had been made for 45 children. From the 21 institutions and agencies able to refuse admission to certain applicants, there had been 47 rejections and 37 acceptances. Several of the 45 children had been rejected by as many as four agencies and were finally placed on probation or sent to the New York State Training School, which could not refuse admission to youths referred by the court.

Kahn (1953) emphasized that he had reviewed only a small percentage of the case records. When the figures he obtained were multiplied 10 or 20 times in the course of a year, the magnitude of the problem became obvious. He described the situation that developed when children had to wait for weeks or months until an appropriate placement could be arranged:

> Rejections often mean a series of court rehearings until an effective plan is made—or until the judge decides to try probation or the New York Training School instead. In the interim, delinquent children wait for weeks and neglected children for weeks, months, or even years in so-called "temporary" facilities, unable to settle down to a routine which permits a feeling of relative stability or to have the advantages of much needed services and programs prescribed for them. (p. 253)

Some of the major reasons for the difficulty in securing appropriate placements were, according to Kahn (1953), the shortage of facilities, restricted intake policies, and the inability of some facilities to assure that the child would receive casework help, psychotherapy, proper grade placement in the residential school, and remedial reading. He criticized the procedure in which it became the probation officer's responsibility to "shop" for an appropriate placement and try to convince the facility to take the juvenile. Probation officers set out to find placements without any coordination or effective communication with other probation officers. This resulted in the more experienced workers, who had developed personal contacts with agencies, making some successful placements while other workers were less successful in that endeavor.

Judge Paul Alexander, who served as president of the National Conference of Juvenile Agencies, attested to the continual pressure placed on juvenile court judges. He was deeply concerned that the unfair burden placed on the judges could have an adverse effect on equitable treatment of delinquent youths. Quoting Alexander's report in the 1944 *National Probation Association Yearbook*:

> I can bear personal witness to the fact that in almost every city of the country the juvenile court judge is the most overworked and harassed of all judges. . . . In only seventeen states can he look forward to a modest pension upon his retirement. . . . His court as well as his children are more often than not housed in dark, dingy, dilapidated, dirty and inadequate quarters. (p. 38)

Alexander continued by talking about the immense pressure that juvenile court judges were under: "When he can give one hour to three cases, and ought to give three hours to one case somebody is going to suffer." He estimated the hours a juvenile court judge works were about double the hours worked by judges in other courts.

The September 1949 issue of *Federal* Probation was published in commemoration of the 50th anniversary of the founding of the first juvenile court. In that issue, Carr compiled a summary of problems facing a considerable number of juvenile courts. Record keeping, he felt, was inadequate. He criticized "sketchy documents called case records, compiled . . . without benefit of any trained caseworkers and sometimes not even compiled" (p. 29). Carr was especially concerned about the lack of qualified professional caseworkers and probation officers to provide needed services to juveniles in trouble.[4] The majority of juvenile courts did not have probation officers. Probation in those cases was merely a matter of "signing the book," assigning youths to their parents for probation (frequently the parents had caused the child's problems in the first place), or using untrained amateurs. Rural areas were particularly devoid of such services because they could not afford to hire professional social workers or probation officers, as could some of the big city juvenile court systems. In addition, the rural areas did not have enough work for full-time personnel (Carr, 1949, pp. 29–30).

Carr's article paid particular attention to the unique problems faced by courts in rural areas. He recognized that individual rural counties did not have the need or the budget to maintain fully staffed juvenile courts; the number of juvenile offenders appearing before a rural court was substantially less than the number appearing before city courts. However, when a juvenile from a rural area was brought into court, Carr believed that the juvenile was entitled to the same (though still too limited) rehabilitative services that would be available to a city youth. He suggested that rather than every rural county having its own juvenile court system, a few counties combine their resources to provide enough work for one well-equipped, technically competent court to replace the 10 or 12 "imitations" then in existence. Carr (1949, pp. 30–31) described the situation as he saw it: "[The rural counties] do not produce enough delinquents to justify fully equipped modern courts; they could not possibly pay for such courts if the business were there; and yet one case mishandled by their well-meaning but untrained officials may cost their states many times the cost of efficient service."

Many of the problem areas delineated by Alexander (1944), Carr (1949), and Kahn (1953) in the 1940s were still apparent in the late 1950s. The organization and policies of juvenile courts continued to vary markedly throughout the United States. In general the large urban areas had a court devoted exclusively to hearing juvenile cases, while in the rural areas the probate judge served also as the juvenile court judge. According to Dunham (1958), the major differences in juvenile court policies in the late 1950s were that (a) the juvenile court judge was elected in some jurisdictions and appointed in others; (b) some judges took a human, personal interest in the youths, while others treated juveniles strictly within the framework of the law; and (c) some juvenile courts had a staff of professional social workers, probation officers, and psychologists, while other courts had only minimal, untrained staff.

Dunham was expressly concerned that there were still a number of juvenile courts across the country that were not oriented toward social work policy. Nevertheless, he recognized that many juvenile courts did utilize social work principles, thereby upgrading the level of service available to juveniles.

Dunham (1955, p. 376) believed that five key factors had served to influence the progressive, social work–oriented juvenile court systems:

> (1) The aggressive social work orientation of the United States Children's Bureau; (2) the broadening jurisdiction of the juvenile court to include not only neglected and dependent children, but all matters of a legal nature involving children; (3) the gradual professionalization of social work; (4) various court decisions involving delinquency; (5) the growing prospects of treatment through the increased acceptance by social workers of psychoanalysis for getting at the roots of conflict which supposedly produce delinquency.

## ■ Early Development of Juvenile Probation

### Volunteers in Probation

The juvenile probation system originated as a volunteer rather than a paid program. John Augustus (1852), a successful bootmaker in Boston, is credited with being the first volunteer and the "father of probation." His voluntary probation work began in 1841, and during the next 18 years, he dedicated himself to helping hundreds of juvenile and adult defendants. He worked primarily with delinquent children. Augustus completed extensive background investigations on most of his potential clients and kept a log of all the cases he worked with, showing their names, dates, addresses, case numbers, and amount of bail, fines, and costs.

Lindner and Savarese (1984) have documented the importance of volunteers in the evolution of probation in Boston, Chicago, and New York City: "Volunteers continued to be important . . . in the evolution of probation with several of them playing very influential roles in having probation legislation enacted in their respective jurisdictions" (p. 7). For example, in Chicago, Julia Lathrop, Alzina Stevens, and Lucy Flower provided direct services to clients on probation and raised money to pay the salaries of probation officers. Dr. Samuel Barrows, David Willard, and Rebecca Salome Foster dedicated themselves to promoting passage of the first probation law in New York.

### Emergence of the Professional Probation Worker

Evaluations of the quality of volunteers' work in the early 1900s uncovered several problems, including "inadequate training and supervision of volunteers" and an irregular work schedule (Lindner & Savarese, 1984, p. 9). In 1905, the New York State Probation Commission criticized the work of volunteer probation officers throughout the state. Even Maurice Parmelee (1918, p. 403), himself a volunteer probation officer who later became a prominent criminologist, registered skepticism about the effectiveness of volunteers: "Much of this probation work has been done by volunteer workers who have been well-meaning, but many of whom, on account of lack of special training and experience and a sentimental point of view have not been very efficient."

One of the harshest critics of probation volunteers was Bernard Flexner (1918, p. 610), who cautioned chief probation officers and other professionals against the "indiscriminate use of volunteers" and recommended that they be limited to working with only one to two probationers at any given time.

Only a few years after the passage of probation legislation (made possible by the noble and strenuous efforts of volunteers), most volunteer probation workers had been replaced by paid professionals. Lindner and Savarese (1984, p. 10) summarized the volunteers' fate in the 1910s and 1920s: "With increased hiring of salaried probation officers, the fate of the volunteer in probation became apparent. Although they would continue to serve in smaller cities and rural areas for a considerable period of time, their overall influence in probation would rapidly diminish."

The use of juvenile probation had been sporadic until a few years after the juvenile court reform movement began. It then spread rapidly to all the states that had passed juvenile court legislation. By 1927, almost all the states had enacted juvenile court laws, and a juvenile probation system had been developed in every state except Wyoming. Probation was to be the alternative disposition that allowed judges to permit juveniles to be treated in their homes. Probation, an arm of the juvenile court, would supervise children in their own communities rather than by placing them in institutions.

According to Kahn (1953), volunteer services working with the juvenile court system (beginning in the 1940s) performed a valuable service to juveniles in trouble. In New York, two of the best known organizations providing volunteer services were the Jewish Board of Guardians and the Catholic Charities (Guidance Institute of Catholic Charities, Youth Counseling Service). These agencies maintained a liaison at the juvenile court to coordinate referrals to appropriate treatment services. Protestant Big Brother and Big Sister movements also worked with the courts in an attempt to arrange a contact for a youth to have a Big Brother or Big Sister. However, Kahn stated that as of the early 1940s these services were generally not available where the need was the greatest—for Protestant Negro youths.

Representatives of the Jewish Board of Guardians and the Catholic Charities, in times of turnover among court personnel, contributed significantly to the orientation of new judges and probation officers. In Kahn's (1953, p. 243) words: "All the voluntary agencies have been excellent friends of the court, interpreting court needs when it has been necessary to turn to authorities or to the public at large in connection with court problems."

By the mid-1960s, probation departments had been established in all 50 states and in hundreds of counties throughout the nation. However, there was a lack of uniformity in the way probation services were delivered in different states and counties. More specifically, a 1967 study by the National Council on Crime and Delinquency (NCCD) for the President's Commission on Law Enforcement and the Administration of Justice found that:

1  In 31 states all counties have probation staff service.
2  A total of 2,306 counties (74% of all counties in the United States) theoretically have such a service. In some of these, however, the service is only token.
3  In 16 states that do not have probation staff coverage in every county, at least some services are available to courts in some counties from persons other than paid, full-time probation officers.
4  In 165 counties in four states, no juvenile probation services at all are available.

Generally, the country's most populous jurisdictions are included among the counties served by probation staff. However, in the smaller counties, service may be expected to be spotty (p. 134).

## ■ Child Guidance Clinics and the Juvenile Courts

At the 1941 National Probation Association Conference, Homer expressed his concern about provision of treatment for juvenile delinquents. He became a strong advocate for a close working relationship between the juvenile courts and child guidance clinics. The first such connection had been established back in 1909 by William Healy, a psychiatrist. Healy's clinic worked in conjunction with the Juvenile Court of Cook County, Illinois, which had become the first juvenile court in the country only a decade earlier. Child guidance clinics received significant impetus for further growth in 1922, when the Commonwealth Fund undertook to sponsor eight demonstration clinics in various parts of the country. St. Louis was selected as the first site (Stevenson, 1934). By the 1930s and 1940s, large numbers of psychiatric social workers had been hired to work in teams with psychiatrists to treat emotionally disturbed children, predelinquents, and delinquents.

Homer's complaint in 1941 was that working relationships between child guidance clinics and juvenile courts were not widespread; in too many areas such a relationship still needed to be formed. He urged prompt attention to the matter, believing that the future of both juvenile courts and child guidance clinics should consist of a close working relationship between the two.

> Any juvenile court which does not use or does not have available child-guidance services most certainly fails to make use of modern techniques for the diagnosis and treatment of behavior disorders in children. The

clinic which is uninterested in delinquent children arbitrarily deprives a large proportion of children of a service which it is peculiarly suited to provide. Furthermore, it is undoubtedly true that small communities unable at present to finance a clinic, could do so with additional support from tax funds which the participation of court agencies would ensure. (Homer, 1941, p. 180)

Although the clinics were usually directed by a psychiatrist, social workers formed the core of clinic operations as they worked with children, families, and school and court personnel. Levine and Levine (1970) found that social workers eventually came to dominate these diagnostic, treatment, and delinquency prevention clinics, if not in status then certainly in numbers and in their significant influence on practice with children exhibiting behavioral disorders. By the late 1950s, the number of child guidance clinics had grown to over 600, most of them located in large cities (Roberts & Kurtz, 1987; Robinson, 1960).

## ■ Probation and the Juvenile Courts

The term *probation*, as defined by Shireman (1971, p. 191) is "a legal status created by order of the sentencing court as an alternative to incarceration." According to Sullenger (1936), the term *probation* is derived from *probare*, meaning "to prove"; that is, it allows the juvenile offender the opportunity to prove himself.

In recent years, probation for juveniles has been thought of in terms of professional probation officers providing juvenile offenders with supportive services and referrals that, depending upon the youth's individual needs, might include individual counseling, group counseling, referral to community mental health centers for outpatient treatment or inpatient psychiatric services, appropriate referrals to addiction treatment programs, family counseling, vocational training, assistance in finding employment, enrolling in alternative education programs, or preparing for the high school equivalency examination. However, the availability of extensive probation services is a relatively recent development.

Massachusetts, in 1878, became the first state to enact legislation providing for probation for juvenile offenders (Teeters & Reinemann, 1950). In the years immediately following passage of this law, the courts did not set up any means of caring for children, initially relying upon existing agencies that volunteered their services. However, the resources provided by these sources were quite limited, necessitating the development of particular probation services to be linked with the court procedure.

Probation practices were greatly extended in the wake of the juvenile court movement 20 years later, but specific practices varied from one jurisdiction to another. By 1902, Rhode Island, Indiana, Minnesota, and New Jersey had followed Massachusetts's lead by passing legislation creating the position of paid state probation officers (Mennel, 1973). In the federal judiciary system, it was not until 1925 that Congress authorized probation and not until 1930 that the federal courts made extensive use of probation as an alternative to incarceration (Teeters & Reinemann, 1950).

Considerable problems with probation practices developed during the early 20th century. Because services provided by probation officers after adjudication can make the difference between whether or not a juvenile will participate in criminal activity in the future, it is appalling to realize the casual attitude and lack of professional standards that characterized probation practices for many years.

According to Mennel (1973, p. 140), the rights of juveniles were not being fully supported because probation officers, "whatever their sympathies for delinquent children, considered themselves servants of the judge of the juvenile court, not defenders of the rights of children." Because the early probation officers did not receive professional training, a multiplicity of problems developed. Most juvenile courts utilized volunteer probation officers, which resulted in representatives from Protestant and Catholic child-saving societies taking on the responsibility of serving as probation officers. Mennel believed that the services these agencies provided should have been in addition to, rather than instead of, trained probation services.

In courts that did have probation officers, concerns were raised because of what Mennel (1973, p. 142) termed an "authoritarian attitude" on the part of the probation personnel. Some workers were said to have exhibited threats in an effort to get youths to straighten out. These actions probably occurred with some frequency because the workers had not received appropriate training for their jobs. The requirements for becoming a juvenile probation officer, entrusted with such heavy responsibility, were unbelievably lax, and they varied from state to state. Until 1913, in New York State (one of the more "progressive" of the states), the ranks of probation officers were made up of "kindly ex-policemen or retired subway guards with political pull." Not until 1928 did the state issue the requirement that probation officers have a minimum of a high school diploma (Robison, 1960, pp. 285–286).

In the 1930s, the U.S. Children's Bureau (Sullenger, 1936, p. 255), recognizing the need for professional standards for probation officers, devised educational and professional standards for minimal qualification as a probation officer working with juveniles:

1 Graduation from college or from a school of social work
2 At least 1 year of experience in casework under supervision
3 A salary comparable to those paid to workers in other fields of social service

The bureau also suggested policies for the handling of juveniles:

1 A child should only be required to report to the probation officer at regular intervals if it seemed clearly to be in the best interest of the juvenile. In any case, such reporting should never be regarded as a substitute for more constructive methods of casework.
2 Reconstructive work with the family should be carried out whenever necessary, either by the probation officer or in cooperation with other social agencies.

As with any other type of national guideline that is not enforceable, these standards and policies were adhered to in some jurisdictions and not in others, depending upon state and local civil service requirements.

In New York State between 1936 and 1948, children's court probation was not part of a civil service program. During those years, because there were no civil service job classifications for these workers, there was no job security, and salary increments were infrequent and inadequate. This resulted in a high turnover rate, with the most qualified workers leaving the system to seek jobs with more security elsewhere, and unqualified or partially qualified workers remaining in their jobs. Not until 1948 did New York State make requirements in line with the standards the U.S. Children's Bureau had set forth more than a decade earlier: a degree from an accredited 4-year college plus 300 credits in social casework or allied courses, in addition to a minimum of 1 year of full-time paid experience in a child welfare or family service agency (Kahn, 1953, pp. 196–197).

Even as New York State was establishing more stringent requirements for becoming a juvenile probation officer, many counties still had no form of probation whatsoever. Teeters and Reinemann (1950) reported on a 1947 study conducted by the National Probation and Parole Association, which revealed that out of a total of 3,071 counties, 1,610 did not have probation services for juveniles. The reasons offered by Teeters and Reinemann (p. 393) were uninformed public, "penny-pinching" fiscal administrators, and judges who lacked social vision.

## ■ Juvenile Court Policies: A Summary

When it was established in Cook County, Illinois, in 1899, the first juvenile court was viewed by the vast majority of social reformers as a milestone in the developmental process of American justice. The purpose and function of the court was to have been rehabilitation rather than punishment.

During the first quarter of the 20th century, the juvenile court movement was warmly and enthusiastically hailed by both the general public and public officials as a panacea for the misbehavior, troubles, and social ills of children and youth. Whitlatch (1987, p. 2), in the 50th anniversary issue of the *Juvenile and Family Court Journal*, summarized the high ideals and overly optimistic promise of the juvenile court legislation:

> It was naively believed that the legislation creating the juvenile court would, of itself, quickly reduce delinquency to an irreducible minimum. . . . Thus, while there was a positive dearth of knowledge, facilities and personnel, there was an over-supply of enthusiasm. The courts were expected to work miracles by judicial pronouncement and without necessary facilities and personnel, repair the damage that resulted from long continued neglect by the home, school and community. Hence, courts were often subject to unjust criticism because they were unable to accomplish the impossible.

It was fervently hoped that through provision of rehabilitation services, the juvenile court system would be successful in stemming the growing tide of juvenile delinquency. However, there have been many problems with this system. From the beginning, juvenile courts have been denied the necessary funds, staff, auxiliary services, and facilities to fulfill their rehabilitative ideal (President's Commission, 1967, p. 23). By the late 1960s and early 1970s, prominent criminologists and sociologists were advancing the belief that juvenile court processing may well damage youths and lead to further delinquency through labeling and the stigma attached to institutional confinement. Since then, major issues affecting juveniles' rights have been argued—issues such as the juvenile being denied due process in court proceedings and the pervasive dearth of treatment resources.

In theory, youthful offenders were supposed to receive comprehensive rehabilitation services intended to replace due process. In actuality, juveniles were sent to institutions where living conditions were as bad as—or worse than—those in adult prisons. Until recently, juveniles faced the risk of imprisonment without benefit of legal counsel and with abridged rights of due process. By the late 1960s and early 1970s, in the aftermath of the *In re Kent* (1966) and *In re Gault* (1967) decisions, many juveniles did finally receive the benefits of either a private attorney or, if the juvenile's family was indigent, a court-appointed public defender. However, because of unwieldy caseloads and the inexperience of some public defenders, juveniles still did not always receive adequate counsel.

Furthermore, the quality and scope of treatment services provided by this system has never equaled the need level of troubled youthful offenders. Only since the mid-1960s has the Supreme Court begun to address the important due process issues in juvenile justice. In the *In re Kent* (1966) and *In re Gault* (1967) decisions, the court held that children could not be denied the right to counsel and protection against self-incrimination–rights guaranteed to adults. In the *In re Winship* (1970) decision, the Supreme Court extended to juvenile court proceedings the "proof beyond a reasonable doubt" standard for conviction in adult proceedings.

We have come a long way in the past four decades, from the time when it was commonplace for juveniles to be ushered into a dimly lit, dingy, and dilapidated detention cell, with no idea about how long they would be detained. The next morning they would be brought into an old courtroom, where they were not told of their right to counsel, their right to remain silent, or their right to appeal. Although progress has been slow, we have seen major achievements, and today the juvenile courts in many jurisdictions are efficient, equitable, and humanistic. Recent developments include continued strengthening of due process safeguards, accelerated case processing and reduced delays in scheduling trial dates, and a greater reliance on alternative sentencing options such as community service and victim restitution, addiction treatments, family counseling, juvenile diversion programs, and short-term secure detention.

Juvenile court judges have the greatest clout in improving the services, alternative programs, and placement options available to juvenile offenders. In recent years, judges and their chief probation officers have advocated for and developed restitution programs in the form of monetary and community work service assignments in order to hold juveniles accountable for their offenses. Juvenile offenders in property-related crimes are the most likely candidates for these restitution programs. In addition, during the current decade the threshold of public tolerance for violent juvenile offenders has decreased considerably. The result has been harsher handling by prosecutors and judges for violent and chronic juvenile offenders. To increase violent juveniles' accountability for their offenses, the strategy used with increasing frequency is the meting out of harsher and more severe penalties.

## Discussion Questions

1   Discuss the concept of *parens patriae.*

2   Discuss the historical development of the juvenile court in the United States.

3   What was the basis for the endorsement given by Judge Edward Lindsey, and other judges, for the establishment of the juvenile court?

4   As of the 1940s, what were the major problems facing juvenile courts and probation?

5   What was the role of child guidance clinics with troubled juveniles?

6   What were the minimum educational and professional standards recommended for new juvenile probation officers by the U.S. Children's Bureau in the 1930s.

7   Which well-known voluntary organization provided volunteer services to New York City's juvenile court in the early 1950s?

8   According to a 1947 national survey, approximately how many counties had probation services for juveniles?

# Notes

1   Not until June 1938 were federal courts given the legal authority to distinguish between juve-
    niles and adults brought before them for violation of federal laws. The Federal Juvenile Delin-
    quency Act included provisions for hearing cases promptly, privately, and without a jury; de-
    tention apart from adult offenders; and greater flexibility in treatment of youths (Teeters &
    Reinemann, 1939, p. 27).
2   By the early 1940s, Connecticut and Wyoming had gone along with the trend and set up
    special courts for juveniles.
3   The age limit of juvenile court jurisdiction varies from state to state. As of 1939, the laws of
    nearly half of the states in the Federal Juvenile Delinquency Act set an age limit of 18 years
    or higher. The trend at the end of the 1930s was in the direction of raising the age limit
    rather than lowering it (Teeters & Reinemann, 1939, p. 29).
4   A 1963 study showed that a particular problem with the juvenile court system was the scar-
    city of qualified judges. Only 71% of the juvenile court judges studied had law degrees. Of
    those judges who were full-time appointees, 72% spent a quarter or less of their time on
    juvenile matters. Thus a juvenile delinquent's future sometimes rested on the decision of a
    judge who may not have had an appropriate legal background or devoted much time to the
    case (McCune & Skoler, 1965).

# References

Abbott, G., Abbott, E., & Breckinridge, S. P. (1938). *The child and the state*. Chicago: Univer-
    sity of Chicago Press.

Addams, J. (1935). *My friend, Julia Lathrop*. New York: Macmillan.

Alexander, P. W. (1944). Speaking as one judge to another. In *National Probation Association
    Yearbook* (pp. 38–39). New York: National Probation Association.

Augustus, J. (1939). *First probation officer*. New York: National Probation Association. (Origi-
    nal work published as *A Report of the Labors of John Augustus*, 1852).

Carr, L. J. (1949). Most courts have to be substandard! *Federal Probation, 13*, 29–30.

Dunham, H. W. (1958). The juvenile court: Contradictory orientations in processing offend-
    ers. *Law and Contemporary Problems, 23*, 371–375.

Flexner, B., & Baldwin, R. (1912). *Juvenile courts and probation*. New York: Century.

Homer, P. (1941). *National Probation Association Yearbook*.

Howe, F. (1913). *The city: The hope of democracy*. New York: Scribner's.

Illinois Board of State Commissioners of Public Charities. (1898). *Fifteenth Biennial Report*
    (p. 63). Springfield, IL: Author.

*In re Gault*, 387 U.S. 1, 12–15 (1967).

*In re Kent*, 383 U.S. 541 (1966).

*In re Winship*, 397 U.S. 358 (1970).

Kahn, A. J. (1953). *A court for children: A study of the New York City children's court*. New York:
    Columbia University Press.

Kamm, E. R., Hunt, D. D., & Fleming, J. A. (1968). *Juvenile law and procedure in California*. Bev-
    erly Hills, CA: Glencoe.

Lemert, E. M. (1971). *Instead of court: Diversion in juvenile justice*. Rockville, MD: National Insti-
    tute of Mental Health, Center for Studies of Crime and Delinquency.

Levine, M. & Levine, A. (1970). The more things change: A case history of child guidance
    clinics. *Journal of Social Issues, 26*, 19–34.

Lindner, C., & Savarese, M. R. (1984). The evolution of probation. *Federal Probation, 48*(2), 3–10.

Lindsey, E. L. (1914). The juvenile court from the lawyer's standpoint. *Annals of the American Academy of Political and Social Sciences, 52,* 145–147.

Lou, H. H. (1927). *Juvenile courts in the United States.* Chapel Hill: University of North Carolina Press.

McCune, S., & Skoler, D. S. (1965). Juvenile court judges in the United States: Part 1. *Crime and Delinquency, 11,* 121–131.

Mennel, R. M. (1973). *Thorns and thistles: Juvenile delinquents in the United States, 1825–1940.* Hanover, NH: University Press of New England.

National Council on Crime and Delinquency. (1967). Data summary from corrections in the United States. In President's Commission on Law Enforcement and the Administration of Justice, *Task Force Report: Corrections* (pp. 134–135). Washington, DC: U.S. Government Printing Office.

Parmelee, M. (1918). *Criminology.* New York: Macmillan.

President's Commission on Law Enforcement and Administration of Justice. (1967). *Task Force Report: Corrections.* Washington, DC: U.S. Government Printing Office.

Roberts, A. R., & Kurtz, L. F. (1987). Historical perspectives on the care and treatment of the mentally ill. *Journal of Sociology and Social Welfare, 4,* 75–94.

Robison, S. M. (1960). *Juvenile delinquency: Its nature and control.* New York: Holt, Rinehart & Winston.

Rothman, D. (1980). *Conscience and convenience: The asylum and its alternatives in progressive America.* Boston: Little, Brown.

Schlossman, S. L. (1977). *Love and the American delinquent: The theory and practice of "progressive" juvenile justice, 1825–1920.* Chicago: University of Chicago Press.

Schlossman, S. L. (1983). Juvenile justice: History and philosophy. In S. H. Kadish (Ed.), *Encyclopedia of crime and justice.* New York: Free Press.

Shireman, C. H. (1971). Crime and delinquency: Probation and parole. In *Encyclopedia of social work* (Vol. 1, pp. 191–196). New York: National Association of Social Workers.

Stevenson, G. S. (1934). *Child guidance clinics.* New York: Commonwealth Fund.

Sullenger, T. E. (1936). *Social determinants in juvenile delinquency.* New York: Wiley.

Teeters, N. K., & Reinemann, J. O. (1950). *The challenge of delinquency.* New York: Prentice-Hall.

U.S. Children's Bureau. (1922). *Proceedings of the conference on juvenile court standards* (Publication No. 97). Washington, DC: U.S. Government Printing Office.

Whitlatch, W. (1987). A brief history of the national council. *Juvenile and Family Court Journal, 38*(2), 1–14.

# 8 The Emergence and Proliferation of Juvenile Diversion Programs

Albert R. Roberts

Juvenile diversion projects emerged as a dominant movement from the late 1960s through the 1970s in cities and towns across the United States. Alternatives included police-based diversion programs, probation diversion, voluntary youth service bureau programs, and community outreach counseling services. The major objective of many of the early diversion programs was to provide a structured, community-based alternative to incarceration so that petty offenders and status offenders would not be exposed to the corrupting influences of the more hardened multiple offenders who populate juvenile institutions.

This chapter begins by defining the term *diversion* and discussing the theory, philosophy, and practicalities on which diversion programs were based. It also discusses the recommendations made by the President's Commission on Law Enforcement and Administration of Justice in 1967 and the influence of several agencies (Law Enforcement Assistance Administration, Office of Youth Development and Delinquency Prevention, and National Advisory Commission on Criminal Justice Standards and Goals) on the establishment of youth service bureaus and other diversion programs. The chapter concludes with a review of the diversion program evaluations that have been conducted.

## ■ Defining Juvenile Diversion

*Juvenile diversion* is defined as any process that is used by components of the criminal justice system (police, prosecution, courts, corrections) whereby youths avoid formal juvenile court processing and adjudication. Diversion refers to "the channeling of cases to noncourt institutions, in instances where these cases would ordinarily have received an adjudicatory (or fact-finding) hearing by a court" (Nejelski, 1976, p. 396).

In a sense, diversion is as old as the juvenile court itself: The major goal of the first juvenile courts, established at the turn of the century, was to provide an alternative to, and thereby divert youths from, the criminal court. The juvenile court was created to avoid the unfair and inhumane treatment to which juveniles were subjected when processed through the criminal court and incarcerated with adult felons.

In the 1930s, crime prevention bureaus were established in several of the larger cities. For example, the Crime Prevention Bureau of the New York City Police Department flourished between 1930 (when it began) and 1934 under the leadership of its first two directors, social workers Virginia Murray and Henrietta Addison. The bureau received police referrals of "wayward minors" and juveniles accused of committing a crime but not arrested. Most of these youths received some sort of social work intervention, usually in the form of diagnosis, counseling, or job placement. For treatment, the bureau generally referred the juveniles to family and children's agencies, hospitals, clinics, and the Bureau of Child Guidance of the Board of Education (Glueck & Glueck, 1936; New York City Police Department, 1932b, pp. 220–222).

Diversion has also existed for a long time in the form of informal station adjustments and discretionary handling by police officers when they have given youths a warning and sent them back home. However, the development of formal programs for the purpose of diverting juveniles from adjudication in the juvenile justice system did not occur until the late 1960s.

## ■ The Labeling Perspective

A basic theme of the labeling perspective is that juveniles and adults who commit minor offenses become habitual offenders because they are singled out from their peers and differentially treated. In the making of a deviant or criminal, Tannenbaum (1938) contends, this official treatment plays a greater role than any other experience.

The labeling approach is not so much concerned with why juveniles commit delinquent acts as with what happens to such individuals when they are officially processed and labeled by the juvenile court. Labeling focuses on societal reactions, the individual's response to those reactions, consequences of the labeling for an individual, and why and how certain behaviors come to be defined as deviant. Societal reactions to what Lemert (1967) calls primary deviance (acts of deviance caused by a combination of etiological factors) often lead to secondary deviance. Secondary deviance involves the development of deviant self-concepts, deviant careers, and deviant acts as a result of the sanctions applied to, and stigmatization of, the individual through agents of social control.

According to the labeling perspective, there is no significant difference between the social-psychological characteristics of those youths labeled delinquent and those who engage in delinquency offenses but never get caught. Sociologists and social psychologists who have advanced the labeling explanation for delinquency have tended to focus on the negative consequences of being labeled.

Lemert (1967) points out that sociologists familiar with the workings and problems of the juvenile court concur that one major and unintended consequence of wardship or adjudication to a correctional institution is stigma. Stigma results in the juvenile being handicapped by the corrupting influences of the institution: "heightened police surveillance, neighborhood isolation, lowered receptivity and tolerance by school officials, and rejections of youth by prospective employers" (p. 92). Thus, juvenile court wards often become stigmatized and labeled by probation officers, judges, and police as the type of youth "destined for failure" (p. 93).

In addition, data indicate that the more a youth is engulfed in the juvenile justice system, the greater the chances of future arrests for serious delinquency acts (President's Commission on Law Enforcement and Administration of Justice, 1967). As aptly pointed out by Empey (1982, p. 410), diversion programs were based on the underlying belief that the "evils of children have been overly dramatized." Therefore, to avoid the inevitable effect of labeling and stigma, juveniles with the potential of being processed through the justice system "should be diverted away from the juvenile justice system into other less harmful agencies—youth service bureaus, welfare agencies, or special schools."

## ■ Federal Initiatives

By the mid-1960s, the number of crimes committed by juveniles had escalated far beyond the increased number of youths in the 10 to 18 age group, and the surge in juvenile crime was obvious to correctional administrators, judicial officials, and criminologists. In 1966, more than 1 million arrests were made of persons under the age of 18. Blumstein (1967) estimated that 27% of all male juveniles could expect to be arrested before they reached their 18th birthday. Approximately half of all juveniles arrested were referred to the juvenile court.

With increased evidence of the criminal justice system's ineffectiveness in rehabilitating juvenile offenders during the 1950s and 1960s, President Johnson, in July 1965, established the Commission on Law Enforcement and Administration of Justice. Its mission was to conduct a comprehensive analysis of crime in America and the ways in which each component of the criminal justice system was handling the crime problem. The commission's objective was to develop recommendations and a national strategy for creating "a safer and more just society."

In the area of crimes committed by juveniles, the President's Commission (1967, p. 81) recommended that the juvenile justice system and community agencies jointly develop alternative methods of treating juveniles: "In place of the formal system, dispositional alternatives to adjudication must be developed for dealing with juveniles, including agencies to provide and coordinate services and procedures to achieve necessary control without unnecessary stigma." The commission recommended development of a nationwide program that would divert thousands of youths each year from formal processing through the juvenile courts.

Aware that most existing community social service and youth-serving agencies would be unable to provide these large numbers of youths with the needed services, the commission proposed the establishment of a new type of agency—the youth service bureau—as an alternative to juvenile court. Through federal grants (primarily from the Law Enforcement Assistance Administration [LEAA] and the Office of Youth Development and Delinquency Prevention) and smaller matching grants from state and county governmental agencies, hundreds of youth service bureaus were developed nationwide. (See chapter 6 for an extensive review of the development of youth service bureaus.) LEAA funding also resulted in the development of alternative schools, job development and training programs, police social work programs, and family counseling programs for youths referred by the police, schools, and court intake personnel.

## ■ Program Expansion in the 1970s

During the 1970s, diversion programs continued to receive significant support from the federal government. In 1973, LEAA's National Advisory Commission on Criminal Justice Standards and Goals (1973b) was sufficiently convinced of the value of diversion programs that it recommended the following:

> Many of the problems considered as delinquency or predelinquency should be deferred to the family, educational or welfare programs, and diverted away from the juvenile court into other community agencies such as youth service bureaus. (p. 58)

> Each State should enact necessary legislation to fund partially and to encourage local establishment of youth service bureaus as a voluntary diversion resource by agencies of the juvenile justice system. (p. 83)

To meet "the goal of minimizing the involvement of adolescence in the juvenile justice system," the National Advisory Commission (1973b, pp. 23–25) proposed that the 1973 rate of both delinquency and status offender cases processed by the juvenile courts be cut in half by 1983. Furthermore, the commission indicated that since processing a youth through the court and confining him in a training school cost approximately $6,000 per year, diversion programs, being nonresidential, would probably also be much less costly than official processing.

The U.S. Juvenile Justice and Delinquency Prevention Act of 1974 provided another major boost to the development of social services for diverted youths, particularly status offenders (such as runaways). With the passage of Title III of the act, know as the Runaway Youth Act, millions of dollars in federal funds were allocated for the establishment of runaway shelters, youth telephone hotline services, and crisis counseling services (P.L. 93-415, 1974).

As a direct result of the passage of the Runaway Youth Act, federal funds were used to develop runaway programs across the country. They provide emergency services such as food, shelter, and counseling services in a safe and wholesome environment that is separate from the law enforcement and juvenile justice systems. Sixty-six grants were awarded in 1975 during the first funding cycle to support programs in 32 states, Puerto Rico, Guam, and the District of Columbia (Roberts, 1987, pp. 8–9).

In 1976, the Office of Juvenile Justice and Delinquency Prevention

(OJJDP) made $10 million available for the funding and development of 11 diversion programs in different parts of the United States and Puerto Rico (Dunford, Osgood, & Weichselbaum, 1982).

# ■ Four Early Programs

Four of the early diversion programs shared the common goals of (a) intervening with first offenders before court processing and commitment to an institution and (b) treating youths in a community-based program. However, the underlying philosophy, methods, and services provided differ.

## Project Crossroads

This diversion program (also known in those days as a pretrial intervention program) was located in Washington, D.C. It was highly structured and provided multiple services and opportunities for youthful offenders. Funded by the U.S. Department of Labor, the project was guided by the philosophy that, given adequate counseling, academic skills, and vocational training, youthful offenders can acquire a sense of self-pride and self-worth that will enable them to become productive and responsible members of society. It consisted of a 90-day, community-based program of manpower services, including counseling, remedial education, job training, and employment.

Project Crossroads's main objective was to provide vocational services to youthful first offenders between the ages of 16 and 26. The eligibility criteria were (a) agreeing to participate in the project, (b) having no prior convictions, (c) having been charged with a nonviolent crime, and (d) being "presently unemployed, underemployed, or in jeopardy of losing a current job" because of the arrest, only marginally enrolled in school, or a dropout (Trotter, 1970, p. 5).

The average age of the participants was 18. The youths and their families often needed various social services but lacked the knowledge of how to obtain them. Project Crossroads established liaisons with several social service organizations, which provided the needed services. If the first attempt at job placement was not successful, repeated efforts were made until a suitable placement was found. Participants were informed that they would be terminated from the project if they neglected to attend job interviews or if they demonstrated a general lack of cooperation.

## The St. Louis Diversion Program

The primary objective of this program (begun in 1971) was to provide home detention for juveniles who would otherwise have been confined to the overcrowded St. Louis Detention Center. A secondary objective was to increase the effectiveness of probationary services by assigning smaller caseloads to probation officers (Keve & Zamtek, 1972).

The staff person responsible for providing intensive supervision to the juveniles was a paraprofessional worker called a community youth leader (CYL). Each CYL had daily field contact with a caseload of five detainees who were given home detention during the period between their arrest and a court hearing. The CYL was responsible for working with the youth, his family, the school, and other involved organizations to help the youth "stay out of trouble." This included serving as a Big Brother by supervising and participating in a variety of sports activities designed to provide alternatives to delinquent activities.

A 1972 evaluation of the home detention program (Keve & Zamtek, 1972) showed that of the first 308 juveniles enrolled in the St. Louis program, only 13 (5%) committed a new offense, and none of those offenses was of an assaultive nature. An additional 53 youths (21%) were returned to detention because they (and often their parents) were uncooperative. Cost-effectiveness data revealed a substantial savings from this program. The estimated average daily cost for home detention was $4.85, compared with a daily cost of $17.54 for secure detention (J. Hubbard, personal communication, 1974).

## Baltimore's Diversion Project

In 1971, a pretrial diversion project, financed by the U.S. Department of Labor, was initiated in Baltimore, Maryland. Eligibility was limited to multiple offenders between the ages of 15 and 17 who were not accused of capital offenses such as murder or rape. Because the program's emphasis was on job counseling and placement, program staff were particularly interested in working with juveniles who were school dropouts and unemployed.

The project operated under the belief that the people best equipped to steer youths straight were ex-inmates, who had been through the criminal justice process and knew why it must be avoided. Thus, in addition to providing employment and counseling services to selected youths at the pretrial stage, Baltimore's project also provided employment for ex-prison inmates. Director Eddie Harrison, himself an ex-inmate, described his views on the aim of counseling: "If a boy is sent off to a state training school the only thing he learns is how to become a better crook. He comes out and he's too old to return to school and statistics show that three out of four will commit another crime. Only this time he becomes a convicted felon" (Eddie Harrison, personal communication, March 1975).

## The Sacramento County 601 Diversion Project

This experimental diversion project, based in Sacramento, California, began in October 1970. The project's objective was to show that a diversion program that focused on providing family crisis intervention and counseling early in the handling of a case would result in lower costs and less recidivism. Counseling services were provided by six deputy probation officers who had received special training in crisis intervention techniques and family counseling. In the first 9 months of operation, the program treated 803 youths and their families (Baron, Feeney, & Thornton, 1973).

Many of the youths selected for the project were habitual runaways, beyond the control of their parents, or truant from school. They had all been designated as offenders under Section 601 of California's Welfare and Institution Code. In 1972, however, the project was expanded to include juveniles who had committed juvenile delinquency offenses (Section 602, offense category).

Juveniles were referred to the project by police, family members, or schools. Within 1 to 2 hours after the referral to the probation intake unit, the probation counselor arranged a family meeting. During this first session, the counselor focused on helping the family recognize that the problem needed to be worked on by the whole family. If the relationship between the youth and parents was too volatile for the young person to return home, an alternative placement was arranged with a volunteer family, a relative, or temporary foster care. The sessions were usually from 1 to 2½ hours in length. The maximum number of sessions was five per family.

Seven months after the initial handling by the diversion project, follow-up data was collected: 35% of the project group had been rearrested, compared to 45.5% of the control group (Baron et al., 1973). More significant was the difference in serious repeat offenses involving criminal conduct (Section 602). In this category, the recidivism rate for the diverted group was 15.3%, compared with 23.4% for the control group. The evidence indicated that diversion to a family crisis counseling project can be effective in reducing recidivism, as well as costs. Since the project made use of existing probation staff, additional personnel resources were not needed.

## ■ Case Example

It is March 1974, and George, age 16, is arrested for stealing a car. The juvenile court judge refers him to a local youth diversion program. During the intake interview, the social worker who coordinates the program learns that George has a troubled home life. His mother is presently institutionalized at a hospital for the mentally ill, and his father travels during the week and is rarely home. George is the youngest of three children, and both older siblings live out of town.

The initial action is to remove George from the neglectful home environment, where he receives no adult love or guidance. Immediate shelter is needed, and the social worker refers George to an emergency youth shelter.

She now has a few weeks to find George a stable living arrangement, probably in a local group home for adolescent boys. The social worker also arranges for George to be given achievement tests in math and English. Although the youth was getting Ds and Fs in public school, achievement test results show that his abilities are good enough for him to obtain a high school equivalency diploma.

George tells the social worker that he has been angry at the boys in his neighborhood because they repeatedly taunt him, saying his mother is "crazy" and "off her rocker" because she is in a mental hospital. He feels embarrassed and ashamed. The social worker provides short-term crisis counseling to help the boy cope with his feelings. She also helps him understand that the neighborhood boys' cruelty results from immaturity and callousness and that if a person had a broken ankle he would receive appropriate medical treatment; similarly, someone with heavy emotional problems has to go to a hospital to get well.

George expresses interest in being trained to work in the automobile repair field. Since the diversion project has access to a vocational evaluation program, George is able to participate in 3 weeks of evaluation to determine his vocational potential. During the vocational evaluation, the youth exhibits good ability for small engine repair as well as for carpentry and bench assembly. However, because of his expressed interest in car repair, the vocational evaluator recommends that George enter a 6-month automobile repair program offered by the state rehabilitation center, where he can prepare for the high school equivalency exam in addition to receiving vocational training.

The Sacramento diversion project was replicated in a number of other counties, including 11 in California (Palmer, Bohnstedt, & Lewis, 1978). For status offenders as well as juveniles with a history of criminal offenses, these programs provided family counseling, group counseling, behavioral contracting, and parent education. Follow-up studies indicated that the replicated programs also reduced recidivism, although to a lesser extent than the original project.

## ■ Effectiveness of Diversion Programs

The main objectives of juvenile diversion were to (a) avoid labeling, (b) reduce unnecessary detention and incarceration, (c) reduce repeat offenses, (d) provide counseling and other services, and (e) lower justice system costs (Palmer & Lewis, 1980). However, it was unrealistic to expect one type of intervention to be a panacea and meet all five objectives for all troubled juveniles.

Viewed on a continuum, there are two groups of youths (those at the end points) for whom juvenile diversion did not seem to be appropriate. At one end were juveniles who committed an occasional childish prank or a deviant act, but as part of maturational development would be likely to outgrow their deviance without any involvement in a diversion program. These youths, were it not for the existence of a diversion program, would probably be released with no further action or involvement with the justice system. At the opposite end of the continuum were juveniles who committed violent offenses such as rape or aggravated assault and who required intensive treatment in a secure and highly structured facility. Although almost all diversion programs recognized that the violent juvenile offender was not suited for diversion, a controversy arose over the practice of referring to such programs youths who committed status or minor offenses. Over the years many evaluations of diversion programs have been conducted. Evidence shows that some programs succeeded in their aims while others fell far short of stated objectives.

Palmer and Lewis (1980), in reporting on the evaluation of juvenile diversion programs for the California Youth Authority, concluded that no single approach is appropriate for all youths. They recommended that several types of diversion alternatives be available so that juveniles could be matched to the alternative that most closely met their needs. In general, Palmer and Lewis found that individual counseling was beneficial to the juveniles and that family counseling was not helpful. They did note, however, that one program that relied on a family treatment approach was successful.

Bohnstedt (1978), discussing the same study on which Palmer and Lewis reported, elaborated on the one successful family counseling program—the Stockton project—which utilized the conjoint family therapy model originated by Virginia Satir. The follow-up study showed that of the 11 projects studied, the Stockton program had the largest difference in recidivism rates between the treatment group (26%) and the comparison group (61%).

Pogrebin, Poole, and Regoli (1984), in reporting on the Adams County Juvenile Diversion Project in Colorado (1977–1979), found a slightly lower rate of recidivism in the experimental project group (6%) than the recidivism rate of 11.5% for the control group. In this study of 560 juveniles, recidivism measures were calculated each month for an 18-month period. The target population was first- or second-time juvenile offenders referred by the intake counselor at the district attorney's office. Violent juveniles were not accepted for the project.

Collingwood and Wilson (1976) reviewed 107 community juvenile diversion projects throughout the United States. The project auspice varied from police diversion to probation diversion to youth service bureau. The focus of the programs varied as well, with different types of services provided. They included individual counseling, recreational programs, and parenting education. The results showed wide variance in recidivism among projects. Most of the studies, however, were based on subjective reports and lacked an experimental design based on true randomization.

Williams (1984) reported on the first offender program of the Dallas Police Department's youth section. This diversion project, utilizing a behavioral contracting program, focused on teaching youths interpersonal and decision-making skills and teaching their parents effective parenting, discipline, and home management skills. Williams found a significantly lower recidivism rate among the approximately 20,000 youths who completed the program (20.7%) than among the youths in the comparison group (64%).

Finally, Dunford, Osgood, and Weichselbaum (1982) conducted a national evaluation of 11 federally funded diversion programs located throughout the United States. Four of the 11 projects were selected for an in-depth experimental analysis, primarily because those sites had formal agreements with their local juvenile justice agencies to (a) randomly select and assign youths to treatment and control groups and (b) ensure that an adequate number of juvenile cases were included in the sample pool for random assignment. The researchers concluded that three of the four projects studied had "reduced the penetration of youth through the justice system." However, it was also found that diversion programs were "no more successful in . . . improving social adjustment, or reducing delinquent behavior than normal justice processing or outright release" (p. 16).

It is important to note that all four of the diversion programs emphasized brokering and referral to community agencies. In addition, some of the programs also provided 1 month of case advocacy or recreation-oriented services. Even the one project that frequently provided individual or family counseling served as a brokering agency, referring youths to appropriate community counseling or recreation agencies and monitoring service delivery by the community agencies. Therefore, while the study findings may support the need to abandon diversion programs with a brokering or recreational role as their primary focus, these findings should not be generalized to all diversion programs. The successful programs already mentioned provide direct services, including intensive family counseling, parenting education, and behavioral contracting, which differentiate them from the projects studied by Dunford, Osgood, and Weichselbaum (1982).

## Summary

The growth of diversion programs in the decade between 1967 and 1977 underscores the fact that this was more than an experiment. These programs became a viable alternative to official processing in the reform-oriented states in this country. The effectiveness of diversion, as measured by program evaluations and follow-up studies, varied widely from one program to the next. Although criminal justice officials may continue to recognize the fact that diversion programs were never fully operationalized as intended—as a total alternative for avoiding contact with the juvenile justice system—that no longer is the overriding concern. The issue is whether diversion will survive the federal and state budget cuts. Several states (e.g., California and Colorado) already have passed laws authorizing and appropriating funds for juvenile diversion programs, while other states failed to support the continuation of diversion programs once the federal funding ended.

## Discussion Question

1  Define the term *juvenile diversion*.

2  Why were the juvenile diversion programs developed?

3  What is the basic theme underlying the labeling perspective?

4  According to Lemert, what is one of the major and unintended consequences of wardship or adjudication to a correctional institution?

5  Summarize the major diversion recommendations made in 1967 by President Johnson's Commission on Law Enforcement and the Administration of Justice.

6  Discuss the objectives and content of one of the four diversion programs described in this chapter.

7  Researchers Palmer and Lewis reported on the evaluation of juvenile diversion programs for the California Youth Authority. What was their major conclusion regarding a differentiated approach to diversion?

## References

Baron, R., Feeney, F., & Thornton, W. (1973). Preventing delinquency through diversion: The Sacramento County 601 diversion project. *Federal Probation, 37*, 13–18.

Blumstein, A. (1967). Systems analysis and the criminal justice system. *Annals of the American Academy of Political and Social Sciences.*

Bohnstedt, M. (1978). Answers to three questions about juvenile diversion. *Journal of Research in Crime and Delinquency, 15*(1), 109–123.

Collingwood, T. R., & Wilson, R. D. (1976). *National survey of diversion projects.* Dallas, TX: Dallas Police Department.

Dunford, F. W., Osgood, D. W., & Weichselbaum, H. F. (1982). *National evaluation of diversion projects.* Washington, DC: U.S. Department of Justice, Office of Juvenile Justice and Delinquency Prevention.

Empey, L. T. (1982). *American delinquency: Its meaning and construction.* Chicago: Dorsey.

Glueck, S., & Glueck, E. (1936). *Preventing crime: A symposium.* New York: McGraw-Hill.

Keve, P. W., & Zamtek, C. S. (1972). *Final report and evaluation of the home detention program, St. Louis, Missouri.* McLean, VA: Research Analysis.

Lemert, E. M. (1967). The juvenile court: Quest and realities in the President's Commission on Law Enforcement and Administration of Justice. In *Task force report: Juvenile delinquency and youth crime* (pp. 91–106). Washington, DC: U.S. Government Printing Office.

National Advisory Commission on Criminal Justice Standards and Goals. (1973b). *Task force on community crime prevention.* Washington, DC: U.S. Government Printing Office.

Nejelski, P. (1976). Diversion: The promise and the danger. *Crime and Delinquency, 22*(4), 393–410.

New York City Police Department. (1932b). *Manual of procedure of the police department.* New York: New York City Police Department.

Palmer, T., Bohnstedt, M., & Lewis, R. (1978). *The evaluation of juvenile diversion projects: Final report.* Sacramento: California Youth Authority, Division of Research.

Palmer, T. B., & Lewis, R. V. (1980, July). A differential approach to juvenile diversion. *Journal of Research in Crime and Delinquency*, pp. 209–227.

President's Commission on Law Enforcement and Administration of Justice. (1967). *Task force report: Juvenile delinquency and youth crime*. Washington, DC: U.S. Government Printing Office.

Roberts, A. R. (1987). *Runaways and nonrunaways*. Chicago: Dorsey.

Tannenbaum, F. (1938). *Crime and the community*. New York: Columbia University Press.

Trotter, J. A., Jr. (1970). *Final report. Phase I, Project Crossroads: January 15, 1968–May 15, 1969*. Washington, DC: National Committee for Children and Youth.

Williams, L. (1984). A police diversion alternative for juvenile offenders. *Police Chief, 51*(2), 54–57.

# III

# Juvenile Justice Processing

# 9  Police Work With Juveniles

## Discretion, Model Programs, and

## School Police Resource Officers

William J. Flynn and Brian McDonough

CAROLE ROBERTS

**K**nowing how and when to invoke the law is a complicated and delicate task faced by the 21st-century police officer. When considered in the context of juvenile offenders, the situation becomes more difficult to navigate because of the philosophical and procedural differences between the adult and juvenile justice systems. Successful police professionals exercise discretion in a manner that satisfies the needs and goals of both systems and provides the community at large with security and a positive feeling for the police. Officers must also take steps to ensure that their actions, or inactions, follow the guidelines of their department regarding professional police behavior and conduct.

This chapter defines *discretion* in the context of street-level encounters between the police and juveniles and explains some variables influencing a police officer's decision to take one particular action in favor of another. Also discussed is antigang community policing that assists police in their decision making, positively influences their youth contacts, enhances their use of juvenile justice resources, and reduces youth violence.

Model crime prevention programs discussed include the Birmingham, Alabama, School Resource Officer Program; the New Brunswick, New Jersey, Police Juvenile Aid Bureau Program; the antigang initiative G.R.E.A.T. Program; and the Boston Police Department's Operation Ceasefire program. Boston's Operation Ceasefire is a fully coordinated program with collaboration between criminal justice practitioners (police, prosecutor, probation) and community leaders (religious leaders, school and health officers) teamed together to reduce juvenile gang violence and provide social opportunities for those who otherwise seem to be following a path to delinquency.

Each of the programs is discussed at length to demonstrate that by transforming a few tenets of community policing as practiced in a controlled environment like the Birmingham, Alabama, school system or in neighborhood "gang turf" areas like Boston, crime can be reduced, resources to improve police decision making can be attained, and police–youth community relations can be improved. Criminal justice research evaluation results are provided and discussed to substantiate that programs are effective and practical for police agencies to implement.

## ■ Discretion

The most critical element of police authority and power is the ability to exercise discretion. The police possess absolute control of individuals who come in contact with them during the performance of their duties. Many decisions routinely made by street-level police officers have the potential to foster positive relationships between the police and the communities they serve or to exacerbate the misunderstanding and ill will some police agencies and neighborhoods already share.

*Webster's* defines *discretion* as follows: "ability to make responsible decisions; individual choice or judgment; power of free decision or latitude of choice within certain legal bounds." An operational definition for *police discretion* is an official action taken by a criminal justice official based on the individual's judgment about the best course of action. This decision-making process involves value judgments, situational factors, personality characteristics (of officers and offenders), available resources, political climate, geography, and departmental policy. It is generally accepted that situational factors have the most profound effect on the officer's decision-making process. Some of the situational factors that are believed to influence an officer's decision to arrest are explained next (Cole & Smith, 1998).

## Seriousness of the Crime

Police understand that they have limited options when an individual stands accused of a violent offense. In fact, the likelihood of arrest seems to be directly proportional to the seriousness of the crime.

## Strength of the Evidence

Police officers often are conditioned to assess the likelihood of a successful prosecution as soon as an arrest becomes an option. Most officers rapidly learn that shabby evidence is likely to result in a considerably uncomfortable cross-examination in court and, more important, an acquittal. The effect of weak evidence can be minimized, however, if the officer decides to take advantage of the different options available.

## Preference of the Victim

Most police officers will take formal action against a juvenile offender when a complaining witness is present and willing to fully cooperate with the police. However, when a victim shows any sign of hesitation about bringing formal charges, the officer is likely to seize the opportunity to relate the negative, time-consuming aspects of getting involved in a legal proceeding and suggest that perhaps the victim could better handle this unofficially. A hesitant complainant at the scene is likely to be a "no-show" complainant when the case is scheduled for court. In this scenario, the police officer has wasted an incredible amount of time completing reports, and the juvenile goes unpunished. More important, the juvenile perceives the process as a sham and may boast to his associates that he "got over" on the system.

## Relationship Between Victim and Suspect

If a juvenile is apprehended in a stolen vehicle that belongs to his next-door neighbor, it is very likely the situation will be handled without an arrest. This assumes, of course, that the neighbors are on good terms and it is an isolated incident. Conversely, an "outsider" who has crossed into unfamiliar territory to steal a car and gets caught will feel the full weight of the law for the misdeed. Simply put, arrests are more likely when the victim and offender are strangers.

## Demeanor of the Suspect

The suspect's attitude has a profound influence on an officer's decision to arrest or not arrest. Most juveniles feel a need to save face in the presence of their friends, and this more often than not results in their arrest. When police encounter juveniles in groups engaged in unacceptable behavior, very often one member of the group emerges as uncooperative and openly defiant. Words are exchanged, and the officer may issue an ultimatum to the group to disperse or face the consequences. The defiant youth may continue to challenge the officer's authority in the hopes of gaining respect and status with those friends. Ultimately, the youth offends or pushes the officer to the limit, and the decision to arrest is made. The same juvenile would probably act differently had the encounter been one on one with the police officer. There would be no need to impress anyone, and the juvenile would act accordingly, resulting in no official action on the part of the officer.

There are other factors that affect an officer's decision-making process. The officer's mood, life and work experiences, and moral values all have an impact on the choices made during the course of any given workday. Another factor that may, at times, have an effect on what type of enforcement action might be used is geography.

The residents of one neighborhood or "section" of a large, diversely populated city may embrace different values than residents across town and therefore will have dissimilar expectations about how the police behave when responding to calls for service. A good police officer realizes this and understands that, at least with regard to nonserious offenses, it is the community that actually dictates what enforcement action, if any, a police officer should take when working in their neighborhood.

This relationship between community values and police behavior has been put into proper perspective by Kelling (1999): "policing that reflects a neighborhood's values and sense of justice and that understands residents' concerns is more likely to do justice than policing that strictly follows a rule book." The problem this creates for the police requires careful examination.

Officers are routinely charged with mediating situations involving participants not only from different neighborhoods but also with different backgrounds from different parts of the world and with cultural norms and behaviors unfamiliar to the officer. It is not unreasonable to expect that in such cases officers may revert to strict application of the law to remedy the situation and keep themselves in good favor with supervisors. As an illustration of the connection between community values and police responses, consider the following scenario:

> A group of five African American male juveniles are engaged in a game of c-low (gambling with dice) at 1:30 A.M. on a moderately traveled street in their own neighborhood. There is a group of onlookers, and a small stack of cash is visible on the sidewalk near the players. A portable radio is providing music for the group, and the conversation is loud and somewhat boisterous.
>
> Since it is summertime, residents in the area have their windows open. No one has called the police to complain, but a police officer, riding alone, turns the corner and observes the activity. One of the players notices the marked car and grabs the cash off the sidewalk, and the players mingle with the rest of the crowd. Someone has turned the music down to a reasonable level.

What type of response from the officer would be considered responsible and sensitive to the values of the community? Do you believe that the maintenance of harmonious relationships between the community and the police is the officer's priority at this point? An experienced, competent police officer would immediately recognize one very critical fact when confronted with this situation. The potential exists for things to get dangerously out of control in a very short period of time.

The officer may decide that the best course of action is to ignore the situation and hope to make it through the shift without any problems from the group. Remember, the juveniles view the officer as an uninvited guest in the neighborhood. They are likely to interpret any intervention as harassment. Still, the officer would be justified in deciding to exit the vehicle and approach the group. An officer may feel that a proactive response is what is required after concluding that it will only be a matter of time before a call is made to headquarters and a police officer is dispatched to disperse the group of loud and unruly juveniles. After all, the department has been advocating community policing and problem solving.

This officer recalls that only 4 months ago a juvenile was shot during an argument over gambling in the same neighborhood. Before the officer decides to exit the vehicle and enter a very volatile situation, there are a number of conditions to consider: How many police are available in the event the crowd turns on the officer? What is the likelihood of a favorable outcome in this case if the officer decides to make an arrest? How will supervisors and other patrol officers feel about this officer being "out of service" just prior to the busiest time in the shift, as the bars are closing and the calls for service are starting to back up? An infinite number of intervening variables could affect the officer's decision in this scenario. What about the wishes or values of the residents in the community? Should the officer assume that, since no residents have complained, the community at large is willing to accept or tolerate the juveniles' behavior? Or do the residents feel isolated and disenfranchised because they interpret the decision to ignore the incident by a responding officer as insensitive to their problems? Finally, do most officers possess the experience, knowledge, and skill necessary to walk such a fine line?

Although there are boundaries to the use of discretion by the police, it remains the most difficult aspect of law enforcement to control. The street-level patrol officer wields the greatest discretionary power of any member of the criminal justice system, and the work environment of police supports the use of discretion. Patrol officers conduct most of their business alone or with a single partner. Only on rare occasions or by request do supervisors directly observe the actions of their subordinates. In most cases, police–citizen encounters do not attract the attention of the general public. The exercise of police discretion is, therefore, invisible. It is not available for review because it is not memorialized in reports or discussed with supervisors. As long as the encounter goes smoothly, the entire event becomes unrecorded history.

The improper use of discretion brings about undesirable and often illegal results. Denial of due process, equal protection under the law, poor police–community relations, and dangerous working conditions are just a few of the negative consequences of misguided or uncontrolled discretion. Some social researchers and police administrators have advocated the development of guidelines and policies to assist well-intentioned officers with their decisions and at the same time deter those officers who tend to abuse discretion.

This movement toward policy formulation related to the use of discretion was initially met with skepticism and ridicule. Opinions, however, have changed. Administrators and street-level officers alike have admitted the utility of a well-written policy or training bulletin. Admittedly, the task is complex and daunting, considering the range of encounters and situations the police are exposed to at any given time or place. The goal of any such policy or guideline is to teach or suggest how an officer should think about a problem and then select a solution.

The City of New Haven Police Department's Order Maintenance Training Bulletin clearly conveys the philosophy and criteria for the exercise of police discretion by members of the department. The bulletin, available in the appendix of Kelling's (1999) *"Broken Windows" and Police Discretion,* is comprehensive and, more important, practical. Most police officers view formal, written operating procedures as either useless because they fail to address real-world situations or as a means to discipline an officer if the outcome of a situation is unfavorable to the citizen and a complaint is lodged.

Researchers have been examining the way police officers exercise discretion long before most police administrators have admitted to the use of such discretion. Piliavin and Briar (1964) observed all juvenile officers in one department over a 9-month period. Their findings, as described next, illustrate the profound consequences an officer's decision to arrest a juvenile have on an individual.

> The observations made in this study serve to underscore the fact that the official delinquent, as distinguished from the juvenile who simply commits a delinquent act, is the product of a social judgment, in this case a judgment made by the police. He is a delinquent because someone in authority has defined him as one, often on the basis of the public face he has presented to officials rather than the kind of offense he has committed.

This study was able to identify a pattern, by the police, of targeting certain groups of youths based on skin color and manner of dress. The authors concede that their data (notes and records) would not withstand a "qualitative assessment of reliability and validity" but when considered, along with interviews of the officers, reasonable inferences can be drawn about the practice of what we now call "racial profiling."

We have examined in some detail the subject of street-level discretion and recognize that not every officer is suited to work with juvenile offenders. Police administrators responsible for making personnel assignments must ensure that qualified individuals are placed in these sensitive positions and are able to interact with a wide range of juvenile justice resources.

The following described programs show how police are interacting with community resources (schools, neighborhood activists, religious leaders, child protection advocates, etc.) to improve decision making, reduce youth violence, and improve police–youth community relations. The programs discussed are the School Resource Officer Program, the Juvenile Aid Bureau Program, the G.R.E.A.T. Program, and the Operation Ceasefire program.

## ■ Established Youth Programs: Examples

Following are overviews of programs serving heavily populated jurisdictions. These programs typically offer more specialized services and target specific issues such as runaways, juvenile prostitution, and gangs (adapted from Muraskin, 1998).

### Port Authority of New York and New Jersey

- ☐ The Youth Services Unit is headquartered at the Port Authority bus terminal in the heart of Manhattan.
- ☐ The staff consists of a police supervisor and three officers, three social workers, and a statistician. The officers' schedule is flexible, depending on activity.

☐ The mission of the unit is to provide crisis intervention, referral services, short- and long-term counseling, and diversion.

## Nassau County, New York

The Nassau County Police Department's Youth Services Unit has two components:

☐ Juvenile Aid Bureau: responsible for traditional enforcement duties associated with delinquent behavior. Members assigned generally work on referrals from officers in other units.
☐ The Youth Projects Bureau maintains close contact with the courts and community resources for juveniles (such as the Police Activities League). This close relationship affords the officers some discretion when working with the youths.
☐ The unit's caseload in 1993 was 5,950.

## City of New Brunswick, New Jersey

The New Brunswick Police Department has a Juvenile Aid Bureau (JAB) staffed by four officers and one supervisor. Two more officers, under the command of the Operations Division, teach one of the more popular anti-gang initiative programs, the G.R.E.A.T. program. The JAB is under the command of the Criminal Investigation Division. Another officer, working in plain clothes and under the command of the Planning and Training Bureau, is designated the school resource officer.

The members of the JAB have the responsibility of investigating all juvenile-related incidents, including missing and runaway children. The unit works primarily on referrals or follow-ups from the patrol division, but they also patrol frequently and get involved in self-initiated activity.

The juvenile officers acknowledge and encourage the use of discretion by uniformed patrol officers when dealing with juveniles. One of the major flaws in the system, according to one officer assigned to the JAB, is that there is no policy or standard operating procedure (SOP) for documenting the number of occasions any one juvenile may have received a "station-house adjustment" or a "curbside warning" by a patrol officer. As a result, there is no way a juvenile officer would have access to accurate information regarding an individual's encounters with the police. Not having this information puts the juvenile officer at a disadvantage when considering formal or informal action for the offender. A simple solution would be to issue a directive to all police personnel to document all contacts with juveniles and forward them to the JAB. More paperwork, however, is not welcomed by busy police officers. It would be very difficult for supervisors to enforce this policy. If the supervisor is not on the scene when the encounter takes place, there is no reason to expect that the officer will generate a report unless the incident goes beyond a field interview or curbside warning.

The majority of information exchange between the patrol division and the JAB occurs through informal means. A phone call or a random meeting at headquarters provides an opportunity for a patrol officer to mention that a particular 14-year-old has a brand new wardrobe and has been associating with a recently paroled adult who did time for selling drugs by using juvenile runners. This relationship between the patrol and juvenile officers is funda-mentally critical to the business of policing juveniles. Relying solely on infor-mation from formal police reports does not allow the juvenile officer to keep abreast of what is going on in the community.

But what we do know from national statistics is that violent crimes by juveniles during school days peak in the afternoon between 3 P.M. and 4 P.M. The hourly peak period is also when the most middle school students are receiving drug and gang resistance training. In 2001, the New Brunswick Police Department's D.A.R.E program graduated 529 fifth-graders from the city's 11 public and parochial schools; 530 seventh- and eighth-graders completed the G.R.E.A.T. program in the same year.

The G.R.E.A.T. program is intended through education to reduce juvenile crime and victimization. The initials are an acronym for gang resistance edu-cation and training. It is a national school-based gang prevention program in which uniformed law enforcement officers teach a 9-week curriculum of skills training to middle school students. The goal of the program is to teach students how to reduce adolescent involvement in criminal behavior and gangs, resist peer pressure, and refrain from gang membership.

Students receive instruction in the development of personal skills, resil-ience skills, resistance skills, and social skills. Other subject matters discussed are crime and its impact on schools and neighborhoods, drugs and neighbor-hoods, responsibility and goal setting, cultural sensitivity, prejudice, and con-flict resolution. Theoretically, these skills will instill a sense of confidence in the youngsters and encourage them to become more self-sufficient as they inevitably face decisions with high-risk or low-risk choices (Esbensen & Os-good, 1997).

The National Institute of Justice (Esbensen & Osgood, 1997) reports that students, after completing the G.R.E.A.T. program course, recorded lower rates of delinquency, lower rates of gang affiliation, more negative attitudes about gangs, and more positive attitudes toward the police. The positive attitude may be attributed to the increased time officers spend with the students, exchanging ideas and thoughts, getting to know one another, and discussing delinquency and crime, its impact on the school and community, cultural differences, sub-stance abuse, and social responsibility.

School resource officers (SROs), while teaching the G.R.E.A.T. program or patrolling the hallways, are becoming more knowledgeable of students' be-havioral patterns, social problems and needs, neighborhood patterns and culture, the social resources available to redirect delinquent student behavior, and more important, the identity of the gang members.

The G.R.E.A.T. program traces its origin to the state of Arizona, which was dealing with a large youth gang population. In 1991 police officers from the Phoenix Police Department, Mesa Police Department, and ATF (Alcohol, Tobacco, and Firearms) joined together to attempt to prevent youth gang membership.

Although the National Institute of Justice has given the G.R.E.A.T. program a favorable rating, one research team gave the program a mixed review. Arizona State University criminal justice researchers reported that the program has only a small impact on students' attitudes and resistance skills and no impact on the percentage of students who say they or their friends are members of gangs.

Palumbo and Ferguson (1995) commented that the G.R.E.A.T. program bears the same political symbolism as D.A.R.E., with two signs of progress. After completing the course, almost 5% of the students felt more confident talking to their peers, and almost 8% of the students reported they declined gang membership if asked by a friend. The authors commented that many of the students realized that gang membership is not socially acceptable, causing fewer members to admit they are gang members.

Palumbo and Ferguson (1995) added further that the overall resistance of students was higher than before the program's implementation and that students after completing the curriculum also developed a more positive feeling toward police officers. According to Jackson (2003), the officers teaching the G.R.E.A.T. program play a pivotal role in prevention because this officer may be the only guardian who talks with the youths about gangs and gang prevention strategies before they are actually approached by a member to join a gang.

## ■ Gangs and Police Responses

Cities across the nation have recently begun to acknowledge, some reluctantly, that juvenile gangs are negatively affecting the quality of life for residents and driving up rates of violent crime. National statistics reflect that on school days 19% of all juvenile violent crimes occur in the 4 hours between 3 P.M. and 7 P.M. Analyses of the FBI National Incident-Based Reporting System (NIBRS) data highlighted the fact that juveniles are at highest risk of being the victim of a violent crime in the 4 hours following the end of the school day, roughly 2 P.M. to 6 P.M. (Office of Juvenile Justice, 1999). Many of the assaults are reportedly related to gang violence.

It is estimated that 4,881 youth gangs flourish in the nation's 79 largest cities (Muraskin & Roberts, 1999). Moore and Cook (1999) have documented that 29% of gang members in the United States in 1998 were between 15 and

17 years old and 11% were under 15 years old. In the city of Boston, it was once estimated that there were 1,300 gang members, ranging in age from 14 to 24. Boston youth gang members were reportedly engaged in a wide range of illicit activity, ranging from minor property and disorder crimes to serious and violent offenses (assaults, robberies, gun possession, and criminal homicide).

The violent crime rate for this age group skyrocketed when youth homicide increased 230% for victims, from 22 homicides in 1987, peaking in 1990 at 73, and leveling off to a yearly average of 44 homicides between 1991 and 1995 (Braga & Kennedy, 2002). To stem the rising tide of crime, the Boston Police Department (BPD) in the early 1990s initiated an intervention project, code-named Operation Ceasefire.

The police-sponsored project focused on a small number of chronically offending gang-involved youths responsible for much of Boston's youth homicide problem. To suppress the gang activity, the police patrol the streets, disrupting "open market" drug locations, imposing a zero-tolerance enforcement action toward all crime and disorder complaints, visiting neighborhood blocks where youth gangs congregate, arresting offenders with open warrants, and interviewing gang members hanging on the corner.

In the homes, police and juvenile probation officers joined together to visit probationers who had court-imposed curfews. Probation visits sent a message to probationers that they were being closely monitored for regulatory violations. Counseling was available, but contempt of court would be applied if they were not at home when the court reported they should be. Probationers were also monitored for their school attendance and drug use.

Also being regulated was the attendance of probationers and parolees who through court supervision were required to attend a community forum. At these meetings were BPD police officers and other criminal justice representatives (prosecutor, probation, community activists, religious leaders) communicating a message to known gang and nongang members that their illicit activities are being closely monitored and that violence would not be tolerated. Open discussion of current crime activity and its impact was solicited, and counseling services that were available were made known.

Also joining the team were community activists and religious leaders after a gang-related shooting ended on a ministry's doorsteps. Braga and Kennedy (2002) report that the activists and members of the religious Ten Point Coalition vocalized their support for law enforcement and offered gang and nongang members opportunities for social service information, educational and recreational resources, substance and alcohol abuse intervention programs, food, and shelter.

The concerted effort by criminal justice officials and community leaders (political and religious) resulted in a reduction of gang violence. The result of the intervention project was phenomenal. Braga and Kennedy (2002) indicate there was a 63% drop in homicides, a 32% decrease in calls about shots fired, a 25% decrease in Boston gun assaults, and a 44% decrease in youth gun assault incidents in one high-risk neighborhood.

Homicides declined from an estimated 44 per year to 26 in 1996, 15 in 1997, 18 in 1998, and 15 in 1999. According to Braga and Kennedy (2002), research suggests that the significant reduction in youth homicide associated with Operation Ceasefire was distinct when compared with youth homicide trends in most major New England and U.S. cities.

## ■ School Resource Officers

Students and teachers no longer feel safe in America's schools. As a response, many law enforcement agencies are assigning their officers to work as school resource officers (SROs) in middle and high schools. The uniformed officers assigned to the schools are expected to enforce the law, deter violators, and serve as mentors and role models.

The National Association of School Resource Officers estimates there are approximately 10,000 SROs nationwide assigned to middle schools and high schools (National Association of School Resource Officers, n.d.). The purpose of their presence is to assist school administrators in improving or maintaining school security, reducing and preventing crime, and deterring criminal gang activity. Some officers acting as liaisons make regular, informal contacts with students, staff, and parents while providing crime and drug prevention information and counseling students as needed.

In the Birmingham, Alabama, public school system, many of its SROs are fulfilling this assignment. Johnson (1999) reports in her abstract that the placement of police officers in the Birmingham city middle schools and high schools is having a positive impact on school violence and disciplinary infractions. Eighteen police officers have been working in the schools since 1995.

The placement of police officers in public schools is not a new police phenomenon (Johnson, 1999). For at least 25 years, the law enforcement agency where one of the authors works has been assigning at least eight police officers to each of the city's four public high schools. Although we do not have access to the city's school crime rate, it is fair to say the problems in existence for the last quarter of a century are as present today, the only difference being more pronounced gang activity.

The influx of gangs in and around schools has inspired a number of federally funded antigang initiatives. Financial funding for these initiatives were made possible by the Violent Crime Control and Law Enforcement Act, a Crime Act bill that authorized more than $3 billion to hire and train officers primarily for community-oriented policing. The bill also allocated more than $100 million for programs aimed specifically at reducing gang activity. It is one of the largest commitments of federal dollars (more than $15 billion) in the history of the United States (Jackson, 2003).

Since the bill's enactment in 1994, a number of enforcement initiatives and prosecutorial strategies have been initiated to stem criminal gang activity and membership. New Jersey enacted a statute that prescribes a sentence of up to 18 months for anyone who actively recruits gang members (New Jersey's Online Gang Free Community, 2003). In California, the Street Terrorism Enforcement and Prevention (STEP) Act allows for the prosecution of gang members on conspiracy charges. And Chicago passed a city ordinance prohibiting gang loitering that authorized its city police officers to arrest gang members who create a menace on public property (Jackson, 2003).

In 1999, however, in the case of *Chicago v. Morales*, the U.S. Supreme Court invalidated Chicago's Gang Congregation Ordinance, ruling that it was impermissibly vague and failed to provide adequate standards to guide police discretion (Schmalleger, 2001). Even though the intent of the ordinance was noble, police suppression activity may not affect gang membership or the conditions that create gangs (Fritsch, Caeti, & Taylor, 1999).

Suppression patrol is practiced by police to deter crowd congregations and prevent disorderly activity. However, this type of patrol has been subject to criticism because of its short-term impact on gang activity. Some strategies that demonstrate their long-term impact and are worthy of review by police managers are research evaluations of Boston's Operation Ceasefire, the G.R.E.A.T. program, and SROs. A review would help to determine which program would have merit in a particular community.

One program that received a favorable rating is the School Officer Resource Program in Birmingham, Alabama. Johnson (1999) reports that many Birmingham school students have come to accept the uniformed police presence as a basic necessity of personal security. The Birmingham students' willingness to accept the SROs as an extension of school guardianship may be attributed to the community-policing principles suggested by Lee Brown, former police commissioner of New York City and Houston: permanent assignments, beat officer empowerment, and power sharing (Brown, 1989).

Officers assigned to specific beats over a long period tend to become more familiar with the stakeholders (in this case, school officials and students) and the cultural norms of the community. Rather than simply patrolling the beat, the officers make an effort to learn about the environment, its physical drawbacks, its residents, and, most important, who is breaking the law and disrupting order.

As a practitioner, the second author worked in a large public housing complex and participated in a problem-oriented policing program. Through the community policing effort and partnership with key stakeholders of the housing authority, we were credited with improving police–community relations and reducing crime and disorder (McDonough, 2002).

Today, members of the police department are encouraged to patrol their beats and sectors proactively by examining the underlying cause of recurring incidents of crime and disorder. The problem-solving process helps officers to identify problems, analyze them completely, develop effective response strategies, and assess the results (Peak & Glensor, 2002).

According to More (1998), problem-solving or problem-oriented policing is a proactive philosophy that promotes the concept that incidents consuming patrol and investigative time can be dealt with more effectively when consideration is given to underlying problems. It also assumes that the expertise and creativity of line officers are reliable sources for developing solutions to problems. Officers who use their problem-solving skills to develop effective solutions and responses may be more likely to consider responses more appropriate for the student offenders' welfare and safety.

Officers who become SROs receive extensive training for their assignment. Although the training is not as specialized as that of juvenile officers because of the difference in juvenile laws and procedures, their role is just as influential (Jackson, 2003). SROs in Birmingham reported they counseled at least 30% of the students at their assigned schools and that the focus of the counseling session was academic performance, followed by school fighting and drug-related behavior (Johnson, 1999).

The SROs have expanded their role from the security monitor into a role model, a guidance counselor, a teacher, a problem solver, and a disciplinarian. According to Johnson (1999), the presence of uniformed police officers and their expanded security role appear to be deterring both violent and nonviolent crime, having a calming effect on students, and promoting respect and a sense of understanding between police officers and students.

According to Johnson (1999), the majority of the school officials stated that parents and teachers were very supportive of the SROs' public school police duties and rated their performance as excellent. SROs reported positive contacts with parents when investigating matters related to school fights, gang activities, and disrespect of teachers.

After interviewing Birmingham's SROs, Johnson (1999) reported that while working in the schools the officers became interested in getting to know the students and in establishing a trusting relationship with them. While on patrol in the schools' hallways, SROs reported they looked for the positive in young people, encouraged students to excel, and congratulated them when they accomplished their goals.

Among school officials and students, the SROs are credited for contributing to a noticeable drop in school violations, ranging from inciting or participating in a major student disturbance to wearing secret society apparel. In a 2-year period, the total number of intermediate and major offenses in high school and middle school suspensions decreased from 3,267 in 1994–95 (before the school resource officers were permanently assigned to city schools) to

2,717 in 1995–96 (after the school resource officers were permanently assigned to city schools) (Johnson, 1999).

The SROs' arrest data were recorded for one 5-month period. The officers arrested 145 students for drug and weapon offenses from January 1996 through May 1996. More important, SROs reported on their patrol sheets that they responded to 157 gang-related activities without incident and counseled 74 at-risk youths. SROs reported the most common topics for discussion were academic performance, school fights, drug-related behavior, leaving school grounds without authorization, and gang-related behavior (Johnson, 1999).

Johnson concludes, based on a review of the data and survey opinions, that program components are in place and appear to be working smoothly. In the Birmingham school system, while the officers were present there was an increased visible police presence, increased student counseling services, increased community police support by school officials, parents, and students, and, most important, a reduction in school violence (Johnson, 1999).

## ■ Specialized Training

Events such as those at Columbine High School have forced police departments to raise their level of preparedness. A majority of supervisors and patrol officers from the New Brunswick Police Department have attended "tabletop" exercises that deal with tactical decision-making scenarios. A tabletop model of New Brunswick High School and surrounding environs was created, and a facilitator introduced a tactical problem at the school, along with random obstacles. Supervisors deployed personnel and managed the scene. After each exercise, the response was critiqued. This training received high marks from all who attended.

## ■ Policies and Youth Programs That Work

Controlling discretion can be a problem for police administrators. Remington and Goldstein (1967) describe two options management has for confronting the issue. One way would be to rely on tradition and make decisions and adjustments as situations arise. The authors refer to this as "unarticulated improvisation." The second method is to acknowledge and use the policy formulation process as a proactive measure to address issues before they become problems.

The immediate challenge when formulating policy for law enforcement is finding the balance between effectiveness and utility. Discretion exercised by police personnel prior to the adjudication process is not easily managed. If street-level officers are not convinced a policy on discretion is practical, they simply choose not to use it, and supervisors are none the wiser. This is in contrast to a policy on report writing, where a supervisor can review a report, note any errors, and discipline or retrain the officer.

Joseph Ryan (2003), former New York City Police captain and expert on community policing and violence, suggests that for community policing to be effective and to deal proactively with crime and disorder, police agencies need to employ three separate strategies: engage in partnerships, initiate problem-solving strategies, and make use of these partnerships to develop joint crime prevention strategies (Roberts, 2003). We concur and suggest that if more police agencies adopt some basic tenets of school-based community policing initiatives such as the Youth Program, Juvenile Aid Bureau, School Resource Officer program, or the G.R.E.A.T. program and transformed these principles into neighborhood-based initiatives, then police officers may improve their decision-making ability and encounter less juvenile crime, less juvenile victimization, and less resistance to authority.

## References

Braga, A. A., & Kennedy, D. M. (2002). Reducing gang violence in Boston. In W. L. Reed & S. H. Decker (Eds.), *Responding to Gangs: Evaluation and Research*. Washington, DC: National Institute of Justice.

Brown, L. (1989).*Community policing: A practical guide for police officials*. Washington, DC: U.S. Department of Justice.

Cole, G. F., & Smith, C. E. (1998). *The American system of criminal justice*. Belmont, CA. Wadsworth.

Esbensen, F.-A., & Osgood, D. W. (1997). *National evaluation of G.R.E.A.T.* Washington, DC: National Institute of Justice.

Fritsch, E., Caeti, T. J., & Taylor, R. W. (1999). Gang suppression through saturation patrol, aggressive curfew, and truancy enforcement: A quasi-experimental test of the Dallas anti-gang initiative. *Crime and Delinquency, 45*, (1), 122–139.

Jackson, M. S. (2003). Law enforcement officers' response to illegal street gang activity. In A. R. Roberts (Ed.), *Critical issues in crime and justice* (2nd ed.). Thousand Oaks, CA: Sage.

Johnson, I. (1999). School violence: The effectiveness of a school resource officer program in a Southern city. *Journal of Criminal Justice, 27*(2), 173–192.

Office of Juvenile Justice and Delinquency Prevention. (1999, November). Violence after school. *Juvenile Justice Bulletin*. Retrieved June 22, 2003, from *http://www.ncjrs.org/html/ ojjdp/9911_11contents.html*

Kelling, G. L. (1999). *"Broken Windows" and Police Discretion*. Washington, DC: National Institute of Justice Research Report.

McDonough, B. (2002) Crime prevention in public housing. In D. M. Robinson (Ed.), *Policing and crime prevention*. Englewood Cliffs, NJ: Prentice-Hall.

Moore, J. P., & Cook, I. L. (1999). *Highlights of the 1998 national youth gang survey* (Fact sheet No. 123). Washington, DC: U.S. Department of Justice, Office of Justice Programs, Office of Juvenile Justice and Delinquency Prevention.

More, H. W. (1998). *Special topics in policing* (2nd ed.). Cincinnati, OH: Anderson.

Muraskin, R. (1998). Police work and juveniles. In A. R. Roberts (Ed.), *Juvenile justice: Policies, programs, and services* (2nd ed.). Chicago: Nelson-Hall.

Muraskin, R., & Roberts, A. (Eds.). (1999). *Visions for change: Crime and justice in the twentieth first century* (p. 53). Englewood Cliffs, NJ: Prentice-Hall.

*National Association of School Resource Officers.* Retrieved June 22, 2003, from *http://www .nasro.org/home.asp*

New Jersey's Online Gang Free Community. *Gang recruitment, threats and intimidation* (New Jersey 2C:33-28. Solicitation, recruitment to join criminal street gang; crime, degrees). Retrieved June 21, 2003, from http://www.state.nj.us/lps/dcj/njgangfree/njenhanced4.htm

Palumbo, D. J., & Ferguson, J. L. (1995). Evaluating gang resistance education and training (GREAT). *Evaluation Review, 19*(6).

Peak, K. J., & Glensor, R. W. (2002). *Community policing and problem solving: Strategies and practices* (3rd ed.). Englewood Cliffs, NJ: Prentice-Hall.

Piliavin, I., & Briar, S. (1964). Police encounters with juveniles. *American Journal of Sociology, 70*, 206–214.

Remington, F., & Goldstein, H. (1967). Law enforcement policy: The police role. In *Task force report: The police*. Washington, DC: U.S. Government Printing Office.

Roberts, A. R. (2003). *Critical issues in crime and justice* (2nd ed.). Thousand Oaks, CA: Sage.

Ryan, J. F. (2003). Community policing and the impact of the COPS program: A potential tool in the local war on terrorism. In A. R. Roberts (Ed.), *Critical issues in crime and justice* (2nd ed.) (pp. 134–147). Thousand Oaks, CA: Sage.

Schmalleger, F. (2001). *Criminal justice today: An introductory text for the twenty-first century* (6th ed.). Englewood Cliffs, NJ: Prentice-Hall.

# 10 Juvenile Detention

Issues for the 21st Century

David W. Roush

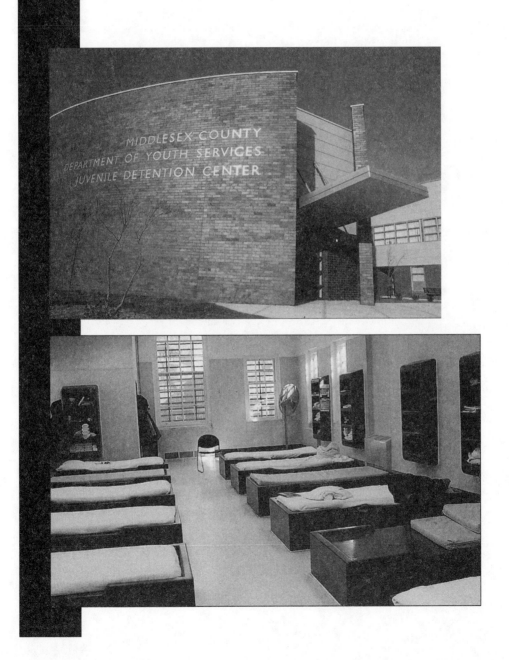

Juvenile detention practitioners have struggled to comprehend the times, especially these times. In that regard, the aftermath of the September 11 terrorist attacks has been a wake-up call. Difficult economic times have pushed us into a sense of our own time and out of our fashionable "out-of-it-ness." For the spirit of juvenile detention to exist beyond this moment, we must thrive and inspire in this moment. We must know the rules, speak the language, and understand the measurements of success. We must be open to and participate in the evolving "best knowledge and practices," adapting them, incorporating them into our operations, and highlighting the successes of our distinctively different system. We are guardians of hope. Discussed in the following pages are selected concepts and issues relevant to juvenile detention's ability to thrive in the 21st century.

Juvenile detention is regularly ignored, maligned, and misunderstood (Hughes & Reuterman, 1982; Kihm, 1981; Roush, 1999a). It is embattled, abused, neglected, underfunded, understaffed, and overcrowded. Juvenile detention is expected to be all things to all segments of juvenile justice (Hammergren, 1984), including mental health, special education, detoxification, shelter care, and maximum security. It is used in lieu of long-term treatment but denied proper resources to provide it. It is pushed and pulled by changing politics and media hyperbole. The problems associated with juvenile detention result, in large part, from its lack of a commonly accepted definition.

Juvenile detention's role and function began through its link to the juvenile court. Juvenile detention is a manifestation of the power of the juvenile court. The court enacts custody through varying degrees of restrictiveness to prevent reoffending (protect public safety), to prevent harm to and by the juvenile (protect self and others), and to ensure the juvenile's presence at court hearings (prevent runaways). This also means providing custody while the court decides and implements postdispositional placements or services. Despite these basic principles, there has been a long-standing confusion about the role and function of juvenile detention (Roush, 1996c), which makes it difficult to define. Hughes and Reuterman (1982), in their second national survey of juvenile detention, noted that juvenile detention provides both care and custody but that practitioners gave mixed responses about which was the priority role and what was an appropriate emphasis on each in daily operations.

On October 31, 1989, following 3 years of work on the subject, the Board of Directors of the National Juvenile Detention Association (NJDA) unanimously adopted the following definition:

> Juvenile detention is the temporary and safe custody of juveniles who are accused of conduct subject to the jurisdiction of the court who require a restricted environment for their own or the community's protection while pending legal action.
> Further, juvenile detention provides a wide range of helpful services that support the juvenile's physical, emotional, and social development.

> Helpful services minimally include education, visitation, communication, counseling, continuous supervision, medical and health care services, nutrition, recreation, and reading.

> Juvenile detention includes or provides for a system of clinical observation and assessment that complements the helpful services and reports findings.

The NJDA definition incorporated the program elements outlined in American Correctional Association (ACA) standards (Smith, Roush, & Kelley, 1990). The collaboration between ACA and NJDA led to a definition statement grounded in professional agreement.

Several responses in defense of programming require consideration. First, programs are a legitimate component of detention. Two requirements for programs are case law (Bell, 1996; Soler et al., 1990) and professional standards (American Correctional Association, 1991; National Commission on Correctional Health Care, 1999). Second, detention contains elements and experiences that are detrimental to youths (Frazier, 1989). Therefore, the profession has an obligation to address, remedy, mediate, or restore the harm done by incarceration, and programs are one way this is accomplished. Third, the objection to programs sent a mixed message. On the one hand, child advocates criticized detention facilities because of poor conditions of confinement and, on the other hand, opposed programs—that is, reliable methods to improve conditions of confinement.

## ■ Understanding Juvenile Detention

### Detention as Process and Place

"Detention as process" focuses on the juvenile court's power to detain (arrest, prevent, control, or stop) a juvenile pending legal action (Dunlap & Roush, 1995). However, "detention as process" asks, "What level of restrictive custody must the court exercise with the juvenile to fulfill the detention function: preventing the juvenile from reoffending, preventing the juvenile from failing to appear for a court hearing, and preventing the juvenile from inflicting harm to self or others?" Because not every juvenile is alike, and because not every juvenile requires secure custody, "detention as process" calls for a range of detention alternatives or a continuum of detention alternatives that is available to the court and that matches the custody needs of a particular juvenile with an appropriate detention option. "Detention as place" emphasizes a secure facility with (a) controlled ingress and egress; (b) security hardware and locks on windows and doors; (c) cement, steel, and cinder block construction; (d) and communications and technology systems representative of secure correctional facilities.

### Professional Standards as Important Guidelines for Effective Practice

The U.S. Department of Justice, through its Office of Juvenile Justice and Delinquency Prevention (OJJDP), altered the course of juvenile detention standards development by conducting a congressionally mandated study of conditions of confinement in juvenile facilities. Abt Associates from Cambridge, Massachusetts, won the competitive award and conducted a comprehensive survey of conditions of confinement in 984 public and private juvenile facilities in the United States (Parent et al., 1994). The findings affirmed what many juvenile confinement practitioners assumed: There was, at best, only a weak relationship between compliance with ACA standards (ACA, 1991) and conditions of confinement. One statement in the report's executive summary was particularly critical of the current version of professional juvenile standards: "Conformance to procedural standards had no discernible effect on conditions within facilities" (Parent et al., 1994, p. ES13). Abt challenged the validity of the standards, and juvenile justice practitioners turned their attention to a new strategy known as "performance-based standards."

What is a performance-based standard? Performance-based standard (PbS) stressed the objectification of outcomes (the use of objective and empirical measures), the verification of outcomes (measurable changes in daily practice), and dynamic or continually improving criteria for acceptability. Loughran and Godfrey (2000) described PbS as a "new wave" in juvenile corrections. Invariably, standards development focuses on outcomes. Outcome measures are important for several reasons. First, outcome measures help staff make specific decisions about program changes. Second, outcomes that are closely linked to day-to-day management can be used routinely to monitor strengths, weaknesses, or trouble spots. This requires ongoing assessments of the conditions of confinement. Third, outcome measures provide assurance to administration, staff, and the public that the total program functions with reasonable effectiveness.

Why is PbS important? PbS remains a very popular concept that an increasing number of juvenile detention administrators view as an effective strategy to improve conditions of confinement. The PbS language continues to permeate the juvenile justice vocabulary, and it has become associated with larger concepts, such as continuous quality improvement and total quality management. Juvenile detention administrators appear to understand PbS, and it holds the promise of becoming an important method of gauging effective practices. Its outcomes orientation and compatibility with data-driven decision models parallel new initiatives within the Office of Justice Programs to strengthen juvenile justice program development.

The Council of Juvenile Correctional Administrators (CJCA) Performance-Based Standards in Juvenile Corrections and Detention Facilities Project, funded by OJJDP, is the leader in PbS development. Their standards have many strengths:

1 The vision statement—"Every juvenile detention and corrections facility in America should be run as if your only child were the next youth to be admitted" (Loughran & Godfrey, 2001)—is quintessential "bright line" between adult and juvenile perspectives on institutions. It is as close to a perfect vision statement as a standards-generating organization for juvenile confinement can express.

2 PbS starts with a definition of the desired outcome. Once the desired outcome is defined, the PbS process moves to the development of policy and procedure that support the production and verification of the desired outcome. For juvenile justice facility administrators, it allows the construction of new and unique visions for their facilities.

3 PbS is theory-driven. The CJCA PbS Project developed a theoretical framework for conditions of confinement based on the work of Logan (1993, p. 27), which defined eight measures of prison performance: security, safety, order, care, activity, justice, conditions, and management. CJCA revised the model to include components that more accurately fit juvenile facilities, such as safety, order, security, health, mental health, programming, justice, and reintegration.

4 PbS promotes the use of good information to inform daily practice. Good information, collected regularly, permits internal and external comparisons regarding operational performance. The continuous improvement system, referred to as the facility improvement plan (FIP) uses (a) regular data collection on specific outcomes, especially those related to safety; (b) regular reporting, monitoring, and sharing of outcomes on other measures, such as assessments and intake-related information; (c) a communications strategy that includes a quality check; (d) use of data to revise an agency's goals and mission; (e) presentation of outcomes to the legislature and elected officials; and (f) internal and external evaluations, the external evaluation being the annual PbS review (Loughran & Godfrey, 2001).

5 PbS enables users to identify their own weaknesses and to create systems to correct them.

Juvenile detention facilities may never engage in accreditation in large numbers. There are many ways to explain this phenomenon, but one key factor is the absence of resources, particularly staff and money, to implement a series of comprehensive standards. Until that day occurs, juvenile justice practitioners will look for useful methods to enhance the quality of care to incarcerated youths. A popular option is the self-improvement or self-assessment process (Burrell & Warboys, 1997; Wildavsky, 1979). This self-correcting and self-evaluating element requires a dynamic approach to setting standards, including benchmarks and criteria. Data-driven systems cannot be static. Standards must have sufficient flexibility to reflect changes in the empirical evidence that informs their definitions of acceptability. For

PbS, the self-evaluating process permits regular adjustments of internally generated benchmarks.

## Crowding and Juvenile Detention Reform

Nearly half of the youths confined in juvenile detention centers, reception centers, training schools, and ranches in 1991 throughout the United States were detained in overcrowded facilities (Parent et al., 1994). This statistic was alarming for two reasons. First, it meant that literally hundreds of thousands of youths were held in facilities operating beyond their design capacity. Second, it may represent a phenomenon that has not yet reached its peak.

The OJJDP-funded study of conditions of confinement (Parent et al., 1994) represented the most comprehensive examination of conditions in juvenile facilities ever undertaken in this country. Some of the most compelling findings pertained to crowding of juvenile facilities:

1 A substantial number of juvenile facilities were extremely crowded. Nearly one out of three confined youths was in a facility operating at more than 120% of design capacity. As a result, one third of confined youths slept in living units with more than 26 juveniles, and one third of confined youths slept in rooms that were smaller than required by national standards.

2 Living in crowded dormitories increased the incidence of injury to staff and juveniles. A positive correlation existed between crowded conditions in training schools and injuries inflicted by juveniles on other juveniles, as well as injuries by juveniles on staff.

3 Facilities operating above their rated capacity had higher rates of suicidal behavior. The data suggested that crowding affects the ability of staff to meaningfully screen potentially suicidal youths, to supervise them, and to intervene effectively.

These findings received widespread review and discussion among juvenile justice stakeholders, underscoring the need for comprehensive reform efforts to reduce and prevent detention crowding.

### Juvenile Detention Alternatives Initiative (JDAI)

To demonstrate that jurisdictions could establish more effective and efficient systems to accomplish the purposes of juvenile detention, the Annie E. Casey Foundation established the Juvenile Detention Alternatives Initiative (JDAI) in 1992. In the largest detention reform effort to date, JDAI sought to reduce the inappropriate detention of youths in selected metropolitan jurisdictions around the country. JDAI staff found in many jurisdictions that (a) statutory criteria for detention were unclear or inappropriately applied; (b) detention decisions by police, probation officers, and judges were often subjective and unrelated to an objective need for detention; (c) unnecessary detention often occurred because of a lack of programmatic alternatives; and (d) systemic inefficiencies (such as a failure to do sufficient preliminary investigation at intake) caused unnecessary detention. This misuse of detention had an obvious impact on crowding.

JDAI had four basic objectives: (a) to eliminate the inappropriate or unnecessary use of secure detention, (b) to minimize failures to appear and the incidence of delinquent behavior, (c) to redirect public finances from building new facility capacity to responsible alternative strategies, and (d) to improve conditions in secure detention facilities (Lubow, 1999b, p. 18). The initiative produced a valuable model for juvenile detention reform, which the foundation published in its Pathways monographs (Annie E. Casey Foundation, 1999). The information contained in the Pathways series, highlighted by the successes from Cook, Multnomah, and Sacramento counties (Rust, 1999), provided juvenile justice with a wealth of information about reform strategies. Beyond that, JDAI staff offered some key lessons that the project taught its participants: (a) Collaboration was foreign and difficult but worth it, (b) judicial leadership was essential, (c) capacities for reform must be grown, (d) the dearth of data could be deadly, (e) significant change was possible, and (f) detention reform was very fragile (Lubow, 1999a, pp. 45–47). A central theme that emerged from the JDAI interventions was the importance of the "collaborative" (a core group of key stakeholders). JDAI employed many tactical strategies for the prevention and reduction of detention crowding, but it also demonstrated that successful reform was synonymous with strategic and systemic change.

### Jurisdictional Planning Assistance (JPA)

Through a joint OJJDP award, NJDA and the Youth Law Center (YLC) outlined a project that applied most of the JDAI concepts and principles to juvenile confinement reform for smaller, rural-urban jurisdictions. The NJDA-YLC project adopted the JDAI principles, but it differed from JDAI in several ways (Roush, 1999b). First, it focused on the smaller, rural-urban jurisdiction. Second, the NJDA-YLC project focused on juvenile confinement—that is, the full range of juvenile custody facilities. This expanded the intervention and reform process to include statewide systems and training schools. Finally, resources available for a strategic intervention were significantly less in the NJDA-YLC project. This meant that the goal of sustainability had to be accomplished through a more time-limited intervention with greater precision in its scope. This proved to be a very important distinction.

The delivery of the NJDA-YLC technical assistance interventions yielded some important lessons:

1 Without some type of motivation, even crisis (severe crowding, the threat of litigation, budget deficits, or strategic uncertainties), it was often difficult to engage a jurisdiction in a strategic planning or corrective process.

2 Change was too often dependent on an effective leader who champi-

oned the reform. If the leader left, changed jobs, or adjusted priorities, the efforts to reform the system stalled.

3 In each jurisdiction, some key staff often attempted to "wait out" the reform-minded leader. Experience again taught that, given the local political process, leaders of agencies and court systems came and went with alarming regularity, as did their plans for improving a system. Again, evidence mounted for a shift in responsibility for sustaining change from the leader to the core stakeholder group.

4 In the absence of credible state and local support for change, it was difficult to connect technical assistance (strategic and change-oriented tools and models developed from a national perspective) to actual reform efforts. Many thought that litigation needed to be an external factor pushing the change. However, litigation required a long-term commitment of resources, which the project did not possess, and the creation of an adversarial relationship, which the project deemed to be counterproductive.

What had become abundantly clear was the necessity for internal factors to drive and sustain reform. Through the jurisdictional planning assistance, NJDA-YLC provided the tools and technical assistance to jurisdictions that wanted to reform their system but did not know how. In each jurisdiction, dramatic changes occurred following a 2-day workshop (Miesner & Roush, 2003).

## Programs and More Programs, People and More People

In the face of prolonged and severe crowding, former Oklahoma County (Oklahoma) Juvenile Bureau Chief Ray Bitsche reaffirmed his belief that "the best security is built on programs and more programs, people and more people" (Burrell, Roush, & Sanniti, 1977; Previte, 1997, p. 77). Several reasons justify programs (Roush, 1999a). First, the empowering statute or legislation that creates juvenile detention in each state usually includes an expectation or requirement for programs and services. Second, Bell (1996) claims that programs are required by the U.S. Supreme Court as a method of meeting the constitutional rights of detained juveniles. Third, the traditions of juvenile justice (Taylor, 1992) and its professional associations, such as ACA and NJDA, identify a wide range of programs as one of the essential distinctions between adult and juvenile detention (Roush, Dunlap, & Rinella, 2002). Fourth, practitioners report that helpful programs make the job easier, more effective, and more enjoyable. This translates into a safer environment for both residents and staff.

### A Vision Statement

An important first task in any successful endeavor is the development of a clear and direct vision statement. The Center for Research & Professional Development (CRPD) vision statement reflects its three core values:

The most efficient way to return a juvenile to a healthy, law-abiding lifestyle is through healthy relationships with healthy adults in healthy environments.

### Healthy Relationships

The essence of juvenile justice is public safety, and the most elegant way to ensure public safety is through the strengthening of prosocial bonds between the community and the offender. The strengthening of these bonds is a function of the ability to repair broken relationships and to enhance healthy relationships, especially those that exist primarily in the community. This requires knowledge of best practices regarding juvenile offenders and a comprehensive approach to delinquency that embraces the community, the victim, and the offender in a restorative manner (Moeser, 1997, 1999).

### Healthy Adults

In every phase of work with troubled youths, those juveniles who succeeded and who became productive members of society invariably attributed their success to one or more influential adults who had a significant impact in their lives. In virtually every phase of the juvenile institution, success is attributable to the quality and character of the direct care staff members.

### In Healthy Environments

Environments exert powerful influences on human behavior, and research indicates that these environmental influences are more pronounced on children and adolescents. Staff who work with youths in confinement settings frequently lose sight of all of the environmental influences within that setting. This occurs because work with juvenile offenders is challenging and demanding, and the range of environmental influences can be complex. These environments or conditions of confinement are tools for staff to make their interactions with youths more effective. An understanding of conditions of confinement also helps juvenile confinement practitioners to understand an environmental continuum and to look at the importance of all environments (home, neighborhood, family, friends, faith-based, and work) as important parts of the juvenile justice process.

If a good institution is a function of good people, the most promising strategy to develop good people is to increase professional development opportunities for all juvenile care workers. However, limited resources plague juvenile detention and corrections facilities, and this constrains training opportunities. For this reason, NJDA, with the support of OJJDP, provides a wide range of staff development programs and strategies for juvenile detention facilities (Brooks, 2000, 2001; Brooks & White, 2000; Gaseau, 2002; Jones & Roush, 1995; Kielas & Roush, 1999; Porpotage, 1996; Roush, 1996a, 1996b, 1996c; Roush, Brooks, & Kielas, 1998; Roush & Jones, 1995; Roush & McMillen, 2000; Roush & Wyss, 1994; Wolford & Brooks, 1999).

### Juvenile Offender Reentry

Another important initiative is juvenile offender reentry (JOR). The U.S. Department of Justice's Office of Justice Program (OJP) has reintroduced reentry as a priority for effective justice services. Many publications address this concept, and OJP has articulated the principles of reentry (Office of Justice Programs, 2002, p. 2). In general terms, reentry applies to the return of the offender from a placement outside the home community back to the home community. For the juvenile justice community, reentry expands the concept of reintegration introduced by Altschuler and Armstrong (1998). Reentry resonates with juvenile justice practitioners because the overwhelming majority of youths released from juvenile facilities return home. Detention must address the physical and emotional components of reentry (Loughran, 2002, p. 2) because both are important to the crafting of a successful outcome.

Reentry suggests that community-based organizations should be included throughout the juvenile confinement process. The public knows and trusts these community-based programs, and their involvement with the juvenile confinement facility enhances the public's cooperation with reentry programs. A systematic involvement of community-based programs throughout incarceration enhances the likelihood of successful community reintegration. This involvement is particularly important for those organizations providing services and outreach in the juvenile's immediate neighborhood or community. Juvenile confinement programs should identify how such organizations can be involved in existing reentry strategies and, if they are not currently included, what strategies can be employed to secure their involvement. Community-based organizations that include faith-based groups can provide a wide variety of services, such as mentoring, tutoring, and counseling, both within the community and within the juvenile confinement setting.

### Detention Education

Juvenile justice experts, child advocacy attorneys, leading detention educators, and case law agree that education is fundamental to the success of juvenile justice interventions with at-risk and delinquent youths (Carbone, 1990; White, 2002). However, detained youths generally have long histories of public school frustrations and failures, particularly academic achievement reports that are consistently 1 or more years below expected grade levels (Foley, 2001). The National Center on Education, Disability, and Juvenile Justice (EDJJ) supported this finding and further reported that most incarcerated youths (a) lag 2 or more years behind their age peers in basic academic skills and (b) have higher rates of grade retention, absenteeism, and suspension or expulsion (Leone & Miesel, 2001). In addition, Burrell and Warboys (2000) noted that, on any given day, 30% to 70% of detained youths are eligible for special education services as defined in the Individuals with Disabilities Education Act (IDEA) of 1997.

LeBlanc, Pfannenstiel, and Tashjian (1991) found that simply duplicating the programs and practices of the public schools yields ineffective education in juvenile confinement facilities. Yet, many detention education programs continue to match their curricula, standards, assessments, units of credit, scheduling, and instructional strategies with those of the public schools. This makes it more difficult to reignite the desire and confidence to learn in educationally disenfranchised students. Likewise, "more of the same" does not adequately prepare students for their transitions to home, public schools, work, community, or other placements. Brooks (2001) concluded that these data mean that detention education programs must "educate differently" or run the risk of repeating the same cycle of failure as their public school predecessors.

An increasing number of detention education program operators, however, subscribe to the philosophy that effective education must be more than rote academic maintenance and that detention education should respond to the juvenile's needs (Leone, Rutherford, & Nelson, 1991; Wolford & Koebel, 1995). In detention, where lengths of stay vary from days to months and occasionally even longer, "educating differently" requires a change in focus from content standards, assessment tests, and Carnegie units to the academic and behavioral needs of individual students in transition. Presented with students at multiple levels and with multiple needs, a high-quality detention education curriculum should provide a continuum of academic services, ranging from special education to GED preparation to postsecondary options. In addition, the detention education curriculum should teach and reinforce prosocial behaviors that translate into success for the student at home, at school, in the community, or in a future placement (Coffey & Gemignani, 1994). Youths in juvenile detention facilities need instruction in communication, problem solving, decision making, interpersonal relationships, values, critical thinking, and healthy lifestyle choices.

## ■ Examples of Promising Programs in Juvenile Detention

### Case Study 1: DuPage County Juvenile Detention Center, Wheaton, Illinois

In February 2000, the DuPage County Juvenile Detention Center, a 96-bed division of the 18th Judicial Circuit Court's Department of Probation and Court Services, implemented a comprehensive intervention program for its residents. The 18th Circuit encompasses all of DuPage County, which sits directly west of Chicago and Cook County and has a population approaching 1 million residents. The average daily population of the center is about 50 residents, with some cyclical variation. The average length of stay is 23 days. A sophisticated intake screening process deflects many would-be residents to detention alternatives.

The new program was implemented as part of the new vision and mission of the Department of Probation and Court Services. Two "pillars" support this vision and mission: restorative justice (Bazemore & Umbreit, 1994, 1998; Maloney, Romig, & Armstrong, 1988; Pranis, 1997) and the "what works" research in criminal justice (Andrews & Bonta, 1994; Andrews et al., 1990; Gendreau, Little, & Goggin, 1996; Kazdin & Weisz, 1998; Lipsey, 1995). The program philosophy has the following beliefs: (a) all human beings have intrinsic value and are worthy of respect; (b) no one loses the ability to make change; (c) we are all responsible for our choices and therefore our behaviors; (d) actions speak louder than words; (e) before a behavior is expected, we need to make sure that it has been taught; and (f) working with juveniles is a challenging, sometimes frustrating, but always worthwhile endeavor.

## Program Structure and Activities

### School Program

All residents are in classes appropriate to their age level and/or cognitive functioning, including middle school, high school, or GED preparation (Leone & Miesel, 2002). Additional tutoring is provided for those who have learning disabilities or other deficits. Improvements in basic skills are monitored as part of the detention center's total quality management plan. Older residents who have completed their high school education are often used to assist in the classroom with more impaired, younger residents.

### Pod-Based (Living Unit) Programs

Small groups of residents, no more than 10 per pod or living unit, live and do everything together (groups, school, meals, recreation). This allows better monitoring of their behavior and enables them to develop effective relationships with their staff and each other. Residents from pods do not mix, except those residents who have attained Level 3 privileges (see later, Behavior Modification System) have mixed recreation on weekend evenings. Forcing accountability among a small group of residents in this way practically eliminates all gang problems, since residents are randomly mixed into pods and have to learn to deal with each other.

### Cognitive-Behavioral Focus

If behavior change is to be "portable"—that is, carry past the detention center program—residents need to make fundamental changes in how they see the world, themselves, and their response to situations around them. The cognitive focus shows residents how their thinking (their beliefs and attitudes) affects their behavior (Bush & Bilodeau, 1997; Bush, Glick, & Taymans, 1997). The goal is to help residents change their thinking and thus their behavior. The model of cognitive intervention used at DuPage is rational behavior training (RBT) (Goodman & Maultsby, 1974; Walen, DiGiuseppe, & Wessler, 1980).

Residents attend five RBT groups each week, where they learn the general cognitive model: Perceptions and interpretations of any situation, which result from deeply held core beliefs, are expressed in "self-talk" or statements about the situation. These lead to feelings, which in turn result in behavior and ultimately consequences or outcomes. Residents are taught how to identify their self-talk and core beliefs and then test them for rationality and reasonableness. They review the outcomes that result from past irrational thinking and learn how changing their thinking can help them take control of their feelings and behavior and, ultimately, their life course.

### Behavior Modification System

The primary element of an effective behavior management system is the systematic reinforcement of appropriate behaviors. DuPage accomplishes this objective through the use of a point system. Residents earn points in five skill areas:

1 Ignore (ignore others' inappropriate behavior, focus on current task, avoid distractions)
2 Talk (effectively articulating what the resident knows in group and classes; appropriate use of language, such as no inappropriate talk or swearing)
3 Cooperate/Participate (follow all directives and expectations, help out, and take initiative)
4 Area (rooms are orderly and neat; residents have prepared materials for group and class; homework is done)
5 Gestures (no gang signing, inappropriate touching; good touching, e.g., patting on the back, shaking hands when meeting someone new and introducing oneself)

These areas are evaluated through six 3-hour time blocks each day. Points range from 0 to 5 in each category, per 3-hour period, for a total of 150 points per day. New appropriate behaviors immediately receive a coupon, with which items can be purchased at the commissary (candy, pop, higher-grade toiletries, writing paper, note cards). Coupons are also given for continued long-term demonstration of good behavior or "heroic" behavior done in a challenging situation.

The focus is on "shaping" new behaviors by reinforcing "small steps" along the process of change. The entire system is based on earning; nothing is taken away, but all privileges (type of visitation, bedtime, use of recreational items, amount and type of items allowed in room) must be earned. On Friday nights, points are totaled, and the level for the next week assigned (from 1 to 3). Those privileges are maintained for the next week regardless of particular behavior during that week. For example, Level 1 residents may only have two books and bedding in their room and visit only parents in a noncontact process behind a glass panel. Level 3 residents may have a plant and a battery-powered radio and have visits from parents and extended family members in a private, nonmonitored conference room.

### Teaching Youths to Set Goals

In the final group of the week, residents receive weekly behavioral goals, which are evaluated three times per day during the following week. At this goal-setting group, residents and staff work together on developing goals for each resident. For a new resident, the goal may be a simple as "Participate three times in each group or class." Once the staff and resident become aware of particular issues, these become more focused, such as "Will follow social skill #5 in taking 'no' for an answer. The steps include. . . ." Behavioral goal writing, which results in goals that are specific, measurable, and objective, is not easy and requires consistent staff training. Juveniles receive a plus mark on their point sheets for each goal achievement in the past period between groups; if they achieve sufficient "pluses" for their level, they go to a "pod plus activity" on Saturday (refreshments and recreational activity). Those residents who did not meet their goals are locked down during this time. Currently, 80% of residents attain their weekly goals.

### Responding to Inappropriate Behavior

No punishment is used in the program. Inappropriate behavior is consequenced by an extinction process using time-outs. Extinction, in behavioral terms, is the removal of stimulus information from the resident's immediate area. Every inappropriate behavior gets a 5-minute time-out. Staff do not warn, nag, and threaten. They simply say, "Please take a time-out." The resident goes to the nearest wall and faces it for 5 minutes. At the end of that time, staff ask the resident why he or she is in time-out. After indicating the inappropriate behavior, the resident returns to regular programming. After five time-outs during a 3-hour grading period, the resident will get only a proportion of earned points for that period. To get full points for a grading period, the resident must be in program and not in time-out. Failure to complete the time-out, or refusal to take it, results in a room time-out (either a sterile time-out room or the resident's own room with everything removed, including bedding) for 30 minutes. This is called a 30-5. The resident who follows expectations for this 30-minute period then returns to program and completes the original 5-minute time-out. Completion of the 30-5 requires 30 minutes of continuous appropriate behavior, or the clock starts again. The resident remains in time-out until he or she chooses to complete it. All behavior during this time is ignored: Threats, screaming, yelling, and pounding are not consequenced. For aggressive, violent, or destructive behavior, a 30-30-5 results. This is a 30-5 with an additional 30-minute period. The last 30 minutes involves doing a rational self-analysis (RSA) or another RBT tool.

### Groups

Each pod of residents attends three groups each day or 21 groups each week. All detention staff have completed a week of training on group dynamics, cognitive behavior interventions, teaching basic skills, and behavior modification. They serve as group leaders, although whenever possible, residents are encouraged to lead groups also. Occasionally, during the group, posters are made to illustrate key concepts. These posters are hung in the pods, and as residents leave, older posters are rotated out into the common areas, with new posters constantly being created. Also, residents carry 3 x 5 cards with them at all times that illustrate learned social skills and key program concepts. Different types of groups include:

☐ Social Skills Training. Using both the Boys Town Basic Skills for Youth and Skillstreaming for Adolescents, residents are taught eight basic skills (e.g., how to introduce themselves, how to take no for an answer, how to follow directions, how to accept positive criticism) and more than 300 other skills. The results of this training can be very powerful: Visitors are amazed that residents come up to them, look them in the face, smile, shake hands, and introduce themselves.

☐ Anger Management. Using a specially created manual, *My Anger Is My Friend*, residents follow a cognitive-behavioral model to understand the source of their anger and learn skills for using anger appropriately. The approach integrates RBT tools and concepts.

☐ Girls' Growth Group. This group is geared to address specific issues for female residents. Twelve topical areas are covered in two groups per week, adapting the cognitive methodology to issues particular to adolescent females.

☐ Addiction. Using a specially created manual, *Why Can't I Stop*, residents examine the dynamics of addiction and ways to deal with it. An estimated 80% to 85% of the residents use, abuse, or are addicted to alcohol or drugs. The approach is based on the cognitive-behavioral model, with use of motivational enhancement tools. This process does not support traditional approaches to drug and alcohol treatment, such as 12 Step or AA and NA models.

☐ Restorative Justice. Using a specially created manual, *The Restorative Justice Guide*, residents look at the implications of bad choices and irresponsible behavior. They look at what harm they may have caused to themselves and to their friends, family, teachers, and the community. They learn skills to make better decisions, understand the ripple effects of their choices and behaviors, and develop a relapse prevention plan to keep them away from bad choices and precriminal and criminal behavior.

- ☐ Moral Decision Making. This group uses the approach from the Skill-streaming/Aggression Replacement Training Model. Residents learn the four stages of moral decision making (based on Kohlberg) and then talk through real-life problem situations, determining what they would do and how this reflects a particular stage of moral decision making. The goal is to move their decision making to higher stages of moral appropriateness, from power/control to concern for society and systems.

- ☐ Forgiveness and Healing. Most residents at the detention center have experienced some trauma in their lives, and many have become stuck with thoughts and feelings about what happened to them that affects their current behavior. Most people can often forgive in small ways every day (accepting apologies, excusing someone who bumped into us). Sometimes the hurt and pain are more extreme, and forgiveness seems out of the question. Sometimes individuals just cannot shake off the past. This curriculum provides a way for beginning the process of forgiveness, which is essential to the process of healing or becoming whole again. The goal is not to dredge up and make public difficult issues but to enable residents to find ways of thinking and feeling about trauma that is not crippling to them. They may not choose to normalize relationships with those who have hurt them, but they can forgive and get on with their lives.

- ☐ Relationship Group. This group is geared for the young residents' pod (10- to 14-year-olds) and looks at various aspects of relationships: family, peers, authority figures, and so on. In this group, youths examine their own relationship styles, those within their families, and ways to communicate and listen to peers and adults more effectively.

JL, who is 17, was released in May. He completed his GED (obtaining a nearly perfect score!), is working several jobs, and is registered at College of DuPage. He has a long history of crime and incarceration, including in the state of California. This is an excerpt from his presentation at the third annual Illinois Detention Symposium, in June 2002:

> When I came to the detention center, my family wrote me off. I had no family. I had nothing. In California, when I was locked up, I was treated like an animal. No one asked me how I was doing. No one cared where I was going. I came to the DuPage Detention Center. The staff became like family to me. They asked how they could help me. They showed me positive things about myself. They taught me skills: how to look at my behavior; how to make changes in my life; how to think positively. I was able to take pride in myself for the first time in my life. I never had any successes. I saw myself as a failure. The detention center taught me how to be successful. I was never able to get along with my family. My father and I hated each other. Last week he told me he was proud of me, and we hugged.

## Case Study 2: Calhoun County Juvenile Home, Marshall, Michigan

The most reliable barometer on the status of Michigan's children reported a noteworthy decrease in juvenile crime in Calhoun County during the period when W. K. Kellogg Foundation funds created a model program for the most criminally active juveniles in the county.

The 42-bed Calhoun County Juvenile Home was a division of the Calhoun County Juvenile Court. In 1989, the Juvenile Court received funding from the W. K. Kellogg Foundation to implement the Holistic Environmental Life-skills Project (HELP). Conceived as a collaborative response to the major problems affecting the future of troubled youths (Roush & Roush, 1993), HELP strengthened, integrated, and expanded the court's continuum of services to its increasingly more difficult offenders. Evaluations of the project resulted in two national distinctions for HELP, the 1992 Gould/Wysinger Award for exceptional programming from the Office of Juvenile Justice and Delinquency Prevention and the 1992 Exemplary Program Award from the National Association of Counties (NACo). The 1994 transfer of the juvenile home operations to the executive branch of county government and changes in facility leadership led to the current demise of programs. Written materials and program resources remain (cf. Roush, 1998), along with replications of the Calhoun County model in Amarillo, Texas, and Wheaton, Illinois.

HELP had four components: (a) social skills training, (b) computer-assisted instruction, (c) creative arts education, and (d) parenting skills education. Each component had its own active and viable citizens' advisory committee to generate innovative ideas, community support, and encouragement.

### Social Skills Training (SST)

Social skills training (SST) addressed social skills and self-esteem, two factors that consistently correlated with delinquency. The literature contained some examples of SST in training school settings (see Roush, 1996e, for review of the research) but no references to similar programs in juvenile detention or juvenile probation. Juvenile Court and W. K. Kellogg Foundation staff selected the Skills for Adolescence (SFA) curriculum (Lions Clubs International and Quest International, 1992; Sprunger & Pellaux, 1989) as the social skills intervention and integrated SFA classes into the detention education and group living components of the detention facility.

SFA was a nontraditional educational program for adolescents that emphasized life skills, such as effective listening, decision making, and positive personal relationships. SFA had been part of public school curricula for many years, but until recently it had not been introduced in a detention center.

#### New Admissions

As new students entered detention, they were involved immediately in the SFA group by having residents who participated in the previous day's sessions review what was done so that new youths were aware of what to expect. New residents were given a chance to feel comfortable and to observe some of the lessons before they were asked to participate. Pressure to participate was rarely put on new students on the first day, even though new residents usually felt comfortable enough to participate by the end of the first session.

SFA materials were repeated and still maintained a high impact on both first-time and repeat residents. Although program staff expressed initial reservations about the high levels of resident turnover in detention, the transient nature of the population may actually have strengthened the impact of repeat lessons because the group of youths in the SFA class became new and dynamic with each admission or release.

Anecdotal and other qualitative sources consistently described student responses in positive terms (Roush, 1996e; Roush, Christner, Lee, & Stelma, 1993). Detained youths enjoyed structured group discussions about important issues in their lives. They were respectful of others in this environment, and the appropriate release of the emotional stress associated with adolescence and secure confinement had a positive effect on behavior in other parts of the detention program. The pattern that emerged regarding student responses was very positive, and it strongly supported the assumption that troubled youths in juvenile detention centers would respond very favorably to a systematic and structured approach to helpful programming.

## Computer-Assisted Instruction

The computer-assisted instruction (CAI) also had a similarly positive impact on detained youths. In the face of opposition from traditional juvenile justice personnel who stated that delinquent youths cannot benefit from computers, CAI proved successful on all evaluation measures. Exit interviews with youths revealed that CAI was one of the most enjoyable components of HELP. Also, empirical measures indicated statistically significant increases in reading skills and appropriate classroom behaviors through the introduction of computers.

Residents averaged 6.7 hours of computer time per week. When asked whether they preferred learning from a computer or a teacher, residents' responses were almost evenly split. Differences in learning styles (auditory or visual) accounted for much of the divergence in opinion. Comments included:

☐ Teachers could answer specific questions.
☐ Teachers have compassion and are interested in the subjects they teach.
☐ Computers go straight to the point.
☐ Computers give immediate feedback.
☐ Students can spend more time with a computer.

### Reading Performance

Computer-assisted instruction had a positive impact on academic performance, particularly reading, as measured by the Woodcock Reading Mastery Test.

Between 1991 and 1992, 36 detainees participated in the Chapter 1 remedial reading program, using CAI reading programs. Their scores demonstrated a statistically significant increase between pretest and posttest ($t = 7.25$; $df = 35$; $p < .0001$). The Woodcock Reading Mastery scores showed an average increase in reading levels of 8.2 months or a 2.2-month increase in reading scores for every month in the CAI reading program.

### Classroom Behavior

Do classroom behaviors improve in a computer lab, as compared with a regular classroom? Twenty residents were selected randomly, and the points on their token economy for classroom behavior were monitored for an 8-week period. Neither the teachers nor the students were aware of this monitoring. At the end of 8 weeks, 17 of the 20 residents earned higher points in the computer lab. A statistically significant difference existed in classroom behavior points between the computer lab and other classrooms ($t = 4.84$; $df = 18$; $p < .0001$).

## Creative Arts Education

This component provided youths with alternative forms of expression to help build self-esteem. Various fine arts were taught, such as drama, art, dance, and music. Through linkages with SST, fine arts instruction emphasized cultural diversity and ethnic sensitivity. Students averaged 5 hours of creative arts instruction per week, and numerous local artists generously volunteered their time to assist in creative arts instruction.

## Parenting Skills Education

Family breakdown was a strong correlate of juvenile delinquency within the county (Roush & Roush, 1993), so parenting skills education was a top priority. It proved to be the most successful component of HELP and served as an example of how innovative ideas become reality. Three initiatives made up parenting skills education.

> **I** Active parenting at the juvenile home. Parents of detained juveniles participated with their children in an active parenting of teens class and in lively activities that promoted parent–child interaction. A parent or guardian at these parents' night activities represented more than half of the detained youths. Ongoing parenting groups were a regular part of the programs and services.
>
> The percentage of parents involved with youth and staff in on-site and parents' night activities and programs reached 72.7% by the third year. Prior to HELP, slightly more than half of juvenile home residents indicated that one or more parents visited regularly. Four years later, 88.7% of juvenile home residents reported regular visits by parents. This was an increase of 59.8%. The majority of the residents claimed that their attitudes toward their parents had changed. The two most frequently reported changes were an increase in appreciation for their par-

ents and a recognition that their parents were watching out for their best interests.

2 Leader certification workshops (LCWs). To reach more parents of detained youths, the citizens' advisory committee suggested that HELP sponsor LCWs for a variety of helping professionals and concerned citizens with the requirement that they conduct free parenting skills education training for at least 10 parents of at-risk children over the subsequent 2 years.

The LCW idea was very popular, and the demand for parenting programs was so great that LCW graduates and HELP staff recorded more than 19,000 hours of community participation in parenting programs during the first 18 months of the LCW strategy. The LCWs also led to the introduction of new programs for teen parents and for children. More than 530 children from area public schools completed new self-esteem programs during 1992. HELP staff verified more than 34,000 hours of community participation in parenting programs. (Someone assigned the full-time job of conducting parenting skills programs would have needed 16.8 years to compile these hours.)

3 Countywide parenting education program. The citizens' advisory committee recommended another redirection of parenting education funds to develop a countywide parenting program to make full use of the LCW concept. The HELP budget was revised to fund the first year of the 2-year project, and the foundation honored the request for expanded parenting education.

### Case Study 3: Kalamazoo County Juvenile Home, Kalamazoo, Michigan

The Kalamazoo County Juvenile Home adopted a conflict resolution and peer mediation strategy. The conflict resolution program started in the detention school program under the leadership of Carol Cramer Brooks, who taught the principles of conflict resolution to detainees in the detention education program. Peer mediation principles were taught to group care staff for implementation and practice during nonschool hours. This division of program responsibilities increased the investment of both staffs in the success of the project. However, initial efforts demonstrated that effective conflict resolution was contingent upon the acquisition of other ancillary or prerequisite skills that included social skills, anger management skills, stress management skills, and healthy lifestyles. Once these skills-based modules were included, the program experienced greater success.

#### Examples of Mediation and Social Skills Training

Practitioners know relatively little about the use of mediation in institutions such as training schools and short-term detention settings. Crawford and Bodine (1996) prepared a very helpful resource for juvenile confinement practitioners about the efficacy of mediation in the institutional setting. Following are two interesting scenarios from staff experiences in Kalamazoo (Nitz, 1996).

### Peer Mediation

Zane, a 14-year-old, White, emotionally impaired (E.I.) male, had been living in detention for several weeks and barely meeting the minimum requirements for rising in the behavioral management program established for all residents. Danny, a 14-year-old, Black, E.I. male, joined the detention population and was assigned to the same living unit as Zane. After the usual few days of settling into the culture of the facility, direct care staff observed a growing friction between the two youths and concluded that race and prejudice were primary issues that need to be observed and discussed with them because of name-calling and racial slurs.

Before an arranged mediation could be held, the two boys engaged in a physical altercation immediately following a lunch period. No fists were thrown, but rather a test of strength (wrestling manner) was the chosen aggressive style. The youths were separated and given the opportunity to cool down and compose themselves. Staff and a trained peer mediator then engaged them in a mediation session to help all involved parties better understand the feelings and thinking that cause critical behavior problems. During the mediation process, Zane shared (a) that he used racial slurs because he had always used them at home and it did not mean anything to call Danny names and (b) that Danny was his same size, thought the same, and was a competitor on the living unit and in the school setting. Danny voiced similar feelings and discovered that his short-tempered nature was causing his behavioral outbursts. He said that he felt better talking directly to Zane with other adults around because it helped him think about what he was saying without getting all worked up. Over the next 3 weeks, Zane and Danny asked to mediate their differences with other residents on two separate occasions and between themselves on one other occasion. Both have told staff that being able to sit and share their feelings helped them get their behaviors under control.

### Social Skills

Diane, a 14-year-old, thin, African American female had been living in detention for several weeks, and, although meeting the minimum requirements of the behavioral management program, she was quiet and socially introverted, preferring to be alone. Viola, a 14-year-old, heavyset, African American female, full of self-esteem, joined the detention population and was assigned to the same living unit as Diane. Immediately, Viola noticed Diane and began to bully her, telling her, with obvious sarcasm, "Shut your mouth, girl, you're too loud." At one point, Viola attempted to push Diane down the stairs on the way to afternoon recreation class. Staff noticed that race and the age-old pecking order were apparent issues affecting these two girls.

Staff decided that respect and prejudice were primary issues that needed to be reviewed because of this bully-type behavior. Approaching Diane one day, Tom, the social worker, asked Diane if Viola was bothering her. "Yes," replied Diane. "She is always watching me at lunch, and the other day, she tried to push me down the stairs." Tom said, "I can tell you two sure steps to make Viola like you. The first step is to let Viola know you want to know all about her. The best way to do that is by asking questions, just about her. What she likes to do, what her favorite foods are, anything. You and I will sit here and think up five questions to ask Viola. The second step is to avoid an argument with her at all costs. If she says, 'Your mother was a stupid whore,' you say, 'Well, my mom worked for a big corporation, but she is no more of a whore than the rest of the people who let big business tell them what to do.' " Tom explained that one way to make friends is to practice these skills, and this practice occurs in the detention unit's daily small group sessions on social skills. Here youths can practice and get ideas from other residents, and everyone can learn together.

## Case Study 4: The New Mexico Model of Mediation and Conflict Resolution in Juvenile Detention

Mediation programs, combined with social skills training in juvenile corrections and detention settings, teach and reinforce communication and conflict resolution skills. The experience of the New Mexico Center on Dispute Resolution led to the development of a program model that includes establishing mediation systems in which residents and staff are trained to mediate disputes that occur in the facility (Smith, 1995). Youths put conflict resolution skills into practice by helping other residents resolve disputes in the facility. Conflict resolution and social skills were also taught to all residents as part of the educational program.

The program approach was designed to model and reinforce conflict resolution, problem-solving, and social skills. By giving residents a model for positive expression and resolution of problems, they learned how to avoid violent and self-defeating behaviors. The mediation process was introduced not to replace but to supplement existing disciplinary policies and procedures. The program reduced the number and seriousness of conflicts and rule infractions.

In both New Mexico and California, facilities implementing the conflict resolution and peer mediation program found reductions in the number of disciplinary problems, a decrease in staff time dealing directly with resident conflicts, and improved relations between staff and residents. A formal evaluation conducted by the University of New Mexico (Steele, 1991) analyzed (a) pretests, posttests, and follow-up instruments administered to youths receiving the conflict resolution curriculum and mediation training, (b) interviews with staff and youths, (c) deportment records from living units and on-site schools, and (d) surveys of success in community integration of the program participants. The results showed that youths receiving the conflict resolution curriculum and those trained as mediators were able to sustain their knowledge of conflict resolution and apply it to situations they encountered at the facilities. There was a 37% decrease in disciplinary infractions among youth mediators compared with 12% for youths who were not trained as mediators. With respect to recidivism, youths who were trained as mediators had an 18.3% lower recidivism rate during the first 6 months after return to the community than a control group without mediation training.

Youth corrections facility staff recognized the importance of this work and the relationship of conflict to delinquency, violence, and gang membership. Interviews with facility staff indicated that the program's impact on the institution included reduced personal conflict, improved resident behavior, increased job satisfaction, and better working conditions, including job safety (Smith, 1995).

### Case Study 5: Pathfinder Detention Education Program, Lincoln, Nebraska

In 1999, the Lancaster County Board, Lincoln, Nebraska, made the decision to build a new detention facility. Meetings with architects and visits to detention centers throughout the Midwest led quickly to the discovery that detention education programs vary greatly in the quality of their education staff, curriculum offerings, and program delivery. An intensive literature review revealed very little, and most did not answer the questions posed by the education staff, the architects, and the county board.

The 2½-year study for the development of a model education program included contact with NJDA's Center for Research & Professional Development (CRPD), which resulted in technical assistance through training programs and through help to build Pathfinder's basic philosophy, mission statement, curriculum, and staffing needs for a high-performance, high-quality education program for the new facility. Three Pathfinder staff completed the NJDA National Educators Training Curriculum. As program development continued, additional teachers were trained in the NJDA curriculum so that everyone had the same background information. This laid the foundation for the intensive study necessary to plan and implement the education program.

The study process demonstrated that an effective education program should have a wide array of curriculum options, with many threads or strands being "hooked on" continuously throughout a class period and school day. Some of these hooks include student assessments about the education program, a multicultural gender-based program for girls, fine arts (including art, vocal and instrumental music, and poetry), reading, character education, decision making, and life skills/life lessons programming. Effective detention education programs have to be flexible, adaptable, and able to make instructional decisions continuously throughout a class period and school day, as well as to improvise and adjust daily as students cycle through the facility quickly. The students coming to the program were alienated, the disenfranchised, dropouts, multiage and multigrade, with varied cultures and backgrounds and a wide disparity of basic skills. The necessity of building quick, personal relationships and hooking the juveniles into a school setting and presenting topics that would be both interesting and educational became the top priority.

Bringing community resources and special activities into the education program was also important, as many detainees are detached from most community activities and services. Friday afternoons were set aside for "specials." The specials included speakers, performances by groups or individuals, community groups, universities and colleges, special holidays, special events, winter and summer Olympics, and whatever else someone expressed an interest in doing as a special. Examples included Black American drummers and dancers, a blues and jazz guitarist, University of Nebraska football, basketball, cheer squads representatives, and of course the mascot "Lil Red," archeologists, ghosts, and best-seller books. This past December, staff located a Pearl Harbor survivor who shared his personal experiences. Students have made bird feeders and special snack packs for a retirement center, animal snack packs for the humane society holiday cards, posters, and signs; studied Earth Day; and saw movies that describe everyday life, entertainment, and history of the world. Specials have been successful, but they require extra time and planning, as safety and security are always a primary consideration.

The desire for continuous professional and personal improvement and the need to hold all of this together and to continue to move forward has led Pathfinder to do some very different and unique things with staff development. Pathfinder has an extensive professional library that emphasizes "a search to the edges" of educational strategies to support the belief that detention education programs must look past the mainstream or regular school literature in order to build expertise and gather tools that are more effective. Additionally, each Pathfinder staff member has a working personal and professional development plan that is in consonance with the school district's evaluation process. Student and teacher surveys allow Pathfinder to do frequent monitoring of what students and teachers are thinking and feeling about the education program. In the future, more comprehensive program assessment and evaluation will provide the direction for future growth of the education program.

## Summary

These are not the first detention centers to demonstrate the advantages of programs. Cognitive-based interventions such as conflict resolution, peer mediation, social skills, and anger management programs and other group-based interventions are ideas that have enjoyed success for decades (Granello & Hanna, 2003). However, until the juvenile detention profession views these approaches as viable components of daily programs, the programs described here must continue to reiterate the advantages of helpful strategies for residents and staff. If these interventions do not make sense logically, some other external and significant event, such as litigation or suicide or chaos, may be necessary to prompt their full exploration. The juvenile detention community has widely embraced the custodial model of supervision in response to public and political pressures to treat juveniles more like adults. This model abandons social competency training and group-based interventions, and many adult detention administrators have been critical of the custodial model's inability to control resident behavior and protect staff safety. Several of the nation's largest juvenile detention centers, including the New York City Department of Juvenile Justice, recently changed back to a caregiver model with an interactive and helping strategy to replace the custodial model.

Giovanni (2002), in the latest assessment of the perceived wants and needs of juvenile detainees in a large, urban jurisdiction (mostly minority youths), revealed the continuing desire on the part of incarcerated adolescents to learn (a) how to make better choices, (b) anger management, (c) computers, and (d) social activities. Youths wanted more involvement with staff, expressing a long-standing assumption on the part of juvenile justice practitioners that delinquent youths sorely lack relationships with healthy, caring adults. Giovanni's research reaffirms the assumptions underlying this chapter and the motivations of the individuals who participate in the programs described.

The experiences and findings from these programs affirm a common set of underlying assumptions that constitute the critical factors for developing group processes in detention. First, the effective implementation of programs is paradoxical. Programs require staff to loosen institutional controls, which ultimately leads to greater controls over youths. Control in this instance should not be equated with structure, order, and regularities, because effective programs contain sufficient order, structure, and regularities to provide safety and security within the process. Control issues in juvenile detention refer to the ability to influence a youth's behavior. The outcome of the group process is a stronger relationship between staff and residents, and the stronger the relationship between staff and youths, the more control staff have over a youth's behavior.

Second, in situations of shrinking resources and crowding, detention faces very difficult times. Public demands for punishment, accountability, and reduced government expenditures contribute to situations in which an inadequate number of staff are pitted against large groups of angry and aggressive detainees. Programs can counteract this phenomenon. It is important to the safety of residents and staff to empower residents to create and maintain appropriate behaviors within the institution. To accomplish this feat, residents must be included in the decision-making processes of the institution, and inclusion begins with structured opportunities for expression, an element of most effective programs.

Third, the current anger expressed by today's violent youths can be partially linked to societal reinforcement of portrayals of these youths as gangsters, worthless, dangerous, and incorrigible. Self-esteem may be at an all-time low for most adolescents, and the transition from feeling bad about yourself to anger is very easy. Institutions that reinforce this language of despair are only asking for problems. Structured, cognitive-based programs serve to dispel these types of stereotypes about young people, provide a release for emotional stress and anxiety, and allow a forum for exploring hopeful and encouraging perspectives on life.

Fourth, programs with a helpful or social skills orientation reinforce the importance of staff who advocate programs and services in juvenile detention. Most detention administrators describe two classifications of staff members: those who do things "to" kids and those who do things "for" kids. Institutional problems generally arise from the interactions between detained youths and the first category of staff. Programs help break down many barriers held by staff members who wish to implement rigid and punitive operations.

## References

American Correctional Association. (1991). *Standards for juvenile detention facilities* (3rd ed.). Laurel, MD: Author.

Andrews, D. A., & Bonta, J. (1994). *The psychology of criminal conduct.* Cincinnati, OH: Anderson.

Andrews, D. A., Zinger, I., Hoge, R. D., Bonta, J., Gendreau, P., & Cullen, F. T. (1990). Does correctional treatment work? A psychologically informed meta-analysis. *Criminology, 28,* 369–404.

Annie E. Casey Foundation. (1999). *Pathways to juvenile detention reform* Baltimore: Annie E. Casey Foundation, Juvenile Detention Alternatives Initiative.

Armstrong, T. L., & Altschuler, D. M. (1998). Recent developments in juvenile aftercare: Assessment, findings, and promising programs. In A. R. Roberts (Ed.), *Juvenile justice: Policies, programs and services* (2nd ed., pp. 448–472). Chicago: Nelson-Hall.

Bazemore, G., & Umbreit, M. (1994). *Balanced and restorative justice: Program summary.* Washington, DC: Office of Juvenile Justice and Delinquency Prevention, U.S. Department of Justice.

Bazemore, G., & Umbreit, M. (1998). Balancing the response to youth crime: Prospects for a restorative juvenile justice in the twenty-first century. In A. R. Roberts (Ed.), *Juvenile justice: Policies, programs and services* (2nd ed., pp. 371–407). Chicago: Nelson-Hall.

Bell, J. R. (1996). Rights and responsibilities of staff and youth. In D. W. Roush (Ed.), *Desktop guide to good juvenile detention practice.* Washington, DC: U.S. Department of Justice, Office of Juvenile Justice and Delinquency Prevention.

Brooks, C. C. (2000, March). *Detention education.* Presentation at the Illinois Juvenile Detention Alternatives Initiative symposium, Oak Brook, IL.

Brooks, C. C. (2001, May). *Applying BARJ principles and practices in confinement education programs.* Presentation at the OJJDP/ACA Juvenile Detention and Corrections forum, San Diego, CA.

Brooks, C. C., & White, C. (2000, February). *National training curriculum for educators of youth in confinement* (OJJDP fact sheet). Washington, DC: U.S. Department of Justice, Office of Juvenile Justice and Delinquency Prevention.

Burrell, S., Roush, D., & Sanniti, C. (1997). *Quality of life: An assessment of the social climate* and conditions of confinement at the Oklahoma County Juvenile Detention Center. Richmond, KY: National Juvenile Detention Association.

Burrell, S., & Warboys, L. (1997). Working together: Building local monitoring capacity for juvenile detention centers. San Francisco: Youth Law Center, California Juvenile Hall Self-Inspection Project.

Burrell, S., & Warboys, L. (2000). Special education and the juvenile justice system (Juvenile Justice Bulletin). Washington, DC: Office of Juvenile Justice and Delinquency Prevention.

Bush, J., & Bilodeau, B. (1997) Cognitive self-change: A training manual. Washington, DC: National Institute of Corrections.

Bush, J., Glick, B., & Taymans, J. (1997) Thinking for a change: Integrated cognitive behavior change program. Washington, DC: National Institute for Correction.

Carbone, V. J. (1990). Education is rehabilitation. Journal for Juvenile Justice and Detention Services, 5, 32–37.

Coffey, O., & Gemignani, R. J. (1994). Effective practices in juvenile correctional education: A study of the literature and research 1980–1992. Washington, DC: Office of Juvenile Justice and Delinquency Prevention.

Crawford, D., & Bodine, R. (Eds.). (1996). Conflict resolution education: A guide to implementing programs in schools, youth-serving organizations, and community and juvenile justice settings. Washington, DC: U. S. Department of Justice, Office of Justice Programs, Office of Juvenile Justice and Delinquency Prevention.

Dunlap, E. L., & Roush, D. W. (1995). Juvenile detention as process and place. Juvenile and Family Court Journal, 46, 3–16.

Foley, R. M. (2001). Academic characteristics of incarcerated youth and correctional educational programs: A literature review. Journal of Emotional and Behavioral Disorders, 9(4), 248–259.

Frazier, C. E. (1989). Preadjudicatory detention. In A. R. Roberts, Juvenile justice: Policies, programs, and services. Chicago: Dorsey.

Gaseau, M. (2002, July 29). Improving juvenile education: Elements of success. The Corrections Connection News Center, pp. 1–9. Retrieved http://www.corrections.com/news/feature/index/html

Gendreau, P., Little, T., & Goggin, C. (1996). A meta-analysis of the predictors of adult offender recidivism: What works! Criminology, 34(4), 575–607.

Giovanni, E. (2002). Perceived needs and interests of juveniles held in preventive detention. Juvenile and Family Court Journal, 53, 51–63.

Goodman, D. S., & Maultsby, M. (1974). Emotional well-being through rational behavior training. Springfield, IL: Charles C. Thomas.

Granello, P. F., & Hanna, F. J. (2003). Incarcerated and court-involved adolescents: Counseling an at-risk population. Journal of Counseling and Development, 81, 11–18.

Hammergren, D. R. (1984). Juvenile detention: Becoming all things to all segments of the juvenile justice system. The Rader Papers: A Journal of Juvenile Detention Services, 1, 1–3.

Hughes, T. R., & Reutermann, N. A. (1982). Juvenile detention facilities: Summary report of a second national survey. Juvenile and Family Court Journal, 33(4), 3–14.

Jones, M. A., & Roush, D. W. (1995). Developing the NJDA juvenile detention care giver training curriculum. Journal for Juvenile Justice and Detention Services, 10, 62–71.

Kazdin, A. E., & Weisz, J. R. (1998). Identifying and developing empirically supported child and adolescent treatments. Journal of Consulting and Clinical Psychology, 66, 19–36.

Kielas, C. M., & Roush, D. W. (1999, December). Internet training evaluation. East Lansing, MI: National Juvenile Detention Association.

Kihm, R. C. (1981). Juvenile detention administration: Managing a political time bomb. Federal Probation, 45(1), 9–13.

LeBlanc, L. A., Pfannenstiel, J. C., & Tashjian, M. D. (1991). Unlocking learning: Chapter 1 in correctional facilities. Washington, DC: U.S. Department of Education.

Leone, P., & Miesel, S. (2002). *Juvenile correctional education programs: The case for quality education in juvenile correctional facilities.* Retrieved August 28, 2003, at http://www.edjj.org/education.html

Leone, P. E., Rutherford, R. B., & Nelson, C. M. (1991). *Special education in juvenile corrections.* Reston, VA: Council for Exceptional Children.

Lions Clubs International and Quest International. (1992). *Skills for adolescence: Curriculum manual* (3rd ed.). Granville, OH: Quest International.

Lipsey, M. W. (1995). What do we learn from 400 research studies on the effectiveness of treatment with juvenile delinquents? In J. McGuire (Ed.), *What works: Reducing reoffending.* Chichester, England: Wiley.

Logan, C. H. (1993). Criminal justice performance measures for prisons. In J. J. Dilulio Jr., J. Q. Wilson, et al. (Eds.), *Performance measures for the criminal justice system.* Washington, DC: U.S. Department of Justice, Bureau of Justice Statistics, and Princeton University Study Group on Criminal Justice Performance Measures.

Loughran, E. J. (February, 2002). Two parts to re-entry. *Council of Juvenile Correctional Administrators,* p. 2.

Loughran, E. J., & Godfrey, K. (2000). Performance-based standards for juvenile facilities: The wave of the future. *Corrections Today, 62,* 91–96.

Loughran, E. J., & Godfrey, K. (2001). *Performance-based standards: A system of continuous improvement.* South Easton, MA: Council of Juvenile Correctional Administrators.

Lubow, B. (1999a). Lessons learned from the Juvenile Detention Alternatives Initiative. In D. W. Roush (Ed.), *Crowding in juvenile detention centers: Practitioner perspectives on what to do about it.* Richmond, KY: National Juvenile Detention Association and Youth Law Center.

Lubow, B. (1999b). Successful strategies for reforming juvenile detention. *Federal Probation, 63,* 16–24.

Maloney, D., Romig, D., & Armstrong, T. (1988). Juvenile probation: The balanced approach. *Juvenile and Family Court Journal, 39,* 1–63.

Miesner, L., & Roush, D. W. (2003). *The prevention and reduction of overcrowding in juvenile confinement facilities: A close-out report.* Washington, DC: Office of Juvenile Justice and Delinquency Prevention.

Moeser, J. P. (1997). Implementing the balanced and restorative justice approach in juvenile detention. *Journal for Juvenile Justice and Detention Services, 12,* 47–52.

Moeser, J. P. (1999). Reclaiming juvenile justice for the 21st century: Balanced and restorative justice. *Reclaiming Children and Youth: Journal of Emotional and Behavioral Problems, 8,* 162–165.

National Commission on Correctional Health Care. (1999). *Standards for health services in juvenile detention and confinement facilities.* Chicago: Author.

Nitz, D. (1996). *The power of mediation and social skills training* (unpublished report). Kalamazoo County Juvenile Home, Kalamazoo, MI.

Office of Justice Programs. (2002). *The serious and violent offender reentry initiative* (fact sheet). Washington, DC: U.S. Department of Justice, Office of Justice Programs. Retrieved August 28, 2003, from http://www.ojp.usdoj.gov/reentry

Parent, D., Leiter, V., Kennedy, S., Livens, L., Wentworth, D., & Wilcox, S. (1994, August). *Conditions of confinement: Juvenile detention and correctional facilities* (research report). Washington, DC: U. S. Department of Justice, Office of Juvenile Justice and Delinquency Prevention.

Porpotage, F. M. (1996, July). *Training of staff in juvenile detention and correctional facilities* (fact sheet No. 37). Washington, DC: Office of Juvenile Justice and Delinquency Prevention.

Pranis, K. (1997). *Guide for implementing the balanced and restorative justice model.* Washington, DC: U. S. Department of Justice, Office of Juvenile Justice and Delinquency Prevention.

Previte, M. T. (1997, February). Preventing security crises at youth centers. *Corrections Today*, pp. 76–79.

Roush, D. D., & Roush, D. W. (1993, March 17). Holistic Environmental Life-skills Project: A public-private partnership to provide helpful services to youths in a juvenile detention facility. *Juvenile Justice Digest*, pp. 4–6.

Roush, D. W. (1996a). A comprehensive strategy for implementing the NJDA careworker training curriculum. *JERITT Bulletin, 7*, 1–4.

Roush, D. W. (1996b). A juvenile justice perspective. In C. M. Nelson, R. B. Rutherford, & B. I. Wolford (Eds.), *Comprehensive and collaborative systems that work for troubled youth: A national agenda*. Richmond, KY: National Coalition of Juvenile Justice Services.

Roush, D. W. (Ed.). (1996c). *Desktop guide to good juvenile detention practice*. Washington, DC: U.S. Department of Justice, Office of Juvenile Justice and Delinquency Prevention.

Roush, D. W. (1996e). Social skills training in juvenile detention: A rationale. *Juvenile and Family Court Journal, 47*, 1–20.

Roush, D. W. (1998). The importance of comprehensive skills-based programs in juvenile detention and corrections. In A. R. Roberts (Ed.), *Juvenile justice: Policies, programs and services* (2nd ed.). New York: Nelson-Hall.

Roush, D. W. (1999a). Helpful juvenile detention. *Reaching Today's Youth, 3*, 63–68.

Roush, D. W. (Ed.). (1999b). *Crowding in juvenile detention centers: Practitioner perspectives on what to do about it*. Richmond, KY: National Juvenile Detention Association and Youth Law Center.

Roush, D. W., Brooks, C. C., & Kielas, C. (1998). Accountability-based training for line staff in juvenile confinement and custody facilities. *Journal for Juvenile Justice and Detention Services, 13*, 85–93.

Roush, D. W., Christner, J. K., Lee, L. K., & Stelma, M. B. (1993). Implementation of social skills training in a juvenile detention center. *Journal for Juvenile Justice and Detention Services, 8*, 32–50.

Roush, D. W., Dunlap, E. L., & Rinella, J. (2002). Arguments against the incarceration of juveniles with adult offenders. In S. Decker & L. Alarid (Eds.), *Controversial issues in juvenile justice*. Los Angeles: Roxbury.

Roush, D. W., & Jones, M. A. (1996). Juvenile detention training: A status report. *Federal Probation, 60*, 54–60.

Roush, D. W., & McMillen, M. (2000, January). *Construction, operations, and staff training for juvenile confinement facilities* (JAIBG bulletin). Washington, DC: U.S. Department of Justice, Office of Juvenile Justice and Delinquency Prevention.

Roush, D. W., & Wyss, T. (Eds.). (1994). *Effective and innovative programs: Resource manual*. Washington, DC: U.S. Department of Justice, Office of Juvenile Justice and Delinquency Prevention.

Rust, B. (1999, Fall/Winter). Juvenile jailhouse rocked. *Advocasey: Documenting programs that work for kids and families*. Retrieved August 28, 2003, from *http://www.aecf.org/publications/advocasey/winter99/juv/juv.pdf*

Smith, J. S., Roush, D. W., & Kelley, R. (1990, January 14). *Public correctional policy on juvenile services: Juvenile detention* (committee report). Laurel, MD: American Correctional Association, Juvenile Detention Committee.

Smith, M. (1995, November). *Implementing mediation and conflict resolution in juvenile detention and corrections facilities*. Albuquerque: New Mexico Center for Dispute Resolution.

Soler, M. I., Shotton, A., Bell, J., Jameson, E., Shauffer, C., & Warboys, L. (1990). *Representing the child client*. New York: Matthew Bender.

Sprunger, B., & Pellaux, D. (1989). Skills for adolescence: Experience with the International Lions–Quest program. *Crisis, 10*, 88–104.

Steele, P. D. (1991). *Youth corrections mediation program: Final report of evaluation activities*. Albuquerque: New Mexico Center for Dispute Resolution.

Taylor, W. J. (1992). Overview of the juvenile justice system. In *Juvenile careworker resource guide*. Laurel, MD: American Correctional Association.

Walen, S. R., DiGiuseppe, R., & Wessler, R. L. (1980). *A practitioner's guide to rational-emotive therapy*. New York: Oxford University Press.

White, C. (2002, April). Reclaiming incarcerated youths through education. *Corrections Today*, pp. 174–178, 188.

Wildavsky, A. (1979). The self-evaluating organization. In H. C. Schulberg & F. Baker (Eds.), *Program evaluation in health fields* (Vol. 2). New York: Human Sciences Press.

Wolford, B., & Brooks, C. C. (1999). Juvenile justice education administrator: An occupational analysis. *Journal for Juvenile Justice and Detention Services, 14*, 87–98.

Wolford, B. I., & Koebel, L. L. (1995, Winter). Reform education to reduce juvenile delinquency. *Criminal Justice*, pp. 2–6, 54–56.

# Juvenile Court

## Bridging the Past and the Future

Carrie J. Petrucci and H. Ted Rubin

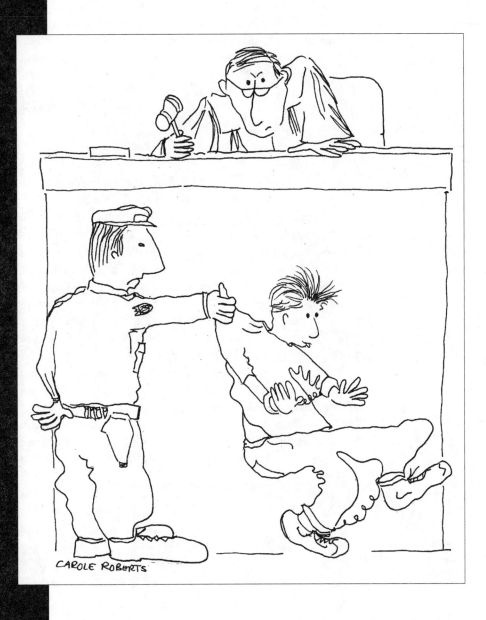

CAROLE ROBERTS

A typical case as described by a juvenile court judge in a juvenile drug court:

> A case is filed for abuse or neglect. In 75% of these petitions, substance abuse by one or both parents is alleged. Neglect or abuse of the children occurs in conjunction with it. On the first day it comes in, which is usually within 48 hours of the child being removed, we identify right up front whether or not there is a substance abuse problem. We identify the fathers of the children. We set up a blood test for children if a father's name is not on the birth certificate. We identify whether or not there are any relatives that are capable of taking care of the children. We do preadoptive home studies because we don't want to place the children in environments where they can't stay permanently if the parent doesn't comply with the court orders. We identify whether there are any special needs for the children. We order psychological exams for the children if needed. For children under age 4, we order developmental screens. We refer the children to Head Start or Healthy Start. So we do all that on the first day.

A typical day as described by a juvenile court judge in dependency court:

> At 7:00 A.M., I come to work. I have meetings every day at 7:30 A.M. or 8:00 A.M. that go for about an hour. These are with court-related people about administrative issues. Sometimes I'll have a meeting scheduled with a countywide committee for domestic violence or child abuse. There is always a stack of papers and about 50 e-mails to respond to. There are always people in line outside my office waiting to talk to me. At 9:30 A.M. I hit the bench, until about noon. I may get a 5-minute break. Then I have a noon meeting. Before 1:30 P.M., a few people come in and see me while the trials get ready. The trials start and go until somewhere between 3:30 P.M. and 5:00 P.M. Then I try to read mail in the middle of all this. I might run off the bench to take a phone call or make a few calls myself. I take home reports for the next day and anything from mail delivery that I couldn't read. It's about 200 pages a night. I spend around 2 hours preparing for the next day because there's no time at work to prepare since other things are happening. If I'm lucky, my trial finishes early, and I'll read the reports before I go home. Then I'll take other materials home, like articles.

A typical case and a more complicated case as described by a judge in delinquency court:

> *A typical case*: A 13½-year-old boy comes to court for an allegation of stealing—typically shoplifting. His family life is complicated. He is living with his single mom, who has three other children. She did not finish high school and has had a series of failed jobs and difficult

relationships. The jobs are all entry level and have not provided stable employment or a sufficient number of hours to include health and dental benefits. Her kids cause enough problems in her life that any employer tires of the interruptions to her timeliness and attendance, typically contributing to her losing her job shortly after getting it. It is the same with her living situation. She falls behind in rent or utilities and has to move. Her relationships are equally chaotic and disruptive: different partner, different rules in the home, inconsistent support and contact. She loses, and so do the kids. The frequent moves and chaotic environments wreak havoc with the school, and despite being in eighth grade, this 13-year-old reads at a fifth-grade level and is only slightly better in math. The circumstances have spiraled into suspension, which gets him further behind and more likely to be put in special classes or even expelled. He is now with the "wrong" crowd and has stolen a coat while at the mall. He is arrested, brought to detention, and released for court to answer the allegations and see what happens to the family.

*A more complex case*: A 13½-year-old boy is arrested for molest. He has had inappropriate physical contact with a 7-year-old girl that includes digital penetration and some indication of more intimate contact. It is discovered that he was molested by one of his mother's live-in mates at the age of 10 and that he has had some fire-setting activities. One of the mother's evictions was for a small fire he set in the hallway. It is further learned that he has a low-functioning IQ in the 65 range that the school system has neither addressed nor discovered. From the ages of 1 to 3, he was left alone for extended periods with little stimulus from his mother or others. Mom would leave him in a crib with a bottle of milk because she was busy with the other children—one older and one younger. Her live-in mate at the time was demanding, abusive, and controlling and didn't like this boy because he was not "his." At 13, he is very small of stature and seems to have a very flat affect, with little recognition of the seriousness of the situation or understanding of the process in which he is about to be a part.

Today's juvenile courts process well over 2 million cases a year. Estimates are that 61% of the cases are delinquency proceedings, which center on criminal actions committed by juveniles that would also be considered criminal if committed by adults. Another 19% are cases generated as a result of children being victims of abuse. Of the remainder, 16% are for status offenses, which are offenses that would not be illegal if committed by an adult, such as curfew violations or truancy (Ostrom, Kauder, & LaFountain, 2001). As the excerpts that begin this chapter reveal, however, often the line between delinquency and dependency cases becomes blurred in practice. Juvenile court cases include a complex array of childhood, family, and societal issues that continue to challenge the expertise of professionals working in juvenile courts.

The last century has seen considerable change in the structure and intent of the children's court. The court began as an informal process based on a social welfare model, emphasizing the best interests of the child. A focus on due process emerged in the 1960s with two key Supreme Court decisions (*Kent v. United States* and *In re Gault*) that emphasized due process rights for juveniles. Many credit this time period with the increasing "criminalization" of the juvenile court (Edwards, 1992; Lederman, 1999; Shepherd, 1999; Snyder & Sickmund, 1999). The 1990s brought an emphasis on accountability and punishment (Kurlychek, Torbet, & Bozynski, 1999; Lederman, 1999). The battle rages on as to how juvenile court ought to operate: on an individualized basis with rehabilitation as its primary intent, as it was originally conceived (Edwards, 1992; *The Janiculum Project,* 1998; Krisberg & Austin, 1993; Lederman, 1999; Lewis, 1999), or disbanding at least the delinquency portion of the juvenile court and creating an "integrated court" with the existing adult criminal court system (Feld, 1999).

The structure of juvenile courts also continues to evolve. In many states, juvenile courts have become family courts, handling all legal issues within the family, including delinquency, child welfare, divorce, and custody (Cooper & Bartlett, 1998; Whitcomb & Hardin, 1996). Many other types of specialized courts are being tested, such as juvenile drug courts and teen courts (Butts, Hoffman, & Buck, 1999; Cooper, 2001). These more specialized court environments are thought to have the potential to address accountability and punishment, as well as incorporate a rehabilitative ideal. They explicitly bring a network of treatment under the umbrella of the court to handle youths, dealing with mental health issues and substance abuse problems or merging adult criminal cases alongside child welfare or delinquency cases. Underlying many of these specialized court approaches is a practice-based legal reform theory called therapeutic jurisprudence (Wexler & Winick, 1991), which considers the law as a therapeutic agent, a concept consonant with the original intent of the juvenile court.

Many concerns surround the day-to-day operations of today's juvenile court. Primary among these are racial and ethnic disparities and discrimination, the criminalization of the juvenile court, and the rising number of girls entering the juvenile justice system (Sickmund, 1994; Snyder & Sickmund, 1999). African American youths in particular are disproportionately represented at all stages of the juvenile justice system, despite their minority status in the overall population. For example, in 1996, African American youths made up 46% of cases waived to criminal court (Snyder & Sickmund, 1999). The jurisdiction of juvenile cases is also changing. More and more juvenile delinquency cases are being waived, deferred, or legislatively mandated to adult court (Sickmund, 1994). The ongoing focus on making the juvenile court more like the adult system has brought close scrutiny to how well juveniles are represented in proceedings, with discouraging results (Burruss & Kempf-Leonard, 2002;

Dodge, 1997; Feld, 1988). The number of females involved in delinquency cases has also increased at an alarming rate (Snyder & Sickmund, 1999).

This chapter discusses some of these current issues and concerns surrounding today's juvenile court. The primary focus here is the juvenile court process itself as it relates to delinquency and child welfare populations. This includes discussions of the court's structure and intent, racial and ethnic disparities, and the more recent practices of specialized courts and therapeutic jurisprudence. A discussion of what juvenile court leaders had to say at the 100th anniversary of the court is also included. Throughout this discussion, it should be remembered that there is no "one" juvenile court type. Juvenile courts vary from state to state and from one jurisdiction to another within states. To the extent possible, a broad view is taken here, highlighting important similarities when they exist but stressing some important differences as well. For further reading, a list of Web sites for national resources for juvenile courts is included at the end of this chapter.

## ■ 100 Years of the Juvenile Court

The late 1990s saw numerous symposiums and conferences dedicated to discussions of the future of juvenile courts. Many juvenile court experts reflected on the purpose of juvenile court and how best to carry out the mandates of the court. Highlights of some of these discussions are presented here.

### The Janiculum Project Recommendations

In 1997, the National Council of Juvenile and Family Court Judges (NCJFCJ) convened 50 juvenile court professionals to discuss the court's strengths and weaknesses. The group's findings were published in *The Janiculum Project Recommendations* in 1998. The name is based on Janus, the mythical god of gates and doorways. Janus is personified with two faces: one looking forward and one looking backward, analogous to what the 50 experts were doing. Most notably, the participants concluded that a separate juvenile court is still needed to handle the special needs of children and families. Furthermore, due process should be the means by which individualized justice is administered. A balanced approach was advocated. This includes attention to the protection of the community, constructive sanctions, accountability, and competency development for youths. The mission statement maintains a similar focus on delinquency, dependency, and neglect, as well as on preserving and strengthening families. Specific recommendations were made in four areas: jurisdictional and structural, procedural, program, and system accountability.

Several of the areas discussed in the report—including the jurisdiction of serious offenses in delinquency court and judicial discretion in determining where these cases are heard, the unification of juvenile and family courts, the qualifications and ongoing training of judges, and the placement of juvenile court within the larger trial court system—remain controversial and are far from settled. Also hotly debated are the procedural rights of youths and families, including the right to a well-trained attorney for the youth and, in the matter of termination of parental rights cases, for the parent (Edwards, 1992).

## A Collaborative, Multidisciplinary, Individualized Juvenile Court

Leading juvenile court judges have also contributed to the dialogue of the future of juvenile courts (Burnett, 2000; Edwards, 1992; Lederman, 1999; Lewis, 1999). California Judge Leonard P. Edwards (1992) makes several recommendations to strengthen the juvenile court. First, he discusses the structure of the juvenile court. Juvenile court is often in a separate jurisdiction from other courts and is therefore relegated to an inferior position. This makes it difficult to attract competent judges, his second key area noted. Retaining competent judges is the third area. Fourth, a unified family court, which combines the legal needs of children and families in one court, could increase the status of the court, as well as counter some of the burnout issues inherent to dealing with abuse, neglect, and delinquency cases. Fifth, Judge Edwards calls for clarification of the purpose of juvenile law. He points out that one key purpose ought to be to contribute to raising children as productive citizens and another is the importance of strengthening families as a first response for children at risk. Sixth and last, adequate resources are needed for the court, its personnel, and the services needed by children and families (Edwards, 1992).

The cornerstone of juvenile court, according to Florida Supreme Court Judge Cindy Lederman, is to administer individualized case dispositions that emphasize accountability as well as the best interests of each youth. She sees the juvenile court as the "most effective prevention tool" in the juvenile justice system. However, the "adultification" of the juvenile court system that has occurred despite a concomitant decrease in juvenile crime in the 1990s has limited judicial discretion and authority, impeding a judge's ability to administer justice therapeutically and on an individualized basis. According to Judge Lederman, juvenile court judges can and must focus on three areas simultaneously: due process, swift and appropriate punishment, and rehabilitation. Furthermore, a juvenile justice response needs to be collaborative and interdisciplinary, with recognition of the relationship between delinquency and dependency and of how violence, substance abuse, and other high-risk behaviors can affect youths. Tomorrow's juvenile court must emphasize the need for interdisciplinary knowledge on the part of judges, to include expertise in assessment and child development; just knowing the law is not enough when intervening in children's lives. Judges must also be proactive in prevention and become involved in program evaluation that provides evidence for ongoing practice. A nonadversarial approach should be emphasized that focuses on the best interests of the child. Finally, the rights of youths can be protected without duplicating the adult criminal court model (Lederman, 1999).

Former NCJFCJ President Judge J. Dean Lewis echoes themes related to Judge Lederman's. In addition, Judge Lewis emphasizes an expanded role for judges that puts them in a more proactive role, as educators of the community and advocates for services for children and as responsible for recruiting and training other court professionals, including attorneys, guardians ad litem, and children's advocates. She, too, points out that judicial discretion has been limited because of misperceptions of juvenile crime. Successful alternatives to incarceration need to be child centered, family focused, community based, multiagency, and multidisciplinary (Lewis, 1999).

District of Columbia Superior Court Judge Arthur Burnett Sr. has a slightly different take, particularly on how to handle juvenile delinquency cases. Similar to Judges Lederman and Lewis, he, too, emphasizes that juvenile justice policy has been based on the public's misperception of juvenile justice, which overemphasizes the actions of the less than 10% of juveniles who commit the worst crimes. Juvenile justice policy for all cases should not be based on the behavior of the smallest proportion and most violent cases. Like Judge Edwards, he calls for more resources so that judges can maintain innovative and revitalized courts that achieve the purposes set out for the court. He also believes that children do require special protection under the law and that a judge, in addition to knowing the law, must maintain interdisciplinary knowledge on child behavior and child development and be sensitive to cross-cultural issues (Burnett, 2000).

Unlike Judges Lederman and Lewis, however, Judge Burnett advocates the use of blended sentences, which allow a juvenile court judge to simultaneously sentence a youth to both juvenile and adult sentences. Judge Burnett sees several advantages to this method. Substantial punishment can be imposed, rather than the proverbial "slap on the wrist," if a serious offense remains within the jurisdiction of juvenile court. If the decision to transfer a youth to adult court could be made based on his or her response to the juvenile court, this could create incentives for rehabilitation at the juvenile court level. The high cost of further incarceration could be avoided when youths respond to their juvenile court sentence. Further, if juveniles do respond to rehabilitative programs, society is protected from future criminal behavior (Burnett, 2000).

## An Integrated Juvenile and Adult Court

At the other end of the spectrum is Minnesota law professor and researcher Barry Feld's argument for an integrated juvenile and adult court to handle delinquency proceedings, eliminating delinquency cases at the juvenile court level entirely. In his view, since *Gault,* the current juvenile delinquency court has become a second-class criminal court that fails to provide rehabilitation and denies youths the same due process rights afforded adults. He sees the juvenile court's dual social welfare and punishment purposes at fatal odds with each other. According to Feld, the juvenile court has been doomed to fail not because of poor implementation or insufficient resources, as many have argued, but because, conceptually, social welfare and social control are an inherent contradiction and cannot coexist in the same institution (Feld, 1999).

In formulating his argument, Feld points out the deficiencies in two competing options: the individualized justice model originally conceived by juvenile court pioneers and a juvenile criminal court modeled after the adult court. Individualized justice was the hallmark of the early juvenile court. This concept refers to giving the judge wide discretion in handling cases so that the focus can be on the best interests of the child rather than strictly on matters of law. An informal approach to court proceedings goes hand in hand with the individualized social welfare approach. Feld argues that individualized justice fosters lawlessness because the treatment philosophy is without a scientific basis. Judges use their own discretion in decision making under this approach, leaving the court open to unchecked discriminatory judicial decision making. The rehabilitative ideal that goes along with the individualized approach is also meaningless, according to Feld, because in order to get services, youths must break the law, making the clientele of the juvenile court unsympathetic to the public and to policy makers. Resources will always be insufficient, he argues, because of public antipathy toward the poor, disadvantaged, and minority children and families that are processed by the court (Feld, 1999).

A juvenile version of the adult criminal court would not work, according to Feld's argument, mostly because it would be redundant and without a rationale for existence. If youths who commit crimes are going to be processed and sentenced in a manner similar to adults, then it calls into question the very notion of delinquency and diminished capacity due to age. Feld argues, if all the same procedural safeguards are to be put in place, then why would it be necessary to have a separate juvenile criminal court? (Feld, 1999).

Feld points out five benefits to an integrated adult court that handles all criminal matters regardless of age. Youths tried in the court would have increased legal protection. Juvenile and adult criminal records could be integrated so that young adults with serious juvenile records would receive more severe sentencing if they continued to come before the court as adults. A coherent sentencing policy with attention to chronic offenders could be implemented because juvenile records would not be sealed. Sentencing disparities associated with juveniles waived to adult court would be eliminated because all youths would be handled the same way. Finally, racial, gender, and geographic disparities due to an individualized approach would be eliminated (Feld, 1999).

An integrated court would allow the youthfulness of an offender to be taken into account as a mitigating factor in sentencing. Feld proposes two key components of a youth sentencing policy. First, he presents a rationale for less severe consequences for young offenders. Youths are seen as having sufficient cognitive capabilities to take responsibility for their behavior but not to the same degree as adults. Knowledge of developmental psychology, jurisprudence, and criminal sentencing policy serves as the rationale for less severe consequences. Second, Feld suggests a "youth discount" to sentencing. Based on a youth's age, he or she might be sentenced to 75% of the sentence allowed for adults. Feld maintains that correctional facilities should be age-segregated and that resources for self-improvement should be provided, particularly to youthful offenders, most of whom will eventually be released from prison.

Feld lists several virtues of his proposed integrated court:

- It could accomplish what blended sentences attempt to do but in a more consistent manner.
- Similar consequences would be given to similar offenders.
- Time-consuming transfer hearings would be eliminated.
- The "punishment gap" in which the same offense might get very different sentences in the adult and juvenile systems would be eliminated. (Feld, 1999)

## The "Public Health" Model Juvenile Court

Juvenile justice researcher Barry Krisberg suggests a very different strategy than Feld's outright abolition of juvenile delinquency court. Krisberg and Austin (1993) outline four key components of a reinvention of the juvenile court. First, they suggest making delinquency a public health issue. In so doing, they argue, a focus on prevention would result. Juveniles could be understood in a larger context of being victimized as well as becoming victimizers. Environmental factors could also be considered in a public health approach, as well as community organizing and self-help approaches. Second, a developmental perspective must be implemented, so that professionals are aware of how youth development affects their behavior and outlook. Third, better legal protection is needed for youths, including providing youths with real access to justice, improving the quality of juvenile judges, opening up proceedings to the public, and getting more funding for legal representation of youths. Fourth, they advocate treating the whole child, regardless of whether the youth has one or a multitude of issues, such as mental health problems, learning disabilities, substance abuse problems, extreme poverty, or status as a dependent of the court; resources must be shared and efficiently administered. Professional turf wars must be set aside, and the reduction of categorical funding for children's programs might be helpful toward this goal (Krisberg & Austin, 1993).

Krisberg and Austin (1993) make a key point to consider in thinking about juvenile justice. Most of us don't consider that "our own children" might ever become involved in the juvenile justice system; it is always "someone else's children" we imagine. Feld (1999) makes a similar point in his work. Juvenile justice advocate and practitioner Jerome Miller (1998) refers to this as the "we–them dichotomy" typical of the corrections field. All three pose the question: How different would the discussion of conditions in juvenile justice be if we imagined our own children before the judge rather than someone else's (Feld, 1999; Krisberg & Austin, 1993; Miller, 1998)?

As this discussion has shown, there are several areas of agreement across various juvenile justice experts, as well as polemic disagreements. Most experts agree that judges and court professionals need to take a multidisciplinary approach that includes knowledge of child development and child behavior beyond what is known about juvenile law. Practical applications of this knowledge is where experts differ: Feld sees a criminalized approach with lesser sentences based on age as a logical outcome, while the remaining experts see a rationale for an individualized social welfare approach to justice, permitting judicial discretion to accommodate both punishment and rehabilitative goals. A focus on due process is also undisputed. Whether it can happen within a juvenile court setting is cause for contention. Outright disagreement emerges on whether the juvenile court can handle both punishment and rehabilitation purposes. Feld vehemently says no, while many judges clearly state yes. These debates will not be resolved here but are likely to continue as future policy decisions mold the changing structure of the juvenile court.

## ■ The Court's Structure and Intent

We now turn to a discussion of some key definitions and to the structure and intent of the juvenile court, followed by a description of the stages of the court process.

### Juvenile Delinquency

Juvenile delinquency is a violation of state or federal law or municipal ordinance by a minor that, if committed by an adult, would constitute a crime. National standards call for a maximum age of 17 for jurisdiction with delinquency matters.[1] Currently, this is the most common age and applies to all states except Connecticut, New York, and North Carolina, which call for a maximum age of 15, and Georgia, Illinois, Louisiana, Massachusetts, Michigan, Missouri, New Hampshire, South Carolina, Texas, and Wisconsin, which call for a maximum age of 16. In many states, juvenile courts can maintain jurisdiction over youths past age 18 and up to age 24. Minimum ages have also been determined in 16 states and range from age 6 (North Carolina), 7 (Maryland, Massachusetts, New York), and 8 (Arizona) to age 10 (Arkansas, Colorado, Kansas, Louisiana, Minnesota, Mississippi, Pennsylvania, South Dakota, Texas, Vermont, Wisconsin) (Snyder & Sickmund, 1999).

The fundamental jurisdictional policy for delinquency, as well as for adult crimes, is a state matter that is not subject to a federal uniformity. Therefore, 16- and 17-year-olds in Connecticut are not considered juveniles, while their peers in Pennsylvania are. Within a state, however, the maximum ages for boys and girls must be the same.[2]

## Exceptions to State Juvenile Court Jurisdiction

### Waivers and Transfers

Not all offenders of juvenile court age are processed in a juvenile court. Three mechanisms exist to transfer juvenile cases to adult court: judicial waivers, concurrent jurisdiction, and statutory exclusion. Judicial waivers are the most common and can occur three ways: at the discretion of the judge, on a presumptive basis with the waiver assumed unless it is determined otherwise, and on a mandatory basis when certain criteria have been met. Concurrent jurisdiction is less common and refers to a case having original jurisdiction in both juvenile and adult court, with discretion left to the prosecutor to decide where to file the case. As of 1997, 15 states allowed concurrent jurisdiction. Statutory exclusion is also known as legislative exclusion and refers to cases that are defined in state law as automatically being referred to adult criminal court. As of 1997, 28 states had exclusion laws focusing on criteria such as use of weapon and a youth's "amenability to treatment." Thirty-one states have a "once an adult, always an adult" provision; any subsequent cases must be tried in adult court once a youth is convicted in adult court (Snyder & Sickmund, 1999).

### Native American Juveniles

Reservation-based Native American juveniles caught offending on a reservation are handled in tribal courts for misdemeanors but in federal courts for what U.S. law terms "major crimes."[3] If their offense occurs off-reservation, they are processed in state juvenile courts. Native American youths who live off-reservation are also handled in state juvenile courts.

### Federal Law Violations

Federal crimes committed by juveniles may be handled by U.S. district courts. Examples include mail theft, interstate transportation of a stolen automobile, and certain drug offenses. Recent federal legislation has made offenses such as juvenile handgun possession federal crimes. However, state juvenile courts still carry the fundamental workload for cases of this type.[4]

## Child Abuse and Neglect and Termination of Parental Rights

Child abuse cases include physical abuse, sexual abuse, emotional abuse, and neglect of children by their caretakers (U.S. Department of Health and Human Services, 2001). Anyone can report a suspected case of child abuse or neglect, including professionals who work with children, such as teachers and psychologists, as well as anonymous callers, including neighbors or family members. Often professionals are "mandated reporters," meaning they are required by law to report any suspected child abuse. Once a report comes in, it is investigated by the local child protective services (CPS) agency. However, in the case of extended removal from a family, only a juvenile court has jurisdiction to remove a child. When children have been removed, parents have a right to a court hearing within usually 48 hours (Ostrom et al., 2001).

Juvenile courts have recently come under considerable pressure to administer justice amid rising numbers of child abuse and neglect cases and dwindling resources. Just under 1 million child victims are reported nationally each year (U.S. Department of Health and Human Services, 2001). The role of juvenile courts has also changed, from focusing on determining whether a child has been abused or neglected and needs to be removed from a family, a reasonably short-term involvement, to taking a more long-term goal of assuring a safe, stable, and permanent home for every abused and neglected child. With the Adoption Assistance and Child Welfare Act of 1980, court responsibilities became more involved because of these long-term goals, the greater number of hearings needed for each case, the complexities of multiproblem families, and the numerous people involved, including the child or children, the parents, the foster parents, the attorneys, and a guardian ad litem or child advocate. Not surprisingly, many courts have had and continue to have difficulty in managing these difficult cases. In response to this, the National Council of Juvenile and Family Court Judges developed national guidelines for child abuse and neglect cases (NCJFCJ, 1995).

The guidelines identify five key principles to assure comprehensive and timely judicial intervention: avoiding unnecessary separation of children from their families by supporting families, focusing on reunification when children have been removed, finding permanent homes when reunification simply is not feasible, making timely decisions in litigation so children are not left in temporary situations for extended periods, and maintaining an oversight role over the case for the juvenile court, focusing on the CPS agency casework and parental behavior. As these guidelines suggest, one of the most important judicial concerns is to focus on treatment, rehabilitation, family preservation, and permanency planning (NCJFCJ, 1995).

Judges are encouraged to practice a "one family, one judge" model, also referred to as direct calendaring. Master calendaring, by contrast, refers to different judges being assigned to different stages of a child's case. Direct calendaring is believed to result in more consistent decision making because judges are more familiar with the complexities of the family situation, what the family needs, and the expectations for the family. Direct calendaring is also thought to make the family less likely to feel that a stranger who is not familiar with their situation is making life-altering decisions on their behalf. Judges may also feel a stronger sense of ownership. A one-judge approach is recommended because of the length of involvement the court might have with a family—often over a year—as well as the complexity of child abuse and neglect investigations (NCJFCJ, 1995).

All children under 18 who may need the court's protection come under the juvenile court's jurisdiction over child abuse and neglect. Characteristically, court jurisdiction over a dependent child will terminate no later than the 18th birthday. When additional time is needed to complete an education or if the youth has a mental or physical handicap, the court may retain jurisdiction until the 21st birthday.

Abuse and neglect cases may lead to court consideration of a petition to terminate a parent's rights to a child and to the child's adoption. A number of states give juvenile or family court jurisdiction over termination proceedings. Doing so has the advantage of allowing a judge familiar with the case to hold this hearing. In locales where termination hearings are held in a different court, the judgment will not be influenced by prior case familiarity.

The codes of numerous American Indian tribes provide for jurisdiction over abuse and neglect that occur on a reservation. The Indian Child Welfare Act, passed by Congress in 1978,[5] requires notification to a tribe when an identifiable Indian child with reservation ties or enrollment eligibility is brought into state court in an abuse or neglect proceeding. The tribe then has the option of either requesting transfer of jurisdiction to the tribal court or intervening in state court. There have been numerous appellate court decisions in this area.[6] Perceived state trial court noncompliance with this act is a major concern (Rubin, 1990).

## Status Offenses

Status offenses can be defined as conduct illegal only for children, or noncriminal misbehavior. Unlike a delinquent, a status offender has not committed an act that, if committed by an adult, would constitute a crime. Examples include running away from home, truancy, curfew violations, and underage drinking (Snyder & Sickmund, 1999). The distinction between a status offense and a delinquent offense did not enter into juvenile justice policy consciousness until the early 1960s. Before that time, state definitions of delinquency also encompassed what are now called status offenses, and status offenders were handled as delinquent offenders. In 1974, the Juvenile Justice and Delinquency Prevention Act "decriminalized" status offenses, making it illegal to put youths in secure detention for status offenses (Snyder & Sickmund, 1999).

The three most common status offenses—truancy, running away from home, and incorrigibility—constituted major court workloads through much of the 1970s (Murray, 1983; Teitlebaum & Gough, 1977). Currently, youths who commit status offenses may be processed by the juvenile court or by child welfare agencies, depending on what state they are in, making accurate counts difficult to maintain. In 1996, about one in five status offense cases was formally handled by the juvenile courts. This came to approximately 162,000 cases, with underage drinking constituting the largest percentage of cases (28%), followed by truancy cases (24%), other cases including curfew, smoking tobacco, and violations of a court order (20%), and runaways (16%). The juvenile court caseload for status offenses is on the rise, more than doubling between 1987 and 1996 (Snyder & Sickmund, 1999).

## Adoption

Many juvenile courts grant adoption decrees. Exceptions include the adoption authority of the separate nonjuvenile probate courts in Alabama, Connecticut, Maine, New Hampshire, and Vermont. Adoptions arise from several primary sources: (a) the voluntary relinquishment or surrender of permanent custody by both parents or the sole parent, (b) court-ordered termination of parental rights, (c) sole parent consent to a stepparent or relative adoption, and (d) privately arranged adoptions, some of which involve children from other countries.

## Additional Types of Cases

Some juvenile courts may handle such additional matters as juvenile traffic offenses, guardianships, commitment procedures for juveniles with mental illness or developmental disabilities, contributing to the delinquency of a minor, consent to an abortion or marriage, and paternity and child support proceedings.

## ■ Stages in the Juvenile Justice Process

Let us now examine the critical processing stages of the juvenile justice process: detention screening, intake screening, adjudication, and dispositions and treatment.

## Detention Screening

### Separate Pretrial Holding Facilities

A goal of early reformers was the creation of juvenile detention centers to replace adult jails for holding alleged juvenile offenders pending a court hearing. The intent was to provide secure care with specially trained child care staff who could assist youngsters, help evaluate them, and prepare youths for return to their families or alternative placements, as determined by the court. Medical evaluation, arrangements for medical treatment, and a school program were other features.

In American communities, there are hundreds of detention centers, many of them constructed along with courtrooms and probation offices in a juvenile court center located some miles from a downtown area. Detention centers can be administered locally or at a state level. State-administered facilities often serve a geographical region rather than a single county. Locally administered centers may house juveniles from nearby counties where no facility exists; payment is made for this service.

Rural areas and less populous communities frequently lack a juvenile detention center. There, juveniles are often housed in jails, either in a separate juvenile cell unit or, still today, mixed with adult offenders. Although serious efforts have been mounted in a number of states in recent years to bar the placement of juveniles in adult jails, perhaps 300,000 youngsters annually are held in these settings. Although regulations seek to ensure that sight and sound separation from adult offenders is provided for juveniles, the requirement is often violated.

### The Decision to Detain

Historically, police or sheriff's officers held the key to the detention center door. If these officials wanted a youth admitted, that youngster was admitted. More recently, detention screening, most often conducted by probation officers, has been inserted in the process. They review whether a law enforcement request for detention should be accepted. Juvenile courts serving populations in excess of 500,000 persons often maintain 24-hour, on-site detention screening. Other communities have this service on-site either 8 or 16 hours daily. In some communities, senior detention center staff perform this screening function. Elsewhere, probation officers perform screening part of the day, with detention center staff performing this function during night-shift hours. Another variation is the assignment of a probation officer to screen on an on-call rather than an on-site basis when the court is closed.

Typically, the law enforcement official hands in a police incident report when he or she delivers a youth to the center. The law enforcement agency is to notify the youth's parents to come to the detention facility to meet with their youngster and the screening officer. Sometimes a youth is releasable, but parents either are not available or reject release.

The detention screener examines the police report and may talk to the police officer about the offense. Age and county of residence are checked out, along with record information as to whether the youth is at present awaiting hearing on another offense or is on probation or parole status. The screener is aware of statutory criteria that allow detention; of court or departmental guidelines that help operationalize statutory criteria; of juvenile justice system norms as to who must, may, or shall not be detained; and of a preference for use of the least restrictive alternative when deprivation of freedom is considered.

The criterion on which most juveniles are detained is that the juvenile is dangerous to self or others if released. Less often used criteria are that detention is necessary to ensure the youth's attendance at court hearings or that no parent is available who can provide suitable care and supervision. Juveniles not released to their parents may, under certain circumstances, be placed in a non-secure shelter facility. A well-regarded detention alternative, home detention or home supervision, is in place in a number of communities, but youngsters more typically are placed into this close surveillance release program following a night or two in detention. With home detention, youngsters are on strict rules, leave home only for school or work or for other activities with parent or staff member approval, and are seen by staff four or more times weekly to maintain controls over the juveniles' activities. Detention screeners may decide that a drug- or alcohol-using youth should be taken to a health facility for special care. Youngsters presenting severe emotional disturbance may be taken to an emergency psychiatric facility.

Many youngsters, following police apprehension, are not taken to a detention facility. Further, police may or may not refer the youngster to the intake arm of the court for screening as to the need for formal court proceedings. About 25% of police apprehensions of juvenile offenders are handled by police, with the remaining 75% of cases referred to the juvenile court for further processing consideration (Snyder & Sickmund, 1999).

Increasingly, statutes provide that if a child is detained, a formal petition must be prepared within a very brief time period. Every state has now legislated that a detention hearing shall be held by a judge or other hearing officer within 24 to 72 hours of admission. The detention hearing reviews the need for further detention. As many as 50% of detained juveniles are released at the detention hearing. Probation officers who perform detention screening are often part of the department's intake division. Intake officers also play an important role in determining whether a referral shall be handled by formal court petition. (For a thorough review of the potential for abuse in detention decisions and the harmful effects of preadjudicatory detention, see the previous chapter.)

## Intake Screening

### The Decision to Petition

In making the filing decision, intake probation officers are often guided by very broad statutory criteria. A statute may provide only that a preliminary inquiry shall be conducted to determine whether the interests of the child or the community require further court action.

Intake is an office procedure, not a field procedure. The most frequently cited statement of the intake purpose is:

> It permits the court to screen its own intake not just on jurisdictional grounds, but, within some limits, upon social grounds as well. It can

cull out cases which should not be dignified with further court processes. . . . It ferrets out the contested matters in the beginning and gives the opportunity for laying down guidelines for appointment of counsel and stopping all social investigation and reporting until the contested issues of fact have been adjudicated. It provides machinery for referral of cases to other agencies when appropriate and beneficial to the child. It gives the court an early opportunity to discover the attitudes of the child, the parents, the police, and any other referral sources. It is a real help in controlling the court's caseload. (Waalkes, 1964, p. 117)

If the referral is not formally petitioned, the case is dismissed, redirected to another agency for service, or handled with an informal probation agreement that usually provides only limited supervision by probation staff. A variation is a consent decree procedure, where a petition is filed but a judge approves an agreement similar to an informal probation agreement. It allows dismissal of the petition following compliance with requirements over a 3- or 6-month interval.

In dismissing a case, an intake probation officer warns a juvenile that a further violation of law will be handled formally and bring serious court sanction. Depending on the seriousness of a subsequent offense and the amount of time lapse between offenses, the threat may or may not be exercised.

Knowledge of community agency resources is particularly important for intake probation officers. With lesser law violations and with status offenses, referrals can be made to different youth-serving, family, mental health, or other community agencies. Aided by federal funding, an extensive number of youth agency services were created during the 1970s to serve as alternatives to court processing. The term used, descriptive of the referral process, was *diversion*. Diversion could be either true diversion or diversion to minimize penetration into the juvenile justice system. True diversion meant that if a juvenile failed to follow through on the diversion referral, nothing would happen. Juveniles diverted to reduce penetration had a string attached: If they failed to fulfill the requirements of the diversion agency, the original charge could be resurrected and a formal petition filed.

In recent years, by statute or by practice, monetary and community work service restitution has been utilized in a growing number of juvenile courts as a strategy for informal case resolution. When a youth pays back a victim for losses sustained in the offense, a charge can be dismissed. Alternatively, as when no victim loss is sustained, performance of an agreed number of community work service hours can result in the dismissal of the charge. These restitution approaches are consistent with an accountability philosophy that holds a juvenile responsible to the victim—or to the community as the symbolic victim—for the injury that was done and sanctions a juvenile in proportion to the severity of the harm that was done.

### The Growing Prosecutor Role

Rising juvenile crime rates in the early 1970s precipitated another development that has affected intake screening substantially. By statute, by agreement with the court, or by assertion that their responsibilities include the intake decision-making role, prosecuting attorneys moved into an influential position at this processing stage (Rubin, 1980). Prosecutor entry has taken different forms, among them:

1  Intake officers make the file, no-file decision. With cases filed, the prosecutor reviews all petitions for legal sufficiency and accuracy. This is the weakest of prosecutor approaches.
2  An intake probation officer cannot dismiss or divert a felony charge without prosecutor concurrence. The prosecutor approves the content of a petition.
3  Intake probation officers recommend for or against filing; prosecutors must approve all recommendations. A prosecutor can dismiss a charge for which a formal petition was recommended or file a charge that had been targeted for dismissal or diversion. The prosecutor approves the content of the petition.
4  More serious charges bypass the intake probation office. They are reviewed by a prosecutor, with the expectation of a formal petition. The prosecutor may remand certain charges to intake for informal resolution. The prosecutor approves the content of any petition.
5  All police referrals bypass intake and go directly to a prosecutor. Decision making is performed by the prosecutor, who exclusively determines whether to prepare a petition for the court.

Prosecutors now dominate the intake-processing stage in many jurisdictions. It should not be assumed that prosecutors, by definition, favor formal petitions more than intake probation officers do. Certainly there are courts where prosecutor entry has led to a substantial increase in formal petitions. But prosecutors generally restrict formal petitioning for status offenses more than do intake officers, and they are not very inclined to bring a first misdemeanor offense before a judge. They do want serious and chronic offenders brought formally before the court.

In 1996, juvenile courts formally processed 56% of referred delinquency cases, a 78% increase since 1987. In the same period, formal juvenile court filings for drug law violations went up 183%, person offenses went up 121%, public order offenses went up 104%, and property offenses formal court filings went up 44%. There are also differences based on age of the offender. Youths 14 or older had 59% of their cases result in formal court processing, as opposed to 44% for youths under 14 (Snyder & Sickmund, 1999).

## Adjudication

### Implementation of the Right to Defense Counsel

Despite the legalization of the juvenile court, few trials occur. Probably fewer than 5% of petitioned juveniles undergo a trial, with its requirement of legal proof. The absence of formal trials is common to other courts as well; only infrequently do adult felony courts record trials with more than 12% to 15% of their cases.

Following the filing of a formal juvenile court petition, an arraignment or initial appearance hearing is conducted. Here, advisement is made of the right to counsel and to free counsel, the right to trial, the right to have witnesses in support of the juvenile subpoenaed, and the opportunity for the juvenile or his attorney to cross-examine adverse witnesses. Vast numbers of juveniles admit to their offenses at this stage, waiving the right to counsel and to trial. Others request counsel, go outside the courtroom for 5 to 10 minutes to talk with an attorney, and then come back in to admit their offense or request a continuance of the case to enable more extended investigation by the lawyer.

Most urban juvenile courts are serviced by public defenders who establish reputations as strong advocates for the juveniles, although their heavy workloads place real constraints on case investigations and time available for the conduct of trials. When the evidence against a youth is weak, defenders ask the prosecutor to dismiss the case, negotiate with the prosecutor for a favorable plea bargain, or go to trial. Trials are more commonly held when a juvenile faces institutionalization if found guilty, since for these cases prosecutors provide little plea-bargaining leeway.

Juvenile courts rely on the appointment of private attorneys to represent juveniles in the absence of a public defender system. Many of these attorneys provide good defense service, although the limited payment provided, together with the usual maximum payment lid, may discourage more comprehensive defense challenges. Some juveniles are represented by lawyers paid by their parents. This may slant lawyer performance toward negotiation and plea in order to lower the lawyer's bill.

Judges can reduce the number of trials they need to conduct by continuously appointing lawyers whose basic approach is to bargain with the prosecutor, avoid trial, and then argue for the least restrictive disposition. Other judges want rigorous defense advocacy and appoint lawyers who are not hesitant to go to trial or challenge the system.

The *Gault* (1967) decision required notification of the right to counsel and free counsel if institutionalization may occur. The decision did not require counsel, only notification of this right. Some states and any number of local jurisdictions have imposed a stronger requirement. New York law requires a defense attorney when there is a formal petition. Iowa will not permit a child to waive counsel from the detention hearing stage onward. A number of local juvenile courts, particularly those serviced by public defenders, mandate a lawyer for every juvenile. Almost universally, hearings concerning transfer of a juvenile to criminal court processing require a lawyer for the youth. Still, the extent of overall defense representation in many courts fails to exceed 15%.

The quality of defense representation is another issue. Though many defense attorneys perform extremely well in this forum, public defenders may be the newest recruits to that office, and private attorneys may have little knowledge of the complexities of the juvenile justice system that could be used advantageously in behalf of their youngsters. A study of the legal representation of children in New York State family courts entered discouraging findings: 45% of representation reflected either seriously inadequate or marginally adequate representation; 27% reflected acceptable representation; 4% effective representation; 24% of observations lacked sufficient information to be coded. Specific problems centered around lack of preparation and lack of contact with juveniles prior to and during a hearing. This research included courtroom observations and transcript analysis of both trials and other courtroom proceedings (Knitzer & Sobie, 1984, p. 8).

### The Juvenile Court Trial

The trial process is similar to criminal court proceedings except for the generalized absence of jury trials. Prosecutors present their evidence; defense attorneys cross-examine prosecution witnesses. The defense may impanel defense witnesses; the defendant may or may not testify. Prosecution may use rebuttal witnesses. The ruling is pronounced. Far more juveniles are found guilty than are found innocent.

Prior to the entry of the prosecutor into the juvenile court, probation officers sometimes performed this function—at a substantial disadvantage when there was defense counsel. Alternatively, judges awkwardly tried to elicit the evidence against a child and, when there was no defense attorney, also sought to help bring out a juvenile's defense. Today's lawyer-oriented system represents a significant improvement.

Probation officers tend to be present at initial appearance hearings, particularly in those courts that move into a dispositional hearing immediately following entry of a plea admitting the offense. In more adversarial juvenile courts, dispositional hearings take place from 3 to 5 weeks following the entry of the plea or the finding of guilt.

A notable development is the growing requirement that juvenile cases be processed speedily. These requirements, imposed by statute or by state or local court rule, mandate swifter processing time for detained juveniles than for those who are not detained. Speedy processing is sought in order to reduce witness memory problems, lead to a faster delivery of intervention services, shorten pretrial deprivation of liberty, or, alternatively, secure the removal of a juvenile from the community to an institution so that new intervention efforts can be initiated.

## Disposition and Treatment

### The Dispositional Hearing

Probation officers have a substantial impact on judicial or referee decisions that sanction a juvenile and set in place a "treatment plan." The social study, or predisposition report, is prepared by a probation officer, who interviews the juvenile and his or her parents during a home study, obtains a school report, contacts other agencies that have worked with the youth, and chronicles a juvenile's prior history with the court; victim loss statements are secured for monetary restitution considerations. Copies of the predisposition report are distributed to the judicial hearing officer and to prosecution and defense counsel. The report may be shared with the youth and the parents, a practice that is troublesome for some probation departments as the report may include critical comments regarding the parents and the probation officer's recommendations may be challenged. But this is good practice.

The actual hearing usually begins with an oral summary of the report by the probation officer. The rules of evidence are relaxed for this hearing: Hearsay statements are permitted, although, for example, when a psychological evaluation has been conducted, a defense attorney may require that the psychologist be present for cross-examination rather than rely on the written report. Psychological and even psychiatric evaluations are commonly conducted in larger juvenile courts with cases involving chronic delinquency, violence, sexual offenses, arson, or the appearance of significant emotional disturbance. Substantial weight is given to these reports, although the predictability of their recommendations arouses skepticism. Frequently, they point to the need for greater structure in a youth's life and recommend residential care to provide that structure.

Different courts have different dispositional norms. Urban juvenile courts tend to retain reoffending juveniles in the community longer than do courts serving less populous districts, since over time and with greater need the urban systems have developed more resources and institutional alternatives. Courts serving less populous jurisdictions "pull the string" quicker and send less serious delinquency cases off to state care. But everywhere, except for very serious offenses, probation is the first resort and usually the second as well.

### The Probation Supervision Function

Counseling is a major stock-in-trade of the probation officer. But probation is a mixture of many things and many styles. It includes warnings, rule clarification, humanized interest and advice, a search for probation causation, advocacy, examination of a juvenile's adjustment and achievement in various environments, connection with external individuals and agencies that might be of positive help, encouragement to undertake constructive experiences, surveillance checks, psychic probes, and more. Probation counseling is a theoretical melting pot that encompasses Freud, reality therapy, smatterings of each new therapeutic approach that has rippled through the nation (almost annually) for the past several decades, some sociological notions, simplified behavior modification, and common sense. Underneath it all is the strategy for the probation officer to gain a relationship with the youth and to serve as a model embedded in the child's mind and conscience, particularly at times of critical choices.

Relatively little family counseling is conducted by probation officers except at investigation stages and at moments of crisis. Juveniles and their families are referred to external family counseling and mental health services. A juvenile's education is an important focus: School counselors may be encouraged to transfer a youth to other classes that are more interesting or hold out the potential for greater success. Tutoring may be arranged. A youth may be transferred to an alternate school for youngsters experiencing difficulty with the regular curriculum.

Probation officers find jobs for youngsters, arrange summer camp opportunities, and facilitate scholarships for wilderness adventure programs. Drug and alcohol recovery services—residential, educational, and counseling—have been drawn on more extensively in recent years. Educational programs may be targeted at juvenile shoplifters.

In many juvenile courts, the frequency of probation contact remains largely intuitive. Juveniles perceived as needing more frequent contact are seen more often than other youths. More serious and more chronic offenders fall into that category. Many probation officers begin seeing new probationers either weekly or biweekly, tapering off to fewer contacts after several months if no special problems are evident. Juvenile probation agency caseloads usually are substantially lighter than adult agency caseloads, affording greater individualization. While some departments average fewer than 40 youngsters on a probation caseload, other departments average 75 or even 100 cases per officer.

A number of probation agencies schematize frequency of contact something like the following: New probationers are seen weekly or biweekly for 3 months unless there are indications that this extent of frequency is unnecessary. After 3 months, the frequency is reduced to a monthly basis unless there are indications that this is insufficient. The protocol provides for collateral contacts with parents, school, and other involved agencies on a declining frequency basis.

At present, there is considerable interest in a more rigorous approach to classification for supervision intensity (Gottfredson & Snyder, 2002; Griffin & Torbet, 2002). Assessment is an important step in this process. Assessing both risks and needs is a common approach to developing an appropriate supervision plan. Frequency of direct and collateral contacts is scheduled for minimum, medium, and maximum supervision levels. The juvenile's assessment point total presumptively places her or him in one of these supervision levels, but agency policy (as with a particularly serious offense) may place the youth in the maximum supervision level even though the point score would fall into a lower supervision class. And probation officers assessing the youth are authorized to recommend overriding the presumptive level and to justify this. This overall approach provides for periodic reassessment of supervised juveniles and then upward or downward movement in intensity level following approval by a staff supervisor. Well-managed departments validate their risk and needs criteria prior to initiating such an approach and periodically thereafter.

## Restitution

Restitution has become an important dimension of the probation experience. It is ordered in both diverted and adjudicated cases and for both first-time and repeat offenders. Initially realized in two forms, monetary restitution and community work service restitution (hereinafter referred to as "community service") are the most common (Rubin, 1988). In a recent nationwide survey, these two types of restitution were found in more than 90% of programs. A third type of restitution has also emerged, direct services to victims, occurring in about 40% of restitution programs (Schneider & Finkelstein, 1998).

Monetary restitution involves paying back the victim for losses or damage suffered. The actual loss amount is not always ordered. Statutes tend to provide that the actual total needs to be ameliorated by a youth's ability to earn this amount within a reasonable period of time. To help with repayment, enlightened juvenile courts have instituted job skill preparation classes to train youngsters to find jobs and hold them. Some programs have courted the private and public sectors for jobs where these youngsters can work, earn, and repay victims. Nationally, about 75% of ordered restitution is repaid, totalling an estimated $44.5 million based on 1991 figures (Schneider & Finkelstein, 1998). Juveniles who fail to make reasonable efforts to obtain work may be returned to a court hearing for review and possible sanction. And many youngsters complete all other probation conditions satisfactorily, but their probation term is extended because they have not completed restitution payments. A small number of courts use "sole sanction restitution" as a disposition with lesser offenses. Violators do not go onto regular probation caseloads; instead, the sole requirement of the court is repayment. With repayment, the case is terminated.

For community service, juveniles are ordered to perform a given number of work hours at a private nonprofit or governmental agency. Average completion rates of community service programs are as high as 88%, with an estimated total of 17.1 million hours of work performed nationwide (Schneider & Finkelstein, 1998). Larger communities have more than 100 sites where this work may be performed. The sites typically include public libraries and parks, animal shelters, nursing homes, community centers, youth agencies, daycare centers, and YMCAs. Youths may participate in supervised work crews in which groups of juveniles go out to a site and work under the direction of a staff member. Many courts have wisely developed a matrix that is used to require more hours for more serious offenses or offense patterns than with less serious offenders, a dimension of proportionality and just deserts. Again, failure to cooperate with the work program can result in a return to court.

Direct services to victims generally occur within victim–offender reconciliation programs (VORPs), in which trained staff bring the victim, if willing, together with the offender. The most common occurrences within these meetings have been the offender apologizing to the victim or negotiating a form of reparation, such as repairing damaged property (Schneider & Finkelstein, 1998).

A national evaluation found lower recidivism (24%) among youths who completed restitution than in youths who failed to complete restitution (46%) (Schneider & Finkelstein, 1998). Another study that compared youths with a restitution order versus youths with probation only found 32% of youths in the restitution group recidivated in a 2-year follow-up, compared with 43% of the probation-only group (Sudipto, 1995). Restitution is often studied in conjunction with victim–offender reconciliation programs. When comparing results from six VORP evaluations in California, five of six evaluations revealed a 10% reduction in recidivism (Evje & Cushman, 2000). A recent four-state study that analyzed victims' and judges' concerns about the juvenile court process found that restitution remains of primary concern to victims (Bazemore, Seymour, & Rubin, 2000). Restitution in either money, community service, or direct services to victims will probably remain a key component for juvenile offender accountability.

Now that the foundation of how a juvenile court operates has been laid, the discussion turns toward some of the current issues and innovations in juvenile courts.

## ■ Racial and Ethnic Disparities

Is the juvenile justice system characterized by racial and ethnic discrimination? This issue continues to be hotly debated among juvenile justice experts. Since its inception, juvenile court caseloads have consisted primarily of disadvantaged youths of racial or ethnic minority status who were also living in poverty. Initially, juvenile court caseloads included large numbers of Irish and Italian immigrants (Krisberg & Austin, 1993). Now African American, Latino, and Native American youths constitute disproportionate numbers at all stages (arrest, detention, disposition, and sentencing) of the juvenile justice system. In 1997, these youths accounted for almost two thirds of youths in the juvenile justice system that were detained and committed but only one third of the general population at large (Snyder & Sickmund, 1999). Do the statistics alone present sufficient evidence to suggest discrimination exists? An understanding of some key terminology is helpful as a first step in furthering this discussion.

*Discrimination* refers to being treated differently based on a group status rather than on one's behavior or qualifications. Discrimination due to race or ethnicity occurs when youths from one group are treated differently than youths from another group, based wholly or in part on their race or ethnicity. In other words, a youth's individual behavior is not the determining factor. It is difficult to prove that discrimination exists in any system because there can be many other competing causes present in juvenile justice decision making (Snyder & Sickmund, 1999; Walker, Spohn, & DeLone, 2000).

Discrimination can be envisioned on a continuum, with systematic discrimination, in which all decisions at all stages are characterized by discrimination, on one end and pure justice, in which discrimination is totally absent, on the other. Three categories of discrimination exist within the two extremes. Institutionalized discrimination suggests that rules or policies result in discriminatory outcomes for racial or ethnic groups, but this discrimination may not be intentional. An example is having an employment requirement for bail. If employment is less available to those of a racial or ethnic minority than to the White population, then the employment requirement becomes a form of institutionalized discrimination. The discrimination is a by-product of the requirement. Contextual discrimination refers to discrimination that occurs in certain situations. An example would be aggressive police patrolling in a low-socioeconomic area inhabited primarily by people who are racial and ethnic minorities. Again, this would result in racial and ethnic disparities, although this may not have been the original intent. Finally, there is individual discrimination. This refers to individual decision makers within the juvenile justice system making decisions that can be linked specifically to race or ethnicity (Walker et al., 2000).

Disparity refers to different groups having different probabilities for a particular outcome because of their group status. For example, minority youths are more likely to end up in a secure facility than White youths. It is important to note that the presence of disparity does not necessarily mean that discrimination exists. Disparity can be due to legal factors, such as previous criminal record or seriousness of offense, or to extralegal factors, such as race or ethnicity. Racial and ethnic disparities have been well documented in the juvenile and adult criminal justice systems (Pope & Feyerherm, 1995; Snyder & Sickmund, 1999; Walker et al., 2000).

Disparity can lead to overrepresentation of youths of specific racial and ethnic groups at various stages of juvenile justice processing. Overrepresentation refers to a larger number of youths of a particular racial or ethnic group being represented in the juvenile justice system than would be expected based on their proportion in the general population. Overrepresentation of youths who are African American, Latino, and Native American has also been well documented in the juvenile and criminal justice systems (Pope & Feyerherm, 1995; Snyder & Sickmund, 1999; Walker et al., 2000).

Where do leading juvenile justice researchers stand on the presence, absence, or degree of discrimination in juvenile justice? Walker, Spohn, and DeLone (2000) argue that prior to the Civil Rights era, the criminal justice system as a whole was characterized by systematic discrimination. Currently, however, they argue it can be characterized by contextual discrimination, which is one step closer to the middle ground than systematic discrimination. Other experts believe that racial bias "clearly exists" in some juvenile justice systems (Devine, Coolbaugh, & Jenkins, 1998) and that "racial status does make a difference" in decision making (Pope & Feyerherm, 1995). At the national level, Snyder and Sickmund (1999) conclude that the data are simply not comprehensive enough to be sure that discrimination exists, but overrepresentation and disparity are clearly evident.

Much of what is known today about racial and ethnic disparities in the juvenile justice system is a consequence of the 1988 reauthorization of the Juvenile Justice and Delinquency Prevention Act of 1974. This federal legislation brought the question of racial and ethnic disparities in juvenile secure confinement to the forefront by funding a national initiative on disproportionate minority confinement (DMC). Part of this research focused on analytic strategies to determine the presence of differential processing after an exhaustive literature review (Pope & Feyerherm, 1995).

The literature review found that disproportionate treatment at some or all decision points was evident in two thirds of the studies, with no evidence for disparity found in one third of the studies. In those studies in which disproportionate treatment was found, the effects were often cumulative, meaning that racial differences, even small ones, that occurred earlier in the process (at intake, for example) affected decisions at a later point in case processing (at sentencing), putting youths at an increased disadvantage as they got further into the system (Pope & Feyerherm, 1995).

Pope and Feyerherm (1995) developed two analytic strategies to pinpoint the presence of disproportionate processing based on the race or ethnicity of youths. The first strategy, referred to as the "simplified model," conceptualizes the juvenile justice system as a series of five decision points. These decision points were selected because they are common to virtually all juvenile justice systems, despite local variations. The decision points are listed next and, as can be seen, are structured as either-or (dichotomous) decisions:

☐ Decision to arrest: Decision to arrest or order to appear in court without arrest
☐ Intake decision: Handle the case at intake or submit the case for further processing
☐ Placement decision: Detain the youth or allow the youth to remain home prior to adjudication

☐ Petition decision: File a formal petition or use an informal resolution to the case

☐ Resolution decision: Resolve the case through probation or custody

This model is best understood graphically. Each of the five decision points for each racial or ethnic group can be conceptualized as a vertical bar, depicting how many youths from each group are processed at each stage. Dramatic increases or decreases from one decision point to another and across groups suggest differential treatment of racial and ethnic groups (Figure 11.1). Bars of approximately equal length across decision points in proportion to each other suggest a lack of differential treatment (Figure 11.2). Differential treatment, if it exists, can be pinpointed at particular processing stages by different trends in the height of the bars for each racial group. Shortcomings of this approach, as noted by the authors, are that it does not allow calculation of the odds of moving from one stage to another for different groups, nor does it consider how one decision point might affect another. Further, this strategy does not provide evidence for discriminatory practices; it merely highlights where disproportionate numbers of racial and ethnic minority groups exist as a step toward further exploration (Pope & Feyerherm, 1995).

The second analytic strategy allows the calculation of odds as well as consideration of a cumulative effect. In this model, a decision tree is built, based on the actual numbers of youths processed at each decision point, so that the number of youths in each racial or ethnic group is tracked through the multiple stages of juvenile justice processing. In this way, cross-comparisons can be made, and odds can be calculated. Again, this strategy

**Figure 11.1    Disproportionate decision making.**

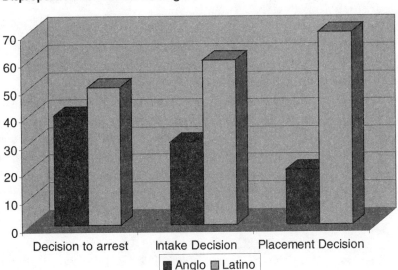

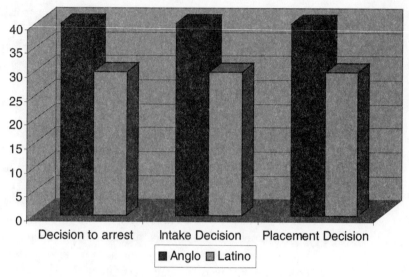

**Figure 11.2    Proportionate decision making.**

does not prove discrimination and only suggests where it might be present (Pope & Feyerherm, 1995).

Rates of overrepresentation can also be calculated by using a fairly straight-forward equation:

$$\frac{\text{\% of minority youths in juvenile justice population}}{\text{\% of minorities in overall population}} = \text{rate of representation}$$

A result larger than 1 suggests overrepresentation, a result less than 1 suggests underrepresentation, and a result close to 1 suggests a proportional representation. This calculation assumes accurate data on the entire juvenile population for a specified geographic area, plus the number of total youths in the juvenile justice population broken down by race and ethnicity. Practical application of this has found that accurate data of this sort are not always available (Devine et al., 1998).

Also part of the disproportionate minority confinement initiative was funding for research by five pilot states to assess their own systems and then develop and implement strategies to reverse any disproportionate trends that were found. A national evaluation then synthesized all the findings. All five states (Arizona, Florida, Iowa, North Carolina, and Oregon) found over-representation of minorities in some or all of the five main decision points. States then developed various strategies to counteract the disproportionate processing, including developing community-based programs for at-risk populations and focusing resources on the intake process, citing this as the most influential stage on disproportionate processing. Interventions that were advocacy-oriented, collaborated with community-based organizations, and developed alternative resources such as prevention and diversion were seen as the most promising (Devine et al., 1998). The importance of focusing on local solutions was also emphasized, since juvenile justice is administered at the local level. Conducting systematic data analysis at the local level, ongoing monitoring, and carefully examining decision points with evidence of disproportionality were all emphasized. Finally, if race bias is found, proposed strategies to eliminate it included staff training to address cultural issues, moving toward group decision making, and careful evaluation of decision-making criteria (Pope & Feyerherm, 1995).

Another important contribution of this national study was the analysis of contributing factors to overrepresentation of racial and ethnic groups. Based on interviews with juveniles in the juvenile justice system and their families, interviews and surveys of juvenile justice staff, public forums, and case file reviews, the following four interrelated domains were determined to be among the more important underlying factors to disproportionate processing:

- The juvenile justice system itself
- The educational system
- The family
- Socioeconomic conditions

Racial and ethnic bias was identified within the juvenile justice system, although it was not necessarily seen as intentional. A lack of diversion programs and culturally appropriate services for minority youths was also noted as a contributing factor in the juvenile justice system. The educational system was often seen as failing many minority youths on account of a lack of culturally specific approaches, as well as higher levels of minorities who were truant, suspended, expelled, and dropouts. The family was the most controversial of the factors. Family functioning and family composition were seen as contributing factors within the family. Single-parent homes and out-of-home placements were noted as occurring disproportionately for youths of racial and ethnic minorities, and this may contribute to their higher incidence in juvenile justice. Finally, poor socioeconomic conditions for many minority youths were also seen as a contributing factor. This included fewer job opportunities, low incomes, and lack of social opportunities. Each of these four areas was recommended for consideration in developing intervention strategies (Devine et al. 1998).

Overall, the most important finding from this work was that overrepresentation of minority youths is an important consideration in the juvenile justice system that can occur at any of the key decision points. In addition, the phenomenon is complex and not easily captured or resolved. Ongoing collaborative strategies are needed to continually monitor progress and maintain intervention strategies that address local needs (Devine et al., 1998; Pope & Feyerherm, 1995). One point remains clear: Disproportionate minority confinement characterizes the juvenile justice system at the national level and results in part from disparities that occur earlier in the juvenile justice system (Snyder & Sickmund, 1999). Causes may include anything from outright discrimination to differences based on rural-urban and suburban case processing, family background, or other organizational or environmental influences (Pope & Feyerherm, 1995). Continued research is needed to further delineate the extent to which overrepresentation is due to discrimination or to other factors and ultimately to ameliorate it through effective intervention strategies.

# ◼ Specialized Courts

## Drug Courts, Mental Health Courts, and Assessment

Concomitant with the focus on accountability that characterized the 1990s was the growing popularity of various types of specialized courts, including juvenile drug courts (Cooper & Bartlett, 1988), mental health courts (Arredondo et al., 2001), and teen courts (Godwin, 2000). Model courts for dependency cases that advocate a one-family, one-judge approach, as well as more efficient and effective case management, are also being practiced (Mentaberry, 1999). In general, specialized courts handle similar cases based on a particular problem or offense. They are credited by some with having the ability to handle the dual focus on accountability and individualized treatment under close judicial monitoring (Lederman, 1999; Lewis, 1999).

Juvenile drug courts and mental health courts are newest on the scene. As of 2001, there were an estimated 140 juvenile drug courts nationwide, with 125 more in the planning stages (Cooper, 2001). The Juvenile Accountability Incentive Block Grant (JAIBG) program administered through OJJDP supports the establishment of juvenile drug courts. Under the auspices of JAIBG, best practices are shared for planning and development of juvenile drug courts. Juvenile drug courts are intended to provide intensive substance abuse services to delinquent and status offender youths as well as to coordinate other needed support services. The primary purpose of juvenile courts is to hold youths accountable for their substance abuse behavior by eliciting swift, sure, and consistent consequences. Key elements of juvenile drug courts have been identified as:

☐ Establishing a juvenile drug court team that usually includes the judge, prosecutor, defense attorney, treatment provider, evaluator, and school representative
☐ Timely intervention after initial contact and ongoing status hearings
☐ A court-supervised program of substance-abuse treatment and other core services
☐ Treatment and service coordination
☐ Ongoing monitoring of the youth's progress

☐   Immediate judicial response to noncompliance
☐   A concerned judge able to respond sensitively and in a culturally appropriate way and who is also familiar with child development, substance abuse, and pharmacology
☐   A program philosophy that focuses on strengths (Cooper, 2001)

To accomplish these goals, certain enhancements to the existing juvenile court process have been recommended as follows:

☐   Comprehensive intake assessment with periodic follow-up assessments
☐   Integration of assessment information with case–processing decisions
☐   A focus on family functioning and how the juvenile is being affected
☐   Coordination between the court, the treatment program, the school, and any other support services
☐   Training all appropriate professionals involved with the court on adolescent development (Cooper, 2001)

It is still too soon to know the full impact of juvenile drug courts. Several areas have been indicated as promising, however, by existing programs: reduced recidivism, reduced drug use as evidenced by urinalysis testing, improved school progress, improved family functioning, and improved life skills of youth offenders (Cooper, 2001).

Juvenile mental health courts are even newer on the scene. According to Arredondo et al. (2001), the first juvenile mental health court began in February 2001 in Santa Clara County, California. This court represents the partnership between mental health and juvenile justice. The goal of the court is to identify and treat youths with serious mental health issues, thereby enhancing community safety through appropriate service provision for these youths. The target population is arrested youths who present with a serious mental illness. This includes a specific list of illnesses that are biologically determined. Eligible illnesses range from major depression, bipolar disorder, schizophrenia, and severe attention-deficit/hyperactivity disorder, to developmental disabilities and severe head injury. A multidisciplinary team, including representatives from mental health, probation, the district attorney, the defense attorney, and the court, oversees the treatment plans. The judge conducts periodic progress reviews at least every 90 days via court hearings with the youths. Youths are required to complete 1 year of probation. Termination of probation can occur if the youth commits another crime. This court was set up with existing funds and staffing. Case studies suggest the potential positive impact that appropriate diagnosis and service provision may have with this population of youths (Arredondo et al., 2001).

The onset of the first juvenile mental health court coincides with an increasing concern about mental health issues as a contributing factor to juvenile justice involvement. The Office of Juvenile Justice and Delinquency Prevention has recently launched a mental health initiative in which it is funding several

277

major projects around the nation that focus on assessment, multigenerational issues, and service delivery models (McKinney, 2001). One notable project in Chicago is focusing on the occurrence of alcohol, drug, and mental disorders among a random sample of detained juveniles and on whether youths received services while in custody. A portion of the sample will be followed longitudinally to document persistence and change in the disorders, concomitant drug use, violence, and HIV-AIDS risk behaviors, as well as services received over time. Preliminary results suggest that as many as two thirds of the youths presented with one or more alcohol, drug, or mental disorders. These data suggest that as many as 670,000 youth in the juvenile justice system nationwide may need mental health services (Teplin, 2001).

Community assessment centers (CACs) are also being developed as a means of early prevention and intervention with youths at risk of involvement with juvenile justice or youths who have been detained (Oldenettel & Wordes, 2000). These centers are intended to streamline assessment and service provision so that duplication of services can be avoided, conduct high-quality assessments of the risks and needs of youths, quickly link youths to services, and facilitate collaboration across agencies through information sharing. Four key elements have been identified:

1 A 24-hour centralized single point of entry or "one-stop shop" or, in some-cases, a "virtual" single point of entry in which several assessment centers with the same procedures accommodate youths across a wide geographic span.
2 Immediate and comprehensive assessments that focus on both risks and needs. Risk assessment deals primarily with public safety issues and what type of placement is best suited to juveniles. Needs assessments look at the problems and strengths of youths and provide the foundation for a service plan.
3 A management information system (MIS) is a computerized database system that tracks important information on each youth, including demographics, case processing, and follow-up. The MIS system is intended to monitor the progress of youths, allow analysts to look at overall trends, and share data across agencies.
4 Integrated case management assigns one case manager to coordinate and implement what was learned in the assessment process, create a treatment plan, monitor that plan, and conduct follow-ups as necessary.

The CAC model is in place in four sites and is currently being evaluated (Oldenettel & Wordes, 2000).

## Teen Courts

As of 1998, there were between 400 and 500 youth courts handling approximately 65,000 cases per year (Butts et al., 1999). Four years later in 2002, the estimate had risen to 800 teen courts nationwide that probably handled approximately 100,000 cases per year (Butts, Buck, & Coggeshall, 2002). Teen courts were based on the notion that if peer pressure can lead youths into delinquent behavior, perhaps it can also be used to turn delinquent behavior around (Butts et al., 2002). The underlying philosophy includes three key components: holding youths accountable, educating youths about the legal process to enhance their respect for it, and empowering youths to be active players in problem solving (Godwin, 2000). Teen courts are distinguished by the fact that most or all of the players in the court are youths. Youths take on the roles and responsibilities of judges, attorneys, bailiffs, and jury members. Youths referred to teen court are typically first-time offenders who have been arrested for nonviolent offenses such as theft, minor assault, disorderly conduct, alcohol possession, and vandalism (Butts & Buck, 2000; Godwin, 2000).

Teen courts vary in how they are implemented and at what stage of the case they occur. Four primary models of teen courts have been identified. The adult judge model has an adult as the judge and youths in all other roles, including prosecuting and defense attorneys, clerks, bailiffs, and jurors. Based on a 1998 nationwide survey, this model handled 60% of all teen court cases. The youth judge model is similar to the adult judge model except that a youth acts as the judge. This model handled 7% of teen court cases in 1998. The youth tribunal model has three youths on a judicial panel who decide the case; these courts handled 7% of all 1998 teen court cases. The peer jury model is similar to a grand jury panel in which youths on a jury listen to testimony and ask questions directly of the youth defendant. The peer jury model handled 22% of all 1998 teen court cases (Butts & Buck, 2000; Butts et al., 1999; Godwin, 2000). Teen courts may serve as a diversion alternative, actually adjudicate the facts of the case through a trial process, or determine only the sentence. Except in the case of adjudication, youth offenders must take responsibility for the offense before being referred to teen court. Involvement is voluntary. In the case of diversion, if youth offenders complete the sentence, the arrest is removed from their record. If they do not comply with the sentence, their case is referred back to juvenile court, as it would be with any other diversion program (Butts et al., 1999).

Most teen courts operate with sentencing guidelines that match particular offenses with a recommended sanction or sentence. Based on a 1998 survey, the most common sentencing component ordered was community service, used in almost all (99%) teen courts. Victim apology letters were the second most used sanction (86%), followed by an essay (79%). A youth offender could be ordered to serve on a teen court jury as part of a sentence (74%). Drug or alcohol classes were recommended in 60% of courts, followed by monetary restitution (34%). Victim awareness classes were ordered in 16% of teen courts, and driving or traffic classes were ordered in 14% of courts (Butts & Buck, 2000).

Teen courts are most often administered by the juvenile court or probation office (37%), followed by private agencies (25%), other types of agencies (19%), law enforcement (12%), schools (5%), and prosecutor or district attorney (3%). Costs are usually covered by state and local budgets. About one third of all teen courts utilize private funding but only on a limited basis. Youths involved in the court are volunteers. Most programs (80%) have a small paid staff that may include a program coordinator. Most teen courts (73%) operate year-round, and others are tied to the school year (Butts & Buck, 2000).

Teen courts' legal authority is informal as a diversion program within the juvenile justice system. As of 2001, only one state (Alaska) specifically mentioned teen courts in their statutes, giving them authority to determine guilt or innocence in a case. The vast majority of states did not mention teen court at all in their statutes. Seven states (Arkansas, Florida, Illinois, Kansas, Minnesota, New Mexico, Rhode Island) specifically mentioned teen courts in their statutes without indicating any procedures for implementation. An additional 14 states (California, Colorado, Iowa, Mississippi, North Carolina, Oklahoma, Tennessee, Texas, Utah, Vermont, Washington, West Virginia, Wisconsin, Wyoming) regulate when teen courts can be used and what type of cases they ought to handle (Butts et al., 2002).

Teen courts enjoy substantial support from others working within the juvenile justice system. In a national survey, 71% of program directors of teen courts indicated that judges were "very supportive." Court intake and probation staff were also very supportive (67%), as were law enforcement personnel (viewed as "very supportive" in 56% of responses). A National Youth Court Center was established in 1999 through funding by OJJDP. This center, administered by the American Probation and Parole Association in Kentucky, has been responsible for writing and distributing national guidelines for teen courts, providing technical assistance and training to new and developing programs, and also acting as an information clearinghouse by maintaining a nationwide database (Vickers, 2000).

The existing research on teen courts suggests that these courts have low recidivism, comparable to other diversion programs, but definitive research on the effectiveness of teen courts is still needed (Butts & Buck, 2000; Garrison, 2001; Harrison, Maupin, & Mays, 2000; LoGalbo & Callahan, 2001). OJJDP funded a nationwide evaluation of teen courts, carried out by researchers at the Urban Institute (Butts et al., 2002). Four sites were examined in four different states using four different models. At all sites, teen courts had been in operation a minimum of 3 years. Teen courts in Arizona and Maryland operated a combination of adult judge and peer jury models, the Alaska teen court operated a youth tribunal model, and the Missouri teen court utilized the youth judge model. Comparison groups were constructed for each site. Recidivism, defined as either another referral to juvenile court or an arrest within 6 months after the teen court appearance, was the primary outcome variable. Across all four sites, approximately 500 youths were followed in the teen court sample, and an equal number were tracked in the comparison groups.

Six-month recidivism rates in the teen court group were as low as 6% and as high as 9%; recidivism in the comparison groups ranged from 4% to 28%. Two sites (Alaska and Missouri) had lower recidivism rates than their comparison sites (6% versus 23% in Alaska and 9% versus 28% in Missouri). A third site (Arizona) had lower recidivism than the comparison site (9% versus 15%), but the difference was not found to be statistically significant. In the fourth site (Maryland), the comparison group had a lower recidivism rate (4%) than the teen court group (8%). This was believed to be due to the high quality of the diversion programs operating in the Maryland comparison site, providing as much individual attention and monitoring as teen court. Perhaps the most interesting distinction of the Alaska and Missouri sites is that the teen courts in each could find offenders guilty rather than requiring that youth offenders admit guilt prior to coming to the court. The authors hypothesized that youth offenders may have been more influenced by a process that gave this amount of authority and responsibility to youths (Butts et al., 2002).

The authors of the national evaluation discuss the fact that the actual mechanism or theory that can be linked to the effectiveness of teen courts has not yet been determined. The findings of the national evaluation are an excellent case in point. It cannot yet be clearly explained why one court might be more effective than another. Seven possible theoretical perspectives are proposed as models for further exploration: peer justice, procedural justice, deterrence, labeling, restorative justice, law-related education, and skill building (Butts et al., 2002). Harrison, Maupin, and Mays (2000) link the teen court explosion to another theory, therapeutic jurisprudence, which is discussed next.

## Therapeutic Jurisprudence

Therapeutic jurisprudence principles may provide an answer to the "how" of the teen court process, and the juvenile court process more generally, with its emphasis on how therapeutic interests can converge with justice interests, while still considering due process (Schiff & Wexler, 1996; Wexler, 1992). A legal reform theory that looks at how legal actors, legal procedures, and legal rules can affect therapeutic and antitherapeutic consequences (Wexler & Winick, 1991, 1996), therapeutic jurisprudence has been linked to adult drug courts and domestic violence courts (Hora, Schma, & Rosenthal, 1999; Keilitz, 2000; Rottman & Casey, 1999; Simon, 1995; Tsai, 2000), as well as to mental health law, criminal law, family law, tort law, and corrections (Wexler & Winick, 1996). An interdisciplinary enterprise, therapeutic jurisprudence calls for the incorporation of empirical research into the legal process to answer key questions (Wexler, 1992; Wexler & Winick, 1992). It also seeks to consider emotional and psychological well-being alongside due process considerations (Slobogin, 1996; Wexler, 1994).

For example, in their analysis of teen courts using a therapeutic jurisprudence lens, Schiff and Wexler (1996) emphasize how the teen court process can benefit not only youths who are defendants but also youths who serve as attorneys, judges, and juries. Through participation in the legal process, these youths may "inoculate" themselves against later law-breaking behavior because of their enhanced understanding and increased respect for the legal system. The authors recommend defendants serving on the jury or even as defense or prosecuting attorneys themselves as a "perspective-taking" exercise. By allowing former youth defendants to participate in another role, the stigmatization or labeling that the youths may have of themselves might be reduced, contributing to a more law-abiding self-image. They further suggest incorporating the use of a victim's attorney, preferably filled by a former defendant, as an emphasis on empathy training for defendants and as a therapeutic experience for victims.

These methods need not be limited to teen court. Wexler (2000) suggests the incorporation of a "relapse-prevention plan" utilizing a cognitive-behavioral approach and problem-solving skill building for all youths appearing in juvenile courts. With the assistance of a probation officer or social worker, youths would be responsible for developing their own relapse prevention plan that would include identifying the thinking patterns that got them into trouble, stating how they would change these thinking patterns, and coming up with a plan of what they will do when they encounter similar high-risk situations. They would then present their relapse prevention plan in a hearing before the juvenile court judge and a "youth advisory jury" trained in problem-solving techniques. This "youth advisory jury" would include volunteers as well as youths who had been before the judge themselves. Their advisory role would consist of asking questions about the proposed plan and suggesting possible flaws or improvements, under the supervision of the juvenile court judge. Youth advisory jury members who had been before the judge themselves could be very effective in spotting disingenuous or inadequate relapse prevention plans. Whether these techniques were used in the juvenile court or a teen court, a more positive problem-solving approach to the court process could be emphasized, rather than running the risk of emulating an adversarial court process that discourages acceptance of responsibility. Research could then determine the effectiveness of this approach (Schiff & Wexler, 1996; Wexler, 2000).

This therapeutic jurisprudence analysis is an example of how different questions are asked when the therapeutic aspects of the court process are considered. Taken broadly, therapeutic jurisprudence asks, How is the teen court or juvenile court process experienced by youths? and What impacts might legal actors or legal procedures have? The answers lead to a discussion of techniques, rather than simply asking whether teen courts or juvenile courts "work." The example also highlights the interdisciplinary nature of therapeutic jurisprudence and how it encourages the incorporation of techniques drawn from the social sciences—in this case, youth advisory juries and relapse prevention planning—to achieve outcomes that are both therapeutic and just (Wexler, 1992). Given the juvenile court's expressed desire for both accountability and rehabilitation of offenders, therapeutic jurisprudence may provide the lens through which juvenile justice practice and policy can be meaningfully understood and enhanced.

## Conclusion

The last 100 years of the juvenile court have called into question its very existence but have also initiated careful rethinking of the underlying assumptions and stark realities of juvenile court practice. Many judges remain committed to the rehabilitative ideal and its effectiveness, while also acknowledging the need for more uniform due process for all youths. Other experts disagree. The pressing concern of racial and ethnic disparities at all decision-points of the juvenile court process has been acknowledged, with the next important step being how to turn this trend around. Specialized juvenile courts focusing on pervasive drug problems and mental health issues are being tested as one method to simultaneously address public safety and the treatment needs of youths. Teen courts that put youths in the roles of judge, jury, and attorney are not new but are growing in popularity, though their effectiveness remains to be seen. Therapeutic jurisprudence may provide a useful lens through which to better understand and analyze not only specialized courts but also the dual therapeutic and justice goals of the juvenile court process as a whole.

## Discussion Questions

1 Can the juvenile court focus on both a rehabilitative function and a punishment function and perform both functions well? In developing your answer, consider other instances in which a person or an organization takes on both functions, and whether it was successful.

2 Do you think all juveniles under 18 years old should be handled initially in a juvenile court, an adult court, or both? How would you determine whether a juvenile case ought to be heard in adult or juvenile court?

3 Compare and contrast how a juvenile property offender's case might be handled in a juvenile court that utilizes a public health model, an integrated juvenile court, a juvenile court that utilizes blended sentencing, and a collaborative juvenile court.

4 Do you think juveniles should be sentenced to the same length of sentences as adults for serious crimes in which a victim is severely harmed or killed? Give reasons why or why not.

**5** Should juveniles with the same offense and offense histories receive the same disposition? Why or why not?

**6** How does a probation officer balance an interest in restitution to a victim with a juvenile's inability to earn money for victim repayment?

**7** What are the key decision points in the juvenile court process? How can individual decision makers avoid making decisions that result in racial or ethnic disparities?

**8** Consider the definitions of individual, contextual, and institutional discrimination. Give examples of how each might occur in a juvenile court setting.

**9** Define discrimination, disparity, and overrepresentation as they relate to the juvenile justice system. Give an example of each.

**10** Describe the four models of teen court. What are the advantages and disadvantages of each model? Which do you think would be most effective from the youth defendant's perspective?

## Notes

1  Institute of Judicial Administration, American Bar Association. (1980). *Juvenile delinquency and sanctions*. Cambridge, MA: Ballinger. Standard 2.1. See also note 8, National Advisory Committee on Criminal Justice Standards and Goals, Standard 3.115. Both sets of standards also recommended a minimum delinquency age of 10 years.

2  See the Oklahoma case of *Lamb v. Brown*, 456 F.2d 18 (10th Cir. 1972); see also *A. v. City of New York*, 286 N.E.2d 432 (N.Y. Ct. App., 1972). A New York statute that allowed status offense jurisdiction for girls to extend 2 years longer than for boys was overturned.

3  See 23 Stat. 362, 386 (1885), now found at 18 U.S.C. § 1153 (1994). However, prosecution of felonies, or major crimes, by juveniles or adults, that take place on Indian reservations is often not pursued in the federal courts. See also Thorne, W. A. (1993, September 18–22). *An assessment of the problems confronting tribal and state courts in the quest for improved relationships*. Paper presented at the Leadership Conference to Develop a National Agenda to Reduce Jurisdictional Disputes Between Tribal, State, and Federal Courts, National Center for State Courts, Santa Fe, NM.

4  Violent Crime Control and Law Enforcement Act, Public Law 103-322, 108 Stat. 1796, § 150001 (1994).

5  Indian Child Welfare Act, 25 U.S.C. § 1901 (1978).

6  *Mississippi Band of Choctaw Indians v. Holyfield*, 109 S. Ct. 1597 (1989); *Matter of Custody of S.E.G.*, 541 N.W.2d 357 (Minn. 1994).

## Juvenile Court Web Sites

*Government Agencies and Research*

National Criminal Justice Reference Service
   http://www.ncjrs.org

National Center for State Courts
    http://www.ncsconline.org/
Office of Juvenile Justice and Delinquency Prevention
    http://www.ojjdp.ncjrs.org

### Other Web Sites

ABA Center on Children and the Law
    http://www.abanet.org/child/
American Judges Association
    http://aja.ncsc.dni.us
National Center for Youth Law
    http://www.youthlaw.org
National Council of Juvenile and Family Court Judges
    http://www.ncjfcj.org
National Youth Court Center
    http://www.youthcourt.net
Office of Justice Programs, U.S. Department of Justice
    http://www.ojp.usdoj.gov
Therapeutic Jurisprudence
    http://www.therapeuticjurisprudence.org

## References

Arredondo, D. E., Kumli, K., Soto, L., Colin, E., Ornellas, J., Davilla Jr., R. J., et al. (2001). Juvenile mental health court: Rationale and protocols. *Juvenile and Family Court Journal 52*, 1–19.

Bazemore, G., Seymour, A., & Rubin, T. (2000). *Victims, judges, and juvenile court reform through restorative justice*. Washington, DC: U.S. Department of Justice, Office of Justice Programs, Office for Victims of Crime.

Burnett Sr., A. L. (2000). What of the future? Envisioning an effective juvenile court. *Criminal Justice Magazine 15*, 1. Retrieved August 28, 2003, from http://www.abanet.org/crimjust/cjmag/15-1/burnett.html

Burruss Jr., B. W., & Kempf-Leonard, K. (2002). Questionable advantage of defense counsel in juvenile court. *Justice Quarterly 19*, 1, 37–68.

Butts, J. A., & Buck, J. (2000). *Teen courts: A focus on research* (NCJ 183472). Washington, DC: U.S. Department of Justice, Office of Justice Programs, Office of Juvenile Justice and Delinquency Prevention.

Butts, J. A., Buck, J., & Coggeshall, M. B. (2002). *The impact of teen court on young offenders*. Washington, DC: Urban Institute.

Butts, J. A., Hoffman, D., & Buck, J. (1999). *OJJDP fact sheet: Teen courts in the United States: A profile of current programs* (FS-99118). Washington, DC: U.S. Department of Justice, Office of Justice Programs, Office of Juvenile Justice and Delinquency Prevention.

Cooper, C. S. (2001). Juvenile Drug Court Programs. (NCJ 184744). Washington, DC: U.S. Department of Justice, Office of Justice Programs, Office of Juvenile Justice and Delinquency Prevention.

Cooper, C. S., & Bartlett, S. (1998). *Juvenile and family drug courts: Profile of program characteristics and implementation issues* (NCJ 171142). Washington, DC: U.S. Department of Justice, Office of Justice Programs.

Devine, P., Coolbaugh, K., & Jenkins, S. (1998). *OJJDP juvenile justice bulletin. Disproportionate minority confinement: Lessons learned from five states* (NCJ 173420). Washington, DC: U.S. Department of Justice, Office of Justice Programs, Office of Juvenile Justice and Delinquency Prevention.

Dodge, D. C. (1997). *Fact sheet 49: Due process advocacy* (FS-9749). Washington, DC: U.S. Department of Justice, Office of Justice Programs, Office of Juvenile Justice and Delinquency Prevention.

Edwards, L. E. (1992). The juvenile court and the role of the juvenile court judge. *Juvenile and Family Court Journal, 43,* 2, 1–45.

Evje, A., & Cushman, R. C. (2000). *A summary of the evaluations of six California victim offender reconciliation programs.* Sacramento, CA: Judicial Council of California, Center for Families, Children and the Courts.

Feld, B. C. (1988). *In re Gault* revisited: A cross-state comparison of the right to counsel in juvenile court. *Crime and Delinquency, 34,* 393–424.

Feld, B. C. (1999). *Bad kids: Race and the transformation of the juvenile court.* New York: Oxford University Press.

Garrison, A. H. (2001). An evaluation of a Delaware teen court. *Juvenile and Family Court Journal, 52*(3), 11–21.

Godwin, T. M. (1996). *OJJDP fact sheet 45: A guide for implementing teen court programs.* Washington, DC: U.S. Department of Justice, Office of Justice Programs, Office of Juvenile Justice and Delinquency Prevention.

Godwin, T. M. (2000). *National youth court guidelines.* Washington, DC: U.S. Department of Justice, Office of Justice Programs, Office of Juvenile Justice and Delinquency Prevention.

Gottfredson, D. M., & Snyder, H. N. (2002). *OJJDP fact sheet 2: Statistical approaches to assessing risk.* Washington, DC: U.S. Department of Justice, Office of Justice Programs, Office of Juvenile Justice and Delinquency Prevention.

Griffin, P., & Torbet, P. (Eds.). (2002). *Desktop guide to good juvenile probation practice: Mission-driven, performance based, outcome-focused.* Washington, DC: National Center for Juvenile Justice.

Harrison, P., Maupin, J. R., & Mays, G. L. (2000). Are teen courts an answer to our juvenile delinquency problems? *Juvenile and Family Court Journal, 51,* 27–35.

Hora, P. F., Schma, W. G., & Rosenthal, J.T.A. (1999). Therapeutic jurisprudence and the drug treatment court movement: Revolutionizing the criminal justice system's response to drug abuse and crime in America. *Notre Dame Law Review, 74,* 439.

The Janiculum project: Reviewing the past and looking toward the future of the juvenile court (1998, September 28–October 1). Sponsored by the National Council of Juvenile and Family Court Judges, Reno, NV.

Keilitz, S. (2000). *Specialization of domestic violence case management in the courts: A national survey.* Williamsburg, VA: National Center for State Courts.

Knitzer, J., & Sobie, M. (1984). *Law guardians in New York state: A study of the legal representation of children.* New York: New York State Bar Association.

Krisberg, B., & Austin, J. F. (1993). *Reinventing juvenile justice.* Newbury Park, CA: Sage.

Kurlychek, M., Torbet, P., & Bozynski, M. (1999). *Focus on accountability: Best practices for juvenile court and probation* (NCJ 177611). Washington, DC: U.S. Department of Justice, Office of Justice Programs, Office of Juvenile Justice and Delinquency Prevention.

Lederman, C. S. (1999). The juvenile court: Putting research to work for prevention. *Juvenile Justice, 6*(2), 22–31.

Lewis, J. D. (1999). An evolving juvenile court: On the front lines with Judge J. Dean Lewis. *Juvenile Justice, 6*(2), 3–12.

LoGalbo, A. P., & Callahan, C. M. (2001). An evaluation of a teen court as a juvenile crime diversion program. *Juvenile and Family Court Journal, 52*(2), 1–11.

McKinney, K. (2001). *OJJDP fact sheet 30: OJJDP mental health initiatives* (FS-200130). Washington, DC: U.S. Department of Justice, Office of Justice Programs, Office of Juvenile Justice and Delinquency Prevention.

Mentaberry, M. (1999). *Model courts serve abused and neglected children* (OJJDP fact sheet 90). Washington, DC: U.S. Department of Justice, Office of Justice Programs, Office of Juvenile Justice and Delinquency Prevention.

Miller, J. G. (1998). *Last one over the wall: The Massachusetts experiment in closing reform schools* (2nd ed.). Columbus: Ohio State University Press.

Murray, J. P. (1983). *Status offenders: A sourcebook.* Boys Town, NE: Boys Town Center.

National Council of Juvenile and Family Court Judges. (1995). *Resource guidelines: Improving court practice in child abuse and neglect cases.* Reno, NV: Author.

Oldenettel, D., & Wordes, M. (2000). *OJJDP juvenile justice bulletin: The community assessment concept* (NCJ 178942). Washington, DC: U.S. Department of Justice, Office of Justice Programs, Office of Juvenile Justice and Delinquency Prevention.

Ostrom, B. J., Kauder, N. B., & LaFountain, R. C. (2001). *Examining the work of state courts, 2001.* Williamsburg, VA: National Center for State Courts.

Pope, C. E., & Feyerherm, W. (1995). Minorities and the juvenile justice system: Research summary. Washington, DC: U.S. Department of Justice, Office of Justice Programs, Office of Juvenile Justice and Delinquency Prevention.

Rottman, D. B., & Casey, P. (1999, July). Therapeutic jurisprudence and the emergence of problem-solving courts. *NIJ Journal,* pp. 12–19.

Rubin, H. T. (1980). The emerging prosecutor dominance of the juvenile court intake process. *Crime and Delinquency, 26*(3), 299–318.

Rubin, H. T. (1988). Fulfilling juvenile restitution requirements in community correctional programs. *Federal Probation, 52*(3), 32–42.

Rubin, H. T. (1990). Tribal courts and state courts: Disputed civil jurisdiction concerns and steps toward resolution. *State Court Journal 14,* 9–15.

Schiff, A. R., & Wexler, D. B. (1996). Teen court: A therapeutic jurisprudence perspective. *Criminal Law Bulletin, 32*(4), 342–357.

Schneider, P. R., & Finkelstein, M. C. (1998). *RESTTA national directory of restitution and community service programs* (NCJ 166365). Bethesda, MD: Pacific Institute for Research and Evaluation. Retrieved August 28, 2003, from http://ojjdp.ncjrs.org/pubs/restta/index.html

Shepherd Jr., R. E. (1999). The juvenile court at 100 years: A look back. *Juvenile Justice, 6*(2), 13–21.

Sickmund, M. (1994). *Juvenile justice bulletin: How juveniles get to criminal court* (NCJ 150309). Washington, DC: U.S. Department of Justice, Office of Justice Programs, Office of Juvenile Justice and Delinquency Prevention.

Simon, L. M. J. (1995). A therapeutic jurisprudence approach to the legal processing of domestic violence cases. *Psychology, Public Policy and Law, 1*(1), 43–79.

Slobogin, C. (1996). Therapeutic jurisprudence: Five dilemmas to ponder. In D. B. Wexler & B. J. Winick (Eds.), *Law in a therapeutic key: Developments in therapeutic jurisprudence* (pp. 763–794). Durham, NC: Carolina Academic Press.

Snyder, H. N., & Sickmund, M. (1999). *Juvenile offenders and victims: 1999 national report.* Washington, DC: Office of Juvenile Justice and Delinquency Prevention.

Sudipto, R. (1995). Juvenile restitution and recidivism in a midwestern county. *Federal Probation, 59*(1), 55–63.

Teitelbaum, L. E., & Gough, A. R. (1977). *Beyond control: Status offenders in the juvenile court.* Cambridge, MA: Ballinger.

Teplin, L. A. (2001). *OJJDP fact sheet 02: Assessing alcohol, drug, and mental disorders in juvenile detainees* (FS-200102). Washington, DC: U.S. Department of Justice, Office of Justice Programs, Office of Juvenile Justice and Delinquency Prevention.

Tsai, B. (2000). Note: The trend toward specialized domestic violence courts: Improvements on an effective innovation. *Fordham Law Review, 68,* 1285–1327.

U.S. Department of Heath and Human Services, Administration on Children, Youth and Families. (2001). *Child maltreatment 1999*. Washington, DC: U.S. Government Printing Office.

Vickers, M. (2000). *OJJDP fact sheet 07: National youth court center*. Washington, DC: U.S. Department of Justice, Office of Justice Programs, Office of Juvenile Justice Delinquency Prevention.

Waalkes, W. (1964). Juvenile court intake: A unique and valuable tool. *Crime and Delinquency, 10*(2), 117–123.

Walker, S., Spohn, C., & DeLone, M. (2000). *The color of justice: Race, ethnicity, and crime in America* (2nd ed.). Scarborough, Ontario, Canada: Wadsworth.

Wexler, D. B. (1992). Justice, mental health, and therapeutic jurisprudence. *Cleveland State Law Review, 40*(¾), 517–526.

Wexler, D. B. (1994). An orientation to therapeutic jurisprudence. *New England Journal on Criminal and Civil Confinement, 20*, 259–264.

Wexler, D. B. (2000). Just some juvenile thinking about delinquent behavior: A therapeutic jurisprudence approach to relapse prevention planning and youth advisory juries. *University of Missouri at Kansas City Law Review, 69*, 93–105.

Wexler, D. B., & Winick, B. J. (1991). *Essays in therapeutic jurisprudence*. Durham, NC: Carolina Academic Press.

Wexler, D. B., & Winick, B. J. (1992). Therapeutic jurisprudence and criminal justice mental health issues. *Mental and Physical Disability Law Reporter, 16*(2), 225–231.

Wexler, D. B., & Winick, B. J. (1996). *Law in a therapeutic key: Developments in therapeutic jurisprudence*. Durham, NC: Carolina Academic Press.

Whitcomb, D., & Hardin, M. (1996). *Coordinating criminal and juvenile court proceedings in child maltreatment cases*. Washington, DC: U.S. Department of Justice, Office of Justice Programs, Office of Juvenile Justice and Delinquency Prevention.

## Cases

*A. v. City of New York*, 286 N.E.2d 432 (N.Y. Ct. App., 1972).

*In re Gault*, 387 U.S. 1 (1967).

*Kent v. United States*, 383 U.S. 541 (1966).

*Lamb v. Brown*, 456 F.2d 18 (10th Cir. 1972).

Matter of Custody of S.E.G., 541 N.W.2d 357 (Minn. 1994).

*Mississippi Band of Choctaw Indians v. Holyfield*, 109 S. Ct. 1597 (1989).

# 12 Mental Illness and Juvenile Offending

Lisa Rapp-Palicchi and Albert R. Roberts

**Psychologist, social worker, and school principal—Mental health team meeting with juvenile offender, N.J. Training School**

One of the most overlooked areas of juvenile justice practice is the assessment, treatment, and research of juvenile offenders with mental disorders, particularly comorbid psychiatric disorders. The interest in intervening on behalf of juvenile offenders with emotional and behavioral disorders began in the early 1900s. As discussed in the historical chapter on the juvenile court and probation services, the point of departure is the first juvenile court clinic established in 1909 in Cook County, Illinois, by a psychiatrist, William Healy. By the mid-1920s, eight additional child guidance clinics had been developed in close collaboration with local juvenile courts in major cities throughout the United States. Prior to the child guidance and juvenile court clinic movement, most inner-city troubled juveniles were being sent to adult prisons or were wandering the streets, rejected by families and society. The efforts from psychiatric social workers, child advocates, legislators, and judges helped begin the child guidance movement, which established clinics and worked in conjunction with juvenile courts to assist juveniles and their families (Roberts, 1998; Thomas & Penn, 2002). By the 1950s there were more than 600 child guidance clinics throughout the United States (Roberts, 1998). Unfortunately, the child guidance clinics in the large cities were integrated with the juvenile courts, while the smaller and medium-sized city clinics and courts rarely coordinated rehabilitation efforts. Juveniles were removed from adult prisons, and judges, working with police and social workers, attempted to help without the use of incarceration. More than 100 years later, we are still facing the same problem: Delinquent and mentally ill youths are often not given the comprehensive case management services they so desperately need. Instead of rehabilitating youths, society often punishes, detains, incarcerates, and in some instances sentences repeat juvenile offenders to death. Fortunately, over the past 100 years, we have substantially increased our knowledge about the nexus between juvenile offending and mental illness. This knowledge should assist advocates, administrators, and legislators in funding more appropriate evidence-based mental health services to these youths and their families in the important years ahead. This chapter discusses the scope of the problem, the relationship between juvenile offending and mental illness, assessment tools, and both effective and contraindicated, even harmful, interventions for juvenile offenders.

## ■ Scope of the Problem

There is a growing recognition that youths who are placed and served in the juvenile justice system have multiple and complex problems beyond delinquent and aggressive behaviors. In many communities throughout North America, research estimates have indicated that the majority of juvenile offenders have one or more diagnosed or undiagnosed mental disorders. In fact, recent studies indicate that at least two thirds of juvenile detainees have one or more mental disorders (Teplin, Abram, McClelland, Dulcan, & Mericle, 2002) and as many as 20% have a severe disorder (MacKinnon-Lewis, Kaufman, & Frabutt, 2002). Specifically, Pliszka, Sherman, Barrow, and Irick (2000) found that 15% to 42% of detained youths had major affective disorders, such as bipolar disorder and depression. In another study, 40% of males and females met criteria for disruptive behavior disorders. Cauffman, Feldman, Waterman, and Steiner (1998) found that female juvenile delinquents were nearly 6 times more likely to suffer from PTSD, both currently and at some time in their lives, than the general population and were 50% more likely to exhibit current symptoms of PTSD than male delinquents. Other research indicates a strong correlation between violent and homicidal juvenile offenders and psychotic disorders. For example, a study evaluating juvenile murderers indicated that up to 96% of the youths met criteria for at least one diagnosis, and 71% had a history of psychotic symptoms (Myers, Scott, Burgess, & Burgess, 1995). According to a study by McGarvey and Waite (2000), 40% of incarcerated youths met the criteria to receive special education, and nearly 50% of their sample scored 6 years below their chronological age on language achievement scores. Also, 20% to 46% of juvenile offenders meet the criteria for attention-deficit/hyperactivity disorder, while 50% to 90% meet the criteria for conduct disorder (Otto, Greenstein, Johnson, & Friedman, 1992). Studies of incarcerated youths have also shown high prevalence rates of current suicidal ideation (20%) (Rohde, Seeley, & Mace, 1997); especially at risk are juveniles who are depressed and conduct-disordered (Rapp & Wodarski, 1997).

The little research that does exist on juveniles who access both the mental health and juvenile justice systems suggests that these youths are more likely to abuse substances, to have been physically abused, to be a minority, and to have a parent who has had criminal involvement (Rosenblatt, Rosenblatt, & Briggs, 2000). In general, comorbid youths tend to have a worse prognostic picture, more peer rejection, and a higher risk for adult criminality, and they report more dangerous, impulsive, and illegal activities (McConaughty & Skiba, 1993)

These statistics present the clinical reality of the juvenile justice population. It is easy to surmise that most youths being seen in this system have multiple problems and do not fit neatly into a single diagnostic category. Even though these youths present with multiple problems, including suicidal ideation, few receive adequate screening, assessment, services, or treatment (MacKinnon-Lewis et al., 2002). These youths have frequently been shunted to the juvenile justice system, which cannot assess, contain, or treat them (Cocozza & Skowyra, 2000). At other times, these youths are dumped into the mental health system, which is also ill prepared to handle their complex problems. Some are literally transferred back and forth between systems, as neither system is able to fully address the needs of these youths and their families (Scott, Snowden, & Libby, 2002). Instead of integrated services from the mental health and juvenile justice systems, a revolving door may more aptly describe the current system.

At first look, the populations of the juvenile justice and mental health systems may appear the same; however, closer inspection indicates that youths who eventually end up in the juvenile justice system are more likely to be from minority or economically disadvantaged backgrounds (Murphy, 2002). Managed care organizations have severely limited the services in the mental health system for impoverished youths and their families (Atkins et al., 1999). Therefore, youths with the same symptoms are treated in different systems. Though neither system has good service delivery, those juveniles dumped into the juvenile justice system have more stigma and long-term ramifications (such as difficulty in obtaining employment) than those in the mental health system.

## ■ Relationship Between Mental Illness and Juvenile Offending

A diagnosis of a mental illness or juvenile offending alone is problematic for practitioners in the mental health and juvenile justice systems because research regarding the etiology, course, and treatment of these problems in children and youths lags significantly behind the problems of adults. However, comorbid conditions, in which a juvenile has two separate and distinct problems at the same time, pose significant theoretical, conceptual, diagnostic, and treatment planning difficulties. Add to the problem that the comorbid conditions bridge two fragmented delivery systems (juvenile justice and mental health or special education), and that problem becomes disastrous.

Comorbid conditions spawn confusion and questions regarding the course of the disorders. For example, are observed symptoms part of one disorder or both? How does one disorder affect the occurrence or onset of another disorder? Did the disorders begin at the same time, or should one be considered primary? Treatment issues also muddy the waters. For instance, should both disorders be treated simultaneously, or should one disorder be treated first? If so, which one, and with which types of interventions? In addition, how can disorders that seem to be polar opposites occur in an individual at the same time? Depression and conduct disorder have very different symptomatology, yet they occur together frequently and warrant concern. (See chapter 15 for application of biopsychosocial assessment and treatment planning with comorbid Axis I disorders and juvenile offending.)

## ■ Mood Disorders and Offending Behavior

Despite the advances in our understanding of mood disorders in children and adolescents, juvenile depression remains seriously underdiagnosed and undertreated (Ryan, 2001). According to Cicchetti and Toth (1998), 70% of depressed adolescents do not receive treatment. Depression, especially untreated, can seriously hinder appropriate development in juveniles, and acute episodes interfere with children's ability to function competently (Kovacs, 1996). Youths with comorbid depression and offending behaviors are at significant risk for suicide attempts and completions. Studies suggest that 75% of adolescent suicide attempters and completers have a psychiatric disorder, most notably mood disorders (Rohde et al., 1997).

Unlike adults who suffer from depression, youths often "act out" their depression through disruptive and aggressive behaviors. Some have termed this "masked depression." Depression can also impair social functioning, peer relationships, and information processing, which can result in poor judgment and delinquent behaviors (Ryan, 2001). Youths with bipolar disorder, which includes cycles of depression and mania, may exhibit delinquent and risk-taking behaviors during the manic phase. During this phase, youths often feel invincible and cannot comprehend any future consequences of their behavior. Effective treatment of juveniles' mood disorders may reduce delinquent and offending behaviors, but the delinquency has to be addressed also (Ryan, 2001). There is no guarantee that all offending behaviors will cease when the mood disorder is treated. In fact, some mood disorders, especially depression, can begin after the onset of delinquency. This may be the case when a youth is first sentenced or incarcerated. Staff in the juvenile justice system should not minimize this depression because these juveniles are at serious risk for dangerous and impulsive behaviors. Youths with symptoms of mood disorders need to be screened immediately and given adequate treatment. Although these youths need limit setting and consequences for offending behavior, correctional facilities are often not equipped to provide the comprehensive treatment these youths need (Ryan, 2001).

## ■ Attention-Deficit/Hyperactivity Disorder, Conduct Disorder, and Offending Behaviors

Attention-deficit/hyperactivity disorder (ADHD) is characterized by inattention, disorganization, hyperactivity, and impulsivity. Juveniles with this disorder often evince poor school performance, poor social relationships, poor problem-solving skills, and difficulty in attending to stimuli (Lexcen & Redding, 2000).

Youths with conduct disorder (CD) persistently violate norms or rules and disregard the rights of others. They may be aggressive toward animals and people and destroy property. These juveniles also have deficits in social skills and problem-solving skills, and they tend to see others' interactions with them as hostile. They are also impulsive and tend to lack empathy (Lexcen & Redding, 2000).

These two disorders are often termed disruptive behavior disorders, and

30% to 50% of youths diagnosed with ADHD also receive a diagnosis of CD (Lexcen & Redding, 2000). Youths with deficits in social skills, problem-solving skills, and increased impulsivity are prone to have problems with law-abiding behavior. Faced, like everyone else, with daily temptations to break the law, these youths are unable to control their initial impulses or think clearly about the pros and cons and future consequences of their behavior. They are also more likely to surround themselves with negative peers and have difficulty in resisting peer pressure. Both disorders place youths at risk for school failure. Juveniles with ADHD have difficulty attending to and acquiring basic academic information, while CD youths' behaviors (e.g., fighting, refusing to follow adults' directives) interfere with their academic performance. Juveniles with both ADHD and CD have been found to have lower intellectual functioning and poorer academic skills, and they enter the juvenile justice system earlier (Foley, Carlton, & Howell, 1996). Youths exhibiting these behaviors should be screened initially and then given a thorough evaluation by a mental health professional. Several medications have been found effective for treating ADHD, and other interventions such as cognitive-behavioral therapy, multisystemic therapy, and parent training are effective for CD youths and their families.

## ■ Learning Disabilities and Offending Behaviors

Studies have found a relationship between learning disabilities and delinquency. Children with disabilities, especially those with cognitive impairments affecting verbal abilities, are more likely than their nondisabled peers to engage in delinquent or offending behavior (Block, 2000). McGarvey and Waite (2000) found that one third of children with disabilities will be arrested within 3 to 5 years of graduating from high school, and 40% of detained youths should be classified as learning disabled. The term *learning disability* here includes specific learning disabilities, mental retardation, emotional disturbance, and health impairments (such as ADHD and epilepsy). Children who qualify for this category are eligible for special education services in the least restrictive environment possible. Most schools provide special education services and classes within their school building; however, some schools utilize alternative schools for children who have a disability but are also exhibiting disruptive or offending behaviors. Juveniles exhibiting severe behaviors are often removed completely from the school system and placed in the juvenile justice system. However, threatening comments, disruptive behavior, refusal to follow adult directives, and aggression are often a manifestation of learning disabilities (Block, 2000). Juveniles who cannot comprehend information, laws, or rules or who are impulsive are going to have problems abiding by school rules and societal laws. Unfortunately, society's response to this group of disabled youths is to thrust them into the juvenile justice system, which is ill equipped to handle youths with serious academic needs. Schools, on the other hand, are equipped to handle educational difficulties but tend to have a very limited repertoire—that is, suspension and expulsion—in handling disruptive behaviors.

Professionals in the juvenile justice system must be further educated regarding learning disabilities and their causes and effects to assist these youths in obtaining the services they require. Likewise, schools need to become more creative and adaptive in handling disruptive behaviors from special education students. Increasing use of the juvenile justice system is not the answer.

## ■ Posttraumatic Stress Disorder and Offending Behaviors

Posttraumatic stress disorder (PTSD) is usually caused by an overwhelming traumatic event outside the range of ordinary human experience. After the event, individuals suffer from intrusive recollections, avoidant or numbing symptoms, and hyperarousal for at least 1 month (Cauffman et al., 1998). Previous research has found 1% to 14% of the general population currently suffering from PTSD, but higher lifetime incidence rates of PTSD have been found among urban and incarcerated youths (Cauffman et al., 1998). This is not surprising because studies have indicated a relationship between traumatic events, mental health problems, and delinquent behavior. Schwab-Stone, Ayers, and Kasprow (1995) found that delinquent behavior was a direct or indirect reflection of past victimization, and other studies have indicated that victims of violence and perpetrators are often one and the same (Rapp-Paglicci & Wodarski, 2000).

Juveniles who suffer a trauma often later evince problem behaviors, emotional difficulties, academic failure, suicidal behavior, and health problems. Others experience depression, anxiety, low self-esteem, and disturbances in socioemotional adjustment (Steiner, Garcia, & Matthews, 1997). Victimization and trauma, especially when untreated and combined with other risk factors, can result in offending behaviors. Youths with symptoms of PTSD and those who disclose previous abuse should be screened immediately upon entrance to the juvenile justice system. A comprehensive mental health evaluation should be conducted if needed. Juveniles with PTSD and offending behaviors have shown improvements after cognitive-behavioral therapy. However, incarceration, where further abuse or trauma could result, is certainly contraindicated for this subgroup of vulnerable juveniles. It should also be noted that youths who are having intrusive recollections or memories about the trauma may exhibit unpredictable behaviors that may be dangerous to themselves or others.

## ■ Assessment

Because so many youths entering the juvenile justice system have concurrent mental health issues, it is imperative that all youths are thoroughly assessed to identify any mental health problems or learning disabilities. Many youths show acute psychological and emotional distress, particularly at the preadjudicatory stage, but some have serious mental illness that has gone undetected or untreated for years (Cocozza & Skowyra, 2000). Youths with undetected mental health problems who are placed in the juvenile justice system can decompensate over time, especially in a stressful environment like detention, incarceration, or boot camp. They can also be at risk for suicide or violent behavior toward other youths and staff, particularly if they are found to be impulsive and depressed.

The juvenile justice system is in dire need of trained mental health professionals to assist with assessment and treatment. Preferably, these professionals should conduct extensive assessments; however, until trained professionals are hired and incorporated into this system, the onus of assessment will continue to lie with juvenile justice personnel.

The formal assessment before a youth is placed within the juvenile justice system should include a thorough history of the youth's development from birth to current age and the family, psychological, social, and academic history. Details regarding child abuse, alcohol and drug problems, lethality, family violence, traumas, and previous mental health issues are crucial. A formal assessment by the school for learning disabilities that may have previously gone unnoticed is also a must. The offending behavior must be explicitly identified in order to assess the severity and chronicity of the offenses. Professionals should consider the known risk factors for delinquency and mental health problems (see Tables 12.1 and 12.2). These risk factors can assist personnel in understanding the severity and potential severity of problems a youth may have. For instance, a youth who has only two risk factors for mental illness will have less of a chance for developing these problems than one who has seven risk factors. The age of the youth in combination with the known risk factors should shed light on where the youth should be placed and treated.

**Table 12.1    Risk Factors for Juvenile Delinquency**

| | |
|---|---|
| Individual | Substance Abuse |
| | Mental health problems, particularly ADHD and Depression |
| | Poor social problem-solving skills |
| | Learning Disabilities |
| | Cognitive Impairments especially affecting verbal abilities |
| Family | Poor parental supervision |
| | Ineffective discipline practices |
| | Exposure to Domestic Violence |
| School | Truancy |
| | Poor academic achievement |
| | Untreated learning disabilities |
| Peer | Association with delinquent peers |
| | Gang membership |
| Community | Exposure to violence |
| | Exposure to drug dealing |

**Table 12.2**   **Risk Factors for Mental Illness**

| Family | Large family size or overcrowding |
|---|---|
| | Paternal criminality |
| | Maternal psychiatric disorder |
| | Severe marital discord |
| Community | Poverty |

Source: Rutter, 1990.

Because of budget cuts and a lack of interest in youths in the juvenile justice system, many states do not have trained mental health professionals in the juvenile justice system. However, there are mental health screening instruments that can be utilized by untrained staff to obtain information quickly and accurately. These mental health screening instruments have the potential to readily and easily assess juveniles and offer important possibilities for the juvenile justice system. For instance, they can reduce the risk of harm to the youths and others, prevent and alleviate suffering, provide the necessary information for appropriate referrals, and reduce potential legal liability (Reppucci & Redding, 2000). The following two instruments show promise as brief screening instruments for staff who are not mental health professionals.

## Massachusetts Youth Screening Instrument

The Massachusetts Youth Screening Instrument (MAYSI-2; Grisso, Barnum, Fletcher, Cauffman, & Peuschold, 2001) was designed specifically for evaluating psychological distress of youths entering the juvenile justice system. It does not focus on psychological diagnoses but rather on situational and characterological distress in youths who are in the juvenile justice system. The instrument has seven subscales: alcohol and drug use, angry-irritable, depressed-anxious, somatic complaints, suicidal ideation, thought disturbance, and traumatic experiences. Scores above the cutoff warrant mental health referrals. The instrument has been proven reliable and valid with youths in the juvenile justice system and, with only 52 items, can be completed in 10 minutes. It is also very easy to score.

## Brief Symptom Inventory

The Brief Symptom Inventory (BSI; Derogatis, 1979) was designed to measure current psychological symptoms and render a diagnosis. The instrument can be administered in 10 minutes and is easily scored. It has established reliability and validity and is available in several languages. The inventory does not have a specific suicide subscale, nor does it assess alcohol use, drug use, or aggression (Reppucci & Redding, 2000). The BSI is useful for a quick psychological screening; however, other instruments would need to be utilized with it for a comprehensive assessment.

Although screening instruments are helpful tools to rapidly screen for mental health and behavioral problems, they should be used with caution. Youths with mental health problems and certainly offending youths often minimize or deny problems. Therefore, assessments must include information from parents or guardians, relatives, teachers, school personnel, counselors, probation officers, religious leaders, and anyone else who may have information regarding the youths. In addition, previous juvenile justice, probation, medical, counselor, and academic records should be reviewed to obtain and corroborate all necessary information. The accuracy of the assessment is of great concern because appropriate referrals cannot be completed and treatment will not be effective without the initial step of assessment.

## ■ Effective Treatment Approaches

Given the complexity of the issue of mental illness and offending behaviors, it is no wonder that practitioners, juvenile justice personnel, and researchers consider these youths among their greatest challenges. Attempts to intervene with these youths have met with numerous barriers, including the following:

1 Inadequate screening and assessment of youths entering the juvenile justice system
2 Lack of training of juvenile justice personnel regarding mental illness and lack of staffing to deliver services
3 Ineffective or nonexistent services for juvenile offenders with combined mental illness and offending behaviors
4 Confusion and arguments across social service agencies and the juvenile justice system regarding which agency is responsible for assisting these youths
5 Lack of empathy for all juvenile offenders in light of the recent "get tough" policies regarding juveniles
6 Arguments between professionals regarding which problem to treat first and how to treat it

Despite these concerns, researchers have begun to identify a clear set of comprehensive strategies for effectively reducing delinquency and ameliorating the symptoms of mental illness in youths. Effective interventions usually begin early (well before youths become involved with the juvenile justice system), when youths are younger and have exhibited only a few risk factors. In fact, the Office of Juvenile Justice and Delinquency Prevention advocates for prevention programs targeted to at-risk youths (Redding, 2000). Typically, there is not just one cause of a juvenile's problems. To this end, effective programs need to address multiple risk factors (i.e., individual, family, and community) and intervene at multiple levels (with the youth, family, and larger systems). Interventions that have been shown to be effective are ones that can be tailored to address the particular risk factors present for that youth and that youth's situation. Additionally, interventions must be of sufficient duration to produce change. Although brief treatment is currently in vogue and demanded by managed care organizations, seriously mentally ill and delinquent youths require intense and ongoing assistance. Studies have suggested that short-term treatments with no follow-up or booster sessions are usually inadequate (Cocozza & Skowyra, 2000). Finally, community-based programs have generally been found to be more effective than incarceration in reducing recidivism.

The following are some examples and explanations of programs or interventions that have been found to be effective.

## Cognitive-Behavioral Approaches

Cognitive-behavioral approaches have fast become some of the most effective treatment protocols for conduct disorder, violent behaviors, depression, and anxiety, for youths as well as adults. The cognitive-behavioral theory suggests that cognitions are determinants of affect and behavior (Dodge, 1993). Kendall (1993) indicates that this mode of treatment attempts to train participants to identify and then alter their cognitions. Because depressed, anxious, and offending youths all manifest distortions in attributions, self-evaluations, locus of control, and perceptions of events, this approach is especially conducive for work with offending youths with mental health problems (Kendall, 1993; Rapp & Wodarski, 1997).

Cognitive-behavioral approaches can include social skills training, parenting skills training, anger management, problem-solving skills, and behavioral contracting. Teaching multiple skills tailored to a youth's and family's particular needs has been found to be the most efficacious approach (Bray, Heiserman, & Hosley, 2002). The "skillstreaming" component teaches a progression of very specific prosocial skills through performance feedback, role playing, and modeling. The anger control element helps youths learn what triggers their anger and how to modify and control it. Problem-solving components teach strategies for identifying problems, alternative actions, and pros and cons of actions. Parenting skills training helps guardians learn to develop behavior modification plans, utilize various reinforcement schedules, and problem-solve creative discipline for youths. These components have been found to be effective with children and youths, as well as with families dealing with mental illness and offending behavior.

## Education

Educational rehabilitation is often an essential part of treatment for any offender, but it is especially pertinent for those youths who suffer from developmental or learning disabilities. Many times, children with learning disabilities go undiagnosed or misdiagnosed for years. Children with these disabilities often have a more difficult time following directions, obeying rules, controlling their impulses, and understanding expectations (Block, 2000). Therefore, they frequently violate rules at school. Expulsion or transfer to an alternative school has been the de facto practice of most schools; however, this procedure does not assist youths and rather sets up youths for future academic and employment failure. Schools that file charges against learning disabled students are using the juvenile court system to criminalize learning disabilities. On the other hand, schools have been criticized for not addressing dangerous students prior to a crisis (such as school shootings). Schools have been placed in a "damned if they do, damned if they don't" position. The bottom line remains the same: Special education services are desperately needed by many juvenile offenders, and they decrease offending behaviors when delivered to youths with learning disabilities (Lexcen & Redding, 2000). The best location for the delivery of these services is certainly in the juvenile's own school; however, if the youth's behaviors warrant an alternative placement, these special education needs must be addressed in the least restrictive environment possible, preferably in conjunction with other community services.

## Motivational Interviewing and Solution-Focused Treatment

Predelinquent and delinquent youths with ADHD, conduct disorder, oppositional defiance disorder, or intermittent explosive anger seem to do well with a combination of strengths-based treatment planning and stimulant medications or selective serotonin reuptake inhibitors (SSRIs) for impulsivity, acting-out behaviors, ADHD symptoms, and anger outbursts. More specifically, a therapeutic alliance needs to be developed between the counselor or social worker and the juvenile. With solid rapport and a therapeutic bond established, juvenile justice treatment staff are more likely to facilitate positive behavior change. The most effective treatment approaches seem to be a combination of the stages of change model, motivational interviewing, solution-focused therapy, cognitive-behavioral treatment, and parent management training (Corcoran & Springer, in press). It is important to start where the juvenile is and match the treatment modality to the juvenile's diagnosis and corresponding treatment goal. In addition, it is critically important to understand the stage of change where the juvenile is when entering treatment, whether it is precontemplation, contemplation, preparation, action, or adaptation/maintenance (Prochaska & Norcross, 1999).

## Functional Family Training

Functional family therapy (FFT) has been found to be an effective mental health practice with families and youths. It has also been shown to reduce recidivism in youths involved in corrections, substance abuse, and very serious juvenile offenders. Additionally, FFT has also been found effective with diverse youths in various geographic areas. Sexton and Alexander (2000) noted reductions in recidivism rates from 25% to 60%.

Trained therapists utilizing FFT work to modify the family's functioning and therefore the youth's symptoms, which are thought to be a symptom of problematic family functioning. The emphasis for change and treatment is on the family, as opposed to singling out or blaming the youth for all of the problems of the family.

## Multisystemic Therapy

One approach that has repeatedly demonstrated positive outcomes is multisystemic therapy (MST) (Henggeler, 1997). MST is an intensive, multimodal, family-based treatment approach focusing on the juvenile and the juvenile's family, peers, school, and community networks. MST aims to improve parental discipline practices and family relations, decrease the youth's contact with deviant peers, improve the youth's academic performance, and develop support systems to maintain the changes. The approach uses intensive case management and a team of other professionals to target multiple problems (Ellis & Sowers, 2001). The team is available to the family 24 hours a day and 7 days a week and utilizes various therapies in addition to multiple concrete services to meet the needs of the youth and family. Again, the main goal is to divert the youth from juvenile justice and mental health residential placements and help the youth and the family progress toward their life goals. Studies have shown that serious juvenile offenders completing MST had recidivism rates of 22% as compared with 71% for those completing outpatient therapy (Borduin et al., 1995; Tate, Reppucci, & Mulvey, 1995). Even juveniles completing only a portion of the MST program had lower recidivism rates (41%) (Redding, 2000). This intervention is especially beneficial to juveniles who have a mental health diagnosis in addition to problems with offending.

## Community-Based Alternatives

Because of the serious concerns for mentally ill offenders placed in typical youth facilities with few resources or supports and the serious problem of overcrowding in youth facilities, there are currently attempts to divert mentally ill and seriously disturbed youths from the system and provide efficacious and cost-effective services in the community. Graduated community-based sanctions involve a continuum of sanctions and treatment alternatives tailored to youths' offenses and particular needs. Intensive supervision is utilized, with incarceration only as a last resort. Instead of incarceration, group homes, house arrest, detention, restitution programs, day treatment, intensive supervision, and aftercare are utilized alone or in combination, based on the needs of the juvenile, his or her family, the community, and the offense. According to Redding (2000), this approach reduces costs, increases accountability by the juvenile and the community, and addresses the individual needs of the juvenile. Another study found this approach the most effective for preventing recidivism, even in violent offenders (Tate et al., 1995). The community-based treatment needs to be long term, which can be costly; however, this approach is still less expensive than incarceration.

## Wraparound Programs

Wraparound services provide an array of formal and informal services to youths and their families while maintaining youths in their community. These programs are effective for low-risk or first-time offenders, because community safety must always be assured. The wraparound programs focus on the youth's and family's strengths and build on the natural supports within the family. They expect family involvement in the treatment and utilize individualized service plans. Kamradt (2000) found that recidivism dropped to as low as 17% for youths and families using wraparound programs. In addition, residential treatment decreased by 60%, inpatient hospitalization decreased 80%, and the average overall cost of care per child decreased by at least $3,300 per month. These figures suggest strong support for these diversion services.

Although the use of community-based services is a promising approach for the effective treatment of mental illness and offending behaviors, it requires intense interagency collaboration and planned integration of services. In other words, various agencies within the community must work together smoothly and comprehensively. Few professionals in any field would reject the notion of collaboration, yet in actual practice it is uncommon and difficult (Murphy, 2002). However, with the increasing number of mentally ill juvenile offenders in multiple systems, no one agency can control, house, or rehabilitate them alone. Community agencies—including schools, adolescent mental health, adult mental health, probation, group homes, substance abuse agencies, CPS, social services, and juvenile justice—have no choice but to collaborate. Agencies need to have good working relationships with each other, clear goals for the juvenile and the family, and a clear understanding of their scope, the scopes of other agencies, and the programs developed to serve this population effectively. Communities intent on developing community-based programs also need to address the differing philosophies of agencies, funding questions, record and data integration, and citizen support (Redding, 2000). Without this integration, the community-based approach will fail. Borum and Modzeleski (2000) also emphasize that graduated sanctions in the community must include early intervention and have a proactive stance. Agencies shouldn't wait to intervene until a serious offense occurs but rather should identify and respond to beginning, minor offenses or to early signs of mental illness with the intent to prevent further and escalating offenses and serious mental illness.

# ■ Contraindicated Treatment Approaches

Along with knowing which programs and treatment interventions are effective with youths who are mentally ill and exhibiting offending behaviors, it is also vital that ineffective treatments are understood. In the past, it was thought that any intervention would be better than nothing. However, research studies have shed light on this inaccurate claim and provide data to prove that some interventions are not only ineffective but also contraindicated. In other words, some interventions make the youth, the family, and the situation worse than no treatment at all. Obviously, this is not the intent of services and programs, but these studies should remind us that research is always necessary to identify whether a procedure, treatment, or program is effective and safe.

## Adult Facilities

The very first interventions for youths were adult prisons. Unfortunately, many young juveniles are still sent to adult facilities because of the offenses they committed or because of mandatory sentencing laws. Although juveniles are supposed to be incarcerated separately from adults, some older adolescents are housed with adults and receive very little if any treatment or vocational or educational rehabilitation. Clearly, this is not a particularly effective route to changing youths' behaviors or reducing mental illness (Ellis & Sowers, 2001). In fact, several large-scale studies have found higher and faster recidivism rates for juveniles transferred to adult facilities than for nontransferred juveniles (Myers, 1999; Winner, Lanza-Kaduce, Bishop, & Fazier, 1997).

Juveniles in adult facilities often learn more criminal behaviors and attitudes from adult inmates, are isolated or sent to lockdown, are abused or neglected by other prisoners and guards, lose ties with family, peers, and community, and come out of adult facilities worse than when they entered (Redding, 2000; Seltzer, 2001). Juveniles also have poorer chances of future employment after adult criminal justice system processing, according to Freeman (1992).

## Boot Camps

Boot camps are used as a type of diversion for youths from typical residential facilities. Often they are used for first offenders in an attempt to shock or scare them into appropriate behavior. The boot camps are usually 3 to 6 months long and based on a military schedule and discipline. Rigorous physical training is part of the foundation, along with education, but most programs do not provide therapy, vocational training, or life skills training. Most studies have not found support for these types of programs for offenders who are not mentally ill (Ellis & Sowers, 2001). Boot camps are contraindicated for mentally ill offenders because of the intense stress induced and the lack of treatment (Seltzer, 2001).

## Incarceration Alone

Programs that have relied on punishment alone without any programming or services have overwhelmingly been ineffective and have exacerbated youths' problems. Many youths have been abused and neglected in their homes and communities, and incarceration is often seen as a continuation of this process. Youths often feel distrustful and blatantly oppositional when faced with staff whose focus is harsh punishment and retribution. Ironically, a study conducted by Sherman (1993) found that punishment actually encouraged future lawbreaking, as juveniles focused on "doing their time" as opposed to the harm they had caused to the victim and the community. Deterrence programs administering punishment alone, including isolation or physical restraints, have repeatedly been very ineffective for youths (Ellis & Sowers, 2001). Furthermore, administering abusive conditions to youths who are learning disabled or mentally ill only exacerbates their conditions and should, in all reality, be considered child abuse.

Juveniles who are suffering from depression are especially at risk when incarcerated without treatment. According to Ryan (2001), incarceration usually increases feelings of hopelessness and despair, which are precursors to suicide. The death rate from suicide is 4.6 times higher in juvenile detention centers than in the general population (Sheras, 2000). Juvenile facilities also lack the adequate staffing necessary to provide sufficient supervision for suicidal youths. The serious lack of funding prohibits hiring and training more staff and prevents mental health services from being developed within these facilities.

## Unspecified and Nondirective Counseling Modalities

Juveniles who engage in offending behaviors and who may have learning disabilities and mental illness have not benefited from nondirective therapy, and in some instances this therapy has been harmful to them (Losel, 1996). Because research studies have repeatedly identified cognitive-behavioral approaches as effective, this modality should be utilized. Unspecified modalities, based on weak theoretical foundations and not supported by research, are contraindicated for juvenile justice clients. Psychodynamic interventions are also not supported by the current research literature and should not be used with this population.

It is obvious from this discussion that there is a substantial body of research on interventions for juvenile offenders. This research should guide practitioners as well as juvenile justice programs in beginning to develop effective interventions and programs for juveniles who have both offending behaviors and mental illness or learning disabilities. It is clear what procedures and programs do not work.

## Conclusion

The research, although still sparse, has indicated that at least two thirds of juvenile detainees have a mental disorder in addition to their offending behaviors. These youths have complex and serious problems. However, current approaches by two fragmented systems—namely, the juvenile justice and mental health systems—are inadequate and in many cases harmful to these juveniles. Mentally ill juveniles and their families require thorough assessment and integrated and multifaceted strategies for intervention. Clearly, advocacy for this very vulnerable population should be at the top of our agenda within the juvenile justice system.

## References

Atkins, D., Pumariega, A., Rogers, K., Montgomery, L., Nybro, C., Jerrers, G., et al. (1999). Mental health and incarcerated youth: I. Prevalence and nature of psychopathology. *Journal of Child and Family Studies, 8,* 193–204.

Block, A. (2000). Special education law and delinquent children: An overview. In *Juvenile justice fact sheet.* Charlottesville: Institute of Law, Psychiatry, and Public Policy, University of Virginia.

Borduin, C., Mann, B., Cone, L., Henggeler, S., Fucci, B., Blaske, D., et al. (1995). Multisystemic treatment of serious juvenile offenders: Long-term prevention of criminality and violence. *Journal of Consulting and Clinical Psychology, 63,* 569–578.

Borum, R., & Modzeleski, W. (2000). *U.S.S.F. safe school initiative: An interim report on the prevention of targeted violence in schools.* Washington, DC: U.S. Secret Service, National Threat Center.

Bray, C., Heiserman, M., & Hosley, C. (2002). Providing community-based interventions to juveniles with mental health disorders: The uniting networks for youth program. *Juvenile Justice Update, 8*(4), 1–15.

Cauffman, E., Feldman, S., Waterman, J., & Steiner, H. (1998). Posttraumatic stress disorder among female juvenile offenders. *Journal of the American Academy of Child and Adolescent Psychiatry, 37*(11), 1209–1216.

Cicchetti, D., & Toth, S. (1998). The development of depression in children and adolescents. *American Psychologist, 53*(2), 221–241.

Cocozza, J., & Skowyra, K. (2000). Youth with mental health disorders: Issues and emerging responses. *Juvenile Justice, 7*(1), 3–13.

Corcoran, J., & Springer, D. W. (in press). Treatment of adolescents with disruptive behavior disorders. In J. Corcoran (Ed.), *Strengths and skills-based interviewing.* New York: Oxford University Press.

Derogatis, L. (1979). *Brief symptom inventory.* Minneapolis, MN: National Computer Systems.

Dodge, K. (1993). Social-cognitive mechanisms in the development of conduct disorder and depression. *Annual Reviews of Psychology, 44,* 559–584.

Ellis, R., & Sowers, K. (2001). *Juvenile justice practice: A cross-disciplinary approach to intervention.* Belmont, CA: Brooks/Cole.

Foley, B., Carlton, C., & Howell, R. (1996). The relationship of attention deficit hyperactivity disorder and conduct disorder to juvenile delinquency: Legal implications. *Bulletin of the American Academy of Psychiatry and Law, 24*(3), 333–345.

Freeman, R. (1992). Crime and employment of disadvantaged youth. In G. Peterson & W. Vroman (Eds.), *Urban labor markets and job opportunity* (pp. 201–238). Washington, DC: National Academy Press.

Grisso, T., Barnum, R., Fletcher, K., Cauffman, E., & Peuschold, D. (2001). Massachusetts Youth Screening Instrument for mental health needs of juvenile justice youths. *Journal of American Academy of Child and Adolescent Psychiatry, 40*(5), 541–548.

Henggeler, S. (1997). Multisystemic therapy: An overview of clinical procedures, outcomes, and policy implications. *Child Psychology and Psychiatry Review, 4*(1), 2–10.

Kamradt, B. (2000). Wraparound Milwaukee: Aiding youth with mental health needs. *Juvenile Justice, 7*(1), 14–23.

Kendall, P. (1993). Cognitive-behavioral therapies with youth: Guiding theory, current status, and emerging developments. *Journal of Consulting and Clinical Psychology, 61*(2), 235–247.

Kovacs, M. (1996). Presentation and course of major depressive disorder during childhood and later years of the life span. *Journal of the American Academy of Child and Adolescent Psychiatry, 35*(6), 705–715.

Lexcen, F., & Redding, R. (2000). Mental health needs of juvenile offenders. In *Juvenile justice fact sheet.* Charlottesville: Institute of Law, Psychiatry, and Public Policy, University of Virginia.

MacKinnon-Lewis, C., Kaufman, M., & Frabutt, J. (2002). Juvenile justice and mental health: Youth and families in the middle. *Aggression and Violent Behavior, 7*(4), 353–363.

McConaughty, S., & Skiba, R. (1993). Comorbidity of externalizing and internalizing problems. *School Psychology Review, 25,* 687–691.

McGarvey, E., & Waite, D. (2000). Profiles of incarcerated adolescents in Virginia: 1993–1998. *The national longitudinal study: A summary of findings.* Washington, DC: Office of Special Education Programs, U.S. Department of Education.

Murphy, R. (2002). Mental health, juvenile justice, and law enforcement responses to youth psychopathology. In D. Marsh (Ed.), *Handbook of serious, emotional disturbance in children and adolescents* (pp. 351–374). New York: Wiley.

Myers, D. (1999). *Excluding violent youths from juvenile court: The effectiveness of legislative waiver.* Unpublished doctoral dissertation, University of Maryland.

Myers, W., Burgess, S., & Burgess, A. (1995). Psychopathology, biopsychosocial factors, crime characteristics, and classification of 25 homicidal youths. *Journal of the American Academy of Child and Adolescent Psychiatry, 34,* 1483–1489.

Pliszka, S., Sherman, J., Barrow, M., & Irick, S. (2000). Affective disorder in juvenile offenders: A preliminary study. *American Journal of Psychiatry, 157,* 130–132.

Rapp, L., & Wodarski, J. (1997). The comorbidity of conduct disorder and depression in adolescents: A comprehensive interpersonal treatment technology. *Family Therapy, 24*(2), 81–100.

Rapp-Paglicci, L., & Wodarski, J. (2000). Antecedent behaviors of male youth victimization: An exploratory study. *Deviant Behavior, 21,* 519–536.

Redding, R. (2000a). Barriers to meeting the mental health needs of offenders in the juvenile justice system. In *Juvenile justice fact sheet.* Charlottesville: Institute of Law, Psychiatry, and Public Policy, University of Virginia.

Redding, R. (2000b). Characteristics of effective treatments and interventions for juvenile offenders. In *Juvenile justice fact sheet.* Charlottesville: Institute of Law, Psychiatry, and Public Policy, University of Virginia.

Redding, R. (2000c). Graduated and community-based sanctions for juvenile offenders. *Juve-*

*nile justice fact sheet*. Charlottesville: Institute of Law, Psychiatry, and Public Policy, University of Virginia.

Redding, R. (2000d). Recidivism rates in juvenile versus criminal court. In *Juvenile justice fact sheet*. Charlottesville: Institute of Law, Psychiatry, and Public Policy, University of Virginia.

Reppucci, N., & Redding, R. (2000). Screening instruments for mental illness in juvenile offenders: The MAYSI and BSI. In *Juvenile justice fact sheet*. Charlottesville: Institute of Law, Psychiatry, and Public Policy, University of Virginia.

Rohde, P., Seeley, J., & Mace, D. (1997). Correlates of suicidal behavior in a juvenile detention population. *Suicide and Life Threatening Behavior, 27*, 164–175.

Rosenblatt, J., Rosenblatt, A., & Briggs, E. (2000). Criminal behavior and emotional disorder: Comparing youth served by the mental health and juvenile justice systems. *Journal of Behavioral Health Services and Research, 27*, 227–237.

Rutter, M. (1990). Psychosocial resilience and protective mechanisms. In A. Rolf, A. Masten, D. Cicchetti, K. Nuechterlein, & S. Weintraub (Eds.), *Risk and protective factors in the development of psychopathology*. New York: Cambridge University Press.

Ryan, E. (2001). Mood disorders in juvenile offenders. In *Juvenile justice fact sheet*. Charlottesville: Institute of Law, Psychiatry, and Public Policy, University of Virginia.

Schwab-Stone, M., Ayers, T., & Kasprow, W. (1995). No safe haven: A study of violence exposure in an urban community. *Journal of American Academy of Child and Adolescent Psychiatry, 34*, 1343–1352.

Scott, M., Snowden, L., & Libby, A. (2002). From mental health to juvenile justice: What factors predict this transition? *Journal of Child and Family Studies, 11*(3), 299–311.

Seltzer, R. (2001). Juveniles with mental disabilities: When incarceration makes youth worse. *Juvenile Justice Update, 7*(2), 9–10.

Sexton, T., & Alexander, J. (2000). Functional family therapy. In *Juvenile justice bulletin*. Washington, DC: Office of Juvenile Justice and Delinquency Prevention.

Sheras, P. (2000). Depression and suicide in juvenile offenders. In *Juvenile justice fact sheet*. Charlottesville: Institute of Law, Psychiatry, and Public Policy, University of Virginia.

Sherman, L. (1993). Defiance, deterrence, and irrelevance: A theory of the criminal sanction. *Journal of Research in Crime and Delinquency, 30*, 445–473.

Steiner, H., Garcia, I., & Matthews, Z. (1997). Postraumatic stress disorder in incarcerated juvenile delinquents: The relation to criminal behavior and recidivism. *Journal of American Academy of Child and Adolescent Psychiatry, 36*, 357–365.

Tate, D., Reppucci, N., & Mulvey, E. (1995). Violent juvenile delinquents: Treatment efficacy and implications for future action. *American Psychologist, 50*, 777–785.

Teplin, L., Abram, K., McClelland, G., Dulcan, M., & Mericle, A. (2002). Psychiatric disorders in youth in juvenile detention. *Archives of General Psychiatry, 59*, 1133–1143.

Thomas, C., & Penn, J. (2002). Juvenile justice mental health services. *Child and Adolescent Psychiatric Clinics of North America, 11*, 731–748.

Winner, L., Lanza-Kaduce, L., Bishop, D., & Frazier, C. (1997). The transfer of juveniles to criminal court: Reexamining recidivism over the long term. *Crime and Delinquency, 43*(4), 548–563.

# 13 A Matter of Years

## The Juvenile Death Penalty and

## the United States Supreme Court

Kenneth C. Haas

Carole Roberts

Twenty-two states permit the execution of people convicted of capital crimes they were charged with committing when they were 16 or 17 years old. The execution of juvenile offenders is not a new practice in the United States. It is, however, a practice that was not clearly constitutional until the late 1980s, when the U.S. Supreme Court announced two landmark decisions. In *Thompson v. Oklahoma* (1988) and *Stanford v. Kentucky* (1989), the Court in effect drew a line that bans the execution of offenders under the age of 16 but permits executions for crimes committed at the age of 16 or older. However, on June 20, 2002, the Court announced that the Eighth Amendment would no longer be construed to permit the execution of mentally retarded offenders. In *Atkins v. Virginia*, the Court reasoned that because such offenders typically have diminished capacities to control impulses, process information, and learn from mistakes, it would be unconstitutional to subject them to the death penalty. Four months later, in *In re Stanford*, four justices asserted that the logic of *Atkins* should be extended to 16- and 17-year-old offenders. It thus may be merely a matter of time before the Court takes that step and bans the execution of juvenile offenders. After a brief look at the history and current status of the juvenile death penalty, this chapter reviews the case law prior to 1988 and analyzes the opinions issued in *Thompson* and *Stanford*. The chapter concludes with a discussion of the impact of *Atkins v. Virginia* on the future of the juvenile death penalty.

## ■ History and Current Status of Juvenile Executions

Condemning juvenile offenders (those convicted of capital crimes committed when they were 16 or 17 years old) to death is not a new practice in the United States, but the actual execution of condemned juveniles has been quite rare. The first documented juvenile execution in the American colonies occurred in 1642, when 16-year-old Thomas Graunger was executed in Plymouth Colony, Massachusetts, for the crime of bestiality (Streib, 1988, p. 251). This was the first of 365 satisfactorily documented juvenile executions in American history. These executions account for 1.8% of the total of approximately 20,000 American executions since 1608 (Streib, 2002).

Today, 40 jurisdictions—38 states, the U.S. military, and the federal government—have death penalty laws authorizing capital punishment for certain forms of murder.[1] Seventeen states have set the minimum age of eligibility for the death penalty at 16,[2] and five states permit the execution of children as young as 17.[3] Eighteen jurisdictions (16 states and the 2 federal jurisdictions) have expressly chosen age 18 at the time of the crime as the minimum age for the maximum penalty (Streib, 2002).[4]

The highest number of juvenile executions came in the 1940s, when 53 juvenile offenders—4.1% of all those executed—were put to death. After the 1940s, the number of juvenile executions dropped precipitously. Only 16 juveniles were executed in the 1950s (2.2% of all executions) and only 3 in the 1960s (1.6%) (Streib, 1987, p. 25). All executions ended temporarily in 1967, as the nation waited for an expected U.S. Supreme Court holding on the constitutionality of capital punishment, and then resumed on January 17, 1977, with the execution of Gary Gilmore in Utah.

Twenty-one executions for juvenile crimes have been carried out since 1976, when the U.S. Supreme Court's holding in *Gregg v. Georgia* made it clear that the death penalty, in and of itself, was not always an unconstitutional punishment. As Table 13.1 indicates, all of the post-*Gregg* executions of juvenile offenders have been imposed by southern states, and Texas is responsible for 13 of the 21 executions. All of those executed have been male, and 20 of the 21 were 17 years old when they committed the crime that led to their execution. As of December 31, 2002, these 21 executions constituted approximately 2.6% of the 820 executions carried out in the post-*Gregg* era.

**Table 13.1**  **Executions of Juvenile Offenders: January 1, 1973, through December 31, 2002**

| Name | Date of Execution | Place of Execution | Race | Age at Crime | Age at Execution |
|------|-------------------|--------------------|------|--------------|------------------|
| Charles Rumbaugh | 9-11-1985 | Texas | White | 17 | 28 |
| J. Terry Roach | 1-10-1986 | South Carolina | White | 17 | 25 |
| Jay Pinkerton | 5-15-1986 | Texas | White | 17 | 24 |
| Dalton Prejean | 5-18-1990 | Louisiana | Black | 17 | 30 |
| Johnny Garrett | 2-11-1992 | Texas | White | 17 | 28 |
| Curtis Harris | 7-1-1993 | Texas | Black | 17 | 31 |
| Frederick Lashley | 7-28-1993 | Missouri | Black | 17 | 29 |
| Ruben Cantu | 8-24-1993 | Texas | Latino | 17 | 26 |
| Chris Burger | 12-7-1993 | Georgia | White | 17 | 33 |
| Joseph Cannon | 4-22-1998 | Texas | White | 17 | 38 |
| Robert Carter | 5-18-1998 | Texas | Black | 17 | 34 |
| Dwayne Allen Wright | 10-14-1998 | Virginia | Black | 17 | 24 |
| Sean Sellers | 2-4-1999 | Oklahoma | White | 16 | 29 |
| Douglas Christopher Thomas | 1-10-2000 | Virginia | White | 17 | 26 |
| Steven Roach | 1-13-2000 | Virginia | White | 17 | 23 |
| Glen McGinnis | 1-25-2000 | Texas | Black | 17 | 27 |
| Shaka Sankofa (Gary Graham) | 6-22-2000 | Texas | Black | 17 | 36 |
| Gerald Mitchell | 10-22-2001 | Texas | Black | 17 | 33 |
| Napoleon Beazley | 5-28-2002 | Texas | Black | 17 | 25 |
| T. J. Jones | 8-8-2002 | Texas | Black | 17 | 25 |
| Toronto Patterson | 8-28-2002 | Texas | Black | 17 | 24 |

Source: Streib, V. L. (2002). *The juvenile death penalty today: Present death row inmates under death sentences and executions for juvenile crimes, January 1, 1973, to December 31, 2002.* Retrieved September 15, 2003, from http://www.deathpenaltyinfo.org/juvchar.html

As of that same date, 80 of the approximately 3,700 death row inmates in the United States were people convicted of a crime committed when they were younger than 18 (Streib, 2002).

## Early Eighth Amendment Holdings

It is interesting to note that 3 of the 21 post-*Gregg* executions of juvenile offenders were carried out in 1985 and 1986—a time when the constitutionality of executing juvenile offenders was very much an unsettled issue. As this chapter will demonstrate, the U.S. Supreme Court would not reach a decision on this issue until it announced its holding in *Stanford v. Kentucky* on June 26, 1989.

Most of the Supreme Court's holdings on the constitutionality of capital punishment laws have begun with the Eighth Amendment to the U.S. Constitution: "Excessive bail shall not be required, nor excessive fines imposed, nor cruel and unusual punishments inflicted." In its earliest death penalty decisions, the Court held that although the cruel and unusual punishment clause does not prohibit capital punishment, it does ban the physical torture of offenders and barbaric forms of execution, such as crucifixion or burning at the stake (*Wilkerson v. Utah,* 1879; *In re Kemmler,* 1890).

At the turn of the 20th century, the Court expanded the historical interpretation of the Eighth Amendment by stating that it prohibits "all punishments which, by their excessive length or severity, are greatly disproportionate to the offense charged" (*Weems v. United States*, 1910, at 367). In 1958, the Court broadened the scope of Eighth Amendment protection by stressing that the constitutional ban on cruel and unusual punishment must be interpreted not in an inflexible or unchanging manner, but in light of the "evolving standards of decency that mark the progress of a maturing society" (*Trop v. Dulles,* 1958, at 101). The *Trop* Court, however, declared that capital punishment "cannot be said to violate the constitutional concept of cruelty in a day when it is still widely accepted" (*Trop* at 99).

## The *Furman* and *Gregg* Decisions

The modern era of death penalty jurisprudence began with the Supreme Court's *Furman v. Georgia* decision in 1972. *Furman* held that all *then existing* state and federal death penalty laws violated the Eighth Amendment because of the arbitrary and discriminatory manner in which they were imposed. Two of the five justices who constituted the *Furman* majority would have gone much further. Justice Brennan and Justice Marshall concluded that capital punishment, under all circumstances, violates the cruel and unusual punishment clause of the Eighth Amendment. Both justices argued that the evidence was overwhelming not only that the death penalty was inflicted unfairly and capriciously but also that it was no more effective than lengthy imprisonment in achieving the legislative goals of deterrence and retribution (*Furman* at 270, quoting *Trop* at 101).

The three remaining concurring opinions by Justices Douglas, Stewart, and White avoided the issue of the constitutionality of the death penalty itself. Instead, they focused on the infirmities in the capital sentencing laws then in effect. None of these laws, it was asserted, gave sentencing judges or juries clear and fair legal guidelines to follow when determining whether to impose the death penalty. The result, as Justice Douglas put it, was that the death penalty was being "disproportionately imposed and carried out on the poor, the Negro, and the members of unpopular groups" (*Furman* at 249–250). It was also apparent, according to the concurring justices, that death sentences often were imposed not upon those who had committed the most heinous crimes but upon a capriciously selected handful of defendants who were in the wrong place at the wrong time. In the memorable words of Justice Stewart, "These death sentences are cruel and unusual in the same way that being struck by lightning is cruel and unusual" (*Furman* at 309). Justice White added that the "contemporary phenomenon" of the discriminatory and arbitrary application of the death penalty was clearly attributable to the excessive and extraordinary amount of discretion allotted to judges and juries in capital cases (*Furman* at 314). Stressing that the death penalty can have little, if any, deterrent or retributive effect under a system in which it is wantonly, freakishly, and rarely imposed, Justice White made it clear that he did not want to intimate that "there is no system of capital punishment that would comport with the Eighth Amendment" (*Furman* at 310–311).

*Furman* had the effect of invalidating the death penalty laws of 39 states, the District of Columbia, and the federal government. In the next 4 years, the legislatures of 35 states enacted new capital punishment statutes in an effort to meet the *Furman* concerns. All of these new statutes were written in one of two ways. First, 10 states made the death penalty mandatory for certain crimes. Second, 25 states established a two-stage trial procedure for capital cases: a guilt adjudication stage, during which the jury (or if the right to a jury trial is waived, the judge) decides the defendant's guilt, and a sentencing stage, during which the jury (or in a few states, the judge) determines the punishment for those found guilty. In this sentencing phase, the jury was to consider certain statutorily defined aggravating and mitigating circumstances relating to the nature of the crime and the character of the defendant. Although there were wide variations among these 25 laws, most of them specified that a death sentence could be imposed only if the sentencing authority found at least one of the statutorily prescribed aggravating circumstances to be present and determined that the aggravating circumstances outweighed any mitigating circumstances that were also present (Irvin & Rose, 1974).

The death penalty laws enacted in response to *Furman* were tested in a series of cases decided on July 2, 1976. In *Woodson v. North Carolina* and *Roberts v. Louisiana*, the Court invalidated the mandatory death penalty laws, reasoning that such laws resulted in "blind infliction of the penalty of death" (*Woodson* at 304). These laws thus were inconsistent with "the fundamental respect for humanity underlying the Eighth Amendment" because they did not permit individual consideration of the circumstances of the crime or the character of the defendant (*Woodson* at 304).

However, in *Gregg v. Georgia* and its companion cases, the Court bestowed its approval on the basic approach most states had taken in response to *Furman*. The plurality opinion in *Gregg*, written by Justice Stewart, concluded that the death penalty is not unconstitutional as a punishment for the crime of murder so long as proper procedures are followed in reaching the decision to impose it (*Gregg* at 186–187). Justice Stewart explained that a procedure under which the death penalty is imposed only after the sentencing authority has considered specific and relevant aggravating and mitigating circumstances would ensure that capital punishment would not be arbitrarily or discriminatorily imposed (*Gregg* at 206–207).

The Georgia statute at issue in *Gregg* listed 10 specific aggravating circumstances and no specific mitigating circumstances. The defense, however, was permitted to introduce any mitigating evidence concerning the evidence, the nature of the crime, and the character of the defendant, and the sentencing jury was to consider this evidence before imposing the death penalty (*Gregg* at 163–165). Justice Stewart praised this statute for focusing the jury's attention on "the particularized nature of the crime and the particularized characteristics of the defendant" (*Gregg* at 206–207).

It is particularly noteworthy that Justice Stewart specifically suggested the age of the offender as an appropriate mitigating factor for jury consideration (*Gregg* at 197). This was both good news and bad news for those who were particularly opposed to the execution of juvenile offenders. On the one hand, the *Gregg* plurality implied that a defendant's youth was one of the more important factors to be weighed. On the other hand, the plurality, in effect, made it clear that, at least for the time being, the Eighth Amendment would not be construed as prohibiting the execution of juveniles.

## ■ Relevant Post-*Gregg* Decisions

In 1978, the Court again recognized the issue of minors and the death penalty. In *Lockett v. Ohio*, the Court struck down an Ohio statute that permitted the sentencing authority to consider only three specific statutory mitigating circumstances: the victim's possible role in inducing or facilitating the murder; the extent to which the defendant was under duress, coercion, or strong provocation; and the extent to which the defendant suffered from mental illness or mental deficiency. Writing for the majority, Chief Justice Burger declared that the Eighth Amendment could not tolerate a statutory scheme that so sharply limits the number and type of mitigating factors to be considered by a sentencing judge or jury (*Lockett* at 604–605). Stressing the importance of treating each defendant "with that degree of respect due the uniqueness of the individual," the chief justice criticized the Ohio law for not permitting the sentencer to consider such critical factors as the defendant's youth or relatively minor role in the crime (*Lockett* at 605). *Lockett* made it clear that sentencing judges and juries must be permitted to consider all pertinent mitigating evidence offered by the defense, including the youth of a juvenile offender, before imposing capital punishment.

Three years later, the Court for the first time agreed to hear the specific issue of the constitutionality of capital punishment for an offense committed when the defendant was only 16 years old (*Eddings v. Oklahoma*, 1981, at 1040). However, when the Court decided *Eddings v. Oklahoma* the following year, it sidestepped the direct constitutional issue. Citing *Lockett*, the justices sent the case back to the trial court, instructing it to give full consideration to all mitigating factors, including the defendant's youth (*Eddings v. Oklahoma*, 1982, at 117). The majority pointedly observed that "the chronological age of a minor is itself a relevant mitigating factor of great weight" (*Eddings* at 116). Although those opposed to the juvenile death penalty certainly were pleased with the Court's action, there would be no premature celebration. Four justices—Chief Justice Burger, Justice Blackmun, Justice Rehnquist, and Justice White—lamented the majority's unwillingness to reach the ultimate constitutional issue and declared that they would have voted to reject any constitutional bar to the execution of 15-year-olds (*Eddings* at 120).

## ■ *Thompson v. Oklahoma* (1988)

It would take another 6 years for the Court to confront the question of the constitutionality of capital punishment as applied to juvenile offenders. On June 29, 1988, the Court announced its decision in a case brought by death row inmate William Wayne Thompson, who was 15 years old when he participated with three older men in the murder of his former brother-in-law. In *Thompson v. Oklahoma*, the Court ruled in favor of Thompson, holding that the execution of someone who was under the age of 16 when he committed his offense would violate the Eighth Amendment prohibition against cruel and unusual punishments. The *Thompson* holding came in an unusual 4-1-3 plurality opinion. Justice Stevens authored the plurality opinion, and Justice O'Connor added the fifth vote on narrower grounds. Justice Scalia wrote on behalf of three dissenters, and Justice Kennedy did not take part in the case.

Justice Stevens's plurality opinion began by applying the "evolving standards of decency" test to the issue at hand (*Thompson* at 821–822). The proper way to do this, he declared, was to examine (a) current state legislation on the acceptance or rejection of the death penalty for offenders younger than certain age limits, (b) the willingness of juries to impose death sentences on juvenile offenders when authorized, and (c) the recommendations of informed organizations and the views of other nations on the acceptability of the juvenile death penalty (*Thompson* at 822–831).

It was especially important, according to Justice Stevens, that all 18 states that had established a minimum age in their death penalty statutes had chosen an age of at least 16 (*Thompson* at 829). He acknowledged that the remaining 19 states with death penalty laws had established no minimum age for imposition of capital punishment (*Thompson* at 826–827). He asserted, however, that "it is reasonable to put this group of statutes to one side because they do not focus on the question of where the chronological line should be drawn" (*Thompson* at 826–829). It was also relevant, according to Justice Stevens, that all 50 states had enacted legislation designating the maximum age for juvenile court jurisdiction at no less than 16 and that the vast majority of states barred 15-year-olds from voting, driving, gambling, serving on a jury, purchasing pornography, or marrying without parental consent (*Thompson* at 824). This legislation, he pointed out, "is consistent with the experience of mankind, as well as the long history of our law, that the normal 15-year-old is not prepared to assume the full responsibilities of an adult" (*Thompson* at 824–825).

Next, Justice Stevens considered the behavior of juries in juvenile death penalty cases. Noting that death sentences for juvenile offenders and actual executions of them have been rare throughout American history, Justice Stevens pointed out that the last execution of a person for a crime committed under age 16 was in 1948, when Louisiana executed a 15-year-old offender (*Thompson* at 832). He also found it noteworthy that of the 1,393 persons sentenced to death by American courts from 1982 through 1986, only 5 were less than 16 years old at the time of the offense—5 young offenders who "received sentences that are cruel and unusual in the same way that being struck by lightning is cruel and unusual" (*Thompson* at 832–833, quoting *Furman* at 309). The extreme rarity of the juvenile death penalty in the United States demonstrates that the execution of 15-year-old offenders "is now generally abhorrent to the conscience of the community" (*Thompson* at 832). He added that the decreasing use of the juvenile death penalty in the United States was in line with its rejection by other nations that "share our Anglo-American heritage" and by such respected professional organizations as the American Bar Association and the American Law Institute (*Thompson* at 830–831).

Justice Stevens concluded the plurality opinion by emphasizing that although the judgments of legislatures and juries "weigh heavily in the balance," the Supreme Court is the ultimate arbiter of the Constitution (*Thompson* at 833). It was therefore left to the justices themselves to determine whether the execution of juvenile offenders measurably contributes to the two social purposes of capital punishment found to be legitimate by the *Gregg* Court: retribution and deterrence (*Thompson* at 833). The plurality answered this question in the negative. Juveniles have less culpability for their crimes than do adults, and this factor, combined with society's fiduciary obligations to its children and the adolescent's significant capacity for growth, makes retribution "simply inapplicable to the execution of a 15-year-old offender" (*Thompson* at 835–837). The deterrence rationale, added Justice Stevens, was similarly inapplicable in this context because adolescents as a class are less self-disciplined and more impulsive than adults (*Thompson* at 834–837). Consequently, the likelihood that the teenage offender will engage in "the kind of cost–benefit analysis that attaches any weight to the possibility of execution is so remote as to be virtually nonexistent" (*Thompson* at 837). Because the imposition of the death penalty for offenses committed by persons 15 years old or younger cannot be expected to make any meaningful contribution to the retributive and deterrent purposes of capital punishment, it is "nothing more than the needless imposition of pain and suffering [and] thus an unconstitutional punishment" (*Thompson* at 838, quoting *Coker v. Georgia* at 592).

The fifth vote to spare Wayne Thompson's life was cast by Justice O'Connor. Her concurring opinion stressed the importance of looking to the decisions of American legislatures for signs of a national consensus forbidding the execution of any person for a crime committed before the age of 16 (*Thompson* at 848–849). As Justice O'Connor saw it, these decisions tended to support the plurality's contention that there is a national consensus against executing 15-year-old offenders (*Thompson* at 849–852). "The single most salient statistic that bears on this case is that every single American legislature that has expressly set a minimum age for capital punishment has set that age at 16 or above" (*Thompson* at 849).

Justice O'Connor, however, thought that it would be premature to infer the existence of such a national consensus while there were 19 states, including Oklahoma, that had authorized capital punishment without setting any statutory minimum age (*Thompson* at 850–852). Indeed, she added, if it were clear that each of these 19 state legislatures had deliberately chosen to authorize capital punishment for 15-year-old offenders, "one could hardly suppose that there is a settled national consensus against the practice" (*Thompson* at 850). There was, however, no evidence that the Oklahoma Legislature or any of the remaining 18 legislatures had rendered a considered judgment approving the imposition of the death penalty on children below the age of 16 (*Thompson* at 852). Consequently, there was a real possibility that these legislatures did not realize their actions would have the effect of making 15-year-old offenders eligible for the death penalty (*Thompson* at 857). Under these unique circumstances, Justice O'Connor concluded that her only choice was to vote against permitting the execution of Wayne Thompson or any other 15-year-old offender who was sentenced to die under a "statute that specifies no minimum age at which the commission of a capital crime can lead to the offender's execution" (*Thompson* at 857–858).

Thus, Justice O'Connor ultimately voted with the plurality to vacate

Wayne Thompson's death sentence, but she refused to provide the fifth vote necessary to establish a majority decision on the broader Eighth Amendment question. Moreover, she pointedly noted that she was persuaded neither that all 15-year-olds are incapable of possessing the moral blameworthiness that would justify capital punishment nor that all 15-year-olds are incapable of being deterred by the threat of the death penalty (*Thompson* at 853). Justice O'Connor's fifth vote drew a line that still prohibits the execution of any person who was under the age of 16 at the time of the offense. She did not intend this line to be permanent, however. If enough state legislatures were to revise their statutes in such a way as to make it clear that 15-year-old (or younger) defendants are eligible for capital punishment, Justice O'Connor would almost certainly vote to uphold these statutes. In fact, she concluded her opinion by inviting "the people's elected representatives" to decide the ultimate moral issue at stake (*Thompson* at 858–859).

In dissent, Justice Scalia, joined by Chief Justice Rehnquist and Justice White, described the plurality and concurring opinions as "obviously designed to nullify rather than effectuate the will of the people of Oklahoma" (*Thompson* at 876). According to Justice Scalia, both Justice Stevens and Justice O'Connor correctly looked to legislative enactments as the most reliable indicators of how our society views a punishment, but they had misinterpreted the legislative evidence (*Thompson* at 865–868). What the survey of state laws unequivocally proved, Justice Scalia asserted, was that the majority (19) of the 37 states that permit capital punishment have *not* set an age limit but instead allow the age at which a juvenile can receive the death penalty to be the same as the age at which the juvenile can be transferred to the adult system (*Thompson* at 868). Moreover, the plurality and concurring justices had ignored evidence of a recent trend of lowering rather than raising the age at which juvenile offenders could be transferred to adult court (*Thompson* at 867). Taken as a whole, therefore, the legislative evidence supported the idea that American society does not abhor or condemn the execution of 15-year-old offenders "when individuated evidence of the particular case warrants it" (*Thompson* at 868).

As Justice Scalia saw it, Oklahoma, like the majority of capital punishment states, had intentionally established a system in which juvenile offenders could be punished with death only in those rare cases in which a juvenile defendant was transferred from the juvenile system to the adult system *and* a jury had considered his young age before imposing a death sentence (*Thompson* at 863). This system was fair in that it required individualized consideration of the offender's maturity and moral responsibility (*Thompson* at 863). Furthermore, it demonstrated the absence of a societal consensus that "no criminal so much as one day under 16 . . . can possibly be deemed mature and responsible enough to be punished with death for any crime" (*Thompson* at 859, 868).

The dissenting opinion also addressed the plurality's reliance on the behavior of juries in juvenile death penalty cases (*Thompson* at 868–872). Although it was true that there had been a decline in the execution of 15-year-old offenders in this century, this showed only that society feels that executing a minor under 16 should be rare (*Thompson* at 870). The rarity of such executions, however, should not have been interpreted by the plurality as evidence of a societal consensus demanding that execution of a juvenile should *never* occur (*Thompson* at 870). The plurality also erred, Justice Scalia added, when it asserted that it is ultimately the Court's responsibility to determine whether a punishment is cruel and unusual (*Thompson* at 872–873). The Court's sole responsibility, he argued, was to measure the "evolving standards of decency" evidenced by the contemporary behavior of state legislatures and sentencing juries (*Thompson* at 872–873). Going further than this "suggests that the plurality is inappropriately acting in a legislative rather than a judicial capacity" (*Thompson* at 872).

Justice Scalia was sharply critical of Justice O'Connor's concurring opinion. Professing that he found the concurring opinion difficult to understand, Justice Scalia proceeded to summarize it as follows:

> Although we cannot actually *find* any national consensus forbidding execution for crimes committed under 16, there may *perhaps* be such a consensus . . . [thus] the Oklahoma statutes plainly authorizing the present execution by treating 15-year-old felons (after individuated findings) as adults, are not adequate, and what is needed is a statute explicitly stating that "15-year-olds can be guilty of capital crimes." (*Thompson* at 874–875)

Justice O'Connor's concurrence, Justice Scalia charged, was deliberately fashioned to make it more difficult to enact legislation resulting in capital punishment for murderers under age 16. Just as it would be difficult to pass a law saying explicitly that "blind people can be executed" or that "white-haired grandmothers" can be executed, it is difficult to pass a law that explicitly states that "15-year-olds can be executed" (*Thompson* at 876). Thus, although Justice O'Connor claimed that her concurring opinion was more respectful of states' rights than was the plurality opinion, her approach was actually "much more disdainful" than the plurality's approach (*Thompson* at 877).

Justice Scalia also assailed Justice O'Connor for attempting to create an unprecedented and unprincipled principle of Eighth Amendment jurisprudence—one that would automatically invalidate virtually all death sentences meted out to 15-year-olds, 75-year-olds, those of extremely low intelligence, or any other appealing groups as to which the existence of a national consensus regarding capital punishment may be in doubt (*Thompson* at 877). Justice Scalia sarcastically characterized Justice O'Connor's approach as "a Solomonic solution" to the problem of how to prevent Wayne Thompson's execution without actually holding that the execution of 15-year-old offenders is categorically unconstitutional (*Thompson* at 878). "I reject that approach," he declared, "and [I] would prefer to it even the misdescription of what constitutes a national consensus favored by the plurality" (*Thompson* at 878).

## ■ *Stanford v. Kentucky* (1989)

Although many legal scholars praised the practical result of the *Thompson* holding—a ban on executing those 15 years old or younger at the time of their crimes—they also lamented the Court's failure to address the question of the constitutionality of executing juveniles under the age of 18 at the time of their offenses (Biele, 1990; Clark, 1990; Garner, 1994; Leahy, 1989; Nanda, 1993). However, not quite 1 year after *Thompson*, on June 26, 1989, the Supreme Court ended years of issue evasion by holding that the Eighth Amendment does not prohibit the imposition of the death penalty on individuals for crimes committed at age 16 or 17. The Court's announcement came in *Stanford v. Kentucky*, a case in which the Court consolidated two different death sentence appeals, one brought by 16-year-old Heath Wilkins and one brought by 17-year-old Kevin Stanford.

Heath Wilkins, then 16 years and 6 months of age, killed 26-year-old Nancy Allen by stabbing her seven times as he and an accomplice robbed the convenience store she co-owned with her husband in Avondale, Missouri. Wilkins was charged with first-degree murder, tried as an adult, and sentenced to death. The Missouri Supreme Court affirmed the sentence, rejecting the argument that the punishment violated the Eighth Amendment prohibition of cruel and unusual punishment. Kevin Stanford, then 17 years and 4 months old, murdered 20-year-old Baerbel Poole in Jefferson County, Kentucky, after robbing the gas station where the victim worked. Stanford and his accomplice raped and sodomized Poole at the gas station and then drove her to a desolate country road, where Stanford shot her to death. The Kentucky juvenile court transferred Stanford's case to an adult trial court, which convicted him of capital murder and sentenced him to die. The Kentucky Supreme Court upheld the death sentence, finding that he had no constitutional right to be placed in a rehabilitation program and that he had been appropriately certified for trial as an adult (*Stanford* at 364–368). The U.S. Supreme Court granted review in both cases to decide whether the Eighth Amendment prohibits capital punishment for crimes committed at 16 or 17 years of age (*Stanford* at 364–365).

The consolidated *Stanford* case produced another plurality decision; this time the Court divided on a 4-1-4 basis. As in *Thompson*, it was Justice O'Connor who wrote a separate concurring opinion that did not fully support the reasoning of the plurality opinion but did provide the crucial fifth vote on the side of the plurality justices. In *Stanford*, however, the plurality consisted of the three *Thompson* dissenters—Chief Justice Rehnquist, Justice Scalia, and Justice White—plus Justice Kennedy, who did not participate in the *Thompson* case. On the other hand, the same four justices who had made up the *Thompson* plurality—Justices Blackmun, Brennan, Marshall, and Stevens—now found themselves in the dissenting position. This, of course, did not bode well for Heath Wilkins and Kevin Stanford. Indeed, the *Stanford* holding reaffirmed the death sentences of both petitioners and rejected the argument that the Eighth Amendment prohibits the execution of 16- and 17-year-old offenders.

Justice Scalia wrote on behalf of the *Stanford* plurality and began by asserting that only two legitimate Eighth Amendment arguments are available to prisoners who challenge their death sentences. The Eighth Amendment, he explained, requires death-sentenced inmates to prove either that their sentence would have been considered cruel and unusual in 1789 when the Bill of Rights was adopted or that there now is a clear national consensus that the sentence violates our society's contemporary standards of decency (*Stanford* at 368–370). Neither Wilkins nor Stanford could make the first argument, Justice Scalia declared, because at the time the Bill of Rights was adopted, "the common law set the rebuttable presumption of incapacity to commit any felony at the age of 14, and theoretically permitted capital punishment to be imposed on anyone over the age of 7" (*Stanford* at 368). Consequently, the only question left to be resolved was whether the original Eighth Amendment standard had "evolved" to the point that imposing the death penalty on 16- or 17-year-old offenders is presently "contrary to the 'evolving standards of decency that mark the progress of a maturing society' " (*Stanford* at 369).

Answering this question in the negative, Justice Scalia expanded upon many of the same points he had made in his *Thompson* dissent. Any "evolution" must be manifested primarily in "the statutes passed by society's elected representatives" (*Stanford* at 370), and as far as Justice Scalia was concerned, the evidence was clear:

> Of the 37 States whose laws permit capital punishment, 15 decline to impose it upon 16-year-old offenders and 12 decline to impose it on 17-year-old offenders. This does not establish the degree of national consensus . . . sufficient to label a particular punishment cruel and unusual. (*Stanford* at 370–371)

Noting that the dissenting justices had taken issue with the plurality's failure to include the states that do not authorize capital punishment among the states precluding the death penalty for juveniles, Justice Scalia responded that while the number of non–death penalty states may bear upon the question of whether there is a consensus against capital punishment altogether, it is "quite irrelevant" to the specific issue in this case: "not whether capital punishment is thought to be desirable but whether persons under 18 are thought to be specifically exempt from it" (*Stanford* at 370). The dissent's position, he added, "is rather like discerning a national consensus that wagering on cockfights is inhumane by counting within that consensus those States that bar all wagering" (*Stanford* at 370). Justice Scalia accused the *Stanford* dissenters (who had, of course, made up the *Thompson* plurality) of "again [working] statistical magic by refusing to count among the States that authorize capital punishment of 16- and 17-year-old offenders those 19 States that set no minimum age in their death penalty statute and specifically permit 16- and 17-year-olds to be sentenced as adults" (*Stanford* at 371).

The attorneys for Wilkins and Stanford had argued, however, that even if the state laws themselves did not establish a settled consensus, the application of these laws—the reluctance of prosecution and juries to impose the death penalty on minors in actual cases—did demonstrate such a consensus (*Stanford* at 373). But the plurality found this evidence to be inconclusive at best, in that it reflected more than anything else the fact that a very small percentage of capital crimes are committed by juvenile offenders (*Stanford* at 374). Justice Scalia further opined that evidence of this nature did not establish a national consensus against the death penalty for minors; it merely established a national consensus that the death penalty should *rarely* be imposed on offenders under 18 (*Stanford* at 374).

The primary thrust of the *Stanford* plurality opinion essentially ended at this point, for Justice Scalia went on to reject virtually all of the other arguments and evidence advanced by the dissenters—arguments and evidence that had carried the day for the *Thompson* plurality. First, stressing that only American conceptions of decency should be considered by the Court, Justice Scalia dismissed the juvenile sentencing practices of other nations as irrelevant to the inquiry at hand (*Stanford* at 369). Second, he rejected the relevance of state laws setting 18 or higher as the minimum age for engaging in such activities as drinking, driving, gambling, voting, or serving on a jury. These kinds of non–death penalty laws, he contended, were not helpful in ascertaining "evolving standards of decency because they operate 'in gross' and do not give individualized consideration to each offender as is constitutionally required in capital punishment cases" (*Stanford* at 374–377). Next, Justice Scalia questioned the relevance of public opinion polls and other social science evidence offered by the petitioners. Such "socioscientific" evidence, he declared, was too uncertain and unreliable to serve as a basis for constitutional analysis (*Stanford* at 377–378). Justice Scalia also ignored the views of various professional organizations and interest groups, suggesting that such groups should advocate their positions to legislative bodies, not to the courts (*Stanford* at 377).

Finally, and most significantly, Justice Scalia repudiated the *Thompson* plurality's assertion that the Court itself is the ultimate judge of whether a particular punishment violates the Eighth Amendment. The issues in this case, he argued, do not permit the justices to apply "one's own informed judgment" as to whether executing juvenile offenders makes a measurable contribution to the goals of retribution and deterrence or whether there is a proportionate relationship between the punishment imposed and the offender's blameworthiness (*Stanford* at 378–379). By declaring that "it is for us ultimately to judge whether the Eighth Amendment permits the [execution of minors]," the

*Thompson* plurality—and the *Stanford* dissenters—had overstepped the boundaries of the judicial role (*Stanford* at 379). Our job, Justice Scalia stressed, "is to identify the 'evolving standards of decency'; to determine not what they *should* be, but what they *are*" (*Stanford* at 378).

Justice Scalia added that he questioned the validity of social science evidence showing that the execution of juvenile offenders served no valid retributive or deterrent purpose (*Stanford* at 377–378). Even if such evidence were 100% trustworthy, however, it would still be irrelevant to the Court's inquiry (*Stanford* at 378). The proper audience for these arguments, he concluded, is the American people and their elected representatives, and that audience has not yet been persuaded that imposing the death penalty on 16- and 17-year-old offenders violates contemporary standards of decency (*Stanford* at 378). Accordingly, the plurality concluded that "such punishment does not offend the Eighth Amendment's prohibition against cruel and unusual punishment" (*Stanford* at 380).

Justice O'Connor's concurring opinion provided the necessary fifth vote to uphold the death sentences, but she noted her disagreement with two parts of the plurality opinion. First, she maintained that the Court *is* obligated to make its own judgment as to whether there is a proportional relationship between the punishment imposed and the defendant's blameworthiness (*Stanford* at 382). Second, she disputed Justice Scalia's contention that state laws distinguishing juveniles from adults for noncriminal purposes (e.g., driving, drinking, voting) were irrelevant to the Court's proportionality analysis (*Stanford* at 382).

Nevertheless, for Justice O'Connor, the fact that "every single American legislature that has expressly set a minimum age for capital punishment has set that age at 16 or above" was sufficient to distinguish *Stanford* from *Thompson* (*Stanford* at 381). The core of her *Thompson* concurrence, she explained, was her view that the Eighth Amendment requires a specific, express minimum age in the pertinent death penalty statute before a juvenile offender can be executed unless "it is clear that no national consensus forbids the imposition of capital punishment for crimes committed at [a particular age]" (*Stanford* at 380). The plurality's most compelling point, she declared, was that the majority of the states that authorize capital punishment permit it to be imposed for crimes committed at the age of 16 (*Stanford* at 381). Under these circumstances, "unlike the peculiar circumstances at work in *Thompson*," she did not find it necessary to require a state legislature to specify that 16- or 17-year-old offenders could be executed for a capital crime (*Stanford* at 381).

Writing for the dissenters, Justice Brennan acknowledged that the Court must begin the task of assessing the constitutionality of a punishment by reviewing state laws concerning capital sentencing (*Stanford* at 383). Justice Scalia's plurality opinion, however, "gives a distorted view of the evidence of contemporary standards that these legislative determinations provide" (*Stanford* at 384). Ignoring Justice Scalia's argument that states with no death penalty laws should not be considered in assessing legislative views on the execution of minors, Justice Brennan pointed out that 12 death penalty states had enacted laws prohibiting offenders under the age of 18 from being sentenced to death and that 15 jurisdictions—14 states and the District of Columbia—have banned capital punishment altogether (*Stanford* at 384). He therefore counted 27 state and local jurisdictions as having concluded that "no one under 18 should face the death penalty" (*Stanford* at 384).

Justice Brennan also noted that an additional three states refused to permit death sentences to be imposed on 16-year-old offenders, thus making a total of 30 states that would not permit the execution of Heath Wilkins (*Stanford* at 384). Furthermore, 19 of the states that permit offenders under the age of 18 to face the death penalty do so only because of the congruence in those states of laws permitting juvenile offenders under certain circumstances to be transferred to state court systems and laws permitting those state courts to impose death sentences (*Stanford* at 385). The legislatures of these 19 states had not truly made "a conscious moral choice to permit the execution of juveniles" (*Stanford* at 385). Thus, only a few jurisdictions "have explicitly set an age below 18 at which a person could be sentenced to death," and it was premature for the plurality to conclude that there was no national consensus against the execution of juvenile offenders (*Stanford* at 385).

Justice Brennan chided Justice Scalia for downplaying the significance of the fact that capital juries rarely sentence juveniles to death. He noted that only 30 out of the total of 2,186 inmates then on death row were under 18 at the time of their crimes and that only 41 of the 1,813 death sentences imposed between 1982 and 1988 were for juvenile crimes (*Stanford* at 386–387). Juvenile offenders, he added, were significantly less likely to receive the death penalty than were adult offenders. A Florida study, for example, showed that between 1982 and 1988, adults arrested for murder were more than 3 times as likely to receive a death sentence than were juveniles arrested for murder (*Stanford* at 387). There could be no doubt, Justice Brennan declared, that "both in absolute and relative terms, imposition of the death penalty on adolescents is distinctly unusual" (*Stanford* at 386). It was therefore difficult to fathom how the plurality could deny that a sentence so rarely imposed is "unusual" within the meaning of the cruel and unusual punishment clause (*Stanford* at 387).

The plurality, according to Justice Brennan, had also discarded other important evidence offered by the petitioners—evidence that he saw as highly relevant to the "evolving standards of decency" at issue. He reasoned, for example, that the opinions of respected professional organizations were valuable as objective indicia of public opinion and therefore clearly relevant in the Court's inquiry (*Stanford* at 388–389). He also reminded the plurality that in the past—indeed, as recently as *Thompson*—the Court had recognized legislation in other countries as relevant to ascertaining "evolving standards of decency" (*Stanford* at 389). Many countries, he explained, have abolished capital punishment, and the majority of the nations that retain it specifically prohibit the execution of juvenile offenders (*Stanford* at 389). Equally important, since 1979 there had been only eight executions of offenders under 18 throughout the world, three in the United States and the rest in Pakistan, Bangladesh, Rwanda, and Barbados (*Stanford* at 389). It was clear, he concluded, that the imposition of the death penalty for juvenile crimes was "overwhelmingly disapproved" within the world community (*Stanford* at 390).

Justice Brennan reserved his harshest criticism for Justice Scalia's assertion that the Court's Eighth Amendment analysis is complete once state statutes and jury verdicts are examined. The judgments of legislatures and juries are important, Justice Brennan conceded, but Justice Scalia's approach—rejecting the principle that it is ultimately the Court's responsibility to determine whether a punishment is cruel and unusual—would amount to an abandonment of the Court's proper role in American government (*Stanford* at 392). Noting his agreement on this issue with Justice O'Connor's concurring opinion, Justice Brennan declared that the Eighth Amendment forbids punishments that make no measurable contribution to the goals of retribution and deterrence and that are "wholly disproportionate to the blameworthiness of the offender" (*Stanford* at 393).

If the plurality justices had conducted a proper proportionality analysis, Justice Brennan continued, they would have found it difficult to show that executing those who lack full responsibility for their actions makes a meaningful contribution to the goal of retribution (*Stanford* at 402–403). It is because children under 18 are less self-disciplined and more impulsive than adults, Justice Brennan pointed out, that all 50 states recognize the age of majority as 18 or older and forbid those below 18 to vote or to serve on a jury (*Stanford* at 394). These kinds of age-based classifications make it clear, he argued, that "18 is the dividing line that society has generally drawn, the point at which it is thought reasonable to assume that persons have an ability to make, and a duty to bear responsibility for their judgments" (*Stanford* at 396).

According to Justice Brennan, juveniles not only lack the necessary culpability to be executed but also lack the level of maturity and responsibility that presumably make adults capable of being deterred by the threat of capital punishment. Whereas adults are presumed to base their actions on a careful calculation of potential gains and losses, adolescents have less capacity to think in long-range terms and are highly unlikely to engage in a careful cost–benefit analysis that includes the possibility of a distant and uncertain punishment (*Stanford* at 404). Moreover, many years of research had shown that juveniles have much less fear of death than do adults "because they have a profound conviction of their own omnipotence and immortality" (*Stanford* at 404–405).

Perhaps even more compelling, according to the dissenters, was a study of adolescents on death row that was recently published in the *American Journal of Psychiatry*.[5] A team of psychiatrists, Justice Brennan explained, had performed detailed diagnostic evaluations of 14 juveniles on death rows in four states. The findings made it unmistakably clear that the juvenile offenders typically sentenced to die are extraordinarily impulsive, immature, and psychologically disturbed (*Stanford* at 398). "Seven of the adolescents sentenced to die were psychotic when evaluated or had been so diagnosed in earlier childhood; four others had histories consistent with diagnoses of severe mood disorders; and the remaining three experienced periodic paranoid episodes, during which they would assault perceived enemies" (*Stanford* at 398). Furthermore, 8 of the 14 had suffered severe head injuries during childhood, 9 of the 14 suffered from serious neurological abnormalities, and 12 had IQ scores below 90 (*Stanford* at 398). To make matters even worse, violence, alcoholism, drug abuse, and psychiatric disorders were commonplace within the families of these children, and in fact, 10 had been physically abused and 5 sexually abused (*Stanford* at 388). This study, Justice Brennan emphasized, demonstrated that the death penalty is greatly disproportionate to the typical death-sentenced juvenile's likely capacity of judgment and level of blameworthiness (*Stanford* at 398). It also makes a mockery, he added, of the plurality's disingenuous assurances that "individualized consideration at transfer and sentencing ensure that only exceptionally mature juveniles, as blameworthy for their crimes as an adult, are sentenced to death" (*Stanford* at 398–399).

Justice Brennan concluded by summarizing the position of the dissenting justices in two sentences:

> There are strong indications that the execution of juvenile offenders violates contemporary standards of decency: a majority of States decline to permit juveniles to be sentenced to death; imposition of the sentence upon minors is very unusual even in those States that permit it; and respected organizations with expertise in relevant areas regard the execution of juveniles as unacceptable, as does international opinion. These indicators serve to confirm [our] conclusion that the Eighth Amendment prohibits the execution of persons for offenses they committed while below the age of 18, because the death penalty is disproportionate when applied to such young offenders and fails measurably to serve the goals of capital punishment. (*Stanford* at 405)

## ■ The *Thompson–Stanford* Aftermath: Conflict and Confusion

The *Stanford* ruling elicited a mixture of praise and criticism from legal analysts. Some complimented the Court for formulating "an appropriate response to Kevin Stanford's and Heath Wilkins' brutality" (Frank, 1990, p. 560) and for "properly placing the present and future responsibility to define contemporary standards of decency in the collective hands of state legislatures" (Strugatz, 1990, p. 245). Others characterized the *Stanford* holding as "judicial callousness" (Scott, 1990, p. 867), as "not responsive to the changing views of Americans toward capital punishment" (Perfecky, 1990, p. 672), and as ignoring the fact that "the Eighth Amendment was intended to protect political minorities from legislative enactments promulgated by political majorities" (Lanier, 1994, p. 1107). Perhaps the only thing that is irrefutable in the aftermath of *Thompson* and *Stanford* is that the justices—and the American people—remain deeply divided on the issue of applying the death penalty to minors.

In at least one respect, the combined effect of *Thompson* and *Stanford* is unmistakable: The Court drew a bright line establishing the constitutionally mandated minimum age for capital punishment at 16. The failure of a clear majority to coalesce in either decision, however, left many important questions unanswered. Justice O'Connor's pivotal concurring vote, in effect, transformed the *Thompson* dissenting opinion into the *Stanford* plurality opinion. As a result, *Stanford* can be seen as a fragile decision that needs further review.

It is especially telling that five justices have not yet agreed on the fundamental issue of *how* the constitutionality of the juvenile death penalty is to be judged. Although Justice O'Connor cast the crucial fifth vote in *Stanford*, allowing states to execute 16-year-old offenders, she refused to join the plurality justices' assertion that the blameworthiness of the defendant and the proportionality of the punishment are irrelevant to Eighth Amendment analysis. She also disagreed with the plurality—and agreed with the dissenters—on the issue of whether age-status statutes on such matters as drinking, driving, and voting should be considered when determining whether a societal consensus exists to ban the execution of juvenile offenders.

As a result, we have had more than a decade of confusion and unpredictability on a question that is both morally troubling and legally significant. On the one hand, five justices voted to set the minimum constitutional age limit for death penalty eligibility at 16. On the other hand, one of the five sided with the four justices who would have drawn the minimum-constitutional-age line at 18 with respect to questions that may very well prove to be determinative the next time the Court addresses the constitutionality of executing juvenile offenders. The *Stanford* decision certainly cannot be said to rest on solid ground.

## ■ *Atkins v. Virginia* (2002)

After 13 years of ignoring the issue, the Supreme Court in 2002 suddenly opened the door for revisiting the question of the constitutionality of the juvenile death penalty. On June 20, 2002, the Court announced its opinion in *Atkins v. Virginia*, a case that raised the question of whether the execution of mentally retarded offenders violates the Eighth Amendment. Interestingly, in 1989, on the same day the Court decided *Stanford v. Kentucky*, the same five justices who made up the *Stanford* majority (Justices O'Connor, Kennedy, Rehnquist, White, and Scalia) concluded in *Penry v. Lynaugh* that the Eighth

Amendment did not prohibit the execution of mentally retarded offenders. In *Penry*, Justice O'Connor wrote the majority opinion, emphasizing that as of 1989 only two states—Georgia and Maryland—had passed laws exempting mentally retarded offenders from death sentences (*Penry* at 333–334). In the *Penry* majority's view, these 2 states, even when added to the 14 states that at that time had no capital punishment laws, did not provide sufficient evidence of a national consensus against executing mentally retarded offenders (*Penry* at 334).

Thirteen years later, however, Justice O'Connor joined (along with Justices Kennedy, Souter, Ginsburg, and Breyer)[6] in Justice Stevens's *Atkins* majority opinion, which, after referring to the legal landscape in 1989, declared, "Much has changed since then" (*Atkins* at 2248). The *Atkins* majority pointed out that between 1989 and 2002, 16 more states with capital punishment laws enacted legislation prohibiting the execution of mentally retarded persons, bringing the total number of states banning such executions to 30: the 12 states that do not authorize capital punishment and 18 of the 38 states that do authorize capital punishment (*Atkins* at 2248–2249).

The *Atkins* dissenters (Chief Justice Rehnquist, Justice Scalia, and Justice Thomas) rebuked the majority for discerning a national consensus against executing mentally retarded offenders in the face of the fact that 20 states still had laws permitting such executions (*Atkins* at 2252). But Justice Stevens explained that the majority had been impressed by "the consistency of the direction of change" (*Atkins* at 2249). He noted that even in an era when anti-crime laws are far more popular than laws designed to protect the rights of defendants, every state that had changed its laws in this area had elected to forbid executions of mentally retarded offenders. No state, on the other hand, had decided to reinstate such executions (*Atkins* at 2249).

It was also significant, according to Justice Stevens, that executions of mentally retarded offenders were very rare in most states and that in the years after *Penry*, only five states—Alabama, Texas, Louisiana, South Carolina, and Virginia—executed any offenders known to be mentally retarded (*Atkins* at 2249). "The practice, therefore, has become truly unusual and it is fair to say that a national consensus has developed against it" (*Atkins* at 2249).

This consensus, Justice Stevens added, was bulwarked by an even broader public, professional, and international consensus (*Atkins* at 2249, n. 21). Public opinion polls showed that the majority of Americans believed that it was wrong to execute the mentally retarded (*Atkins* at 2249, n. 21). A number of respected professional and religious organizations, including the American Psychological Association and the United States Catholic Conference, were on record as opposing such executions (*Atkins* at 2249, n. 21). The majority also took into account the fact that "within the world community, the imposition of the death penalty for crimes committed by mentally retarded offenders is overwhelmingly disapproved" (*Atkins* at 2250, n. 21).

The *Atkins* majority next advanced an argument that, on its face, would seem to apply to the question of the constitutionality of executing juvenile offenders as well as mentally retarded offenders:

> Mentally retarded persons frequently know the difference between right and wrong and are competent to stand trial. Because of their impairments, however, by definition they have diminished capacities to understand and process information, to communicate, to abstract from mistakes and learn from experience, to engage in logical reasoning, to control impulses, and to understand the reactions of others. . . . There is abundant evidence that they often act on impulse rather than pursuant to a premeditated plan, and that in group settings they are followers rather than leaders. Their deficiencies do not warrant an exemption from criminal sanctions, but they do diminish their personal culpability. (*Atkins* at 2250–2251)

These kinds of deficiencies, Justice Stevens contended, made it difficult to square the practice of executing the mentally retarded with much of the Court's past death penalty jurisprudence (*Atkins* at 2251). In *Gregg v. Georgia* (1976), the Court upheld the constitutionality of capital punishment largely because it was believed that the death penalty served two legitimate social goals: retribution and deterrence (*Atkins* at 2251). But the purpose of retribution—making sure that a criminal gets his "just deserts"—cannot be truly achieved by executing people who have an impaired ability to control impulses and understand the consequences of their actions (*Atkins* at 2251). Similarly, the goal of deterrence is not likely to be achieved by threatening to execute people who have diminished abilities to learn from experience and "process the information of the possibility of execution as a penalty and, as a result, control their conduct based on that information" (*Atkins* at 2251). Because the execution of mentally retarded offenders cannot measurably advance the goals of retribution or deterrence, such punishment is little more than the purposeless infliction of suffering and violates the Eighth Amendment's ban on cruel and unusual punishments (*Atkins* at 2252).

## ■ *Atkins* and the Future of the Juvenile Death Penalty

The *Atkins* holding already has generated speculation by legal scholars that the Supreme Court will abolish the juvenile death penalty in a matter of years. One commentator has detailed the many ways in which both the holding and the reasoning of the *Atkins* Court will open new paths in death penalty litigation and could lead not only to the end of the juvenile death penalty but also to the judicial abolition of capital punishment in the United States (Steiker, 2002). Another has argued forcefully that the *Atkins* decision "requires" the Supreme Court to hold that the execution of 16- and 17-year-old offenders violates the Eighth Amendment (Power, 2002, p. 94).

By far the most important post-*Atkins* development is that four of the justices who constituted the *Atkins* majority have made it unmistakably clear that they believe that the juvenile death penalty cannot stand in light of the Court's decision in *Atkins*. On October 21, 2002, Justices Stevens, Souter, Ginsburg, and Breyer announced their position in a written opinion dissenting from a five-to-four vote declining to hear a new appeal brought by Kevin Stanford, the losing petitioner in *Stanford v. Kentucky*. Ordinarily, if four justices vote to hear an appeal, the Court will grant review. However, Stanford's new appeal came in a habeas corpus petition brought directly to the Court rather than through the lower courts. Such petitions are relatively infrequent and require five votes rather than the usual four.

Stanford, still residing on Kentucky's death row, asked the Court to take his case in order to reconsider the question of the constitutionality of executing those who committed their crimes at age 16 or 17. However, in *In re Stanford* (2002), the three *Atkins* dissenters—Justices Rehnquist, Scalia, and Thomas—joined with Justices Kennedy and O'Connor in refusing to review the case. A denial of review does not constitute a decision on the constitutional merits of the case. The Court's action, however, was significant because of the opinion issued by the dissenting justices. The majority justices declined review without comment, but the four dissenters used strong language to explain why they would have liked to have heard the case.

Writing for the dissenting justices, Justice Stevens described the practice of executing juvenile offenders as "a shameful practice" and "a relic of the past [that] is inconsistent with evolving standards of decency in a civilized society" (*In re Stanford* at 475). Much of the dissenting opinion quoted at length from key portions of Justice Brennan's dissenting arguments in *Stanford v. Kentucky*, which Justice Stevens asserted "are just as forceful and correct as they were in 1989" (*In re Stanford* at 473–474).

According to the dissenters, the case for abolition of the juvenile death penalty is even stronger today than it was in 1989. Justice Stevens contended that a growing body of neuroscientific evidence shows that "adolescent brains are not fully developed" (*In re Stanford* at 474). Such evidence, he maintained, strengthened Justice Brennan's 1989 argument that many important emotional and psychological changes in the maturation process do not occur until people are in their early 20s (*In re Stanford* at 474). Thus it is simply not fair to hold juveniles to adult levels of criminal responsibility (*In re Stanford* at 474).

As the dissenting justices saw it, the most significant development since 1989 was *Atkins v. Virginia*:

> The reasons supporting that holding, with one exception, apply with equal or greater force to the execution of juvenile offenders. The exception—the number of States expressly forbidding the execution of juvenile offenders (28) is slightly fewer than the number forbidding the execution of the mentally retarded (30)—does not justify disparate treatment of the two classes. (*In re Stanford* at 472)

The dissenting justices also found it noteworthy that no states have lowered the age of eligibility for the death penalty since *Stanford v. Kentucky* (*In re Stanford* at 474). Indeed, since 1989, five states—Indiana, Montana, New York, Kansas, and Washington—have raised the age of eligibility to 18 (*In re Stanford* at 472–473). The *Atkins* Court found it significant that all legislative change on the question of executing the mentally retarded since 1989 was in the same direction—toward abolition—and the same logic should apply to the question of executing juvenile offenders (*In re Stanford* at 474). Thus, the time had come to reverse *Stanford v. Kentucky* and bring juvenile executions to an end (*In re Stanford* at 474–475).

On January 27, 2003, the Supreme Court declined to hear still another constitutional challenge to the juvenile death penalty. In *Hain v. Mullin*, the Court, without comment, dismissed an appeal brought by Scott Hain, an Oklahoma death row inmate convicted of committing murder in the course of a carjacking when he was 17 (Greenhouse, 2003, p. A19). As in *In re Stanford*, the Court's denial of review did not set a binding precedent. It is noteworthy, however, because it suggests that the four justices who would like to announce a constitutional ban on executing juvenile offenders are hesitant to press the issue for now. Unlike Stanford's appeal, Hain's case was brought as an ordinary petition for a writ of certiorari, under which the four justices who oppose the juvenile death penalty could have granted review on their own. It thus appears that they are not confident that they will be able to get a fifth vote if full review is granted in a juvenile death penalty case.

A fifth vote, of course, would be most likely to come from Justice Kennedy or Justice O'Connor, both of whom joined in the *Atkins* majority. It seems reasonable to speculate that the four dissenting justices from *In re Stanford* lack confidence that they can move Justice Kennedy or Justice O'Connor into their corner. Accordingly, they may have decided that it is preferable to avoid the issue for now rather than risk a decision that would entrench the holding of *Stanford v. Kentucky*.

It is quite possible that another strategic consideration was the public attention focused on the fall 2002 sniper killings in the Washington, D.C., area and the subsequent arrests of 17-year-old Lee Boyd Malvo and his adult companion, John Muhammad. Supporters of the juvenile death penalty have cited Malvo's case as evidence that the juvenile death penalty should be retained for particularly heinous crimes (Lane, 2003, p. A4). Some of the justices may believe that it is best to wait a while in the hope that anger about the sniper shootings abates and that more states may pass legislation banning capital punishment for offenders under 18.

## Conclusion

As this book is going to press, four justices of the U.S. Supreme Court have taken what appears to be an unyielding position against the practice of executing juvenile offenders. Justices Stevens, Souter, Ginsburg, and Breyer need only one more vote to put an end to such executions. Moreover, in 2002, two of the remaining five justices—Kennedy and O'Connor—joined these four in ending the legally comparable practice of executing mentally retarded offenders. Only Chief Justice Rehnquist and Justices Scalia and Thomas appear to be intractably opposed to the position that executing juvenile offenders violates the cruel and unusual punishment clause of the Eighth Amendment.

What happens over the next few years obviously depends on a variety of factors, including internal debates among the justices, the evolving views of Justices Kennedy and O'Connor, and the possibility of one or more changes in the composition of the Court. Chief Justice Rehnquist and Justice O'Connor are considered the most likely of the justices to retire in the near future, but Justice Stevens, who has been on the Court since 1975 and is 82 years old, may be considering it as well. Because President Bush would be likely to appoint a justice who subscribes to a judicial philosophy that includes support for the constitutionality of death penalty laws, the departure of the chief justice would leave the current split over the juvenile death penalty unchanged. But if either Justice Stevens, the harshest critic of juvenile executions, or Justice O'Connor, who must be considered a "swing voter" on the issue, were to leave the Court, the odds in favor of abolition would go down.

All things considered, however, the momentum still seems to be going in the direction of invalidating juvenile death penalty laws. If either Justice O'Connor or Justice Stevens were to announce retirement, Senate Democrats would undoubtedly mount a particularly strong campaign against a nominee viewed as a doctrinaire conservative. For that matter, no one can predict the outcome of the 2004 elections at this point. Moreover, the logic and reasoning underlying *Atkins* clearly weigh in favor of abolishing juvenile executions and seem to reflect a recent shift in public attitudes and concerns about capital punishment. Regardless of changes in the composition of the Court or the vagaries of American politics, the practice of executing juvenile offenders may very well come to an end in a matter of years.

## Discussion Questions

I   The United States is the only Western democracy to retain capital punishment, and it is one of only three nations that retain the juvenile death penalty. The other two are Iran and the Democratic Republic of Congo. Why hasn't the United States joined the vast majority of nations that condemn the execution of juvenile offenders? Is there something unusual in our culture, our attitudes toward children, our beliefs about the value of human life, or perhaps in our political system that can explain why the United States persists in a practice that has been so overwhelmingly rejected by most of the rest of the world? Could it be that we are right and that the vast majority of other nations are wrong on this issue? Is the death penalty a just and effective way to combat juvenile crime?

**2**  In his plurality opinion in *Stanford v. Kentucky* (1989), Justice Scalia argued that public opinion polls, social science studies, the practices of other nations, and the positions taken by experts, learned societies, and professional organizations were irrelevant to the Court's decision. Do you agree? Why or why not?

**3**  Justice Scalia also rejected the relevancy of the many state laws that set a minimum age of 18 as the legal age for engaging in such activities as drinking, gambling, voting, and serving on a jury. Do you agree with Justice Scalia? Why or why not?

**4**  Since 1976, the Supreme Court has held that the death penalty, because of its severity and finality, can be used only when it serves a valid penological purpose that a lesser sentence could not. The Court has cited retribution and deterrence as the two acceptable penological goals served by a valid capital punishment statute. But does executing juvenile offenders make a measurable contribution to the goal of retribution? If minors do not have the same levels of maturity and responsibility that we presume in adults, doesn't it follow that they are less culpable and blameworthy for their actions than are adults?

**5**  Does the execution of juvenile offenders make an acceptable or measurable contribution to the goal of deterrence? According to Justice Brennan's dissenting opinion in *Stanford v. Kentucky*, juveniles typically lack the level of maturity and responsibility that presumably make adults capable of being deterred by the threat of capital punishment. Therefore, he argues, there is little or no deterrent justification for the juvenile death penalty; minors can be adequately punished through the lesser sentence of lengthy imprisonment. Do you agree? Why or why not?

**6**  In his dissenting opinion in *In re Stanford* (2002), Justice Stevens argued that the Supreme Court's decision in *Atkins v. Virginia* (2002) to ban the execution of mentally retarded offenders compels the Court to find the juvenile death penalty unconstitutional as well. But are nonretarded 16- and 17-year-olds truly comparable with mentally retarded adults? The American Association of Mental Retardation currently defines the mentally retarded individual as someone who has "significant subaverage intellectual function" *as well as* significant limitations in at least two of the following areas: communication, self-care, home living, social skills, community use, self-direction, health and safety, functional academics, leisure, and work. Clearly, the vast majority of 16- and 17-year-olds cannot be said to have "significant subaverage intellectual function." Does this weaken the case for abolishing the juvenile death penalty?

**7**  The *Stanford* plurality and the *Atkins* majority disagree as to whether the Supreme Court should consider the following factors when it determines the constitutionality of capital punishment laws: (a) the laws and practices of other nations, (b) the opinions of national professional organizations, and (c) public opinion polls. Which of these factors, if any, should the Supreme Court take into account when assessing the constitutionality of the juvenile death penalty?

## Notes

1  The 13 jurisdictions that do not authorize capital punishment are the District of Columbia and the states of Alaska, Hawaii, Iowa, Maine, Massachusetts, Michigan, Minnesota, North Dakota, Rhode Island, Vermont, West Virginia, and Wisconsin. (NAACP, 2002, p. 1).

2  The 17 states that allow the execution of 16-year-olds are Alabama, Arizona, Arkansas, Delaware, Idaho, Kentucky, Louisiana, Mississippi, Missouri, Nevada, Oklahoma, Pennsylvania, South Carolina, South Dakota, Utah, Virginia, and Wyoming (Streib, 2002).

3  The five states that have chosen the age of 17 as the minimum age for capital punishment are Florida, Georgia, New Hampshire, North Carolina, and Texas (Streib, 2002).

4  The 18 jurisdictions that use 18 as the minimum age for the death penalty are the U.S. government, the U.S. military, and the states of California, Colorado, Connecticut, Illinois, Indiana, Kansas, Maryland, Montana, Nebraska, New Jersey, New Mexico, New York, Ohio, Oregon, and Tennessee (Streib, 2002).

5  See Lewis et al. (1988). Neuropsychiatric, psychoeducational, and family characteristics of 14 juveniles condemned to death in the United States. *American Journal of Psychiatry, 145*, 584–616.

6  Justice Ruth Bader Ginsburg replaced Justice White in 1993, and Justice Stephen Breyer replaced Justice Blackmun in 1994. Both were appointed by President Clinton. Since then, the composition of the Court has remained unchanged.

## References

Bieler, G. M. (1990). Death be not proud: A note on juvenile capital punishment. *New York Law School Journal of Human Rights 7*, 179–213.

Clark, J. D. (1990). Juveniles and the death penalty: A square peg in a round hole. *Mississippi College Law Review 10*, 169–192.

Frank J. R. (1990). *Stanford v. Kentucky*: Did the Court bite the constitutional bullet. *Akron Law Review 23*, 547–560.

Garner, M. E. (1994). Capital punishment for minors. *Journal of Juvenile Law 15*, 150–167.

Greenhouse, L. (2003, January 28). Justices deny inmate appeal in execution of juveniles. *New York Times*, p. A19.

Irvin, C., & Rose, H. E. (1974). The response to *Furman*: Can legislators breathe life back into death? *Cleveland State Law Review 23*, 172–189.

Lane, C. (2003, January 28). Justices spurn case on juvenile executions. *Washington Post*, p. A4.

Lanier, T. S. (1994). Juvenile offenders and the death penalty: An analysis of *Stanford v. Kentucky*. *Mercer Law Review 45*, 1097–1108.

Leahy, G. A. (1989). The execution of a child under the age of sixteen years at the date of the offense is unconstitutional according to the Eighth and Fourteenth Amendments. *Suffolk University Law Review, 23*, 890–896.

NAACP Legal and Educational Defense Fund. (2003, Winter). *Death Row U.S.A.* New York: NAACP Legal and Educational Defense Fund.

Nanda, V. P. (1993). The United States reservation to the ban on the death penalty for juvenile offenders. *DePaul Law Review, 42*, 1311–1340.

Perfecky, T. M. (1990). Children, the death penalty, and the Eighth Amendment: An analysis of *Stanford v. Kentucky*. *Villanova Law Review, 35*, 641–673.

Power, E. P. (2002). Too young to die: The juvenile death penalty after *Atkins v. Virginia*. *Capital Defense Journal, 15*, 93–114.

Scott, M. S. (1990). Evolving standards of decency and the death penalty for juvenile offenders: The contradiction presented by *Stanford v. Kentucky*. *Capital University Law Review, 19*, 851–867.

Steiker, C. (2002). Things fall apart but the center holds: The Supreme Court and the death penalty. *New York University Law Review, 77*, 1475–1490.

Streib, V. L. (1987). *Death penalty for juveniles*. Bloomington: Indiana University Press.

Streib, V. L. (1988). Imposing the death penalty on children. In K. C. Haas & J. A. Inciardi (Eds.), *Challenging capital punishment: Legal and social science approaches* (pp. 245–267). Newbury Park, CA.: Sage.

Streib, V. L. (2002). *The juvenile death penalty today: Present death row inmates under death sentences and executions for juvenile crimes, January 1, 1973, to December 31, 2002*. Retrieved September 2, 2003, from *http://www.deathpenaltyinfo.org/*juvchar.html

Strugatz, M. D. (1990). Juvenile capital punishment and evolving standards of decency. *Suffolk University Law Review, 24*, 237–245.

## Cases

*Atkins v. Virginia*, 122 S. Ct. 2242 (2002).
*Coker v. Georgia*, 433 U.S. 584 (1977).
*Eddings v. Oklahoma*, 450 U.S. 1040 (1981).
*Eddings v. Oklahoma*, 455 U.S. 104 (1982).
*Furman v. Georgia*, 408 U.S. 238 (1972).
*Gregg v. Georgia*, 428 U.S. 153 (1976).
*Hain v. Mullin*, 123 S. Ct. 993 (2003).
*In re Kemmler*, 136 U.S. 436 (1890).
*In re Stanford*, 123 S. Ct. 472 (2002).
*In re Stanford*, 123 S. Ct. 472 (2002).
*Lockett v. Ohio*, 438 U.S. 586 (1978).
*Penry v. Lynaugh*, 492 U.S. 302 (1989).
*Roberts v. Louisiana*, 428 U.S. 325 (1976).
*Stanford v. Kentucky*, 492 U.S. 361 (1989).
*Thompson v. Oklahoma*, 487 U.S. 815 (1988).
*Trop v. Dulles*, 356 U.S. 86 (1958).
*Weems v. United States*, 217 U.S. 349 (1910).
*Wilkerson v. Utah*, 99 U.S. 130 (1879).
*Woodson v. North Carolina*, 428 U.S. 280 (1976).

# IV

## Research and Innovative Treatment Programs

# 14 Principles and Evidence of the Effectiveness of Family Treatment

Carrie J. Petrucci and Albert R. Roberts

CAROLE ROBERTS

Family-based interventions in juvenile justice have been an accepted approach for several decades but until recently lacked convincing and methodologically rigorous research to support them as an effective strategy. Because of comprehensive national research agendas in the 1980s and 1990s, a vast improvement in available practice-based research on family treatment strategies occurred, which, in turn, has increased the popularity of these programs. Several federal agencies have contributed to this growing knowledge base, including the Office of Juvenile Justice Delinquency and Prevention (OJJDP), the Center for Substance Abuse Treatment at the Substance Abuse and Mental Health Services Administration (SAMHSA), and the National Institute of Drug Abuse (NIDA).

The information in this chapter draws largely from an extensive review of the professional literature and the research from two national programs: the Causes and Correlates of Juvenile Delinquency program, funded by OJJDP, and the Strengthening America's Families project, funded by a collaborative effort between OJJDP and SAMHSA. As will be shown, in some instances family treatment programs were a primary focus of the research, and at other times family issues and family programs emerged as a valuable component alongside other important structures.

Several recent studies have found family treatment with juvenile offenders to be effective in reducing recidivism (Henggeler, 1997; Henggeler, Clingempeel, Brondino, & Pickrel, 2002; Sexton & Alexander, 2000). These outcome studies were carefully designed and included follow-up periods of 6 months to several years. In addition, the very positive rehabilitative impact of family therapy on juvenile delinquents and their families has been demonstrated in several meta-analyses. Meta-analysis is a research technique in which researchers review a number of outcome and follow-up studies to determine whether specific types of programs are successful in changing or modifying delinquent behavior. Andrews and associates' (1990) meta-analysis yielded 154 statistical comparisons of the magnitude and direction of treatment impact on recidivism and found that effective intervention methods reduced recidivism by more than 50%. Two of the criminologists in the six-member research team summarized the importance of this study as having documented "why some programs worked while others did not. . . . There is good reason why some programs are effective while others produce no effect or, in fact, increase recidivism" (Gendreau & Andrews, 1990, pp. 177–178). The answer rests in what the program specifically does and how appropriately the rehabilitation or treatment component is matched to client needs (Gendreau & Andrews, 1990). Furthermore, in their meta-analysis of the effect sizes of nine different treatment modalities, Roberts and Camasso (1991) concluded that family treatment programs consistently had the largest effect sizes. In addition, the

positive effect sizes of family counseling held up under close scrutiny. The typical study of the effectiveness of family counseling had strong and rigorous research designs including samples of 200 to 225 cases, multivariate statistical analysis, and follow-up periods of 12–15 months post-treatment. (Roberts & Camasso, 1991, p. 437)

This chapter first presents an overview of family systems theory to explain how interventions at the family level are effective. Special emphasis is given to the co-occurrence of child abuse and delinquency. Next is a discussion of what is known about the risk and protective factors related to juvenile delinquency, followed by key principles of family treatment programs. We then look briefly at the early beginnings of family counseling for juvenile offenders by describing some model programs. Types of current family treatment programs are then presented. We conclude the chapter with a review of several promising, proven family treatment programs. This final section includes family treatment as the main intervention focus, family treatment within a more comprehensive approach, and parenting programs. The abundance of current programs reveals a renewed interest in family treatment to deal effectively with juvenile behavior problems and delinquency.

## ■ The Family and Juvenile Delinquency

Family systems theory is the foundation of the majority of family treatment programs. This theory states that the family is the major socializing agent that influences and helps shape the child's attitude, values, behavior, and personality (Howes & Cicchetti, 1993; Minuchin, 1985). It therefore has a significant impact on the development of the child, in contrast to approaches that focus solely on the individual child. Many child development experts, sociologists, psychologists, and criminologists concur that the family often exercises the greatest influence on the child's early life. The early life experiences of the child lay the foundation for acquired attitudes, values, and behavior patterns. The child may develop maladaptive coping behaviors such as delinquency and other behavioral disturbances as a result of intense family conflict, tension, and disruption. Several researchers have documented the influence of these variables as contributors to delinquency (Abrahamson, 1960; Andry, 1960; Biron & LeBlanc, 1977; Freeman & Savastano, 1970; Glueck & Glueck, 1968; Kumpfer, 1999; Norland, Shover, Thornton, & James, 1979; Rodman & Grams, 1967).

In their discussion of Minuchin's (1985) work, Howes and Cicchetti (1993) outline six basic principles of family systems theory:

1 The family must be seen as an "organized whole," with each member interdependent upon the others. This assumes that when one member changes or responds differently, it affects other family members.
2 Family patterns of interaction should be visualized as actions and reactions in a circular rather than a one-way, linear fashion. In other words,

the actions and reactions of family members play off one another rather than being a one-way communication.

3 Many family systems are resistant to change because they desire to maintain their ongoing patterns of relating, the status quo. Family systems change only when change will meet the needs of one of its members.

4 Well-functioning family systems are constantly adapting their patterns of interaction to meet the needs of its members, rather than resisting change. Their patterns of interaction change as the developmental level of the family changes.

5 Family systems are made up of subsystems, such as the parents subsystem and the parent–child subsystem.

6 Individuals and famil subsystems are separated by boundaries. How family members interact acress these boundaries are governed by rules and consistent behavior.

A family systems approach looks to intervene with the entire family as a means to address the behavior problems of the child (Howes & Cicchetti, 1993; Minuchin, 1985; Robbins & Szapocznik, 2000). The change can occur by addressing either the entire family or one person within the family (Robbins & Szapocznik, 2000).

Family intervention researchers emphasize effective parenting as the best means to reduce or prevent childhood emotional and behavioral problems leading to delinquency (Kumpfer, 1999). Taking an approach that strengthens families is the preferred approach among these researchers and the emphasis in the Strengthening America's Families program funded by OJJDP. Another key aspect of a family approach is to consider the larger social context that influences the family, which in turn influences the child (Kumpfer, 1999).

Given this discussion of the family's influence on the child's development, it should come as no surprise that child abuse and delinquency co-occur among delinquent youths and that child abuse is therefore of increasing concern.

## Child Abuse and Delinquency

Does child abuse or neglect have a cause–effect relationship with delinquency? This question still cannot be answered definitively through current research. In their review of existing studies, Wiebush, Freitag, and Baird (2001) point out that children who have been abused are more likely to become involved in delinquent behavior and to continue in it and that delinquent children have a much higher prevalence of abuse. Several studies highlight that child abuse or neglect is more prevalent among delinquent youths than among youths in the general population (Kelley, Thornberry, & Smith, 1997; Lemmon, 1999; Lewis, Mallouh, & Webb, 1989; Smith & Thornberry, 1995; Widom, 1989,

1992). A similar pattern is seen at the adult level. A Bureau of Justice Statistics prison survey of state inmates revealed that 14% of male inmates and 37% of female inmates reported abuse prior to age 18, compared with an expected prevalence of child abuse in the general population of about 4%. For inmates who reported living in foster care, 44% of males and 87% of females reported child abuse. State prison inmates who were abused were also more likely to be serving time for a violent offense (Harlow, 1999).

The relationship between child abuse and delinquency or adult criminality has been noted to be "complex," meaning it cannot be assumed that all children who are abused will go on to become delinquents (Lewis et al., 1989; Widom, 1989). Both child maltreatment and delinquency are thought to be caused by multidimensional risk factors that may not be the same across youths. More-over, the same risk factor may be related to both child maltreatment and delinquency, making it difficult for researchers to disentangle these effects. Prospective studies with large sample sizes and long follow-ups are needed to definitively determine causal pathways (Lemmon, 1999).

Researchers have found that both childhood physical abuse and neglect (e.g., abandonment and severe malnutrition) result in a greater likelihood for later arrest for a violent crime (Lemon, 1999; Widom, 1992). Cathy Spatz Widom's (1992) prospective study tracked 1,575 children from childhood into young adulthood. The study group was 908 substantiated cases of either child physical abuse or neglect processed by the courts between 1967 and 1971 and followed through official records for almost 20 years. A comparison group of 667 children was matched to the abuse cases (study group). The major finding of this important prospective study was that childhood abuse or neglect "in-creased the odds of future delinquency and adult criminality overall by 40 percent" (Widom, 1992, p. 1). The study sample came from a metropolitan area in the Midwest and was limited to children between 6 and 11 years old at the time of the reported abuse or neglect (Maxfield & Widom, 1996). Wi-dom's (1992) research implies that attention should be paid to neglect cases and that out-of-home placement in an appropriate setting may not present a greater risk to some children.

The Rochester Youth Development Study, part of OJJDP's Causes and Correlates of Delinquency program, also analyzed several aspects of child abuse and neglect and the connection to delinquency. The stratified study sample of 1,000 subjects was selected from seventh- and eighth-grade students in Roch-ester during spring 1988. Data collection consisted of a multiwave panel ap-proach, in which the juvenile and one of the parents were interviewed every 6 months over a 4½-year period. According to Smith and Thornberry (1995), a history of child maltreatment had a significant effect on both the prevalence and frequency of official delinquency; specifically, 45% of the maltreated youths had an arrest record, compared with 32% of the youths with no history of child maltreatment (Smith & Thornberry, 1995). In a later analysis of the same data, a history of child abuse was found to be a significant risk factor for the frequency of serious delinquency and for official delinquency but not for minor delinquency. In addition, youths with a history of child maltreatment were more likely to have problems with drugs, school, mental illness, and teen pregnancy (Kelley et al., 1997). The variables of social class and family structure revealed significant differences related to childhood maltreatment. Poor children and those being reared by single parents had significantly higher maltreatment prevalence rates before the age of 12 than children residing with both biological parents in economically stable homes. Finally, the more frequently and severely maltreated children had consistently higher scores for official and self-reported serious and violent delinquency (Kelley et al., 1997; Smith & Thornberry, 1995).

Many previous studies have emphasized and attempted to explain the relationship of child abuse, maltreatment, and neglect to the deviant behavior of children and youths (Alfaro, 1981; Helfer & Kempe, 1968; Kratcoski, 1982; Mouzakitis, 1981). Violence in the home encourages physical aggression and abuse as a means for solving problems. It prevents youths from feeling empathy for others. It also decreases the ability of children and youths to cope with stress. Exposure to severe physical battering early in life provides a foundation and breeding ground for violent and antisocial behavior. According to Helfer and Kempe (1968): "The effects of child abuse and neglect are cumulative. Once the developmental process of a child is insulted or arrested by bizarre child rearing patterns, the scars remain. One should not be surprised then to find that the large majority of delinquent adolescents indicate that they were abused as children" (pp. xvii–xviii).

These studies suggest that childhood maltreatment is associated with higher rates of delinquency and violent crime. The implications of the current research are that intensive family preservation and multisystemic treatment approaches should be used with maltreated children at a young age to break the intergenerational cycle of violence. Extensive longitudinal research is needed in different jurisdictions to determine under what conditions out-of-home group home placements, home-based family preservation services, foster care, and/or multisystemic treatment works best in preventing adolescent involvement in delinquency.

## ■ Risk and Protective Factors

Several researchers have identified risk factors and protective factors for delinquency. Risk factors are believed to place a youth at "risk" for delinquent behavior. Protective factors are believed to "protect" a youth from delinquency by lessening the impact of a risk factor. These factors are important because if they represent something that is malleable, or can be changed, they can often serve as the targets for intervention. Contrast a parent's coping style as a risk factor compared with one's age or gender (Hawkins et al., 2000; Lipsey & Derzon, 1998). There is not universal agreement on the most important risk and protective factors. What is most interesting about this discussion that relates to this chapter is that family factors often emerge as important.

In a project funded by OJJDP, 22 leading juvenile researchers were brought together for 2 years to form the Study Group on Serious and Violent Juvenile Offenders. The group's task was to analyze current risk and protective factors related to violent juvenile offending (Hawkins et al., 2000). In their meta-analysis of 66 longitudinal studies focusing on youths who had committed acts of physical violence or had threatened to do so, the study group identified a series of "malleable predictors" of violence in five domains:

☐ Individual
☐ Family
☐ School
☐ Peer-related
☐ Community/neighborhood

Of greatest interest in this chapter are the family factors, which were further broken down as follows:

☐ Parental criminality
☐ Child maltreatment
☐ Poor family management practices
☐ Low parental involvement
☐ Poor family bonding and family conflict
☐ Parental attitudes favorable to substance use and violence
☐ Residential mobility
☐ Parent–child separation (Hawkins et al., 2000, p. 3)

A key point made in this research was that a single risk factor is seldom the cause of delinquency. Rather, several risk and protective factors are often present in combination, creating a multidimensional and complex array of factors contributing to delinquency. Interventions are more likely to be effective if they address multiple factors (Hawkins et al., 2000).

Moreover, youths present with different combinations of risk and protective factors, so a one-size-fits-all approach in interventions is not likely to achieve success (Browning & Huizinga, 1999; Lipsey & Derzon, 1998). In their meta-analysis, Lipsey and Derzon (1998) found different rankings for predictors and risk factors for delinquency based on the age of the youths. For example, having a juvenile offense was the strongest predictor for youths aged 6 to 11 but was ranked third among predictors for youths aged 12 to 14. Lack of social ties was the strongest predictor for youths aged 12 to 14 but was ranked fourth for youths aged 6 to 11. Nor should protective factors be quickly defined as the opposite of risk factors (Wasserman, Miller, & Cothern, 2000).

When the same study group also focused on the most important factors related specifically to prevention, once again interventions that focused on family were more effective than those that did not (Wasserman et al., 2000).

The Causes and Correlates of Delinquency Research program is a longitudinal study of approximately 4,000 youths from three cities (Denver, Pittsburgh, and Rochester) who were randomly selected and interviewed either once or twice a year, along with one parent, beginning in 1986. All three sites found the family to be a key influence as a risk or protective factor for delinquent behavior (Browning & Huizinga, 1999; Browning & Loeber, 1999; Browning, Thornberry, & Porter, 1999). Table 14.1 lists each study's findings relating to risk and protective factors. The Denver study focused more obviously on what constituted a "successful adolescence." This was defined as "minimal involvement in serious delinquencies, minimal problems resulting from drug use, age-appropriate grade in school or graduation from high school, and good self-esteem/self-efficacy" (Browning & Huizinga, 1999, p. 1). As can be seen, a stable family and good parental monitoring were noted as key factors in successful adolescence. The Pittsburgh and Rochester studies both identified family factors within a constellation of comprehensive factors. Like Denver,

**Table 14.1    Risk and Protective Factors Highlighting Family Factors for the Denver, Pittsburgh, and Rochester Youth Studies**

| Factors | Denver | Pittsburgh | Rochester |
| --- | --- | --- | --- |
| Risk/protective factors | Conventional friends | Individual | Family |
| | Stable family | Family | School |
| | Good parental monitoring | Macro level (socioeconomic) | Peer influences |
| | Positive expectations for the future | Cumulative effect | Gang membership |
| | Not having delinquent peers | | Structural position (social class and community) |
| | Number of protective factors must exceed number of risk factors for youth to be "successful" | | |
| Family factors | Stable family | Poor supervision | Quality of parent–child relationship: attachment and involvement |
| | Good parental monitoring | Poor parent–son communication | Bidirectional relationship between family process factors and delinquency |
| | | Physical punishment by the mother | Influence of family variables lessened as youth got older |

Source: Browning & Huizinga, 1999; Browning & Loeber, 1999; Browning, Thornbury, & Porter, 1999.

the Pittsburgh study highlighted the importance of poor supervision, which was found to have the greatest influence on delinquency, increasing the risk. Poor communication between parent and son (the Pittsburgh study included only boys) and physical punishment administered by the mother were also influential factors on delinquency (Browning & Loeber, 1999). The Rochester study focused on the parent–child relationship. They found that stronger attachment and involvement of parents with their children reduced the likelihood of delinquency. However, the impact of family variables decreased as the youths passed through adolescence. They also found a bidirectional relationship between family process variables and delinquency, meaning that each factor influenced the others (Browning et al., 1999).

As part of the Strengthening America's Families project, Karol Kumpfer (1999) conducted an extensive literature review, identified a list of family risk factors, and broke these down into four general categories as follows:

☐ Family history (further broken down in the next list).
☐ Family management problems: A family's ability to manage a child's behavior. Problems can occur when the family must manage a difficult child with, for example, hyperactivity. The parent responds ineffectively, which contributes to increased aggressiveness by the child, creating a cycle of a poor relationship between parents and the child. This category also includes lack of supervision and monitoring.
☐ Family conflicts: Conflicts between family members may increase a child's risk for crime and violence.
☐ Family poverty: Poverty, along with economic loss and structural disadvantage, may affect family interactions because it lowers a parent's ability to provide consistent and involved parenting.

Family history risk factors were noted as follows:

☐ Family history: The child witnessing a behavior problem of the parent or a sibling
☐ Poor socialization practices: Failing to teach the child key competencies such as life, social, and academic skills
☐ Poor supervision of the child: Supervision by a sibling or lack of parental monitoring of child's activities
☐ Poor discipline skills: Lax, inconsistent, excessive; unrealistic expectations of the child; harsh punishment
☐ Poor parent–child relationship: Lack of parental bonding, caretaker loss, or parent rejects child
☐ Excessive family conflict and marital discord: Verbal, physical, or sexual abuse
☐ Family disorganization: Including chaos and stress due to poor family management skills or poverty
☐ Poor parental mental health: Including depression or irritability

☐ Family isolation: Lack of extended family networks that are supportive and lack of community supports

☐ Differential family acculturation: Parents lose control of their children because parents are less acculturated than the children (Kumpfer, 1999, pp. 9–10)

Looking more specifically at protective factors, Kumpfer and Alvarado (1998) identified five major areas:

☐ Supportive parent–child relationships
☐ Positive discipline methods
☐ Monitoring and supervision
☐ Families who advocate for their children
☐ Parents who seek information and support (p. 3)

Based on these meta-analyses and comprehensive literature reviews, it is evident that various aspects of parenting are key correlates as risk or protective factors for subsequent delinquent behavior. The advantage in identifying these factors is that those that are malleable or amenable to change can then be built into targeted interventions to reduce the risk of delinquency or to change delinquent behavior.

## ■ Key Components and Principles of Effective Family Programs

Kumpfer and Alvarado (1998) identified 12 key principles of effective family programs based on their review of family-focused treatments:

☐ Comprehensive interventions: The most effective programs are comprehensive in that they address multiple dimensions of the child (cognitive, behavioral, social, emotional, physical, and spiritual) at multiple levels (family, peer group, school, community).

☐ Family-focused programs: Programs need to focus on the family as a whole, rather than only on the child or only on the parent. Comprehensive treatments that address the needs of the child, parent, and family have been found to be the most effective for youths with antisocial behaviors.

☐ Long-term programs: A short-term program may provide only a "bandage" to the family problems. Long-term programs are needed to address the needs of high-risk families.

☐ Intensity of programs: Programs must be of sufficient length and intensity to address family needs. In addition, families must have time to develop rapport and trust with the therapist, the family's needs must be determined, support services must be located, and the problems need to be addressed comprehensively.

☐ Cultural traditions: Interventions must fit the cultural traditions of families. This has been found to improve recruitment, retention, and outcome effectiveness.

☐ Developmentally appropriate interventions: Programs need to be structured to meet the developmental needs of children, but programs also need to consider a parent's readiness to change.

☐ Family dynamics: Programs that change how a family interacts have the greatest chance of long-term effectiveness. Improving parenting skills can be key in maintaining positive family dynamics over time.

☐ An early start: Particularly in the case of dysfunctional families, interventions that start earlier in a child's life can be more effective.

☐ Program components: Address family relations, communication, and parental monitoring.

☐ Recruitment and retention: Research has shown that families can be recruited and retained in programs when transportation needs are addressed, meals or snacks are included, child care is available; the location is nonthreatening, and participating families perceive the provider as genuine and caring.

☐ Use of videos: Videotapes can be effective modeling tools if good and bad parenting is shown and if the actors reflect the ethnicity, culture, and background of the families watching the video.

☐ The trainer: The efficacy of the trainer or staff person administering the program to families is believed to be extremely important. Staff who clearly share the program philosophy are also viewed as more effective.

Several key staff characteristics have been identified (Kumpfer & Alvarado, 1998):

☐ Communication skills in presenting and listening
☐ Warmth, genuineness, and empathy
☐ Openness and willingness to share
☐ Sensitivity to family and group processes
☐ Dedication to, care for, and concern about families
☐ Flexibility
☐ Humor
☐ Credibility
☐ Personal experience with children as a parent or child care provider (p. 10)

The challenge now becomes applying these principles in real-world programs that must provide services in an environment of limited resources. There may be much at stake. With family factors playing such a pivotal role in delinquent behavior, could parenting practices that contribute to delinquent behavior be passed on from one generation to another? Some studies suggest this may be the case. In a longitudinal study of 109 parents and their male children, Pear and Capaldi (2001) looked at whether parents' history of being abused was associated with being abusive toward their own children. After a 10-year follow-up, parents who had been abused were significantly more likely to have abused their own children, as reported by the children themselves (now 10 years older). In 1998, the National Institute of Mental Health and OJJDP funded a 5-year study to analyze intergenerational transmission of antisocial behavior among the 1,000 youths from the Rochester Youth Development Study (the Intergenerational Transmission of Antisocial Behavior project). Forty percent of these youths have now become parents. Carolyn Smith and her colleagues are looking for factors that might mediate delinquency for integration into prevention programs. It will take these kinds of prospective, longitudinal studies to begin to make informative recommendations about this issue. The key point is that families are influential in a child's socialization, as most people might guess and as rigorous research continues to support. Before moving to the discussion of proven programs, we will step back to take a look at some early family treatment programs to illustrate how these programs have evolved.

## ■ Early Treatment Approaches

Family treatment has been available in many different forms since the 1970s: short-term crisis intervention, a family systems approach, behavioral contracting, education on effective parenting for the juveniles' parents, and various combinations of these. We will highlight short-term intervention and behavioral contracting, both of which often incorporated elements of a system approach and/or parent education. Programs were generally developed to provide treatment for the family unit in whatever form it took (e.g., mother, father, juvenile-in-need, and sibling; mother, grandmother, juvenile, foster parents, juvenile-in-need, and siblings). Occasionally, programs are geared toward treating parents in groups separate from the youths, although treating only the parent or the youth has since been found to be less effective (Kumpfer & Alvarado, 1998).

### Short-Term Crisis Intervention

An important characteristic of this type of treatment is the counselor's immediate response to referrals (Stratton, 1975; Wade, Morton, Lind, & Ferris, 1977), which is still effective today (Robbins & Szapocznik, 2000). The goal of this type of treatment is to initiate services as soon as possible after the juvenile's arrest, when the family may be more receptive to such intervention. Most families—particularly those who have previously experienced the delays and inefficiencies characteristic of bureaucracies—are pleased by the immediate availability of a counselor.

According to Roberts (2000) in the *Crisis Intervention Handbook*, a crisis can be a turning point in a person's life. Timely and rapid assessment and intervention is critical to mobilize the previously hidden strengths, capacities, and coping skills of the juvenile and his or her family. Crisis intervention requires the display of acceptance and hopefulness, "sensitivity, active listening skills, and empathy on the part of the crisis intervenor. . . . If the crisis counselor, social worker, or psychologist is able to establish rapport with the person in crisis soon after the acute crisis episode, many months of later treatment may be averted" (Roberts, 2000; p. 8).

Wade et al. (1977) discussed the Intensive Intervention Project (IIP), which was developed in Honolulu, Hawaii, as a diversion program for first-time juvenile offenders, most of whom were referred for status offenses (49% were runaways and 36% were incorrigibles). The primary aspects of this project's treatment program were:

1 Responding immediately to referrals
2 Providing intensive, short-term counseling services with flexible scheduling of sessions to accommodate each family's needs
3 Emphasizing "the family as a system which is functioning maladaptively and which requires changes as a unit" (p. 45)
4 Pairing counselors in male–female teams and assigning them to clients of similar ethnic backgrounds to increase the likelihood of the family relating well to the staff
5 Using graduate student volunteers to supplement the small paid staff, which consisted of a clinical coordinator, a full-time counselor, and a half-time secretary
6 Making referrals to community agencies to follow up on the changes begun through intensive counseling

The crisis intervention techniques the counselors utilized in this project were a combination of the family systems and crisis intervention techniques of Ackerman (1962), Langley and Kaplan (1968), and Satir (1967). Those techniques are summarized briefly in Wade et al. (1977, p. 46).

Another program providing families with short-term crisis intervention was based in San Fernando, California (Stratton, 1975). It had an experimental design in which juveniles who were picked up by the police for committing a status offense were randomly assigned to an experimental or control group, each with 30 individuals. Those in the experimental group received short-term family crisis intervention. In most cases, the initial family counseling session was held within an hour of the juvenile's arrival at the police department. All families were expected to attend at least one follow-up meeting, and additional counseling sessions were available as needed. Families were seen an average of 2.5 times.

Many of the families were resistant to the family-focused approach, as evidenced by their missing scheduled appointments. Frequently they attempted to deny any responsibility for their adolescents' actions. According to

Stratton (1975, p. 16), "they preferred the police or counselor to talk only to the child, and wanted them to give the child specific instructions about what he could or could not do. The parents not only did not want to be present, they often wanted to abdicate any responsibility for what happened to him."

After 6 months, the two groups were examined with regard to rearrests, the number of days juveniles were detained in juvenile hall, and the program costs. The total number of youths rearrested was almost the same for both groups (9 from the experimental group versus 10 from the control), but those in the control group had committed twice as many total offenses (24 offenses compared with 12 for the experimental group).

An examination of cost-effectiveness showed that the cost for the traditional method ($7,497) was more than double that of the family counseling program ($3,541). If the counselor felt that agreement had been reached during the initial session (held at the police station), the youth was released to the parent and avoided detention at juvenile hall. The greatest savings were realized from lower detention costs for the family counseling group.

A short-term family treatment program was provided for the families of 40 juveniles who had been arrested for status offenses and were referred by the juvenile court in Salt Lake City to the University of Utah's Family Therapy Clinic (Parsons & Alexander, 1973). A major goal of this project was to strengthen patterns of communication in the home. In Parsons and Alexander's view, parents frequently establish too many rules and do not respond consistently when those rules are broken. This results in a lack of structure at home, which fosters a climate for acting-out behavior. The family members were given training in "solution-oriented communication patterns." In addition, they were asked to read a behavior modification manual that described the increase and decrease of behaviors on a systems level. (The reading material was an updated version of the 1968 Patterson and Gullion manual.) The therapy sessions were conducted by graduate students in clinical psychology.

The families were divided into one experimental group, two comparison groups, and one no-treatment control group. The study found that "treatment families became less silent, talked more equally, and experienced an increase in both the frequency and duration of simultaneous speech" (Parsons & Alexander, 1973, p. 199); the control families showed no improvement in these areas. The researchers concluded that a focus on family members per se is not sufficient to improve communication patterns. Instead, intervention should focus on specific communication processes, in particular those that enable the family to adjust to stress rather than continue patterns leading to dysfunction.

## Behavioral Contracting

Behavioral contracting was another form of early family intervention. A program utilizing such techniques was developed in Dallas, Texas, for youthful offenders and their parents under the auspices of the Youth Services Program of the Dallas Police Department (Douds, Engelsgjesd, & Collingwood, 1977). Parents and juveniles initially participated in separate groups for 15 hours of skills training in which parents were taught the methods and underlying principles of behavioral contracting. Families then attended monthly meetings to help them incorporate contracting into their household routine.

Douds, Engelsgjesd, and Collingwood (1977) determined that a common characteristic among these families is an inconsistent approach to child rearing. The parents often vacillated "between punitiveness and permissiveness until they reach a point of helplessness where the youth is in control." Behavioral contracting deals specifically with such issues as being consistent, clarifying one's expectations, and changing the family system from utilizing punishment to introducing rewards to improve the juvenile's behavior.

The Dallas program used the following guidelines in developing a contract (Douds et al., 1977, p. 412):

1 Explore the existing problems and needs to change.
2 Have parents and youths list what they think the responsibilities and the privileges of each should be.
3 Narrow the lists of responsibilities and select appropriate rewards for carrying them out.
4 Develop the written agreement.
5 Implement the agreement.
6 Review the results and repeat the steps as appropriate.

The researchers found that parental authority in the home increased and recidivism was markedly decreased. Of the juveniles who completed the program, the recidivism rate for those in the treatment group was 10.7% compared with 42.7% for those in the control group.

## ■ Types of Family Programs

One of the most notable changes about family treatment programs is that they have become more comprehensive. Several researchers have identified groupings or types of family programs. Family-focused treatment programs are sometimes one component within a comprehensive intervention approach that may include an emphasis on individuals, schools, or communities, or family treatment programs can be the primary focus of the intervention.

In their 1995 program summary, OJJDP identified "programs that work" to prevent delinquency (U.S. Department of Justice, 1995). Programs were organized in two ways: by developmental stage of the child or applicable to all ages and based on the implementation strategy, including community-based, family-based, or school-based. For programs organized by developmental stage, family programs are the primary intervention in the first three stages of the child's life, covering prenatal and perinatal (emphasizing the health of the child), birth to age 4 (emphasizing the parent–child bond, parenting skills, and cognitive development of the child), and ages 4 to 6 (emphasizing learning readiness and social competence of the child). For the last two stages, youths ages 7 to 12 (emphasizing family support and youth's commitment to school) and adolescents 13 to 18 (emphasizing peers, education, employment), family treatment is then conducted in conjunction with school, peer, and community interventions (U.S. Department of Justice, 1995).

Effective family-centered approaches have also been categorized into three groups: behavioral parent training, family therapy, and family skills training or behavioral family therapy (Kumpfer & Alvarado, 1998). In later work, Kumpfer (1999) grouped effective family-focused programs into two groups: family prevention approaches and parenting approaches. Family prevention approaches include family skills training programs, family education programs, family therapy, family services, family preservation programs, and surrogate family approaches. Parenting approaches include behavioral parent training programs, parent education programs, parent support groups, parent aid or in-home parent education, parent involvement in youth groups, and Adlerian parenting programs (Kumpfer, 1999). Thus, these two categorizations represent more of a merging of the major categories (family-focused and parent-focused) with more distinct subgroups identified. For purposes of discussion of effective programs presented later in this chapter, three groupings are utilized: family approaches, parenting approaches, and comprehensive approaches.

Review of the most effective family treatment programs reveals several common themes (Kumpfer & Alvarado, 1998). First, programs that "improve family relations, parental monitoring and supervision, and parent-child attachment" (p. 6) have been effective in preventing delinquency. Second, because there are no simple solutions, complex and multidimensional programs are the most successful. Comprehensive programs that encourage change at the level of the family, school, and community are preferred. Third, skills training programs that allow family members to practice new skills have longer lasting effects than information-sharing-only types of education programs. Fourth, programs that combine life skills and social skills for youths to address social and academic competencies alongside parent training programs are more effective than programs that address only the youth or child. This combined approach contributes to better parental supervision and nurturance that can affect multiple risk and protective factors. Fifth, programs must be implemented by highly skilled and well-trained professionals to be the most effective. Table 14.2 compiles the most effective programs in Kumpfer and Alvarado's (1998) comprehensive review.

**Table 14.2    Top Family Treatment Programs as Identified by the Strengthening America's Families Program**

| Name | Type |
|------|------|
| *Exemplary Programs* | |
| Functional Family Therapy | Family therapy |
| Helping the Noncompliant Child | Parent training |
| Iowa Strengthening Families Program for Families with Pre and Early Teens | Family skills training |
| Multisystemic Therapy Programs | Comprehensive |
| Parents and Child Training Series | Comprehensive |
| Prenatal and Early Childhood Nurse Home Visitation Program | Family in-home support |
| Preparing for the Drug Free Years | Parent training |
| Raising a Thinking Child: I Can Problem Solve Program | Parenting training |
| Strengthening Families Program | Family skills training |
| Structural Family Therapy | Family therapy |
| Treatment Foster Care | Parent training |
| *Model Programs* | |
| Center for Development, Education, and Nutrition (CEDEN) Healthy and Fair Start Program | Family in-home support |
| Effective Black Parenting Program | Parent training |
| Families and Schools Together (FAST) | Comprehensive |
| Focus on Families | Parent training |
| Healthy Families Indiana | Comprehensive |
| Home Instruction Program for Preschool Youngsters (HIPPY) | Family in-home support |
| Home-Based Behavioral Systems Family Therapy | Family therapy |
| HOMEBUILDERS | Comprehensive |
| MELD | Parent training |
| Nurturing Parent Program | Family skills training |
| Parents Anonymous | Comprehensive |
| Parent Project | Parent training |
| Parenting Adolescents Wisely | Parent training |
| Strengthening Hawaii Families | Family skills training |
| *Promising Programs* | |
| Bethesda Day Treatment | Comprehensive |
| Birth to Three | Parent training |
| Families in Focus | Family skills training |
| Family Support Program | Parent training |
| First Steps | Family in-home support |
| Health Start Partnership | Comprehensive |
| Home Base Program | Comprehensive |
| Project SEEK (Services to Enable and Empower Kids) | Comprehensive |
| Strengthening Multi-Ethnic Families and Communities | Parent training |

*Source:* Kumpfer & Alvarado, 1998, Table 1, p. 4.

*Definitions of categories per OJJDP:* Exemplary and model programs have rigorous research and evaluation to support the effectiveness of the program; promising programs have some research and evaluation support but lack a sufficient amount (OJJDP Program Summary, 1995).

## ■ Examples of Proven Programs

### Family Programs

#### Brief Strategic Family Therapy

Brief strategic family therapy (BSFT) began at the Spanish Family Guidance Center in the 1970s at the University of Miami School of Medicine, Department of Psychiatric and Behavioral Sciences (see Robbins & Szapocznik, 2000). The program was originally conceived to deal with an increase in behavior problems among primarily Cuban youths. A comprehensive study on value orientations was undertaken to assure the program's cultural appropriateness. The main finding of the study was that Cuban families expected a family intervention approach. The stress of acculturation was also evident. Structural family therapy was developed with two main strategies: treatment was to be problem-focused and pragmatic (strategic) and time-limited. This approach evolved into brief strategic family therapy (BSFT), which integrates theory, research, and clinical practice. The target population is Hispanic youths age 8 to 17 at risk for behavior problems or already exhibiting them, including conduct disorder, delinquency, and alcohol and substance abuse problems (Robbins & Szapocznik, 2000).

Family systems theory is BSFT's theoretical foundation. BSFT sets out to improve problem behavior by improving the family relationship and by improving relationships between the family and the other systems that influence the family. It seeks to mitigate risk factors including the stresses resulting from immigration, to reduce family conflict, and to consider the multiple systems relationships of the family living in the inner city, while enhancing protective factors, including developing positive relationships with extended families and building a strong family focus. Length of treatment is usually 12 to 15 sessions over a 3-month period. It is process oriented, taking a close look at how families interact. The three components of the intervention are joining (addresses the family's engagement in therapy and deals with resistance), diagnosis (the therapist identifies the family's interactional patterns), and restructuring (the therapist works with the family to reframe their interactions). BSFT has been expanded to be culturally appropriate for African American families and for Latino families from geographic regions other than Cuba (Robbins & Szapocznik, 2000).

Several other programs have developed out of BSFT, including bicultural effectiveness training (helps families learn bicultural skills to lower acculturation-related stress), family effectiveness training (combines bicultural effectiveness training with BSFT), multicultural effectiveness training (addresses the needs of non-Cuban Hispanic parents), and one-person family therapy (focuses therapy on one family member when barriers or resistance keep the entire family from participating in therapy). BSFT and its consequent programs have been rigorously tested with experimental designs, and it is among the exemplary programs identified by OJJDP. It has been found to be effective in improving youth behavior, reducing recidivism, and improving family relationships (Kumpfer, 1999; Robbins & Szapocznik, 2000). Moreover, it engages hard-to-reach families at a much higher rate than typical programs. In a clinical trial, 57% of the comparison group did not participate in treatment compared with 7% in the strategic family therapy program. Looking at completion rates, 25% of the comparison group families completed the program and 77% completed structural family therapy (Robbins & Szapocznik, 2000; Szapocznik et al., 1988).

### Functional Family Therapy

Functional family therapy (FFT) began in 1969 at the University of Utah's Psychology Department Family Clinic to serve at-risk adolescents and their families from diverse populations (see Sexton & Alexander, 2000). It targets youths age 11 to 18 from all ethnic and cultural backgrounds. It combines clinical theory and experience into a flexible and culturally sensitive intervention with families. FFT emphasizes the family's strengths as a first step toward problem solving. It is multidimensional in that it focuses on the individual, the family, and the treatment system. The therapist engages in a three-stage clinical process: engagement and motivation (helping a family reframe their thinking into more positive terms), behavior change (implementing a long-term behavior change plan tailored to the family's needs), and generalization (applying positive family change and connecting with community resources to sustain change). FFT usually involves 8 to 12 sessions over a 3-month period, involving usually 30 hours of direct service (Sexton & Alexander, 2000).

Over the last 30 years, FFT has been rigorously tested. Across several studies that utilized comparison groups with no treatment, traditional juvenile court services, and other types of family treatment, rearrests for youths participating in FFT were reduced by 20% to 60%. FFT has also been found to be cost-effective, saving as much as $14,000 per family (Sexton & Alexander, 2000).

## Parenting Programs

### Preparing for the Drug Free Years

The Preparing for the Drug Free Years program (PDFY) originated at the University of Washington in Seattle in 1984, with the goal of helping parents of youths age 8 to 14 to use parenting skills to reduce risk factors and enhance protective factors to prevent drug abuse (see Haggerty, Kosterman, Catalano, & Hawkins, 1999). The program grew out of a comprehensive review of risk and protective factors related to substance abuse, focusing on parental supervision, poor communication, unclear rules and expectations, inconsistent discipline, family conflict, favorable attitudes of family members to drug and alcohol use, and parental substance abuse. Identified protective factors include parental support for a child's competencies, warmth and affection, and clear behavior standards. PDFY was developed to be applicable to families of diverse backgrounds and has been implemented with families of diverse racial and ethnic backgrounds, low-income families, and single-parent families. It has been extensively tested and disseminated, trained over 120,000 families, and is currently operating in more than 30 states (Haggerty et al., 1999).

The theoretical base of PDFY is the social development model. This model emphasizes bonding at several levels (family, school, and peers) and emphasizes positive prosocial bonds as a means to help youths avoid delinquent behavior. Three critical factors are considered for a youth to bond positively to the family: how much positive interaction occurs in the family; family skills in problem solving, completing tasks, and interacting; and rewards and punishments. The program targets these critical factors by increasing positive interaction and involvement between the parent and child, teaching skills to counter peer pressure, teaching parents how to be consistent in their family management, and dealing with family conflict. The program is a standard curriculum with five sessions, 2 hours each, with specific content. It can also be implemented in 10 1-hour sessions. Discussion and practice are built into each session so there is flexibility in the length of time for implementation (Haggerty et al., 1999).

Evaluation efforts have focused on whether the program reduces risk factors and enhances protective factors and on whether substance abuse by youths is reduced. In an evaluation in Iowa, 175 parents completed the program (84% of those that started it). Parents self-reported on knowledge and attitudes and were also videotaped. Intervention-specific parenting skills were found to have increased in the PDFY group compared with the comparison group. Mothers reported giving rewards, communicating rules, punishing more appropriately, restricting their child's alcohol use, having greater expectations that their child would refuse beer from a peer, having less conflict with spouses, and being more involved with the child. Fathers were more likely to communicate rules and were more involved with the child. Communication and better relationships between each parent and the child were also found. In another experimental study in which 360 families participated, similar findings occurred, and positive results were found to sustain themselves over a 1- to 2-year follow-up period. Youths were also found to have reduced smoking and drinking behaviors compared with youths whose parents did not receive PDFY (Haggerty et al., 1999). PDFY is a showcase program at CSAP and has also been recognized by NIDA (Kumpfer, 1999).

## Comprehensive Programs

### Multisystemic Therapy

Another exemplary program that is empirically supported and cost-effective is a family preservation home-based services approach referred to as multisystemic therapy (MST). MST is targeted toward youths with serious antisocial behavior and is intended to avoid out-of-home placement (see Henggeler, 1997). MST programs are based on the belief that the most effective method of helping a troubled antisocial youth is by helping the youth and the family improve their psychosocial functioning. It borrows from both family systems theory (Minuchin, 1974) and Urie Bronfenbrenner's ecological theory (1979), which considers the individual within systems that impact at the individual level, the family level, and the societal level. It is comprehensive in that it intervenes at the individual level with the youth (problem solving), the family (appropriate discipline), and the larger context, including peers (promoting prosocial peers), school (academic performance), neighborhoods, and communities. There are four critical aspects of service delivery: length of service (usually 3 to 5 months, with 60 contact hours), staffing patterns (using a highly trained team with low caseloads), hours of service (staff are available 7 days a week, 24 hours a day for emergencies), and location of services (usually in the home). In most cases, during the first 30 days of treatment, contact with the case manager or master's-level therapist occurs daily.

MST has been extensively evaluated (see Borduin et al., 1995; Henggeler, 1997; Kumpfer, 1999). Longitudinal follow-up studies of MST in Missouri and South Carolina indicate lower recidivism rates (including fewer arrests and commitments to juvenile facilities) for the experimental groups receiving MST than for comparison groups receiving traditional court-ordered services (e.g., curfew, mandatory school attendance, and/or probation supervision) (Borduin et al., 1995; Henggeler, 1997). Quasi-experimental research by Borduin et al. (1995) in South Carolina and Missouri has demonstrated the long-term effectiveness of MST in reducing criminal activity among chronic and violent juvenile offenders. In a 4-year follow-up of delinquent youths with substance abuse problems, youths who received MST had lower aggressive criminal activity than youths who received usual community services, but there was no difference in property crimes (Henggeler et al., 2002). MST has also been found to be cost-effective (Henggeler, 1997). Several randomized clinical trials are currently under way that will evaluate MST integrated into juvenile drug court and with youths who have a dual diagnosis of mental health and substance abuse.

Research from the past 30 years has provided evidence that in order to provide effective remedies for emotionally disturbed and violence-prone juveniles, it is critical that all members of families be strengthened through strategic family therapy, family systems treatment, family preservation services, solution-based therapy, and/or multisystemic therapy.

## Conclusion

The family system exerts tremendous influence on the growth and development of children. The dysfunctional family often does great harm when it imparts negative attitudes and values and antisocial behavioral patterns to its children. In sharp contrast, the well-functioning family has great power to nurture and heal its children while transmitting socially acceptable attitudes, a sense of responsibility and commitment to hard work, humanitarian values, and prosocial behavior patterns. Many families, including dysfunctional ones, have a strong desire to be supportive and caring. Through family counseling, more families can begin to learn improved methods of communication, supportiveness, and effective limit setting and discipline.

## Discussion Questions

1　What are the key principles of family systems theory? What similarities and differences do you see between these principles and the risk and protective factors for youth behavior problems?

2　Is child abuse an antecedent to juvenile delinquency? Support your position with research evidence.

3　Do you think that individual factors or family factors are more important when creating interventions for delinquent youths? Give reasons for choosing one or the other.

4　What are the primary risk factors for juvenile delinquency?

5　What are the primary protective factors for juvenile delinquency?

6　Discuss the relationship between the key components of effective family programs and risk and protective factors for juvenile delinquency.

7　What similarities and differences do you see in the early family treatment programs and the proven programs?

8　What are three categories of family-centered approaches? Describe what targeted behaviors each addresses.

## References

Abrahamson, D. (1960). *The psychology of crime.* New York: Columbia University Press.

Ackerman, N. W. (1962). Adolescent problems: A symptom of family disorder. In *Family process.* New York: Basic Books.

Alfaro, J. D. (1981). Report of the relationship between child abuse and neglect and later socially deviant behavior. In J. R. Hunner & Y. E. Walker (Eds.), *Exploring the relationship between child abuse and delinquency* (pp. 175–219). Montclair, NJ: Allenheld, Osmun.

Andrews, D. A., Zinger, I., Hoge, R. D., Bonta, J., Gendreau, P., & Cullen, F. T. (1990). Does correctional treatment work? A clinically relevant and psychologically informed meta-analysis. *Criminology, 28*, 369–404.

Andry, R. G. (1960). *Delinquency and parental pathology*. London: Methuen.

Biron, L., & LeBlanc, M. (1977). Family components and home-based delinquency. *British Journal of Criminology, 17*, 157–168.

Borduin, C. M., Mann, B. J., Cone, L. T., Henggeler, S. W., Fucci, B. R., Blaske, D. M., et al. (1995). Multisystemic treatment of serious juvenile offenders: Long-term prevention of criminality and violence. *Journal of Consulting and Clinical Psychology, 63*, 569–578.

Bronfenbrenner, U. (1979). *The ecology of human development: Experiments by nature and design*. Cambridge, MA: Harvard University Press.

Browning, K., & Huizinga, D. (1999). *Highlights of findings from the Denver Youth study* (OJJDP fact sheet 106; NCJ FS-99106). Washington, DC: U.S. Department of Justice, Office of Justice Programs, Office of Juvenile Justice and Delinquency Prevention.

Browning, K., & Loeber, R. (1999). *Highlights of findings from the Pittsburgh Youth Study* (OJJDP fact sheet 95; NCJ FS-9995). Washington, DC: U.S. Department of Justice, Office of Justice Programs, Office of Juvenile Justice and Delinquency Prevention.

Browning, K., Thornberry, T. P., & Porter, P. K. (1999). *Highlights of findings from the Rochester Youth Development Study* (OJJDP fact sheet 103; NCJ FS-99103). Washington, DC: U.S. Department of Justice, Office of Justice Programs, Office of Juvenile Justice and Delinquency Prevention.

Douds, A. F., Engelsgjesd, M., & Collingwood, T. R. (1977). Behavior contracting with youthful offenders. *Child Welfare, 56*, 409–417.

Freeman, B., & Savastano, G. (1970). The affluent youthful offender. *Crime and Delinquency, 16*(3), 264–272.

Gendreau, P., & Andrews, D. A. (1990). Tertiary prevention: What the meta-analysis of the offender treatment literature tell us about "what works." *Canadian Journal of Criminology, 32*, 173–184.

Glueck, S., & Glueck, E. (1968). *Delinquents and nondelinquents in perspective*. Cambridge, MA: Harvard University Press.

Haggerty, K., Kosterman, R., Catalano, R. F., & Hawkins, J. D. (1999). *Preparing for the drug free years* (NCJ 173408). Washington, DC: U.S. Department of Justice, Office of Justice Programs, Office of Juvenile Justice and Delinquency Prevention.

Harlow, C. W. (1999). *Prior abuse reported by inmates and probationers* (NCJ 172879). Washington, DC: U.S. Department of Justice, Office of Justice Programs, Bureau of Justice Statistics.

Hawkins, J. D., Herrenkohl, T. I., Farrington, D. P., Brewer, D., Catalano, R. F., Harachi, T. W., et al. (2000). *Predictors of youth violence* (NCJ 179065). Washington, DC: U.S. Department of Justice, Office of Justice Programs, Office of Juvenile Justice and Delinquency Prevention.

Helfer, R., & Kempe, C. H. (Eds.). (1968). *Battered child*. Chicago: University of Chicago Press.

Henggeler, S. W. (1997). *Treating serious anti-social behavior in youth: The MST approach* (NCJ 165151). Washington, DC: U.S. Department of Justice, Office of Justice Programs, Office of Juvenile Justice and Delinquency Prevention.

Henggeler, S. W., Clingempeel, W. G., Brondino, M. J., & Pickrel, S. G. (2002). Four-year follow-up of multisystemic therapy with substance-abusing and substance-dependent juvenile offenders. *Journal of the American Academy of Child and Adolescent Psychiatry, 41*(7), 868–874.

Howes, P. W., & Cicchetti, D. (1993). A family/relational perspective on maltreating families: Parallel processes across systems and social policy implications. In D. Cicchetti & S. L. Toth (Eds.), *Child abuse, child development, and social policy* (pp. 249–299). Norwood, NJ: Ablex.

Kelley, B. T., Thornberry, T. P., & Smith, C. A. (1997). *In the wake of child maltreatment* (NCJ 165257). Washington, DC: U.S. Department of Justice, Office of Justice Programs, Office of Juvenile Justice Delinquency Prevention.

Kratcoski, P. C. (1982). Child abuse and violence against the family. *Child Welfare, 61*(7), 435–444.

Kumpfer, K. L. (1999). *Strengthening America's families: Exemplary parenting and family strategies for delinquency prevention.* Washington, DC: U.S. Department of Justice, Office of Justice Programs, Office of Juvenile Justice Delinquency Prevention.

Kumpfer, K. L., & Alvarado, R. (1998). *Effective family strengthening interventions* (NCJ 171121). Washington, DC: U.S. Department of Justice, Office of Justice Programs, Office of Juvenile Justice Delinquency Prevention.

Langley, D. G., & Kaplan, D. M. (1968). *Treatment of families in crisis.* New York: Grune & Stratton.

Lemmon, J. H. (1999). How child maltreatment affects dimensions of juvenile delinquency in a cohort of low-income urban youths. *Justice Quarterly, 16*(2), 357–376.

Lewis, D. O., Mallouh, C., & Webb, V. (1989). Child abuse, delinquency, and violent criminality. In D. Cicchetti & V. Carlson (Eds.), *Child maltreatment: Theory and research on the causes and consequences of child abuse and neglect* (pp. 707–721). New York: Cambridge University Press.

Lipsey, M. W., & Derzon, J. H. (1998). Predictors of violent or serious delinquency in adolescence and early adulthood. In R. Loeber & D. P. Farrington (Eds.), *Serious and violent juvenile offenders: Risk factors and successful interventions* (pp. 86–105). Thousand Oaks, CA: Sage.

Minuchin, S. (1974). *Families and family therapy.* Cambridge, MA: Harvard University Press.

Minuchin, P. (1985). Families and individual development: Provocations from the field of family therapy. *Child Development, 56,* 289–302.

Mouzakitis, C. M. (1981). An inquiry into the problem of child abuse and juvenile delinquency. In J. R. Hunner & Y. E. Walker (Eds.), *Exploring the relationship between child abuse and delinquency.* Montclair, NJ: Allenheld, Osmun.

Norland, S., Shover, N., Thornton, W. E., & James, J. (1979). Intrafamily conflict and delinquency. *Pacific Sociological Review, 22,* 223–240.

Parsons, B., & Alexander, J. (1973). Short-term family intervention: A therapy outcome study. *Journal of Consulting and Clinical Psychology, 41,* 195–201.

Patterson, G. R., & Gullion, M. E. (1968). *Living with children. New methods for parents and teachers.* Champaign, IL: Research Press.

Pear, K. C., & Capaldi, D. M. (2001). Intergenerational transmission of abuse: A two-generational prospective study of an at-risk sample. *Child Abuse and Neglect, 25*(11), 1439–1461.

Robbins, M. S., & Szapocznik, J. (2000). *Brief strategic family therapy* (NCJ 179285). Washington, DC: U.S. Department of Justice, Office of Justice Programs, Office of Juvenile Justice and Delinquency Prevention.

Roberts, A. R. (Ed.). (2000). *Crisis intervention handbook: Assessment, treatment, and research* (2nd ed.). New York: Oxford University Press.

Roberts, A. R., & Camasso, M. J. (1990). Juvenile offender treatment programs and cost-benefit analysis. *Juvenile and Family Court Journal, 42*(1), 37–47.

Roberts, A. R., & Camasso, M. J. (1991). The effect of juvenile offender treatment programs on recidivism: A meta-analysis of 46 studies. *Notre Dame Journal of Law, Ethics, and Public Policy, 5*(2), 421–441.

Rodman, H., & Grams, P. (1967). Juvenile delinquency and the family: A review and discussion. In President's Commission on Law Enforcement and Administration of Justice, *Task force report: Juvenile delinquency and youth crime* (pp. 188–221). Washington, DC: U.S. Government Printing Office.

Satir, V. (1967). *Confronting family therapy.* Palo Alto, CA: Science and Behavior Books.

Sexton, T. L., & Alexander, J. F. (2000). *Functional family therapy* (NCJ 184743). Washington, DC: U.S. Department of Justice, Office of Justice Programs, Office of Juvenile Justice and Delinquency Prevention.

Smith, C., & Thornberry, T. P. (1995). The relationship between childhood maltreatment and adolescent involvement in delinquency. *Criminology, 33*(4), 451–481.

Stratton, J. G. (1975). Effects of crisis intervention counseling on predelinquent and misdemeanor juvenile offenders. *Juvenile Justice, 26,* 7–18.

Szapocznik, J., Perez-Vidal, A., Brickman, A. L., Foote, F. H., Santisteban, D. A., Hervis, O. E., et al. (1988). Engaging adolescent drug abusers and their families into treatment: A strategic structural systems approach. *Journal of Consulting and Clinical Psychology 56,* 552–557.

U.S. Department of Justice, Office of Justice Programs, Office of Juvenile Justice and Delinquency Prevention. (1995). *Delinquency prevention works program summary* (OJJDP program summary). Washington, DC: OJJDP Program Summary.

Wade, T. C., Morton, T. L., Lind, J. E., & Ferris, N. R. (1977). A family crisis intervention approach to diversion from the juvenile justice system. *Juvenile Justice, 28*(3), 43–45.

Wasserman, G. A., Miller, L. S., & Cothern, L. (2000). *Prevention of serious and violent juvenile offending* (NCJ 178898). Washington, DC: U.S. Department of Justice, Office of Justice Programs, Office of Juvenile Justice and Delinquency Prevention.

Widom, C. S. (1989). Child abuse, neglect, and adult behavior: Research design and findings on criminality, violence, and child abuse. *American Journal of Orthopsychiatry, 59*(3), 355–367.

Widom, C. S. (1992). *The cycle of violence* (NCJ 136607). Washington, DC: U.S. Department of Justice, Office of Justice Programs, National Institute of Justice.

Wiebush, R., Freitag, R., & Baird, C. (2001). *Preventing delinquency through improved child protection services* (NCJ 187759). Washington, DC: U.S. Department of Justice, Office of Justice Programs, Office of Juvenile Justice and Delinquency Prevention.

# 15 Evidence-Based Treatment of Juvenile Delinquents With Externalizing Disorders

## Conduct Disorder and Explosive Anger Case Exemplar

David W. Springer

CAROLE ROBERTS

Juvenile delinquents with externalizing disorders are a challenging, yet rewarding, population to treat. The externalizing disorders—namely, attention-deficit/hyperactivity disorder (ADHD), conduct disorder (CD), and oppositional defiant disorder (ODD)—are some of the most common encountered by practitioners working with juvenile delinquents (Kazdin, 2002; Kronenberger & Meyer, 2001). In studies of community and clinic samples, a large percentage (e.g., 45% to 70%) of youths with CD or ADHD also met criteria for the other disorder (Fergusson, Horwood, & Lloyd, 1991), and comorbidity between CD and ODD, anxiety disorders, and depression is common as well (Kazdin, 2002). In a recent epidemiological study that examined psychiatric disorders in juvenile delinquents (Teplin, Abram, McClelland, Dulcan, & Mericle, 2002), the most common disorders were substance use disorders and disruptive behavior disorders (oppositional defiant disorder and conduct disorder), with more than 40% of males and females meeting criteria for a disruptive behavior disorder. Accordingly, this chapter presents a case exemplar of treating a juvenile delinquent dually diagnosed with conduct disorder and alcohol abuse.

First, there is a difference between juvenile delinquency and CD. Many readers may be aware of the behaviors associated with a diagnosis of CD, such as aggressive behavior toward others, using a weapon, fire setting, cruelty to animals or persons, vandalism, lying, truancy, running away, and theft (American Psychiatric Association [APA], 2000). The *DSM-IV-TR* allows for coding a client with one of two subtypes of CD: childhood-onset type (at least one criterion characteristic occurs prior to age 10) and adolescent-onset type (absence of any criteria prior to age 10). Although an adolescent may be considered a "juvenile delinquent" after only one delinquent act, to warrant a diagnosis of CD, that same adolescent must be engaged in a pattern of behavior over an extended period (at least 6 months) that consistently violates the rights of others and societal norms. It is critical, therefore, that practitioners take painstaking care in their diagnostic assessments of conduct disorder, as both false positives and false negatives carry potentially serious consequences for both the offender and society (Springer, McNeece, & Arnold, 2003).

Part of what makes treating juveniles with conduct disorder so challenging is the multifaceted nature of their problems. Fortunately, in recent years there have been significant advances in psychosocial treatments for children and adolescents with disruptive behavior disorders. Some of these evidence-based practices are applied to the case example of Matt in this chapter. For purposes here, Rosen and Proctor's (2002) definition of *evidence-based practice* (EBP) has been adopted, whereby "practitioners will select interventions on the basis of their empirically demonstrated links to the desired outcomes" (p. 743).

# ■ Case Example: Matt

Matt is a 16-year-old Anglo male who was recently picked up by a police officer and taken to the local juvenile assessment center for truancy, vandalism (graffiti), and underage drinking. Earlier that morning, Matt had beaten up a classmate at school. This physical altercation was unprovoked. His case was formally adjudicated through the county juvenile drug court. Rather than being expelled, he is now attending the alternative learning center (ALC). Following the recommendation from the multidisciplinary treatment team, the judge has ordered Matt to receive substance abuse and mental health treatment while on probation. Matt lives with his mother and stepfather. Matt's father committed suicide when Matt was 8 years old, and his mother remarried when Matt was 10. His mother and stepfather have been having difficulty in parenting Matt since he was 13. He does not respect the rules at home, such as abiding by curfews and completing chores. Matt often loses his temper and takes little responsibility for his behavior, and he has a pattern of stealing and lying. His IQ falls within the normal range, and his medical history is uncomplicated.

Matt's social worker was interested in helping Matt and his family by using interventions that gave them the best shot at a successful outcome. While there were many interventions from which to choose, the social worker wanted to use only those that had a solid evidence base. Vandiver (2002) outlines seven steps in applying evidence-based practices with clients: (a) Conduct a biopsychosocial assessment, (b) arrive at a diagnosis and select diagnosis-specific guidelines, (c) identify problems, (d) develop goals or planned targets of change, (e) develop an intervention plan, (f) establish outcome measures, and (g) evaluate. As best as she was able, the social worker used these seven steps as a framework to guide her work with Matt and his family.

## Biopsychosocial Assessment

As the first active phase of treatment, a thorough assessment is the cornerstone of a solid treatment plan (Springer, 2002a). During their initial session together, the social worker conducted a complete biopsychosocial assessment with Matt and his parents (cf. Austrian, 2002; Springer, 2002a).

As part of this initial assessment, the Child and Adolescent Functional Assessment Scale (CAFAS) (Hodges, 2000) was administered. The CAFAS is a standardized multidimensional assessment tool that is used to measure the extent to which the mental health or substance use disorders of youths age 7 to 17 impair functioning. It is completed by the clinician and requires specialized training. A major benefit of the CAFAS in helping practitioners determine a youth's overall level of functioning is that it covers eight areas: school/work, home, community, behavior toward others, moods/emotions, self-harmful behavior, substance use, and thinking. The adolescent's level of impaired functioning in each of these eight domains is scored as severe (score of

30), moderate (20), mild (10), or minimal (0). Additionally, an overall score can be computed. These scores can be graphically depicted on a one-page scoring sheet that provides a profile of the youth's functioning. An appealing feature of recent versions is that the CAFAS now includes strength-based items. Although these items are not used in the scoring, they are useful in treatment planning (Springer, McNeece, & Arnold, 2003). The psychometric properties of the CAFAS have been demonstrated in numerous studies (cf. Hodges & Cheong-Seok, 2000; Hodges & Wong, 1996). One study on the predictive validity of the CAFAS supported the notion that this scale is able to predict recidivism in juvenile delinquents (Hodges & Cheong-Seok, 2000). Higher scores on the CAFAS are associated with previous psychiatric hospitalizations, serious psychiatric diagnoses, restrictive living arrangements, below-average school performance and attendance, and contact with law enforcement (Hodges, Doucette-Gates, & Oinghong, 1999).

The social worker had several reasons for selecting the CAFAS. It is clinician-rated (as opposed to a self-report pencil-and-paper scale), which is especially important, given that adolescents with CD often have low insight and underreport problematic behavior (Kronenberger & Meyer, 2001; Teplin et al., 2002). The CAFAS is standardized, covers several areas of functioning, provides clinical cutting scores, and includes strength-based items. For these reasons, it is used widely across U.S. communities. Of course, other scales would have also been excellent choices, such as the widely used Eyberg Child Behavior Inventory (ECBI), a 36-item parent-rating scale that measures conduct-problem behaviors in children and adolescents (Burns & Patterson, 1990; Robinson, Eyberg, & Ross, 1980).

In addition to the CAFAS, the timeline follow-back procedure (Sobell & Sobell, 1992) was used, specifically to assess Matt's substance abuse history (his primary substance of choice was alcohol). This procedure is a structured interview technique that samples a specific period of time. A monthly calendar and memory anchor points were used to help Matt reconstruct daily use during the past month. Whereas adult studies have found that direct self-report measures have high levels of sensitivity in detecting substance use problems and compare favorably with biomedical measures (blood and urine tests) (National Institute on Alcohol Abuse and Alcoholism, 1990), the timeline follow-back may offer the most sensitive assessment for adolescent substance abusers (Leccese & Waldron, 1994). (As part of his probation, Matt also had to submit random urine screens.)

## Diagnose and Review Corresponding Evidence Base

After ruling out medical causes, and based on the collective results of the biopsychosocial assessment, the CAFAS, and the timeline follow-back, the social worker diagnosed Matt as follows:

| | |
|---|---|
| Axis I. | 312.82 Conduct Disorder, Adolescent-Onset Type, Moderate<br>305.00 Alcohol Abuse |
| Axis II. | V71.09 No diagnosis |
| Axis III. | None |
| Axis IV. | V61.20 Parent–Child Relational Problem; V62.3 Academic Problems;<br>Involvement with juvenile justice system |

After the initial assessment, the social worker began working collaboratively with Matt and his parents to decide the best course of action. Through a search of the literature and key databases (cf. Fonagy, Target, Cottrell, Phillips, & Kurtz, 2002; Kazdin, 2002; http://www.effectivechildtherapy.com; http://www.samhsa.gov), the social worker learned the following.

Several meta-analyses suggest that the most effective approaches for treating juvenile offenders have a cognitive-behavioral component combined with close supervision and advocacy, and more positive treatment effects are realized in community settings than in institutional settings (Deschenes & Greenwood, 1994). Lipsey and Wilson (1998) conducted a meta-analysis of experimental or quasi-experimental studies of interventions for serious and violent juvenile delinquents. They reviewed 200 programs, which were further divided into programs for institutionalized juveniles ($N = 83$) and noninstitutionalized juveniles ($N = 117$). McBride, VanderWaal, Terry, and VanBuren (1999, p. 58) nicely synthesized the findings of Lipsey and Wilson's meta-analysis.

Noninstitutionalized programs that demonstrate good evidence of effectiveness include behavioral therapies (family and contingency contracting), intensive case management (including system collaboration and continuing care), multisystemic therapy (MST), restitution programs (parole and probation based), and skills training. Institutionalized programs that demonstrate good effectiveness include behavioral programs (cognitive mediation and stress inoculation training), longer term community residential programs (therapeutic communities with cognitive-behavioral approaches), multiple services within residential communities (case management approach), and skills training (aggression replacement training and cognitive restructuring).

More specifically, the social worker found expert consensus that treatments with the strongest evidence base (as demonstrated in randomized controlled clinical trials) for treating children and adolescents with conduct disorder are parent management training, multisystemic therapy, cognitive problem-solving skills training, and functional family therapy (Fonagy & Kurtz, 2002; Kazdin, 2002).

## Parent Management Training

Parent management training (PMT) is a summary term that describes a therapeutic strategy in which parents are trained to use skills for managing their child's problem behavior (Kazdin, 1997), such as effective command giving, setting up reinforcement systems, and using punishment, including taking away privileges and assigning extra chores. Although PMT programs may differ in focus and the therapeutic strategies used, they all share the common goal of enhancing parental control over children's behavior (Barkley, 1987; Cavell, 2000; Eyberg, 1988; Forehand & McMahon, 1981; Patterson, Reid, Jones, & Conger, 1975; Webster-Stratton & Herbert, 1994). To date, parent management training is the best treatment for youth with oppositional defiant disorder (Brestan & Eyberg, 1998; Hanish, Tolan, & Guerra, 1996), and the effectiveness of parent training is well documented and, in many respects, impressive (Serketich & Dumas. 1996).

Yet, studies examining the effectiveness of PMT with adolescents are equivocal, with some studies suggesting that adolescents respond less well to PMT than do their younger counterparts (Dishion & Patterson, 1992; Kazdin, 2002). In Brestan and Eyberg's (1998) review of studies that examined the effectiveness of psychosocial interventions for child and adolescent conduct problems, two interventions were considered to be "well-established treatments" according to the stringent criteria set forth by the Division 12 (Clinical Psychology) Task Force on Promotion and Dissemination of Psychological Procedures: the videotape modeling parent training program (Spaccarelli, Cotler, & Penman, 1992; Webster-Stratton, 1984, 1994) and parent training programs based on Patterson and Gullion's (1968) manual *Living with Children* (Alexander & Parsons, 1973; Bernal, Klinnert, & Schultz, 1980; Wiltz & Patterson, 1974). These two approaches target parents with children ages 3 to 8 years and 3 to 12 years, respectively.

## Multisystemic Therapy

Multisystemic therapy (MST) (Henggeler & Borduin, 1990; Henggeler, Schoenwald, Borduin, Rowland, & Cunningham, 1998) is a family- and community-based treatment approach that is theoretically grounded in a social-ecological framework (Bronfenbrenner, 1979) and family systems (Haley, 1976; Minuchin, 1974). A basic foundation of MST is the belief that a juvenile's acting out or antisocial behavior is best addressed by interfacing with multiple systems, including the adolescent's family, peers, school, teachers, neighbors, and others (Brown, Borduin, & Henggeler, 2001). Thus, the MST practitioner interfaces not only with the adolescent but also with various individuals and settings that influence the adolescent's life. Services are delivered in the client's natural environment, such as the client's home or a neighborhood center. There have been numerous studies demonstrating the effectiveness of MST with high-risk youth (cf. Borduin et al., 1995; Brunk, Henggeler, & Whelan, 1987; Henggeler et al., 1986). According to Brown et al. (2001), "To date, MST is the only treatment for serious delinquent behavior that has demonstrated both short-term and long-term treatment effects in randomized, controlled clinical trials with violent and chronic juvenile offenders and their families from various cultural and ethnic backgrounds" (p. 458).

## Problem-Solving Skills Training

Problem-solving skills training (PSST) (Spivak & Schure, 1974) is a cognitively based intervention that has been used to treat aggressive and antisocial youth (Kazdin, 1994). The problem-solving process helps clients learn how to produce a variety of potentially effective responses when faced with problem situations. Regardless of the specific problem-solving model used, the primary focus is on thought processes to help adolescents address deficiencies and distortions in their approach to interpersonal situations (Kazdin, 1994). A variety of techniques are used, including didactic teaching, practice, modeling, role playing, feedback, social reinforcement, and therapeutic games (Kronenberger & Meyer, 2001). The problem-solving approach typically includes five steps for the practitioner and client: (a) defining the problem, (b) brainstorming, (c) evaluating the alternatives, (d) choosing and implementing an alternative, and (e) evaluating the implemented option (Kazdin, 2003). Several randomized clinical trials (type 1 and 2 studies) have demonstrated the effectiveness of PSST with impulsive, aggressive, and conduct-disordered children and adolescents (cf. Baer & Nietzel, 1991; Durlak, Furhman, & Lampman, 1991; Kazdin, 2000; cited in Kazdin, 2002).

## Brief Strategic Family Therapy

Brief strategic family therapy (BSFT) developed out of a programmatic series of studies with Hispanic youths (Coatsworth, Szapocznik, Kurtines, & Santisteban, 1997; Szapocznik & Kurtines, 1989). With its strong grounding in a cultural frame of reference, this approach considers factors such as family cohesion, parental control, and communication. Treatment strategies focus on changing concrete interaction patterns in the family, with the therapist challenging interaction patterns to help the family consider alternative ways of dealing with one another. A unique aspect of this approach is that Szapocznik and his colleagues assert that family therapy is a way of conceptualizing problems and interventions but that seeing the entire family may not be necessary (Kazdin, 2002). Several studies (type 1 and 2) have demonstrated improvements in child and family functioning compared with other treatment and control conditions (cf. Coatsworth et al., 1997; Szapocznik & Kurtines, 1989).

## Functional Family Therapy

Functional family therapy (FFT) (Alexander & Parsons, 1973, 1982), like MST, is an integrative approach that relies on systems, behavioral, and cognitive views of functioning. Clinical problems are conceptualized in terms of the function they serve for the family system and for the individual client. Research underlying FFT has found that families with delinquents have higher rates of defensiveness and blaming and lower rates of mutual support (Alexander & Parsons, 1982). The goal of treatment "is the achievement of a change in patterns of interaction and communication, in a manner that engenders adaptive family functioning" (Fonagy & Kurtz, 2002, p. 158). Treatment is grounded in learning theory. FFT has clinically significant and lasting effects on recidivism. In nine studies conducted on FFT between 1973 and 1997, a 25% to 80% improvement was found in recidivism, out-of-home placement, or future offending by siblings of the treated youth (Fonagy & Kurtz, 2002).

## Select Intervention Plan

According to Gambrill (1999), in EBP "social workers seek out practice-related research findings regarding important practice decisions and share the results of their search with clients. If they find that there is no evidence that a method they recommend will help a client, they so inform the client and describe their theoretical rationale for their recommendation. Clients are involved as informed participants" (p. 346). Accordingly, the social worker shared as much as she knew about all of these approaches with Matt and his parents, with the decision making taking place as follows. Given that Matt was 16 years of age, that the outcome findings on PMT with adolescents were equivocal, and that his pattern of behavior was rather entrenched, the social worker and his parents decided against PMT as a primary treatment option. Although MST is probably the most effective treatment available for treating high-risk juvenile offenders like Matt, MST was not being used in the social worker's setting, or even in the local community. Thus, this treatment was not considered an option for Matt's family. Both PSST and FFT were implemented with Matt and his family. Both of these approaches have been demonstrated effective with clients like Matt, and the social worker had been trained in both approaches. While BSFT was also considered, the social worker was not trained in this sophisticated family therapy approach.

## Establish Treatment Goals and Targets for Change

Once the primary interventions, PSST and FFT, had been selected, treatment goals had to be established. The following guidelines are helpful in establishing treatment goals. The goals should be clearly defined and measurable, feasible and realistic, be set collaboratively by the practitioner and the client, stem directly from the assessment process, and be stated in positive terms, focusing on client growth.

The practitioner worked collaboratively with Matt and his parents to come up with the following treatment goals:

I Matt's parents will set firm and consistent limits, using natural rewards and consequences.

**2** Matt and his parents will improve communication and establish a behavioral contract.

**3** Matt will follow the rules at home, as spelled out in the behavioral contract, at least 90% of the time.

**4** Matt will follow the rules at school, as evidenced by earning 3 points a day in every class for doing so.

**5** Matt will meet all the terms of his probation.

**6** Matt will learn alternative ways of dealing with his anger.

**7** Matt will abstain from using alcohol or other drugs.

Matt and his family agreed to these terms for a 2-week period, at which time they would be reexamined and modified if needed. The 2-week time limit on these goals was set because doing something for 2 weeks seems more feasible to many adolescents than agreeing to such conditions indefinitely. For an example of a more detailed and comprehensive treatment plan, see Springer (2002b).

### Implement Intervention Plan

With treatment goals in place, the social worker began working with Matt and his family in family therapy. In the early phase of treatment, the social worker engaged all of the family members in the therapeutic process, in part by using a "nonblaming message." The social worker stressed the need for active participation from everyone in the family and addressed the effect that Matt's behavior had on the entire family system.

The patterns of blaming in the family were first addressed. Matt often got blamed for all of the family's problems. In other words, Matt has assumed (or been assigned) the family role of "scapegoat." Matt's behavior was reframed: He was praised by the social worker for doing too good a job of acting out the family's problems, and he was relieved of this responsibility for the time being. The social worker introduced cognitive aspects commonly associated with the FFT approach, including behavioral components, communication skills training, behavioral contracting, and contingency management. Positive reinforcement was also encouraged among family members.

It was also important for the social worker to provide Matt with as much one-on-one time as possible early on in treatment to establish therapeutic rapport (cf. Todd & Selekman, 1994). By joining with Matt, the social worker did not lose him when it came time to empower his parents to set limits. To this end, she also used empathy and humor with Matt.

As Matt's family progressed through treatment, they sometimes had difficulty in translating their treatment goals into actions. For example, when Matt's behavior began to improve, issues that the family had been pushing aside began to surface. The social worker helped the family gradually shift toward more interpersonal issues. Recall that a key assumption of the FFT approach is that clinical problems are couched in terms of the function that they serve for the family and for the individual. During one session, Matt shared that he sometimes wondered if his dad had the right idea (by killing himself). The family had never discussed the suicide of Matt's father. This was explored at length in the next couple of family therapy sessions, which served several purposes. It allowed all of them to express their thoughts surrounding this tragic event, but it also gave the family an opportunity to practice some of the new communication skills that they had learned by discussing a sensitive and emotionally charged topic.

As the family examined Matt's alcohol abuse, the social worker avoided the use of labels such as addict or alcoholic, which often do more harm than good with adolescent offenders (Todd & Selekman, 1994). Instead, during individual sessions (with Matt) and family sessions, techniques common in PSST (e.g., role playing, feedback, and in vivo practice) were used to help Matt generate alternative solutions to interpersonal problems (e.g., becoming angry with others) that triggered his drinking.

To help specifically with anger management, which many of her other clients at the ALC also struggled with, the social worker started an anger management therapy group. The Substance Abuse and Mental Health Services Administration's Center for Substance Abuse Treatment (Reilly & Shopshire, 2002) has issued a 12-week cognitive-behavioral anger management group treatment manual, *Anger Management for Substance Abuse and Mental Health Clients: A Cognitive Behavioral Therapy Manual*, which is available at no cost from the National Clearinghouse on Alcohol and Drug Information (NCADI) (http://www.samhsa.org). This group treatment is an evidence-based combined cognitive-behavioral therapy (CBT) approach that employs relaxation, cognitive, and communication skills. The approach presents clients with options that draw on these different interventions and then encourages them to develop individualized anger control plans that use as many of the techniques as possible. The social worker used this treatment manual to successfully facilitate the anger management group with her clients at the ALC. Note that only a couple of the adolescents in this group had a diagnosis of conduct disorder. Having too many conduct-disordered youths in the same treatment group can be countertherapeutic (Feldman, Caplinger, & Wodarski, 1983).

Matt's anger management plan reflects many of the interventions used in the 12-week group therapy manual: five primary treatment goals, along with corresponding interventions. See Table 15.1 for a listing of the treatment goals and a sampling of the corresponding interventions related to Matt's anger management plan. Of course, this list of interventions is not exhaustive, and there is some overlap across treatment goals and interventions. For a more detailed example of an anger management plan that includes long-term goals and corresponding short-term objectives and interventions, see Dulmus and Wodarski (2002).

**Table 15.1    Matt's CAFAS Results: Intake and Termination**

| CAFAS Domain | Intake | Termination |
| --- | --- | --- |
| School/work | 30 | 10 |
| Home | 30 | 10 |
| Community | 30 | 0 |
| Behavior toward others | 30 | 10 |
| Moods/emotions | 20 | 10 |
| Self-harmful behavior | 0 | 0 |
| Substance use | 30 | 10 |
| Thinking | 10 | 0 |
| Overall functioning | 180 | 50 |

## Monitor Treatment Progress

As the termination of treatment approached, the social worker introduced longer intervals between sessions. She treated the final sessions as once-a-month maintenance sessions for the family to report on how things were going. Matt and his family made considerable progress on the desired treatment outcomes, which are "the targets toward which interventions are directed" (Rosen & Proctor, 2002, p. 744). Over the course of 4 months, progress was evidenced across several areas of functioning. Matt performed well enough at the ALC that he was allowed to transition back into his mainstream school. For the most part, he continued to meet the terms of probation and produced clean urinalyses. However, on two separate occasions, Matt did report drinking a six-pack of beer at a party. On both occasions, Matt was angry at his parents. Using a harm-reduction approach to substance abuse treatment (cf. McNeece, Bullington, Arnold, & Springer, 2002), the social worker encouraged the family to view this as a normal part of the treatment process. She worked with Matt on identifying the anger that triggered his drinking and, using PSST, problem-solved with him on what he could do differently the next time he was feeling angry. Matt had no incidents of physical violence at school or in the neighborhood, although he did sometimes still lose his temper at home when his parents enforced rules.

Matt's therapeutic gains were also monitored with the CAFAS, which was administered at intake and at termination (see Table 15.2). Based on the scores for each domain, Matt's impairment in functioning could be interpreted as follows: severe (score of 30), moderate (score of 20), mild (score of 10), or minimal (score of 0). The overall scores can also be computed as severe (140–240), marked (100–130), moderate (50–90), mild (20–40), or minimal to no (0–10) impairment in functioning. In sum, then, it seems that Matt made significant progress over the course of treatment, moving from "severe im-

**Table 15.2    Treatment Goals and Corresponding Interventions for Matt's Anger Management Plan**

| Treatment Goals | Interventions |
|---|---|
| 1. Become aware of intense anger outbursts. | 1. Monitor anger using the "Anger Meter." <br> 2. List positive "pay-offs" that Matt gets from angry outbursts and aggressive actions. |
| 2. Stop violence or the threat of violence (physical and verbal). | 1. Explore events that trigger anger and cues to anger. <br> 2. Explore, role-play, and practice alternative coping strategies (e.g., take a timeout, exercise, deep breathing, conflict resolution model, progressive muscle relaxation). |
| 3. Develop self-control over thoughts and actions. | 1. Review the aggression cycle. <br> 2. Use Ellis's A-B-C-D model of cognitive restructuring. <br> 3. Model and practice thought stopping. |
| 4. Accept responsibility for own actions. | 1. Confront Matt in group when he does not accept responsibility for his actions, and reward him when he does. <br> 2. Record at least two irrational beliefs during the week, and how to dispute these beliefs, using Ellis's A-B-C-D model. |
| 5. Receive support and feedback from others. | 1. Use the here-and-now of the group experience to provide feedback to Matt. <br> 2. Discuss Matt's progress in family therapy sessions. |

pairment in functioning" at intake to the low range of "moderate impairment in functioning" 4 months later.

## Conclusion

In the treatment of adolescents, cognitive-based interventions are generally most effective when combined with behavioral contingencies in the child's natural environment (Ervin, Bankert, & DuPaul, 1996). It makes little sense to treat an adolescent in isolation from his or her natural environment. Pearson, Lipton, Cleland, and Yee (2002) encourage policy makers to consider adopting cognitive skills training programs such as those reviewed in this chapter.

The first three treatments reviewed (PMT, MST, and PSST) have more extensive (type 1 and 2 studies) follow-up data supporting their effectiveness. FFT has controlled clinical trials supporting its efficacy, but the scope of this evidence is not as solid as it is for the other approaches. Nevertheless, these approaches are all quite promising, and their empirical base places them ahead of other approaches available for treating children and adolescents with conduct problems (Kazdin, 2002). It is worth noting that all but PSST place a primary emphasis on the family.

Despite the promising treatment effects produced by these interventions, existing treatments need to be refined and new ones developed. We cannot yet determine the short- and long-term impact of evidence-based treatments on conduct-disordered youths, and it is sometimes unclear what part of the therapeutic process produces change. In the meantime, practitioners can use the existing knowledge base to guide their work with this complex and challenging population.

## References

Alexander, J. F., & Parsons, B. V. (1973). Short-term behavioral intervention with delinquents: Impact on family process and recidivism. *Journal of Abnormal Psychology, 81*, 219–225.

Alexander, J. F., & Parsons, B. V. (1982). *Functional family therapy.* Monterey, CA: Brooks/Cole.

American Psychiatric Association. (2000). *Diagnostic and statistical manual of mental disorders* (4th ed., text revision). Washington, DC: Author.

Austrian, S. G. (2002). Guidelines for conducting a biopsychosocial assessment. In A. R. Roberts & G. J. Greene (Eds.), *Social workers' desk reference* (pp. 204–208). New York: Oxford University Press.

Baer, R. A., & Nietzel, M. T. (1991). Cognitive and behavioral treatment of impulsivity in children: A meta-analytic review of the outcome literature. *Journal of Clinical Child Psychology, 20*, 400–412.

Barkley, R. A. (1987). *Defiant children: A clinician's manual for parent training.* New York: Guilford.

Bernal, M. E., Klinnert, M. D., & Schultz, L. A. (1980). Outcome evaluation of behavioral parent training and client-centered parent counseling for children with conduct problems. *Journal of Applied Behavior Analysis, 13*, 677–691.

Borduin, C. M., Mann, B. J., Cone, L. T., Henggeler, S. W., Fucci, B. R., Blaske, D. M., et al. (1995). Multisystemic treatment of serious juvenile offenders: Long-term prevention of criminality and violence. *Journal of Consulting and Clinical Psychology, 63*, 569–578.

Brestan, E. V., & Eyberg, S. M. (1998). Effective psychosocial treatments of conduct-disordered children and adolescents: 29 years, 82 studies, and 5,272 kids. *Journal of Clinical Child Psychology, 27*, 180–189.

Bronfenbrenner, U. (1979). *The ecology of human development: Experiences by nature and design.* Cambridge, MA: Harvard University Press.

Brown, T. L., Borduin, C. M., & Henggeler, S. W. (2001). Treating juvenile offenders in community settings. In J. B. Ashford, B. D. Sales, & W. H. Reid (Eds.), *Treating adult and juvenile offenders with special needs* (pp. 445–464). Washington, DC: American Psychological Association.

Brunk, M., Henggeler, S. W., & Whelan, J. P. (1987). A comparison of multisystemic therapy and parent training in the brief treatment of child abuse and neglect. *Journal of Consulting and Clinical Psychology, 55*, 311–318.

Burns, G. L., & Patterson, D. R. (1990). Conduct problem behaviors in a stratified random sample of children and adolescents: New standardization data on the Eyberg Child Behavior Inventory. *Psychological Assessment, 2*, 391–397.

Cavell, T. A. (2000). *Working with parents of aggressive children: A practitioner's guide.* Washington, DC: American Psychological Association.

Coatsworth, J. D., Szapocznik, J., Kurtines, W., & Santisteban, D. A. (1997). Culturally competent psychosocial interventions with antisocial problem behavior in Hispanic youths. In D. M. Stoff, J. Breiling, & J. D. Maser (Eds.), *Handbook of antisocial behavior* (pp. 395–404). New York, Wiley.

Deschenes, E. P., & Greenwood, P. W. (1994). Treating the juvenile drug offender. In D. L. MacKenzie & C. D. Uchida (Eds.), *Drugs and crime: Evaluating public policy initiatives* (pp. 253–280). Thousand Oaks, CA: Sage.

Dishion, T. J., & Patterson, G. R. (1992). Age effects in parent training outcomes. *Behavior Therapy, 23*, 719–729.

Dulmas, C. N., & Wodarski, J. S. (2002). Parameters of social work treatment plans: Case application of explosive anger. In A. R. Roberts & G. J. Greene (Eds.), *Social workers' desk reference* (pp. 314–319). New York: Oxford University Press.

Durlak, J. A., Furhman, T., & Lampman, C. (1991). Effectiveness of cognitive-behavioral therapy for maladapting children: A meta-analysis. *Psychological Bulletin, 110*, 204–214.

Ervin, R. A., Bankert, C. L., & DuPaul, G. J. (1996). Treatment of attention-deficit/hyperactivity disorder. In M. A. Reinecke, F. M. Dattilio, & A. Freeman (Eds.), *Cognitive therapy with children and adolescents* (pp. 38–61). New York: Guilford.

Eyberg, S. (1988). Parent–child interaction therapy: Integration of traditional and behavioral concerns. *Child and Family Behavior Therapy, 10*, 33–45.

Feldman, R. A., Caplinger, T. E., & Wodarski, J. S. (1983). *The St. Louis conundrum: The effective treatment of antisocial youths.* Englewood Cliffs, NJ: Prentice Hall.

Fergusson, D. M., Horwood, L. J., & Lloyd, M. (1991). Confirmatory factor models of attention deficit and conduct disorder. *Journal of Child Psychology and Psychiatry, 32*, 257–274.

Fonagy, P., & Kurtz, A. (2002). Disturbance of conduct. In P. Fonagy, M. Target, D. Cottrell, J. Phillips, & Z. Kurtz (Eds.), *What works for whom? A critical review of treatments for children and adolescents* (pp. 106–192). New York: Guilford.

Fonagy, P., Target, M., Cottrell, D., Phillips, J., & Kurtz, Z. (2002). *What works for whom? A critical review of treatments for children and adolescents.* New York: Guilford.

Forehand, R. L., & McMahon, R. J. (1981). *Helping the noncompliant child: A clinician's guide to present training.* New York: Guilford.

Gambrill, E. (1999). Evidence-based practice: An alternative to authority-based practice. *Families in Society: The Journal of Contemporary Human Services, 80*, 341–350.

Haley, J. (1976). *Problem solving therapy.* San Francisco, CA: Jossey-Bass.

Hanish, L. D., Tolan, P. H., & Guerra, N. G. (1996). Treatment of oppositional defiant disorder. In M. A. Reinecke, F. M. Dattilio, & A. Freeman (Eds.), *Cognitive therapy with children and adolescents* (pp. 62–78). New York: Guilford.

Henggeler, S. W., & Borduin, C. M. (1990). *Family therapy and beyond: A multisystemic approach to treating the behavior problems of children and adolescents.* Pacific Grove, CA: Brooks/Cole.

Henggeler, S. W., Rodick, J. D., Borduin, C. M., Hanson, C. L., Watson, S. M., & Urey, J. R. (1986). Multisystemic treatment of juvenile offenders: Effects on adolescent behavior and family interactions. *Developmental Psychology, 22*, 132–141.

Henggeler, S. W., Schoenwald, S. K., Borduin, C. M., Rowland, M. D., & Cunningham, P. B. (1998). *Multisystemic treatment of antisocial behavior in children and adolescents.* New York: Guilford.

Hodges, K. (2000). *The Child and Adolescent Functional Assessment Scale self training manual.* Ypsilanti: Eastern Michigan University, Department of Psychology.

Hodges, K., & Cheong-Seok, K. (2000). Psychometric study of the Child and Adolescent Functional Assessment Scale: Prediction of contact with the law and poor school attendance. *Journal of Abnormal Child Psychology, 28*, 287–297.

Hodges, K., Doucette-Gates, A., & Oinghong, L. (1999). The relationship between the Child and Adolescent Functional Assessment Scale (CAFAS) and indicators of functioning. *Journal of Child and Family Studies, 8*, 109–122.

Hodges, K., & Wong, M. M. (1996). Psychometric characteristics of a multi-dimensional measure to assess impairment: The Child and Adolescent Functional Assessment Scale. *Journal of Child and Family Studies, 5*, 445–467.

Kazdin, A. E. (1994). Psychotherapy for children and adolescents. In A. E. Bergin & S. L. Garfield (Eds.), *Handbook of psychotherapy and behavior change* (4th ed., pp. 543–594). New York: Wiley.

Kazdin, A. E. (1997). Parent management training: Evidence, outcome, and issues. *Journal of the American Academy of Child and Adolescent Psychiatry, 36,* 1349–1356.

Kazdin, A. E. (2000). *Psychotherapy for children and adolescents: Directions for research and practice.* New York: Oxford University Press.

Kazdin, A. E. (2002). Psychosocial treatments for conduct disorder in children and adolescents. In P. E. Nathan & J. M. Gorman (Eds.), *A guide to treatments that work* (2nd ed., pp. 57–85). New York: Oxford University Press.

Kazdin, A. E. (2003). Problem-solving skills training and parent management training for conduct disorder. In E. E. Kazdin & J. R. Weisz (Eds.), *Evidence-based psychotherapies for children and adolescents* (pp. 241–262). New York: Guilford Press.

Kronenberger, W. G., & Meyer, R. G. (2001). *The child clinician's handbook* (2nd ed.). Boston: Allyn & Bacon.

Leccese, M., & Waldron, H. B. (1994). Assessing adolescent substance abuse: A critique of current measurement instruments. *Journal of Substance Abuse Treatment, 11,* 553–563.

Lipsey, M. W., & Wilson, D. B. (1998). Effective intervention for serious juvenile offenders: A synthesis of research. In R. Loever & D. Farrington (Eds.), *Serious and violent juvenile offenders: Risk factors and successful interventions* (pp. 313–344). London: Sage.

McBride, D. C., VanderWaal, C. J., Terry, Y. M., & VanBuren, H. (1999). *Breaking the cycle of drug use among juvenile offenders.* Retrieved October 24, 2002, from http://www.ncjrs.org/pdffiles1/nij/179273.pdf

McNeece, C. A., Bullington, B., Arnold, E. M., & Springer, D. W. (2002). The war on drugs: Treatment, research, and substance abuse intervention in the twenty-first century. In R. Muraskin & A. R. Roberts (Eds.), *Visions for change: Crime and justice in the twenty-first century* (3rd ed., pp. 11–36). Upper Saddle River, NJ: Prentice Hall.

Minuchin, S. (1974). *Families and family therapy.* Cambridge, MA: Harvard University Press.

National Institute on Alcohol Abuse and Alcoholism. (1990). *Seventh special report to the U.S. Congress on alcohol and health.* Rockville, MD: U.S. Department of Health and Human Services.

Patterson, G. R., & Gullion, M. E. (1968). *Living with children: New methods for parents and teachers.* Champaign, IL: Research Press.

Patterson, G. R., Reid, J. B., Jones, R. R., & Conger, R. E. (1975). *A social learning approach to family intervention: Vol. 1. Families with aggressive children.* Eugene, OR: Castalia.

Pearson, F. S., Lipton, D. S., Cleland, C. M., & Yee, D. S. (2002). The effects of behavioral/cognitive-behavioral programs on recidivism. *Crime and Delinquency, 48*(3), 476–496.

Reilly, P. M., & Shopshire, M. S. (2002). *Anger management for substance abuse and mental health clients: A cognitive behavioral therapy manual.* Washington, DC: U.S. Department of Health and Human Services, Substance Abuse and Mental Health Services Administration.

Robinson, E. A., Eyberg, S. M., & Ross, A. W. (1980). The standardization of an inventory of child conduct problem behaviors. *Journal of Clinical Child Psychology, 9,* 22–29.

Rosen, A., & Proctor, E. K. (2002). Standards for evidence-based social work practice: The role of replicable and appropriate interventions, outcomes, and practice guidelines. In A. R. Roberts & G. J. Greene (Eds.), *Social workers' desk reference* (pp. 743–747). New York: Oxford University Press.

Serketich, W. J., & Dumas, J. E. (1996). The effectiveness of behavioral parent training to modify antisocial behavior in children: A meta analysis. *Behavior Therapy, 27,* 171–186.

Sobell, L. C., & Sobell, M. B. (1992). Timeline follow-back: A technique for assessing self-reported alcohol consumption. In R. Z. Litten & J. P. Allen (Eds.), *Measuring alcohol consumption: Psychosocial and biochemical methods* (pp. 41–72). Totowa, NJ: Humana.

Spaccarelli, S., Cotler, S., & Penman, D. (1992). Problem-solving skills training as a supplement to behavioral parent training. *Cognitive Therapy and Research, 16*, 1–18.

Spivak, G., & Shure, M. B. (1974). *Social adjustment of young children.* San Francisco, Jossey-Bass.

Springer, D. W. (2002a). Assessment protocols and rapid assessment instruments with troubled adolescents. In A. R. Roberts & G. J. Greene (Eds.), *Social workers' desk reference* (pp. 217–221). New York: Oxford University Press.

Springer, D. W. (2002b). Treatment planning with adolescents: ADHD case application. In A. R. Roberts & G. J. Greene (Eds.), *Social workers' desk reference* (pp. 731–738). New York: Oxford University Press.

Springer, D. W., McNeece, C. A., & Arnold, E. M. (2003). *Substance abuse treatment for criminal offenders: An evidence-based guide for practitioners.* Washington, DC: American Psychological Association.

Szapocznik, J., & Kurtines, W. M. (1989). *Breakthroughs in family therapy with drug-abusing problem youth.* New York: Springer.

Teplin, L. A., Abram, K. M., McClelland, G. M., Dulcan, M. K., & Mericle, A. A. (2002). Psychiatric disorders in youth in juvenile detention. *Archives of General Psychiatry, 59,* 1133–1143.

Todd, T. C., & Selekman, M. (1994). A structural-strategic model for treating the adolescent who is abusing alcohol and other drugs. In W. Snyder, & T. Ooms (Eds.), *Empowering families, helping adolescents: Family-centered treatment of adolescents with alcohol, drug abuse, and mental health problems* (pp. 79–89). Rockville, MD: U.S. Department of Health and Human Services, Center for Substance Abuse Treatment.

Vandiver, V. L. (2002). Step-by-step practice guidelines for using evidence-based practice and expert consensus in mental health settings. In A. R. Roberts & G. J. Greene (Eds.), *Social workers' desk reference* (pp. 731–738). New York: Oxford University Press.

Webster-Stratton, C. (1984). Randomized trial of two parent-training programs for families with conduct-disordered children. *Journal of Consulting and Clinical Psychology, 52,* 666–678.

Webster-Stratton, C. (1994). Advancing videotape parent training: A comparison study. *Journal of Consulting and Clinical Psychology, 62,* 583–593.

Webster-Stratton, C., & Herbert, M. (1994). *Troubled families—problem children.* New York: Wiley.

Wiltz, N. A., & Patterson, G. R. (1974). An evaluation of parent training procedures designed to alter inappropriate aggressive behavior of boys. *Behavior Therapy, 5,* 215–221.

# 16 Understanding the Impact of Trauma on Female Juvenile Delinquency and Gender-Specific Practice

Scott K. Okamoto and Meda Chesney-Lind

CAROLE ROBERTS

In recent years, there has been increased attention in the literature on the patterns of behavior and models of practice related to female youths (e.g., Alder & Hunter, 1999; Belknap, Dunn, & Holsinger, 1997; Chesney-Lind & Okamoto, 2003; Okamoto & Chesney-Lind, 2003). Much of this literature has highlighted the sexism inherent in the juvenile justice and mental health systems and the unique treatment needs of girls in these systems. While this literature has been useful in identifying broad, important issues related to girls at risk, it is somewhat limited in elucidating the etiology of female delinquency and offending. Belknap, Holsinger, and Dunn (1997) suggest that sexual and nonsexual physical abuse are important factors in explaining the etiology of female delinquency and the gender differences in offending behavior. In what ways does abuse affect girls differently than boys, and how do girls' abuse histories affect practitioners working with this population in the treatment setting?

The focus of this chapter is the impact of girls' trauma, primarily in the forms of physical and sexual abuse, on their behavior in juvenile justice and mental health treatment settings. Specifically, this chapter argues that understanding the childhood trauma of girls is central to understanding their behavior in the treatment setting and is a major component of gender-specific practice. In this chapter, the dimensions of physical and sexual abuse of girls are examined, the relationship of girls' trauma histories with their manifestations of emotionality and aggressive behavior in the treatment setting is explored, and practice implications are discussed.

## ■ Dimensions of Physical and Sexual Abuse of Girls

### Prevalence

In 2000, national statistics estimated that, of the 879,000 reported cases of child maltreatment, 19.3% were for physical abuse and 10.1% were for sexual abuse (U.S. DHHS, 2002). Although male and female youths have similar rates of victimization for physical abuse, the rate of sexual abuse for girls is substantially higher than for boys (female-to-male ratio of 1.7:0.4). Other estimates have corroborated these statistics. Finkelhor and Baron (1986), for example, estimate that roughly 71% of the victims of child sexual abuse are female. Physical and sexual abuse rates for girls in juvenile justice and mental health settings are substantially higher than those within the general population. Acoca (1998), for example, found that 81% of girls in California's juvenile justice system had experienced one or more incidents of physical or sexual abuse. Forty-five percent of these girls reported having been beaten, and 56% of them reported having experienced one or more forms of sexual abuse. Similarly, Green, Russo, Navratil, and Loeber (1999) found that nearly two thirds (63.3%) of clinic-referred girls in their study reported physical or sexual abuse, with approximately a quarter (26.5%) of the girls experiencing both types of abuse.

In terms of perpetrators, both male and female parents account for similar proportions of physical abuse (28.2% and 32.1%, respectively). However, male parents account for a substantially higher proportion of sexual abuse incidents than female parents (21.5% versus 3.9%; U.S. DHHS, 2002). In terms of sexual abuse, the rates of male perpetrators are much higher in juvenile justice and mental health settings than those within the general population. Fontanella, Harrington, and Zuravin (2000), for example, examined 74 cases of clinic-referred preschoolers and found that 82% of the perpetrators in these cases were male. Lamb and Garretson (2003) examined the forensic interviews for 672 cases of child sexual abuse in three different countries (Britain, Israel, and the United States) and found that male perpetrators were involved in 98% of the alleged incidents of abuse. As illustrated later in this chapter, the over-representation of male sexual abuse perpetrators most likely has an impact on the behavior of girls in the treatment setting, particularly in their interactions with male practitioners.

## Correlates to Physical and Sexual Abuse in Girls

Research has identified relationships between girls' physical and sexual abuse and child and adolescent disorders such as conduct problems (Gore-Felton, Koopman, McGarvey, Hernandez, & Canterbury, 2001; Green et al., 1999), running away (Green et al., 1999; Siegel & Williams, 2003), truancy (Green et al., 1999), and depression (Green et al., 1999). In particular, some research has supported the hypothesis that sexual abuse leads girls to run away in order to escape the abuse experienced at home (McCormack, Janus, & Burgess, 1986). Siegel and Williams (2003), for example, examined the medical and family court records of 206 victims of reported child sexual abuse and compared them with a matched comparison group. They found that all but one of the girls arrested for running away were in the sexually abused group. Similarly, Dembo, Sue, Borden, and Manning (1995) examined a large cohort of youths ($N = 2,104$) in Florida and found that girls' problem behaviors (such as running away) often were related to an abusive, traumatizing home life. Once on the street, it is further hypothesized that girls are exposed to prostitution, drug abuse, and drug selling as a means of survival (Belknap, Holsinger, et al., 1997). As support for this hypothesis, McCormack et al. (1986) found that sexually abused female runaways were significantly more likely than their nonabused counterparts to engage in delinquent or criminal activities, such as substance abuse, petty theft, and prostitution. DeKeseredy (2000) also describes how prostitution functions as a survival strategy for some runaway adolescent females in Canada. He notes that they are in higher demand as prostitutes than adult females within the street culture, allowing them to make a living in a "gender-stratified society."

## Attributions

Recent literature has examined the unique attributions of girls related to their abusive experiences. Kolko, Brown, and Berliner (2002) examined the different dimensions of child abuse attributions and found distinct differences between boys and girls. Girls had higher scores for items related to the abuser's negative intentions and for perceived victimization consequences. In other words, compared with boys, girls tended to feel more strongly that their abuser was malicious and lacked remorse. More so than boys, they also felt that they had a lot of problems related to the abuse and needed "a lot of help." Consistent with these findings, Bugental and Shennum (2002) found that childhood victimization had an impact on girls' perceived powerlessness in relationships with adults. Maltreated boys, on the other hand, did not reveal any differences in their attributions based on their abuse history. These findings point to the unique gender-based cognitions related to abuse and to the need to address these cognitions in the treatment setting.

In addition to the literature focused on broad social problems and cognitive attributions related to girls, specific behavioral manifestations of abuse in girls have been discussed in the literature and have direct implications for the treatment setting. Three of these manifestations are discussed in the next section: girls' discomfort with men, girls' emotionality, and girls' aggression.

## ■ Manifestations of Abuse in Girls

### Discomfort with Men

Perhaps because of the documented overrepresentation of male sexual abuse perpetrators, research has suggested that sexually abused girls have an initial discomfort in working with male practitioners (Fowler & Wagner, 1993; Fowler, Wagner, Iachini, & Johnson, 1992; Moon, Wagner, & Fowler, 1993; Trowell & Kolvin, 1999). This effect appears to be particularly pronounced with younger sexually abused girls (Moon et al., 1993). Lamb and Garretson (2003) found that practitioner gender influences the quality and quantity of responses from sexually abused girls. They found that girls provided more details to directive questions (i.e., who, what, where, when, and why questions) related to abuse incidents from female interviewers than from male interviewers. Some research suggests that girls' initial discomfort toward male practitioners might dissipate throughout the therapeutic process. Fowler and Wagner (1993) found that 20 sexually abused girls referred for individual counseling in their study all expressed interest in working with a female counselor. However, by the end of the six-session program, the girls who were treated by male counselors stated that they were comfortable with them and were more likely to feel comfortable with a male counselor in the future. Although the impact of practitioners' gender is an important factor related to therapeutic progress, Lamb and Garretson (2003) suggest that the effects of practitioner gender are mitigated by the use of evidence-based practice guidelines, such as the National Institute of Child Health and Human Development structured interview protocol for forensic interviews.

## Emotionality

Research has indicated that female youths receiving juvenile justice and mental health services, unlike their male counterparts, often display extreme levels of emotions. Observations by both youth-serving practitioners and female youth clients suggest that girls' complex issues, and the emotional way in which they are expressed, can be very challenging to address in the therapeutic setting (Alder & Hunter, 1999; Baines & Alder, 1996). Much of this research frames girls' emotionality in a negative context. For example, youth-serving practitioners in Baines and Alder's study frequently referred to young women as "hysterical." One of the youth workers in their study provides a shocking example of girls' "hysteria."

> We've had kids in the laundry, sort of holding knives against their
> breasts, and you know that they're not going to do it, but they've been
> in there yelling and screaming and it's been very, I'll use the loaded
> term, hysterical. (p. 476)

More recently, Belknap, Winter, and Cady (2003) have described similar findings in their focus group study. Practitioners in their study described girls as "emotional," "erratic," or "histrionic." While they acknowledge the frustrations experienced by practitioners working with girls, they also point to the inherent sexism in these descriptions and caution that some of these perceptions are "to a degree based on labels that may translate into expectations of girls' behavior" (p. 222), which in turn may have a negative impact on the efficacy of gender-specific practice.

Nonetheless, some research has identified a relationship between emotional dysregulation and sexual abuse. Shipman, Zeman, Penza, and Champion (2000) examined how sexual abuse influenced the emotion management skills of 6- to 12-year-old girls receiving services through Child Protective Services. Their findings suggest that maltreated girls have less emotional understanding (i.e., the causes and consequences of emotional experiences) and less emotional self-awareness. They also found that maltreated girls tended to be more prone than nonmaltreated girls to inappropriate affective displays, such as angry outbursts or the "hysterical" behaviors described in the Baines and Alder (1996) and Belknap et al. (2003) studies.

Although the majority of the research focuses on pathological forms of female emotionality, some research describes the positive functions of this personality trait. In their study of youth workers' perceptions and feelings in working with girls, Chesney-Lind and Freitas (1999) found that the emotional nature of girls made it easier for some youth workers to engage with the population and establish rapport. Some of the practitioners indicated that the "expressive nature" of girls promoted mutual emotional support among girls in milieu-based programs. One practitioner in their study described the ways in which girls supported each other in the treatment setting.

> And so in group we hear one another, we validate one another, we hug each other. And the more we do that, even my girls that are dual diagnosis, you start to touch them from a place of respect and honor [and] they'll just really come around. It's just wonderful to see it. (p. 11)

The literature on female youth emotionality suggests unique implications for gender-specific programming. Youth-serving practitioners in the Baines and Alder (1996) and Belknap et al. (2003) studies indicated or suggested that dealing with the emotionality of female clients was demanding and time-consuming. Their findings suggest that programs for girls should be structured with low staff-to-client ratios in order to meet their demands and needs (Chesney-Lind & Okamoto, 2003). This would most likely have a positive impact on the therapeutic relationship-building process with girls, thereby enhancing therapeutic engagement and possibly clinical outcomes.

## Aggression

Research has described a relationship between physical aggression and victimization of girls. Siegel and Williams (2003), for example, found that 13.6% of the sexually abused female youths in their study were arrested for violent offenses, compared with 6.3% of the nonabused female youths in their comparison group. Further, they found that the rate of violent offenses as adults for the sexually abused group was more than twice as high as for the nonabused group (9.3% versus 4.4%). Artz's (1998) ethnographic study of girls in Canada provides insight into the relationship between aggression and victimization of girls. The girls in her study stated that they learned at home that "might makes right" and engaged in "horizontal violence" directed at other powerless girls (often with boys in the audience). Her findings illustrate not only the learned aspect of girls' violent behavior but also the patriarchal context in which it exists.

In addition to research on physical aggression, the topic of girls and relational aggression has also been appearing in the popular and academic literatures (e.g., Crick & Grotpeter, 1995; Wiseman, 2002). Crick et al. (1998) define *relational aggression* as "behaviors that harm others through damage (or threat of damage) to relationships or feelings of acceptance, friendship, or group inclusion" (p. 77). Examples of these types of behaviors include gossiping, spreading rumors, or ignoring someone with the intent to exclude them from a social group. The majority of research on relational aggression focuses on peer-to-peer interactions in the school setting. However, recent research has suggested a link between prior victimization and relational aggression in the treatment setting.

Okamoto (2002, in press) examined the use of relational aggression in the treatment setting between male practitioners and female youth clients. Respondents in these studies suggested gender-specific manifestations of sexual abuse in the treatment setting that, when resisted, may lead to girls' anger and subsequent relational aggression. Specifically, respondents stated that the framework for cross-gender relationships for female youth clients is often sexual in nature, because of their past history of sexual abuse by men. In other words, girls' initial behaviors toward male practitioners in the therapeutic setting function to re-create the pattern of past victimization by men (Okamoto, 2002). Respondents indicated that, when sexual behaviors were resisted, the result was anger from the female youth clients. Anger manifested itself in a variety of relationally aggressive behaviors: ignoring the practitioner, refusing to attend sessions, or spreading rumors about the practitioner.

Practitioners stated that one of the most severe forms of rumor spreading from girls in treatment was to make a sexual abuse allegation toward the practitioner (Okamoto, 2002, in press). One respondent described this phenomenon.

> There was a time when a girl was mad at me. She was claiming that I was acting more favorably toward another, because she wasn't having as many problems. She started out saying that the girl had a crush on me. And, then when that didn't get anywhere, she stepped it up. "She's flirting with [respondent's name], she likes [respondent's name]." She [went] all the way to saying that we had some sort of a fling. That almost resulted in a complete investigation. (Okamoto, 2002, p. 263)

Respondents in these studies indicated that the consequences of these allegations were severe, because they have the potential to damage a practitioner's professional reputation and career (Okamoto, in press). Although these studies elucidate the unique manifestations of relational aggression in the treatment setting, they also must be interpreted with caution, as they do not suggest that sexual abuse allegations should automatically be attributed to relational aggression. In fact, this terrain is particularly complex because so many girls have experienced sexual abuse in foster care and other institutional settings (see Chesney-Lind & Shelden, 2003, for review).

It is also important to note that relationally aggressive behaviors in the treatment setting most likely reflect girls' powerlessness within the juvenile justice and mental health service systems and in the overall society. Okamoto and Chesney-Lind (2002) describe how these behaviors function as a way for the powerless (i.e., female youth clients) to punish the "bad" behaviors of the powerful (i.e., male practitioners). Because some research has illustrated practitioners' inappropriate use and abuse of power toward girls in the juvenile justice system (e.g., Acoca, 1998), relational aggression from girls in these settings and situations might function as a form of protection.

## ■ Implications for Practice

The literature on female youth victimization highlights several important implications for gender-specific practice in juvenile justice and mental health settings. The act of physical and sexual abuse represents not only a severe form of trauma but also a severe violation of the trust within significant relationships in girls' lives. Therefore, working with girls should focus on developing healthy interpersonal relationships. Calhoun (2001) describes the importance of this process.

> Female juvenile offenders travel a different pathway to delinquency than male juvenile offenders. A large part of this different path can be understood by taking into consideration the importance and role of relationships in a female's life and development. (p. 94)

Further, a study focused on sexually abused female youths' recommendations for postabuse services suggests that girls themselves *want* to develop healthy therapeutic relationships with practitioners (Potter, Holmes, & Barton, 2002). Specifically, the girls in this study stated that the main aspect they wanted from treatment was someone to talk to about the effects of the trauma on their lives. Finally, as some of the research suggests, the process of developing healthy interpersonal relationships for girls is particularly significant in relationships with the opposite sex. As Okamoto (2002) states, for many sexually abused girls, the female youth client's experience with an emotionally supportive and caring male can be an extremely powerful intervention in itself.

Gender-specific treatment should also focus on promoting emotional regulation. Emotional regulation is a focus of one gender-specific treatment model called dialectical behavioral therapy (DBT) (Linehan, 1993; Linehan & Wagner, 1990). Research focused on the use of the model with severely disturbed female juvenile offenders found that it was effective in reducing certain behavior problems (e.g., aggression, parasuicidal behavior) with the population (Trupin et al., 1999). Although the effectiveness of DBT has recently been challenged in the literature (Kendall & Pollack, 2003), the model's focus on emotional regulation is consistent with existing research on girls and victimization (Shipman et al., 2000). Future research should explore various ways to promote emotional regulation in the treatment setting.

Finally, working with girls should focus on practitioners' feelings and perceptions toward the population and the need for appropriate boundary setting. The feelings and perceptions toward female youth clients should be incorporated into practitioners' ongoing training and supervision. Some qualitative research has described horrific and abusive treatment of female juvenile of-fenders by youth workers (e.g., Acoca, 1998; Kersten, 1990). These events may be related to a lack of consistent supervision that holds practitioners accountable for their behavior while simultaneously focusing on their honest reactions toward their female youth clients. Ideally, good supervision should also focus on promoting practitioners' self-awareness in working with girls. This is particularly important for male practitioners working with the popu-lation (Okamoto, 2002; St. Germaine & Kessell, 1989). Further, male practi-tioners need specialized training in boundary setting with female youth clients (Belknap et al., 2003; Okamoto, 2003). Belknap et al. (2003) state, "Girls need to learn how to interact appropriately with males and establish healthy rela-tionships with them" (p. 227). Male practitioners who set appropriate bound-aries with their female youth clients can facilitate these processes.

## Gender-Specific Model Programs

A national review of model programs for girls illustrates effective responses to girls' trauma and delinquent behaviors that reflect many of the issues discussed in this chapter. The Office of Juvenile Justice and Delinquency Prevention (OJJDP, 1998) conducted an elaborate process to identify and select the most promising gender-specific programs in the United States. Programs were eval-uated on multiple criteria, such as their inclusion of gender-specific issues in their program goals or the mission of their agency, their assessment and treat-ment of sexual abuse, and their incorporation of ongoing gender-specific vic-timization training. Of nominations received from 212 programs across the country, 16 programs were identified as the most promising programs for girls (see OJJDP, 1998, for a review of these programs). The programs targeting the female juvenile offender population have several commonalities. First, all of these programs incorporated individual and/or group counseling focused on issues of victimization, particularly physical and sexual abuse. For example, the Harriet Tubman Residential Center in Auburn, New York, incorporates a curriculum component in the program that addresses victimization issues and promotes abuse awareness, prevention, and personal empowerment. Second, most of these programs are careful in their incorporation of male practitioners. Caritas House, a residential treatment facility in Pawtucket, Rhode Island, has male administrators but incorporates only female staff on site. The Staff-Secured Detention Program for Female Juvenile Offenders in Philadelphia has a policy that male staff members may never spend time alone with female clients. Finally, many of these programs focus on relationship building for girls. For example, Alternative Rehabilitation Communities (ARC), a residential treatment facility in Harrisburg, Pennsylvania, incorporates training for girls in conflict resolution, assertiveness, and decision making in order to promote positive interpersonal skills. An examination of gender-specific model programs (such as those outlined by OJJDP) is the first step toward identifying effective practice principles in working with girls and may also provide direction in program development for future gender-specific programs.

## Conclusions

This chapter examined the impact of girls' physical and sexual abuse on their attributions and behaviors in juvenile justice and mental health treatment settings. As described in this chapter, abuse accounts for many of the aggressive and emotional behaviors of girls and therefore is arguably one of the primary reasons for their entry into the juvenile justice and mental health systems. Because of their unique reactions to abuse, female youths require specialized services, and practitioners working with these youths require specialized training and supervision. As this chapter suggests, it is no longer sufficient to assume that female youths will benefit from programs that have been developed and evaluated specifically for boys' social and behavioral issues.

More research is needed to further elucidate the unique aspects of gender-specific programs. For example, research might differentiate between situations when girls' emotionality enhances therapeutic relationships and when it becomes pathological to treatment. Further, little is known about effective training methods and supervision techniques for practitioners working with girls. More research is needed that focuses on gender-specific aggressive behaviors and effective practice principles that can be used to address them. Finally, more research focused on the prevention and intervention of physical and sexual abuse is critical in order to enhance the well-being of female youths.

## Discussion Questions

1   In what ways does this chapter illustrate the differences in delinquency between boys and girls?

2   What do you think is the connection between girls' trauma and predominant forms of female juvenile delinquency (e.g., prostitution)?

3   What special difficulties do male practitioners face in working with girls in juvenile justice programs? In light of these issues, should only female practitioners be allowed to work with girls? Why or why not?

4   Do you feel that relational aggression is a serious form of aggressive behavior, or is it merely a concept that "pathologizes" the normal behavior of girls? Explain.

5   In what ways are the treatment needs of girls different from those of boys? If you could design a model program for girls, what would it look like?

# References

Acoca, L. (1998). Outside/inside: The violation of American girls at home, on the streets, and in the juvenile justice system. *Crime and Delinquency, 44*(4), 561–589.

Alder, C., & Hunter, N. (1999). *"Not worse, just different"? Working with young women in the juvenile justice system.* Melbourne, Australia: University of Melbourne, Criminology Department.

Artz, S. (1998). *Sex, power, and the violent school girl.* Toronto: Trifolium.

Baines, M., & Alder, C. (1996). Are girls more difficult to work with? Youth workers' perspectives in juvenile justice and related areas. *Crime and Delinquency, 42*(3), 467–485.

Belknap, J., Dunn, M., & Holsinger, K. (1997). *Moving toward juvenile justice and youth-serving systems that address the distinct experience of the adolescent female.* Cincinnati, OH: Gender Specific Services Work Group.

Belknap, J., Holsinger, K., & Dunn, M. (1997). Understanding incarcerated girls: The results of a focus group study. *Prison Journal, 77*(4), 381–404.

Belknap, J., Winter, E. J., & Cady, B. (2003). Professionals' assessments of the needs of delinquent girls: The results of a focus group study. In B. Bloom (Ed.), *Gendered justice: Addressing female offenders* (pp. 209–239). Durham, NC: Carolina Academic Press.

Bugental, D. B., & Shennum, W. (2002). Gender, power, and violence in the family. *Child Maltreatment, 7*(1), 56–64.

Calhoun, G. B. (2001). Differences between male and female juvenile offenders as measured by the BASC. *Journal of Offender Rehabilitation, 33*(2), 87–96.

Chesney-Lind, M., & Freitas, K. (1999). *Working with girls: Exploring practitioner issues, experiences and feelings* (Rep. No. 403). Honolulu: University of Hawaii at Manoa, Social Science Research Institute.

Chesney-Lind, M., & Okamoto, S. K. (2003). Gender matters: Patterns in girls' delinquency and gender responsive programming. In B. Bloom (Ed.), *Gendered justice: Addressing female offenders* (pp. 241–266). Durham, NC: Carolina Academic Press.

Chesney-Lind, M., & Shelden, R. (2003). *Girls, delinquency and juvenile justice* (3rd ed.). Belmont, CA: Wadsworth.

Crick, N. R., & Grotpeter, J. K. (1995). Relational aggression, gender, and social-psychological adjustment. *Child Development, 66,* 710–722.

Crick, N. R., Werner, N. E., Casas, J. F., O'Brien, K. M., Nelson, D. A., Grotpeter, J. K., et al. (1998). Childhood aggression and gender: A new look at an old problem. In D. Bernstein (Ed.), *Gender & motivation: Vol. 45. The Nebraska Symposium on Motivation* (pp. 75–141). Lincoln: University of Nebraska Press.

DeKeseredy, W. S. (2000). *Women, crime and the Canadian criminal justice system.* Cincinnati, OH: Anderson.

Dembo, R., Sue, S. C., Borden, P., & Manning, D. (1995, August). *Gender differences in service needs among youths entering a juvenile assessment center: A replication study.* Paper presented at the annual meeting of the Society of Social Problems, Washington, DC.

Finkelhor, D., & Baron, L. (1986). Risk factors for child sexual abuse. *Journal of Interpersonal Violence, 1,* 43–71.

Fontanella, C., Harrington, D., & Zuravin, S. J. (2000). Gender differences in the characteristics and outcomes of sexually abused preschoolers. *Journal of Child Sexual Abuse, 9*(2), 21–40.

Fowler, W. E., & Wagner, W. G. (1993). Preference for and comfort with male versus female counselors among sexually abused girls in individual treatment. *Journal of Counseling Psychology, 40*(1), 65–72.

Fowler, W. E., Wagner, W. G., Iachini, A., & Johnson, J. T. (1992). The impact of sex of psychological examiner on sexually abused girls' preference for and anticipated comfort with male versus female counselors. *Child Study Journal, 22*(1), 1–10.

Gore-Felton, C., Koopman, C., McGarvey, E., Hernandez, N., & Canterbury, R. J. (2001). Relationships of sexual, physical, and emotional abuse to emotional and behavioral problems among incarcerated adolescents. *Journal of Child Sexual Abuse, 10*(1), 73–88.

Green, S. M., Russo, M. F., Navratil, J. L., & Loeber, R. (1999). Sexual and physical abuse among adolescent girls with disruptive behavior problems. *Journal of Child and Family Studies, 8*(2), 151–168.

Kendall, K., & Pollack, S. (2003). Cognitive behavioralism in women's prisons: A critical analysis of therapeutic assumptions and practices. In B. Bloom (Ed.), *Gendered justice: Addressing female offenders* (pp. 69–96). Durham, NC: Carolina Academic Press.

Kersten, J. (1990). A gender specific look at patterns of violence in juvenile institutions: Or are girls really "more difficult to handle"? *International Journal of the Sociology of Law, 18*, 473–493.

Kolko, D. J., Brown, E. J., & Berliner, L. (2002). Children's perceptions of their abusive experience: Measurement and preliminary findings. *Child Maltreatment, 7*(1), 42–55.

Lamb, M. E., & Garretson, M. E. (2003). The effects of interviewer gender and child gender on the informativeness of alleged child sexual abuse victims in forensic interviews. *Law and Human Behavior, 27*(2), 157–171.

Linehan, M. M. (1993). *Cognitive-behavioral treatment of personality disorder.* New York: Guilford.

Linehan, M. M., & Wagner, A. W. (1990). Dialectical behavior therapy: A feminist-behavioral treatment of borderline personality disorder. *Behavior Therapist, 13*(1), 9–14.

McCormack, A., Janus, M. D., & Burgess, A. W. (1986). Runaway youths and sexual victimization: Gender differences in an adolescent runaway population. *Child Abuse and Neglect, 10*, 387–395.

Moon, L. T., Wagner, W. G., & Fowler, W. E. (1993). Counselor preference and anticipated comfort ratings for a clinic sample of sexually abused versus non-abused girls. *Journal of Child and Family Studies, 2*(4), 327–338.

Office of Juvenile Justice and Delinquency Prevention. (1998, October). *Guiding principles for promising female programming.* Retrieved September 8, 2003, from http://www.ojjdp.ncjrs.org/pubs/principles/contents.html

Okamoto, S. K. (2002). The challenges of male practitioners working with female youth clients. *Child and Youth Care Forum, 31*(4), 257–268.

Okamoto, S. K. (2003). The function of professional boundaries in the therapeutic relationship between male practitioners and female youth clients. *Child and Adolescent Social Work Journal, 20*(4), 303–313.

Okamoto, S. K. (in press). Relational aggression of girls in treatment: A challenge for male practitioners. *Residential Treatment for Children and Youth.*

Okamoto, S. K., & Chesney-Lind, M. (2002, October–November). Girls and relational aggression: Beyond the "mean girl" hype. *Women, Girls, and Criminal Justice, 3*(6), 81–82, 90.

Okamoto, S. K., & Chesney-Lind, M. (2003). "What do we do with girls?" The dimensions of and responses to female juvenile delinquency. In A. R. Roberts (Ed.), *Critical issues in crime and justice* (2nd ed., pp. 244–252). Thousand Oaks, CA: Sage.

Potter, R., Holmes, P., & Barton, H. (2002). Do we listen or do we assume? What teenagers want from a post-abuse service. *Psychiatric Bulletin, 26*, 377–379.

Shipman, K., Zeman, J., Penza, S., & Champion, K. (2000). Emotion management skills in sexually maltreated and nonmaltreated girls: A developmental psychopathology perspective. *Development and Psychopathology, 12*, 47–62.

Siegel, J. A., & Williams, L. M. (2003). The relationship between child sexual abuse and female delinquency and crime: A prospective study. *Journal of Research in Crime and Delinquency, 40*(1), 71–94.

St. Germaine, E. A., & Kessell, M. J. (1989). Professional boundary setting for male youth workers with female adolescent clients. *Child and Youth Care Quarterly, 18*(4), 259–271.

Trowell, J., & Kolvin, I. (1999). Lessons from a psychotherapy outcome study with sexually abused girls. *Clinical Child Psychology and Psychiatry, 4*(1), 79–89.

Trupin, E. W., Stewart, D., Boesky, L., McClurg, B., Beach, B., Hormann, S., et al. (1999, February). *Evaluation of dialectical behavior therapy with incarcerated female juvenile offenders.* Paper presented at the 11th annual research conference, A system of care for children's mental health: Expanding the research base, Tampa, FL.

U.S. Department of Health and Human Services (DHHS), Administration on Children, Youth, and Families. (2002). *Child maltreatment 2000.* Washington, DC: U.S. Government Printing Office. Retrieved September 8, 2003, from http://www.acf.hhs.gov/programs/cb/publications/cm00/cm2000.pdf

Wiseman, R. (2002). *Queen bees and wannabes.* New York: Crown.

# 17 Structured Wilderness Experiences

## Camping, Environmental, and Other

## Outdoor Rehabilitation Programs

Albert R. Roberts

ithin the context of juvenile justice, a distinction can be made between alternatives that are intended primarily to meet rehabilitation goals (such as structured wilderness treatment programs) and alternatives intended primarily to meet social control goals (such as juvenile training schools and military-oriented boot camps). This chapter begins with an introductory statement on the origins of wilderness programs and some current promising models and then compares them with traditional training schools. An examination of the similarities and differences among the various established wilderness programs follows, with descriptions and outcome data on the effectiveness of 11 of the most widely known wilderness treatment and rehabilitation programs. Some of the more critical programmatic components are reviewed, including therapeutic camping, rock climbing, wagon train, ocean quests, an overnight solo experience, alternative school, and family counseling. The chapter concludes by examining outcome data, including follow-up studies and program evaluations, on the effectiveness of wilderness programs.

## ■ Origins of Wilderness Programs

Wilderness programs usually provide adjudicated and troubled youths with a rigorous physical and emotional challenge unlike anything they have ever known. In small, closely supervised groups, the juvenile offenders learn to follow instructions and work cooperatively with other youths to accomplish a series of difficult physical challenges, thereby enhancing their own self-esteem. Most programs also strive to strengthen the youths' academic skills by incorporating aspects of learning directly related to outdoor living (e.g., map reading and compass skills).

The present-day wilderness programs for juvenile offenders evolved from two separate directions: forestry camps for youthful offenders and the Outward Bound model created in Wales during World War II. The earliest outdoor program for juvenile delinquents was established in the 1930s in the Forestry Department in Los Angeles County by Karl Holton. Typical work projects youths (boys only) performed at forestry camps were "conservation, park development, road construction, safety programs, and farming; these projects [were] supplemented by individual and group counseling, recreational, educational and religious programs" (Robison, 1960, p. 329). The usual length of stay did not exceed 6 months. The original purpose of Outward Bound was to train merchant seamen in accomplishing rigorous physical challenges, as well as to develop group pride and a shared trust as the group worked together to achieve strenuous goals (William & Chun, 1973).

A modern version of the Civilian Conservation Corps and Youth Forestry Camps of the 1930s was planned in 1993 and 1994 as a result of passage of the National and Community Service Trust Act of 1993, the AmeriCorps Program, and the Youth Environmental Service (YES) program (Cronin, 1996).

The start of a national network of environmental work programs for juvenile offenders was implemented in 1994 with the endorsement of Attorney General Janet Reno.

By 1996, six pilot programs had been developed in three areas of the United States: Florida, Utah, and Washington, D.C. The two programs in Washington, D.C., are nonresidential. They are held in 6-week cycles and target both at-risk youths (8 to 14 years old) and adjudicated youths 16 years of age and older. The other four programs are residential and serve adjudicated males age 12 to 18 in Utah and Florida. The Utah programs are short term, lasting from 1 to 4 months, while the two Florida programs have a duration of 4 to 6 months and 12 to 13 months, respectively. All of the programs combine educational classes with structured opportunities for at-risk, inner-city youths and adjudicated youths to become involved in environmental work, parks and forestry work, refuge ecology, and wilderness experiences. Work crews handle such tasks as lawn mowing, trail building, clearing trash, removing old fencing, beach cleanup, exotic vegetation control, maintenance of equipment, seed mixing, building corrals for wild horses, building visitor centers and picnic areas in public parks, and preservation and restoration of wetlands (Cronin, 1996).

These types of programs help instill a work ethic among juvenile offenders while providing important national and community service opportunities. Federal land managers and the National Park Service have been struggling to preserve, maintain, and clean up vast land tracts, forests, wetlands, and parks nationwide on limited budgets. With a backlog of environmental and conservation projects, the Youth Environment Service (YES) is a promising partnership between the Office of Juvenile Justice and Delinquency Prevention (OJJDP) of the Department of Justice and the Department of the Interior. In addition, these programs seem to be successful in helping juvenile offenders earn money so they can repay their victims. For example, the Genesis Youth Center, a 72-bed community-based residential facility located near Salt Lake City, Utah, works cooperatively with the state restitution program. The youth participants are paid minimum wage, and their earnings are allocated to the Utah Department of Youth Services and to the juvenile courts to pay victim restitution. During the first 6 months of the program's operation, 178 participating youths "earned a total of $103,789 in victim restitution" (Cronin, 1996, p. 19).

Two recently recognized model wilderness programs are the Gulf Coast Trades Center's Conservation Corp in Texas and the Florida Environmental Institute, also referred to as the Last Chance Ranch, located in the Everglades. Both of these model programs include 2 hours of daily academic education and a full day of vocational trades and outdoor conservation work. The Gulf Coast Trades Center was honored by the Texas Youth Commission and the Texas Governor's Office in 1997 and 2002, and in 2001 it won an award from the U.S. Forest Service. This model program provides juvenile offenders with the opportunity to learn a trade and work intensively in clearing and maintaining forests, as well as working on construction, preservation, and trail maintenance projects throughout the 1,300 miles of trail in the Sam Houston National Forest, the Double Lakes National Recreation Area, and a few other state parks. In addition, the Gulf Coast YouthBuild program teaches the youths how to lay a foundation, frame a house, put up Sheetrock, and construct a roof, as well as build toolsheds, outdoor shelters, and picnic areas in state parks. The average length of stay is 6 to 9 months. During 1999–2000 there was a low rearrest rate of 16%, and the recidivism rate for 1998–1999 was 19%. This is considerably lower than the 50% to 70% recidivism rate among youths released from many of the state juvenile correctional facilities that do not emphasize academic, vocational, and career education for all juvenile felons. The Florida Environmental Institute seems to have rehabilitated some of the most serious felony juvenile offenders in Florida. The youths committed to this small therapeutic facility learn to clean and maintain wetlands and swamps in the Everglades; dig up tree stumps and clear land; cut grass, weed, and grow corn, peas, and cucumbers on the ranch grounds; and raise cattle, pigs, and horses. These adjudicated juvenile offenders also have the responsibility of repairing and renovating ranch buildings and in some cases constructing new buildings. The centerpiece of this program and of other associated Marine Institute programs is a strict behavior management protocol. The youths are assessed five times each day on seven areas of behavior, including appearance, attitude, punctuality, participation, enthusiasm, and manners. There are also cumulative weekly rankings from which the juveniles earn point cards that ultimately provide credits toward going home. Fighting, breaking the rules, and/or disobeying instructions result in extra tough physical chores and a lengthening of the youth's stay. Youths released from the Last Chance Ranch in 1997–1998 averaged 32 prior charges, including 11.7 felony charges prior to arrival at the facility. The recidivism rate from 1997 through 2000 was extremely low; only 15.8% of juvenile offenders released from the Last Chance Ranch were adjudicated for a new offense within 12 months after release. The recidivism rate was even lower in 2000, when only 1 of the 21 youths (4.6%) released from the Last Chance Ranch were reconvicted for a new offense. This is a small facility housing 22 youths at one time; it is minimum security, with an intensive behavior management point system for the youths to earn credits toward early release. Finally, the program has an intensive aftercare supervision program.

## ■ Traditional Training Schools Versus Wilderness Adventure Programs

Typically, the interaction between staff and juveniles in a juvenile institution is restricted to custodial duty such as taking a head count as the youths move from one place in the institution to another, maintaining order, and carrying out professional responsibilities such as requiring the juveniles' participation in academic education, vocational education, or weekly group counseling sessions.

The ratio of juveniles to staff members varies from institution to institution, but the range is usually one counselor for 50 to 100 youths. Most of the contacts between staff and youths are brief and superficial, and there is little opportunity for ongoing, meaningful interaction in which the staff person is perceived as a genuine role model by the youths.

In sharp contrast, it is not uncommon for a wilderness program to have a staffing ratio ranging from one adult for five youths to almost a one-on-one relationship at intervals during the day. Youths who have become adept at conning and manipulating the institutional system quickly discover that they are not able to get away with ignoring their responsibilities or giving only half-hearted effort to a task. The wilderness model, essentially a back-to-basics approach, strips away the trappings of modern society (on which we have all come to depend) and focuses on the essential primary needs of food and shelter, with the goal of fostering the development of self-confidence and socially acceptable coping mechanisms for the participants. Youths in the group are required to interact cooperatively with each other to accomplish daily tasks. For example, when the only place to sleep is a tent that the group is responsible for setting up, the entire group quickly learns that they need to work together to erect their shelter. Likewise, when the only food to eat is that which the group prepares, then the entire group participates. When problems arise, they are dealt with immediately by the ever-present staff.

Although staff salaries for employees of privately run wilderness programs are usually well below the rate paid to institutional staff and state-operated facilities, these outdoor programs tend to attract a corps of dedicated, hard-working individuals who take a genuine interest in each youth. The fact that the adults are subjecting themselves to the same physical challenges as the juveniles makes a significant impression on the youths.

Often the small group of juveniles assigned to one adult is viewed as a substitute family unit in which the staff serve as role models who continually demonstrate mature, caring, socially acceptable behaviors. Many of the staff are hired because of their expertise in an outdoor activity such as canoeing or mountain climbing; their mastery of an adventurous outdoor skill that the youths know nothing about earns them a measure of respect at the outset. However, burnout and a high rate of staff turnover occur at many of the wilderness camps because of the low salary and the round-the-clock nature of the job.

## ■ Outdoor Program Comparisons

### Similarities

Despite many variations in the structure of wilderness programs, most programs share several commonalities:

☐ Providing a well-organized program focusing on the mastery of difficult physical challenges

☐ Creating an opportunity for heightened self-respect among youths who have a history of repeated failures in school, difficulty in social relationships, and problems with family members

☐ Using the outdoors and the reality of ensuring one's own survival as the setting for teaching academic subjects

☐ Learning how to work cooperatively with others to complete a task

Most wilderness programs include the following components:

1 An *orientation phase* in which the youth is introduced to the expectations and requirements for successful completion of the program.

2 A series of increasingly difficult *physical challenges* that take into account the juvenile's desire for risk and excitement in an environment—the outdoors—that cannot be conned or manipulated. Typical challenges include rock climbing, rappelling, canoeing, backpacking, hiking, cross-country skiing, and cave exploring.

3 An *educational component* directly related to the camp experience.

4 A "*solo*" (ranging in length from one overnight to 3 days) in which each participant is required to survive alone in the wilderness using the skills acquired during the program.

5 A *final event*, generally a marathon run of several miles.

6 A *celebration ceremony* signifying the successful completion of the program, at which the participants may be awarded a diploma or certificate of completion.

### Differences

The many areas in which camps differ are:

☐ *Eligibility criteria.* Most programs do not accept juveniles who have committed violent offenses. Status offenders, adolescents with a history of drug abuse, youths adjudicated for property offenses, and predelinquent juveniles meet the eligibility requirements set forth by various programs. Some programs are coed; others are restricted to only boys.

☐ *Program auspices.* Programs are administered by private nonprofit or for-profit organizations, as well as by a state office, usually a division of youth services.

□ *Point of entry.* Some youths are sent directly to a program by a judge (or probation officer). Others enter the camp after serving time in a training school as a condition of prerelease. Still others are sentenced to a training school but given the option of volunteering for a wilderness program experience: If successful, they avoid the training school; if unsuccessful, they are sent to a training school.

□ *Duration of program.* The length of each program ranges from 26 days to 18 months.

□ *Involvement of family members.* While not a usual requirement, a few programs strongly encourage parents to attend counseling sessions with their child or participate in parents' groups.

□ *Type and frequency of counseling.* Some of the programs have no formal counseling component, and others have group, family, and/or individual counseling one or more times per week.

□ *Aftercare.* Some programs provide continuity by having community-based follow-up services. Others end the relationship when the youth returns home. The most promising and effective aftercare program is Associated Marine Institutes (AMI), which operates 22 residential and 29 nonresidential day programs in eight states and one foreign country. AMI provides approximately 3 years of aftercare to its graduates, including AMI alumni meetings for recent graduates; trips, picnics, and special events for alumni; a job bank; a mentoring program; and continuing care retreats.

## ■ Model Programs

Although wilderness programs exist in many states, descriptions of these programs are only rarely reported in professional journals and textbooks on delinquency and juvenile justice. For this book, I collected information on wilderness camps from many of the publicly and privately operated programs across the United States, provided they have outcome data measuring program effectiveness. Table 17.1 summarizes information on selected wilderness programs. Seven programs that provide challenging wilderness experiences to juvenile delinquents are described in more detail in this section.

### Associated Marine Institutes

The Associated Marine Institutes (AMI) contracts with state divisions for youth in many different areas of the United States to provide intensive programming for male and female adolescents age 15 to 18. Established in 1969, with headquarters in Tampa, Florida, AMI serves approximately 2,000 youths annually in Florida, Georgia, Arkansas, Louisiana, South Carolina, Texas, Delaware, Virginia, and the Cayman Islands. The participants have been adjudicated for

**Table 17.1    Selected Wilderness Programs: Summary of Data on Staff, Programs, and Follow-up Studies, 1984 and 2002**

| Program and Location | Program Characteristics | Year Program Began | Number of Youths Completing Program | Number of staff | Staff: Youth Ratio | Evaluation/Follow-up |
|---|---|---|---|---|---|---|
| Associated Marine Institutes Programs, located in Florida, South Carolina, and Delaware<br><br>In 7 states and the Cayman Islands—over 50 institutes | 6–9 month stay<br>Focus on developing socially appropriate behavior and learning academic and social skills while learning to repair boats and engines<br>Activities include scuba diving, seamanship/boating, and planting | 1969 | 2,300 in 2000 | 500 | 1:7 | Low recidivism rates, approximately 12% to 28% in 1998, 1999, 2000 after 3-year follow-up (recidivism varied with location) |
| Camp Woodson, North Carolina's Division of Youth Services, Fairview, North Carolina | Precamp component<br>Trail life<br>Solo experience<br>7 weeks | 1976 | 130 in 1984 | 19 | 1:7 | None |
| Eagle Nest Camp Experiential Reintegration Program, New Mexico | Progressive (3-stage) program designed to strengthen self-responsibility | 1980 | 110 in 1984 | | | None |
| Eckerd Foundation Wilderness System Program, Florida, Georgia, New Hampshire, North Carolina, Rhode Island, Tennessee, and Vermont (39 different programs) | Wilderness camping<br>Transitional classroom phase<br>Family counseling and 18-month aftercare services<br>10 youths per 2 teacher-counselors | 1968 | 579 in 1984<br>1,619 in 1996 | 116<br>160 | 1:5<br>1:5 | None<br>Follow-up study 12 months after completion of program (June 1996) showed 19% of graduates had a conviction for delinquency or a criminal offense within 12 months after release; 12 month follow-up study<br>Post treatment in 2002 indicated a low recidivism rate of 26% despite 11 month Average stay in program. Average academic gain of 1.3 school yrs in reading & general Knowledge. |

402

| Program and Location | Program Characteristics | Year Program Began | Number of Youths Completing Program | Number of staff | Staff: Youth Ratio | Evaluation/Follow-up |
|---|---|---|---|---|---|---|
| Hurricane Island Outward Bound, Florida | 18-day wilderness trip and a 10-day follow-up component for youths and their families | 1983 | 132 in 1996 | 19 | 1:7 | 19% recidivism rate<br>81% of youths who successfully completed the program had no rearrests one year later in 1996 |
| OceanQuest (a VisionQuest program), Ft. Mifflin, Pennsylvania | Advanced program usually requiring completion of at least 2 months on VisionQuest's wagon train<br>Instruction in water safety, oceanography, map/compass skills<br>Group home<br>Family involvement in support group | Reinstituted in 1984 | — | 11 | 1:1.2 | 1999 Univ. of Pennsylvania follow-up study of 1,230 youths who graduated from VisionQuest's residential treatment program in PA between 1992 and 1995. After reviewing state and county court and arrest records, low recidivism rate of 37.6% was reported. Oklahoma VisionQuest found that only 7% of the violent juveniles committed a new violent felony offense in 1999 study. |
| Spectrum Wilderness program, Carbondale, Illinois | 30-day program, including a 2-week expedition into a wilderness site<br>Program concludes with a 3-day "solo" experience | | 130 in 1990 | - | 1:11 | The youths who successfully completed the program had a 50% reduction in arrest rates; but those who did not successfully complete the program had no reduction in arrest rates in 1990 |
| Stephen L. French Youth Wilderness (Homeward Bound) program, Massachusetts Division of Youth Services, Brewster, Massachusetts | Wilderness experience<br>Group counseling<br>Community service assignments<br>3-day solo experience<br>26 days | 1970 | 350 | | 1:8 | Experimental group 20.8% Recidivism rate versus 42.7% recidivism rate for control group |

(continued)

**Table 17.1    Selected Wilderness Programs: Summary of Data on Staff, Programs, and Follow-up Studies, 1984 and 2002 (continued)**

| Program and Location | Program Characteristics | Year Program Began | Number of Youths Completing Program | Number of staff | Staff: Youth Ratio | Evaluation/Follow-up |
|---|---|---|---|---|---|---|
| Thistledew Camp, Togo, Minnesota | 2.5 months of school in a forest area 3 weeks of challenge involving rock climbing, high ropes, and wilderness expeditions 12 to 16 hours per day of intensive structured programming for all youths concludes with a 4-day solo experience | 1973 | 195 in 1996 | 46 | 1:2 | 30% rearrest rate for 16 and 17 year olds 62% rearrest rate for 13 to 15 year olds in 1996 |
| VisionQuest Tucson. Arizona | 6-day wilderness adventure 3-day solo experience Wagon train 12–15 months | 1973 | | | 1:1 | 43% rearrest rate (but no follow-up time frame specified) |
| Wilderness Camping Program, Alabama Youth Services Division | Group work Wilderness camping, stressing teamwork and mutual problem solving | 1982 | 57 in 1994 | | | Follow-up study 9 months after completion of program: only 17% rearrested |
| Wolfcreek Wilderness School, Georgia Division of Youth Services Atlanta, Georgia | Intensive and relatively short in duration (26 days) Enhances self-image by providing success experiences Small staff-youth ratio of 2 instructors for each group of 10 youths | 1978 | 108 in 1984 | 2 | 1:5 | None |

| Program and Location | Program Characteristics | Year Program Began | Number of Youths Completing Program | Number of staff | Staff: Youth Ratio | Evaluation/Follow-up |
|---|---|---|---|---|---|---|
| Youth Challenge Wilderness Expedition Program, Middletown, Connecticut | Team-building approach to problem solving Bolstering self-esteem through backpacking, canoeing, and mountain climbing | 1978 | 683 in 1984 | | | None |
| RedCliff Ascent, Enterprise, Utah | The Trek-hiking thru the red rocks & high desert terrain, experiential learning such as building a shelter, campfire, and cooking. Studying plant and animal life, geography and map-reading, astronomy and physical education. | 1993 | 145 in 2002 | 8 | 1:3 | Pre and Post measures—baseline on admission and 6 months later indicated that 91% of the youths completing the program demonstrated significant clinical improvement in mental health status. Youths seemed to be recovered from depression, substance abuse, oppositional defiance disorder, rage, low self-esteem, paranoia, irresponsibility, and dishonesty |

either status offenses (e.g., truancy) or more serious delinquency offenses such as breaking and entering, auto theft, assault, and armed robbery. Most have a long history of contacts with the police (with an average of 8 to 12 arrests). The average age of the adjudicated youths upon admission to the program varies between 15.9 and 16.2 years of age between 1988 and 2001. The average age at first offense varied was 14.6 to 15.8 years of age. It declined starting after 1995, when the average age was 15.3, to 2001, when the average age was 14.6 (in 1988 it was 15.8, and in 1989 it was 15.5).

Youths take an average of 6 to 9 months to complete the AMI program; they learn how to work with engines, make boat repairs, clear and maintain trails in state parks, and scuba dive. The overriding goals are to improve the youths' educational and vocational skills and to teach them to behave in a socially appropriate, law-abiding manner. The staff work with youths individually and in small groups to improve their reading comprehension and math levels in preparation for the GED, as appropriate. The current student to academic instructor ratio is 7:1.

According to the AMI recidivism study completed in 2001, AMI has impressive follow-up statistics on the success of its programs, with some locations reporting an extremely low rearrest rate of only 12%, while other locations report a 28% rearrest rate within 1 year after completion of the program. The 2001 AMI follow-up study included 2,741 students. Slightly over half (53.7%) of the study sample had been adjudicated for a felony offense prior to program enrollment. The recidivism rate for these serious juvenile offenders was only 28.7% 1 year after completing the program, compared with an average recidivism rate of 65% for felony-type juvenile offenders released from juvenile institutions.

## VisionQuest

One of the most publicized and widely known outdoor adventure program is VisionQuest, a for-profit organization based in Tucson, Arizona. VisionQuest began in 1973 headed by Robert Burton, a controversial figure who has generated high praise as well as considerable criticism for his unorthodox treatment methods. VisionQuest (VQ) operates several types of programs: group homes, wilderness camps, residential programs, HomeQuest (a home-based family counseling program), OceanQuest, and the Wagon Train—considered the most visible of all the VQ programs.

The usual length of stay at the coed program is 12 to 18 months, considerably longer than most other wilderness programs. Before entering the program, the youths make a commitment that includes a pledge to abstain from drugs, alcohol, and sex; to complete at least two "high-impact" programs during a 1-year stay; and to remain with the program until discharge (Sweeney, 1982).

Greenwood, Lipson, Abrahamse, and Zimring (1983) determined that the key to the program's success was the close and frequent interaction between the juvenile offender and staff members, combined with the primitive conditions of the wilderness, which serve to "inspire a degree of intimacy, trust and mutual respect that goes far beyond that found in traditional institutions" (p. 86).

VisionQuest operates two wilderness camps, one in the mountains of New Mexico and the other in Franklin, Pennsylvania. Included in the wilderness experience are a "blind walk," for which the youths are blindfolded, and a solo that requires each participant to spend 3 days alone in the wilderness with only minimal food and water. There is also a 6-day adventure featuring rock climbing and rappelling, culminating in a 6-mile run.

VisionQuest's wagon trains, which travel 15 to 20 miles per day, have transported youths thousands of miles cross-country in much the same way as the early settlers explored the new frontier. The adolescents must all work together to keep the wagon train on its scheduled course. Staff and youths live and work side by side in a family atmosphere. Each "family" has responsibility for its own wagon, horses, mules, and equipment. The ratio of staff to youths approaches one to one. The daily schedule was described in a VisionQuest newsletter: The youths and staff awake at 6 A.M. each day. Morning activities include watering and feeding the animals and taking down the tepees. When the wagons leave the campsite, the task of the "campjacks" is to clean up the campground and then proceed to the next location to make preparations for that night. They are responsible for setting up the tepees, digging the fire pit, and making a picket line for the animals. When the chores have been completed, the youths concentrate on the educational program.

The usual bedtime is 8 P.M., but it may be later to accommodate such activities as group or individual counseling, tutoring, or a special event. There are some breaks in the grueling schedule. One day out of every five or six is allotted for making equipment repairs, doing laundry, and having a shower. Sometimes the staff use this time to accompany the youths on a recreational outing such as a trip to a local point of interest, a sports event, a movie, or dinner in a restaurant.

A youth who wants to ride a horse or a mule must be willing to care for the animal. If an animal is not treated properly, the juvenile forfeits the privilege of riding and must walk beside the wagon train.

Parents are permitted to visit their children at various places on the wagon train's route.

## Confrontations and Discipline

Because of the close contact between staff and youths, the con games and the peer pressure to be a troublemaker rarely get started. Youths are always under the watchful eye of the staff. The adolescents learn to follow the rules because they are directly related to their safety. They learn to work as a team because the activities (such as setting up tepees) require a team effort. As distinct from a reformatory, where a troublemaker gains status and approbation from his peers, youths sentenced to VQ only provoke the anger of their peers if they refuse to do or are careless in doing their share of the work (Greenwood et al., 1983).

However, misbehavior does occur, and the adolescents are held accountable for their actions. Misbehavior is dealt with by a direct confrontation between senior staff members and the youth. The controversy surrounding the VQ program has arisen mainly because of the unorthodox methods used in the confrontation process:

> The staff may observe that a youth is beginning to talk back to staff, neglect duties, or provoke incidents with other youths. The senior staff decides that a confrontation is in order. It is triggered by a specific incident; perhaps the youth tries to get another youth to do his or her job, or performs a chore sloppily. The confrontation begins with loud and direct verbal confrontation, with the staff member and the youth nose to nose. Two or three more staff now gather around. The youth is continuously challenged. What is he up to? Who does he think he is? What is his problem? The youth may answer back in kind, or shrink into silence, or burst into tears, or even become physical. The staff stays on him until he works through a crisis. As things calm down, the discussion becomes more rational. Specific suggestions are made or orders given. By the time it is all over, they all go about their business as if nothing happened; the air is cleared. The staff may talk about how it went at their nightly meeting.

Although some may see the confrontational approach as unnecessarily harsh, the youths seem to recognize its value. The following comments were made by Wayne, a 16-year-old participant from Pennsylvania whose mother was a prostitute. Wayne had a history of auto thefts, gang fights, burglaries, drug abuse, and running away from placements prior to being sent to VisionQuest:

> They surround you to make sure you don't hurt anyone. Then you're screaming and yelling and getting out frustrations and cussing them off the wall. Then they let you up off the ground, and you talk about things that are really bothering you. Usually things with your family. . . .
>
> I feel like I've got better control now. . . . Things that happen that pissed me off before don't anymore. I've learned to discipline myself, to sit down and talk about things with the staff. I feel as if I know them and feel comfortable around them. (Sweeney, 1982, p. 20)

Wayne continued his comments with a comparison of VisionQuest with juvenile detention centers to which he had been sent previously:

> At detention centers I had no rights whatsoever. We just sat around and watched TV and then went to bed. If you got out of control, they'd sock

it to you—choke you and grab you by your arms and legs and get you so you couldn't move. They'd grab you by your head and squeeze you. VQ is different. (Greenwood et al., 1983, p. 59)

Unacceptable actions are also handled by losing privileges or being assigned additional chores. For example, while on the wagon train a juvenile who tries to run away might be "put in the pit," which means that he is required to remain in the middle of the circle of wagons and tepees (remaining there to sleep as well) next to the fire pit so that he is under continual surveillance.

## OceanQuest

Programs such as VisionQuest are not without risk. One VQ component, OceanQuest, was temporarily discontinued in 1980 after a boating accident resulted in nine deaths (seven youths and two counselors) during a storm. A Coast Guard investigation of the accident found no evidence of misconduct, but the report cited several factors that contributed to the disaster: the crew's lack of experience; the extreme weather conditions; the fatigue of the persons on board, who had been at sea for approximately 40 hours; and the failure of the other vessels to conduct a timely search for the missing boat (Sweeney, 1982).

Ocean voyages were reinstituted in 1984 with a 130-foot schooner, the *Western Union*, which had been used by the Western Union Telegraph Company for laying and repairing underwater telegraph cables until 1973, when the arrival of satellites made a cable ship unnecessary. The current headquarters for the sailing program is Fort Mifflin in Pennsylvania. The *Western Union* crew is 11 staff and 13 youths. Before juveniles are permitted to embark on an OceanQuest, they are generally required to complete the wilderness program and at least 8 weeks on a wagon train. In addition, they need to receive the endorsement of the wagon master. Thus, youths who are given permission to enter the sailing program have worked hard and demonstrated their commitment to VisionQuest. Prior to sailing, the crew is given instruction in seamanship, swimming, and water safety, as well as ocean-related education on such topics as marine ecology, oceanography, and map and compass skills.

## Group Home Program

Following the successful completion of two "high-impact" programs, youths become eligible for one of the program's group homes as a way of integrating them into the community. Group homes are geared to meet the needs of the individual, such as offering younger youths a home that utilizes a nurturing family approach, while the emphasis in a home for older adolescents is preparation for independent living.

## Case Examples

The following are excerpts from a January 27, 1985, *Los Angeles Times* article written by 18-year-old Tawny Allen, who had successfully completed the

VisionQuest program and felt that it had made a vital difference in her life. At the time the article was written, she was an assistant manager of a fast-food restaurant.

Tawny mentioned that during the Quest she had tried to con the others by pretending she had hurt her ankle; the other participants carried her for 8 miles. However, the staff learned of her deception and required her to undergo the Quest a second time. Her account of her experience is as follows:

> I finished Quest on my second attempt with flying colors and felt so good about myself. For once in my life I had accomplished something.
>
> After that, I went to Wagon Train. It was hard, but that's the whole idea. Doing things so hard really makes you feel good once you complete them.
>
> The Wagon Train was a very good experience for me. I got close to a lot of staff and kids. It seems the more I began to like myself, the closer I got to other people.
>
> "Residential" in Tucson was my last VisionQuest stop. There you live in houses and work on the "Direction." I needed to finish my high school and go back home because I was only 16. So, I earned my way into public school and—except for a D in algebra—got all As and Bs, which was something I'd never done before.
>
> Whenever any one of the girls in my group had a problem or needed to deal with something, we'd all circle up and help her resolve it. Most of the time other people's feelings would come out too. There were things that all us kids needed to get out that we never could before. Things like being raped or abused or being put aside by our parents.
>
> One thing that was so good about the staff in VQ was that they never gave up on us. Even though we didn't give a damn about ourselves. They helped me to grow up. I faced a lot of things while I was in there and it hurt sometimes, but that's the only way you can get rid of bad feelings: Facing them and talking about them. That's what I was taught there, and it worked.
>
> When I got out, I was two years behind in school but very interested in getting my diploma. I finished it all in time to graduate the year I was supposed to—and worked at a Burger King at the same time.
>
> That was a year and a half ago. Now I'm 18, living on my own and working.
>
> My time at VisionQuest was the best time in my life. Also the hardest. VisionQuest probably saved my life, and I'm glad I was there.

### Family Involvement

Family members are encouraged to attend individual counseling and support groups to discuss issues related to raising a child who has delinquent behavior.

The counselors who interviewed the juvenile prior to program entry also keep the family apprised of the individual's progress at VisionQuest. The counselors invite family members to visit while their child is participating in various aspects of the overall program.

## Stephen L. French Youth Wilderness Program (Homeward Bound)

The Stephen L. French Youth Wilderness Program, located in Brewster, Massachusetts, on the inner coast of Cape Cod, is under the jurisdiction of the Massachusetts Division of Youth Services (DYS). Originally the site was utilized by DYS for a youth forestry camp. Its purpose was to provide delinquent adolescents with a work therapy program in which they were assigned such tasks as building campsites and clearing trails (Willman & Chun, 1973). In 1970 there was a reorganization, and the superintendent of the forestry camp, Alan A. Collette, developed the rigorous wilderness education program now known as Homeward Bound.

Homeward Bound is one of the few state-run outdoor experiential programs to have achieved prominence beyond its regional boundaries. The recognition it has received is due in large part to the dedication of Collette, who continues to serve as the chief administrator. The stated goal of the program is "to present its participants with the opportunity to increase self-respect through self-discipline and to experience the satisfaction of overcoming challenging physical and psychological obstacles through individual and group effort" (Collette, n.d.).

The courts refer approximately 350 boys (age 14 to 17) to the program annually. At the beginning of the 26-day wilderness experience, the youths are placed in groups of eight, called brigades. Initially their time is spent participating in community service assignments, taking short hikes and runs, and completing obstacle courses. A counselor works with each boy individually in planning for release from the program. After the boys have been oriented to survival skills, they embark on a particular wilderness experience involving such activities as rock climbing, rappelling, canoeing, camping, cross-country skiing, and pullboating (Willman & Chun, 1973; Collette, n.d.). The program also provides "individual and group counseling; psychological, educational, and vocational testing; and tutoring" (Collette, n.d.).

A 10-day trip along the Appalachian Trail, often through snow 4 feet deep, is an example of the excursions in which the youths participate. The culmination of the program (and the most difficult assignment) is a 3-day solo experience in the wilderness with only "a few matches, a plastic sheet, a cooking pail and water" (Willman & Chun, 1973).

Because Homeward Bound is under the jurisdiction of the state DYS, it is not able to initiate an aftercare component that would provide much-needed continuity. Community-based follow-up activities are handled by regular DYS caseworkers (Greenwood & Zimring, 1985).

## Jack and Ruth Eckerd Foundation Therapeutic Wilderness Program

Through the Eckerd Foundation, wealthy Florida businessman Jack Eckerd has established a number of nonprofit therapeutic and educational camping programs to treat troubled and delinquent youths. The foundation developed its first therapeutic wilderness camping program in Brooksville, Florida, in 1968. Additional camps followed, and Eckerd currently has 16 programs: 5 in Florida, 5 in North Carolina, 2 in Georgia, 1 in New Hampshire, 1 in Tennessee, 1 in Rhode Island, and 1 in Vermont. These camps serve children age 10 through 17, with more than two thirds of the participants between the ages of 13 and 15. At the Eckerd camps, the emphasis is on helping children develop improved ways of dealing with their emotions and on teaching them realistic methods for solving problems. As of June 2003, there were 39 Eckerd Youth Alternative Programs that have provided services to more than 50,000 troubled youths over the past 35 years. The latest recidivism study indicated a rate of approximately 26% 1 year posttreatment.

The foundation describes its program in terms different than those used to describe many of the other wilderness programs. It is referred to as residential treatment and therapeutic wilderness camps, with emphasis on the therapeutic aspect. While other programs highlight the various types of wilderness activities and mention a counseling component only in passing, the Eckerd program literature emphasizes "an individualized, experience-based educational process aimed at developing a self-directed, self-assured learner."

In comparing the extent and rigor of the physical challenges at Vision-Quest, Homeward Bound, and Eckerd, Greenwood and Zimring (1985) concluded that Eckerd's program was less "physically oriented" than the others, with more emphasis on education. They also found that many of the youths who are referred to Eckerd camps have less serious emotional and behavioral problems than youths who attend the other two programs.

The children participate in a highly structured program in which outdoor experiences are used to motivate the youths to succeed in academic education and interpersonal relationships (Greenwood & Zimring, 1985). Since 1977, the program has been accredited as an alternative school by the Southern Association of Colleges and Schools.

Although their referrals do not come solely from the court, as is the case with many other wilderness programs, a sizable percentage of campers do have a record of juvenile delinquency offenses. In 1984, 57% of the participants in the program in Florida and 95% of those in Vermont were adjudicated as juvenile offenders. In 1995–1996, 55% of the 1,619 youths served by the Eckerd wilderness programs had been adjudicated for a delinquency offense. Youths are referred to an Eckerd camp by different sources, most frequently the state division of youth services or a court order. Other referral sources include the public school system and the county mental health center (Jack and Ruth Eckerd Foundation, 1984, 1997).

The offenses committed by youths prior to referral range from running away and truancy to drug offenses, breaking and entering, auto theft, and burglary. The two crime categories with the greatest percentage of referrals are theft/larceny and breaking and entering.

Campers are placed in a living environment with 10 children and two teacher–counselors. Each individual is dependent on the group for activities of daily living such as constructing the shelter, gathering wood for cooking, deciding on a meal plan, and recreational activities (Jack and Ruth Eckerd Foundation, Eckard Youth Alternatives, at http://www.eckerd.org).

## Educational Program

The educational program is presented in two phases: the experiential program and the transitional classroom. Individualized education plans are developed for each camper. In the first phase, the campers develop improved language and math skills in the course of completing a project such as developing trip and menu plans, preparing a budget, constructing the shelter, and working on the camp newspaper.

A youth is ready to enter phase two when he or she has demonstrated the ability to handle a more formalized educational environment. Phase two is seen as a "bridge" between the residential program and the mainstream educational system to which the youth will return. The emphasis shifts from experiential learning to formal academic instruction.

## Family Counseling

One of the important differences between the Eckerd program and other wilderness camps is the family counseling component. In making their decisions on admission of new applicants, the Eckerd staff request that the child's family (or a family substitute) agree to participate actively in the camper's treatment. While the child is participating in the camp activities, the parent(s) attend group meetings with other parents. Periodically, the camper returns home for a 4-day visit. Following each home visit, the social worker meets with the family to discuss what has taken place. According to the program literature, the family worker provides follow-up services for 18 months after the camper's graduation from the program.

## Camp Woodson

Camp Woodson, located in Fairview, North Carolina, is a therapeutic, adventure-based wilderness program for adjudicated juvenile offenders. Emphasis is placed on helping youths gain self-confidence through achievement of progressively more difficult tasks. The program, which began in 1976, has 130 male and female campers per year and 19 staff. The camp serves youths who have been sent to one of the Division of Youth Services (DYS) training schools in North Carolina. The juveniles are considered eligible for the outdoor program when they have demonstrated acceptable behavior at the training school.

The camp is typically comprised of adolescents age 13 to 16 who have either revoked probation or been adjudicated for nonviolent offenses such as breaking and entering, auto theft, or shoplifting. The program has four main elements: precamp, trail life, solo experience, and therapy.

## Precamp

The goal of the 4-week precamp component is to initiate the group building process. During precamp, the youths participate in four activities (e.g., day hikes, ropes course, swim tests) geared to assess their physical conditioning and emotional adjustment and learn food preparation, rope management, hygiene, clothing care, and communication tools. At the conclusion of precamp, individuals are assigned to a tent and activity group on the basis of staff observations and recommendations.

## Trail Life

Campers participate in a variety of outdoor activities, including rock climbing, whitewater canoeing, hiking, backpacking, caving, and horseback riding. All physical challenges are, according to one program description, "designed in gradual levels of difficulty in order to progressively develop skill and trust levels." Each juvenile is assigned to a "tent group" of four or five youths and one staff member. Each group functions independently, living together, doing its own cooking and other housekeeping chores, and looking after its equipment. The groups spend most of their time in the wilderness, returning to the base camp periodically for more food and supplies and to repair equipment.

## Solo Experience

During the last week of the program, each youth is expected to have a solo adventure campout, spending one night alone in the wilderness. The adolescent is told where to camp and provided with the appropriate equipment and supplies. Camp Woodson's solos are different from those of other programs (which emphasize survival in the wilderness with minimal provisions). The purpose is instead to provide an experience that enables the individual to demonstrate recently acquired knowledge of the outdoors. The solo also provides the occasion for reflection and self-examination.

There is also a 2-day final expedition that is more challenging than the previous expeditions. The final event stresses teamwork, decision making, and group cohesiveness. Camp ends with a graduation ceremony at which the campers are honored for their accomplishments. It is attended by family members, court counselors, and camp staff.

## Therapeutic Elements

As with the other wilderness programs, staff are expected to serve as observable role models. The juveniles receive individual counseling twice a week. Sessions focus on articulating specific behavioral goals and developing methods for goal attainment.

## Corvallis House

Corvallis House, located in Salem, Oregon, is a community-based group home program that incorporates wilderness trips (e.g., snow camping, skiing, rock climbing, mountaineering) as an important component of its overall treatment approach. But unlike many other wilderness models, its program is not based totally on outdoor adventures. Corvallis House began its program with a structure similar to the Outward Bound model. It has now evolved into a comprehensive program providing not only wilderness trips but also academic education, work-study, drug and alcohol treatment, and independent living programs.

The majority of the boys at Corvallis House have a history of drug or alcohol abuse. Residents are required to attend classes in which the facts about drugs and alcohol are taught, and treatment to help them deal with past substance abuse is provided. The facility also provides a full program of high school courses.

## Wilderness Probation Program

A wilderness probation program—the Sierra II Wilderness Adventure program—was initiated in Virginia Beach, Virginia, in 1975 (Callahan, 1985). The main components of this model are group meetings for the juveniles twice a month, group sessions for parents twice a month, a wilderness excursion one weekend per month, and a 12-day "primitive expedition" in the summer. This wilderness probation approach operates with only 3 paid staff and 14 volunteers.

The program has the following goals:

1. To learn, through the group process, socially acceptable ways of handling peer pressure in the youths' own environment
2. To learn how to survive in the wilderness
3. To learn productive, challenging activities to occupy the youths' leisure time

The counselors try to relate the struggle in the wilderness to the struggles with which the youths are confronted on a daily basis, such as putting more effort into resolving problems at school or at home. Callahan believes that the adolescents benefit from the weekend trips because, in addition to learning how to work successfully in a group, the excursions provide a cooling-off period during times of family dysfunction.

Included in the 12-day summer excursion are such activities as backpacking, a canoe trip, mountain climbing, and cave exploration. The culmination is a 10- to 12-mile run. Following the marathon run, the group discussion focuses on the individuals' accomplishments during the expedition and how the experience can improve relationships at home and school and with peers. During the excursions, slides and videotapes are made. Shown to parents and youths during later group meetings, the slides and tapes serve to demonstrate the problem-solving skills that should be utilized by parents and children in resolving everyday problems.

## ■ Program Evaluations

There have been only a handful of published follow-up studies on the effectiveness of wilderness programs, and most of the data come from studies conducted in the 1970s. There is a need for rigorous, methodologically sound research covering various aspects of the wilderness adventure experience. Researchers should study the relationship between later success and such program aspects as length of stay, age of participants, severity of offenses, length of aftercare program, and involvement of parents in aftercare counseling.

The most recent longitudinal follow-up study was the Associated Marine Institutes, Inc. (AMI) 2001 and 2002 Recidivism study, which includes both rearrest and readjudication data from the programs in all eight states and the Cayman Islands. What is most impressive is that more than 70% of the graduates of these programs were successful as defined by the fact that they were in school or employed and had not been rearrested 1 year after program completion. Depending on the program and on whether the juveniles were felony versus status or misdemeanor offenders, rearrest rates ranged from 12% to 28%. The Florida-based programs with status and misdemeanant offenders fared the best, with only a 12% recidivism rate. The implications are that it seems to be beneficial to intervene early with runaways, truants, reckless drivers, and vandals before these youths escalate to committing chronic felony offenses.

The second study was completed in 1997 by Professors Smith, Switzer, Sturkie, and Campbell of Campbell University: 425 of the Eckerd wilderness educational system graduates in 1996 were studied 3, 6, 9, and 12 months after graduation to collect data on recidivism. Nineteen percent had recidivated—a new adjudication or conviction—within 12 months after release from placement.

Of the few studies conducted, one of the most widely cited is a 1-year follow-up conducted by Kelly and Baer (1971). They studied 120 boys who had come in contact with the Massachusetts DYS. The researchers developed two matched groups with 60 boys in each. The experimental group was boys who attended one of the Outward Bound schools (located in Minnesota, in Colorado, or on Hurricane Island, 10 miles off the Maine coast). The boys in the comparison group were given routine processing by DYS: Some youths were sent to an institution while others were immediately paroled. The two groups were matched by age at time of selection for the study, offense for which the youth was committed, and number of prior DYS commitments (p. 438).

The boys were between the ages of 15 and 17 and healthy, with no severe psychopathology or physical disability. They had no history of violent or sexually assaultive behavior, and all had agreed to participate in the program.

Kelly and Baer (1971, p. 438) defined *recidivism* as "a return to a juvenile institution or commitment to an adult institution for a new offense within one year after parole." The 1-year follow-up data showed that the experimental group had a 20% recidivism rate, while the comparison group had a 42% rate. It should be noted that there were program differences among the three Outward Bound schools studied. The Colorado and Hurricane Island programs emphasized "severe physical challenge, felt danger, and high excitement" (p. 440) and made only minimal efforts to provide the participants with a verbal interpretation of the wilderness experience. Those were the schools that had the lower recidivism rates: Colorado's program had a zero recidivism rate; Hurricane Island's was 11%. Conversely, the Minnesota program, although it did stress physical challenge, was described by the researchers as having a "relatively low objective danger and excitement level" and focusing attention on interpersonal relationships and "development of a spiritual attitude" (p. 440). The recidivism rate for Minnesota's school was 42%.

Kelly and Baer's study produced other noteworthy findings. Their study showed that the average age of a juvenile's initial court appearance was significantly lower for those who recidivated (12.8 years) than for those who did not (14.3 years). This finding would indicate that Outward Bound may be more effective for juveniles whose first appearance in court occurred when they were somewhat older.

The experimental group of juveniles in Kelly and Baer's (1971) 1-year follow-up was the focus of another report 5 years after their Outward Bound experience. Baer, Jacobs, and Carr (1975) examined the relationship between the characteristics exhibited by youths during their 26-day stay at Outward Bound and recidivism during the following 5 years. At the completion of the Outward Bound course, those youths who had demonstrated personal growth and completed all course requirements had been awarded a certificate. In addition to ascertaining the 5-year recidivism rate for the group as a whole, Baer et al. examined the differences between the youths who had received a certificate of completion and those who had not. (A certificate had been awarded to only 50 of the 60 participants.) Of the 60 youths studied, a total of 24 had recidivated. The recidivism rate for those who had successfully completed the program requirements was 30%; in contrast, the recidivism rate for those who had not received a certificate was 90%. From this study, it appears that the important indicator with regard to later recidivism is not a juvenile's having been assigned to Outward Bound but the way the juvenile handled the rigorous program requirements.

Behar and Stephens (1978) conducted an evaluation of a wilderness camping program for emotionally disturbed children (many of whom had also committed delinquent acts) in North Carolina. They conducted a follow-up of 46 boys who had been released from the Carolina Boys' Camp between 1972 and 1975. A variety of posttreatment factors were examined, including school adjustment, leisure time activities, interpersonal problems, problems at home, and delinquency.

The clients showed considerable improvement in all areas with the exception of juvenile delinquency. The researchers found that the percentage of boys whose adjustment in school was considered "adequate" rose from 27% to 73%. Similarly, before attending the camp 56% to 71% of the boys were having interpersonal problems with parents, siblings, and/or teachers. This figure decreased to 15% or lower after discharge from the camp program.

The one area in which no improvement was found was delinquency. The same percentage of parents (55%) reported that their child "had been arrested or in trouble with the law" before the program as after the program. Behar and Stephens did find an association between length of stay at the camp and subsequent delinquency: Youths who were delinquent had been in the program only three fourths as long as the nonlawbreaking juveniles (318 days versus 421).

The Alabama Department of Youth Services (DYS) (n.d.) conducted a follow-up on 65 boys who had participated in the Wilderness Camping Program at Oak Mountain State Park between May 1982 and September 1983. Of the 40 boys for whom data were obtained, only 7 (17%) had been rearrested during the first 9 months after discharge from DYS. Most of the boys who had been assigned to the wilderness program had committed property offenses. Slightly more than half of the youths were sent to an aftercare program following the wilderness experience, while the rest of the boys were discharged. The report stated that none of the boys who participated in aftercare was rearrested. Although the rearrest rate is quite low, it should be noted that the researchers attempted to follow up 65 youths but obtained data on only 40 of them. Although the status of the missing 25 boys was not known, it may well be that at least some did have further trouble with the law.

Greenwood et al. (1983) reported on follow-up research of VisionQuest's program that had been conducted by Behavioral Research Associates in 1979. That study found a rearrest rate of 43% for youths who had been released from the program for at least 13 months prior to the study.

Willman and Chun (1973) conducted a follow-up study of the Homeward Bound program run by the Massachusetts DYS. They found a recidivism rate (the term *recidivism* was not defined) of 20.8% for the Homeward Bound youths versus a 42.7% recidivism rate among the control group.

A major stumbling block in comparing various follow-up studies is the inconsistent way in which the term *recidivism* is defined. Some researchers equate recidivism with rearrest, others use recidivism to mean a new commitment to a correctional facility, and still others speak of the recidivism rate without defining it at all. Thus, for example, the reader is cautioned that the 43% recidivism (i.e., rearrest) rate at VisionQuest (Greenwood et al., 1983) should not be compared with the 20% recidivism (i.e., recommitment) rate of Kelly and Baer's (1971) Outward Bound research, because the basis for determining recidivism in those two studies was not the same. Another factor that should also be considered is the previous history of the juveniles in the various programs. Some programs select only first-time offenders while others, such as VisionQuest, state that their programs recruit chronic juvenile delinquents.

## Summary

Wilderness programs have been found by several researchers to be at least as effective as institutionalization and in some studies considerably more effective. This chapter has documented wilderness programs as a preferred alternative for juvenile offenders that is much more cost-effective, humane, and replicable than institutional treatment.

Detailed descriptions were provided of the common features and programmatic differences among seven of the well-established wilderness adventure programs. Characteristic program components are therapeutic camping, canoeing, an overnight solo experience, an alternative school program, and a family counseling component.

The chapter concludes by reviewing follow-up studies on the effectiveness of wilderness programs. A major stumbling block to determining the effectiveness of these programs is the dearth of systematic longitudinal studies and the inconsistent way in which the term *recidivism* has been defined. There is a need for carefully planned longitudinal studies based on an experimental design and conducted simultaneously in several parts of the country. Only after further systematic research is completed will we be able to identify and recommend for replication those programs that work best with specific offender groups.

## Discussion Questions

1 What was the name and purpose of the earliest outdoor wilderness program, which was established for juvenile offenders in the 1930s in Los Angeles?

2 Outline the differences between traditional training schools and structured wilderness challenge programs.

3 List the four common features of the established wilderness programs for juvenile offenders.

**4** What are the focus and major strengths of the AMI Florida Environmental Institute and the Gulf Coast Trades Center Conservation Program?

**5** Discuss the objectives and major activities, staffing pattern, and average length of stay at VisionQuest or the Eckerd Foundation's Therapeutic Wilderness Camps.

**6** Discuss the findings and their implications from the Kelly and Baer (1971) and the Baer et al. (1975) follow-up studies of participants in the Outward Bound programs.

**7** Outline the type of study design needed to conduct a methodologically sound, longitudinal follow-up study of juvenile offenders.

## References

Alabama Department of Youth Services. (n.d.). *Wilderness program evaluation report: May 1982–September 1983*. Mt. Meigs, AL: Division of Planning, Research, and Development.

American Marine Institutes. (2001 and 2002). *AMI recidivism study*. Tampa, FL: Author.

Baer, D. J., Jacobs, P. J., & Carr, F. E. (1975). Instructors' ratings of delinquents after Outward Bound survival training and their subsequent recidivism. *Psychological Reports, 36*, 547–553.

Behar, L., & Stephens, D. (1978). Wilderness camping: An evaluation of a residential treatment program for emotionally disturbed children. *American Journal of Orthopsychiatry, 48*, 644–653.

Callahan, R., Jr. (1985). Wilderness probation: A decade later. *Juvenile and Family Court Journal, 36*, 31–35.

Center for the Study of Youth Policy. (1999). *VisionQuest follow-up study of 1,230 high-risk youth*. Philadelphia: University of Pennsylvania Center for the Study of Youth Policy.

Collette, A. A. (n.d.). *Program description*. Stephen L. French Youth Wilderness Program.

Cronin, R. C. (1996). Youth Environmental Service in action: Program summary. Washington, DC: Office of Juvenile Justice and Delinquency Prevention, U.S. Department of Justice.

Florida Department of Juvenile Justice. (2000). Program accountability measures for DJJ commitment programs: A two-year analysis, FY 1999–2000 (management report No. 2000-9). Tallahassee: Author.

Greenwood, P. W., Lipson, A. J., Abrahamse, A., & Zimring, F. E. (1983). *Youth crime and juvenile justice in California: A report to the legislature*. Santa Monica, CA: Rand.

Greenwood, P. W., & Zimring, F. E. (1985). *One more change: The pursuit of promising intervention strategies for chronic juvenile offenders*. Santa Monica, CA: Rand.

Jack and Ruth Eckerd Foundation. (1997). *Annual descriptive summary 1997*. Clearwater, FL: Eckerd Foundation.

Jack and Ruth Eckerd Foundation. (n.d.). *Therapeutic wilderness camping program brochure*. Clearwater, FL: Eckerd Foundation.

Kelly, F. J., & Baer, D. J. (1971). Physical challenge as a treatment for delinquency. *Crime and Delinquency, 17*, 437–445.

Robison, S. M. (1960). *Juvenile delinquency: Its nature and control*. New York: Holt, Rinehart, and Winston.

Sweeney, P. (1982, February). VisionQuest's rite of passage. *Corrections Magazine*, pp. 22–32.

VisionQuest. (n.d.). Program descriptions.

VisionQuest. (1982). Wagon Train.

VisionQuest. (n.d.). *Western Union* (newsletter). Tucson, AZ: Visionquest.

Willman, H. C., Jr., & Chun, R. X. E. (1973, September). Homeward Bound: An alternative to the institutionalization of adjudicated juvenile offenders. *Federal Probation*, pp. 52–58.

# 18 Juvenile Homicide Encapsulated

Kathleen M. Heide

The March 24, 1998, massacre at a middle school in Jonesboro, Arkansas, occurred in a small, rural Southern community and quickly became a global event. *Time* and *Newsweek* featured the two young killers, Andrew Golden, age 11, and Mitchell Johnson, age 13, on their magazine covers. These two "kids" were subsequently convicted of killing 4 girls and a teacher and wounding 10 more in an ambush of their fellow students. They were not the first young killers to murder their classmates senselessly in recent years, and tragically these boys were not the last ones to participate in acts of mass destruction. In May 1998, 15-year-old Kip Kinkel killed his parents and then opened fire on his classmates, killing 2 and wounding 23 in Springfield, Oregon (McGee & DeBernardo, 1999). In April 1999, 17-year-old Dylan Klebold and 18-year-old Eric Harris went on a killing spree in their Littleton, Colorado, high school that left 13 dead and more than 20 others wounded before they turned their guns on themselves, ending their lives (Franz & Moser, 2000).

Mass shootings characterized by multiple victims, often randomly targeted, by unhappy, angry, and alienated youths using high-powered weaponry represent the most extreme form of juvenile violence. Although there is some evidence that incidents of this nature are increasing (Meloy et al., 2001), fortunately they remain rare events involving little more than a dozen youths over the last 10 years (Heide, 1999a). In contrast, the number of homicide arrestees known to be under 18 during the 10-year-period 1991–2000 averaged 2,150 per year (Federal Bureau of Investigation, 1992–2001).

## ■ Putting Youth Murder in Perspective

The issue of juvenile homicide has been headlined repeatedly in the news all over the United States and abroad since the early 1990s. While it is difficult to assess the exact number of murders committed by juveniles because the age of the killer is not specified by the arresting authority in as many as a third of the cases (Snyder, 2001), murders by young people have risen over the last two decades. Dramatic increases in youths being arrested for homicide beginning in the early 1980s are apparent, whether the frame of reference is youths under 18 or those in their middle to late teens (Heide, 1999b).

The term *youths* is a broad concept that encompasses both juveniles and adolescents. Although these words are often used interchangeably in the media and in the professional literature, they can be distinguished. Juvenile or minority status is determined on the basis of age and is a legislative decision (Butts & Snyder, 1997; Heide, 1992). The federal government and the majority of the states, for example, designate youths under 18 as juveniles (Bortner, 1988; Sickmund, 1994). The Federal Bureau of Investigation (2001) classifies arrests of "children 17 and under" as juvenile arrests.

Adolescence, in contrast to juvenile status, is based on human development and varies across individuals. It is a stormy period characterized by hormonal changes, growth spurts, psychological changes, and enhancement of intellectual abilities and motor skills. According to child development experts, adolescence begins with puberty, which typically commences by age 12 or 13 but may start earlier (Solomon, Schmidt, & Ardragna, 1990; see also Lee, Lee, & Chen, 1995). Adolescence extends through the teen years to age 19 or 20 (Solomon et al., 1990). The term *children* is commonly used to refer to pre-pubescent youths.

Analysis of crime patterns clearly indicates that youth involvement in homicide remains a serious problem in the United States in the 21st century. Homicide arrests of juveniles rose every year from 1984 through 1993. The dramatic escalation in murders by juveniles during this time frame put the country in the grips of fear. In 1993, the number of juveniles arrested for murder—3,284—was 3 times higher than the number arrested in 1984 and had reached an all-time high (Heide, 1999b). The rate at which juveniles were arrested for murder also increased substantially during this time frame. The juvenile murder rate peaked in 1993 at 14 per 100,000, which was more than twice the level of the early 1980s (6 per 100,000) (Snyder, 1997). The significant rise in murders committed by those under 18 during this time frame cannot be attributed to an increase in the juvenile population during this period. In fact, the percentage of young Americans in the population during this time frame had generally been declining (Blumstein, 1995; Ewing, 1990; Fox, 1996; Gest & Friedman, 1994; Heide, 1994b).

Although the numbers of minors arrested for murder decreased over the period 1994 through 2000, it would be wrong to conclude that the crisis in lethal youth violence is over. The percentage of all homicide arrests involving juveniles in 2000, after 7 years of decline, is still higher than it was in 1984, when juvenile homicide was just beginning to increase. In 1984, 7.3% of all homicide arrestees were juveniles; in 2000, 9.3% of those arrested for murder were under 18. The mean percentage of homicide arrestees who were juveniles during the 10-year period of escalation (1984–1993) was 11.6%; the comparable mean percentage during the 7-year period of decline (1994–2000) was 13.0%.

The seriousness of the youth homicide problem is underscored when the unit of analysis is 15- to 19-year-olds. Smith and Feiler (1995) computed the *absolute* and *relative* levels of youth involvement in arrests for murder during the period 1958–1993. Examination of trends in arrest rates revealed a very striking escalation in homicides by youths in their late teens beginning in the mid-1980s. The arrest rates for 15- to 19-year-olds recorded in 1992 (42.4 per 100,000) and 1993 (42.2) were the highest recorded for *any* age group during the 36 years covered by the data. Similarly, the researchers concluded that "the ratio for 15- to 19-year-olds in 1993 marks the greatest relative involvement in murder arrests for any age group during the period under study" (Smith & Feiler, 1995, p. 330). Recent follow-up data revealed that youth involvement remained highest, even when the analyses were extended to encompass data through 1999 (Feiler & Smith, 2000).

Two recently released government reports concluded that, despite the decreasing trends, youth homicide and youth violence have not abated. The U.S. Surgeon General in a January 2001 report on youth violence made the following observations:

> Since 1993, when the epidemic peaked, youth violence has declined significantly nationwide, as signaled by downward trends in arrest records, victimization data, and hospital emergency room records. But the problem has not been resolved. Another key indicator of youth violence— youths' confidential reports about their violence behavior—reveals no change since 1993 in the proportion of young people who have committed physically injurious and potentially lethal acts. (American Psychological Association, 2001, p. 1)

The Bureau of Justice Statistics in a March 2000 report noted: "Despite the encouraging improvement since 1993, the levels of gun homicide by juveniles and young adults are well-above those of the mid-1980's" and "the levels of youth homicide remain well-above those of the early and mid-1980's" (Fox & Zawitz, 2000, pp. 1, 2). The report of the U.S. Surgeon General ended with the following warning:

> This is no time for complacency. The epidemic of lethal violence that swept the United States from 1983 to 1993 was funneled in large part by easy access to weapons, notably firearms. If the sizable numbers of youths still involved in violence today begin carrying and using weapons as they did a decade ago, this country may see a resurgence of the lethal violence that characterized the violence epidemic. (American Psychological Association, 2001, p. 2)

## ■ Youths Who Kill: A Synthesis of the Literature

When youths kill today, adults ask why, just as they have for centuries (Zagar, Arbit, Sylvies, Busch, & Hughes, 1990). The question, however, has become more complex since the mid-1980s because there are really two issues involved: Why are youths killing, and why have we seen more youths killing today in the United States than in previous generations? This chapter synthesizes the literature on clinical and empirical findings related to youth homicide. Then it addresses factors operating today that appear to be contributing to the escalation in murders by youths.

Many clinicians and researchers have examined cases of youths killing over the last 50 years in an effort to determine the causes of juvenile homicide. Two excellent critiques of the literature by University of Virginia Professor

Dewey Cornell and SUNY Professor Charles Patrick Ewing have been previously published (Cornell, 1989; Ewing, 1990). Both scholars cited a number of methodological problems with most of the available studies on juvenile homicide and suggested that reported findings be viewed with caution.

Much of the difficulty with this literature stems from the fact that most published accounts of young killers are case studies. The cases reported were often drawn from psychiatric populations referred to the authors for evaluation and/or treatment after the youth committed a homicide. The conclusions drawn from these cases, while interesting and suggestive, cannot provide us with precise explanations regarding why youths kill because it is unknown to what extent the youths examined are typical of the population of juvenile murderers. In addition, in the absence of control groups of any kind, we cannot know in what ways these young killers differ from nonviolent juvenile offenders, violent juvenile offenders who do not kill, and juveniles with no prior records.

Research on juvenile murderers has been primarily descriptive. Not surprisingly, psychogenic explanations (e.g., mental illness, defective intelligence, childhood trauma) have largely predominated in the literature, given the professional background of many of the authors. Biopsychological explanations (e.g., neurological impairments, brain injury) have been investigated, as have data on important sociological variables (e.g., family constellation, gang involvement, drug and alcohol use, participation in other antisocial behavior, peer associations). Sociological theories of criminal behavior (e.g., strain/anomie, subcultural, social control, labeling, conflict and radical theories; see Bynum & Thompson, 1999, for discussion of sociological theories), however, have not been systematically investigated in the literature on youth homicide.

Statements about juvenile murderers in the professional literature are typically about male adolescents who kill. Although some studies of adolescent homicide have included both females and males (e.g., Dolan & Smith, 2001; Labelle, Bradford, Bourget, Jones, & Carmichael, 1991; Malmquist, 1990), most research has focused on male adolescents because they are the overwhelming majority of juvenile homicide offenders.

## Girls Who Kill

A few publications report case studies of girls who have murdered (e.g., Benedek & Cornell, 1989; Ewing, 1990; Gardiner, 1985; Heide, 1992; McCarthy, 1978; Medlicott, 1955; Russell, 1986). These studies reveal that girls are more likely than boys to kill family members and to use accomplices to effect these murders. Girls are also more likely to perform secondary roles when the killings are gang related or occur during the commission of a felony, such as robbery. Their accomplices are generally male. Pregnant unmarried girls who kill their offspring at birth or shortly thereafter, in contrast, often appear to act alone. Girls' motives for murder are varied. Instrumental reasons include ending abuse meted out by an abusive parent, eliminating witnesses to a crime, and concealing a pregnancy. Expressive reasons include acting out psychological conflict or mental illness, supporting a boyfriend's activities, and demonstrating allegiance to gang members (Ewing, 1990).

## Homicides Involving Young Children as Offenders

Research specifically investigating "little kids" who kill has also been sparse, partly because of the low incidence and the difficulty of obtaining access to these youths (e.g., Bender, 1959; Carek & Watson, 1964; Ewing, 1990; Goetting, 1989, 1995; Petti & Davidman, 1981; Pfeffer, 1980; Shumaker & Prinz, 2000; Tooley, 1975). The importance of distinguishing between preadolescents and adolescents in understanding what motivates youths to kill and in designing effective treatment plans was recognized by clinicians as early as 1940 (Bender & Curran, 1940). Subsequent investigators, however, have not consistently used age as a criterion in selecting samples of youths who kill (Easson & Steinhilber, 1961; Goetting, 1989; Myers, Scott, Burgess, & Burgess, 1995; Sargent, 1962). In one frequently cited report, for example, the young killers ranged in age from 3.5 to 16 years old (Sargent, 1962).

Although recent research suggests that preteen and adolescent murderers may share some commonalities (Shumaker & Prinz, 2000), the differences between the two groups cannot be ignored. Physically healthy children under 9 who kill, in contrast to older youths, typically do not fully understand the concept of death (Bender & Curran, 1940; Cornell, 1989; Heide, 1992; O'Halloran & Altmaier, 1996). They have great difficulty in comprehending that their actions are irreversible (Bender & Curran, 1940). Prepubescent children who kill often act impulsively and without clear goals in mind (e.g., Adelson, 1972; Carek & Watson, 1964; Goetting, 1989). Preadolescent murderers are also more likely than older youths to kill in response to the unstated wishes of their parents (e.g., Tooley, 1975; Tucker & Cornwall, 1977). In addition, the incidence of severe conflict (e.g., Bernstein, 1978; Paluszny & McNabb, 1975) or severe mental illness (Bender, 1959; Heide, 1984; "Incompetency standards in death penalty and juvenile cases," 1984; Pfeffer, 1980; Tucker & Cornwall, 1977; Zenoff & Zients, 1979) tends to be higher among younger children who kill than among their adolescent counterparts. Adolescent killers are more likely to kill because of the lifestyles that they have embraced or in response to situational or environmental constraints that they believe to be placed on them (Heide, 1984, 1992; Sorrells, 1977; Zenoff & Zients, 1979).

## Case Study Research Pertaining to Adolescent Murderers

The literature here highlights findings from studies of youths who typically ranged in age from 12 to 17, although some research included adolescents in their late teen years. In recognition of reporting practices in the professional literature, the terms *juvenile* and *adolescent* are treated as equivalent terms in the discussion that follows. Similarly, the terms *murder* and *homicide* are used synonymously, though the intended legal meaning is that of *murder*. Accordingly, terms such as *juvenile homicide offender*, *adolescent murderer*, and *young killer* are used interchangeably throughout the remainder of this chapter.

The following sections address various areas covered in case studies of adolescent murderers. Keep in mind the caveats discussed previously regarding the shortcomings of this body of literature.

## Psychological Disorder and Youth Homicide

Several scholars have also synthesized existing scientific publications relating to various types of juvenile homicide offenders (Adams, 1974; Busch, Zagar, Hughes, Arbit, & Bussell, 1990; Cornell, Benedek, & Benedek, 1987b, 1989; Ewing, 1990; Haizlip, Corder, & Ball, 1984; Lewis, Lovely, et al., 1985, 1988; Myers, 1992; and, with respect to preadolescent murderers, Shumaker & Prinz, 2000), including youths who commit sexual murders (Myers, 1994; Myers et al., 1995; Myers, Burgess, & Nelson, 1998). Much of the literature, particularly during the 1940s, 1950s, 1960s, and 1970s, suggested that psychodynamic factors propelled youths to kill (Lewis et al., 1985). These factors included impaired ego development, unresolved Oedipal and dependency needs, displaced anger, the ability to dehumanize the victim, and narcissistic deficits (Cornell, 1989; see, e.g., Bender & Curran, 1940; Mack, Scherl, & Macht, 1973; Malmquist, 1971, 1990; McCarthy, 1978; Miller & Looney, 1974; Scherl & Mack, 1966; Smith, 1965; Washbrook, 1979).

Many studies have investigated the extent of severe psychopathology, such as psychosis, organic brain disease, and neurological impairments (Cornell, 1989; Ewing, 1990). The findings, particularly with respect to the presence of psychosis among juvenile homicide offenders, are mixed and may be the result of how the samples were generated. Individuals who are diagnosed as psychotic have lost touch with reality, often experience hallucinations (seeing or hearing things that are not occurring) and delusions (bizarre beliefs), and behave inappropriately. Most studies report that juvenile homicide offenders are rarely psychotic (e.g., Bailey, 1994; Corder, Ball, Haizlip, Rollins, & Beaumont, 1976; Cornell, 1989; Cornell et al., 1987b, 1989; Dolan & Smith, 2001; Ewing, 1990; Hellsten & Katila, 1965; Kashani, Darby, Allan, Hantke, & Reid, 1997; King, 1975; Labelle et al., 1991; Malmquist, 1971; Myers & Kemph, 1988, 1990; Myers et al., 1995; Patterson, 1943; Petti & Davidman, 1981; Russell, 1965, 1979; Shumaker & McKee, 2001; Sorrells, 1977; Stearns, 1957; Walshe-Brennan, 1974, 1977; Yates, Beutler, & Crago, 1984; with respect to adolescent mass murderers, see Meloy, Hempel, Mohandie, Shiva, & Gray, 2001). Some studies, however, do posit a high incidence of psychosis (e.g., Bender 1959; Lewis, Pincus, et al., 1988; Rosner, Weiderlight, Rosner, & Wieczorek, 1978; Sendi & Blomgren, 1975), episodic psychotic symptomatology (Lewis et al.,

1985; Lewis, Lovely, et al., 1988; Myers et al., 1995; Myers & Scott, 1998), and other serious mental illness, such as mood disorders (Lewis, Pincus, et al., 1988; Malmquist, 1971, 1990).

Several case reports have suggested that young killers suffered from a brief psychotic episode, which remitted spontaneously after the homicides (e.g., Cornell, 1989; McCarthy, 1978; Miller & Looney, 1974; Mohr & McKnight, 1971; Sadoff, 1971; Smith, 1965). This phenomenon, initially introduced by the renowned psychiatrist Karl Menninger and one of his colleagues 40 years ago, is known as "episodic dyscontrol syndrome" and is characterized by incidents of severe loss of impulse control in individuals with impaired ego development (Menninger & Mayman, 1956). Diagnosing psychosis in homicide offenders who kill impulsively, brutally, and apparently senselessly, in the absence of clear psychotic symptoms, has been strongly challenged by some of the leading experts on juvenile homicide (e.g., Cornell, 1989; Ewing, 1990).

The literature shows considerable variation in diagnoses given to adolescent murderers within (e.g., Labelle et al., 1991; Malmquist, 1971; Myers & Scott, 1998; Rosner et al., 1978; Russell, 1979) as well as across studies. Personality disorders and conduct disorders rank among the more common diagnoses (Bailey, 1994; Dolan & Smith, 2001; Ewing 1990; Labelle et al., 1991; Malmquist, 1971; Myers et al., 1995, 1998; Myers & Kemph, 1988, 1990; Rosner et al., 1978; Russell, 1979; Santtila & Haapasalo, 1997; Schmideberg, 1973; Sendi & Blomgren, 1975; Sorrells, 1977; Yates, Beutler, & Crago, 1983; and, with respect to preteen murderers, Shumaker & Prinz, 2000). Attention-deficit/hyperactivity disorder (ADHD) has also been noted with some frequency (Myers & Scott, 1998; Myers et al., 1995; Santtila & Haapasalo, 1997; and, with respect to preteen murderers, Shumaker & Prinz, 2000).

## Neurological Impairment and Youth Homicide

Significant disagreement also exists with respect to the prevalence of neurological problems in juvenile killers (Cornell, 1989; Ewing, 1990), which may be partly due to differences in the assessment and reporting practices used by various clinicians (Podolsky, 1965; Restifo & Lewis, 1985; Thom, 1949). Neurological impairment may be indicated by brain or severe head injuries, past and present seizure disorders, abnormal head circumferences or electroencephalogram (EEG) findings, soft neurological signs, and deficits on neurological testing (Myers, 1992). Several researchers have found significant neurological impairment or abnormalities among young killers (e.g., Bailey, 1996; Bender, 1959; Busch et al., 1990; Lewis et al., 1985; Lewis, Lovely, et al., 1988; Michaels, 1961; Myers, 1994; Myers et al., 1995; Woods, 1961; Zagar et al., 1990), particularly those on death row (Lewis, Pincus, et al., 1988). Others maintain that neurological difficulties are absent or rare among the juvenile murderers assessed in their studies (e.g., Dolan & Smith, 2001; Hellsten & Katila, 1965; Labelle et al., 1991; Petti & Davidman, 1981; Russell, 1986; Scherl & Mack, 1966; Walshe-Brennan, 1974, 1977).

## The Intelligence of Young Homicide Offenders

The findings with respect to intelligence are also mixed. Several studies reported mentally retarded youths (IQ score below 70) among their samples of adolescent homicide offenders (Bender, 1959; Busch et al., 1990; Darby, Allan, Kashani, Hartke, & Reid, 1998; Labelle et al., 1991; Lewis, Pincus, et al., 1988; Patterson, 1943; Solway, Richardson, Hays, & Elion, 1981; Zagar et al., 1990). There is a consensus across many studies, however, that few young killers are mentally retarded (Ewing, 1990).

In contrast, there is disagreement regarding the intelligence of the majority of young killers (e.g., Ewing, 1990). Some researchers reported that the typical IQ scores of the juvenile homicide offenders in their samples were in the below average range (70–99) (Busch et al., 1990; Darby et al., 1998; Hays, Solway, & Schreiner, 1978; Labelle et al, 1991; Lewis, Pincus, et al., 1988; Petti & Davidman, 1981; Solway et al., 1981; Zagar et al., 1990). Others, however, have found that the IQ scores were typically average to above average (100–129) (Bender, 1959; Kashani et al., 1997; King, 1975; Patterson, 1943).

The literature on juvenile homicide offenders indicates that, regardless of intelligence potential, many struggle in educational settings. As a group, they tend to perform poorly academically (Bernstein, 1978; Hellsten & Katila, 1965; Myers & Scott, 1998; Myers et al., 1995; Scherl & Mack, 1966; Sendi & Blomgren, 1975; Shumaker & McGee, 2001; Stearns, 1957), have cognitive and language deficits (King, 1975; Myers & Mutch, 1992), experience severe educational difficulties (Bailey, 1994; Busch et al., 1990; Zagar et al., 1990), suffer from learning disabilities (Bender, 1959; Darby et al., 1998; Dolan & Smith, 2001; Hardwick & Rowton-Lee, 1996; King, 1975; Lewis, Pincus, et al., 1988; Myers & Scott, 1998; Myers et al., 1995; Patterson, 1943; Sendi & Blomgren, 1975), and engage in disruptive behavior in the classroom (Bailey, 1996; Myers et al., 1995).

## Home Environments of Youths Who Murder

In-depth analyses of the families of young killers have been lacking (Crespi & Rigazio-DiGilio, 1996). Case studies of adolescents who killed biological parents and stepparents have appeared far more often in the professional literature than other types of juvenile homicide offenders (Ewing, 1990; Zenoff & Zients, 1979; see also, e.g., Anthony & Rizzo, 1973; Cormier, Angliker, Gagne, & Markus, 1978; Duncan & Duncan, 1971; Heide, 1992; Kalogerakis, 1971; Kashani et al., 1997; McCully, 1978; Mones, 1985, 1991; Mouridsen & Tolstrup, 1988; Post, 1982; Russell, 1984; Sadoff, 1971; Sargent, 1962; Scherl & Mack, 1966; Tanay, 1973, 1976; Wertham, 1941). These studies have indicated that youths who killed parents or stepparents, particularly fathers or stepfathers, were typically raised in homes where child abuse, spouse abuse, and parental chemical dependency were common (Heide, 1992, 1995). Research on the adopted child syndrome suggests that adopted youths who kill

their fathers may be driven by other psychodynamic factors, including unresolved loss, extreme dissociation of rage, hypersensitivity to rejection, and
confusion about their identity (Kirschner, 1992).

With few exceptions (e.g., Fiddes, 1981; King, 1975), published research
and case studies report that the majority of adolescent homicide offenders are
raised in broken homes (Darby et al., 1998; Ewing, 1990; see also, e.g., Easson
& Steinhilber, 1961; Labelle et al., 1991; McCarthy, 1978; Patterson, 1943;
Petti & Davidman, 1981; Rosner et al., 1978; Russell, 1986; Scherl & Mack,
1966; Smith, 1965; Sorrells, 1977; Woods, 1961). Some more recent studies
suggest that the majority are likely to come from criminally violent families
(Busch et al., 1990; Zagar et al., 1990). Parental alcoholism, mental illness,
and other indicators of parental psychopathology are commonly found in the
histories of juvenile murderers (Ewing, 1990; see also, e.g., Bailey, 1994, 1996;
Corder et al., 1976; Dolan & Smith, 2001; Heide, 1992; Hellsten & Katila,
1965; Labelle et al, 1991; Lewis, Lovely, et al., 1988; Lewis, Pincus, et al.,
1988; Lewis et al., 1985; Myers et al., 1995, 1998; Petti & Davidman, 1981;
Santtila & Haapasalo, 1997; Sorrells, 1977). Child maltreatment and spouse
abuse are also repeatedly encountered in the homes of adolescent homicide
offenders (Dolan & Smith, 2001; Ewing, 1990; Myers et al., 1995, 1998).
Young killers as a group (e.g., King, 1975; Myers & Scott, 1998; Woods, 1961)
and in particular youths who kill parents (Corder et al., 1976; Duncan &
Duncan, 1971; Heide, 1992, 1994a; Malmquist, 1971; Patterson, 1943; Post,
1982; Russell, 1984; Sargent, 1962; Tanay, 1976) have frequently witnessed
one parent, typically the mother, being abused by the other parental figure.
Juvenile murderers (e.g., Bailey, 1994, 1996; King, 1975; Lewis et al., 1985;
Lewis, Pincus, et al., 1988; Myers & Scott, 1998; Myers et al., 1995; Santtila
& Haapasalo, 1997; Sendi & Blomgren, 1975), especially adolescent parricide
offenders (e.g., Corder et al., 1976; Duncan & Duncan, 1971; Heide, 1992,
1994a; Malmquist, 1971; Scherl & Mack, 1966; Tanay, 1976), have often been
physically abused. Sexual abuse has also been documented in the lives of
juvenile murderers (e.g., Bailey 1994, 1996; Corder et al., 1976; Dolan &
Smith, 2001; Lewis, Pincus, et al., 1988; Sendi & Blomgren, 1975), including
those who kill parents (Heide, 1992, 1994a).

### Involvement in Other Antisocial Behavior

Juvenile homicide offenders had engaged in several types of deviant behavior
prior to committing homicide (Ewing, 1990). Several studies have reported
that the majority of adolescent murderers have had a prior arrest or offense
history (e.g., Bailey, 1996; Cornell, Benedek, & Benedek, 1987a; Darby et al.,
1998; Dolan & Smith, 2001; Ewing, 1990; Fiddes, 1981; Labelle et al., 1991;
Myers et al., 1995, 1998; Rosner et al., 1978; Sorrells, 1977). Findings regarding whether young killers have had a lengthy history of fighting and other
violent or antisocial behavior have been mixed. Some researchers have reported
extensive antisocial behavior (e.g., Darby et al., 1998; Lewis et al., 1985; Lewis,

Lovely, et al., 1988; McCarthy, 1978; Myers et al., 1995, 1998); others have uncovered little or none (Malmquist, 1971; Patterson, 1943; Walshe-Brennan, 1974); still others found that previous delinquency varied significantly by the type of juvenile homicide offender (e.g., Zenoff & Zients, 1979) or the nature of the relationship between the offender and the victim (Corder et al., 1976). Gang participation has also been found among juvenile homicide offenders (Busch et al., 1990; Darby et al., 1998; Zagar et al., 1990).

## Substance Abuse

The literature on substance abuse among juvenile homicide offenders has been sparse (Ewing, 1990). Available studies suggest that the percentages of juvenile homicide offenders who reported abusing substances or being substance dependent have increased over the last 20 to 30 years (Ewing, 1990; Myers, 1992; see also, e.g., Busch et al., 1990; Lewis, Pincus, et al., 1988; Myers & Kemph, 1990; Zagar et al., 1990). Earlier studies indicated that between 20% and 25% of young killers abused alcohol or drugs (Corder et al., 1976; Malmquist, 1971). Cornell et al. (1987a) reported that more than 70% of the 72 juvenile murderers in their Michigan sample drank alcohol or used drugs. Robert Zagar and his colleagues (1990) compared alcohol abuse among 101 juvenile murderers with 101 matched nonviolent delinquents in Cook County, Illinois. They reported that juvenile murderers were significantly more likely to abuse alcohol than the control group (45% vs. 28%). Myers and Kemph (1990) reported that half of the 14 homicide youths in their study were diagnosed as substance dependent. In a later study of 18 juvenile murderers, Myers and Scott (1998) found that 50% were substance dependent. Psychiatrist Susan Bailey (1996) reported that, of the 20 juvenile murderers in the United Kingdom she treated, 75% abused alcohol and 35% abused drugs. Dolan and Smith (2001) found that 50% of the 46 juvenile homicide offenders referred to an adolescent forensic unit in Britain during 1986–1996 had a history of alcohol abuse, manifested in binge drinking, and 39.1% had a history of illicit drug use. Researchers in Finland reported in 1997 that 10 of the 13 young homicide offenders in their study were dependent on alcohol (Santtila & Haapasalo, 1997).

In addition to increases in substance abuse and dependence, there is evidence that the percentage of those who indicated that they were "high" at the time of the murder has also risen since the 1970s. Sorrells's study of juvenile murderers in California published in 1977 indicated that approximately 25% (8 of 31) of juvenile homicide offenders were under the influence of drugs and alcohol at the time of the homicidal event (Sorrells, 1977). Cornell et al. noted 10 years later that more than 50% (38 of 72) of their sample of juvenile killers had killed while they were intoxicated (Cornell et al., 1987a). A U.S. Department of Justice study, also published in 1987, indicated that 42.5% of juvenile murderers were under the influence of alcohol, drugs, or both at the time of the incident (U.S. Department of Justice, 1987). Fendrich and his colleagues compared substance involvement among 16- and 17-year-old juvenile murderers with that of four different age groups of adult murderers incarcerated in New York State prisons in a 1995 publication. The groups were compared in terms of regular lifetime use, substance use during the week preceding the homicide, and use at the time of the crime. In general, the juvenile murderers had relatively "lighter" use and lower levels of drug involvement than adults in the sample. Of the 16 juvenile homicide offenders, 8 indicated that they were "substance affected" (intoxicated, crashing, sick, or in need of a substance) at the time of the murder. Of these 8, 5 acknowledged using alcohol and 3, marijuana. Only 3 young killers reported using cocaine, heroin, or psychedelics. The research team cautioned against concluding that substance use does not present a special risk for violent, homicidal behavior among juveniles (Fendrich, Mackesy-Amiti, Goldstein, Spunt, & Brownstein, 1995).

> Analysis of respondent substance use attribution patterns suggests that when 16–17 year old perpetrators use substances, the substances they use tend to have considerably more lethal effects than they do on perpetrators in older age groups. Thus, our study suggests that a focus on ingestion and involvement rates may underestimate the risk posed by substances for homicidal behavior among juveniles. (p. 1363)

### Other Social Difficulties

Studies have indicated that a significant proportion of juvenile murderers do not attend school regularly (Ewing, 1990) because of truancy (e.g., Bailey, 1994, 1996; Dolan & Smith, 2001; Myers et al., 1998; Shumaker & McGee, 2001; Smith, 1965), dropping out, or suspension/expulsion (e.g., Cornell et al., 1987a; Myers et al., 1998; Shumaker & McGee, 2001). Running away is a common response of adolescent parricide offenders (e.g., Heide, 1992; Sadoff, 1971; Scherl & Mack, 1966; Tanay, 1976). Enuresis (bedwetting) (e.g., Dolan & Smith, 2001; Easson & Steinhilber, 1961; Michaels, 1961; Myers et al., 1995; Russell, 1986; Sendi & Blomgren, 1975) and difficulties in relating to peers (e.g., Corder et al., 1976; Marten, 1965; Zenoff & Zients, 1979) have also been found in the histories of youths who kill.

## ■ Summary: A Case Study Portrait of Adolescents Who Kill

Given the methodological problems in the literature cited earlier, generalizations from many of these studies to the population of juvenile murderers must be made with caution. Some consensus among the studies reported, however, suggests that a portrait of the typical adolescent murderer can be drawn. Most youths who possess these characteristics do not commit murder, but available data suggest that today's young killer tends to be a male who is unlikely to be psychotic or mentally retarded, to do well in school, or to come from a home where his biological parents live together in a healthy and peaceful relationship. Rather, he is likely to have experienced or to have been exposed to violence in his home and to have a prior arrest record. He is increasingly more likely to use/abuse drugs and alcohol than juvenile homicide offenders in the past.

## Empirical Studies of Juvenile Homicide Offenders

Well-designed empirical studies of juvenile murderers that attempt to compensate for the weaknesses of case studies do exist. However, they are relatively few in number and typically also suffer from methodological limitations related particularly to sample selection and size. Hence, generalizations from these studies also must be made with caution.

In one study, for example, 71 adolescent homicide offenders were matched with 71 nonviolent delinquents with respect to age, race, gender, and socioeconomic class. Both groups were selected from a group of 1,956 juveniles referred for evaluation by the juvenile court. The sample of juvenile murderers represented all youths convicted of homicide in the referral sample. The control group was a subset of the larger sample. Accordingly, the samples were retrospective and nonrandom and reflected the selection bias in the referral and adjudication process.

Both groups were assessed on numerous educational, psychiatric, psychological, social, and physical dimensions. Four significant differences were found between the two groups. Compared with nonviolent delinquents, juvenile homicide offenders were more likely to come from criminally violent families, to participate in a gang, to have severe educational deficits, and to abuse alcohol (Busch et al., 1990). The same results were obtained when the study was repeated by using different groups of juveniles obtained and matched in the same way (Zagar et al., 1990).

Dorothy Otnow Lewis, a psychiatrist at New York University School of Medicine, and her colleagues have also conducted several investigations of juvenile homicide offenders (Lewis, Lovely, et al., 1988; Lewis, Pincus, et al., 1988; Lewis et al., 1983, 1985). Their research, although groundbreaking, often consisted of small samples of cases referred to the senior author and her team for evaluation. In one study, Lewis et al. compared 13 juvenile murderers evaluated after the homicide with 14 violent delinquents and 18 nonviolent youths. All three groups were incarcerated at the time of the evaluation and were compared with respect to a set of neurological, psychiatric, psychological, and social variables. Analyses revealed that the adolescent homicide offenders did not differ from violent delinquents. However, the juvenile murderers were significantly more likely than the nonviolent delinquents to be neuropsychiatrically impaired, to have been raised in violent homes, and to have been physically abused (Lewis, Lovely, et al., 1988).

A Finnish study was similarly designed to assess whether selected risk factors would differentiate young murderers from other violent offenders and from nonviolent youths. Sample subjects were recruited from among all Finnish male prisoners born after a certain year and ranged in age from 18 to 22 at the time of the study. The pool of volunteers was asked to indicate their prior criminal involvements on a questionnaire. The subjects were then divided into groups from which study participants were randomly chosen. The groups were small: 13 had committed murder or attempted to do so, 13 had committed less serious assaults, and 11 reported no violent crimes in their offending history. Several reliable differences were found. Members of the homicide group were significantly more likely to admit having been cruel to animals than members of the two other groups. Members in the murderer group began abusing alcohol at a significantly younger age than those in the nonviolent group. Relative to the nonviolent offenders, the homicide offenders were significantly more likely to have been physically abused and to be dependent on harder drugs, such as cocaine, speed, stimulants, and tranquilizers. Although other differences were observable among the groups, the findings did not reach significance, which could have been due to the small sample sizes (Santtila & Haapasalo, 1997).

Two studies published in 2001 explored differences between a group of juvenile murderers and control groups of violent offenders (Shumaker & McGee, 2001) and fire-setters (Dolan & Smith, 2001) by using retrospective case analyses. In the first study, 30 juvenile males charged with murder were compared with 62 boys charged with other violent offenses. These individuals were all referred for pretrial psychiatric evaluation between 1987 and 1997. This study was methodologically superior to earlier studies in several ways. It had a relatively large number of murderers, explored many clinical and offense-related variables, and utilized a control group. In addition, the authors assessed potential differences between youths charged with murder and those charged with battery with intent to kill. Comparisons of the two groups made from existing case files on 33 demographic, historical, clinical, offense, and forensic variables yielded only three differences: Juvenile murderers were significantly less likely to have an Axis I diagnosis of mental disorder than other violent juveniles (63.3% vs. 81.4%). Group differences in the types of diagnoses were discernible. Half of the homicide group was diagnosed as having an adjustment disorder or a substance abuse disorder, whereas 69% of the violent group was diagnosed with a chronic or organically based disorder such as conduct disorder, attention deficit disorder, psychosis, or mood disorder. The homicide offenders were also significantly more likely than the other violent offenders to have acted alone (46.7% vs. 8.1%) and to have committed their crimes in a domestic setting (40% vs. 6.5%) (Shumaker & McGee, 2001).

In the second study, 46 juvenile murderers were compared with 106 fire-setters who were referred to an adolescent forensic center for evaluation in England between 1986 and 1996. The matching of the fire-setters to the young killers on age, ethnicity, socioeconomic data, and criminal history data was an obvious strength of this study. The two samples were also matched in terms of referral to the same unit for assessment on the basis of court adjudications during the same period to ensure that the two groups were evaluated by the same team. Extensive data on demographics, personal and family history, and medical and psychiatric history were extracted from case files; offense-related characteristics were culled from legal depositions and newspaper articles. Juvenile killers were significantly more likely than the arsonists to be male and to have histories of frequent changes of school, alcohol abuse, and alcohol intoxication at the time of the murder. The homicide group was significantly less likely than the fire-setting group to be diagnosed as psychotic, to have had delayed developmental milestones, to have a history in being in care, and to have had previous contact with social, psychological, and psychiatric services. A discriminant function analysis found that psychotic illness, care history, prior psychology contact, and alcohol abuse at the time of the crime successfully differentiated the two groups. Of these four, only alcohol abuse at the time of the offense was more prevalent in the homicide group (Dolan & Smith, 2001).

Other empirical studies have looked for distinguishing characteristics among youths who commit murder (e.g., Corder et al., 1976; Cornell et al., 1987b; Cornell, Miller, & Benedek, 1988). Billie Corder and her colleagues compared 10 youths charged with killing parents, 10 youths charged with killing other relatives or close acquaintances, and 10 youths charged with killing strangers. In addition to the groups being small in size, they were not randomly generated. Individuals in the three groups had been sent to the hospital for evaluation and were matched by age, gender, intelligence, socioeconomic status, and date of hospital admission. The three groups differed significantly on several variables. Those who killed parents, for example, were significantly more likely than those who killed others to have been physically abused, to have come from homes where their mothers were beaten by their fathers, and to have amnesia for the murder (Corder et al., 1976).

## Typologies of Juvenile Murderers and Crime Classification

Several other researchers, as highlighted earlier, have proposed typologies of youths who kill. Attempts to validate typologies of juvenile homicide offenders, however, have often failed because they had small samples or lacked control groups. In contrast, the typology proposed by Cornell, Benedek, and Benedek has shown remarkable promise. This scheme classifies juvenile homicide offenders into three categories based on circumstances of the offense: psychotic (youths who had symptoms of severe mental illness such as hallucinations or delusions), conflict (youths who were engaged in an argument or dispute with the victim when the killing occurred), and crime (youths who killed during the commission of another felony, such as rape or robbery).

The Cornell et al. typology was tested with 72 juveniles charged with murder and a control group of 35 adolescents charged with larceny. Both groups were referred for pretrial evaluation and were assessed with respect to eight composite categories: "family dysfunction, school adjustment, childhood problems, violence history, delinquent behavior, substance abuse, psychiatric problems, and stressful life events prior to the offense" (Cornell et al., 1987b, p. 386). Based on information pertaining to the offense, 7% of the juvenile homicide offenders were assigned to the psychotic subgroup, 42% to the conflict subgroup, and 51% to the crime subgroup.

Analyses revealed significant differences on all eight composite categories between the homicide group and the larceny group. In addition, a number of significant differences emerged among the three subgroups of juvenile homicide offenders. Psychotic homicide offenders were significantly more likely to score higher on the psychiatric history composite and lower on the index of criminal activity than the nonpsychotic groups. In relation to the conflict group, the crime group scored significantly higher on school adjustment problems, substance abuse, and criminal activity and lower on stressful life events. This study provided preliminary support that juvenile homicide offenders could be distinguished from other groups of offenders and from one another. The authors correctly advised that further studies are needed to determine whether the differences among the homicide subgroups will hold up when group assignment is not determined by offense circumstances (Cornell et al., 1987b, 1989).

Subsequent research has found significant differences between the crime and conflict groups. The crime group youths had higher levels of psychopathology on the Minnesota Multiphasic Personality Inventory (an objective measure of personality) (Cornell et al., 1988; for a discussion of various personality measures, see Sarason & Sarason, 1996) than the conflict group youths. The crime group killers also had more serious histories of substance abuse and prior delinquent behavior than the conflict group murderers (Cornell, 1990). The crime group adolescents were more likely to act with others and to be intoxicated on drugs at the time of the murder than the conflict group youths. The crime group homicide offenders also showed poorer object differentiation and more of a victim orientation in responses to the Rorschach (a projective measure of personality) than their conflict group counterparts. The Rorschach responses suggest that crime group youths are more likely to dehumanize other people, to respond violently when frustrated, and to have more severe developmental deficits than conflict group youths (Greco & Cornell, 1992).

Distinctions also emerged within the conflict group between youths who murdered parents and those who killed other victims, none of whom were family members. Juvenile parricide offenders scored lower on school adjustment problems and prior delinquent history than those who killed others but were higher on a family dysfunction measure. Cornell's findings with respect to youths who kill parents are similar to the conclusions reached in clinical case studies and provide further empirical support that these youths may represent a distinct type of homicide offender (Cornell, 1990; Heide, 1992).

Wade Myers and his colleagues classified 25 juvenile homicide offenders by using the FBI *Crime Classification Manual* (CCM). The murderers involved in their study included children and adolescents. The sample size was too small to test differences among the four categories of motives in the CCM. Accordingly, the cases were classified into only two categories: "criminal enterprise" and "personal crime" (Myers et al., 1995).

Important findings from this study included characteristics common to the young killers, as well as those that differentiated the two groups. Ten profile characteristics applied to more than 70% of the total sample: family dysfunction, previous violent acts toward others, disruptive behavior disorder, failed at least one grade, emotional abuse by family member, family violence, prior arrests, learning disabilities, weapon of choice, and psychotic symptoms (Myers et al., 1995, Table 2, p. 1488).

Statistical analyses compared the two crime classification groups with respect to psychiatric diagnoses, psychotic symptoms, biopsychosocial variables, and crime characteristics. Statistically significant differences were found between the criminal enterprise and personal cause groups with respect to victim age, victim relationship, and physical abuse. Youths in the criminal group were more likely than those in the personal group to have been abused and to have killed an adult or elderly victim whom they did not know. Personal group murderers tended to select a child or adolescent victim whom they knew (Myers et al., 1995).

## ◼ Factors Contributing to the Rise in Juvenile Homicide

The existent literature on juvenile homicide rarely addresses the factors that fueled the recent dramatic rise in murders by juveniles beginning in the mid-1980s. Several reasons account for the gap. Most of the studies of adolescent murderers were published prior to 1990. These research efforts were typically restricted to the analysis of individual and family characteristics, which were relatively easy to obtain and verify. These studies were not designed to measure many sociological variables of interest and therefore did not address the phenomenon of juvenile homicide within the context of broad societal changes during the past several decades.

The following section attempts to supplement the existing literature on young murderers with a perspective that offers explanations for the shifts to more juveniles being involved in acts of homicide in the United States, particularly from the mid-1980s to the early 1990s. I am convinced, after evaluating approximately 100 adolescents involved in murder, that many factors often act in concert when youths kill. Some of these factors are more global and difficult to measure in the individual case, yet their effects on society and on a generation of children growing up today are more visible. As depicted in

Table 18.1, these variables can be grouped into five main categories: situational factors, societal influences, resource availability, personality characteristics, and their cumulative effects.

I present these 15 variables in the hope that the discussion sheds light on why youths today are more likely to kill than in prior years and leads to further research into these factors and their interactive effects. Suggestions made with respect to intervention strategies are based on finding solutions to the problems highlighted next.

## Situational Factor

Many of today's youths grow up in families that foster violent and destructive behaviors. Despite a decrease in the number of young Americans, reports of *child abuse* have greatly increased in recent years (e.g., Florida Center for Children and Youth, 1993; Sickmund, Snyder, & Poe-Yamagata, 1997; Snyder & Sickmund, 1995; Willis, 1995). Commentators often ask if the increase is due to a genuine increase in the incidence of abuse or merely reflects an increase in its reporting. Social services personnel and child abuse experts typically reply that some of the increase may be due to the greater willingness of people to report various types of abuse today than in the past. However, they maintain that it is highly unlikely, given the magnitude of the difference, that changes in reporting practices can account for most of the increase. Figures released by the U.S. Advisory Board on Child Abuse and Neglect in 1993, for example, indicated that reported cases of child abuse and neglect had increased from

**Table 18.1    Ingredients for Juvenile Murder in the 1990s**

| | |
|---|---|
| Situational factors | Child abuse |
| | Child neglect |
| | Absence of positive male role models |
| Societal influences | Crisis in leadership and lack of heroes |
| | Witnessing violence |
| Resource availability | Access to guns |
| | Involvement in alcohol and drugs |
| | Poverty and lack of resources |
| Personality characteristics | Low self esteem |
| | Inability to deal with strong negative feelings |
| | Boredom and nothing constructive to do |
| | Poor judgment |
| | Prejudice and hatred |
| Cumulative effect | Little or nothing left to lose |
| | Biological connection |

Source: Herde, 1997b. Copyright John Wiley & Sons, Ltd. Reproduced with permission.

60,000 in 1973 to over 3,000,000 cases in 1993 (U.S. Advisory Board on Child Abuse and Neglect, 1993; Willis, 1995).

Although the majority of children who are victims or witnesses of family violence do not grow up to victimize others (e.g., Gelles & Conte, 1990; Scudder, Blount, Heide, & Silverman, 1993; Smith & Thornberry, 1995), a growing body of research indicates that these children are at greater risk of engaging in delinquent behavior (Dahlberg, 1998; Dahlberg & Potter, 2001; Loeber & Farringon, 2001). Retrospective studies of violent adolescents and young killers have repeatedly found child abuse, neglect, and exposure to parental violence in their backgrounds (e.g., Cornell, 1989; Ewing, 1990; Heide, 1992; Lewis, Shanok, Grant, & Ritvo, 1983; Lewis, Shanok, Pincus, & Glaser, 1979; Lewis et al., 1985; Lewis, Pincus, 1988; Sendi & Blomgren, 1975).

Well-controlled and extensive research conducted in recent years by several professors at the State University of New York at Albany has helped to clarify the nature of the relationship of child maltreatment to delinquency. These studies were prospective by design, meaning that subjects were selected for reasons other than having a delinquent history and followed up several years to determine the extent of their subsequent involvement in criminal or delinquent behavior. Professor Cathy Spatz Widom used official records to compare the criminal and delinquent involvement of maltreated youths with a matched group of nonmaltreated youths. She found that youths who were abused and neglected were at higher risk of becoming juvenile delinquents or adult criminals and of engaging in violent criminal behavior. In comparison with youths with no history of child maltreatment, abused and neglected children committed significantly more offenses, began their delinquent careers earlier, and had a higher percentage of individuals charged with five or more offenses (Widom, 1989a, 1989b, 1989c, 1989d). Those who had been victimized as children were also significantly more likely than the control group to receive a diagnosis of antisocial personality disorder (persistent pattern of violating the rights of others) as adults, even after demographic characteristics and arrest history were taken into account (Luntz & Widom, 1994).

Professors Carolyn Smith and Terence Thornberry investigated the relationship of child maltreatment to involvement in delinquency among students attending public schools in Rochester, New York. Unlike other prospective studies, this research included self-reported measures of delinquency, as well as official records. According to the study design, students from seventh and eighth grade were selected in such a way as to overrepresent those who were at higher risk of delinquency and drug involvement, and these youths were followed over time. Using official measures of delinquency, Smith and Thornberry replicated Widom's findings. More important, they found that "more serious forms of self-reported delinquency, including violent, serious, and moderate forms of delinquency" (Smith & Thornberry, 1995, p. 468) were related to child maltreatment. Subsequent analyses confirmed that these results were genuine and not due to factors such as race or ethnicity, gender, socio-economic class, family structure, or mobility. This study also provided preliminary support to the hypothesis that experiencing more extensive childhood maltreatment was related to more serious forms of delinquency (Smith & Thornberry, 1995).

A growing body of evidence indicates that even young children are traumatized by exposure to parental violence (Osofsky, 1995). Research has also indicated that youths' witnessing of parental violence is associated with subsequent violent behavior (Thornberry, 1994), particularly by men toward their spouses or partners (Briere, 1992; Browne, 1987; Gelles & Conte, 1990; Hotaling & Sugarman, 1986; Howell, Krisberg, & Jones, 1995; Silvern et al., 1994; Thornberry, 1994). Smith and Thornberry (1995) found that children who witnessed and experienced many violent acts in their homes (child abuse, spouse abuse, and family conflict) were twice as likely to engage in violent acts themselves (Howell, Krisberg, & Jones 1995).

Some children who are physically, sexually, verbally, and psychologically abused kill the abusive parent, who often has alcohol or other drug problems (Heide, 1992). Typically, these adolescents have been victims of multiple types of abuse and neglect. They kill because they are afraid or see no other way to escape this situation or to end the abuse. Patty was a 17-year-old girl who, for years, had been physically, verbally, and psychologically abused by her father. In addition, she was sexually abused and forcibly raped by him. After being denied help by the adult figures in her life and failing in earlier attempts to kill herself and run away, Patty believed she had no recourse (Heide, 1992). Early one morning while he slept, she fired a bullet into his head.

Living in households like Patty's, many abused youths fail to bond with others. These adolescents often lack attachments to teachers and conventional peers, as well as to parents. Consequently, they do not develop the values, empathy, and self-concept that foster self-control and could inhibit them from killing others (see Bailey, 1996; Dahlberg, 1998; Hirschi, 1969; Magid & McKelvey, 1987; Reckless, 1961). Malcolm, for example, had been sexually abused and physically, medically, and emotionally neglected from the time he was a child. His father abandoned him as an infant, and his alcoholic mother died when he was 7. At 12, he was living on the streets, making his way by taking what he wanted by threat or force. I first met Malcolm at age 15 after he had been charged with two counts of murder and two counts of attempted murder, each count resulting from separate incidents.

Rather than being passively indifferent toward the lives of others, some abused youths are angry and in pain and vent their rage through destruction and violence (Magid & McKelvey, 1987). One of my clients, José, was sentenced to prison for a murder he committed at age 18. The killing was especially brutal—the victim was beaten beyond recognition. The blows to the victim's skull were so severe that brain tissue was found in several areas of the apartment. José committed the crime with the assistance of three friends.

The four boys all told me that it was José's idea to commit the murder. José acknowledged a long history of violence toward others. He explained that he wanted to hurt others as he had been hurt.

*Neglect* frequently accompanies abuse, but it can also exist independently, often manifesting itself as the common failure of parents to supervise their children (Heide, 1992). Several significant changes in family structures observable during the period 1970 to 1990 probably contributed to decreasing levels of child supervision and have placed adolescents at greater risk of getting into serious trouble.

As one indicator, the number of children born to unmarried mothers nearly tripled—from 398,700 in 1970 to 1,165,384 in 1990. Over the two decades, dramatic increases in illegitimate births are apparent among both White and Black women. For every 1,000 births by White women, the number who were born to unmarried women rose from 57 in 1970 to 201 in 1990. The comparable figures for births to Black unmarried women were 376 in 1970 and 652 in 1990 (U.S. Department of Health and Human Services, 1990, p. 198).

During the same period, the divorce rate (Bynum & Thompson, 1999; U.S. Department of Health and Human Services, 1990) and percentage of single-parent households (Magid & McKelvey, 1987) also increased. Today, more than 50% of all marriages end in divorce. The Carnegie Council on Adolescent Development (1995) noted in its concluding report that more than 50% of all children in the United States in the mid-1990s will be raised, for at least part of their childhood and adolescent years, in a single-parent household, a far greater percentage than a few decades ago. Almost half of the adolescent children of married parents will experience their parents' divorce or remarriage by age 16 (Carnegie Council on Human Development, 1995).

In addition to the rising number of children born to single mothers and the increasing divorce rate and percentage of single-parent families, the number of mothers in the workforce also increased significantly since 1970. In 1970, 30% of married women with children under age 6 were gainfully employed; in 1990, 59% of women in this category were working. The percentage of married women with children ages 6 to 17 who were working rose from 49% in 1970 to 74% in 1990. Figures for single mothers with children are not available for 1970 to permit comparisons across the two decades. However, 1990 data indicate that among single mothers, 49% with children under age 6 and 70% with children ages 6 to 17 were working (U.S. Department of Commerce, Economics and Statistics Administration, Bureau of the Census, 1994; U.S. Bureau of Labor Statistics, 1993, Table No. 626, p. 402). Increases in the percentages of working wives with children was evident among both White and Black women over the last two decades (U.S. Department of Commerce, Economics and Statistics Administration, Bureau of the Census, 1994; U.S. Bureau of Labor Statistics, 1993, Table No. 627, p. 402).

Given these familial changes, the time that youths spend with their parents and the amount of supervision and guidance that they receive have significantly decreased during the past several decades (Carnegie Council on Adolescent Development, 1995, p. 36; Dahlberg, 1998). Experts estimate that children in the 1990s lost an average of 10 to 12 hours per week of parental time, compared with children in 1960 (Resnick et al., 1997). In 1970, 37% of families with children under 18 lacked full-time parental supervision. In 1992, the percentage had risen to 57% (Fox, 1996).

Many of the adolescent homicide offenders I examine are not in school during the day and are out late at night. Their parents do not know where they are, in what activities they are involved, or with whom they are associating.

Often accompanying abuse or lack of supervision is the *absence of positive male role models*. In some cases, the identities or whereabouts of fathers are unknown. In others, fathers are present only to be uninvolved, violent, or both. Boys need same-sex role models to define themselves as male. When fathers are absent, young males are more likely to exaggerate their purported masculinity (e.g., Messerschmidt, 1993; Silverman & Dinitz, 1974).

Mothers, although typically loved and often revered by their sons, all too frequently cannot control their sons' behavior. Case 1004 told me, for example, that his mother was "a nice lady . . . she took care a me when I was out there, ya know, but I would avoid every word she was sayin', that why I'm in here now. I wouldn't do what she say." Case 1005 related that his mother was "a very tiny young lady, but I love her more than anything, ya know, and like, she give me anything I want. I don't have to go out and do wrong, I just did it. She give me anything. She try to tell me what good and what bad for me. But, I just, I didn't listen."

## Societal Influences

On a larger scale, youths who kill today are also affected by our country's *crisis in leadership and lack of heroes*. In the past, U.S. presidents, successful entertainers, and legendary sports figures were presented to the youths of America as people to emulate. In the last two decades, the personal ethics and behavior of many of these individuals have been seriously questioned. Government leaders who break campaign promises and involve themselves in money and sex scandals have shown that many politicians today deny responsibility for their behavior and their decisions. When leaders of our country are no longer expected to keep their word and are not held accountable, some youths become cynical about their futures. When police officers are viewed on nationwide television repeatedly beating an African American in their custody and are proven to be lying on the witness stand in the case of another African American man, adolescents from minority groups increasingly lose faith in a criminal justice system that is supposed to protect them and to dispense equal justice. When world-class boxing champion Mike Tyson and rappers like Snoop Doggy

Dogg (Dunn, 1996) are accused of violent criminal acts, some adolescents feel free to adopt similar courses of behavior.

Adolescent deviance and decreased inhibitions to violence have also been correlated to *witnessing violence* (Bailey, 1996; Prothrow-Stith & Weissman, 1991; Resnick et al., 1997). Although authorities debate whether some individuals are more "susceptible" to engaging in violence after repeated viewings because of personality, biological, or environmental factors, two facts are beyond dispute. First, over the last two decades, films and television shows, including the evening news, have become more and more violent ("Crime may be down, but not on TV news," 1997; Fox & Levin, 1994; Lacayo, 1995; Levin & Fox, 1985; Prothrow-Stith & Weissman, 1991). Second, the American public has become increasingly concerned about the effects of violent programming on people in general and especially on the young (Lacayo, 1995).

Experts estimate that the average youth in the United States watches 45 violent acts on television every day, with most of them committed with handguns (Myers, 1992). A study conducted by the American Psychological Association confirmed that children who view 2 to 4 hours of television violence daily will witness 8,000 murders and 100,000 other acts of violence before finishing elementary school ("Big World, Small Screen," discussed in Wheeler, 1993). The APA Commission on Violence and Youth estimated further that, if the viewing period is extended to the late teens, these youths will have observed about 200,000 violent acts. The commission cautioned that these figures may be even higher for youths who watch cable programs and R-rated movies on home VCRs (Sleek, 1994).

An impressive body of research spanning more than 30 years indicates that exposure to television violence is related to violent behavior (Bushman & Anderson, 2001; Wheeler, 1993). For example, research shows that aggressive children who have difficulty in school and in relating to peers tend to watch more television (Sleek, 1994). Researchers in the physical and social sciences agree that repeated exposure to a stimulus habituates individuals to that stimulus. When habituation to a violent stimulus occurs, for example, more intense violent behaviors are needed for the viewers' bodies to react and to register physiological indicators of distress (Fromm, 1973; Solomon, Schmidt, & Ardragna, 1990). In this context, the increasing popularity of violent video games also becomes a cause for concern (Hardwick & Rowton-Lee, 1996). As noted by psychiatrist Susan Bailey, "Violent video games provide a forum for learning and practicing aggressive solutions to conflict situations. The effect appears to be cognitive in the short term, primary aggressive thoughts in the long term leading to changes in everyday social interactions" (Bailey, 2000, p. 152).

Perhaps even more troubling than the many children watching violent programs and playing violent games are the smaller number of youths who see violence firsthand in their neighborhoods, schools, and homes (Jenkins, 1995; Marans & Berkman, 1997; Osofsky, 1995). Inner-city youths' exposure to violence is particularly alarming (e.g., Jenkins & Bell, 1994). In 1992, Carl

Bell and Esther Jenkins surveyed 203 African American students in a public high school in an inner-city Chicago community. Four of five of these students qualified for some type of public assistance. The area of the school consistently had one of the highest homicide rates and ranked third in homicides during the year the study was conducted. When asked, 43% reported that they had seen a killing, and 59% reported that someone close to them had been killed. The percentages of children who reported exposure to shootings were even higher: 61% had seen a shooting, 66% knew that someone who was close to them had been shot, 48% had been shot at themselves, and 6% had actually been shot (Bell & Jenkins, 1994).

To many children and teens, the world is a violent place. This image is particularly extolled in the music known as gangsta rap. Rappers such as Ice-T, Spice 1, MC Eiht, Eightball and MJG, and Geto Boys sing about robbing, killing, and raping, which they maintain is part of everyday life in "the hood" for low-income members of society, particularly African Americans. The words in gangsta rap music, similar to the scenes in televised violence, seem likely to have a disinhibiting and desensitizing effect on those who listen to them repeatedly. Although the link between gangsta rap music and violence has not been proven, a recent study provided some evidence that misogynous (hate-filled) rap music was related to sexually aggressive behavior against women by men (Barongan & Hall, 1995). In several of my recent cases, violent music lyrics appeared to provide the additional impetus needed for unbonded youths to kill (Heide, 1997a).

Most of the inner-city young homicide offenders whom I have evaluated viewed violence as part of everyday life. They carried guns and were prepared to use them. Case 1002 explained that he brought a gun with him on the day of the homicidal event because "you see, that's a real rough neighborhood and it was rougher than the neighborhood I stayed in, you know, if you don't have a gun around there, something is able to be killed. So I had to bring a gun with me that day."

Life in the project "was like really wild," Case 1005 maintained. There was "a lot of robbing and killing goin' on." People who lived there "growed up in the wild, a faster place, that all they know." Case 2014 stated that there was "a lot of violence" in his neighborhood, "a lot of crime, everyday, fighting, killing." Case 5030 remembered, "One time I was walking, sidewalk, I saw a man get busted in the head, man get shot. They don't want police come there. Whoever did it get away. I seen a lot of, I seen a lot of violence in my time."

Case 2008 explained that he got in trouble because he "found the wrong people, see them do something, then you want to do it." He indicated that watching people in his neighborhood shooting up or at each other had an effect on him: "I wanted to try it." When asked if the homicidal event was the first time he had ever shot at anybody, Case 2008 replied, "No" and indicated that he had shot at people "often." He added, "I really wanted to scare them. . . . They play with me like that, too."

## Resource Availability

Not only do our youths grow up in a world that encourages violence but also those in the United States are increasingly finding themselves surrounded with the tools that make acts of violence quick and easy (Dahlberg, 1998; Sheley & Wright, 1995). Research has demonstrated that youth involvement in violence has been associated with the frequency of carrying a weapon (Resnick et al., 1997). Moreover, the U.S. increase in murders by juveniles in recent years has been tied directly to their use of firearms, particularly handguns (Blumstein, 1995; Fox, 1996; Kennedy, 1997; Sickmund et al., 1997). Analyses by the Federal Bureau of Investigation indicate that gun homicides by juveniles nearly tripled from 1983 to 1991. In contrast, murders by juveniles using other weapons declined during the same period. In 1976, 59% of young homicide offenders killed their victims with a firearm. Twenty-five years later, 78% selected firearms as their weapons of destruction (Howell et al., 1995).

Carnegie-Mellon University Professor Alfred Blumstein has argued that the increase in killings by juveniles is a result of the rapid growth in the crack markets in the mid-1980s. Juveniles who were recruited into illicit drug marketing armed themselves with guns for protection. Other juveniles in these communities, aware of what was happening, armed themselves for protection and for status reasons. Consequently, guns become more prevalent in the larger community. When guns are easily accessible, youths who often are impulsive and unskilled in conflict resolution may use them as a means of retaliation. The presence of firearms increases the likelihood that an act of lethal violence will occur under these circumstances (Blumstein, 1995, 1996; see also Kennedy, 1997).

The majority of juvenile homicide offenders I see used *guns*, which were readily available to them, to kill their victims. At the time Case 1004 was arrested for murder and armed robbery, he had three firearms on his person that he had just gotten from a burglary. Case 1004 related, however, that he did not usually walk around on the street with a gun "on me, but I had some I can get. If I didn't have none, I can get some. I can get one or whatever from a brother or my friend." He explained that most of his friends carried guns "once in awhile, they'll, like on a Friday night, they'll walk around with 'em, you know, in case something jumps off in the neighborhood."

Many of these youths did not have the physical ability or the emotional detachment to use other weapons of destruction, such as knives or fists. At the age of 12, Timmy, a boy from a middle-class family, decided he was going to kill himself. He thought that he would kill his mother, whom he perceived as the person responsible for much of the unhappiness in his family, before killing himself. Although Timmy tried to get his brother to leave the home, his brother did not cooperate. Rather than postpone his plan, Timmy shot his brother with a .357 Magnum. When his mother arrived home, he shot her as well. Overcome by the sight of human carnage, Timmy could not manage to turn the gun on himself. Instead, he aborted his plan and called for help.

Most of the adolescents I have evaluated who were involved in felony homicides were using *alcohol and drugs*. These observations are consistent with findings from a growing number of studies of a substantial relationship between adolescent violence and substance abuse (e.g., Elliott, Huizinga, & Menard, 1989; Johnston, O'Malley, & Bachman, 1993; *National Drug Control Strategy*, 1995; Osgood, 1995). Interestingly, drug use surveys indicate that the rates of illicit drug use by adolescents, which had declined during the 1980s (*Drugs, crime, and the justice system*, 1992; National Criminal Justice Reference Service, 1997; Osgood, 1995), began rising again in the 1990s and was much higher than the rates were a generation ago. This increase was observed among younger as well as older adolescents ("Drug use up, study shows," 1997). The percentage of youths reporting use of marijuana, stimulants, hallucinogens, and inhalants in the past month rose from 1991 through 1994 (*National Drug Control Strategy*, 1995). The Parent Resource Institute for Drug Education (PRIDE) 1993–1994 survey of junior high (grades 6 through 8) and high school students (grades 9 through 12) found a strong link in both groups between use of alcohol and marijuana and several measures of violent behavior, including carrying a gun to school and threatening to harm another person (*National Drug Control Strategy*, 1995).

Although few of the young killers I have evaluated claim that alcohol or drugs caused them to commit murder, it is likely that chemical abuse affected their judgment about engaging in criminal activity and their perceptions during the homicidal event. In addition, it is highly probable, in light of prior research, that the use of alcohol and drugs by many adolescent murderers is "more a reflection of shared influences on a wide variety of deviant behavior than of any causal relationship (Osgood, 1995, p. 32). Several researchers have found that various types of deviant or illegal behaviors are positively related to one another (e.g., Dembo et al., 1992; Elliott et al., 1989; Gottfredson & Hirschi, 1990; Osgood, Johnston, O'Malley, & Bachman, 1988; Resnick et al., 1997).

Another teen I evaluated was Peter, a gentle boy who had a serious drug problem for which he had been hospitalized. Peter was diagnosed as having severe marijuana dependence and a history of alcohol and cocaine abuse. One day, after getting high on marijuana and possibly acid, Peter impulsively entered the home of an elderly man intending to steal his car. When the man unexpectedly appeared, Peter stabbed him with a knife he had picked up moments before in the kitchen. Peter said that he "freaked out" after he saw the victim's blood. He left shortly thereafter in the victim's car and picked up some other kids to go joyriding. Although he knew what he did was wrong, the drugs helped Peter forget about the homicide for a while.

The majority of the young killers I have met are *poor and lacking in resources*. This finding is, to some extent, reflective of the rising percentage of Americans under age 18 being raised in families with incomes below the poverty line (Ewing, 1990; Stephens, 1997). The percentage of children living in poverty in the 1990s increased as a by-product of the changes in family structure over the last two decades. The escalation in single-female-headed households, occasioned by the rise in births to unwed females and the rising divorce rates, has resulted in more children being raised in poverty (Garfinkel & McLanahan, 1986; Wright & Wright, 1995). Research indicates that about three of four households headed by single females live in poverty at least some of the time and that one third are chronically poor. As the 1990s were drawing to an end, it appeared that one of three children under age 6 were living below the poverty line (Stephens, 1997).

Many young killers are from lower-class areas where they are routinely subjected to multiple types of disadvantage, chronic stress, and few positive role models. These are the environments in which unhealthy lifestyles, substance abuse, and violent crimes flourish (Dahlberg & Potter, 2001). Robbery and burglary provide a means to acquire money, drugs, and other goods, as well as an opportunity for fun (see Cloward & Ohlin, 1960; Cohen, 1955; Merton, 1938). When asked how he could afford to buy drugs, for example, Case 5030 stated matter-of-factly that he was "stealing anything that I can get my hands on" from "anyplace."

Case 1002 reported that whenever he was "out there doing wrong," he was trying to help his mother. "Every time I go out and make money, you know, I would bring it to my momma. Tell her to keep the money. She know that it would be stolen or something, you know, and then my momma didn't like stolen money, you know, she would hardly take it." He related that he gave the money to his mother to help her with "bills, help her get some clothes, something she want, anything, food."

## Personality Characteristics

Changes in the personality characteristics of youths over the last two or three decades are difficult to measure. Unlike the variables discussed under situational factors, societal influences, and resource availability, no indicators systematically chart differences in how youths today perceive the world and respond to it, relative to their counterparts 20 and 30 years ago. On the basis of the previous discussion, it seems fair to say that adolescents today in many ways encounter greater challenges at a younger age than youths in the past. Many of these juveniles face these difficulties with parents who cope maladaptively themselves. Other youths confront problems alone. Some youths under such constraints fare well; unfortunately, too many do poorly.

The adolescent homicide offenders I have evaluated generally lack a healthy self-concept. They have deficits in communication skills and decision-making ability. The personalities of youths who kill are almost always marked by *low self-esteem*. They may appear tough and cool, but deep down they typically feel insecure and do not believe they can succeed in conventional activities such as school, sports, or work. Johnny, who was sentenced to life in prison at age 16, did not like violence. He was an obese youth who hung around with some "tough kids." He explained that he went along with their violent escapades, which eventually resulted in his charge of murder, because he "wanted to be somebody."

Another common trait of adolescents who kill is an *inability to deal with strong negative emotions* such as anger or jealousy. Many of these youths, particularly those who are unbonded, have low frustration tolerance (poor self-control) and a fragile self-concept. When wronged, they become consumed with rage and feel compelled to strike back (see Gottfredson & Hirschi, 1990; Magid & McKelvey, 1987; Reckless, 1961). In addressing "the young male syndrome" and homicide, Professors Margo Wilson and Martin Daly at Mc-Master University noted that "the precipitating insult may appear petty, but it is usually a deliberate provocation (or is perceived to be), and hence constitutes a public challenge that cannot be shrugged off" (Wilson & Daly, 1985). To some male adolescents, nothing less than murder is considered an appropriate response. Derek shot the clerk in the convenience store because the man "dissed" him. Derek explained that he had entered the store, pointed the gun at the clerk, and demanded money. When the clerk allegedly laughed and tried to brush Derek's hand away, Derek fired directly into him.

The perceived affronts do not always come from strangers. Jerry methodically planned the execution of his "best friend," who had gone out with Jerry's girlfriend. Jerry believed that "he broke a rule" and deserved to die.

Other youths are more *bored* than angry. Engaging in violent behavior becomes a way to amuse themselves, to pass the time. Many of these young killers I evaluated were neither committed to nor involved in conventional and prosocial activities, such as school, sports, or work. Lacking such "bonds," these youths had the free time and often developed the concomitant belief system needed to commit crime (Hirschi, 1969; see also Sutherland & Cressey, 1943; Sykes & Matza, 1957). They fashioned themselves as "players" in the game of life, and they were out to have "a good time" (Cheatwood & Block, 1990; Heide, 1984).

For these adolescents, robbing and using guns often seemed like fun and a way to reduce boredom. Case 2008 related that he engaged in fewer strong-arm robberies of women as time went on because "that ain't excite me no more. I stop trying to do that. I stop doing that, though I use to do that sometimes to ladies, then I try men like that." Although most of the boys had participated in robberies several times in the past, this time was different. Something happened in the interchange, typically quite unexpectedly, that turned the robbery into a homicide. My clinical observations about the relationship between multiple offenders engaged in concurrent felonies and homicide are consistent with empirical findings reported by Cheatwood (1996).

Some youths simply have *poor judgment*. They became involved in felony homicides not so much out of anger or reckless thrill seeking but because they chose to be at the wrong place at the wrong time. When invited to accompany a group of boys "out for a night of fun," they are sent cues that something bad might happen, but these indications go undetected. One of my clients, Tony, found himself in this kind of situation. Tony was a kid who did not have many friends. One evening, Tony saw some boys from his neighborhood riding around in a nice car. They stopped and asked if he would like to join them. Tony got into the car, which had been stolen shortly before. A few minutes later the boys stopped at a gas station. The next thing Tony knew, he found himself in the middle of a robbery, which ended with one of the boys shooting and killing the attendant.

Although many groups of children and youths commit acts of violence out of generalized anger or for kicks, still others do so out of *prejudice and hatred*. Despite the civil rights movement of the 1960s, the United States has encountered increasing struggles with issues of cultural diversity in recent years. Affirmative action, sexual harassment policies, gender equity, political correctness, and hate-crime statutes were once presented as means to move our nation toward a society of peacefulness and equity. Today, these concepts are interpreted by some Americans as threats, reverse discrimination, and detrimental to First Amendment rights.

Youths today, as in the past, search for their identities through causes in which to believe. Those with fragile self-esteem tend to be attracted to groups that accept and exalt them on the basis of superficial characteristics, such as skin color. Two teenage Caucasian brothers about whom I was consulted were members of a skinhead group. One evening they came across a homeless African American man who had passed out in a public garage. Unprovoked, they beat him until he died.

## ■ The Cumulative Effect in Context

For many youths, the effect of these factors is cumulative. Put succinctly, many young killers growing up during the last two decades have *little or nothing left to lose*. These are the kids who are angry, frequently in pain, and too often unattached to other human beings because of experiences in their home and neighborhood environments. More than in other generations, adolescents today and in the recent past are growing up in an era beset by "an overall decline of the extent and influence of the family from the extended multigenerational family, to the nuclear family, to the single parent family, to the 'no parent' family of street children" (Friedman, 1993, p. 50).

Many of these youths lack self-esteem and the resources to improve their lives. They are living in a society experiencing increases in youths having sex and babies outside of marriage (Friedman, 1992), using drugs, engaging in criminal violence, and dying violently, whether through homicide or suicide. As a result, many juveniles today are living under extreme stress and are severely alienated (e.g., Lerner, 1994; Wynne & Hess, 1986). They do not hold conventional values or dreams. Often chronically bored, they use drugs, alcohol, and sex to anesthetize themselves and commit crimes for fun. They live in the moment. To them, thrills—and lives—are cheap.

Case 3017 described his friends as

> the type that like to party and stuff. None of them would do no hard drugs and that, [they would] smoke a little reefer. I had a few of them that were shooting up, but—a couple of them shooting up, you know, doing some hard drugs. But the rest of the ones I went to school with, they skip school, making bad grades, you know, and do nothing in school but mess with the girls, go to lunch, PE, and that's about it. That's all for school for them. Then, ah, go do some wrong, go break into some houses, robbing, whatever they want to do. Makes them some money. Then they go get high and party. That's about all they do.

When asked, he explained his friends' and his own participation in burglaries and robberies.

> They say that's the only way they can, ah, left to make money, you know. I didn't see it like that 'cause, you know, I [was] used to getting me a job for something like that right there. But since I've got started getting high with them, you know, I didn't want to be called square at all like that, so go along with it. Just do what they do. . . . I'm under the influence, you know, by my friends, you know. They want to do this, you see. I'm drunk, I'm not really thinking about nothing right now. But see, whatever they do, I be game, you know. I be ready to do it with them.

In summary, changes in situational factors, societal influences, and resource availability during the last 20 to 30 years appear to be significant factors in the rising involvement of youths in homicides. These variables probably interact with the personality characteristics of particular adolescents, making some youths more likely to engage in violent behavior than others.

## The Biological Connection

Biological factors have not been considered under any of the variables discussed so far. Yet, in many cases, they may be intricately entwined in the homicidal equation (Roth, 1994a, 1994b, p. 8). Experts agree that all human behavior, including violence and aggression, is the result of intricate processes in the brain (Coccaro, 1995; Moffitt, Lynam, & Silva, 1994; Reiss & Roth, 1993). In reviewing the research on biological perspectives of violence, the Panel on the Understanding and Control of Violent Behavior made the following observations:

Violent behaviors may result from relatively permanent conditions or from temporary states. Relatively permanent conditions may result from genetic instructions, from events during fetal or pubertal development, from perinatal accidents, or from birth trauma. Relevant temporary states may be brought on either by some purely internal activity (e.g., brain seizures) or through responses to external stressors, stimuli that produce sexual arousal, ingestion of alcohol or other psychoactive substance, or some other external stimulus. (Reiss & Roth, 1993, p. 115)

A growing body of research suggests that violent behavior may be linked at least in some cases to genetics, neurological factors, and biochemical reactions (e.g., Eysenck, 1977; Fishbein, 1990; Glueck & Glueck, 1950; Goleman, 1995; Hardwick & Rowton-Lee, 1996; Jeffrey, 1979; Lewis, 1992; Lewis & Yeager, 2000; Mednick & Christiansen, 1977; Moffitt et al., 1994; Pincus, 1993; Reiss & Roth, 1993; Roth, 1994b; Widom, 1991; Wilson & Hernstein, 1985). Recent findings suggesting an association between violent behavior and genetic influences, the neurotransmitter serotonin, and brain dysfunctions are particularly interesting.

Results from two studies conducted in Israel and in the United States and released in January 1996 provided the first replicated association between a particular gene (the D4 dopamine receptor gene) and a specific personality trait, called "novelty-seeking." Those who score high on this trait are characterized as impulsive, curious, excitable, fickle, quick-tempered, and extravagant. These studies in concert demonstrated that this association was independent of ethnicity, age, or gender of the study participants (Benjamin et al., 1996; Ebstein et al., 1996).

Of the 50 known neurotransmitters, serotonin is the one that has been most intensively studied in relation to violent behavior by animal and human subjects. Significant differences in serotonin synthesis, release, and metabolism have been found in violent versus nonviolent animals from a variety of species. Although caution is advised in generalizing from animal studies to human behavior, several researchers have reported an association between low levels of serotonin and impulsive, aggressive, or suicidal behavior in humans (Coccaro, 1995; Lewis & Yeager, 2000; Reiss & Roth, 1993). Some scientists have concluded from these studies that cruelty and brutality to children can lead to changes in brain chemistry. These brain chemistry changes may help to explain why some battered children later become violent adults (Goleman, 1995).

Although no neurophysiological variable has yet been found, several types of indirect data suggest that brain functioning abnormalities increase the likelihood of violent behavior. Many studies have found that neurophysiological deficits in attention, memory, and language and verbal skills are common in youths who demonstrate violent or aggressive behavior. This correlation could indicate a direct relationship between limbic system damage and violent behavior. However, Reiss and Roth reported that "it is more likely to reflect less

**453**

direct results of distorted social interactions with peers resulting from impaired communication skills, or to arise from frustration over the inability to compete successfully with peers in cognitive tasks" (Reiss & Roth, 1993, p. 123; see also Moffitt et al., 1994).

Conclusions drawn with respect to juvenile murderers by Dorothy Otnow Lewis are also consistent with a "diathesis-stress theory" (Sarason & Sarason, 1996) of aggression. She maintained that genetic factors and biological vulnerabilities, particularly when severe, predispose certain individuals to respond violently. Lewis's research findings suggest that if these individuals are subjected to intense psychological, social, and environmental stressors that exceed their ability to cope, violent expression is more likely to result, particularly among males (Lewis, 1992; Lewis et al., 1989, 1991). Lewis's theory of neuropsychiatric vulnerability also received support in a larger study involving urban delinquents in Chicago (Hughes, Zagar, Arbit, & Busch, 1991), in a study of 21 juvenile murderers in England (Bailey, 1996), and in a study of 18 juvenile murderers in Florida (Myers & Scott, 1998). Results from a study of young murderers in Finland were consistent with Lewis's theory, although not as distinct and definite (Santtila & Haapasalo, 1997).

Reversing the trend toward increasing death and destructiveness by juveniles that we have seen in the United States since the mid-1980s is not an easy task. The factors that have contributed to the rise in juvenile homicide must be taken into account in any serious discussion of prevention and meaningful intervention with violent offenders. Realistically speaking, neutralizing or eliminating the variables that contribute to youths becoming involved in homicidal incidents may take a generation or more to accomplish. Efforts to decrease violence must include parents, the educational system, the community, government leaders, the nation, and the media working together to raise a healthier next generation and a more peaceful society (Heide, 1999b, 2000).

## Note

This chapter revises material originally presented in chapters titled "The Phenomenon of Juvenile Homicide" and "Ingredients for Juvenile Murder" published in Heide (1999b). Portions of the section "Factors Contributing to the Rise in Juvenile Homicide" were originally published in the *Stanford Law and Policy Review* (Heide, 1996) and in a special edition of *Behavioral Sciences and the Law* (Heide, 1997b).

## References

Adams, K. A. (1974). The child who murders: A review of theory and research. *Criminal Justice and Behavior, 1*, 51–61.

Adelson, L. (1972). The battering child. *Journal of the American Medical Association, 222*, 159–161.

American Psychological Association. (2001, June). Youth violence: Report from the Surgeon General (executive summary). *The Child, Youth, and Family Services, 34*(2), 1–7.

Anthony, E. J., & Rizzo, A. (1973). Adolescent girls who kill or try to kill their fathers. In E. J. Anthony & C. Koupernik (Eds.), *The Impact of Disease and Death* (pp. 330–350). New York: Wiley Interscience.

Bailey, S. (1994). Critical pathways of child and adolescent murderers. *Chronicle, International Association of Juvenile and Family Court Magistrates, 1*(3), 5–12.

Bailey, S. (1996). Adolescents who murder, *Journal of Adolescence, 19*, 19–39.

Bailey, S. (2000). Editorial: Juvenile homicide. *Criminal Behaviour and Mental Health, 10*, 149–154.

Barongan, C., & Hall, G.C.N. (1995). The influence of misogynous rap music on sexual aggression against women. *Psychology of Women Quarterly, 19*(2), 195–207.

Bell, C. C., & Jenkins, E. (1994, November 29). Statement before the Subcommittee on Juvenile Justice of the Senate Committee on Juvenile Crime: *Breaking the cycles of violence.* Washington, DC.

Bender, L. (1959). Children and adolescents who have killed. *American Journal of Psychiatry, 116*, 510–513.

Bender, L., & Curran, F. J. (1940). Children and adolescents who kill. *Criminal Psychopathology, 1*(4), 297–321.

Benedek, E. P., & Cornell, D. G. (1989). Clinical presentations of homicidal adolescents. In E. P. Benedek & D. G. Cornell (Eds.), *Juvenile homicide* (pp. 37–57). Washington, DC: American Psychiatric Press.

Benjamin, J., Li, L., Patterson, C., Greenberg, B. D., Murphy, D. L., & Hamer, D. H. (1996). Population and familial association between the D4 and dopamine receptor gene and measures of Novelty Seeking. *Nature Genetics, 12*, 81–84.

Bernstein, J. I. (1978). Premeditated murder by an eight year old boy. *International Journal of Offender Therapy and Comparative Criminology, 22*, 47–56.

Blumstein, A. (1995, August). Violence by young people: Why the deadly nexus? *National Institute of Justice Journal*, pp. 2–9.

Blumstein, A. (1996, June). Youth violence, guns, and illicit markets. *National Institute of Justice Research Review*, pp. 1–3.

Bortner, M. A. (1988). *Delinquency and justice.* New York: McGraw Hill.

Briere, J. N. (1992). *Child abuse trauma.* Newbury Park, CA: Sage.

Browne, A. (1987). *When battered women kill.* New York: Free Press.

Busch, K. G., Zagar, R., Hughes, J. R., Arbit, J., & Bussell, R. E. (1990). Adolescents who kill. *Journal of Clinical Psychology, 46*(4), 472–485.

Bushman, B. J., & Anderson, C. A. (2001). Media violence and the American public: Scientific facts versus media misinformation. *American Psychologist, 56*(6–7), 477–489.

Butts, J. A., & Snyder, H. N. (1997, September). *The youngest delinquents: Offenders under age 15* (Juvenile Justice Bulletin). Washington, DC: U.S. Department of Justice, Office of Juvenile Justice and Delinquency Prevention.

Bynum, J. E., & Thompson, W. E. (1999). *Juvenile delinquency: A sociological approach* (4th ed). Boston: Allyn & Bacon.

Carek, D. J., & Watson, A. S. (1964). Treatment of a family involved in fratricide. *Archives of General Psychiatry, 11*, 533–542.

Carnegie Council on Adolescent Development. (1995). *Great transitions: Preparing adolescents for a new century.* New York: Carnegie Corporation of New York.

Cheatwood, D. (1996). Interactional patterns in multiple-offender homicides. *Justice Quarterly, 13*(1), 107–128.

Cheatwood, D., & Block, K. J. (1990). Youth and homicide: An investigation of the age factor in criminal homicide. *Justice Quarterly, 7*(2), 265–292.

Cloward, R. A., & Ohlin, L. E. (1960). *Delinquency and opportunity.* New York: Free Press.

Coccaro, E. F. (1995, January–February). The biology of aggression. *Scientific American Science & Medicine*, pp. 38–47.

Cohen, A. (1955). *Delinquent boys: The culture of the gang.* New York: Free Press.

Corder, B. F., Ball, B. C., Haizlip, T. M., Rollins, R., & Beaumont, R. (1976). Adolescent parricide: A comparison with other adolescent murder. *American Journal of Psychiatry, 133*(8), 957–961.

Cormier, B. M., Angliker, C. C. J., Gagne, P. W., & Markus, B. (1978) Adolescents who kill a member of the family. In J. M. Eekelaar & S. N. Katz (Eds.), *Family violence: An international and interdisciplinary study* (pp. 466–478). Toronto, Canada: Butterworth.

Cornell, D. G. (1989). Causes of juvenile homicide: A review of the literature. In E. P. Benedek & D. G. Cornell (Eds.), *Juvenile homicide* (pp. 3–36). Washington, DC: American Psychiatric Press.

Cornell, D. G. (1990). Prior adjustment of violent juvenile offenders. *Law and Human Behavior, 14*, 569–577.

Cornell, D. G., Benedek, E. P., & Benedek, D. M. (1987a). Characteristics of adolescents charged with homicide. *Behavioral Sciences and the Law, 5*, 11–23.

Cornell, D. G., Benedek, E. P., & Benedek, D. M. (1987b). Juvenile homicide: Prior adjustment and a proposed typology. *American Journal of Orthopsychiatry, 57*(3), 383–393.

Cornell, D. G., Benedek, E. P., & Benedek, D. M. (1989). A typology of juvenile homicide offenders. In E. P. Benedek & D. G. Cornell (Eds.), *Juvenile homicide* (pp. 59–84). Washington, DC: American Psychiatric Press.

Cornell, D. G., Miller, C., & Benedek, E. P. (1988). MMPI profiles of adolescents charged with homicide. *Behavioral Sciences and the Law, 6*(3), 401–407.

Crespi, T. D., & Rigazio-DiGilio, S. A. (1996). Adolescent homicide and family pathology: Implications for research and treatment with adolescents. *Adolescence, 31*(122), 353–367.

Crime may be down, but not on TV news (1997, August 13). *Tampa Tribune* (Nation/World), p. 2.

Dahlberg, L. L. (1998). Youth violence in the United States: Major trends, risk factors, and prevention approaches. *American Journal of Preventive Medicine, 14*(4), 259–272.

Dahlberg, L. L., & Potter, L. B. (2001). Youth violence: Developmental pathways and prevention strategies. *American Journal of Preventive Medicine, 20*(1), 3–14.

Darby, P. J., Allan, W. D., Kashani, J. H., Hartke, K. L., & Reid, J. C. (1998). Analysis of 112 juveniles who committed homicide: Characteristics and a closer look at family abuse. *Journal of Family Violence, 13*(4), 365–375.

Dembo, R., Williams, L., Wothke, W., Schmeidler, J., Getreu, A., Berry, E., et al. (1992). The generality of deviance: Replication of a structural model among high-risk youths. *Journal of Research in Crime and Delinquency, 29*, 200–216.

Dolan, M., & Smith, C. (2001). Juvenile homicide offenders: 10 years' experience of an adolescent forensic psychiatry service. *Journal of Forensic Psychiatry, 12*(2), 313–329.

Drug use up, study shows. (1997, August 14). *Tampa Tribune*, p. 4.

*Drugs, crime, and the justice system: A national report from the Bureau of Justice Statistics.* (1992). Washington, DC: U.S. Department of Justice, Office of Justice Programs, Bureau of Justice Statistics.

Duncan, J. W., & Duncan, G. M. (1971). Murder in the family. *American Journal of Psychiatry, 127*(11), 74–78.

Dunn, M. (1996, February 21). No ordinary trial for no ordinary rapper. *Tampa Tribune*, p. 4.

Easson, W. M., & Steinhilber, R. M. (1961). Murderous aggression by children and adolescents. *Archives of General Psychiatry, 4*, 27–35.

Ebstein, R. P., Novick, O., Umansky, R., Priel, B., Osher, Y., Blaine, D., et al. (1996). Dopamine D4 receptor (D4DR) exon III polymorphism associated with the human personality trait of novelty seeking. *Nature Genetics, 12*, 78–80.

Elliott, D. S., Huizinga, D., & Menard, S. (1989). *Multiple problem youth: Delinquency, substance use, and mental health problems*. New York: Springer-Verlag.

Ewing, C. P. (1990). *When children kill*. Lexington, MA: Lexington Books.

Eysenck, H. J. (1977). *Crime and personality* (3rd ed.). London: Routledge & Kegan Paul.

Federal Bureau of Investigation. (1984–2000). *Crime in the United States* (1985–2001). Washington, DC: U.S. Government Printing Office.

Feiler, S. M., & Smith, M. D. (2000, November). *Absolute and relative involvement in homicide offending: An update*. Paper presented at the meeting of the American Society of Criminology, San Francisco.

Fendrich, M., Mackesy-Amiti, M. E., Goldstein, P., Spunt, B., & Brownstein, H. (1995). Substance involvement among juvenile murderers: Comparisons with older offenders based on interviews with prison inmates. *International Journal of the Addictions, 30*(11), 1363–1382.

Fiddes, D. O. (1981). Scotland in the seventies: Adolescents in care and custody: A survey of adolescent murder in Scotland. *Journal of Adolescence, 4*, 47–58.

Fishbein, D. H. (1990). Biological perspectives in criminology. *Criminology, 28*(1), 27–72.

Florida Center for Children and Youth. (1993). *Key facts about the children: A report on the status of Florida's children: Vol. 4. The 1993 Florida kids count data book*. Tallahassee, FL: Author.

Fox, J. A. (1996). *Trends in juvenile violence*. Washington, DC: U.S. Department of Justice, Bureau of Justice Statistics.

Fox, J. A., & Zawitz, M. W. (2000). Homicide trends in the United States: 1998 update. Washington, DC: USDOT, Bureau of Justice Statistics.

Fox, J. A., & Levin, J. (1994). *Overkill: Mass murder and serial killing exposed*. New York: Plenum.

Franz, C. E., & Moser, R. S. (2000). Youth violence and victimization: An introduction. In R. S. Moser & C. E. Franz (Eds.), *Shocking violence* (pp. 3–17). Springfield, IL: Charles C. Thomas.

Friedman, H. L. (1992). Changing patterns of adolescent sexual behavior: Consequences for health and development. *Journal of Adolescent Health, 13*, 345–350.

Friedman, H. L. (1993). Promoting the health of adolescents in the United States of America: A global perspective. *Journal of Adolescent Health, 14*, 509–519.

Fromm, E. (1973). *The anatomy of human destructiveness*. Greenwich, CT: Fawcett.

Gardiner, M. (1985). *The deadly innocents: Portraits of children who kill*. New Haven, Ct: Yale University Press.

Garfinkel, I., & McLanahan, S. S. (1986). *Single mothers and their children: A new American dilemma*. Washington, DC: Urban Institute Press.

Gelles, R. J., & Conte, J. R. (1990). Domestic violence and sexual abuse of children: A review of research in the eighties. *Journal of Marriage and the Family, 52*, 1045–1058.

Gest, T., & Friedman, D. (1994, August 29). The new crime wave. *U.S. News & World Report*, p. 26.

Glueck, S., & Glueck, E. (1950). *Unraveling juvenile delinquency*. Cambridge, MA: Harvard University Press.

Goetting, A. (1989). Patterns of homicide among children. *Criminal Justice and Behavior, 16*(1), 63–80.

Goetting, A. (1995). *Homicide in families and other special populations*. New York: Springer.

Goleman, D. (1995, October 3). *Early violence leaves its mark on the brain*. Retrieved September 11, 2003, from http://www.cirp.org/library/psych/goleman/

Gottfredson, M. R., & Hirschi, T. (1990). *A general theory of crime*. Stanford, CA: Stanford University Press.

Greco, C. M., & Cornell, D. G. (1992). Rorschach object relations of adolescents who committed homicide. *Journal of Personality Assessment, 59*(3), 574–583.

Haizlip, T., Corder, B. F., & Ball, B. C. (1984). Adolescent murderer. In C. R. Keith (Ed.), *Aggressive adolescent* (pp. 126–148). New York: Free Press.

Hardwick, P. J., & Rowton-Lee, M. A. (1996). Adolescent homicide: Toward assessment of risk. *Journal of Adolescence, 19*, 263–276.

Hays, J. R., Solway, K. S., & Schreiner, D. (1978). Intellectual characteristics of juvenile murderers versus status offenders. *Psychological Reports, 43*, 80–82.

Heide, K. M. (1984, November). *A preliminary identification of types of adolescent murderers.* Paper presented at the 36th annual meeting of the American Society of Criminology, Cincinnati, OH.

Heide, K. M. (1992). *Why kids kill parents: Child abuse and adolescent homicide.* Columbus: Ohio State University Press.

Heide, K. M. (1994a). Evidence of child maltreatment among adolescent parricide offenders. *International Journal of Offender Therapy and Comparative Criminology, 38*(2), 151–162.

Heide, K. M. (1994b). Homicide: 25 years later. In M. Moore (Ed.), *Economic and social issues in the New South: Perspectives on race and ethnicity conference proceedings* (pp. 64–84). Tampa: Institute on Black Life, University of South Florida.

Heide, K. M. (1995). *Why kids kill parents: Child abuse and adolescent homicide.* Thousand Oaks, CA: Sage.

Heide, K. M. (1996). Why kids keep killing: The correlates, causes, and challenge of juvenile homicide. *Stanford Law and Policy Review, 7*(1), 43–49.

Heide, K. M. (1997a). Editorial: Killing words. *International Journal of Offender Therapy and Comparative Criminology, 41*(1), 3–8.

Heide, K. M. (1997b). Juvenile homicide in America: How can we stop the killing? *Behavioral Sciences and the Law, 15*, 203–220.

Heide, K. M. (1999a, June). 1998 keynote address: School shootings and youth violence: What's going on in the U.S.? *Proceedings of the homicide research working group meetings, 1997 and 1998, Sheperdstown, WV, and Ann Arbor, MI* (pp. 116–130). Washington, D.C.: Federal Bureau of Investigation.

Heide, K. M. (1999b). *Young killers.* Thousand Oaks, CA: Sage.

Heide, K. M. (2000). Six concentrated strategies to reduce youth violence in the United States, *Barry Law Review, 1*(1), 143–157.

Hellsten, P., & Katila, O. (1965). Murder and other homicide, by children under 15 in Finland. *Psychiatric Quarterly Supplement, 39*(1), 54–74.

Hirschi, T. (1969). *Causes of delinquency.* Berkeley: University of California Press.

Hotaling, G. T., & Sugarman, D. B. (1986). An analysis of risk markers in husband to wife violence: The current state of knowledge. *Violence and Victims, 1*, 101–124.

Howell, J. C., Krisberg, B., & Jones, M. (1995). Trends in juvenile crime and youth violence. In J. C. Howell, B. Krisberg, J. D. Harvhiss, & J. J. Wilson (Eds.), *A sourcebook: Serious, violent, & chronic juvenile offenders* (pp. 1–35). Thousand Oaks, CA: Sage.

Hughes, J. R., Zagar, R., Arbit, J., & Busch, K. G. (1991). Medical, family, and scholastic conditions in urban delinquents. *Journal of Clinical Psychology, 47*(3), 448–464.

Incompetency standards in death penalty and juvenile cases. (1984). *Mental and Physical Disability Law Reporter, 8*(2), 92–93.

Jeffrey, C. R. (1979). *Biology and crime.* Beverly Hills, CA: Sage.

Jenkins, E. (1995). Violence exposure, psychological distress and risk behaviors in a sample of inner-city youth. In C. R. Block & R. Block (Eds.), *Trends, risks, and interventions in lethal violence: Proceedings of the third annual symposium of the homicide research working group* (pp. 287–298). Washington, D.C.: National Institute of Justice.

Jenkins, E., & Bell, C. (1994). Violence among inner city high school students and posttraumatic stress disorder. In S. Friedman (Ed.), *Anxiety disorders in African Americans* (pp. 76–88). New York: Springer.

Johnston, L. D., O'Malley, P. M., & Bachman, J. G. (1993). *National survey results on drug use* from the Monitoring the Future Study, 1975–1992: Vol. I. Secondary school students. Rock-ville, MD: National Institute on Drug Abuse.

Kalogerakis, M. G. (1971). Homicide in adolescents: fantasy and deed. In J. Fawcett, Dynamics of violence (pp. 93–103). Chicago: American Medical Association.

Kashani, J. H., Darby, P. J., Allan, W. D., Hantke, K. I., & Reid, J. C. (1997). Intrafamilial homicide committed by juveniles: Examination of a sample with recommendations for prevention. Journal of Forensic Sciences, 42(6), 873–878.

Kennedy, D. M. (1997). Juvenile gun violence and gun markets in Boston Washington, DC: U.S. Department of Justice, National Institute of Justice.

King, C. H. (1975). The ego and the integration of violence in homicidal youth. American Journal of Orthopsychiatry, 45, 134–145.

Kirschner, D. (1992). Understanding adoptees who kill: Dissociation, patricide, and the psychodynamics of adoption. International Journal of Offender Therapy and Comparative Criminology, 36(4), 323–334.

Labelle, A., Bradford, J. M., Bourget, D., Jones, B., & Carmichael, M. (1991). Adolescent murderers. Canadian Journal of Psychiatry, 36, 583–587.

Lacayo, R. (1995, June 12). Violent reaction. Time, pp. 24–30.

Lee, A. S., Lee, E. S. & Chen, J. (1995). Young killers. In M. Reidel & J. Boulahanis (Eds.), Proceedings of the 1995 meeting of the homicide research working group (pp. 15–20). Washington, DC: National Institute of Justice Report.

Lerner, R. M. (1994). America's youth in crisis. Thousand Oaks, CA: Sage.

Levin, J., & Fox, J. (1985). Mass murder: America's growing menace. New York: Plenum.

Lewis, D. O. (1992). From abuse to violence: Psychophysiological consequences of maltreatment. Journal of the American Academy of Child and Adolescent Psychiatry, 31(3), 383–391.

Lewis, D. O., Lovely, R., Yeager, C., & Femina, D. D. (1989). Toward a theory of the genesis of violence: A follow-up study of delinquents. Journal of the American Academy of Child and Adolescent Psychiatry, 28, 431–436.

Lewis, D. O., Lovely, R., Yeager, C., Ferguson, G., Friedman, M., Sloane, G., et al. (1988). Intrinsic and environmental characteristics of juvenile murderers. Journal of the American Academy of Child and Adolescent Psychiatry, 27(5), 582–587.

Lewis, D. O., Moy, E., Jackson, L. D., Aaronson, R., Restifo, N., Serra, S., et al. (1985). Biopsychosocial characteristics of children who later murder: A prospective study. American Journal of Psychiatry, 142, 1161–1167.

Lewis, D. O., Pincus, J. H., Bard, B., Richardson, E., Feldman, M., Prichep, L.S., et al. (1988). Neuropsychiatric, psychoeducational, and family characteristics of 14 juveniles condemned to death in the United States. American Journal of Psychiatry, 145, 584–589.

Lewis, D. O., Shanok, S. S., Grant, M., & Ritvo, E. (1983). Homicidally aggressive young children: Neuropsychiatric and experimental correlates. American Journal of Psychiatry, 140(2), 148–153.

Lewis, D. O., Shanok, S. S., Pincus, J. H., & Glaser, G. H. (1979). Violent juvenile delinquents: Psychiatric, neurological, psychological, and abuse factors. Journal of the American Academy of Child Psychiatry, 18, 307–319.

Lewis, D. O., Yeager, C. A., Cobham-Portorral, C. S., Klein, N., Showalter, C., & Anthony, A. (1991). A follow-up of female delinquents: Maternal contributions to the perpetration of deviance. Journal of the American Academy of Child Psychiatry, 30, 197–201.

Lewis, D. O., & Yeager, C. A. (2000). Juvenile violence: Preface. Child and Adolescent Psychiatric Clinics of North America, 9(4), xi–xvi.

Loeber, R., & Farrington, D. P. (2001). Child delinquents: Development, intervention, and service needs. Thousand Oaks, CA: Sage.

Luntz, B. K., & Widom, C. S. (1994). Antisocial personality disorder in abused and neglected children grown up. American Journal of Psychiatry, 151(5), 670–674.

Mack, J., Scherl, D., & Macht, L. (1973). Children who kill their mothers. In A. J. Anthony & C. Koupernik (Eds.), *The child in his family: The impact of disease and death* (pp. 319–332). New York: Wiley Interscience.

Magid, K., & McKelvey, C. A. (1987). *High risk: Children without a conscience.* New York: Bantam.

Malmquist, C. P. (1971). Premonitory signs of homicidal aggression in juveniles. *American Journal of Psychiatry, 128*(4), 461–465.

Malmquist, C. P. (1990). Depression in homicidal adolescents. *Bulletin of the American Academy of Psychiatry and the Law, 18*(1), 23–36.

Marans, S., & Berkman, M. (1997). Child development–community policing: Partnership in a climate of violence. Washington, DC: U.S. Department of Justice, Office of Juvenile Justice and Delinquency Prevention.

Marten, G. W. (1965). Adolescent murderers. *Southern Medical Journal, 58,* 1217–1218.

McCarthy, J. B. (1978). Narcissism and the self in homicidal adolescents. *American Journal of Psychoanalysis, 38,* 19–29.

McCully, R. S. (1978). The laugh of Satan: A study of a familial murderer. *Journal of Personality Assessment, 42*(1), 81–91.

McGee, J. P., & DeBernardo, C. R. (1999). The classroom avenger: A behavioral profile of school based shootings. *Forensic Examiner, 8*(5–6), 16–18.

Medlicott, R. W. (1955). Paranoia of the exalted type in a setting of folie à deux: A study of two adolescent homicides. *British Journal of Medical Psychology, 28,* 205–223.

Mednick, S. A., & Christiansen, K. O. (Eds.). (1977). *Biosocial bases of criminal behavior.* New York: Gardner.

Meloy, J. R., Hempel, A. G., Mohandie, K., Shiva, A., & Gray, B. T. (2001). Offender and offense characteristics of a nonrandom sample of adolescent mass murderers. *Journal of the American Academy of Child and Adolescent Psychiatry, 40*(6), 719–728.

Menninger, K., & Mayman, M. (1956). Episodic dyscontrol: A third order of stress adaptation. *Bulletin of the Menninger Clinic, 20,* 153–165.

Merton, R. (1938). Social structure and anomie. *American Sociological Review 3,* 672–682.

Messerschmidt, J. W. (1993). *Masculinities and crime: Critique and reconceptualization.* Lantham, MD: Rowman & Littlefield.

Michaels, J. J. (1961). Enuresis in murderous aggressive children and adolescents. *Archives of General Psychiatry, 5,* 94–97.

Miller, D., & Looney, J. (1974). The prediction of adolescent homicide: Episodic dyscontrol and dehumanization. *American Journal of Psychoanalysis, 34,* 187–198.

Moffitt, T. E., Lynam, D. R., & Silva, P. A. (1994). Neuropsychological tests predicting persistent male delinquency. *Criminology, 2*(32), 277–300.

Mohr, J. W., & McKnight, C. K. (1971). Violence as a function of age and relationship with special reference to matricide. *Canadian Psychiatric Association Journal, 16,* 29–32.

Mones, P. (1985). The relationship between child abuse and parricide. In E. H. Newberg & R. Bourne (Eds.), *Unhappy families: Clinical and research perspectives on family violence* (pp. 31–38). Littleton, MA: PSG Publishing.

Mones, P. (1991). *When a child kills: Abused children who kill their parents.* New York: Pocket.

Mouridsen, S. E., & Tolstrup, K. (1988). Children who kill: A case study of matricide. *Journal of Child Psychology and Psychiatry, 29,* 511–515.

Myers, W. C. (1992). What treatments do we have for children and adolescents who have killed? *Bulletin of the American Academy of Psychiatry and the Law, 20*(1), 47–58.

Myers, W. C. (1994). Sexual homicide by adolescents. *Journal of American Academy of Adolescent Psychiatry, 33*(7), 962–969.

Myers, W. C., Burgess, A. W., & Nelson, J. A. (1998). Criminal and behavioral aspects of juvenile sexual homicide. *Journal of Forensic Science, 43*(2), 340–347.

Myers, W. C., & Kemph, J. P. (1988). Characteristics and treatment of four homicidal adolescents. *Journal of the American Academy of Child and Adolescent Psychiatry, 27*(5), 595–599.

Myers, W. C., & Kemph, J. P. (1990). DSM-IIIR classification of homicidal youth: Help or hindrance. *Journal of Clinical Psychiatry, 51*, 239–242.

Myers, W. C., & Mutch, P. A. (1992). Language disorders in disruptive behavior disordered homicidal youth. *Journal of Forensic Sciences, 37*(3), 919–922.

Myers, W. C., & Scott, K. (1998). Psychotic and conduct disorder symptoms in juvenile murderers. *Journal of Homicide Studies, 2*(2), 160–175.

Myers, W. C., Scott, K., Burgess, A. W., & Burgess, A. G. (1995). Psychopathology, biopsychosocial factors, crime characteristics, and classification of 25 homicidal youths. *Journal of the American Academy of Child and Adolescent Psychiatry, 34*, 1483–1489.

National Criminal Justice Reference Service. (1997). *Fact sheet: Drug use trends.* Rockville, MD: National Criminal Justice Reference Service, White House Office of National Drug Control Policy, Drug Policy Information Clearinghouse.

*National drug control strategy: Executive summary.* (1995, April). Washington, DC: Office of National Drug Control Policy, Executive Office of the President.

O'Halloran, C. M., & Altmaier, E. M. (1996). Awareness of death among children: Does a life-threatening illness alter the process of discovery? *Journal of Counseling & Development, 74*(3), 259–262.

Osgood, D. W. (1995, January). *Drugs, alcohol, and violence.* Boulder: Institute of Behavioral Science, Regents of the University of Colorado.

Osgood, D. W., Johnston, L. D., O'Malley, P. M., & Bachman, J. G. (1988). The generality of deviance in late adolescence and early adulthood. *American Sociological Review, 53*, 81–93.

Osofsky, J. D. (1995). Children who witness domestic violence: The invisible victims. *Society for Research in Child Development Social Policy Report, 9*(3): 1–16.

Paluszny, M., & McNabb, M. (1975). Therapy of a six-year-old who committed fratricide. *Journal of the American Academy of Child Psychiatry, 14*, 319–336.

Patterson, R. M. (1943). Psychiatric study of juveniles involved in homicide. *American Journal of Orthopsychiatry, 13*, 125–130.

Petti, T. A., & Davidman, L. (1981). Homicidal school-age children: Cognitive style and demographic features. *Child Psychiatry and Human Development, 12*, 82–89.

Pfeffer, C. R. (1980). Psychiatric hospital treatment of assaultive homicidal children. *American Journal of Psychotherapy 34*(2), 197–207.

Pincus, J. H. (1993). Neurologist's role in understanding violence. *Archives of Neurology, 8*, 867–869.

Podolsky, E. (1965). Children who kill. *General Practitioner, 31*, 98.

Post, S. (1982). Adolescent parricide in abusive families. *Child Welfare, 61*, 455–455.

Prothrow-Stith, D., & Weissman, M. (1991). *Deadly consequences.* New York: Harper Collins.

Reckless, W. (1961). A new theory of delinquency and crime. *Federal Probation 25*, 42–46.

Reiss, A. J., & Roth, J. A. (Eds.). (1993). *Understanding and preventing violence.* Washington, DC: National Academy Press.

Resnick, M. D., Bearman, P. S., Blum, R. W., Bauman, K. F., Harris, K. M., Jones, J., et al. (1997). Protecting adolescents from harm: Findings from the National Longitudinal Study on Adolescent Health. *Journal of the American Medical Association, 278*(10), 823–832.

Restifo, N., & Lewis, D. O. (1985). Three case reports of a single homicidal adolescent. *American Journal of Psychiatry, 142*(3), 388.

Rosner, R., Weiderlight, M., Rosner, M. B. H., & Wieczorek, R. R. (1978). Adolescents accused of murder and manslaughter: A five year descriptive study. *Bulletin of the American Academy of Psychiatry and Law, 7*, 342–351.

Roth, J. A. (1994a). *Psychoactive substances and violence* (National Institute of Justice research in brief). Washington, DC: U.S. Department of Justice, Office of Justice Programs.

Roth, J. A. (1994b). *Understanding and preventing violence* (National Institute of Justice research in brief). Washington, DC: U.S. Department of Justice, Office of Justice Programs.

Russell, D. H. (1965). A study of juvenile murderers. *Journal of Offender Therapy, 9*(3), 55–86.

Russell, D. H. (1979) Ingredients of juvenile murder. *International Journal of Offender Therapy and Comparative Criminology, 23*, 65–72.

Russell, D. H. (1984) A study of juvenile murderers of family members. *International Journal of Offender Therapy and Comparative Criminology, 28*(3), 177–192.

Russell, D. H. (1986). Girls who kill. *International Journal of Offender Therapy and Comparative Criminology, 30*, 171–176.

Sadoff, R. L. (1971). Clinical observations on parricide. *Psychiatric Quarterly, 45*(1), 65–69.

Santtila, P., & Haapasalo, J. (1997). Neurological and psychological risk factors among young homicidal, violent, and nonviolent offenders in Finland. *Homicide Studies, 1*(3), 234–253.

Sarason, I. G., & Sarason, B. R. (1996). *Abnormal psychology: The problem of maladaptive behavior.* Upper Saddle River, NJ: Prentice Hall.

Sargent, D. (1962). Children who kill: A family conspiracy? *Social Work, 7*, 35–42.

Scherl, D. J., & Mack, J. E. (1966). A study of adolescent matricide. *Journal of the American Academy of Child Psychiatry, 5*(2), 569–593.

Schmideberg, M. (1973). Juvenile murderers. *International Journal of Offender Therapy and Comparative Criminology, 17*, 240–245.

Scudder, R. G., Blount, W. R., Heide, K. M., & Silverman, I. J. (1993). Important links between child abuse, neglect, and delinquency. *International Journal of Offender Therapy and Comparative Criminology, 37*(4), 315–323.

Sendi, I. B., & Blomgren, P. G. (1975). A comparative study of predictive criteria in the predisposition of homicidal adolescents. *American Journal of Psychiatry, 132*, 423–427.

Sheley, J. F., & Wright, J. D. (1995). *In the line of fire: Youth, guns, and violence in America.* New York: Aldine de Gruyter.

Shumaker, D. M., & McKee, G. R. (2001). Characteristics of homicidal and violent juveniles. *Violence and Victims, 16*(4), 401–409.

Shumaker, D. M., & Prinz, R. J. (2000). Children who murder: A review. *Clinical Child and Family Psychology Review, 3*(2), 97–115.

Sickmund, M. (1994, October). *How juveniles get to criminal court.* Washington, DC: U.S. Department of Justice, Office of Justice Programs, Office of Juvenile Justice and Delinquency Prevention.

Sickmund, M., Snyder, H. N., & Poe-Yamagata, E. (1997, August). *Juvenile offenders and victims: 1997 update on violence.* Washington, DC: U.S. Department of Justice, Office of Juvenile Justice and Delinquency Prevention.

Silverman, I. J., & Dinitz, S. (1974). Compulsive masculinity and delinquency. *Criminology, 11*(4), 498–515.

Silvern, L., Waelde, L. C., Karyl, J., Hodges, W. F., Starke, J., Heidt, E., et al. (1994). Relationships of parental abuse to college students' depression, trauma symptoms, and self-esteem. *Child, Youth, and Family Services Quarterly, 17*(1), 7–9.

Sleek, S. (1994, January). APA works to reduce violence in media. *Monitor*, pp. 6–7.

Smith, C., & Thornberry, T. P. (1995). The relationship between childhood maltreatment and adolescent involvement in delinquency. *Criminology, 33*(4), 451–481.

Smith, M. D., & Feiler, S. M. (1995). Absolute and relative involvement in homicide offending: Contemporary youth and the baby boom cohorts. *Violence and Victims, 10*, 327–333.

Smith, S. (1965). The adolescent murderer: A psychodynamic interpretation. *Archives of General Psychiatry, 13*, 310–319.

Snyder, H. N. (2001). Law enforcement and juvenile crime. Washington, D.C.: U.S. Department of Justice, Office of Justice and Delinquency Prevention.

Snyder, H. N. (1997, November). Juvenile arrests 1996 (Juvenile Justice Bulletin). Washington, DC: U.S. Department of Justice, Office of Juvenile Justice and Delinquency Prevention.

Snyder, H. N., & Sickmund, M. (1995). *Juvenile offenders and victims: A focus on violence*. Washington, DC: U.S. Department of Justice, Office of Juvenile Justice and Delinquency Prevention.

Solomon, E., Schmidt, R., & Ardragna, P. (1990). *Human anatomy and physiology*. Philadelphia: Saunders.

Solway, I. S., Richardson, L., Hays, J. R., & Elion, V. H. (1981). Adolescent murderers: Literature review and preliminary research findings. In J. R. Hays, T. K. Roberts, & K. Solway (Eds.), *Violence and the violent individual* (pp. 193–210). Jamaica, NY: Spectrum.

Sorrells, J. M. (1977). Kids who kill. *Crime and Delinquency, 23,* 313–320.

Stearns, A. (1957). Murder by adolescents with obscure motivation. *American Journal of Psychiatry, 114,* 303–305.

Stephens, G. (1997). *Youth at risk: Saving the world's most valuable resource*. Bethesda, MD: World Future Society.

Sutherland, E. H., & Cressey, D. R. (1943). *Principles of criminology*. Philadelphia: J. B. Lippincott.

Sykes, G. M., & Matza, D. (1957). Techniques of neutralization: A theory of delinquency. *American Sociological Review, 22,* 664–670.

Tanay, E. (1973). Adolescents who kill parents: Reactive parricide. *Australian and New Zealand Journal of Psychiatry, 7,* 263–277.

Tanay, E. (1976). Reactive parricide. *Journal of Forensic Sciences, 21*(1), 76–82.

Thom, D. (1949). Juvenile delinquency and criminal homicide. *Journal of the Maine Medical Association, 40,* 176.

Thornberry, T. P. (1994). *Violent families and youth violence* (fact sheet No. 21). Washington, DC: U.S. Department of Justice, Office of Juvenile Justice and Delinquency Prevention.

Tooley, K. (1975). The small assassins. *Journal of the American Academy of Child Psychiatry, 14,* 306–318.

Tucker, L. S., & Cornwall, T. P. (1977). Mother–son "folie à deux": A case of attempted patricide. *American Journal of Psychiatry, 134*(10), 1146–1147.

U.S. Advisory Board on Child Abuse and Neglect (USABCAN). (1993). *Neighbors helping neighbors: A new national strategy for the protection of children*. Washington, DC: National Clearinghouse on Child Abuse and Neglect.

U.S. Department of Commerce, Economics and Statistics Administration, Bureau of the Census. (1994). *Statistical abstracts of the United States: 1994* (114th ed.) Washington: U.S. Government Printing Office.

U.S. Department of Health and Human Services, Center for Disease Control and Prevention, National Center for Health Statistics. (1990). *Vital statistics of the United States: Vol. 1, Natality*. Washington: U.S. Government Printing Office.

U.S. Department of Justice. (1987). *Bureau of Justice Statistics special report: Survey of youth in custody*. Washington, DC: U.S. Government Printing Office.

Walshe-Brennan, K. S. (1974). Psychopathology of homicidal children. *Royal Society of Health, 94,* 274–276.

Walshe-Brennan, K. S. (1977). A socio-psychological investigation of young murderers. *British Journal of Criminology, 17*(1), 53–63.

Washbrook, R. A. H. (1979). Bereavement leading to murder. *International Journal of Offender Therapy and Comparative Criminology, 23*(1), 57–64.

Wertham, F. (1941). *Dark legend: A study in murder*. New York: Duell, Sloan, & Pearce.

Wheeler, J. L. (1993). *Remote controlled: How TV affects you and your family*. Hagerstown, MD: Review and Herald Publishing Association.

Widom, C. S. (1989a). Child abuse, neglect, and adult behavior: Research design and findings on criminality, violence, and child abuse. *American Journal of Orthopsychiatry, 59*(3), 355–366.

Widom, C. S. (1989b). Child abuse, neglect, and violent criminal behavior. *Criminology, 27,* 251–271.

Widom, C. S. (1989c). Does violence beget violence? A critical examination of the literature. *Psychological Bulletin, 106*(1), 3–28.

Widom, C. S. (1989d). The cycle of violence. *Science, 244,* 160–166.

Widom, C. S. (1991). A tail on an untold tale: Response to "Biological and genetic contributors to violence": Widom's untold tale. *Psychological Bulletin, 109*(1), 130–132.

Willis, D. J. (1995). Psychological impact of child abuse and neglect. *Journal of Clinical Child Psychology, 24*(suppl.), 2–4.

Wilson, J. Q., & Hernstein, R. J. (1985). *Crime and human nature.* New York: Simon & Schuster.

Wilson, M., & Daly, M. (1985). Competitiveness, risk taking, and violence: The young male syndrome. *Ethology and Sociobiology, 6*(1), 59–73.

Woods, S. M. (1961). Adolescent violence and homicide: Ego disruption and the 6 and 14 dysrhythmia. *Archives of General Psychiatry, 5,* 528–534.

Wright, K. N., & Wright, K. E. (1995). *Family life, delinquency, and crime: A policymaker's guide. Research summary.* Washington, DC: U.S. Department of Justice, Office of Juvenile Justice and Delinquency Prevention.

Wynne, E., & Hess, M. (1986). Long-term trends in youth conduct and the revival of traditional value patterns. *Educational Evaluation and Policy Analysis, 8*(3), 294–308.

Yates, A., Beutler, L. E., & Crago, M. (1983). Characteristics of young, violent offenders. *Journal of Psychiatry and Law, 11*(2), 137–149.

Zagar, R., Arbit, J., Sylvies, R., Busch, K., & Hughes, J. R. (1990). Homicidal adolescents: A Replication. *Psychological Reports, 67,* 1235–1242.

Zenoff, E. H., & Zients, A. B. (1979). Juvenile murderers: Should the punishment fit the crime? *International Journal of Law and Psychiatry, 2*(4), 533–553.

# V

# Bridging the Present to the Future

# 19

# Balanced and Restorative Justice

## Prospects for Juvenile Justice in the 21st Century

Gordon Bazemore and Mark Umbreit

Current approaches in juvenile justice, based on a retributive philosophical framework and the individual treatment mission, have failed to satisfy the basic needs of victims, the community, and juvenile offenders. This chapter explores an emerging framework based on the restorative justice philosophy and the balanced approach mission. This framework requires that juvenile justice systems devote primary attention to reparation for harm to victims and the community, increasing offender competencies, and protecting the public through processes in which offenders, victims, and the community are all active participants. Implementing this new approach involves building support for restorative values and for the new mission, articulating new goals and objectives for intervention, reallocating resources, redesigning job descriptions, developing new reporting measures and data collection systems, and giving priority to new programs and practices. Building on existing programs and practices, such as victim offender mediation, creative community service, restitution work experience and other competency development interventions, and innovative strategies for enhancing public safety, balanced and restorative justice reform is an evolutionary process that begins with small pilot projects in jurisdictions wishing to implement systemic change in juvenile justice.

Crime victims, offenders, and community members are often caught in a downward spiral in which crime leads to greater fear and increased isolation and distrust among community members, which leads to even more crime. Community safety depends primarily on voluntary individual restraint conditioned by community norms, which control harmful behavior and reinforce conventional productive behavior. The more connected community members are, the more likely they are to restrain impulses that would be disapproved of by the community. As community bonds are weakened by fear and isolation, the power of community disapproval is reduced, and crime increases.

The effects of this process are magnified with young people. During adolescence, the need to belong, to have a place that is valued, and to be "bonded" to others intensifies (Erickson, 1968). Youths who are not bonded to conventional community institutions such as school, work, and religious and recreational organizations are much more likely to engage in criminal behavior (Hawkins & Catalano, 1992; Hirschi, 1969; Polk & Kobrin, 1972). At the time youths most need to be connected, conventional adults are likely to pull away from them, in part because of extreme styles of dress, music, and language. Media stories about youth crime promote a generalized fear of young people among adults. That fear is deeply disturbing but at the same time provides a sense of power to adolescents and creates image problems even for those who are not engaged in any criminal behavior.

Can the spiral of ever-increasing fear and isolation, which feeds juvenile crime, be broken? Is it possible to respond to juvenile crime in ways that strengthen community bonds while sending clear messages about personal responsibility and accountability? Can victims of crime become actively involved in the process of holding offenders accountable and receiving compensation? Mutual responsibility between the individual and society is the loom on which the fabric of community is woven. Crime, and especially juvenile crime, represents a failure of responsibility—sometimes on one side but often on both. An effective model for reducing juvenile crime would therefore be one that emphasizes and reestablishes mutual responsibility as the central component to interrupt cycles of isolation and disconnectedness among community members while sending a clear message about accountability to youths and the community.

This chapter proposes one such alternative model, based on a new philosophical framework, *restorative justice* (Bazemore & Schiff, 2001; Bazemore & Walgrave, 1999; Umbreit, 1998, 2001; Van Ness & Strong, 2001; Zehr, 1990, 2002), and on a new mission for juvenile justice, the *balanced approach* (Bazemore, 1993, 2001; Maloney, Romig, & Armstrong, 1988). As a new "paradigm" or "lens" for viewing the problem of crime and the response to it (Zehr, 2002), the *balanced and restorative justice* model is garnering interest among a growing number of juvenile justice managers, community leaders, victims' organizations, and youth advocates. A national survey found that restorative justice policies and/or practices were developing in nearly every state, ranging from small pilot projects to major systemic change involving large programs (O'Brien, 2000). Restorative justice is increasingly being viewed as an alternative that holds promise for preserving a separate, distinctive, and significantly reformed and restructured juvenile justice system (Bazemore, 1993; Bazemore & Umbreit, 1995; Bazemore & Walgrave, 1999; Rosenberg, 1993). Ultimately, these reform advocates hope to change the role and image of the juvenile justice system from "receptacle" and "revolving door" to "resource" for enhancing the quality of life in communities through victim and community restoration, youth development and offender competency development, and creative risk management and prevention aimed at improved public safety. The promise of a restorative framework is a justice process that can more effectively serve victims and victimized communities, leaving these communities stronger after juvenile justice system intervention than before (Van Ness, 2001; Zehr, 1990). More than 63 empirical studies in five countries (Umbreit, Coates, & Vos, 2002) of restorative justice mediation, conferencing, and dialogue (Bazemore & Umbreit, 2001) in which victims meet offenders, usually with other support people or parents present, to talk about the impact of the crime and to develop a plan to repair the harm, have been conducted. These studies, which have ranged from quasi-experimental and experimental designs to meta-analyses, have consistently found high levels of victim and offender satisfaction and perceptions of fairness, greater likelihood of restitution completion, and reduced recidivism. A more recent multisite study (Umbreit, Vos, Coates, & Brown, 2003) even found restorative justice through victim–offender dialogue to be quite helpful in responding to the needs of victims of severe violence, including homicide, and the responsible offender. The vast majority of these studies have evaluated the oldest and most widely used form of restorative justice, that of victim–offender mediation (Umbreit, Coates, & Roberts, 2000; Umbreit et al., 2001), with more than 1,400 programs in 18 countries (Umbreit, 2001). This relatively strong empirical grounding of restorative justice theory bodes well for this contemporary justice reform movement that is developing support throughout the world, with recent endorsements by the United Nations (2000) and the Council of Europe (1999).

The purpose of this chapter is somewhat different from the others in this book. Rather than reviewing research and theory pertinent to a specific problem, reporting new research, or describing a specific "program" or series of programmatic interventions for delinquent offenders, our objective is to describe the balanced and restorative justice model as a holistic new approach to strategic reform in juvenile justice systems. Thus, while we discuss program models and practices consistent with this approach, the primary focus of this chapter is a general contrast between the values, goals, and objectives, priorities for practice, and management implications of this relatively new model and those of current juvenile justice systems.

## ■ Why a New Framework?

The juvenile justice system faces a crisis of confidence. Fear of violent juvenile crime and a sense of frustration with the effectiveness of the current system are fueling major changes in juvenile justice across the nation, which, if unchecked, threaten to culminate in the elimination of a separate and distinctive justice system for juvenile offenders (Bazemore & Umbreit, 1995; Feld, 1990). Unable to stem the tide of declining public support and respond to recent legislative assaults on its jurisdiction (e.g., Lemov, 1994), the juvenile justice system finds increasing number of youths removed from its authority and exiting a system whose influence, mandate, and credibility are shrinking (Butts, 1994).[1]

### The Individual Treatment Mission and Retributive Justice: Limited Choices for Juvenile Court Decision Making and Reform

Any group of agencies and organizations that refers to itself as a "justice" system is generally expected to address three needs. These needs, which provide the basic rationale for any criminal justice intervention into the lives of citizens, are (a) the need to sanction those who commit crimes, (b) the need to promote secure communities and enhance public safety, and (c) the need to rehabilitate offenders. In recent years, justice systems have also been asked or required to assume responsibility for helping to restore victim losses.[2] Some are accepting this challenge and discovering a natural linkage between the demand to make victims whole and the need to provide for meaningful sanctioning (Bazemore, 1994; Bazemore & Umbreit, 1995; Schneider, 1985).

Founded as a quasi-welfare agency, the juvenile court has traditionally focused primarily on providing treatment in the "best interests" of the juvenile offender (Melton, 1989; Rothman, 1980). In doing so, the court has often neglected to effectively sanction, denounce, or provide meaningful consequences for offense behavior, and juvenile justice systems have failed to address public safety goals. Little if any attention has been given to the goal of making victims whole. Further, because of limits inherent in the individual treatment mission, juvenile justice has also often failed to meet expectations in achieving rehabilitative objectives (e.g., Lab & Whitehead, 1988). As the traditional *parens patriae* philosophy that originally guided juvenile courts has declined in influence, these failures and widely documented inconsistencies in juvenile justice decision making have brought numerous pressures on juvenile courts for reform.

One attempt to bring rationality to the erratic decision making in the juvenile court and affirm the importance of the sanctioning function is through the application of the "just deserts" philosophy (Schneider & Shram, 1983; von Hirsch, 1976). Though intended in part to reduce arbitrary and excessive use of punishment, the just deserts policies and practices actually *implemented* have resulted in an expansion of punishment. Specifically, adoption of mandatory and determinate sentencing guidelines, codes, and purpose clause provisions that de-emphasized the role of rehabilitation and removed references to the needs of offenders, expanded prosecutorial powers, and allowed fewer restrictions on transfer to adult court (Feld, 1990) led to increased incarceration and longer stays in residential and detention facilities but with no discernible impact on crime rates (Castellano, 1986; McAllair, 1993).

In addition, just deserts reforms in juvenile justice sent several questionable messages to policy makers and the public. First, in giving new priority to punishment, retributive policies gave lower priority to the rehabilitative goal. Second, in failing to address public safety specifically as a juvenile justice goal, retributive reforms tended to confuse community protection with sanctioning objectives. Third, by focusing only on punishment primarily by incarceration and giving new legitimacy to punishment for its own sake, retributive reforms closed off consideration of less harmful and less expensive forms of sanctioning and made these sanctions appear weak and inadequate. This emphasis helped to expand the use of incarceration and fueled what now appears to be an ever-increasing demand to transfer more juveniles into the criminal justice system (Butts, 1994; Feld, 1990).

Today, juvenile justice professionals must respond to the conflicting demands of an increasingly dominant retributive justice philosophy (Bazemore & Umbreit, 1995; Zehr, 1990, 2002) and a weakened individual treatment mission, which nonetheless continues to exert strong influence on the agenda for correctional intervention with juvenile offenders (Palmer, 1992). Neither retributive justice nor the treatment mission provides an adequate framework for preserving and reforming juvenile justice; the punishment choice and the treatment choice provide limited options to decision makers.

## Choosing Punishment

While it may satisfy the public need for retribution, the punitive choice may also have counterdeterrent and other negative side effects. As currently practiced, juvenile court punishment tends to "label the *person* not the *deed* as evil" and often isolates offenders without providing a way for them to regain their self-respect and the respect of the community (Makkai & Braithwaite, 1994, p. 362; Zehr, 1990). Instead, punishment and stigma may encourage lawbreakers to focus on themselves rather than on their victims and the community as they learn to "take the punishment" without taking responsibility for the offense (Wright, 1991).

Other widely documented counterproductive effects of retributive punishment include the tendency for punishment to undermine self-restraint (e.g., Lepper, 1983), to create problems of adjustment for individuals or exacerbate risk factors that encourage further delinquency (Link, 1987), to weaken conventional community bonds by affecting job prospects and family relations (Sampson & Laub, 1993), and to damage conventional peer and adult relations, leading to social rejection and estrangement (Zhang & Messner, 1994). Increasing the severity of punishment may have little or no impact if decision makers have miscalculated the extent to which the offender experiences a sanction such as incarceration as punitive (Crouch, 1993), but it may also increase the probability of this estrangement (Zhang & Messner, 1994) or even drive offenders to greater lengths in order to escape punishment (Wright, 1991).

At the community level, the more often punishment is used and condoned as appropriate, the more demand is created for expanded use of punitive sanctions and for increased severity, especially when it becomes apparent that current levels are not accomplishing sanctioning goals (Christie, 1982; Wilkins, 1991). Moreover, some have argued that increased use of punishment by the justice system reinforces more general use of punishment by creating a climate in which violent responses are viewed as acceptable problem-solving techniques in various community, family, and other interpersonal situations (Christie, 1982; see also Bowers, Pierce, & McDevitt, 1980). Finally, those who continue to assume that punishment enhances social order and community solidarity may wish to heed Durkheim's caution that the more frequently punishment is used, the less effective it becomes, because it tends to destroy whatever shameful feelings or moralistic tendencies offenders and would-be offenders have (Garland, 1990).

On the other hand, as a number of theorists and researchers have observed (Braithwaite, 1989; Garland, 1990; Wilkins, 1991), there are more effective ways to provide consequences for crime and to respond to the legitimate need for communities to affirm positive values and send messages to offenders and would-be offenders that criminal behavior is unacceptable. Although nonpunitive sanctions can serve important expressive and symbolic functions in promoting social control by equating sanctioning with retributive punishment, policy makers may ignore these less expensive and less shameful options:

> Since punishment is reproaching, the best punishment is that which puts the blame . . . in the most expressive but least expensive way possible. . . . It is not a matter of making him suffer . . . or as if the essential thing were to intimidate and terrorize. Rather it is a matter of reaffirming the obligation at the moment when it is violated, in order to strengthen the sense of duty, both for the guilty party and for those witnessing the offense—those whom the offense tends to demoralize. (Durkheim, 1961, pp. 181–182; cited in Braithwaite, 1989, p. 178)

From this perspective, sanctioning aimed at regulating conduct by communicating value-based messages to offenders and the community is more likely to enhance community solidarity than is sanctioning based on vengeance and the intent to inflict pain. Expressive sanctioning may also promote peaceful dispute resolution and order maintenance (Griffiths & Belleau, 1993; Wilkins, 1991), while imposing consequences that make offenders aware of the harm caused by their behavior to individual victims and to the collective.

## Choosing Treatment

Despite its inadequacy, punishment in the public mind is at least somewhat related to the offense and seems to affirm community disapproval of proscribed behavior. Treatment, on the other hand, appears to be related solely to the needs of the offender. From a sanctioning perspective, treatment interventions fail to fulfill societal needs to denounce crime, reaffirm community values, confront the offender, and provide either real or symbolic consequences related to the crime and the nature of the harm caused to victims and the community (Wright, 1991).

On the contrary, it is difficult to convince most citizens that juvenile justice treatment programs provide anything other than benefits to offenders (e.g., services, recreational activities) while asking them for little or nothing in return. Although citizens expect juvenile offenders to be confronted with their crimes and to be made aware of and experience consequences (e.g., Schwartz & Van Vleet, 1992), treatment may appear to excuse and deny responsibility for crime, and there is little in the message of the treatment response that attempts to communicate to offenders that they have harmed someone and should take action to repair damages. Moreover, because treatment often requires little of offenders beyond participating in counseling or remedial services, these interventions typically do little to reinforce conventional community values in offenders (e.g., the work ethic).[3]

## ▧ Asking Different Questions: Toward a New Approach

As Byrne (1989) has observed in assessing the weaknesses of control/surveillance and treatment models in community corrections, both punishment and treatment responses in juvenile justice are practically and conceptually incomplete. Taking a one-dimensional view of the offender, each model operates from a "closed system" logic (see also Reiss, 1986) that targets only offenders for service or punishment and fails to include other parties critical to the resolution of crime. Specifically, victims can rarely count on reparation, assistance, or acknowledgment and typically do not participate in any meaningful way in the juvenile justice process (Galaway & Hudson, 1990). Community members are seldom asked for input or informed of their potentially vital role in meeting sanctioning, rehabilitation, and public safety objectives. In addition, both punitive and therapeutic interventions place offenders in a passive role— as the object of treatment or services on the one hand and of punishment and surveillance on the other (Eglash, 1975)—and few opportunities are provided for lawbreakers to actively make amends for their crimes or to practice productive behavior that might facilitate habilitation and reintegration.

Ultimately, as Wilkins (1991, p. 312) asserts, "It is now generally accepted that the problem of crime cannot be simplified to the problem of the criminal." As atomized responses to delinquent behavior, neither treatment nor punishment is capable of meeting the needs of offender, community, family, and victim (McElrae, 1993; Walgrave, 1993). From the perspective of a growing number of juvenile justice professionals, the decline in community support for juvenile justice is therefore not difficult to understand. Juvenile court sanctions send unclear or ambiguous messages to offenders and fail to provide meaningful consequences related to the offense; supervision strategies often provide little structure to the offender's day and offer few opportunities for active engagement in productive activity; rehabilitation programs and practices do not and should not be expected to rehabilitate because they do nothing to improve an offender's prospects for conventional adulthood and provide little linkage to conventional community groups and institutions. Just as advocates of community policing are beginning to question whether efforts to increase arrests, enhance motorized patrol, and reduce response time are effective in preventing crime (e.g., Sparrow, Moore, & Kennedy, 1990), these juvenile justice professionals, as well as policy makers and citizens, are beginning to ask new questions about the fundamental rationale behind the current response to youth crime (see box).

Such questions suggest that a range of needs—for example, the need to alter the marginal and disenfranchised status of victims, the need for offenders to be held meaningfully accountable for the harm resulting from their crimes, and the need to develop new strategies for promoting safer communities— have been nearly ignored. Other needs—for example, the need for active and structured supervision of offenders, the need to increase prospects for offender

## Rethinking the Business of Juvenile Justice

If the source of the problem of delinquency is in the community, family, and schools, why do all casework strategies target only individual offenders for change, and why are these other institutions so seldom involved in the change process?

If the problem is really that some person and/or community has been harmed and suffered loss by an offender, why are victims and community representatives not directly involved in the sanctioning and the rehabilitation process, and why isn't restoration of victims the primary focus of sanctioning?

If the problem is a lack of integration, rehabilitation, and habilitation, why do correctional strategies focus on isolation of offenders?

If the goal of sanctioning is to send messages to offenders about the consequences and harm caused to others by crime, why are sanctions so unrelated to the offense itself, and why is the sanctioning and rehabilitative process so detached from victims and the offender's community?

If public support is needed to ensure juvenile justice effectiveness (and the continued survival of juvenile justice), why do we continue to send messages to the public that offenders are getting off easy or even being rewarded by the system for their crime (e.g., by referring them to recreational programs and giving low priority to victim and community restoration)?

If the goal is to ensure public safety while offenders are on community supervision, why do we seem to utilize so few options for structuring the offender's time in productive activity, and why do we focus only on offender surveillance rather than promoting strategies for developing safer communities?

If the goal is to make offenders more responsible and accountable, why do we place them in positions (e.g., in most treatment programs) where others assume responsibility for them?

If juvenile justice professionals are experts in delinquent behavior, why are juvenile justice agencies treated only as a receptacle for dumping problem kids rather than a resource for resolving problems in schools and communities?

Source: Bazemore & Washington (1995).

integration or reintegration into productive life in the community, and the need for better strategies to promote direct engagement of citizens and community organizations in addressing these other needs—are inadequately met by the interventions prescribed by the treatment mission and the retributive justice framework.

Previous efforts to reform the system have brought about positive changes, including increased due process protections for juveniles (Rosenberg, 1993), improved classification and risk assessment (Baird, 1985; Clear & Gallagher, 1983), and smaller, less crowded residential facilities (Miller, 1991; Schwartz, Barton, & Orlando, 1991). These reforms in the *structure* and *process* of juvenile justice intervention have done little, however, to change the *content* of intervention. They have also done little to alter the role of victims, community members, offenders, and system professionals in the response to juvenile crime.

Despite their questioning and criticism of the juvenile justice system, most justice professionals and many policy makers remain convinced that a separate and distinctive juvenile justice system—even with its current flaws—will remain more effective in responding to juvenile crime than criminal courts and adult corrections (Bazemore, 1993; Rosenberg, 1993; Butts & Mears, 2001). While most reform in juvenile justice continues to be crisis driven, some juvenile justice managers are responding to inherent problems in their juvenile justice systems by choosing a more long-term, critical, and broadly focused path to reform. In doing so, they join others in state and local government who are reexamining their mission and are not afraid to ask questions that would have been viewed as absurd a decade ago. In the remainder of this chapter, we examine one alternative mission for juvenile justice and consider prospects for a new paradigm for juvenile justice.

## ■ A Balanced Approach Mission in a Restorative Framework

Recent crises in juvenile justice systems in several states brought on by often desperate policy maker reactions to the threat of juvenile crime suggest the possibility of radical transformation toward an even more retributive response to youth crime (e.g., Lemov, 1994). Alternatively, there are also increasing signs that a "paradigm shift" may be under way that could lead to a more responsive, effective, and just approach to juvenile crime. While paradigm shifts often grow out of disruption, failure, and crisis, they also make it possible to challenge old traditions that blind us to new solutions and allow us to begin to articulate new values and goals in an effort to reinvent current systems and organizations (Kuhn, 1962). An effective juvenile justice mission is needed to guide rational reform and help justice professionals and communities restructure their systems in a meaningful way while avoiding fads and quick-fix solutions. As a practical blueprint for action, a mission statement should identify the clients or "customers" of juvenile justice, prioritize services, articulate management values, provide guidelines for resource allocation and programmatic priorities, and articulate roles and responsibilities for staff and the community. The mission should also be actively used as a tool to guide ongoing reform and to help engage the community in the justice process.

### The Balanced Approach Mission

Frustrated by the pendulum swings between policy emphasis on individual treatment and retribution and by unclear or unrealistic expectations from the public, a growing number of juvenile justice professionals are beginning to embrace a practical new performance-based mission for juvenile justice generally and community supervision specifically. As first outlined in a special issue of the *Journal of Juvenile and Family Courts* (Maloney et al., 1988), the balanced approach mission addresses community demands for (a) sanctioning based on accountability measures that restore victims and clearly denounce and provide meaningful consequences for offensive behavior, (b) offender rehabilitation and reintegration, and (c) enhanced community safety and security. It does this by articulating three system goals directed toward the three primary "client/customers" of the system: the victim, the offender, and the community (see Figure 19.1).

These system goals, which also govern the response to each offense, are accountability, competency development, and community protection (Maloney et al., 1988). The general goal of "balance" suggests that policies and programs should seek to address each of the three goals in each case and that system balance should be pursued as managers seek to allocate resources to meet needs and achieve goals associated with each client/customer. Values associated with each goal and each customer are listed in Figure 19.1.

As the primary sanctioning goal in the balanced approach, accountability refers specifically to the requirement that offenders "make amends" for the harm resulting from their crimes by repaying or restoring losses to victims and the community. Competency development, the rehabilitative goal for intervention, requires that youths who enter the juvenile justice system should exit the system more capable of being productive and responsible in the community. The community protection goal explicitly acknowledges and endorses a long-time public expectation that juvenile justice must place equal emphasis on promoting public safety and security at the lowest possible cost. Finally, the mission is founded on the belief that justice is best served when the victim, community, and youths are viewed as equal clients of the justice system.

The balanced approach mission is rooted in and responsive to traditional values in American communities (e.g., making amends to victims and the public; the work ethic). As a result, it provides a strong basis for engaging the

**Figure 19.1    The Balanced Approach**

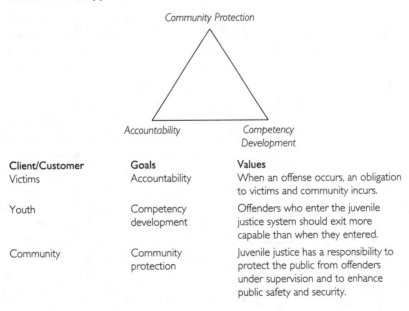

| Client/Customer | Goals | Values |
|---|---|---|
| Victims | Accountability | When an offense occurs, an obligation to victims and community incurs. |
| Youth | Competency development | Offenders who enter the juvenile justice system should exit more capable than when they entered. |
| Community | Community protection | Juvenile justice has a responsibility to protect the public from offenders under supervision and to enhance public safety and security. |

support and participation of the community. To be successful in meeting the needs of the three clients/customers and to avoid being co-opted by the retributive justice agenda or simply used in an effort to win new support for the individual treatment mission, the balanced approach mission must be implemented within a value framework that recognizes crime as harm done to victims and the community, values the participation of victims and community, and prioritizes restoration as a goal of the justice process. Restorative justice provides such a framework.

## The Restorative Justice Framework

Although it draws upon ancient concepts and practices abandoned late in the Middle Ages as formal justice systems emerged and began to define the obligation of offenders as a debt to the king or lord (and later to the state) rather than to victims (Davis, 1992; Schafer, 1970), modern interest in restorative justice has been influenced by several developments in the 1970s and 1980s. Notably, the reemergence of restorative philosophy and practice grew out of experience with reparative sanctions and processes (e.g., restitution, victim–offender mediation) (Galaway & Hudson, 1990; Schneider, 1985; Umbreit & Coates, 1993), the victims' movement, the rise of informal neighborhood justice and dispute resolution processes (Messmer & Otto, 1992), and new thinking on equity and human relationships influenced in part by the women's movement and the peace and social justice movements (Harris & Umbreit, 1993; Pepinsky & Quinney, 1991).

Restorative justice offers a coherent alternative to the increasingly retributive focus of the juvenile court sanctioning process and also moves beyond the limits of individual treatment based on the "medical model." While retributive justice is based on public vengeance and the provision of punishment through an adversarial process, restorative justice is concerned with the broader relationship among offender, victim, and community and gives priority to repairing the damage or harm done to victims and victimized communities (Galaway & Hudson, 1990; Zehr, 1990). Restorative justice differs most clearly from retributive justice (see Table 19.1) in its view of crime as more of government authority. Rather, what is most significant about criminal behavior is the injury to victims, communities, and offenders that is its result.

As Table 19.1 suggests, restorative justice offers a different lens for viewing the problem of crime and provides a new outlook on the appropriate public response to the harm that results when an offense is committed (Zehr, 1990, 2002). As an overall philosophy for the juvenile justice system, restorative justice provides critical guidance to managers and policy makers in rethinking the traditional sanctioning, rehabilitative, and public safety functions of juvenile justice—and in adding the new concern with making victims whole and involving them in the justice process. Neither punitive nor lenient in its focus, restorative justice has as its primary objective reparation of harm done to vic-

**Table 19.1    Contrasting Retributive Justice and Restorative Justice**

| Retributive Justice | Restorative Justice |
| --- | --- |
| Crime is an act against the state, a violation of a law, an abstract idea. | Crime is an act against another person and the community. |
| The criminal justice system controls. | Crime control lies primarily in the community. |
| Offender accountability is defined as taking punishment. | Accountability is defined as assuming responsibility and taking action to repair harm. |
| Crime is an individual act with individual responsibility. | Crime has both individual and social dimensions of responsibility. |
| Punishment is effective:<br>  a. Threat of punishment deters crime.<br>  b. Punishment changes behavior. | Punishment alone is not effective in changing behavior and is disruptive to community harmony and good relationships. |
| Victims are peripheral to the process. | Victims are central to the process. |
| The offender is defined by deficits. | The offender is defined by capacity to make amends. |
| Focus is on establishing blame or guilt, on the past (did he/she do it?). | Focus is on problem solving, on liabilities/obligation, on the future (what should be done). |
| Emphasis is adversarial. | Emphasis is on dialogue and negotiation. |
| Imposition of pain to punish and community is on the sideline. | Restitution as a means of restoring. |
| Response is focused on the offender's behavior. | Response focused on harmful results. |
| Dependence upon proxy professionals. | Direct involvement by participants. |

tims, recognition by the offender of harm caused by the offense, conciliation, and, if appropriate, reconciliation among victim, offender, and community.

While giving primary focus to the needs of victims, restorative justice also speaks directly to the need for societies to make allowances for offender repentance or forgiveness and to make possible and encourage offender reintegration following appropriate sanctioning (Van Ness, 1993; Zehr, 1990, 2002). However, restorative justice does not imply that serious and violent offenders who present significant risks to others should be released into the community. While restorative justice advocates would argue that less reliance on incarceration strictly as a punitive tool, coupled with better strategies to strengthen the prevention capacity of communities, would be likely to reduce incarceration, they would also recognize the need for secure facilities to protect the public from those offenders who represent significant risks to public safety. Although often implemented primarily at the "front end" of the juvenile justice system as part of diversion or probation (e.g., Schneider, 1985; Umbreit & Coates, 1993), restorative justice principles in fact suggest a holistic, systemwide response to crime (Van Ness, 1993; Zehr, 1990, 2002), directed toward even the most serious cases as well as in response to first offenses. At the "deep end" of the system, a restorative response might emphasize victim awareness education to those in secure institutions and would give priority to services and support aimed at addressing the material and emotional needs of the victims of those offenders. On the front end of the juvenile justice system, restorative justice would demand a sanction requiring the offender to make amends to victims and the community. Ideally, all such reparative sanctions (e.g., monetary restitution, community service) would be tied directly to the nature of the harm resulting from the offense and fulfill the fundamental need of communities to denounce criminal behavior, provide meaningful consequences, and send a message to the offender and would-be offender that criminal behaviors are unacceptable.

## A Balanced and Restorative Justice Model

Restorative justice is based on the assumption that none of the essential functions of the justice system—rehabilitation, community protection, sanctioning, and victim restoration—can be effectively accomplished without the joint involvement of victims, offenders, and the community. It is based on the belief and value statement that justice is best served when victims, offenders, and the community receive balanced attention and gain tangible benefits from their interactions with the juvenile justice system.

Grounded in these restorative assumptions and values, the balanced mission provides a blueprint for meeting the traditional needs for sanctioning, rehabilitation, and increased public safety, while serving the overarching goal of restoration of the victim. In meeting these needs, new goals directed at each client or customer of the system then become the basis for developing new performance objectives, identifying new appropriate programs and practices to accomplish objectives, and specifying new roles and responsibilities of juvenile justice staff and other individuals and organizations. Table 19.2 briefly summarizes at the most general level basic differences in values, goals, objectives, preferred practices, and roles between the current paradigm (the retributive justice framework and the individual treatment mission) and the proposed new paradigm (the restorative justice framework and the balanced approach mission).

But while a balanced and restorative model is a prescription for change in values and goals for juvenile justice systems, it is not a "cookbook" that provides generic, panacean solutions to all problems raised by specific crimes committed by specific offenders against specific victims in all communities. Thus, at times difficult questions raised by professionals and policy makers will need to be viewed in the context of what must be acknowledged as a less than perfect resolution of problems of crime in the current system (Van Ness, 1993). Such problems will need to be resolved as communities, victims, and offenders work with juvenile justice professionals to apply the core principles of the balanced and restorative justice framework to unique cases and to obstacles to implementation as they arise. The remainder of this chapter describes

**Table 19.2    How Is It Different? Current Paradigm and Balanced and Restorative Justice Paradigm**

| Current Paradigm | New Paradigm |
| --- | --- |
| *Philosophical Framework and Mission* | |
| Retributive justice and individual treatment. | Restorative justice and the balanced approach. |
| *Clients and Values* | |
| Youthful offender is main client to be tracked, punished, treated, and controlled. | Youth, victim, and community receive balanced attention as client/customers of the system who are both targets of intervention and partners in the response to crime. |
| *System Goals* | |
| Rehabilitation through individual treatment; sanctioning through punishment focused on victims and incarceration; public safety through offender's increased isolation. | Rehabilitation through competency development; sanctioning through accountability to communities; public safety through community security, preventive capacity development, and relationship building. |
| *Performance Objectives* | |
| Administration of punishment; service provision; compliance with rules of supervision; complete treatment; changes in offender attitude; removal of offenders from community; retribution and deterrence. | More competent offenders; reintegration of offenders; restoration of victims and offender awareness of harm; safe and secure citizens engaged in preventive activities; separation of violent, predatory offenders from the community. |
| *Practices* | |
| Incarceration as punishment; monitoring and surveillance, individual casework; counseling programs; and traditional treatment. | Reparative sanctions and processes; victim services; work, service, and learning structuring offender's time; guardians and mentors in the community; use of incarceration for public safety. |
| *Roles* | |
| Active role for juvenile justice professionals; passive role for victims and offenders. | Active role for offenders, victims, and community. |

the differences between these principles and those of retributive justice and the treatment model in more detail. It also outlines changes in current policy and practice needed to address the three goals of justice system intervention in a way that meets the needs of the three customers of the system, while giving new priority to victim restoration.

Offender accountability and consequences relate to the nature and degree of harm resulting from offenses, as well as the relative culpability of the offender in causing this harm. Some writers have recently noted that societies that are most effective in controlling crime provide for a "reintegrative shaming" process, in which citizens and victims are actively involved in an effort to make offenders aware of the harm caused by their behavior to the collective and to affirm community values (Braithwaite, 1989; Haley, 1989; Makkai & Braithwaite, 1994). In these "low crime" societies, sanctioning is a community function in which a denunciation process is generally followed by a process of reparation to victims and the community, reintegration, conciliation, and forgiveness.

Crime is best controlled when members of the community are the primary controllers through active participation in shaming offenders and, having shamed them, through concerted participation in integrating the offender back into the community. Low-crime societies are societies where people do not mind their own business, where tolerance of deviance has definite limits, and where communities prefer to handle their own crime problems rather than hand them over to professionals (Braithwaite, 1989, p. 8).

# ◼ Contrasting Individual Treatment, Retribution, and Balanced and Restorative Justice

### Sanctioning Offenders: Accountability in a Balanced and Restorative Model

A major priority of any justice system is to publicly denounce harmful behavior and to provide consequences for offenders. To accomplish this, a justice system must develop meaningful terms of accountability.

Values

The retributive model gives priority to punishment through incarceration as the primary means of sanctioning offenders for violations against the state. While the fairness, meaningfulness, and appropriateness of sanctions are of legitimate interest to the state, the core values underlying the balanced and restorative model, on the other hand, demand that juvenile justice systems first hold offenders accountable to the victim and the community (Umbreit, 1994b, 1998). By shifting the focus of offender accountability or "debt" from the state to the victim, restorative justice sanctions meet the needs of communities to provide meaningful consequences for crime, confront offenders, and denounce delinquent behavior. Thus, while confinement of offenders may be necessary for public safety reasons, in no case is confinement or restriction of offenders for punitive reasons equated with accountability in restorative justice (see Table 19.3, row 1).

As such, restorative accountability prescribes an obligation or responsibility of the offender to "make amends" by repairing the damage to those who have been harmed or wronged; to the extent that the community is an indirect victim, work service, fines, or other forms of payback are appropriate once the direct victim has received reparation. Victims and community members are

**Table 19.3**     **Sanctioning: Restorative Versus Retributive Accountability**

| | Current System (Retributive Punishment) | Balanced and Restorative System (Restorative Accountability) |
|---|---|---|
| Values and assumptions | Accountability is to the justice system and is defined as the offender taking punishment. | Accountability is to victims and is defined as making amends to victims and the *community. When an offense occurs, an* obligation to victims incurs. Victims have the right to active involvement in the justice process. |
| Performance | Number of offenders punished | Number and proportion of victims restored. |
| Objectives | Swiftness, certainty, and severity of punishment. | Number of victims involved; amount of restitution paid and community service hours worked per amount ordered; offenders made aware of harm due to their offense (hopefully experience remorse); victim satisfaction; number of reparative settlement agreements negotiated and completed: promptness and quality of completion of restorative requirements; quality of service work and quality of overall process. |
| Priorities for practice | Incarceration; electronic monitoring; required treatment; punitive fines and fees. | Restitution; victim-offender mediation; victim impact panels and awareness education; victim services; restorative community service; direct victim service or victim-driven service; restorative fines. |

encouraged to play an active role in holding young offenders accountable through mediation, victim awareness panels, mentoring, and other projects.

Currently, juvenile justice systems are offender driven (Wright, 1991). Thus, an additional value underlying the sanctioning function in systems moving toward restorative justice would be to elevate the role of victims and victim involvement. Although "victims' rights" has become the rallying cry of many politicians and prosecutors, victims' *needs* are not a major concern of retributive justice (Elias, 1993; Zehr, 1990, 2002). Rather, the concerns and interests of prosecutors, judges, defense attorneys, and rehabilitation programs (e.g., in winning cases, processing offenders, or securing clients) all appear to take precedence over the needs of victims (Messmer & Otto, 1992; Wright, 1991). Restorative juvenile justice would thus devote primary attention to the needs of victims—to have their victimization acknowledged, to be allowed to participate in the justice process, and to be given a decision-making role within this process.

## Performance Objectives

Currently, success in juvenile court sanctioning seems to be measured by how much punishment is inflicted (and, to a lesser extent, how much treatment is provided). In contrast, performance objectives for the goal of restorative accountability are driven by the needs of victims for material and emotional restoration and involvement and, simultaneously, the need for offenders to understand the consequences of their actions and actively make amends for the harm done (see Table 19.3, row 2). Because the denunciation of inappropriate behavior is an important function of any justice system, the symbolic message sent by sanctions is also of critical importance (Davis, 1992; Garland, 1990). Performance objectives of restorative sanctioning would take account of the extent to which offenders, victims, and the community understand the purpose and intent of juvenile court sanctions. Table 19.4 contrasts the implicit messages relayed to these customers of the system by treatment, punishment, and restorative sanctions.

### Priorities for Practice

In contrast to the tendency of retributive justice to rely primarily on incarceration and other restrictions to punish offenders, restorative sanctioning would give first priority to practices that promote reparation and victim involvement. Row 3 of Table 19.3 lists programs and practices consistent with restorative goals and values. Restitution, community service, victim impact panels, victim–offender mediation (Schneider, 1985; Umbreit, 1994a; Umbreit & Coates, 1993; Umbreit, Coates, & Vos, 2000), and similar practices are aimed at link-

**Table 19.4**     **The "Messages" of Sanctions**

|  | Individual | Retributive | Restorative |
|---|---|---|---|
| Offender | You are "sick" or disturbed and your behavior is not your fault. We will provide treatment or services in your best interest. | You are a bad person who willfully chose to commit an offense. We will punish you with swiftness and severity to deter you from future offending. | Your actions have consequences; you have wronged someone or the community through your offense. You are responsible for your crime and capable of restoring the victim or repaying the damages. |
| Victim | Our only concern is the needs of the offender. | Our first concern is to make offenders suffer the consequences of their crime. | The juvenile justice system believes you are important and will do its best to ensure that to the degree possible the offender repays the victims and the public for their crimes. |
| Community | We will do our best to rehabilitate offenders through providing appropriate treatment and services. Highly trained professionals will solve the problem—leave it to us. | We will protect you by isolating offenders from the community and will send a message through severe punishment to would-be offenders that crime will not be tolerated. Threats are the best way to control behavior. | We need the help of the community. The community is a key player in holding offenders accountable. |

ing the sanction directly to the crime and the victim (both individual and community) and are meant to ensure that offenders take action toward making amends. These now familiar sanctions can in addition be given a more "victim-driven" (and thus more restorative) focus by allowing for direct victim input. Victims may therefore be asked, for example, to provide input into community service or personal service requirements for offenders, as well as into restitution agreements (Bazemore & Maloney, 1994; Umbreit, 1994a).

## Rehabilitating Offenders: Competency Development in a Balanced and Restorative Model

In the balanced approach, the traditional individual treatment agenda is replaced by a broader emphasis on the goal of competency development, which requires that offenders "exit the system more capable of being productive and responsible in the community" (Maloney et al., 1988). Competency development in the balanced approach emphasizes the need for a broader concern with maturational development, especially by means of acquiring the survival skills required for daily living.

### Values and Assumptions

While individual treatment is based on an assumption of the need to identify deficits and dysfunctions and to provide remedial help, the more preventive and proactive competency development intervention strategy focuses first on identifying individual, family, and community strengths (e.g., Lofquist, 1983). Family members and other conventional adults in the offender's community are viewed as essential resources in this process and would be engaged in efforts to increase offender competency, as well as in efforts to ensure accountability and public safety.

Essentially, the traditional treatment model encourages a view of young offenders as incapable of positive, productive behavior until the offenders' personal and interpersonal problems are judged to be solved through participation in therapeutic or remedial interventions (Pittman & Fleming, 1991).[4] A competency development approach, on the other hand, assumes that most offenders with the right supervision and support can begin immediate involvement in some productive activity (see Table 19.5). Viewing competency as "the capacity to do something well that others value" (Polk & Kobrin, 1972), advocates of a competency development strategy would encourage offenders' ability to be productive and effective in activities that are viewed as important by conventional groups in their own communities and in the larger society. A competency development approach would also address needed changes in the capacity of those community groups and agencies to accommodate diversity, reintegrate offenders, and build on emerging offender strengths, and it should attempt to build family skills and resources.

**Table 19.5    Rehabilitative Intervention: Competency Development Versus Individual Treatment**

|  | Current System | Balanced and Restorative |
|---|---|---|
| Values and assumptions | Primary and initial focus on identifying deficits and on developing ameliorative approaches to correct problems; delinquents defined as in need of services, assumed incompetent, disturbed and incapable of productive, rational action without remedial therapeutic intervention; most offenders need individual adult treatment and benefit from therapeutic interventions. | Primary and initial focus on identifying strengths and building on the positive; youths and families viewed as resources; youths assumed competent and having capacity for positive action; preventive and proactive; emphasis on change in community institutions and adult behavior; offenders learn best by doing; counseling and therapy needed on a limited basis as support for active engagement. |
| Performance objectives | Avoid negative influence of designated people, places, and activities; follow rules of supervision (e.g., curfew, school attendance); attend and participate in treatment activities (e.g., counseling); complete all required treatment and terminate supervision; improvements in attitude and self-concept; psychological adjustment; improved family interaction. | Begin new, positive relationships and positive behavior in conventional roles; avoid placement of youths in stigmatizing treatments; practice competent, conventional behavior; active demonstration of competency through completion of productive activity (service and/or work with community benefit); significant increase in measurable competencies (academic, social, occupational, etc.); improvements in self-image and public image (community acceptance) and increased bonding. |
| Priorities for Practice | Group and family counseling; casework probation; drug therapy and drug education; recreational activities; outdoor challenge programs; mentoring programs; remedial education. | Work experience and employment; youths as drug educators/researchers; youths as recreational aides; youths develop cultural education projects; youths as mediators; recycling and community beautification projects; intergenerational service projects with the elderly; cross-age tutoring (juvenile offenders teach younger children); peer counseling; anger management and decision-making skills training; cognitive restructuring; family living skills. |

## Performance Objectives

Contrary to the treatment model, the primary and initial change sought in the offender in a competency development approach is increased bonding to conventional groups and increased acceptance by these groups and the community generally. Although improvements in self-image are viewed as an important change in the offender, visible participation in productive activity is needed to bring about change in the offender's "public image" (Bazemore, 1991; Polk & Kobrin, 1972). Such improvement in the community's perception of the offender is ultimately needed for effective reintegration, and it requires increasing the offender's ability to function as a productive, responsible citizen.

Many traditional treatment and service interventions (e.g., drug abuse counseling, family crisis intervention) provide valuable support and needed assistance to offenders and would be incorporated into a comprehensive rehabilitative agenda based on competency development. However, unless competency development interventions are given priority, quasi-therapeutic treatment and service programs will continue to consume the majority of staff time and juvenile justice resources (Lofquist, 1983; Pittman & Fleming, 1991).

## Priorities for Practice

Treatment casework typically fails to actively engage young offenders in valued, productive activities. While treatment interventions tend to keep offenders in passive roles as recipients of treatment or services, competency development interventions attempt to engage youths in productive activity with some potential direct benefit to others—which also provides opportunities for them to increase their own skills (Bazemore, 1993). Practices like those listed in Table 19.5 (row 3, column 2), such as work experience, active learning, and creative community service (Bazemore & Maloney, 1994), provide opportunities for skill building, positive interaction between youths and conventional adults, potential for earning money, and a chance for delinquent youths to demonstrate publicly that they are also capable of competent and productive behavior. To develop a legitimate identity, youths must gain a sense that they are useful, that they belong to their community and conventional groups within it, that they are competent and can make meaningful contributions, and that they have some power over what happens to them (Polk & Kobrin, 1972). By allowing offenders to "practice" being competent in new roles, these active and productive competency-building experiences may also change the public image of offenders from liability to resource (Bazemore & Maloney, 1994). In addition, as Table 19.5 suggests, intervention practices and programs such as cognitive restructuring, decision-making skill training, and anger management are needed to reinforce behavioral, experiential programs with efforts to build cognitive skills (e.g., Goldstein & Huff, 1992; also see Table 19.5, row 3, column 2). Delinquent youths involved in competency development interventions could also receive counseling or other treatment and remedial services as needed to address personal and interpersonal problems, but, contrary to the treatment model, these services would be provided as *support* for involvement in productive activity rather than as an end in themselves (Bazemore, 1991).

## Enhancing Public Safety: Community Protection in a Balanced and Restorative Model

Traditionally, juvenile justice professionals have been unable to articulate a clear role for the juvenile justice system in enhancing public safety. As a result, the system has often reacted to public demands for protection by using the limited and expensive strategy of incarcerating individual offenders. As the community policing movement is demonstrating, however, a focus on individual offenders alone is inadequate as a strategy to control and prevent crime and protect the public (e.g., Sparrow, Moore, & Kennedy, 1990). From this perspective, attempting to achieve public safety objectives by incarcerating offenders or by "treating" them through individual casework approaches is equivalent to attempting to "fight cancer with surgery" (Sherman, 1983). Just as community policing has moved from a focus on responding to "incidents" by arrests to broader preventative strategies, the balanced and restorative justice model provides a challenge to juvenile justice managers to define community protection more holistically, to include structuring the offender's time in the community, developing a continuum of sanctions and incentives (Maloney et al., 1988), and building the preventive capacity of community institutions. Protecting the community in a balanced and restorative justice system would thus have both an internal focus on strengthening controls in individual offenders and an external community focus. The community focus would emphasize both prevention and risk management and would target adults and adult institutions, as well as juvenile offenders, for intervention (Lofquist, 1983; Pittman & Fleming, 1991).

### Values and Assumptions

Current extensive use of secure confinement for juvenile offenders often confuses risk management and punishment objectives (Klein, 1993). Although all offenders who disobey court orders or commit crimes deserve sanctions or consequences, only a small portion represent risks to public safety (e.g., Irwin & Austin, 1993). In a balanced and restorative model, a central value guiding the commitment to the community as "client" is that no youths will be released from supervision without juvenile justice professionals doing everything within their power to minimize risks that the offender may pose to citizen safety (Klein, 1993). For some offenders, ensuring public safety will almost inevitably mean reliance on residential confinement for some period of time. For most, however, it will mean that intensive efforts should be made to develop alternative systems to ensure that offenders can be managed safely in their communities. Because youths on community supervision (probation and parole) represent the most immediate risk to public safety presented by known offenders, a balanced approach to community protection would require an increase in resources designated to ensuring strengthened supervision for offenders on probation and those exiting residential programs.

## Performance Objectives

A balanced approach to community protection would demand that public safety goals must not be achieved at the expense of meeting competency development and restorative accountability objectives; on the contrary, achieving the latter goals should enhance public safety. Active involvement in competency-building activities and in reparative processes also protects the public by structuring an offender's time in productive activities while providing direct benefit to offenders and victims and helping to strengthen the offender's internal controls and community bonds (Bazemore & Maloney, 1994). Implementing these practices and achieving these goals are much more difficult in secure residential settings. Thus, offenders who do not present objective risks to public safety should be kept in the community whenever possible, with increased resources invested in ensuring community safety. Preventive public safety objectives also include increasing the capacity of local neighborhoods to supervise youthful offenders and prevent delinquency while improving general feelings of safety and well-being among citizens (see Table 19.6) (Bazemore & Schiff, 1996).

## Priorities for Practice

A balanced and restorative perspective also gives priority to these capacity-building efforts in communities and neighborhood institutions (e.g., schools, housing projects) and emphasizes the need to strengthen internal controls in delinquent youths, as well as external controls in communities. As Table 19.6 suggests, a balanced system for community protection rests on four kinds of practices and policies: a continuum of sanctions, incentives, and consequences; an ongoing effort to ensure that the offender's time is structured around productive activity; an ongoing effort to build community capacity for prevention and guardianship; and residential confinement for high-risk offenders, followed by balanced, intensive aftercare (Armstrong & Altschuler, 1991; Maloney et al., 1988). Ultimately, because the restorative paradigm is based on a view of justice as resolving conflict and reconciling conflicting interests that lead to crime, practices such as alternative dispute resolution directed through schools, religious groups, and other community agencies would be expanded and supported (Umbreit, 1998). Using community guardians to assist parents in completing restorative requirements and to monitor youths under court supervision has also been tried successfully in some jurisdictions.

An immediate challenge for jurisdictions wishing to implement a balanced approach to community protection is to develop a progressive response system (Armstrong, Maloney, & Romig, 1990) that specifies the range of sanctions and risk management requirements appropriate to offenders based on objective risk assessment. Such a system would also clearly articulate a range of preferred, intermediate consequences for failure to comply with conditions of supervision as part of a "progressive" response system (Armstrong et al., 1990).

**Table 19.6**    **Public Safety in the Current System and in a Balanced and Restorative Justice System**

| | Current System | Balanced and Restorative System |
|---|---|---|
| Values and Assumptions | Public safety requires extensive investment in and use of locked facilities; in the community, intensive surveillance and monitoring are the best strategies to protect the public. Community-based risk management viewed as ineffective for most offenders. | Public safety is best achieved by collaborative efforts of justice systems and community groups to develop preventive capacity. Incarceration is a limited, expensive, and a "last resort" solution for most offenders; structuring the offenders time and providing a clear continuum of sanctions and incentives provide the best approach. The public has a right to a safe and secure community. The community has a responsibility to actively promote healing and restoration. |
| Performance objectives | Number of offenders incarcerated and detained; reduced recidivism through deterrence or threat of incarceration. | Reduced recidivism, especially while offenders are under supervision in the community; increase in citizen feelings of safety and confidence in the juvenile justice system; creation of community "guardians" and improved preventive capacity of schools, families, and community agencies; increase in offender bonding and reintegration; direct involvement of community members. |
| Priorities for practice | Extensive use of detention; incarceration; electronic monitoring and surveillance. Absence of intermediate consequences for violation of community supervision; little collaboration or effort to build community prevention; resources invested in facilities versus community safety. | Intensive structuring of offender's time and opportunities for bonding through participation in productive activities involving conventional adults (e.g., work experiences, alternative service); clear policy options for consequences for noncompliance with supervision requirements and incentives for compliance; engage community "guardians" in the process; collaborate with community policing units; school prevention programs such as conflict resolution, mediation, and anger management; parent training and parent child mediation; incarceration for offenders who represent risk to community safety with intensive aftercare; use of volunteer community members. |

Next, preventing recidivism while the offender is on community supervision should begin with a strategic focus on free time, or hours available for involvement in crime, and an effort to impose structure on the offender's time by requiring involvement in productive activity (Klein, 1993). Practices used to accomplish reparative or accountability objectives (e.g., community service) and competency development objectives (e.g., work experience programs) can also reinforce public safety objectives by providing additional means for structuring an offender's time in group activities. Ultimately, as advocates of community policing are demonstrating (Sparrow, Moore, & Kennedy, 1990), new strategies are needed to begin to increase the capacity of community institutions to prevent crime and reintegrate offenders, as well as to challenge the narrow view of community protection that focuses on individual offenders.

# ■ Moving Toward a Balanced and Restorative Model

The balanced and restorative justice model is a holistic approach in which policy and practice simultaneously address the interests of three clients through a balanced allocation of resources. Although the mandate to serve three clients rather than one will provide a challenge to juvenile justice systems that have maintained a one-dimensional focus on the offender, the model assumes that significant long-term offender change is in any case unlikely to occur without the involvement of victims and the community. Because making amends to victims is viewed as a first step in the meaningful rehabilitation (see Table 19.6) and reintegration of offenders (Braithwaite, 1989; Eglash, 1975), meeting rehabilitative objectives is also contingent on meeting reparative obligations and cannot be achieved without the involvement of victims, community, and offenders. Likewise, community protection that does not also engage the community and victims as well as offenders is at best limited to efforts to incapacitate and manage risk presented by known individual lawbreakers. Finally, sanctioning that is not focused on accountability to victims and does not involve victims and communities in the process is likely to be primarily punitive in its focus.

Most juvenile justice systems, though influenced predominantly by retributive justice philosophy and the individual treatment mission, contain some elements of policy and practice that meet restorative objectives. Practices such as restitution, victim offender mediation, and meaningful community service are the building blocks upon which further restorative practices can be developed. In addition, it is now possible to point to emerging programmatic examples that provide potential models for the kind of system reform implied by the balanced and restorative justice model (e.g., Bazemore, 1991; Bazemore & Maloney, 1994; Schneider, 1985; Umbreit, 1994a). The best intervention practices and programs accomplish the overall goals in a way that reconciles the interests and meets the mutual needs of victims, community, and offender by simultaneously addressing sanctioning, rehabilitation, and public safety goals (see examples in appendix A of this chapter).

Unfortunately, despite the potential of these interventions, there are dangers in a primary reliance on innovative programs and practices as the basis for reform. Programmatic or "program-driven" reform often fails to consider the fit between new programs and the existing values, policies, and bureaucratic constraints of criminal justice agencies (McShane & Williams, 1992), and it may confuse systemic reform with one practice or program (e.g., victim offender mediation). Such programs may quickly become marginalized, having little impact on business as usual in juvenile justice, and restorative sanctions may simply be used as punitive or therapeutic "add-ons" in systems that retain a primary emphasis on retribution and individual treatment (Bazemore & Maloney, 1994; Shapiro, 1990).

An effective implementation strategy must therefore quickly begin to address fundamental issues of management and organizational priorities that determine resource allocation, job descriptions, and performance measures (Umbreit & Carey, in press) while also building on the more comprehensive restorative programs in order to "pilot" practices and policies as models for entire systems (Bazemore & Umbreit, 1995). One of the first steps in this process is to begin a critical examination of the traditional roles and responsibilities of staff, offender, victim, and community in the justice process.

## The Challenge of Changing Roles

In most juvenile justice systems today, the task of addressing sanctioning, public safety, and rehabilitative goals is left to professionals; offenders, victims, and citizens remain on the sideline as spectators or passive participants. Juvenile justice caseworkers, for example, are responsible for providing treatment and services, judges and prosecutors determine appropriate punishment, and law enforcement, with the assistance of juvenile justice staff who provide control over offenders in secure settings and surveillance in community settings, are given primary responsibility for public safety. Neither the retributive justice framework nor the individual treatment mission has allowed policy makers to articulate meaningful, active roles for the community, victims, and offenders in the process. As Table 19.7 suggests, balanced and restorative justice defines new roles for each in sanctioning, rehabilitation, and enhancing public safety.

### Restorative Sanctioning Roles

Because balanced and restorative justice assumes that sanctions ultimately derive their meaning, fairness, and effectiveness from the involvement of victims and the community, these parties are encouraged to actively participate in the sanctioning process. Juvenile court judges have traditionally been leaders in the juvenile court and have been assigned primary responsibility for sanctioning juvenile offenders. Judges will continue to play leadership roles in the movement toward the new sanctioning approach and must be involved in developing creative new mechanisms for allowing meaningful victim and community input without jeopardizing the rights of offenders. Table 19.7 lists possible roles for professionals and juvenile justice customer–clients in the sanctioning process.

### Competency Development Roles

Although it is the community—with institutions such as schools and employers—that must allow for and facilitate the reintegrative process necessary for rehabilitation, treatment interventions focus almost exclusively on changing

**Table 19.7    New Roles in the Balanced and Restorative Justice Model**

| Customer | Sanctioning Through Accountability | Rehabilitation Through Competency Development | Enhancing Public Safety |
|---|---|---|---|
| Offender | Actively work to restore loss to victims and community and face victims or surrogate victims. | Actively involved as resource in service roles, which improve quality of life in community and provide new experiences, skills, and self-esteem as productive resources for positive action. | Become involved in constructive competency building and restorative activities in a balanced program; develop internal controls and new peer and organizational commitments. |
| Victim | Active involvement in all stages of the process; document psychological and emotional impact of crime; participate in mediation on a voluntary basis; help determine sanction for offender. | Provide input into the rehabilitative process; suggest community service options for offender. | Provide input regarding continuing safety concerns, fear, and needed controls on offenders; encourage protective support for other victims. |
| Community | Involved as mediators; develop community service and paid work opportunities for offenders with reparative obligations; assist victims and support offenders in completing obligations. | Develop new opportunities for youth to make productive contributions; build competency and a sense of belonging. | Provide "guardianship" of offenders, mentoring, and input to juvenile justice systems regarding safety concerns; address underlying community problems that contribute to delinquency. |
| Juvenile justice professional | Facilitate mediation; ensure that restoration occurs (by providing ways for offenders to earn funds for restitution); develop creative/restorative community service options; engage community members in the process; educate community on its role. | Develop new roles for young offenders that allow them to practice and demonstrate competency; assess and build on youth and community strengths; develop community partnerships. | Develop range of incentives and consequences to ensure offender compliance with supervision objectives; assist school and family in their efforts to control and maintain offenders in the community; develop prevention capacity of local organizations. |

the behavior of individual youths. In so doing, these interventions ignore the need for change in institutions and adult behaviors that limit reintegration and bonding of delinquent youths. A balanced, competency development approach would require that offenders, community members, and victims play active roles in the reintegrative process and that each of these groups also become *targets* of service and intervention. The role of the juvenile justice professional in this process is to create opportunities for youths to demonstrate competence and to build the preventive capacity of families and the community "socializing" institutions—schools, places of work, civic organizations, and churches—that are ultimately responsible for the conventional transition of youths into productive citizens. The role of the community is to provide juveniles with access to roles and activities that allow them to practice and demonstrate competent behavior and to support offenders in reintegrative efforts to ensure the positive development of youths. In the process, juvenile justice systems that put forward clear, objective, and consensus-based performance outcomes based on offender competency development objectives may change their organizational image from one of "tax liability" to one of "community asset."

### Community Protection Roles

A priority for juvenile justice practice aimed at enhancing public safety in the balanced and restorative model is to collaborate with and assist other community agencies. An equally important commitment is that the juvenile justice system should be a general resource for promoting more secure, stable, and capable communities and community organizations rather than simply a repository for warehousing youthful offenders or a social work agency concerned with casework treatment. Table 19.7 also suggests new active roles for offenders, victims, and the community in a balanced focus on public safety.

## The Implementation Process: Guidelines for Changing Focus

The first step in the change process is to develop a vision of where the system should be; the second step is to determine where the system is now in terms of policy and practice consistent with the model. By building on existing practices that fit the model, changes can be made that gradually move juvenile justice systems and agencies away from retributive priorities and toward the restorative end of the justice continuum. The assessment process begins by examining the quality and effectiveness of current practices under each balanced and restorative justice goal: (a) To what extent is the system effective in restoring victims, producing more competent offenders, and enhancing public safety; (b) to what extent are policies and practices consistent with the values of restorative justice; (c) what gaps exist in current programming, and what programs are redundant or inconsistent with the new goals and values; (d) and to what extent are community groups and crime victims involved in the juvenile justice system? Zehr's "Restorative Justice Yardstick" (see appendix B of this chapter) provides vital benchmarks for this assessment of consistency with restorative justice goals.

### Managing Change

The complexity of juvenile justice requires that reform efforts be carefully planned and deliberate and include input from staff as well as all other stakeholders in the system and the community. The balanced and restorative justice model is not a "program." It is a framework to guide every decision and action in the system. Truly balanced systems based on restorative values cannot be constructed overnight, and they cannot be achieved through mandates. Implementing a balanced and restorative justice model should be viewed as a continuous process of strategic improvement in local juvenile justice that engages all of those who are affected by juvenile crime. Although the goals and values of the model are constant, there is no single recipe for operationalizing balanced and restorative justice principles. Thus, each community may find a different way to achieve the goals. The following guidelines will improve prospects for success in implementing the model.[5]

1. Start small. Starting small allows for better management of reform efforts that in fact go against traditional policy and practice. Juvenile justice managers should think in terms of small, well-run, and successful demonstration or pilot projects that can lead to ever-widening system and community efforts.

2. Pick institutional targets and community projects with the potential for wider expansion and ongoing operation. In choosing a pilot project, select programs or probation units that are well managed and neighborhoods where there is a base of support for new approaches. Design projects such as "high-demand" service activities, which, when supported by credible community employers and civic organizations (e.g., the Chamber of Commerce, Kiwanis), have a higher probability of more or less permanent adoption and institutionalization. To ensure that a demonstration effort to build up the competency development capacity of the juvenile justice system, for example, is not viewed as a "one-shot" special project rather than a model for institutional change, include schools and employers as partners and try to have an impact on programs and practices that block reentry of delinquent youths into educational and career ladders.

3. Develop an internal steering committee to set goals and monitor progress. This should be a small management team well acquainted with and committed to the balanced and restorative justice model. Its charge should be to document the "current state" of system investment in balanced and restorative policies and practices, to determine the scope and quality of those policies and practices, and to develop short- and long-term benchmarks and "action steps" for program development, policy reform, and value and cultural change consistent with the reform. The primary goal of the steering committee is to ensure the success of initial pilot efforts and to promote strategic expansion. This group should be involved in the initial diagnostic process and in ongoing assessment to ensure that existing programs and practices are incorporating the principles and values of the new philosophy and mission *and* that no new programs are added that are inconsistent with or do not meet the objectives of the mission.

4. Engage juvenile justice staff and decision makers in values clarification, consensus building, assessment, and goal definition. Although the goals and objectives of the balanced and restorative justice model appeal to

common values, terms such as *accountability* and *community protection* can be interpreted in many different ways. Juvenile justice managers and the steering committee must take the time to present the model to other key decision makers (e.g., judges, prosecutors) as an *alternative* to the current retributive philosophy and individual treatment mission and must begin the effort to build consensus around core underlying values. From these initial efforts, leaders can seek support for new pilot initiatives to demonstrate the effectiveness of the model.

5 Identify at least one victim advocacy organization and/or several individual victims of juvenile crime who can become active sponsors and partners in the overall effort to implement a balanced and restorative justice model. The presence of victims in the overall project is vital precisely because victims are so removed and absent from the current offender-driven juvenile justice system. Victims will also be important partners and political allies in the reform process and will provide meaningful input into the development of rehabilitative and public safety policies and practices, as well as sanctioning processes aimed at restoration.

6 Cultivate ownership and sponsorship of specific projects by conventional community institutions such as employers, victims' groups, and civic organizations. To ensure that projects and activities will be viewed as meaningful, ask these sponsors for ideas about projects important to them. Avoid the standard juvenile justice coalitions limited to directors of agencies focused on youths "with problems." Seek commitment from organizations with clout that can influence conventional growth and development of youths (e.g., through work, education) rather than treatment organizations (e.g., mental health, drug abuse) and service providers. Cultivate victims and members of victim support groups as leaders and spokespersons for restorative approaches. Involve these groups in a community advisory board.

7 In all pilot efforts and planning groups, ensure cultural diversity and focus on having an impact on minority overrepresentation and racial discrimination in juvenile justice. To do this, make sure indigenous minority organizations—businesses and business groups, churches, civic and fraternal organizations—are involved and asked to assume leadership and advocacy roles from the beginning. Whenever possible, select service and action projects that result in improvements in offenders' and victims' own neighborhoods.

8 Build on the power of the group. Group activities and projects allow for peer and adult support and involvement with adolescents in the juvenile justice system. Group projects also enhance youths' skills in working with others.

9 Focus on projects that mix youths and adults, including the elderly. Arrange for service, victim awareness, mediation, work, and leadership projects that allow young people and adults to work together on common problems and solutions (e.g., neighborhood crime prevention,

problems of crime victims). Such projects create a context and provide structure for "mentoring" relationships, help to break down the isolation of youths from the real world of work and politics, and provide positive demonstrations of clear alternatives to individual casework with offenders. Whenever possible, try to include nondelinquent youths, including college students, in positive service and other group projects in order to decrease the stigma associated with these activities as projects for "bad kids" and to provide for positive peer and adult support.

## Sustaining Reform and Using the Mission

The implementation process should be viewed as part of a continual cycle of improvement in achieving system balance and promoting restorative values. The ongoing cycle should generally move from local piloting of the new model to state, regional, and national dissemination and expansion, and then back to additional local piloting and development. Thus, once jurisdictions have begun the initial tasks of education, consensus building, and values clarification, have developed the steering committee, and have established procedures for monitoring progress as discussed previously, the following steps are suggested as a guide to piloting the model: (a) Discuss priorities for practice and policy needed to achieve balanced approach objectives; (b) design and implement a pilot effort to demonstrate how the various components of the approach work together in one part of the system and/or one local community; (c) assign staff roles in the pilot and begin the infrastructure development process, including articulation of new roles for staff and management protocols consistent with the objectives of the model; (d) develop a plan for and begin the reallocation of existing resources and acquisition of new resources; (e) establish action steps based on the assessment of the current policy and goals for policy and programmatic change; and (f) identify training and technical assistance needs linked to each task, focusing first on the pilot or demonstration effort. Appendix C of this chapter provides some additional suggestions about policy and procedural changes that may be needed to facilitate changes implied by balanced and restorative principles.

At the most general level, what is needed in jurisdictions implementing the model is to begin using the mission *actively* on a daily basis. To accomplish significant reform, the balanced and restorative justice model must be understood first as a tool for strategic planning rather than as a new service or program. The policies and practices that grow out of the new mission and framework should generally replace, rather than add to, many existing practices and policies and thus should not add new costs to most juvenile justice systems.

## "Seeds" of Balanced and Restorative Justice Systems

As an emerging new paradigm, balanced and restorative justice will not provide complete solutions to all complex problems facing juvenile justice professionals and policy makers. While juvenile justice systems have demonstrated the potential of restorative programs and research studies have yielded promising empirical results[6] (e.g., Butts & Snyder, 1991; Schneider, 1985, 1986; Umbreit & Coates, 1993), the policy, programs, and practices of restorative justice remain marginalized in most of the country today, and few juvenile justice systems have adopted these as prototypes for systemic reform. However, some juvenile justice managers and their staffs are accepting the challenges of the new model to move toward balance in meeting the needs of victim, offender, and community. These professionals, including several involved in demonstration efforts in local juvenile justice systems in five states, have in recent months begun a long-term process of "reinventing" or restructuring their systems based on the balanced mission and the restorative justice framework. As pilot sites in a national action research project funded by the Office of Juvenile Justice and Delinquency Prevention to implement the balanced and restorative justice model (Bazemore & Umbreit, 1995), local jurisdictions in Oregon, Texas, Florida, Pennsylvania, and Minnesota are using the mission and framework as a guide to strategic planning while initiating pilot programs that demonstrate the principles of the model on a small scale. Although at different stages in their implementation of balanced and restorative practices, each jurisdiction has unique strengths and highlights one or more model policy, program, or process components that promise to point the way toward the systemic change that is their common goal.

Three counties in Oregon (Lane, Deschutes, and Multnomah), for example, which had each adopted the balanced approach mission several years ago and quickly developed model work experience and service components (Bazemore & Maloney, 1994) as well as cognitive skill training curricula for offenders on probation, recently realized that their implementation of the mission lacked a focus on victim input and involvement and required that greater priority be given to completion of reparative sanctions orders. Similarly, Travis County (Austin), Texas, had earlier adopted the mission but recently realized that their juvenile justice system had become "program-driven" and had lost sight of the relevance of programs and practices to larger system goals; management and staff are currently attempting to breathe new life into the mission and using it to scrutinize current practices with an eye to improving victim involvement.

Three jurisdictions new to the model (and receiving more intensive assistance from the project) are building on strengths inherent in their local communities and juvenile justice agencies while also developing components that had been missing or marginally operational. Dakota County, Minnesota, for example, is using the mission and restorative values to restructure management decision-making processes and to revitalize and give greater priority to practices that have been used effectively for a number of years (e.g., community service). Palm Beach County, Florida, has recently implemented a local residential program (which is based on balanced and restorative principles) for some of the most serious offenders in the system (see appendix A of this chapter), and Allegheny County (Pittsburgh), Pennsylvania, is building on the neighborhood focus of its Community Intensive Supervision Project (CISP) to "model" restorative practices for the system as a whole.

## Conclusion

The history of justice reforms in the United States has been one of pendulum swings between an emphasis on punishment and an emphasis on treatment. Similarly, public policy and discourse seem to fluctuate between "It's all society's fault" and "It's all the individual's fault." The public and professionals are increasingly frustrated with such false choices between simplistic options that do not reflect the reality of our life experiences. The balanced and restorative justice model addresses both individual and community responsibility by focusing on repair of harm and requiring that both contribute to that repair.

The current dominance of the retributive model in juvenile justice and an increasingly punitive national climate may make the vision of a balanced and restorative justice model seem distant, even unattainable. However, in the crisis surrounding juvenile justice systems today, apparently utopian visions may be needed to sustain the motivation of those hoping to preserve and also reform a distinctive justice system for juvenile offenders. In this regard, Belgian criminologist Lode Walgrave's comment that, in the case of restorative justice, "there is nothing so *practical* as a good Utopia" seems especially germane (Walgrave, 1993). In fact, all of us can make practical changes within our span of control to move toward the balanced and restorative end of the justice continuum. Small changes in daily work make a big difference. Every community member and every professional who is moved by the vision will be able to find some piece to contribute toward a new juvenile justice. "This [restorative] vision of justice isn't just about saving money or averting prison construction—and it's certainly not about being soft on crime. It's about making things right instead of lamenting what's wrong, cultivating strength rather than perpetuating failure" (*Minneapolis Star Tribune*, 1993).

## Appendix A: Restorative Justice in Action: Programmatic Examples

### Juvenile Reparation Program, Center for Community Justice, Elkhart, Indiana

The Juvenile Reparation Program (JPR) targets older juveniles who may have previously failed in the system and risk continuing their negative behavior into adulthood. The accountability and responsibility of the participants includes understanding and acknowledging the harm, accepting responsibility by finding a solution, and taking concrete actions to make it right. JRP staff assist clients in developing a contract, which routinely includes restitution to the victim, volunteer service as symbolic restitution to the community, and specific self-improvement strategies; it may also include face-to-face mediation. Throughout their involvement with JRP, clients are restricted to their homes except when attending approved activities such as school, employment, or counseling. Volunteer telephone monitors ensure that clients follow these rules, as well as providing added encouragement and accountability.

### Crime Repair Service Crews

In these projects, currently being implemented as community service alternatives for juveniles who have either been diverted from court or assigned to probation service interventions, young offenders confront the real harm to the quality of life of citizens that results from household burglaries. Crews in these programs work with adult supervisors to repair windows, doors, and other damage to the homes of elderly persons victimized by break-ins. Service and accountability are combined with positive learning and some competency development, in an intervention that has the potential for direct positive impact on citizens' feelings of safety.

### The South Florida Youth Environmental Service

This recently opened residential program for serious juvenile offenders, operated by the juvenile justice system in Palm Beach County, Florida, is a holistic attempt to address simultaneously the three primary objectives and the three customers of a restorative correctional intervention. Located in a wildlife preserve surrounded by water and swampland in a national park in the Florida Everglades, this program addresses public safety objectives through the physical and staff security of the program. Public safety in the postprogram phase is addressed by preventive efforts to continue programmatic activities once these youths return to their home communities. The core program is centered around paid work experience, as well as unpaid community service, in which young offenders work with national park staff in maintenance and restoration of portions of the Loxahatchee wildlife preserve. Educational curricula emphasizing environmental preservation and environmental career exploration are incorporated around this competency-building experience. Accountability to victims is addressed by direct payments deducted from offender paychecks (or payment into a victims' fund when original victims cannot be located), and the program is beginning to incorporate victim awareness classes and victim panels.

Finally, in articulating such untraditional performance objectives as measurable improvement in plant growth, ecological diversity, and better public access to Loxahatchee National Wildlife Refuge, program administrators exemplify the broader emphasis of restorative justice on achieving community-oriented objectives. Such objectives go beyond those directed at individual offenders and operationalize the broader goals of restoring victims, restoring offenders, and restoring the community.

## The Eastern Oregon Homeless Project and Abuse Shelter Coalition

These two projects of the Deschutes County, Oregon, Department of Community Corrections are examples of an ongoing effort by the agency director to expand on the "corrections as a resource" theme by utilizing adult and juvenile probationers and parolees to accomplish a variety of human services and public works tasks. In these projects, which the director has described as examples of "community service on its highest plane," young offenders have worked with volunteer builders and carpenters to construct a homeless shelter (after raising money for materials) and a domestic abuse crisis center. Offenders completed community service hours in a way that provided an important long-term benefit to their community, taught them lessons about the needs of other citizens (including those victimized by violent abuse), provided an opportunity for skill development and positive interaction with conventional adults, and ensured that offenders' time on community supervision was occupied for significant portions of the day and evening.

## Bridging the Present to the Future: Family Group Conferences

In these conferences, based on the traditions of the Maori people of New Zealand, the victim and his or her supporters are given the opportunity to speak of how they have been affected by the crime and to condemn the behavior of young offenders. The offender, his or her family or community surrogates, a trained mediator, and the victim then participate in designing appropriate ways for the offender to repair the harm and make amends to the victim and the community.

## Appendix B: A Restorative Justice Yardstick

I Do victims experience justice?

- ☐ Are there sufficient opportunities for them to tell their truth to relevant listeners?
- ☐ Are they receiving needed compensation or restitution?
- ☐ Is the injustice adequately acknowledged?
- ☐ Are they sufficiently protected against further violation?
- ☐ Does the outcome adequately reflect the severity of the offense?
- ☐ Are they receiving adequate information about the event, the offender, and the process?
- ☐ Do they have a voice in the process?
- ☐ Is the experience of justice adequately public?

☐ Do they have adequate support from others?

☐ Are their families receiving adequate assistance and support?

☐ Are other needs—material, psychological, spiritual—being addressed?

**2** Do offenders experience justice?

☐ Are they encouraged to understand and take responsibility for what they have done?

☐ Are misattributions challenged?

☐ Are they provided encouragement and opportunity to make things right?

☐ Are they given the opportunity to participate in the process?

☐ Is there encouragement toward changed behavior (repentance)?

☐ Is there a mechanism for monitoring or verifying changes?

☐ Are their own needs being addressed?

☐ Are their families receiving support and assistance?

**3** Is the victim–offender relationship addressed?

☐ Is there opportunity for a meeting, if appropriate—either direct or therapeutic?

☐ Is there opportunity and encouragement for an exchange of information—about the event, about one another?

☐ Are misattributions being challenged?

**4** Are community concerns being taken into account?

☐ Are the process and outcome sufficiently public?

☐ Is community protection being addressed?

☐ Is there need for some restitution or symbolic action for the community?

☐ Is the community represented in some way in the process?

**5** Is the future being addressed?

☐ Is there provision for solving the problems that led up to this event?

☐ Is there provision for solving problems caused by this event?

☐ Have future intentions been addressed?

☐ Is there provision for monitoring, verifying, and troubleshooting outcomes? (Zehr, 1990)

## Appendix C: Restorative Justice Principles in Action: Implications for Systematic Change

Sample policy and procedure changes:

☐ Development of new mission and goals based on restorative values and the balanced approach mission

☐ Reallocation of resources to achieve new goals

- ☐ Redesign of job descriptions to prioritize restorative task
- ☐ Creation of community advisory boards to guide the juvenile justice system
- ☐ Replacement of current system's reporting requirements with measurements based on reparation, including reporting forms and data collection systems
- ☐ Data collection about victims
- ☐ Predispositional recommendations that specify sentencing recommendations for each component: (a) accountability, (b) competency development, and (c) public safety
- ☐ Notification to the victim of the community service completed by the offender
- ☐ Opportunity for some victim choice in the type of community service required of an offender
- ☐ Funds collected from the offender allocated for restitution to the victim before any other financial obligations
- ☐ Candidates for promotion in juvenile justice systems required to demonstrate knowledge of restorative justice and the balanced approach

## Discussion Questions

**1** List three value differences between a restorative approach to juvenile justice and current approaches.

**2** How does sanctioning differ in a restorative approach to juvenile justice?

**3** List five performance outcomes in balanced and restorative justice.

**4** What does it mean to be a client or "customer" of juvenile justice in balanced and restorative justice? Who are the customers of juvenile justice?

**5** What programs or practices would be emphasized in a balanced approach to offender rehabilitation? How would a balanced approach to public safety differ?

**6** Discuss the role of victims in restorative justice. What are some possible barriers to victim participation? How might these be overcome?

## Notes

This chapter is based on a draft strategy monograph submitted to the Office of Juvenile Justice and Delinquency Prevention (OJJDP) (Grant No. 92-JN-CX-0005). Points of view or opinions expressed in this document are those of the authors and do not necessarily represent the official position or policies of OJJDP or the U.S. Department of Justice. Special thanks to Kay Pranis, restorative justice planner, Minnesota Department of Corrections, for assistance in preparing this chapter. The authors also wish to thank Ted Rubin, Troy Armstrong, and Charles Washington, who provided helpful comments on earlier drafts of the manuscript.

1   Legislative changes mandating fixed sentences in adult prisons for youths meeting minimal age requirements (or no age requirements) in states such as Georgia, Florida, Tennessee, and Oregon (Lemov, 1994), for example, challenge the viability of a separate court and justice system for young persons. Such changes represent only some of the extreme legislative assaults on the jurisdiction of the juvenile court in more than a decade of transformation in policy and procedure. Nationally, the number of delinquency cases transferred to criminal courts increased 65% between 1986 and 1990. Half of all juvenile offenders transferred to U.S. criminal courts in 1992 were property offenders. As documented in chapter 1 of this book, arrest rates for juvenile violent crimes peaked in 1994 and have gone down every year since 1994. Fortunately, a lot has changed since 1994. Specifically, juvenile court judges are adjudicating juveniles to probation dispositions in increasing numbers, from approximately 300,000 in 1994 to more than 400,000 juvenile probation dispositions in 1999.

2   While primary responsibility for addressing the three needs has been assigned to different criminal justice agencies (e.g., the police are assigned primary responsibility for public safety), lines of responsibility are necessarily blurred, and each agency is expected to play an important role in all three. Defining the role of juvenile justice in addressing these needs—especially those that concern sanctioning offenders and enhancing public safety—has been an ongoing challenge. Ironically, law enforcement agencies have begun to define their role more broadly to include rehabilitative and even sanctioning as well as public safety functions. While juvenile justice has attempted to restrict its role, even in the rehabilitative domain juvenile justice agencies are, at the same time, asked to meet unrealistic expectations—in essence, to be "all things to all people" (Maloney et al., 1988).

3   Although the public may not always demand a punitive response and has, at least in surveys, supported a rehabilitative emphasis for juveniles (Doble & Klein, 1989; Schwartz & Van Vleet, 1992; Steinhart, 1988), there are signs that citizens and policy makers may be increasingly skeptical of such traditional services and therapeutically based intervention. As a consequence, increasing support for out-of-home placements after years of emphasis on incarceration alternatives (Schwartz & Van Vleet, 1992), as well as for "shock" and confrontational alternatives with very dubious intervention logics (boot camps), may be due to the fact that these programs provide obvious, immediate, and often explicitly punitive consequences for crime (Gendrau, Cullen, & Bonta, 1994; Morash & Rucker, 1990). As we argue in this chapter, it is possible to envision a more empowering, effective, and "marketable" rehabilitative agenda that is also consistent with a more meaningful, nonretributive approach to sanctioning.

4   Van Ness (1993) suggests that the term *restorative justice* was first coined by Albert Eglash (1975) in a paper in which he distinguished between retributive justice based on punishment, distributive justice based on therapeutic treatment, and restorative justice based on restitution. Though still unfamiliar in the United States, the term is widely used in Europe, where restorative justice has been on the agenda of policy makers and researchers for approximately a decade (Davis, 1992; Messmer & Otto, 1992).

5   The increased reliance on informal processes associated with restorative justice (Umbreit, 1994a; Zehr, 1990, 2002), for example, seems difficult to envision in a system in which formal rules and procedures are in part intended to protect offenders from the abuses of unrestricted retribution and may be especially troubling to youth advocates concerned about further slippage in current due process protections in juvenile courts (e.g., Feld, 1990). Proponents of restorative justice would counter that in most cases the current court process is itself often highly informal rather than truly adversarial (see Eisenstein & Jacobs, 1991; Hackler, 1991) but is based on negotiation and bargaining in the service of the retributive ends of the state (and the professional interests of attorneys) rather than the interests of fairness and due process.

6    Individual treatment as a rehabilitative model has been both fairly and unfairly criticized as ineffective (Lab & Whitehead, 1988; Martinson, 1974), as well as stigmatizing, paternalistic, expensive, inequitable, and lacking in legal safeguards or standards for limiting duration and intensity (Lofquist, 1983; Pittman & Fleming, 1991; Walgrave, 1994). Although treatment practices have changed since the 1970s, when these criticisms were more common (Palmer, 1992), many of the central weaknesses in the logic of the individual treatment model remain relevant today.

7    Although detailed description of program models (e.g., staffing patterns, funding, and program components) is beyond the scope and focus of this overview of the balanced mission and restorative framework, specific guides to implementation of programs that receive priority in the balanced and restorative justice model are readily available. Interested professionals can now find materials on restitution and community service (Schneider, 1985), victim offender mediation (Umbreit, 1994a; Umbreit, Coates, & Roberts, 2000; Umbreit, Coates, & Vos, 2000), victim awareness education and victim panels (English & Crawford, 1989), preventive mediation and dispute resolution (Umbreit, 1998; Umbreit, Coates, & Vos, 2000), work experience and employment (Bazemore, 1991), cognitive skill development (Goldstein & Huff, 1992), and the "family group conference" model (Alder & Wundersitz, 1994; Bazemore & Umbreit, 2001; McElrae, 1993).

8    These guidelines are adapted from Polk (1974).

9    Although a new research agenda should be launched to explore the impact of balanced and restorative interventions on victims and communities as well as offenders, an emerging theoretical base and body of research is supportive of the view that the experience of making amends for harm done to victims and the community through restitution and unpaid service may have positive rehabilitative effects (Butts & Snyder, 1991; Eglash, 1975; Schneider, 1991; Wright, 1991). One clear basis for this expectation is derived from the equity theory idea that individuals in social and political situations tend toward fairness and balance (Schneider, 1991). Schneider's (1991) research in particular tends to support this expected impact of community service and restitution and also suggests that completion of restitution and service was related to a greater sense of citizenship (as reflected in a self-image as a good, honest, law-abiding person) and a greater likelihood to express remorse. These in turn decreased the likelihood of reoffending. Such impacts would, moreover, seem to be more likely and more intensive when these sanctions follow face-to-face encounters between victim and offender in mediation sessions (Umbreit, 1994b; Umbreit, Coates, & Vos, 2000).

## References

Adler, C., & Wundersitz, J. (1994). *Family conferencing and juvenile justice: The way forward or misplaced optimism.* Canberra: Australian Institute of Criminology.

Armstrong, T., & Altschuler, D. M. (1991). Intensive aftercare for the high-risk juvenile parolee: Issues and approaches in reintegration and community supervision. In T. Armstrong (Ed.), *Intensive interventions with high-risk youths: Promising approaches in juvenile probation and parole* (pp. 45–84). Monsey, NY: Willow Tree Press.

Armstrong, T., Maloney, D., & Romig, D. (1990, Winter). The balanced approach in juvenile probation: Principles, issues, and application. *Perspectives*, pp. 8–13.

Baird, C. (1985). Classifying juveniles: Making the most out of an important management tool. *Corrections Today, 47*, 32–38.

Bazemore, G. (1991). New concepts and alternative practice in community supervision of juvenile offenders: Rediscovering work experience and competency development. *Journal of Crime and Justice, 14*, 27–35.

Bazemore, G. (1993). Abolish, preserve or restructure: A case for the balanced approach justice paradigm and a balanced mission. In *The juvenile court: Dynamic, dysfunctional or dead?* (pp. 23–30). Philadelphia: Center for the Study of Youth Policy, School of Social Work, University of Pennsylvania.

Bazemore, G. (1994). *Balanced and restorative justice: Program summary.* Washington, DC: U.S. Dept. of Justice, Office of Juvenile Justice and Delinquency Prevention.

Bazemore, G. (2001). Young people, trouble, and crime: Restorative justice as a normative theory of informal social control and social support. *Youth and Society, 33*(2), 199–226.

Bazemore, G., & Maloney, D. (1994). Rehabilitating community service: Toward restorative service in a balanced justice system. *Federal Probation, 58*(1), 24–34.

Bazemore, G., & Schiff, M. (1996). Community justice/restorative justice: Prospects for a new social ecology for community corrections. *International Journal of Comparative and Applied Criminal Justice, 20*(2), 311–335.

Bazemore, G. & Schiff, M. (2001). *Restorative and community justice: Repairing harm and transforming communities.* Cinncinnati, OH: Anderson.

Bazemore, G., & Umbreit, M. (1995). Rethinking the sanctioning function in juvenile court: Retributive or restorative responses to youth crime. *Crime and Delinquency, 41*(3),296–316.

Bazemore, G., & Umbreit, M. (2001). *A comparison of four restorative justice conferencing models* (Juvenile Justice Bulletin). Washington, DC: Office of Juvenile Justice & Delinquency Prevention, Office of Justice Programs, U.S. Department of Justice.

Bazemore, G., & Walgrave, L. (1999). *Restorative juvenile justice: Repairing the harm of youth crime.* Monsey, NY: Criminal Justice Press.

Bazemore, G., & Washington, C. (1995). Charting the future of the juvenile justice system: Reinventing mission and management. *Spectrum: The Journal of State Government, 68*(2), 51–66.

Bowers, W. J., Pierce, G., & McDevitt, J. (1980). *Legal homicide: Death as punishment in America, 1864–1982.* Boston: Northeastern University Press.

Braithwaite, J. (1989). *Crime, shame and reintegration.* New York: Cambridge University Press.

Butts, J. (1994). *Offenders in juvenile court, 1992.* Washington, DC: U.S. Department of Justice, Office of Juvenile Justice and Delinquency Prevention.

Butts, J. & Mears, D. (2001). Reviving juvenile justice in a get tough era. *Youth & Society, 33*(2): 169–198.

Butts, J., & Snyder, H. (1991). *Restitution and juvenile recidivism.* Pittsburgh, PA: National Center for Juvenile Justice.

Byrne, J. M. (1989). Reintegrating the concept of community into community-based corrections. *Crime and Delinquency, 35,* 471–499.

Castellano, T. (1986). The justice model in the juvenile justice system: Washington state's experience. *Law and Policy, 8,* 479–506.

Christie, N. (1982). *Limits to pain.* Oxford: Martin Robertson.

Clear, T., & Gallagher, K. (1983). Management problems in risk screening devices in probation and parole. *Evaluation Review, 7,* 217–234.

Council of Europe Committee of Ministers. (1999). *Mediation in penal matters.* Recommendation No. R(99)19. Adopted September 15, 1999.

Crouch, M. (1993). Is incarceration really worse? Analysis of offenders' preferences for prison over probation. *Justice Quarterly, 10,* 67–88.

Davis, G. (1992). *Making amends: Mediation and reparation in criminal justice.* London: Routledge.

Doble, J., & Klein, J. (1989). *Prison overcrowding and alternative sentencing: The views of the people of Alabama.* New York: Public Agenda Foundation.

Durkheim, E. (1961). *Moral education: A study in the theory and application of the sociology of education.* Trans. E. K. Wilson & H. Schnurer. New York: Free Press.

Eglash, A. (1975). Beyond restitution: Creative restitution. In J. Hudson and B. Galaway (Eds.), *Restitution in criminal justice* (pp. 91–101). Lexington, MA: Lexington Books.

Eisenstein, J., & Jacobs, H. (1991). *Felony justice: An organizational analysis of criminal courts.* 2nd ed. Boston: Little, Brown.

Elias, R. (1993). *Victims still: The political manipulation of crime victims.* Newbury Park, CA: Sage.

English, S., & Crawford, M. (1989). *Victim awareness education is basic to offender programming* (monograph). Sacramento: California Youth Authority.

Erickson, E. (1968). *Childhood and society.* New York: Norton.

Feld, B. (1990). The punitive juvenile court and the quality of procedural justice: Disjunctions between rhetoric and reality. *Crime and Delinquency, 36,* 443–464.

Galaway, B., & Hudson, J. (Eds.). (1990). *Criminal justice, restitution, and reconciliation.* Massey, NY: Criminal Justice Press.

Garland, D. (1990). *Punishment and modern society: A study in social theory.* Chicago: University of Chicago Press.

Gendreau, P., Cullen, F., & Bonta, J. (1994). Up to speed: Intensive rehabilitation supervision: The next generation in community corrections. *Federal Probation, 58,* 72–78.

Goldstein, A., & Huff, R. (Eds.). (1992). *The gang intervention handbook.* Champaign, IL: Research Press.

Griffiths, C. T., & Belleau, C. (1993, August). *Restoration, reconciliation and healing: The revitalization of culture and tradition in addressing crime and victimization in aboriginal communities.* Paper presented at the meeting of the 11th International Congress on Criminology, Budapest, Hungary.

Hackler, J. (1991). *The possible overuse of not guilty pleas in juvenile justice* (monograph). Edmonton: Centre for Criminological Research, University of Alberta.

Haley, J. (1989). Confession, repentance, and absolution. In M. Wright & B. Galaway (Eds.), *Mediation and criminal justice: Victims, offenders and community* (pp. 195–211). London: Sage.

Harris, K., & Umbreit, M. (1993). *Restorative justice: Back to the future in criminal justice* (working paper). Minneapolis: Minnesota Citizens Council.

Hawkins, J. D., & Catalano, R. F. (1992). *Communities that care: Action for drug abuse prevention.* San Francisco, CA: Jossey-Bass.

Hirschi, T. (1969). *Causes of delinquency.* Berkeley: University of California Press.

Irwin, J., & Austin, J. (1993). *Its about time: America's imprisonment binge.* Belmont, CA: Wadsworth.

Klein, A. (1993). *Community protection as an intervention paradigm in a balanced juvenile justice system.* Unpublished manuscript.

Kuhn, T. (1962). *The structure of scientific revolutions.* Chicago: University of Chicago Press.

Lab, S. P., & Whitehead, J. T. (1988). An analysis of juvenile correctional treatment. *Crime and Delinquency, 34,* 60–83.

Lemov, P. (1994, December). The assault on juvenile justice. *Governing,* pp. 26–31.

Link, B. (1987). Understanding labelling effects in the area of mental disorders: Assessment of the effects of expectations. *American Sociological Review, 47,* 456–478.

Lofquist, W. A. (1983). *Discovering the meaning of prevention: A practical approach to positive change.* Tucson, AZ: AYD Publications.

Makkai, T., & Braithwaite, J. (1994). Reintegrative shaming and compliance with regulatory standards. *Criminology, 32,* 361–385.

Maloney, D., Romig, D., & Armstrong, T. (1988). *Juvenile probation: The balanced approach.* Reno, NV: National Council of Juvenile and Family Court Judges.

Martinson, R. (1974). What works: Questions and answers about prison reform. *Public Interest, 32,* 22–54.

McAllair, D. (1993). Reaffirming rehabilitation in juvenile justice. *Youth and Society, 25*, 104–125.

McElrae, F. W. M. (1993). A new model of justice. In B. J. Brown (Ed.), *The youth court in New Zealand: A new model of justice* (pp. 1–14). Auckland, New Zealand: Legal Research Foundation.

McShane, M., & Williams, F. (1992). Radical victimology: A critique of the concept of victim in traditional victimology. *Crime and Delinquency, 38*, 258–271.

Melton, G. B. (1989). Taking *Gault* seriously: Toward a new juvenile court. *Nebraska Law Review, 68*, 146–181.

Messmer, H., & Otto, H. (Eds.). (1992). Restorative justice on trial: Pitfalls and potentials of victim offender mediation. In *International research perspectives*. Norwell, MA: Kluwer.

Miller, J. (1991). *Last one over the wall.* Columbus: Ohio State University Press.

*Minneapolis Star Tribune.* (1993, July 11). Editorial, p. 10.

Morash, M., & Rucker, L. (1990). A critical look at the idea of boot camp as a correctional reform. *Crime and Delinquency, 36*(2), 204–222.

O'Brien, P. (2000). *Restorative juvenile justice in the states: A national assessment of policy development and implementation.* Boca Raton: Florida Atlantic University.

Palmer, T. (1992). *The re-emergence of correctional intervention.* Beverly Hills, CA: Sage.

Pepinsky, H. E., & Quinney, R. (Eds.). (1991). *Criminology as peacemaking.* Bloomington: Indiana University Press.

Pittman, K., & Fleming, W. (1991, September). *A new vision: Promoting youth development.* Testimony before the House Select Committee on Children, Youth and Families, Washington, DC.

Polk, K. (1974). *Options for institutional reform* (monograph). Eugene: Marion County Youth Study, University of Oregon.

Polk, K., & Kobrin, S. (1972). *Delinquency prevention through youth development.* Washington, DC: Office of Youth Development.

Reiss, A. (1986). Why are communities important in understanding crime? In A. J. Reiss & M. Tonry (Eds.), *Communities and crime* (pp. 1–33). Chicago: University of Chicago Press.

Rosenberg, I. M. (1993). Leaving bad enough alone: A response to juvenile court abolitionists. In *The juvenile court: Dynamic, dysfunctional or dead?* (pp. 14–22). Philadelphia: Center for the Study of Youth Policy, School of Social Work, University of Pennsylvania.

Rothman, D. (1980). *Conscience and convenience: The asylum and its alternatives in progressive America.* New York: HarperCollins.

Sampson, R. J., & Laub, J. H. (1993). *Crime in the making: Pathways and turning points through life.* Cambridge, MA: Harvard University Press.

Schafer, S. (1970). *Compensation and restitution to victims of crime.* Montclair, NJ: Smith Patterson.

Schneider, A. (1985). *Guide to juvenile restitution.* Washington, DC: U.S. Department of Justice, Office of Juvenile Justice and Delinquency Prevention.

Schneider, A. (1986). Restitution and recidivism rates of juvenile offenders: Results from four experimental studies. *Criminology, 24*(3), 533–552.

Schneider, A., & Schram, D. (1983). *A justice philosophy for the juvenile court.* Seattle, WA: Urban Policy Research.

Schneider, P. R. (1991, December). *National restitution program survey.* Presentation to Juvenile Restitution, OJJDP, Washington, DC.

Schwartz, I., Barton, W., & Orlando, F. (1991). Keeping kids out of secure detention. *Public Welfare, 46*, 20–26.

Schwartz, L., & Van Vleet, R. (1992). Public policy and the incarceration of juveniles: Directions for the 1990s. In Ira Schwartz (Ed.), *Juvenile justice and public policy* (pp. 151–164). New York: Lexington.

Shapiro, C. (1990). Is restitution legislation the chameleon of the victims' movement? In B.

Galaway & J. Hudson (Eds.), *Criminal justice, restitution, and reconciliation* (pp. 73–80). Monsey, NY: Willow Tree.

Sherman, X. (1983). Police in the laboratory of criminal justice. In K. Feinberg (Ed.), *Violent crime in America* (pp. 26–43). Washington, DC: National Policy Exchange.

Sparrow, M., Moore, M., & Kennedy, D. (1990). *Beyond 911: A new era for policing*. New York: Basic Books.

Steinhart, D. (1988). *California opinion poll: Public attitudes on youth crime*. San Francisco, CA: National Council on Crime and Delinquency.

Umbreit, M. S. (1994a). *Victim meets offender: The impact of restorative justice and mediation*. Monsey, NY: Criminal Justice Press.

Umbreit, M. S. (1994b, May). Victim empowerment through mediation. *Perspectives* (special edition), pp. 25–30.

Umbreit, M. S. (1998). Restorative justice through victim offender mediation: A multi-site assessment. *Western Criminology Review, 1*(1), 1–27.

Umbreit, M. S., & Coates, R. (1993). Cross site analysis of victim offender mediation in four states. *Crime and Delinquency, 39*(4), 15–25.

Umbreit, M. S., Coates, R. B., & Roberts, A. W. (2000). The impact of victim offender mediation: A cross-national perspective. *Mediation Quarterly, 17*(1), 215–229.

Umbreit, M. S., Coates, R. B., & Vos, B. (2000). The impact of victim offender mediation: Two decades of research. *Federal Probation, 65*(3), 29–35.

Umbreit, M. S., Coates, R. B. & Vos, B. (2002). The impact of restorative justice conferencing: A multi-national perspective. *British Journal of Community Justice, 1*(2), 21–48.

Umbreit, M. S., Vos, B., Coates, R. B., & Brown, K. (2003). *Facing violence: The path of restorative justice and dialogue*. Monsey, NY: Criminal Justice Press.

Van Ness, D. (1993). New wine in old wineskins: Four challengers of restorative justice. *Criminal Law Forum, 4*(2), 251–276.

Van Ness, D., & Strong, K. H. (2001). *Restoring justice* (2nd ed.). Cincinnati, OH: Anderson.

Von Hirsch, A. (1976). *Doing justice*. New York: Hill and Wang.

Walgrave, L. (1993, August). *Beyond retribution and rehabilitation: Restoration as the dominant paradigm in judicial intervention against juvenile crime*. Paper presented at the International Congress on Criminology, Budapest, Hungary.

Walgrave, L. (1994, May 16–19). *Criminological prevention in the city: For a crime prevention that is really criminological prevention*. Paper presented at the 49th International Conference of Criminology, Leuven, Belgium.

Wilkins, L. (1991). *Punishment, crime and market forces*. Brookfield, VT: Dartmouth.

Wright, M. (1991). *Justice for victims and offenders*. Buckingham, U.K.: Open University.

Zehr, H. (1990). *Changing lenses*. Scottsdale, PA: Herald Press.

Zehr, H. (2002). *The little book of restorative justice*. Intercourse, PA: Good Books.

Zhang, L., & Messner, S. F. (1994). The severity of official punishment for delinquency and change in interpersonal relations in Chinese society. *Journal of Research in Crime and Delinquency, 31*, 416–433.

# 20 Juvenile Assessment Centers

An Innovative Approach to Identify and Respond to
Youths With Substance Abuse and Related Problems
Entering the Justice System

Richard Dembo, James Schmeidler, and Wansley Walters

The present chapter discusses juvenile assessment centers, their promise, and the challenges they face in identifying and responding effectively to youth with substance use and related problems who are entering the juvenile justice system. The chapter begins with a discussion of the need for intervention services for troubled youth and the need for centralized intake facilities. A brief history of juvenile assessment centers is then presented, followed by a discussion of key elements of assessment centers and variation among assessment centers. The various opportunities provided by juvenile assessment centers to the communities they serve are then discussed. Following this discussion, challenges presented by assessment centers are considered. We end with a vision for the future in which juvenile assessment centers are seen as contributing to the quality of life within the communities in which they are located and to knowledge development of effective interventions to address the service needs of high-risk youth.

## ■ The Need for Innovative, Cost-Effective Intervention Services

Developing and implementing effective and cost-attractive intervention services for youths with alcohol and other drug use and related problems who have contact with the juvenile justice system remain critical needs (Sherman et al., 1997). There are several reasons for this urgency.

First, there has been an increase in youth crime and its effects, as well as a growing awareness of the magnitude of these and related problems in various high-risk groups (Butts & Harrell, 1998). Although there are recent indications that violent crime among juveniles has decreased, youth crime overall remains at unacceptably high levels. For example, a study in Maricopa County (which includes Phoenix), Arizona, involving 150,000 youths born between 1962 and 1977 who reached age 18 between 1980 and 1995, found that 46% of the males referred to juvenile court intake for the first time and 27% of the females were referred at least one more time—with 19% of the males eventually receiving four or more referrals (Snyder & Sickmund, 1999). The juvenile population is expected to increase substantially in the next 20 years, which threatens to further increase the burden on the juvenile justice system. National drug test studies of arrested juveniles continue to indicate high levels of drug use. Data from the Arrestee Drug Abuse Monitoring Program indicate 35% of arrested and detained juveniles report alcohol involvement, 70% report some other type of drug involvement, and 75% report either alcohol or other drug involvement (National Center on Addiction and Substance Abuse, 2002). This situation, together with the high rate of law violation referrals to juvenile court (a 57% increase between 1980 and 1995), has resulted in an increasingly clogged and backlogged juvenile court system in many jurisdictions throughout the United States, less involvement in case deliberation and supervision, and less effective placement in needed services (Snyder & Sickmund, 1995).

Related to these problems, treatment entry and retention present considerable challenges in treating juveniles with substance abuse and related problems (Battjes, Onken, & Delany, 1999). Many juveniles do not enter treatment, or leave prematurely, with associated high rates of drug use, crime, and health and social problems. Posttreatment relapse rates among adolescents with drug abuse problems (Catalano, Hawkins, Wells, Miller, & Brewer, 1990–1991), particularly those involved in the justice system, remain high (Armstrong & Altschuler, 1998), reflecting the often chronic nature of these problems. In the absence of effective intervention services, all too many juveniles entering the juvenile justice system will move to the adult justice system and consume a large and growing amount of local, state, and national criminal justice and mental health resources as they grow older (Office of National Drug Control Policy, 2001).

Second, service providers are challenged to address the multiple problems that are presented by youths in the juvenile justice system. More younger juveniles are being arrested; they have many serious, interrelated problems, including drug use, educational deficits, emotional issues, abuse, and neglect (Dembo, Schmeidler, Nini-Gough, & Manning, 1998). Research has consistently documented that many juveniles entering the juvenile justice system are experiencing multiple personal, educational, and family problems (Dembo et al., 1996). Among the problems most consistently reported by researchers are *physical abuse* (Dembo, Williams, & Schmeidler, 1998), *sexual victimization* (Dembo, Williams, & Schmeidler, 1998; Dembo et al., 2000), *poor emotional/psychological functioning* (Dembo & Schmeidler, 2003; Teplin, Abram, McClelland, Dulcan, & Mericle, 2002); *poor educational functioning* (Dembo, Williams, Schmeidler, & Howitt, 1991), and *alcohol and other drug use* (Dembo, Pacheco, Schmeidler, Fisher, & Cooper, 1997). In particular, mental health and drug abuse problems are co-occurring with increased frequency among juvenile offenders (Teplin et al., 2002; Winters, 1998). Many of these juveniles' difficulties can be traced to *family alcohol or other drug use, mental health, or crime problems* that began when they were young (Dembo, Williams, Wothke, Schmeidler, & Brown, 1992; Dembo et al., 2000). The interrelationship of these problems makes it urgent that holistic, not one problem at a time, services be developed for these juveniles and their families. Unfortunately, juvenile justice agencies in most jurisdictions have limited resources for providing high-quality screening, assessment, and treatment, and many juveniles entering the juvenile justice system come from families lacking resources to pay for care.

Third, effective intervention services are especially needed by minority (particularly African American and Hispanic) inner-city juveniles and families who have historically been underserved in regard to their mental health and substance abuse service needs (Arcia, Keyes, Gallagher, & Herrick, 1993; Dembo & Seeberger, 2000; Sirles, 1990; Tolan, Ryan, & Jaffe, 1988). These families tend to have lower substance abuse and mental health treatment service utilization rates (for program entry, engagement, and duration), than Anglo families. Among the factors responsible for these differences are the generally lower incomes of Black and Hispanic families (resulting in a reliance on inadequately funded public services), transportation problems, a lack of cultural sensitivity among service providers, and language differences (Arcia et al., 1993). Minority and inner-city juveniles are often socialized in communities and families that are economically and socially stressed. The psychosocial strain experienced by these youths, including their witnessing violence and its effects (Crimmins, Cleary, Brownstein, Spunt, & Warley, 2000), increases their risk of future drug use, delinquency, and crime (Nurco, Balter, & Kinlock, 1994) and impedes their development as socially responsible and productive adults (LeBlanc, 1990).

Fourth, innovative, low-cost, effective efforts are critically needed in which staff working with delinquent juveniles and their families are trained to provide in-home intervention services (to increase family participation) and, where indicated, to link them with other community resources. (As the University of Colorado Center for the Study and Prevention of Violence [1999], asserts, it is important that these intervention programs have been proven effective by evaluation studies.) Such programs hold promise of improving services available to various high-risk juveniles and their families, especially to African American and Latino families.

Fifth, more early-intervention services are seriously needed to work at the front end of the juvenile justice system. Such services hold promise of involving youths and their families in needed services as soon as possible after arrest, while they are open to access help, to reduce treatment entry and engagement problems. Early intervention holds promise of cost-effectively reducing the probability that troubled juveniles will continue criminal and high health-risk behavior into adulthood (Dembo & Schmeidler, 2002; Klitzner, Fisher, Stewart, & Gilbert, 1991).

## ■ The Need for Centralized Intake Facilities

Among the guiding principles in their review of the existing literature on effective programming for drug-involved adolescents, McBride, Vanderwall, Terry, and Van Buren (1999) concluded that (a) intervention must take place early when it has the best chance of reversing or ameliorating problem behaviors, (b) adolescents entering the system must undergo a comprehensive needs assessment in order to tailor interventions to each juvenile's unique needs, and (c) once needs have been identified, adolescents must be provided with a flexible and comprehensive continuum of care that offers the full range of relevant services needed for effective intervention.

Indeed, single intake facilities represent an important opportunity to identify the problems of troubled youths and involve them in helping services and intervention programs. These facilities could recast the front end of the juvenile justice system in the communities in which they operate. As a general model, single intake facilities involve representatives from a range of community agencies, including law enforcement, juvenile justice, and human service agencies, who are colocated at the facility. Successfully operating single intake facilities help overcome major workload and juvenile justice "systemic" problems.

Single intake units, such as juvenile assessment centers or community assessment centers, have been established in many areas throughout Florida and in Kansas, Colorado, and elsewhere in the United States. They represent an exciting, innovative development in juvenile justice. As discussed later, while there are many advantages associated with successfully operating single intake units, these facilities also present several challenges.

## ■ A Brief History of Juvenile Assessment Centers

Following a 15-month development period, involving extensive discussions with various community stakeholders, the first juvenile assessment center (JAC) was established in Hillsborough County (Tampa), Florida, in 1993 (Dembo & Brown, 1994). Funds for the JAC were obtained via competition from Drug Abuse Act of 1998 (Byrne Grant) funds. The Tampa JAC opened its doors to truant youths in January 1993; in May 1993, the JAC began accepting youths arrested on felony and weapons misdemeanor charges. In July 1994, the JAC opened its doors to all arrested youths.

In June 1993, a special session of the Florida Legislature addressed the issue of prison overcrowding. Prior to this special session, the head of the Florida House of Representatives Appropriation Committee visited the Tampa JAC with his wife. He was impressed with the concept and operation of the center and was instrumental in including $1.2 million in the special appropriation budget resulting from this special session to establish three additional JACs. In 1994, the Florida Legislature established the Florida Department of Juvenile Justice and added $2 million to the budget to set up eight more JACs in the state. During the early period, word about the Tampa and other Florida JACs (e.g., Orlando, Tallahassee) spread, and several other states expressed an interest in opening similar facilities in their jurisdictions. For example, Colorado and Kansas began to establish JACs. In contrast to the Colorado experience, where JACs were established by a number of different counties, the Kansas Legislature included these programs as part of the Kansas Youth Authority that was established in 1997. Since this early period, JACs have spread throughout the United States, and they are currently operating in 18 Florida locations.

In light of this momentum, federal agencies became interested in the concept. In 1995, the Office of Juvenile Justice and Delinquency Prevention (OJJDP) held a focus group meeting to review the potential of JACs to serve at-risk youths around the country. The Florida experience was an important component of this discussion. Although the focus group was positive about the JAC concept and established key elements of assessment centers (discussed later), concerns were expressed over their "net widening" potential, over-representation of minorities, and the limited knowledge about the level and type of community support needed for JACs to succeed (OJJDP, 1995; Olde-nettel & Wordes, 2000). In response, OJJDP sponsored a fact-finding study by Cronin (1996) to move the OJJDP assessment center initiative forward. This effort involved visiting a number of JACs, as well as a mail survey of juvenile justice and youth service personnel nationwide, and extensive telephone net-working (Cronin, 1996). Based on these results, OJJDP established a community assessment center (CAC) initiative in 1996 to explore the usefulness of the concept. The CAC demonstration effort involved funding four communities. Denver, Colorado, and Lee County, Florida were designated "planning sites" and received funds to develop new CACs. Jefferson County, Colorado, and Orlando, Florida, were designated "enhancement sites," where funds were to be used to improve their current assessment centers. Additional funds were awarded to the National Council of Crime and Delinquency to evaluate this initiative; and the Florida Alcohol and Drug Abuse Association was funded to provide training and technical assistance to the four funded communities.

In the mid-1990s, the Center for Substance Abuse Treatment (CSAT) became interested in JACs as an effective approach to intervene with juvenile offenders with drug abuse problems. CSAT commissioned James Rivers to complete an assessment of JACs and prepare a summary report on the topic, the Rivers report (1997). Rivers visited five JACs: Orlando (Orange County), Tallahassee (Leon County), and Tampa (Hillsborough County), Florida; Golden (Jefferson County), Colorado; and Olathe (Johnson County), Kansas. He also reviewed available reports and statistics. Although he found considerable variation among JACs in regard to their organization structures, locations, staffing patterns and operating schedules, management information system (MIS) functions, and populations served, Rivers concluded that funding JACs could make a contribution to the mission of CSAT—particularly in the area of knowledge development.

## ◼ Key Elements of Assessment Centers

Although JACs may differ in a number of ways discussed earlier, they generally share a number of common elements. OJJDP has codified four common elements for the CACs they funded (Oldenettel & Wordes, 2000, pp. 1–2):

I Single point of entry: a 24-hour centralized point of intake and assessment for juveniles who have come or are likely to come into contact with the juvenile justice system.

**2** Immediate and comprehensive assessments: service providers associated with the JAC make an initial broad-based and, if necessary, a later in-depth assessment of youths' circumstances and treatment needs.

**3** Management information systems: needed to manage and monitor youths, help ensure the provision of appropriate treatment services, and avoid duplication of services.

**4** Integrated case management services: JAC staff use information obtained from the assessment process and the MIS to develop recommendations to improve access to services, complete follow-ups of referred youths, and periodically reassess youths placed in various services.

The OJJDP is no longer funding CACs (Eric Peterson, personal communication, January 2003). At the same time, the OJJDP "common elements" are useful points of reference in discussing JACs, although there are differences in their implementation. First, JACs represent single points of entry, a centralized location where arrested youths in the community served by the JAC are brought for processing. Second, JACs are sites for preliminary screening of arrested youths for potential problems needing follow-up by in-depth assessments. Although OJJDP CAC criteria include the completion of comprehensive assessments on indicated youths, many JACs, particularly those in urban areas where many youths are processed, do not complete these assessments on-site during the youths' processing. Rather, in-depth assessments are often completed following their JAC processing, in detention centers (for youths placed in these secure facilities) or in various community locations. Third, as noted earlier, JAC MISs vary in their comprehensiveness and sophistication. Fourth, JACs usually provide case management services, although these services are often limited to subsets of processed youths—such as youths placed in diversion programs.

## ▣ Variation Among Juvenile Assessment Centers

Located in diverse areas of the United States with differing resources, service infrastructures, and preexisting arrangements among stakeholder agencies related to juvenile justice functions, JACs differ from one another. These differences are reflected in their (a) days and hours of operation, (b) program components, (c) screening and assessment protocols, (d) type of management information system (MIS), (e) support services, (f) degree of agency colocation, and (g) research activities. Some of these differences were noted in the Cronin (1996) and Rivers (1997) reports. JACs appear to operate as separate entities, with little coordination with other JACs in nearby jurisdictions.

Those JACs serving low-density population areas tend to operate fewer days and hours than JACs in urban locations. JACs also are distinguished by their program components. For example, in addition to booking, screening, and assessment functions, some JACs have a truancy component and also serve children in need of services (CINS) and families in need of services (FINS) cases.

Screening and assessment protocols vary among JACs. Some JACs use state-of-the-art screening and assessment instruments, followed by treatment planning conferences, whereas other JACs use locally prepared screening and assessment forms and make referrals for additional assessment and treatment planning. MIS systems used by JACs vary considerably: Some JACs use highly sophisticated MIS software packages, and other JACs use locally developed forms to record information collected by JAC staff on processed youths and facility operations. Relatedly, research activities at JACs range from none to the preparation of routine reports of selected characteristics of JAC-processed youths (e.g., sociodemographic and arrest charge information) to sophisticated multivariate analyses of JAC-collected data.

Support services also differ among JACs. For example, a number of Florida JACs are located next to juvenile addiction receiving facilities (JARFs). Youths in need of alcohol and other drug detoxification, stabilization, assessment, and referral assistance are brought to these facilities by various referral agencies (e.g., schools), and JAC-processed youths in need of immediate alcohol or other drug services are brought to these facilities for care. Because services beyond core juvenile justice processing differ among JACs, it is not surprising that the number and kinds of agencies colocated at JACs reflect these varia-tions. Hence, some JACs have numerous colocated agencies, whereas some JACs house only agencies providing core juvenile justice functions. For ex-ample, the following agencies are colocated at the Hillsborough County, Flor-ida, JAC: Hillsborough County Sheriff Office (booking functions and super-vision of the secure wing, where processed youths are awaiting movement out of the JAC to the custody of their parents, detention center, etc.), Florida Department of Juvenile Justice detention screening staff, an on-site diversion unit where diversion-eligible youths and their parents are interviewed and recommendations made to the State Attorney's Office for diversion program placement of these youths, and the Hillsborough County School Board truancy program.

## Opportunities Presented by Juvenile Assessment Centers

### A Site for Agencies to Complete Legally Required Functions for Arrested Youths

Juvenile assessment centers provide an opportunity for agencies responsible for dealing with arrested juveniles to carry out their legally mandated respon-sibilities while colocated in the same facility. Such an arrangement facilitates interagency collaborative efforts. Programmatically, single intake facilities pro-vide solutions to (a) problems experienced by law enforcement personnel in achieving expeditious disposition of juveniles, permitting their return to law enforcement functions; (b) problems experienced by juvenile justice agency staff in locating youths not eligible for secure detention and completing screening, assessments, and processing required to support judicial and nonjudicial dispositions; (c) problems experienced by state attorney personnel and juvenile judges in effecting meaningful dispositions without an adequate range of information on youths and dispositional alternatives; and (d) problems experienced by clinical staff in achieving child and family compliance in participating in in-depth assessments that are needed to guide dispositional recommendations to juvenile court. These problems are often not the result of lack of motivation or commitment on the part of these agencies; rather, they reflect infrastructure problems that can be improved considerably by colocating the operations of relevant agencies to permit the simultaneous accomplishment of required legal and social service interventions.

### An Opportunity to Obtain Comprehensive Information on Youths and Refer Them to Needed Services

As noted earlier, research has indicated that many youths entering the juvenile justice system are experiencing multiple personal, educational, and family problems. JACs provide an excellent opportunity to systematically collect sociodemographic data; delinquency, abuse, and neglect history; educational history and needs; and psychosocial functioning (e.g., mental health problems and substance use, including urine testing) information on arrested youths. Such information is essential in determining the various problems these youths may be experiencing in order to refer them for in-depth assessments and improve the quality and appropriateness of referrals. Such information can increase interagency coordination in meeting the needs of troubled youths and their families, reduce duplication of effort, and smooth the transition of youths from one program or agency to another. For example, at the Hillsborough County JAC, comprehensive information, including urine specimens, is collected on processed youths. This information is used by an on-site case management unit to recommend diversion program placement for eligible youths to the State Attorney's Office, as well as to identify specific services the youths may need.

### Assist Communities in Gaining a Better Picture of Troubled Youths and Learn of New, Emerging Problems

One useful consequence of systematically collecting comprehensive information on youths processed at JAC facilities is the ability to inform community leadership and stakeholders on the problems and service needs of these youths and to provide insight into new, emerging problems. This information should be supplied to community leaders and stakeholders on a periodic basis, so they know about any shifts in the types of youths being processed and their problems. Gaining a more complete understanding of processed youths' problems can provide communities with an informed basis upon which to expand existing services or develop new services. This is an important resource when submitting proposals for competitive review to various state and federal agencies. Relatedly, this information can help educate the general public about these issues and facilitate their support for needed programs and services.

Another benefit associated with the collection of systematic information on youths processed at single intake facilities is providing insight into new, emerging youth problems. For example, systematic urine testing can identify new patterns of drug use, such as methamphetamines or heroin, which the community leadership and stakeholder agencies can use to prepare appropriate enforcement and intervention responses.

### Provide Needed Information to Judicial and Juvenile Justice Agencies to Enable Moving Cases Through Disposition and Placement

Judicial and juvenile justice agencies are in critical need of accurate, comprehensive information on arrested youths, so they can make insightful and effective decisions regarding disposition and program placement. For example, the State Attorney's Office may need screening information, together with urine test results, to refer youths to juvenile drug court or another community-based diversion program. Juvenile justice personnel will need intake screening information on youths, together with any in-depth assessments, to make decisions regarding program placement following court disposition of their cases. JACs can serve as a great resource for this information.

### A Focal Point for Early Intervention

Most U.S. juvenile justice jurisdictions are crisis oriented, working with limited fiscal, physical, and personnel resources. Guidry (1991) notes that juvenile justice agencies typically have an episodic interest in troubled youths. Interest is focused on the judicially imposed consequences of illegal behavior, with court-imposed intervention coming only after repeated court appearances. At that point, many youths have developed a long list of failures in informal or loosely structured programs, developed serious problems at school, and established a pattern of delinquent behavior, including drug use.

Reaching these youths in early adolescence provides an excellent opportunity to involve them in health and human service intervention before their problems become more serious. Early intervention can reduce the probability that they will continue criminal and high health-risk behavior into adulthood (Klitzner et al., 1991) and thus the enormous cost to society of crime, drug abuse, and mental illness (Office of National Drug Control Policy, 2001). Community-based services should be a preferred alternative to justice system services for early interventions provided to nonviolent offenders with minor arrest histories (Dembo, Wareham, & Schmeidler, in press). JACs can play a critical role in this service delivery process.

The Tampa JAC has a case management unit whose major purpose is to complete screening of arrested youths who are eligible for diversion programs placement (i.e., assignment to community services in lieu of being sent to juvenile court). JAC case management staff review the arrest histories and current charges of youths arrested on misdemeanor offenses to determine if they can be recommended for placement in a nonjudicial diversion program (Arbitration, Intensive Delinquency Diversion Services [IDDS], Juvenile Drug Court). Case manager recommendations to Arbitration, IDDS, or Juvenile Drug Court are forwarded to the State Attorney's Office (SAO), where they are usually approved. Case management staff carry the files of placed cases until the youths complete or are terminated from the diversion program. In this way, JACs can serve as excellent sites for early intervention services for arrested youths and their families (Dembo & Pacheco, 1999; Dembo & Schmeidler, 2002).

In the Arbitration program, the parent or guardian and the juvenile appear, along with the victim, at a hearing before a trained arbitrator. The arbitrator explores the details of the case by questioning the defendant and listening to information contributed by the parents and victim, then makes a decision as to the most appropriate sanctions (e.g., community service hours, paying restitution) for the particular set of circumstances, and imposes these sanctions on the juvenile. Arbitration staff monitor completion of assigned sanctions. Compliance with program rules (e.g., consistent school attendance, acceptable behavior at home) is also monitored and can result in program extension or failure of a youth. Although program involvement can last up to a year, on average, youths complete the program in 10 weeks. Youths who complete all that is asked of them are deemed program "successes," and their charges are dismissed. Youths who do not complete the assigned sanctions are considered "failures," and their cases are referred back to the SAO for formal prosecution of the original charge(s).

The IDDS program is a 5- to 7-month program designed to serve the higher risk portion of the youth population. Referral criteria target youths who are at high risk of becoming serious or chronic offenders. Contracted case management services are provided to the youths. The continuous and extensive contact with the youth, parents or guardians, school, employer, and assigned case manager, among other service providers, is considered essential to the youth's success in the IDDS program. The JAC is the major source of referrals, with the approval of the SAO, of youths to IDDS. Whether a youth is deemed a "success" or a "failure" depends on the youth's performance in the program, level of progress, and an assessment of future threat to the community. Youths who do not successfully complete the program are referred back to the SAO for formal prosecution of the original charge(s).

Juvenile Drug Court is a structured 9- to 12-month program involving four phases. Phase 1 is detoxification, stabilization, and in-depth assessment (3 to 5 days). Phase 2 is an intensive day treatment program designed to last between 2 and 13 weeks. Clients who do not benefit from the outpatient program can be referred to a residential program by the court. Phase 3 of the program, designed to last 12 weeks, focuses on continued sobriety, with an emphasis on decision-making skills, peer relationships, and educational and vocational issues. Phase 4, the final stage, lasts for the duration of the program. Here, emphasis is placed on the client's continued involvement in support groups and counseling sessions that will sustain drug-free living.

## Implementing and Evaluating New Intervention Services

The JACs are an ideal location to develop, implement, and evaluate the effectiveness of new, innovative service delivery strategies. Innovative services are especially needed by minority and inner-city youths and their families, who have traditionally been underserved (Arcia et al., 1993; Dembo & Seeberger, 2000; Sirles, 1990; Tolan et al., 1988).

### The Youth Support Project

The Youth Support Project (YSP), a family intervention project funded by the National Institute on Drug Abuse that operated out of the Tampa JAC, is an example of such an innovative service. The YSP implemented a 10-week systems-oriented and structural approach to family preservation, a home based family empowerment intervention (FEI) (Dembo & Schmeidler, 2002) delivered by project field consultants in four phases:

*Phase 1: Introduction*

Phase 1 (session 1 or 1–2) is characterized by the introduction of the field consultant and all family members involved, a description of the intervention and supervision design, a review of the intervention procedures (including videotaping or audiotaping family meetings) and timing, and responses to any questions the family may have about the program.

*Phase 2: Consultation*

Phase 2 (ideally sessions 2–3 through 9–12) is characterized by inquiry and participation by the field consultant and demonstration of the methods used for sharing and asking. The field consultant conducts the activities.

*Phase 3: Family Work*

Phase 3 (ideally sessions 10–13 through 27) is characterized by the family members taking the lead in reorganizing ways of communicating, relating, and thinking about family functioning.

### Phase 4: Graduation

Phase 4 (ideally sessions 28–30) is characterized by review of the intervention and preparation for separation from the FEI. It takes place after the field consultant and clinical supervisor have agreed that the family has met the goals of the intervention.

Families involved in the project were randomly assigned to one of two groups: the extended services intervention (ESI) or the family empowerment intervention (FEI) group. ESI group families received monthly phone contacts from project research assistants (RAs), and FEI group families received personal in-home visits from project field consultants. Field consultants visited families to work on the following goals: (a) Restore the family hierarchy (parents, children, etc.); (b) restructure boundaries between parents and children; (c) encourage parents to take greater responsibility for family functioning; (d) increase family structure through implementation of rules and consequences; (e) enhance parenting skills; (f) have parents set limits, expectations, and rules that increase the likelihood that the target youth's behavior will improve; (g) improve communication skills among all family members; (h) improve problem-solving skills, particularly in the target youth; and (i), where needed, connect the family to other systems (e.g., school, church, community activities). It was expected that empowering parents will result in improvements in the client youth's behavior and psychosocial functioning—including reduced recidivism.

The FEI families were expected to participate in three 1-hour family meetings per week for approximately 10 weeks. All household members (i.e., persons living under the same roof as the target youth) were expected to participate in these meetings. Both FEI and ESI families had 24-hour-a-day, 7-day-a-week access to YSP staff and to information on various community resources via a project-developed agency and services resource file. YSP staff provided families with information about different community agencies and assisted them in obtaining appropriate referrals to meet their needs.

A distinctive feature of this intervention is that the families were served by field consultants, who are not trained therapists—although they were trained by, and perform their work under the direction of, licensed clinicians. The choice of paraprofessionals was based on a cost-effectiveness argument and is supported by experimental research indicating that, at least for some treatments, paraprofessionals produce outcomes that are better than those under control conditions and similar to those involving professional therapists (Christensen & Jacobson, 1994; Weisz, Weiss, Han, Granger, & Morton, 1995). Further, by requiring less previous therapy training, the FEI, if proven effective, would be highly attractive to agencies providing services to juvenile offenders, which often operate with financial constraints.

Youths processed at the Hillsborough County JAC (Dembo & Brown,

1994) who were arrested on misdemeanor or felony charges were sampled for inclusion in the project. When openings occurred on the field consultants' caseloads, a listing of recently arrested youths was drawn. A cross-tabulation of these cases was completed in regard to their gender and race or ethnicity (African American, Latino, and Anglo), and equal numbers of youths in each of these six cells were randomly selected to process for enrollment in the YSP. This procedure and large sample size provided good representation of African American, Latino, and Anglo youths of both sexes and their families in the study.

Twelve-month and longer term follow-up analyses indicated very promising results. In regard to official record recidivism, 12-month analyses indicated that youths completing the FEI had significantly lower rates of new charges and new arrests than youths not completing the FEI. The long-term study of official record data on the youths covered 12 to 48 months following their random assignment to the FEI or ESI groups. The results indicated youths completing the FEI had marginally significantly lower cumulative arrest charges and very close to statistically significant lower cumulative new arrests over the 48-month follow-up period than youths not completing the FEI.

Twelve-month follow-up information on the youths' psychosocial functioning, including their self-reported delinquency, was collected by in-depth interviews 1 year following the youth's baseline interview; the long-term self-report data covered events up to 36 months following the youth's baseline interviews. The youth's last available follow-up interview was used as the best measure of long-term outcome. The 12-month follow-up data indicated that youths completing the FEI had a marginally significantly lower rate of engaging in drug sales than ESI youths. Further analyses comparing youths completing the FEI and those not completing the FEI found that FEI completers reported significantly less involvement in crimes against persons, drug sales, and total delinquency and marginally significantly less involvement in theft and index crimes than youths not completing the FEI. The longer term self-report data analyses found that youths completing the FEI reported significantly less involvement in crimes against persons, drug sales, and total delinquency than youths not completing the FEI. In regard to drug use, youths receiving FEI services reported significantly fewer occasions of getting very high or drunk on alcohol and a lower frequency of marijuana use during the 12-month follow-up period than ESI youths; further, youths receiving FEI services had a significantly lower rate of positive hair tests for marijuana than youths receiving ESI services. Longer term outcome analyses indicated FEI completers reported getting very high or drunk on alcohol significantly less often than FEI noncompleters.

It is important to note that the FEI and ESI groups did not differ significantly on a wide variety of demographic, offense history, abuse and neglect history, and baseline psychosocial variables, and neither did the youths who completed the FEI differ from those who did not complete it on these variables.

Thus, the differences in outcome that were found cannot be attributed to baseline differences among the groups.

Further analyses documented the considerable direct cost savings to the juvenile justice system by providing FEI services to diversion-eligible youths in Hillsborough County, Florida. The calculation of justice system costs was based on new arrest rates and incarceration costs for FEI compared with ESI youths (both diversion and nondiversion cases) over a 3-year cumulative period. The results showed that, by the end of the 3-year period, the projected cumulative cost savings to the justice system as a result of providing FEI services was $4.7 million.

### Sexually Transmitted Disease Testing and Intervention

Sexually transmitted diseases (STDs), drug use, and delinquency are associated risk behaviors that reduce the quality of life and health of individuals, families, and communities. Youths who use alcohol or other drugs are even more likely than other youths to engage in sexual intercourse and other sexually risky behaviors. There are an estimated 4 million chlamydia and 1 million gonorrhea infections in the United States each year, and 40% of these infections occur in 15- to 19-year-olds, who represent 6% of the population (Florida Department of Health, n.d.); females have higher rates of chlamydia and gonorrhea than males. Early detection and treatment of STDs is crucial to prevent further transmission and development of chronic, long-term sequelae. The vast majority of chlamydia and gonorrhea infections are asymptomatic; individuals with an undiagnosed STD are 2 to 5 times more likely to become infected with HIV (Fleming & Wasserheit, 1999). The Institute of Medicine (Eng & Butler, 1997) recommended increased STD screening of youths involved in the juvenile justice system (e.g, detention centers), but practice still lags greatly behind need.

In collaboration with the Florida Department of Health (DOH), the Tampa JAC completed a pilot project from November 2000 through mid-February 2001, which screened arrested youths processed at the JAC for chlamydia and gonorrhea, the first STD screening initiative at a JAC facility. The DOH staff was responsible for the voluntary specimen collection, pretest counseling, obtaining informed consent, follow-up and posttest counseling, and treatment of positive cases. Results indicated a 6% to 10% positive rate, which is 2 to 3 times the prevalence rate for these two diseases among youths that age in the general population.

### The Miami–Dade JAC, National Demonstration Project

Another innovative set of front-end juvenile justice system services is represented by the National Demonstration Project. In the middle 1990s, the arrest process for juveniles in Miami–Dade County, Florida, was so dysfunctional that organized crime groups were using juveniles as their labor force and coaching them on how to "trick" the system. In an urban community of more than 2 million, juvenile arrests hit 20,000 in 1995, with dire predictions of further increases. High-profile and violent juvenile offenses were discouraging visitors from all over the world. And in an era when information holds the key, the only information authorities in Miami–Dade County had about the juvenile arrest population was the actual number of arrests. Even that information was difficult to get, with more than 30 law enforcement agencies individually processing arrested juveniles. The Miami–Dade situation required a large, comprehensive, state-of-the-art facility that could serve as a starting point for juvenile system reform.

The Miami–Dade JAC opened in late 1997 as a community partnership under the leadership of the Miami–Dade Police Department (MDPD). (In Miami–Dade, the countywide police department serves as the sheriff's department. Miami–Dade does not have an elected sheriff. This department is not to be confused with the City of Miami Police Department, which is a municipal department serving a population of 2.2 million.) While the resources were provided by the MDPD and the Florida Department of Juvenile Justice, all juvenile justice stakeholders were invited to be members of the JAC partnership. These partners include the Florida Department of Juvenile Justice, the Florida Department of Children and Families, Miami–Dade State Attorney's Office, Miami–Dade Public Schools, Miami–Dade Department of Corrections, Miami–Dade Department of Human Resources, Miami–Dade Administrative Office of the Courts, administrative juvenile judges, and the Miami–Dade Office of the Clerk of the Court. All partners, whether they are physically located at the JAC or not, have been active participants in the planning and implementation of all processes. During the intensive 3-year planning process to develop the JAC, one major goal was critical: The Miami–Dade JAC wanted to do more than simply process arrested juveniles.

The first year of operation was dedicated to the formidable task of defining a new way of doing business. While contending with procedures, turf issues, and the sometimes difficult implementation of advanced technology, the collective agencies at the JAC achieved unprecedented efficiencies. A process that formerly could take up to 6 weeks for a nondetainable juvenile offender now can take less than 2 hours. Police officers who formerly spent an average of 6 hours processing juveniles are in and out of the JAC in an average of 15 minutes, including their profile conference with the State Attorney's Office. Livescan fingerprint technology and a multitiered identification process tell the JAC whether this is a juvenile's first arrest or the fifth. The system allows the Florida Department of Juvenile Justice to administer assessments to 100% of juveniles entering the system, which was not possible before the JAC. The connection with the courts allows the case to be created in the JAC. Last, the complete cooperation of all law enforcement agencies, through the Dade County Chiefs of Police, enables this JAC to be the centralized point of entry into the system. This allows the Miami–Dade JAC to collect critical information on the complete juvenile arrest population.

During the first year of operation, as efficiencies were achieved, two very important observations were made. First, the overall arrest population could be broadly categorized into three groups: (a) youths doing a lot of "kid" things (e.g., loitering, shoplifting, school fights); (b) youths acting out on serious issues in their lives (e.g., substance abuse, family problems, school problems); and (c) serious, habitual, and potentially dangerous juvenile offenders. Second, there was a great deal of high-quality research being conducted throughout the United States in the area of juvenile justice. Unfortunately, no instruction was given on how to apply the principles of the different areas of research in a 24-hour-a-day operation processing a diverse and complex population of children.

This was the basis that led the Miami–Dade JAC to propose a demonstration project, and receive funding from the U.S. Congress, that would partner researchers and operational staff in the reform of an active, functioning system. It would allow Miami–Dade County to develop the foundation needed to effectively plan and strategically apply specialized and research-proven interventions and programs based on the needs of the children in the system. In a time of limited resources, it would ultimately be possible to provide an alternative to the "cookie-cutter" way of dealing with an entire population of juvenile offenders.

For the project to begin to accomplish the objectives, planning needed to take into account the three broad categories of arrested juveniles previously mentioned. Add to this mix ages that range from 8 to 18, gender differences, ethnic composition, and all of the different combinations of factors that these imply, and it became obvious that the project had to begin in the broadest, most comprehensive way. Four initial components were identified that would start to address multiple issues across the scope of the juvenile arrest population that contained both minor and serious offenders.

1  Screening and Assessment: This project identified state-of-the-art screening and assessment instruments and helped establish a clinically informed protocol for processing arrested youths at the JAC.

2  Postarrest Diversion: This is an alternative arrest-processing program that allowed the JAC to keep first-arrest juveniles for minor offenses from entering the juvenile justice system. It also provided an opportunity to study youths at this early point of contact with the justice system, identify risk and protective factors, and develop a personalized diversion program addressing the needs of the child and not the offense. An evaluation of this program made recommendations to strengthen it by incorporating best practices in the field. These recommendations were reflected in a new processing protocol that determined (a) youths' psychosocial problems and needs for mental health, alcohol/other drug use, and family/household relationships services and (b) risk for recidivism, which is in the process of being implemented.

**3** Specialized Program Models: Three projects were established, each focusing on a significant subpopulation of youths processed at the JAC:

  a. Reflecting a concern over the increases in the proportion of female youths processed at the JAC in recent years (22% of 15,088 processed youths in 2001, compared with lower rates in previous years), the gender-specific intervention project sought to identify the gender-specific needs of girls and recommend training and program improvements and developments to more effectively address their needs.

  b. The younger siblings of serious habitual offenders are at high risk for delinquency. The Serious Habitual Offender Siblings (SHOSIB) project was designed to develop a model of prevention for these vulnerable youngsters.

  c. In recognition of the continued, significant overrepresentation of Haitian juvenile arrestees among youths entering the JAC, the Haitian Juvenile Arrestee Prevention Study focused on identifying the service needs and service usage of the Miami–Dade Haitian community, as well as determining key elements of culturally specific and appropriate interventions for these youths.

**4** The Information Resource Center (IRC): Another major component of the national demonstration project was development of an IRC with access to information on youths from multiple agencies (e.g., Miami–Dade Schools, the Criminal Justice Information System [CJIS], the JAC MIS). For the first time, comprehensive information on youths would be available to inform juvenile judges, service providers, researchers, citizens, and public officials on juvenile arrestee psychosocial problems (e.g., drug use) and public safety issues (e.g., rates of arrest, trends in arrests).

Phase 1 of the national demonstration project involved the development of state-of-the-art screening and assessment procedures, program designs, and intervention models. Phase 2, which is currently being implemented, involves the implementation and evaluation of a new postarrest diversion protocol, as well as staff and community training in key areas, such as cultural diversity and gender-specific issues.

## Improve the Community's Infrastructure, Integration of Services, and Continuum of Care

In the process of improving communication, information sharing, and collaboration for youth program referrals or placements among community agencies, single intake facilities contribute to strengthening the community's infrastructure and service delivery system. Increased interaction among the staffs of different agencies helps break down stereotypes and increases mutual trust and respect. Needing to collaborate to screen, refer, and place youths in appropriate services increases agency coordination, reduces duplication of services, and helps smooth the transition of the youths from the judicial system into the community service system. In these ways, single intake facilities can serve as a catalyst for community integration of services and a continuum of care.

## ◼ Challenges Presented by Juvenile Assessment Centers

Single intake facilities have many strengths. At the same time, they are presented with continuing challenges to their successful operation.

### Guarding Against Net Widening

A potential problem with JACs is that youths involved in relatively minor offenses, such as retail theft, will be brought into the juvenile justice system, have a record established on them, and placed in justice system–operated programs and supervision. These experiences can lead these youths to coming to define themselves as delinquent and increase the likelihood that their delinquent behavior will continue and become more serious (Dembo et al., in press). It is important that collaborating agencies work together to ensure that net widening does not occur. It might be good practice to bring youths arrested on misdemeanor charges to single intake facilities for processing only after they have committed more than two minor offenses, with other youths referred to community-based, non-juvenile-justice agencies for services.

### Ongoing Efforts Are Needed to Ensure Continuing Support of Key Stakeholder Agencies

Like other community collaborations, JACs involve dynamic and sometimes shifting relationships among such agencies as law enforcement, juvenile justice, the judiciary, and service providers. There is a need for ongoing efforts to ensure a high level of cooperation among these agencies, particularly in times of reduced funding and changing political alliances. A good vehicle for this process is the establishment of single intake facility advisory committees, on which key stakeholder agencies have membership, to oversee and guide the operation of these facilities. These committees can serve as an important forum where problems in processing youths, identifying their service needs, and moving their cases forward to judicial, juvenile justice, and community service agencies can be presented, discussed, and resolved. JAC advisory committees have been in operation in Florida for several years and have great potential for strengthening community support for local JACs.

## Community Acceptance

Because there are different interest groups relating to each JAC, the success of these programs rests on their ability to meet the needs of its various constituencies. Based on our experience at the Tampa and Miami–Dade JACs, a primary interest of law enforcement personnel is in quickly transferring arrested youths to JAC staff and returning to street duty. Community-based service providers wishing to receive referrals from the JAC will be supportive of the program if they receive appropriate and timely placements. Stakeholder agencies, such as the State Attorney's Office, wish to receive timely summaries of the JAC preliminary screening process, so they can make appropriate decisions regarding placing an arrested youth in a diversion program or filing a delinquency petition. An effective means to address these multiple needs is for the JAC advisory committee to (a) include all agencies bringing or referring youths to the JAC, as well as individuals or agencies receiving referrals or cases from the facility, and (b) hold periodic meetings to address agency-specific needs as well as interface issues. Wherever possible, the advisory committee should exercise oversight over the JAC and not merely serve as an "advisory group." The Tampa JAC advisory committee, for example, has found this to be an effective way of implementing and monitoring changes in the operation of the assessment center.

The families of arrested youths constitute another important consumer group. Yet, they are infrequently consulted in the establishment of JACs or in efforts to evaluate their effectiveness. Interviews with families participating in the YSP indicated a number of important issues facing families whose children were processed at the Tampa JAC: (a) The juvenile courts and other juvenile justice agencies need to make a final disposition on the youth's case in as reasonably short a period of time as possible, (b) youths and their parents or guardians should receive factual information about the movement of their cases through the State Attorney's Office or juvenile court, with a time frame within which major decisions will be made about the case (e.g., arraignment, adjudicatory hearing, disposition hearing), (c) youths should receive high-quality treatment services by caring staff, (d) promises made to youths and their families should be kept, and (e) the families of youths assigned to receive in-depth assessment or treatment services should be contacted promptly by service agencies to increase treatment engagement and retention (Dembo & Schmeidler, 2002).

## Continuing Efforts Are Needed to Maintain a Strong Infrastructure and High-Quality Operation of Single Intake Facilities

Often JACs are administered by local, private, nonprofit agencies. The salaries for line staff in many of these agencies are relatively low, resulting in high rates of staff turnover. This circumstance makes it difficult to maintain a high-quality infrastructure and the operation of these facilities. High staff turnover requires the dedication of considerable effort to hire and train new personnel and educate them regarding processing and referral criteria and practices, and it is bound to cause strains to the effective operation of these facilities. Effort and resources need to be directed to correct these problems where they exist. Unfortunately, in the absence of secure federal, state, or local funding, nonprofit agencies administering JACs face ongoing challenges to maintain adequate funding for high-quality operations. Initial capital expenses may be needed for facility construction or renovation. Ongoing funding is needed for rent, leasing, or mortgage payments. Funds are needed to pay personnel and for facility security, utilities, equipment, and the development and maintenance of management information systems.

### Ongoing Need to Maintain the Original Vision of Single Point of Entry Facilities

When JACs first open, they usually have sufficient funding, considerable stakeholder agency support, and high public visibility. Over time, funding streams may change, and stakeholder agency support may alter as they deal with their own internal issues. It is imperative, however, that the original vision of the JAC be maintained so that it can effectively serve its important community purpose. Maintaining a consistent vision does not mean that assessment centers should be resistant to changes in community concerns, agency mandates, and the problems of processed youths. Effective and community-connected JACs can make appropriate changes to respond to these issues. At the same time, it is important that JACs do not degrade to becoming merely sophisticated booking, fingerprinting, and photo image sites, in neglect of one of their key purposes: identifying and responding to the problems of troubled youths. JAC advisory committees can serve a very important role in this process.

## ■ A Vision for the Future

A major issue in service delivery for at-risk adolescents is that there is so little of it (Physician Leadership on National Drug Policy, 2002; U.S. Public Health Service, 2000). Relatedly, quality research on the effectiveness of service interventions for these youths is distinguished by the fact that it is quite limited (Dembo, Livingston, & Schmeidler, 2002). JACs can address both these needs. As discussed earlier, JACs are ideal locations to effectively place troubled youths in intervention services before their problems become more serious and to collect important information to evaluate the outcomes of these services.

Few service programs divert resources from treatment to evaluate outcomes, especially long-term follow-up. Thus, they cannot distinguish service or client characteristics associated with good outcomes. One strength of JAC programs is the opportunity to collect and analyze large longitudinal data sets that, over time, provide recidivism information in addition to client intake characteristics and referrals (Dembo, Schmeidler, Pacheco, Cooper, & Williams, 1997). The very large sample sizes and the extensive data collection at the JAC can be used to address other important issues (Dembo, Schmeidler, Nini-Gough, Chin Sue, et al., 1998).

It is clear there are many differences among juvenile drug abusers, as well as youths with mental health and other serious problems who are involved with the justice system. However, in the absence of valid in-depth assessment information on their problem areas, a common practice is to refer youths to programs with available slots, rather than to services that address their specific needs. Much more detailed information is needed on these youths' service needs so that better matches of individuals to treatment programs can be made. At the same time, almost all treatment studies involve sample sizes that are too small for meaningful comparisons of differential efficacy among subgroups of youths. If treatment service information were added to a JAC database, the large sample size would permit exploratory analyses of this important issue.

Integration of treatment program data into the JAC database could also provide a solution to a major problem in service delivery. Many youths do not enroll in treatment programs to which they are referred or do not remain in treatment (Battjes et al., 1999). Regular checking of a youth's treatment status on the JAC information system would permit timely intervention to help youths who do not enter treatment or who leave prematurely.

Finally, the identification of drug use is a critical initial step in the treatment of an abuser. Biological testing (urine, hair, and/or saliva) for drug use should be incorporated into the preliminary screening and in-depth assessment processes. Because it provides a more objective evaluation of recent use than a youth's self-report, it may be used to validate the self-reported use or may indicate additional drugs of use that are not reported. Most youths are reluctant to report the use of more socially proscribed drugs like cocaine (Dembo, Shemwell, et al., 1999).

Given the limited resources that are currently directed to troubled youths, we believe a national commitment to help troubled youths continues to be needed if we are to reduce their substance abuse, delinquency, and associated problems, as well as the personal, familial, community, and social costs that are related to them (Physician Leadership on National Drug Policy, 2002). Unfortunately, in the current austere funding environment in which we are living, early-intervention, front-end juvenile justice services in many jurisdictions are being cut or eliminated, while more deep-end, residential programs are being maintained with few if any cuts. These changes reflect a greater reliance on incarceration in long-term residential facilities in the juvenile justice system. In spite of the fact that residential commitment programs for troubled youths have been found to be ineffective in reducing recidivism, there has been an increased tendency to place youthful offenders in these programs (Altschuler & Armstrong, 1991; Greenwood & Zimring, 1985). Residential commitment programs are expensive to build and operate, and they often isolate youths from their families and general society. While there are youths who commit serious crimes and serious habitual offenders who require placement in secure facilities to protect the public, many institutional facilities house nonserious offenders, who would be more effectively, and less expensively, involved in community-based programs. A key way of cost-effectively reducing the development of delinquent careers is to involve nonserious juvenile offenders in early-intervention programs before the trajectories of their offense behaviors escalate (Greenwood, Model, Rydell, & Chiesa, 1998; Rand, 1996).

Drug-involved youths in the justice system continue to consume a large and growing amount of public health and justice system resources. Beyond these economic estimates is the poignancy of young lives lost to useful purpose and the pain and tragedy this failure causes these youths, their families, and the community. Rates of recidivism among juvenile offenders remain unacceptable (Snyder & Sickmund, 1999). Many middle-aged prisoners in state prisons trace their criminal careers to adolescence (U.S. Department of Justice, 1983)—stressing the importance of remediating the problems of juvenile offenders early in life. The issues are clear. Do we have the dedication of purpose and vision to rise to the challenge they present? Although researchers are unable to establish the necessary political infrastructure to accomplish these objectives, they can continue to educate political leaders to gain their commitment to this conceptually based, research-grounded blueprint for improving the quality of life of their constituencies.

## References

Altschuler, D. M., & Armstrong, T. L. (1991). *Intensive community-based aftercare prototype: Policies and procedures* (report prepared for the Office of Juvenile Justice and Delinquency Prevention, U.S. Department of Justice). Baltimore: Johns Hopkins University, Institute for Policy Studies.

Arcia, E., Keyes, L., Gallagher, J. J., & Herrick, H. (1993). National portrait of sociodemographic factors associated with underutilization of services: Relevance to early intervention. *Journal of Early Intervention, 17*, 283–297.

Armstrong, T. L., & Altschuler, D. M. (1998). Recent developments in juvenile aftercare: Assessment, findings, and promising programs. In A. R. Roberts (Ed.), *Juvenile justice* (2nd ed.). Chicago: Nelson-Hall.

Battjes, R. J., Onken, L. S., & Delany, P. J. (1999). Drug abuse treatment entry and engagement: Report of a meeting on treatment readiness. *Journal of Clinical Psychology, 55*, 643–657.

Butts, J. A., & Harrell, A. V. (1998). *Delinquents or criminals: Policy options for young offenders.* Washington, DC: Urban League.

Catalano, R. F., Hawkins, J. D., Wells, E. A., Miller, J., & Brewer, D. (1990–1991). Evaluation of the effectiveness of adolescent drug abuse treatment, assessment of risks for relapse, and promising approaches for relapse prevention. *International Journal of the Addictions, 25*, 1085–1140.

Christensen, A., & Jacobson, N. S. (1994). Who (or what) can do psychotherapy: The status and challenge of nonprofessional therapies. *Psychological Science, 5*(1), 8–14.

Crimmins, S. M., Cleary, S. D., Brownstein, H. H., Spunt, B. J., & Warley, R. M. (2000). Trauma, drugs and violence among juvenile offenders. *Journal of Psychoactive Drugs, 32,* 43–54.

Cronin, R. (1996). *Fact-finding report on community assessment centers (CACs): Final report.* Washington, DC: U.S. Department of Justice, Office of Justice Programs, Office of Juvenile Justice and Delinquency Prevention.

Dembo, R., & Brown, R. (1994). The Hillsborough County juvenile assessment center. *Journal of Child and Adolescent Substance Abuse, 3,* 25–43.

Dembo, R., Livingston, S., & Schmeidler, J. (2002). Treatment for drug-involved youth in the juvenile justice system. In C. Leukefeld, F. Tims, & D. Farabee (Eds.), *Treatment of drug offenders: Policies and issues.* New York: Springer.

Dembo, R., & Pacheco, K. (1999). Criminal justice responses to adolescent substance abuse. In R. T. Ammerman, P. J. Ott, & R. E. Tarter (Eds.), *Prevention and societal impact of drug and alcohol abuse.* Mahwah, NJ: Erlbaum.

Dembo, R., Pacheco, K., Schmeidler, J., Fisher, L., & Cooper, S. (1997). Drug use and delinquent behavior among high risk youths. *Journal of Child and Adolescent Substance Abuse, 6,* 1–25.

Dembo, R., & Schmeidler, J. (2002). *Family empowerment intervention: An innovative service for high-risk youths and their families.* Binghamton, NY: Haworth.

Dembo, R., & Schmeidler, J. (2003a). A classification of high risk youths. *Crime and Delinquency, 49,* 201–230.

Dembo, R., Schmeidler, J., Nini-Gough, B., Chin Sue, C., Borden, P., & Manning, D. (1998). Predictors of recidivism to a juvenile assessment center: A three year study. *Journal of Child and Adolescent Substance Abuse, 7,* 57–77.

Dembo, R., Schmeidler, J., Nini-Gough, B., & Manning, D. (1998). Sociodemographic, delinquency-abuse history, and psychosocial functioning differences among juvenile offenders of various ages. *Journal of Child and Adolescent Substance Abuse, 8,* 63–78.

Dembo, R., Schmeidler, J., Pacheco, K., Cooper, S., & Williams, L. (1997). The relationships between youths' identified substance use, mental health or other problems at a juvenile assessment center and their referrals to needed services. *Journal of Child and Adolescent Substance Abuse, 6,* 23–54.

Dembo, R., & Seeberger, W. (2000). The need for innovative approaches to meet the substance abuse and mental health service needs of inner-city African American male youths involved with the juvenile justice system (commissioned paper by the U.S. Commission on Civil Rights). In U.S. Commission on Civil Rights, *The crisis of the young African American male in the inner cities.* Washington, DC: U.S. Commission on Civil Rights.

Dembo, R., Shemwell, M., Guida, J., Schmeidler, J., Baumgartner, W., Ramirez-Garnica, G., et al. (1999). Comparison of self-report, urine sample, and hair testing for drug use: A longitudinal study. In T. Mieczkowski (Ed.), *Drug testing methods: Assessment and evaluation.* New York: CRC.

Dembo, R., Turner, G., Schmeidler, J., Chin Sue, C., Borden, P., & Manning, D. (1996) Development and evaluation of a classification of high risk youths entering a juvenile assessment center. *International Journal of the Addictions, 31,* 303–322.

Dembo, R., Wareham, J., & Schmeidler, J. (in press). Evaluation of the impact of a policy change on diversion program recidivism. *Journal of Offender Rehabilitation.*

Dembo, R., Williams, L., & Schmeidler, J. (1993). Addressing the problems of substance abuse in juvenile corrections. In J. A. Inciardi (Ed.), *Drug treatment in criminal justice settings.* Newbury Park, CA: Sage.

Dembo, R., Williams, L., & Schmeidler, J. (1998). Key findings from the Tampa longitudinal study of juvenile detainees: Contributions to a theory of drug use and delinquency among high risk youths. In A. R. Roberts (Ed.), *Juvenile Justice* (2nd ed.). Chicago: Nelson-Hall.

Dembo, R., Williams, L., Schmeidler, J., & Howitt, D. (1991). *Tough cases: School outreach for at-risk youth*. Washington, DC: U.S. Department of Education, Office of the Assistant Secretary for Educational Research and Improvement.

Dembo, R., Williams, L., Wothke, W., Schmeidler, J., & Brown, C. H. (1992). The role of family factors, physical abuse and sexual victimization experiences in high risk youths' alcohol and other drug use and delinquency: A longitudinal model. *Violence and Victims, 7*, 245–266.

Dembo, R., Wothke, W., Shemwell, M., Pacheco, K., Seeberger, W., Rollie, M., & Schmeidler, J. (2000). A structural model of the influence of family problems and child abuse factors on serious delinquency among youths processed at a juvenile assessment center. *Journal of Child and Adolescent Substance Abuse, 10*, 17–31.

Eng, T. R., & Butler, W. T. (Eds.). (1997). *The hidden epidemic: Confronting sexually transmitted diseases*. Washington, DC: National Academy Press.

Fleming, D., & Wasserheit, J. (1999). From epidemiological synergy to public health policy and practice: The contribution of other sexually transmitted diseases to sexual transmission of HIV infection. *Sexually Transmitted Infections, 75*, 3–17.

Florida Department of Health. (n.d.).Accessed February 2000. http://www.doh.state.fl.us

Greenwood, P. W., Model, K. E., Rydell, C. P., & Chiesa, J. (1998). *Diverting children from a life of crime: Measuring costs and benefits* (MR-699-1-UCB/RC/IF). Santa Monica, CA: Rand.

Greenwood, P. W., & Zimring, F. E. (1985). *One more chance: The pursuit of promising intervention strategies for chronic delinquent offenders*. Santa Monica, CA: RAND.

Guidry, J. (1991, June 18). Cloak of evil not worn by adults alone. *Tampa Tribune*.

Klitzner, M., Fisher, D., Stewart, K., & Gilbert, S. (1991). *Report to the Robert Wood Johnson Foundation on strategies for early intervention with children and youth to avoid abuse of addictive substances*. Bethesda, MD: Pacific Institute for Research and Evaluation.

LeBlanc, M. (1990, November). *Family dynamics, adolescent delinquency and adult criminality*. Paper presented at the Society for Life History Research conference, Keystone, CO.

McBride, D., Vanderwall, C., Terry, Y., & Van Buren, H. (1999). *Breaking the cycle of drug use among juvenile offenders* (report prepared for the National Institute of Justice). Berrien Springs, MI: Andrews University, Department of Behavioral Sciences.

National Center on Addiction and Substance Abuse. (2002). *Trends in substance use and treatment needs among inmates* (final report to the National Institute of Justice). New York: National Center on Addiction and Substance Abuse at Columbia University.

Nurco, D. N., Balter, M. B., & Kinlock, T. (1994). Vulnerability to narcotic addiction. *Journal of Drug Issues, 24*, 293–314.

Office of Juvenile Justice and Delinquency Prevention. (1995). *Community assessment centers: A discussion of the concept's efficacy* (issue overview). Washington, DC: Author.

Office of National Drug Control Policy. (2001). *The economic costs of drug abuse in the United States, 1992–1998*. Washington, DC: Author.

Oldenettel, D., & Wordes, M. (2000). *The community assessment center concept* (Juvenile Justice bulletin). Washington, DC: U.S. Department of Justice, Office of Justice Programs, Office of Juvenile Justice and Delinquency Prevention.

Physician Leadership on National Drug Policy. (2002). *Adolescent substance abuse: A public health priority*. Providence, RI: Center for Alcohol and Addiction Studies.

Rand. (1996). *Diverting children from a life of crime: What are the costs and benefits?* (RAND research brief). Santa Monica, CA: Author.

Rivers, J. (1997). *Juvenile assessment centers site visits: Executive summary and final report* (prepared for the Center for Substance Abuse Treatment). Miami, FL.: University of Miami School of Medicine, Comprehensive Drug Research Center.

Sherman, L., Gottfredson, D., MacKenzie, D., Eck, J., Reuten, P., & Bushway, S. (1997). *Preventing crime: What works, what doesn't, what's promising?* College Park, MD: University of Maryland, Department of Criminology and Criminal Justice.

Sirles, E. A. (1990). Dropout from intake, diagnostics, and treatment. *Community Mental Health Journal, 26,* 345–360.

Snyder, H., & Sickmund, M. (1995). *Juvenile offenders and victims: A national report.* Washington, DC: Office of Juvenile Justice and Delinquency Prevention.

Snyder, H. N., & Sickmund, M. (1999). *Juvenile offenders and victims: 1999 national report* (NCJ 178257). Washington, DC: Department of Justice, Office of Juvenile Justice and Delinquency Prevention.

Teplin, L. A., Abram, K. M., McClelland, G. M., Dulcan, M. K., & Mericle, A. A. (2002). Psychiatric disorders in youth in juvenile detention. *Archives of General Psychiatry, 59,* 1133–1143.

Tolan, P., Ryan, K., & Jaffe, C. (1988). Adolescents' mental health service use and provider, process, and recipient characteristics. *Journal of Clinical Child Psychology, 17,* 229–236.

U.S. Department of Justice. (1983). *Career patterns in crime* (NCJ-88672). Washington, DC: Bureau of Justice Statistics Bulletin.

U.S. Public Health Service. (2000). *Report of the Surgeon General's conference on children's mental health: A national action agenda.* Washington, DC: Author.

University of Colorado Center for the Study and Prevention of Violence. (1999). Model program selection criteria. Retrieved from ftp://128.138.129.25. File: www.colorado.edu/cspu/blueprints/about/criteria.htm.

Weisz, J. R., Weiss, B., Han, S. S., Granger, D. A., & Norton, P. (1995). Effects of psychotherapy with children and adolescents revisited: A meta-analysis of treatment outcome studies. *Psychological Bulletin, 117,* 450–468.

Winters, K. C. (1998, November). *Substance abuse and juvenile offenders.* Paper presented at the Physicians Leadership for National Drug Policy Conference, Washington, DC.

# 21 Epilogue

## National Survey of Juvenile Offender Treatment Programs That Work

Albert R. Roberts

**Gulf Coast Trade Center, Texas**

With the beginning of the new millennium, there has been a dramatic turn toward accountability and systematic review of evidence-based treatment programs. During the past three decades, several billion dollars were allocated by the federal Office of Juvenile Justice and Delinquency Prevention (OJJDP) through federal and state block grants and state contracts that were based on population, juvenile crime rates, and political influences. This is slowly changing. Society, legislators, and correctional administrators in a growing number of states are requiring juvenile justice officials to plan and implement outcome studies in order to determine program efficacy and effectiveness. Efficacy research refers to those studies that have utilized randomization and control/comparison groups. Effectiveness studies refer to program evaluations that include before and after measures such as rearrest or readjudication data, anecdotal information, and case studies.

In planning this national study, our goal was to identify juvenile offender treatment programs that seem to be effective in reducing recidivism, both short term and long term. We also sought to identify the rationale juvenile justice administrators use to justify identifying a program as a model for the nation and worthy of replication by other jurisdictions. In other words, we gave juvenile justice programs an opportunity for increased visibility and recognition, provided that the programs had demonstrated effectiveness through systematic, longitudinal follow-up studies and/or evidence-based studies.

Over the past century, criminologists and correctional researchers have demonstrated that juvenile prisons, also known as state training schools, are usually ineffective sanctions in rehabilitating juvenile offenders. The fact that most juveniles incarcerated in state facilities are not dangerous felons when they enter the facility yet soon after release frequently commit violent felonies leads to the conclusion that incarceration may well corrupt and harm certain juvenile offenders.

Most studies of youthful offenders released from large state training schools during the past three decades have reported consistently high rates of recidivism. In fact, the past research has indicated that between 55% and 91% of juvenile offenders are arrested within 2 years of release from a juvenile institution. In addition, the overwhelming majority of juvenile offenders in juvenile correctional institutions are not dangerous; they were found guilty of property crimes, not violent felony crimes. Therefore, it was not surprising that 9 of the 10 model programs with very low readjudication rates documented in this national survey were community-based, vocationally oriented, and/or minimum-security, short-term residential programs. More specifically, the four most promising model programs were the Associated Marine Institutes Last Chance Ranch in Florida, the Bethesda Day Treatment Center in Pennsylvania, the Earn-It restitution program in New Hampshire, and the Gulf Coast Trades Center in Texas. Recidivism in terms of readjudications in these four programs ranged from 10.4% to 15.8% within 12 months of release or discharge.

## ■ Survey Methodology

By cross-listing several address lists compiled from the latest American Correctional Association Directory of Institutions and Agencies, the OJJDP Web site, National Criminal Justice Reference Service, and the Google search engine. I developed a list of 145 state and county juvenile justice administrators and mailed to them (along with a cover letter) a detailed two-page questionnaire that we developed and pretested with three administrators of large state juvenile justice departments. The questionnaire contained a combination of structured and open-ended questions. Within 1 month after mailing, the post office returned 15 of the envelopes stamped "address unknown" or "moved with no forwarding address." By June 2001, analyzable responses had been received from 69 respondents, a 53% response rate. In April 2003, we followed up with letters and phone calls to the ten programs selected as model programs to obtain the most recent recidivism data measuring program effectiveness.

All of the 69 respondents indicated that they direct one or more model juvenile offender treatment programs. There was wide variation in how the juvenile justice officials defined a model or successful program. Unfortunately, only 10 or 14% of the respondents understood the importance of well-planned research and outcome studies. The 10 respondents represent a cross section of juvenile justice programs located in urban, suburban, and rural areas in all parts of the United States.

## ■ Results

This survey research indicated that limited funds are allocated for determining efficacy and effectiveness of programs. In fact, the overwhelming majority of responding programs gave as their rationale for selecting their program as a model the following:

> "People like our program."
> "We have the best program in the state because the juveniles tell us they like it."
> "We have a fine program because it is interesting."
> "Our program bolsters self-esteem."
> "Values clarification and forcing responsibility is the key to success."
> "Our program is widely considered to be the nation's oldest juvenile correction program, and therefore the most successful."
> "Our program is best because it has spirit on top of the mechanics of the program."
> "Our program should be replicated because none of the juveniles have committed suicide in the past six months.

In sharp contrast to these non-evidence-based rationales, the 10 programs we chose as model programs have conducted systematic research with outcome measures, including recidivism data 12 months to 36 months after completing the program. These model programs were judged to have demonstrated success by operationally defining *recidivism* in terms of rearrest rates, technical probation or court order violations, or new adjudications. When the model program is compared with traditional institutional programs, recidivism rates were significantly lower for those who completed the programs.

# ■ AMI

AMI (Associated Marine Institutes) is a network of community-based, noninstitutional programs for delinquent youths. The institutes that are collectively known as AMI are autonomous nonprofit organizations with 22 residential programs and 29 nonresidential day programs in seven states and the Cayman Islands. Although they are autonomous, they are all consistent in philosophical outlook, core training programs, activities, and success patterns, based on the systematic documentation of recidivism data.

This program focuses on involving adjudicated youths in marine research projects with an emphasis on vocational training, gaining aquatic knowledge, obtaining a GED or high school diploma, and counseling to encourage core values. There is no general program methodology description other than the program goals, but the recidivism rates for the programs as a whole suggest success in treating youthful offenders. The 2,741 program participants who participated in AMI between 1997 and 2001 were included in the recidivism study, which covered a period of 1 year following release from the program. The results are as follows:

☐ The overall recidivism rate was 28.5% (based on a convicted law violation) More than half of the program participants had received a felony conviction before enrollment in the program, and the recidivism rate for these program participants was 28.7%.

☐ Program participants who were placed in some type of work environment upon release from the program had the lowest recidivism rate of 22.1%, participants released into a combined school–work program had a recidivism rate of 25.6%, and those released to a school program had a recidivism rate of 35.8%.

☐ Only 23% of the female participants recidivated versus 29.2% of the male participants. Those who had been placed into the program as a condition of juvenile probation recidivated at a rate of 32.4%, and those who were directly committed (those who were in legal custody of the state) recidivated at a rate of 27.2%. Program participants who attended

**Table 21.1    Program Comparison of 10 Evidence-Based Model Juvenile Rehabilitation Programs Based on National Survey (Matrix)**

| Program | Location | Program Goals | Treatment | Duration | Population | Outcome | Sample Size |
|---|---|---|---|---|---|---|---|
| Associated Marine Institutes (AMI) | 7 states and the Cayman Islands | • Vocational Training<br>• Improve Academic Level<br>• Emphasizing Core Values | • Involvement in Marine Research Projects, such as aquatics, diving, oceanography, seamanship, marine biology<br>• Education | Ongoing | Adjudicated Youth, 14–18 yrs of age<br>Average of 8–12 offenses before coming to AMI | • 28.5% new adjud.-Recidivism Rate (1 year after release); most common recid.car theft | • 2741<br>• 54% of the 782 youths that recidivated did so within 4 months |
| AMI's Last Chance Ranch | Florida Everglades | • Behavior Management<br>• To Improve Academic Level | • Behavior Modification Program Based on a Point System<br>• Educat, 22 juv.at a time<br>• Physical Labor on the Ranch<br>• Community Service and Involvement in Environmental Projects | Minimum 1 Year (Ongoing) | Adjudicated Youth with Felony Offenses | • 15.8% Recidivism Rate (12 months) as defined as new adjudication. Most common recidivating offense burglary & car theft | • 57 |
| Bethesda Day Treatment Center | West Milton, PA | • Positive Socialization | • Alternative Education<br>• Drug Counseling<br>• Family Systems Counseling<br>• Short-Term Foster Care (Community Based) | 55+ hours a week (Ongoing) | Adjudicated, Non-adjudicated, Avg. Intake Age: 14.1 (10–17 yrs), "High-Risk" status offenders referred for truancy, incorrigibility, running away from home, or theft. IQ: 82% Below Avg. | • 10.4% Recidivism Rate within the first 12 months post discharge-new status offense | • NA |

(continued)

**Table 21.1    Program Comparison of 10 Evidence-Based Model Juvenile Rehabilitation Programs Based on National Survey (Matrix) (cont.)**

| Program | Location | Program Goals | Treatment | Duration | Population | Outcome | Sample Size |
|---|---|---|---|---|---|---|---|
| Earn-It | Keene, NH | • Restitution<br>• Low Cost Operation | • Employment for Restitution (Community Based) Court ordered monthly restitution; arranging work placement & community service | Ongoing | Adjudicated, Avg. Age 15.3 (12–18 yrs), "Low-Risk" Youth, Below Grade Level | • 5 to 14% Recidivism Rate after 12 mo.; Only 5% reoffense rate in all of 2000.<br>• 72% Program Completion | • 105 |
| Eckerd Wilderness Educational System | 18 Facilities (7 States) | • Improve Academic level, Vocational, and Social Skills<br>• Avoid Secure Confinement Costs<br>• Community Reintegration | • Group Activities<br>• Education<br>• Therapy<br>• Community Service | 1 Year (Ongoing) | Adjudicated, Non-adjudicated Avg. Intake Age: 14.5 (11–17 yrs) Below Grade Level | • 85.1% Graduation Rate<br>• 1.3-Year Grade Level Increase<br>• 26.7% Recidivism Rate (21 months) | • 820 eligible<br>• 418 graduates |
| Eckerd Wilderness Educational System (NC) | North Carolina | • Improve Academic level, Vocational and Social Skills<br>• Avoid Secure Confinement Costs<br>• Community Reintegration | • Group Activities<br>• Education<br>• Therapy<br>• Community Service | 1 Year (Ongoing) | Adjudicated, Non-adjudicated Avg. Intake Age: 14.4 (11–17 yr) Avg. IQ: 91.2 | • 84% Graduation Rate<br>• 1.2-Year Grade Level Increase<br>• 19.1%-new adjudication; Recidivism Rate (12 months) | • 406 |

| Program | Location | Components | Program Elements | Duration | Target Population | Recidivism/Outcomes | Number Served |
|---|---|---|---|---|---|---|---|
| Gulf Coast Trades Center (TYC) | New Waverly, TX | • Occupational Training, 9 trades<br>• Academic Skills Training | • Work Placement<br>• Location Monitoring (Community Based) Intensive aftercare and job placement | 6–9 Months | Adjudicated, 13–17 yrs. Of age; 65% of program graduates find employment in their chosen trade | • 15.7% Recidivism Rate, 12 month (Reincarceration) | 249 in 2000<br>311 in 2001<br>262 in 2002 |
| Texas Youth Commission | Texas | • Community Protection<br>• Education<br>• Resocialization<br>• Competency-based research-based system in academic beh. Correctional tx. | • Capital and Serious Violent Offenders Program<br>• Sex Offenders program<br>• Chemical Dependency Program<br>• Emotionally Disturbed Program<br>• ABC Resocialization program | 17–21 Months | Adjudicated, Avg. Age 16, 4–5 Years Below Grade Level, IQ: 75% are Below 90 | • 32.2% Reincarceration Rate for Any Offense (1 year)<br>• 28.9% Reincarceration Rate for Felony Offense (3 years) | • 5524 |
| Missouri Statewide system of residential facilities and group homes | 5 regions throughout Missouri | • Address education<br>• Treatment And rehabilitation needs<br>• small residential facilities and group home<br>• Family Tx. And Aftercare | • Residential and community day treatment, and aftercare by trackers and case managers<br>• Intensive family treatment<br>• 90 minute group therapy sessions 5 days a week | Ongoing | Juveniles with felony adjudications as well as juvenile status offenders | • Recidivism rate of 11% to 29% within 3 years post-release; only 8% recidivism rate-sentenced to adult prisons within 3 yrs release | • Based on 1,386 juvenile offenders released from custody in 1999. |
| Wraparound Milwaukee | Milwaukee, WI | • Address Mental Health, Substance Abuse, Emotional and Behavioral Need<br>• Provide Support in a Non-Residential Setting | • Community Based Care<br>• Family Services<br>• Ongoing Evaluations<br>• Team Driven Servicing for the Child and Family<br>• Strengths based treatment approach | Ongoing | Children and adolescents who have a serious emotional, behavioral or mental health disturbance that must have persisted for 6 months and who are at an immediate risk of residential treatment, psychiatric hospitalization or juvenile corr correctional placement. | • 15% Property Offenses, 5% Assault, 3% Weapons 2% Sex Offenses, 6% for Drug Offenses—One yr. Recidivism Rates | • 490 (based on program participants referred by probation) |

the nonresidential program recidivated at a rate of 31% versus a 31.6% recidivism rate for those who were in the residential program.

The results are indicators of the success of the programs as a whole, with the highest success rate of reduced recidivism for those who were placed in a work environment. The results also show very little difference in the recidivism rate between the residential and nonresidential program participants.

## ■ AMI's Last Chance Ranch

The Florida Environmental Institute (aka Last Chance Ranch) is one of the AMI programs developed for youths with felony offenses. This program is located in the Florida Everglades, and it is a working ranch with no iron bars, handcuffs, or locked cells. It is located 15 miles from the nearest state road and 35 miles from the nearest town.

The ranch accommodates only 22 participants at one time, and its mission is to address the youths' problems and change their behavior. This is a three-phase program that operates on a strict behavior management regimen. The program participants earn points toward going home that are based on their behavior. They are allowed to go home only after they have earned enough "point cards" to progress through the required levels. They are awarded points based on their behavior, being on time, appearance, attitude, leadership, participation, enthusiasm, and manners. The rate at which they are awarded points dictates the length of their stay. If they are well behaved and exhibit a good attitude, then they can complete the program in 1 year. If not, they will stay much longer.

The program has three phases, with phase one lasting approximately 6 months. During this phase, they stay in a dormitory with no television, air conditioning, or other amenities. They receive individualized academic education to make progress toward a GED or diploma. They also are required to perform basic chores and physical labor on the ranch.

Phase two of the program lasts 6 months or longer. During this phase, the youths move into a more comfortable dormitory with air conditioning, television, better furnishings, and a bit of private space. They continue their academic and ranch work and also take part in occasional community service and environmental projects. Toward the end of phase two, participants can earn the right to go back to their hometowns with a Florida Environmental Institute (FEI) staff member in order to begin the process of rebuilding their lives.

Phase three of the program has a heavy focus on the transition to home. During the month prior to leaving the ranch, youths work closely with counselors to develop plans for their return. Once home, the youths receive five visits per week from an FEI community coordinator, plus frequent calls from the case manager on staff at the ranch. Community coordinators may return youths to the ranch if their behavior lapses. The youths receive intensive support at home for 6 months before they are graduated from the program.

The Last Chance Ranch has juveniles with the highest felony rate among the 35 Florida programs serving serious juvenile offenders. During 1997–1998, the average youth from FEI had an average of 32.7 charges and 11.8 felony charges. However, during the 4-year period 1997–2000, only 15.8% (9 of 57) of the serious juvenile offenders released from FEI were found guilty of a new offense in their first 12 months following program completion. The average reconviction rate is more than 40% for all Florida institutions serving serious juvenile offenders. In addition, during the year 2000, only 1 FEI graduate of 21 was found by a court to have committed a new offense during the 12-month follow-up period.

The success rate of FEI's Last Chance Ranch is due in part to the high staff–participant ratio that allows the program to be tailored to the individual's needs. The low recidivism rates for the program indicate success in rehabilitating serious juvenile offenders.

## ■ Bethesda Day Treatment Center

The Bethesda Day Treatment Center program is designed to assist youths of all troubled circumstances, whether adjudicated delinquents, status offenders, or child abuse dependency cases. The program provides a residential setting or day treatment, as well as in-home treatment services (certified social workers and counselors come to the youth's home). The program is designed to work with all youths and provides individualized education, substance abuse counseling, family systems counseling, and short-term foster care. The program offers a wide variety of counseling options and combinations. The program is designed to facilitate reentry into the community.

An interesting aspect to the program is how intensive it is. The program involves the whole family and is integrated into the home, school, community, and peer groups. It may require 55 hours or more per week. The program does not suspend or expel any youths, allowing them to move beyond hostility and aggression. The no suspension policy does not allow the program to exclude difficult youths; thus the counselors do not give up on any youth.

The Bethesda model has 17 treatment modules that are combined and customized to meet the needs of the individual youth. The modules range from psychological counseling, to social counseling, to educational and vocational training. A majority of the youths receive group, individual, family, academic, life skills, and substance abuse counseling.

The client recidivism rate was reported to be 10.4%, overall. Many of the program's youths have prior offenses, with the average age at adjudication around 14.1 years. Two thirds of the youths are below grade level in reading.

This well-rounded program actively treats the most difficult youths (high-risk youths), normally removed from day treatment programs. The diversity of treatment options appears to be a strength of the program, offering solutions that other programs frequently overlook. The psychological and family counseling modules may be the most important for fostering a more self-aware youth and increasing the cohesion and functioning level in the family.

The program evaluation did not assess individual modules of the program. Therefore, the effectiveness of any one module needs to be determined by further study. The family counseling component, for example, is a useful approach and may well help the families of these troubled youths, thereby facilitating change at the root of the problem. Providing the family with new skills and the ability to function at a higher level is promising. The families of adjudicated youths often suffer from considerable disorganization and lack of consistent discipline. Nonadjudicated or diverted youths may fare considerably better because of their families' willing participation and support for the program, and they may be more motivated than the families of the adjudicated youths committed to a state institution.

This program does appear to be effective; it provides the services that are set as goals, and it has a very low recidivism rate of 10.4%. Some authorities claim that juvenile status offenders frequently escalate their lawbreaking pattern to serious crimes starting at the age of 16 or 17. We believe that most status offenders will outgrow their rebellious behavior (e.g. truancy, running away, curfew violations) if they are given the opportunity to participate in structured recreational programs, wilderness programs, alternative education programs, and comprehensive day treatment programs like Bethesda Day Treatment Center.

## ■ Texas Youth Commission

Texas Youth Commission (TYC) serves as the central organization in charge of all of the youths who have been into state custody. The TYC offers a variety of programs that target specific offenders: Capital and Serious Violent Offenders, Sex Offenders, Chemical Dependency, and Emotionally Disturbed.

Each of these programs is designed to provide discipline, promote skills growth, educate, and facilitate individual accountability, in addition to giving the youths social skills that will allow better reintegration into society. Also, the programs focus on specific treatments that address the deficiencies of the youths and the types of crimes they commit.

The Capital and Serious Violent Offender Treatment program (formerly the Capital Offender Treatment program) offers psychological services to the youths. The youths are assisted in understanding the origins of their violent behavior. The treatment also requires role playing of the violent act to help the offender gain empathy for the victim and to understand alternatives to the violent behavior.

The Capital and Serious Violent Offender Treatment program has demonstrated its effectiveness based on rearrest rates. The rearrest rates of treated and nontreated offenders diverge over the 36-month period measured (see Figure 21.1). Rearrest rates for felonies showed an average of a 25.8% difference between the treated and nontreated groups; violent offenses showed a 31% difference. There was a 41.1% difference between the groups for reincarceration.

Based on the rates of recidivism, during this evaluation (1996 to 2000) it is clear that the Capital and Serious Violent Offender program was effective at reducing recidivism. The evaluation also provided data on the youth Sex Of-

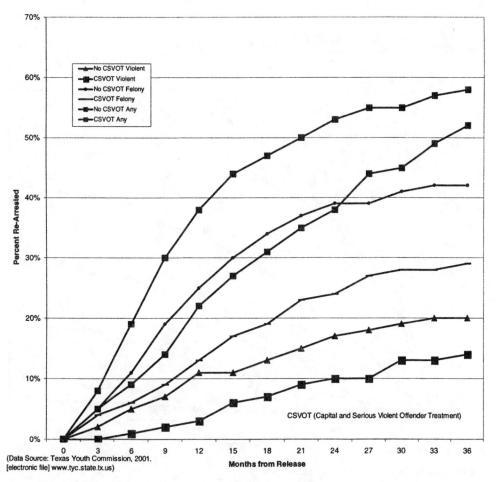

**Figure 21.1**   **Capital and serious violent offender rearrest rates.**

fender treatment program. That data shows that sex offenders were also helped by the TYC's specialized treatment program, as shown in Figure 21.2.

The treatment that sex offenders receive is designed to prevent future sexual offenses. It consists of cognitive-behavioral therapy, in addition to the basic resocialization and educational training offered in all of the programs. Sex offenders who went through the program were rearrested, on average, 61% less than the nontreated youths. The youths completing the program were arrested 12% less on sex offenses than youths who did not receive treatment. Sex offenders, overall, demonstrated improvement after completing the program. There were spikes in reoffending at 3 and 6 months after release. The increase of offenses in the treated group over the nontreated group may indicate that the treatment period should be lengthened by at least 6 months and possibly 1 year. The lengthening of the program may increase the differ-

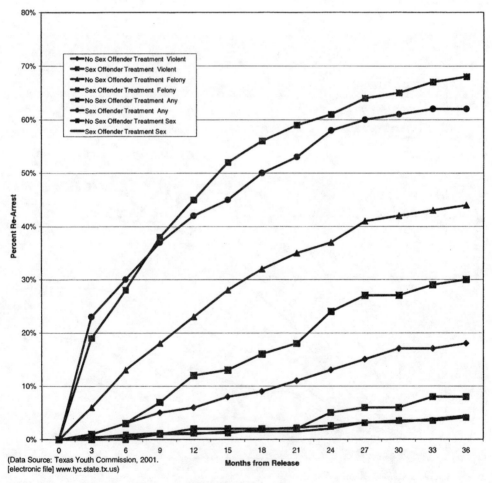

(Data Source: Texas Youth Commission, 2001.
[electronic file] www.tyc.state.tx.us)

**Figure 21.2    Rearrest rates for sex offenders.**

ences between treatment and nontreatment in all rearrest offense categories, including sex and violent offenses.

The TYC also has a special Chemical Dependency program for chemically dependent youths. It consists of social skills and educational training, in addition to a group therapy type of treatment that focuses on understanding the causes and cycles of chemical dependency. This program is divided into two treatment paths, using secure facilities and nonsecure facilities. The youths in each program showed a reduction in rearrest rates. The youths in the secure treatment facilities showed very modest improvement in rearrest categories and were only slightly better in reincarceration categories. The youths in the nonsecure facilities showed more improvement than the secured group. According to the TYC's report, the nonsecured youths were arrested 34% less than nontreated youths and were 32% less likely to be incarcerated for any offense. The report does not provide details about how the offenders were assigned to the secure or nonsecure treatment facilities.

The Emotionally Disturbed youth program is centered on the basics of socialization. Specific areas of focus are family, community, and school integration. The therapy works on short-term behavior management goals, as well as long-term family and community-specific problems. The treatment program is structured like the Chemical Dependency program, with secure and nonsecure treatment facilities. According to the TYC report, violent offense rearrest rates, for nonsecure treatment facility youths, show a 36% greater decrease than nontreated youths and an 8.5% difference for the secure facility treated youths. The reincarceration rates show a more consistent rate of improvement, 12.3% for the nonsecure and 10.4% for the secure treatment facility program over the nontreated groups.

Overall, the TYC's treatment programs are very successful at reducing rearrest and reincarceration rates. Table 21.1 shows the actual rearrest and reincarceration rates. As reported by the TYC, 1-year rearrest rates for violent offenses have declined from 1997 to 2001, dropping from 11.2% to 8.7%,

**Table 21.2    Actual Recidivism Rates for Selected Year**

| Year (number inmates) | Rearrest Violent Offense 1 Year | Rearrest Felony Offense 1 Year | Rearrest Any Offense 1 Year | Reincarceration Any Offense 1 Year | Reincarceration Any Offense 3 Years | Reincarceration Felony Offense 3 Years |
|---|---|---|---|---|---|---|
| 1997 (4561) | 11.2% | 36.9% | 48.9% | 28.9% | 50.8% | 35.3% |
| 1999 (5524) | 8.6% | 36.7% | 54.7% | 26.9% | 50.1% | 31.2% |
| 2001 (5524) | 8.7% | 31.1% | 53.5% | 31.1% | 49.3% | 28.6% |

Data Source: Texas Youth Commission, 2001. Accessed September 17, 2003, at www.tyc.state.tx.us

respectively. In the same period, there has been a 5.8% reduction in 1-year felony rearrests and 6.7% reduction in 3-year felony reincarcerations within the program.

For a better understanding of the programs, consider a few key facts about the average offender entering the programs (as found in the TYC):

☐   90% were boys.
☐   39% were Hispanic.
☐   34% were African American.
☐   26% were Anglo.
☐   42% admitted at intake that they are gang members.
☐   Median age at commitment was 16.
☐   Median reading and math achievement level was fifth or sixth grade (4 to 5 years behind their peers).
☐   75% had IQs below the mean score of 100.
☐   55% had a high need for drug treatment.
☐   43% were severely emotionally disturbed.
☐   Three of four youths had parents who never married or who divorced or separated.
☐   The vast majority had a history of being abused or neglected.
☐   More than half came from low-income homes.
☐   Many had families with histories of criminal behavior.
☐   Many had family members with mental impairments.
☐   More than half (57%) were in juvenile court on two or more felony-level offenses before being committed to TYC.

A composite of the average offender would be a 16-year-old Hispanic male with an IQ of 91. He would have barely completed the eighth grade but be able to read only on a fifth-grade level. He would have probably been arrested for burglary and assault, but that would not have been his first offense. Before being remanded to the Texas Youth Commission, he would have lived in a single-parent household, which in turn had a parent with poor parenting skills and a low income. He was probably one of several children who were frequently left to watch themselves and therefore attended school irregularly.

The TYC would, after referral, provide a specialized treatment program to address his violent behavior. Additionally, he would be taught some of the basic skills that he had not learned at home, such as how to interact with his family in a positive way and how to be socially involved in the community. He will also acquire the basic education that he will need to reintegrate after he is released in 17 to 21 months.

The TYC's youth offender program is one of the most comprehensive. The program's only shortfall is that there is no community-based prevention program. The youths are placed in this program only after being adjudicated on violent or felony-level offenses. Many less serious offenders may benefit from similar intense treatment. For example, the therapy that serious violent offenders receive to deal with their emotions and recognize alternate choices could be applied to many "acting out" and less serious violent offenders.

## ■ Gulf Coast Trades Center (TYC)

The Gulf Coast program fosters "occupational skills/academic skills coupled with work experience," as described in the survey response. In addition to its strong emphasis on academics and vocational training, the Gulf Coast program utilizes many behavioral management and counseling strategies typical in other youth treatment centers. The academic portion of the program is a self-paced study design. The program's youths attain general education degrees (GEDs) at a 60% rate, but there are no group comparisons for educational attainment. Vocational skills are acquired through work placement at nonprofit organizations and government agencies.

All participants in the program are between the ages of 13 and 18, and 80% of program participants are male. Approximately one fifth of the participants are White, and African American and Hispanic youths each are about two fifths of the Gulf Coast population. The youths are housed in on-campus dormitories with no locked cells or physical restraints. A select group of older program participants who are unlikely to return to their family homes reside on an independent living campus.

Supervision of the youths is structured and organized into three phases. The first phase is for 30 days. During this time, the youth attends school and work. Participants spend 2 hours every day in Gulf Coast's Learning Resource Center, where they work on basic skills, study for the GED, or earn high school credits. Students work at their own pace, using individualized plans developed and updated according to extensive pretesting and ongoing assessments. In each vocational track, program participants must demonstrate a mastery of several dozen competencies in order to earn a vocational certificate. During the average stay of 6 to 9 months at Gulf Coast, an average of 80% to 90% of program participants earn this credential, which then allows them to participate in Gulf Coast's work experience activities.

The second phase is for 60 days. This phase resembles a traditional probation arrangement, with strict rules and minimal privileges, in addition to strict monitoring. The final phase is a 90-day period that is the same as the second phase, except there is a 1-hour curfew extension. After completion of the training programs and obtaining on-the-job work experience, Gulf Coast provides extensive aftercare support, including job search and job placement assistance. Approximately half of the graduates take part in an intensive 90-day aftercare program, in which program staff serve as advocates and mentors. These youths are visited in their homes at least three times per week. Another 40% of graduates take part in a more moderate aftercare program, and approximately 10% did not receive aftercare support because of their location.

The most recent readjudication and reincarceration rate is 15.7% within 12 months of completing the program. This is very impressive, considering the fact that 249 youths completed the program in 2000, 311 youths completed the program in 2001, and 262 juvenile offenders completed the Gulf Coast Trades Center program in 2002.

The reincarceration rate for the program from 1989 to 1993 was 27.5%. Figure 21.3 shows the 5-year (1989–1993) reincarceration rate. The decrease between 1991 and 1992 is not explained in the program review. Figure 21.4 shows a 7-year reincarceration rate based on a 1-year period after release from the program. The rates include youths who reached the age of majority during the observational period. The 1991 to 1992 period reflects a similar decrease, as shown in Table 21.1.

Recidivism data for the second half of the 1990s show that only 15.7% of the youths who graduated from Gulf Coast from 1995 through 1999 were incarcerated within 1 year of release. This compares with a 37.6% recidivism rate for Texas youths released from other medium-security residential facilities during this same period. The 3-year recidivism rate for Gulf Coast youths for

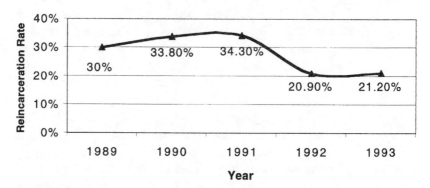

**Figure 21.3**  **Reincarceration rate: 5-year period**
(data source: Gulf Coast Trade Center program evaluation).

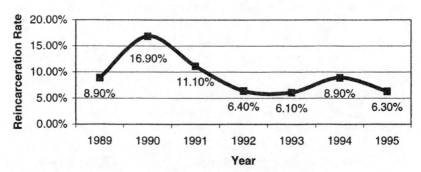

**Figure 21.4**  **Reincarceration rate: 7-year period, 1 year postrelease**
(data source: Gulf Coast Trade Center program evaluation)

the same time period is 18.2% versus 27.4% for other Texas youths in medium-security facilities.

This program provides intense in-community supervision, occupational and/or academic skills, basic behavioral modification techniques, and the possibility for low-wage employment with an aftercare program. This program may be effective for no other reason than serving the function of "grounding" the youth and monitoring the youth's location and activities in the community. The program offers realistic vocational trades training and deterrence through threat of harsher regulations or imprisonment.

## ■ Eckerd Wilderness Educational System

The Eckerd Wilderness Educational System has 18 facilities in seven states. The program provides services to youths who have been adjudicated into the program, as well as others who voluntarily participate (nonadjudicated). The program seeks to improve academic functioning, vocational skills, and emotional and social functioning, including skills that will assist the youths in reintegration into family and community settings. The youths are required to participate in group activities, education, and therapy. Usually, there are camp-specific projects (beautification or expansion) and public service projects (Adopt-a-Highway). The program runs year-round.

The system received 903 admissions during the 1995–1996 year, when there were a total of 1,619 youths program wide. Most of the youths were males, 14 to 15 years old, with an average of an eighth-grade education. Typically, the youths were White and came from single-parent homes (45.1%). About half of the youths in the system were adjudicated into the program. Most of the adjudicated youths were convicted of felony property offenses (52.6%) or persons offenses (17.9%).

Eight of the camps have been evaluated for quality of services. The eight camps received a rating of 81% or better. The area of concern was the inability of the counselors to effectively teach the youths problem-solving and planning skills. This affected the counselors' ability to help the youths reduce unwanted behaviors. Further counselor training in the principles of behavioral therapy and clear communication may remedy this problem.

Of the 820 eligible youths, there was an 85.1% graduation rate, up from 79% in 1994–1995. The average length of stay was 11.6 months for all of the camps, including several specialized program camps that are designed for shorter-duration programs and others that provide specific treatments. While at the camps, the youths averaged a 1.3-year grade level increase per year in reading skills, a one to one improvement in math, and a 1.2-year grade level increase in general knowledge. The camps were inconsistent with improvement on the Moos Family Environment Scale. Vermont was the only state (one sex offender camp) that showed consistent improvement. About 50% of the youths that entered the system were adjudicated, and 73.3% did not recidivate (arrest) within 21 months. No data were provided for the recidivism on adjudicated youths in isolation from the aggregate data. Only 78% of the graduating youths enrolled in any form of the educational system. Of those who graduated, 62.2% were employed in some manner at the 12-month follow-up point. Of the 418 graduates, 42 were receiving mental health care after graduation. The report did not provide outcome results for specific camp locations or programs, nor did it specify the types of mental heath care services being used.

The authors of the report found that the program had begun emphasizing a shorter program stay to increase the number of youths processed. Parents were reported to have complaints about not having contact with their children or children's counselors. Aftercare services were reported to be weak. Counselors were reported to need additional training and ongoing supervision.

The Eckerd Wilderness Educational System seems to be successful at accomplishing its educational goals. The change to a wilderness camp environment for the juvenile offenders also seems to be therapeutic. To strengthen this model program, the director should consider the need for specific individualized treatment plans for each youth entering the program.

## ■ Eckerd Wilderness Educational System (North Carolina)

The Eckerd Wilderness Educational System program provides services to youths who have been adjudicated into the program, as well as to others who voluntarily participate (nonadjudicated). The program seeks to improve academic functioning, vocational skills, and emotional and social functioning, including skills that will assist the youths in reintegration into family and community settings. The youths are required to participate in group activities, education, and therapy. Usually, there are camp-specific projects (beautification or expansion) and public service projects (Adopt-a-Highway). The program runs year-round.

Most of the program's youths are male (85.9% in 2000–2001). The average age at intake is 14.4 (the program accepts youths from ages 11 to 17). The average grade level upon entering is 7.9 (age and grade have remained fairly constant over the evaluated years). In the 2000–2001 year, 55.4% of the entering youths had an offense conviction, up from 52.2% in 1999–2000 and 47.3% in 1989–1999, with the average number of offenses between two and three. Serious offenses were most common (58%). The program saw an 84% graduation rate over the 2000–2001 year (406 youths). The Woodcock-Johnson Revised Achievement Test is used to measure ability upon entry and exit of the program. Reading and math scores both show an improvement for the 2000–2001-year, 1.2% and 0.9%, respectively. The Piers Harris Children's Self-

**Table 21.3**  **Six- and 12-Month Follow-Up Summary Report: North Carolina Graduate Youth July 1, 1999–June 30, 2000**

| Living Status at 6 and 12 Months Post Placement | 6 Months | | 12 Months | |
|---|---|---|---|---|
| | # | % | # | % |
| Both parents (biological or adoptive) | 71 | 22.8 | 79 | 25.9 |
| Single mother, biological, adoptive, or step | 89 | 28.5 | 87 | 28.5 |
| Single father, biological, adoptive, or step | 24 | 7.7 | 15 | 4.9 |
| Parent biological and stepparent/adoptive parent/live-in partner | 83 | 26.6 | 68 | 22.3 |
| Other relative | 22 | 7.1 | 18 | 5.9 |
| Foster home/group home | 8 | 2.6 | 5 | 1.6 |
| Other[a] | 15 | 4.8 | 33 | 10.8 |

[a]*Other* is defined as independent living, friend, mental health placement, or delinquency placement.

Source: Eckerd Wilderness Educational System (North Carolina) Evaluation Report Fiscal year 2000–2001, Eckerd Youth Alternatives.

Concept Scale is used to evaluate youths upon entering and exiting the program. This evaluation has shown a 16% improvement for the 2000–2001 year.

After graduation, the Eckerd Wilderness Educational System of North Carolina keeps track of the graduating youths for 6- and 12-month follow-ups (Table 21.2).

Of the youths who were adjudicated into the program, 8.2% recidivated within 6 months and 15.3% within 12 months. After leaving the program, 1.8% of youths at 6 months and 3.1% at 12 months were receiving residential mental health treatment. At 6 months 13.8%, and at 12 months 19.1%, were receiving nonresidential mental health treatment. Many of the youths were successfully reintegrated into their families and communities (93.7% at 6 months and 87.2% at 12 months), and they were enrolled in school and/or employed. The evaluation did not specify how work or employment determinations were made. The Eckerd Wilderness Educational System is effective at producing positive results in its goal areas of raising academic education levels and reducing reoffending.

## ■ Earn-It

The Earn-It program is a restitution-based youthful offender program. The program is designed to place offenders into jobs that allow them to repay the victim of the crime. The program requires the youth's parents and or employer to consent to the program provisions before a youth is allowed to participate. The program measures success in dollars paid by the youth.

The program does not offer psychological, family, or social skills counseling. The program had a 14% recidivism rate over the observed 6-year period

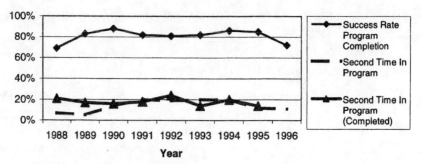

**Figure 21.5   Success rate (program completion)**
(data source: Earn-It program evaluation).

(based on the youths who completed the program). As shown in Figure 21.5, 72% of the participants completed the program in 1996. The program is successful in meeting its goal of a 30% or less recidivism rate. Three percent to 5% of the program's participants were adjudicated to the program instead of a secure confinement facility. For the 1996 year, shoplifting, criminal mischief, and theft were the top offenses for 64 of the 105 participants. In 1996, the program collected $4,940.95 and paid victims $2,430.89. The courts had ordered a total of $7,620.87 in restitution fines, with the average fine being $212.00. The average age of the offender was 15.3 years old, 79% of the youths are male, and a majority of the youths were below average in school; of these, most were coded as "special education."

During the observation period, 18% of the youths in the program had been in the program at least once before. On average, 14% of those complete the program. This program would be strengthened by addressing the youth's problems that led to the criminal behavior in conjunction with restitution. The evaluation did not clarify how the recidivism rate was measured or provide the reasoning behind a target rate of 30% recidivism. With a target rate of 30%, the program obviously is not concerned with providing more to the offender than a punitive correction through required labor. As for the victims, restitution is helpful in recovering monetary losses due to the youth's crime. Unfortunately, only about half of the money earned through the program actually reaches the victim. The Earn-It program is successful in meeting its goal of less than a 30% recidivism rate.

### ■ Missouri Division of Youth (DYS) Statewide Residential and Non-Residential Day Treatment Programs

Unfortunately, the majority of states still rely on large state training schools, also known as juvenile correctional institutions to confine approximately 200 to 2,200 juvenile offenders. The recidivism rates of juveniles released from these large training schools are consistently high, ranging from 55% to 90% within one or two years. For example, recidivism studies from Maryland reported an 82% recidivism rate two years after release, and Washington State reported a 68% recidivism rate two years post-release for incarcerated juveniles. In sharp contrast, the Missouri Division of Youth Services has reported an 11% to 29% recidivism rate, three years post-release, in its statewide juvenile system consisting of small-scale residential facilities, which each house 15 to 33 youths. Missouri also provides extensive treatment including 90-minute group therapy sessions, 5 days a week at all of its residential facilities. They also conduct multi-systemic family treatment including genogram family trees and DYS family therapists regularly meet with all youths and their families. Many of the juveniles in the residential treatment facilities have been adjudicated for felony offenses such as car theft, burglary, and/or drug dealing. In contrast, the juveniles placed in group home settings are usually status offenders in need of more structured supervision than is available in their own homes.

According to a February, 2003 DYS recidivism study, approximately 11% to 29% of youths released from CYS custody in 1999 had recidivated within three years. Most impressive is the finding that only 8 percent were sentenced to adult prisons or short-term 120-day adult confinement programs.

In addition to day treatment transitional programs, DYS has assigned "trackers," usually college seniors majoring in social work or criminal justice to offer support, mentoring and monitoring to approximately 800 delinquent youths in community supervision each day. Another 500 juveniles throughout the five regions of Missouri are in a supervised aftercare status with consistent oversight from the same case manager who took on their case soon after they entered custody. The median length of stay for Missouri juveniles adjudicated by the state to a residential treatment facility is 6 months, followed by 6–12 months of community supervision.

In addition to the residential treatment facilities, Missouri juvenile offenders may be sent to one of 24 group homes located across the state. Six of the group homes are small, with 10 to 12 beds, while the other 18 group homes have a capacity that ranges from 20 to 30 youths. The overwhelming majority of youths in these group homes have committed non-violent offenses, and many are status offenders. During the day they spend considerable time in academic classes, individual and group counseling, computer learning lab, group projects, jobs, field trips, pet therapy, etc.

The DYS focus and orientation on treatment and rehabilitation in small settings, rather than on punishment in large institutions seems to be cost-effective.

The DYS successful outcomes seem to be based on the following:

☐ Systematic screening of juvenile offenders before placement.
☐ Systematic supervision of adjudicated youth.

- ☐ Highly educated and trained staff available 24 hours a day.
- ☐ Family involvement and M.S.W. trained family therapists are an integral component of the residential treatment as well as the home-based after-care.
- ☐ Trackers to mentor and monitor the juveniles who are in aftercare and identify problems as soon as they arise.

Missouri's network of small residential facilities and group homes were selected as models worthy of replication by other jurisdictions because of its intensive treatment orientation, intensive aftercare program, and low recidivism rate of 11% to 29% three years post-release.

## ■ Wraparound Milwaukee

The term *wraparound* is defined as a philosophy of care that includes a definable planning process involving the child and family that results in a set of community services and natural supports individualized for that child to obtain a set of positive outcomes. These services are then said to be "wrapped" around the specific needs of that child and family.

Wraparound Milwaukee is an innovative system of care for children with serious emotional, behavioral, and mental health needs. Its approach emphasizes developing and delivering strength-based, highly individualized, and community-focused services to the children and their families. The program can be described as a public managed care entity that is responsible for meeting all the mental health, substance abuse, social service, and other supportive needs of the youths in the Milwaukee community. Multiple service systems are combined into a single system of care for the program participants and their families, and governance of this program is under the auspices of the Milwaukee County Health and Human Services Department. The program aim is to offer intensive, comprehensive assistance to troubled youths and their families in their own homes, thus avoiding a residential and not as highly individualized "blanket" treatment program. The core elements of Wraparound Milwaukee's approach include:

- ☐ Community-based care
- ☐ Services individualized based on the needs of the client
- ☐ Adherence to culturally competent services and supports
- ☐ Family involvement in the design and delivery of services
- ☐ Team-driven planning process
- ☐ Flexible funding
- ☐ Balance of formal and informal services to support families
- ☐ Collaboration among child servicing systems
- ☐ Unconditional care or never giving up on a child
- ☐ Presence of an ongoing evaluation process

The care coordinators are the cornerstone of this program. They facilitate the process by conducting strengths and needs assessments, by facilitating team planning, by identifying and obtaining treatment resources and supports for the child and family, and by monitoring and evaluating the care plan. They work with small caseloads of up to eight families, and they are intensively trained and certified in the wraparound process by Wraparound Milwaukee. Within the first 30 days of enrollment, the care coordinator will work with the child and family to develop the team that will service the particular child and family. In addition, a care plan is developed by the team in order to determine needs and identify strategies to help the child.

Wraparound Milwaukee targets children and adolescents through age 18 who have a serious emotional, behavioral, or mental health disturbance. The child's condition must have persisted for 6 months and be expected to persist for 1 year or more, and the child must be exhibiting functional symptoms or impairments that place him or her at an immediate risk of residential treatment, psychiatric hospitalization, or juvenile correctional placement. The child must also be receiving services from two or more of the following systems:

☐ Mental health
☐ Social services
☐ Child welfare
☐ Juvenile justice
☐ Special education

These children are placed in Wraparound Milwaukee through a court order that activates the child welfare and juvenile court finding. This court order is flexible in that it gives authority to Wraparound Milwaukee to determine the level of placement needed for each child and allows the program to move the child to a different level of care without having to obtain a new court order.

Pooled funding for Wraparound Milwaukee was created to meet the comprehensive needs of children with serious emotional needs. Funds from various child-serving systems and Medicaid are blended, using case rates and a capitation arrangement to create maximum flexibility and the most sufficient funding base possible. The key child-serving agencies that have collaborated with this program in order to fund services to the targeted children are:

☐ Bureau of Milwaukee Child Welfare, the state-administered, privately operated system overseeing all child protection services in Milwaukee County
☐ Milwaukee County Delinquency and Court Services, the county-operated probation services for delinquent youths
☐ Division of Health Care Financing, a state agency administering all Medicaid services, including all special managed care programs

**Table 21.4**    **Wraparound Milwaukee**

|  | Prior to Enrollment | During Enrollment | Following Enrollment |
|---|---|---|---|
| Property offenses | 40% | 21% | 15% |
| Assaults | 18% | 11% | 5% |
| Weapons offenses | 11% | 4% | 3% |
| Sex offenses | 17% | 4% | 2% |
| Drug offenses | 9% | 6% | 6% |
| Other offenses | 32% | 18% | 14% |

This is based on a sample size of 490 program participants.

☐    Milwaukee County Behavioral Health Division, Children's Branch, which is responsible for overseeing public mental health services for children in Milwaukee and designated to operate Wraparound Milwaukee

In 2001, Wraparound Milwaukee served a total of 869 children and their families meeting the criteria required for program admission. The average daily enrollment during this time was 560 families. Wraparound Milwaukee serves a primarily male population (71%) whose average age is 13.2 years. They are primarily African American, although there is a great deal of ethnic diversity within the program. Nearly half of the program participants live at or below the federal poverty level of $15,000 per year.

For those children who were referred to Wraparound Milwaukee as a condition of their probation, recidivism was measured as a rate of legal reoffense (the sample size used is 490 program participants). The rate of offense for these children decreases during enrollment and continues to decline during the year following completion of the program. Prior to enrollment, each child had an average of 2 offenses, which decreased to an average of 1.1 offenses during enrollment and an average of 0.77 offenses in the 1 year following enrollment. Adjudications were also measured prior to enrollment, during enrollment, and 1 year following completion of the program, with the same results, showing a continuous decrease until 1 year following program completion. Prior to enrollment in the program, there were an average of 1.26 adjudications compared with an average of 0.73 during enrollment and 0.57 in the 1 year following enrollment. Recidivism studies of these children also focused on specific types of offenses committed: property offenses, other offenses (consisting primarily of disorderly conduct), assaults, weapons offenses, sex offenses, and drug offenses. In all cases there was a significant decrease in these offenses during enrollment, with another decline (with the exception of drug offenses, which stayed at the same rate) in the 1 year following completion of the program. Table 21.3 breaks down the percentages of number of offenses committed prior to enrollment, during enrollment, and during the 1 year following enrollment.

Wraparound Milwaukee is a successful program because it has, through its intense individualized treatment structure, contributed to desired outcomes for the children and families involved. This model, which provides strength-based, comprehensive, flexible, and cost-effective alternatives to institutional care for children, has contributed significantly to broad-based and valued outcomes for both the children and their families.

## ■ Conclusion

The 10 programs that were evaluated had many positive features in common, such as lower recidivism rates 12 months after treatment completion and evidence of the acquisition of improved reading and math levels, positive socialization, and enhanced social skills. Several of the programs seemed honest about their limitations and changes they would like to make in the near future with regard to more training of counselors and ongoing built-in evaluations. More specifically, the Eckerd Wilderness Educational System evaluation highlighted that the counselors needed additional training on a quarterly basis. The Bethesda Day Treatment Center program is trying to obtain additional funding for ongoing and regular program evaluations. On the positive side, all of these 10 model programs have provided evidence of attaining short-term, interim, and long-term goals.

As is to be expected, cross-study comparisons were challenging and difficult. It would be useful if federal and state juvenile justice funding sources could agree on standardized outcome measures similar to those recommended in the *Desk Reference of Evidence-Based Practice in Health Care and Human Services*. Standardized outcome and performance measures could evaluate how well the program has achieved its goals, the demographics of the youths coming into and exiting the program, average treatment lengths, evaluation of the individualized treatment aspects in each program, and the rate of reoffending and technical parole violations for all youths who enter the program (completed or not) at 6-, 12-, 24-, and 36-month intervals. Such standardized measurements would allow for an accurate comparison between programs and for the components of any one program to be evaluated separately.

These juvenile offender treatment programs serve a very important function. They provide many youths with a second chance through supportive and caring treatment protocols that can break the cycle of habitual delinquency and criminality. As more juvenile offender treatment models are developed, evaluated, and replicated, the exemplary models will stand out. These programs benefit society by teaching the juvenile offenders an alternative path in life and provide the youths with the mindset and skills necessary to avoid repeating their mistakes or escalating their level of offending, which make all of society a safer and more humane place.

# Glossary

## Evelyn Roberts Levine

**Accountability:** Accountability involves providing information, in useful form, to others who must make decisions or take action regarding a person, case, situation, agency, or community. A social worker may be accountable to a supervisor, community, clients, the court, a board of directors, the profession, and others. Being accountable means being responsible for providing services in accordance with high standards.

**Addams, Jane:** Established Hull House, an early settlement house in Chicago during the 1880s to help wayward youths, homeless families, and new immigrants.

**Adjudication:** A juvenile who is *adjudicated* is judicially determined (judged) by an official juvenile justice agency (e.g., the county juvenile court) to be a delinquent or status offender.

**Adventure Corps:** This character-building organization, similar to Boy Scouts and Girl Scouts, was designed to reach delinquency-prone youths eight to twelve years of age. It provided exciting recreational and educational activities for young people as an alternative to gang membership. Squad leaders and their assistants were neighborhood residents who were paid a stipend.

**Advocacy:** To speak up, to plead the case for another, or to champion a cause, often for individuals and groups that cannot speak out on their own behalf. Types of advocacy include self-advocacy, case advocacy (for an individual client), and class advocacy (advocacy on behalf of a group or category of individuals in similar circumstances).

**Aggression Replacement Training (ART):** A multimodal, psychoeducational intervention to promote skills acquisition and performance, improve anger control, decrease the frequency of acting out behaviors, and increase the frequency of constructive, prosocial behaviors. The primary ART trainers for clients are teachers, counselors, social workers, child-care workers, and others who have direct responsibility for youths who frequently behave aggressively. The intervention is made up of the following three components, each of which the youth attends on a weekly basis: skillstreaming; anger control training; and moral education.

**Anger Control Training (ACT):** Its goal is teaching youths the self-control techniques of anger control. In ACT, each young person is required to bring to each session a description of a recent anger-arousing experience (a hassle), which each records in a binder ("hassle log"). For ten weeks the youngsters are trained to respond to their hassles with a chain of behaviors that include: identifying triggers; identifying cues; using reminders; and using reducers.

Anger management: Juveniles need to learn adaptive ways to manage anger. Techniques based on cognitive-behavioral restructuring are effective in helping individuals to recognize the antecedents of anger and its physiological indicators, to learn alternative coping skills to use when provoked, and to become comfortable using these strategies through role-playing and other exercises.

Anti-bullying programs: Anti-bullying programs have been employed internationally for decades, and provide a model for school violence prevention programs, particularly as bullying is often seen as an early indicator of violent behavior toward others. The manner in which adults in positions of authority respond to reports of victimization impacts on future reports from students. If adult responses do not solve violence problems, students feel unsupported or betrayed by these adults and are vulnerable to more victimization. In essence, the victim is violated twice; once by a bully and once by the system that is supposed to protect them.

Arbitration program: The parent or guardian and the juvenile appear, along with the victim, at a hearing before a trained arbitrator. The arbitrator explores the details of the case by questioning the defendant and listening to information contributed by the parents and victim, then makes a decision as to the most appropriate sanctions (e.g., community service hours, paying restitution) for the particular set of circumstances, and imposes these sanctions on the juvenile. Arbitration staff monitor completion of assigned sanctions. *See also restorative justice and victim-offender mediation.*

Associated Marine Institutes (AMI): Established in 1969, with headquarters in Tampa, Florida, AMI serves approximately two thousand youths annually in Florida, Georgia, Arkansas, Louisiana, South Carolina, Texas, Delaware, and Virginia. The participants have been adjudicated for either status offenses (e.g., truancy) or more serious delinquency offenses such as breaking and entering, auto theft, assault, and armed robbery. They learn how to work with engines, make boat repairs, clear and maintain trails in state parks, and scuba dive. The overriding goals are to improve the youths' educational and vocational skills and to teach them to behave in a socially appropriate, law-abiding manner.

Attention Deficit Hyperactivity Disorder (ADHD): ADHD is characterized by inattention, disorganization, hyperactivity, and impulsivity. Juveniles with this disorder often are easily distracted, inattentive, have difficulty concentrating and have poor organizational skills. They demonstrate poor school performance, little patience, poor problem-solving skills, and difficulty attending to stimuli.

Balanced and restorative justice: This model addresses both individual and community responsibility by focusing on repair of harm and requiring that both contribute to that repair.

Balanced approach: Mission addresses community demands for: (1) sanctioning based on accountability measures that restore victims and clearly denounce and provide meaningful consequences for offensive behavior; (2) offender rehabilitation and reintegration; and (3) enhanced community safety and security. It does this by articulating three system goals directed toward the three primary "client/customers" of the system—the victim, the offender, and the community.

Behavior Modification System: The primary element of an effective behavior management system is the systematic and direct reinforcement of appropriate behaviors. In many systems, the focus is on "shaping" new behaviors by reinforcing "small steps" along the process of change. The entire system is based on earning; nothing is taken away, but all privileges (type of visitation, bedtime, use of recreational items, amount and type of items allowed in room) must be earned.

Bipolar Disorder: *See Mood Disorders.*

Boot camps: Boot camps are used as a type of diversion for youth from typical residential facilities. Often they are used for first offenders to attempt to "shock or scare" them into appropriate behavior. Boot camps are usually from 3–6 months long and based on a military schedule and discipline. Rigorous physical training is part of the foundation along with education, but the majority of programs do not provide therapy, vocational training, or life skills training.

Brief Strategic Family Therapy (BSFT): This treatment modality was developed out of a programmatic series of studies with Hispanic youths. With a strong grounding in a cultural frame of reference, this approach considers factors such as family cohesion, parental control, and communication. Treatment strategies focus on changing concrete interaction patterns in the family, with the therapist challenging interaction patterns to help the family consider alternative ways of dealing with one another.

Brief treatment: An approach to working with clients that acknowledges upfront that there is a time limit to treatment. Models vary and may specify time limits (e.g., up to 12 sessions) or may limit the amount of time e.g., up to three months). In other words, the treatment is not open-ended. *See also the quarterly international journal entitled-Brief Treatment and Crisis Intervention: www.brief-treatment.oupjournals.org and Dr. Roberts's website: www.crisisintervention network.com.*

Brief Symptom Inventory (BSI): BSI was designed to measure current psychological symptoms and result in a diagnosis. The instrument can be administered in ten minutes and is easily scored. It has established reliability and validity and is available in several languages. The inventory does not have a specific suicide subscale, nor does it assess alcohol, drug use, or aggression. The BSI is useful for a quick psychological screening, however other instruments would need to be utilized with it for a comprehensive assessment.

Camp Woodson: Located in Fairview, North Carolina, Camp Woodson is a therapeutic, adventure-based wilderness program for adjudicated juvenile offenders. Emphasis is placed on helping youths gain self-confidence through achievement of progressively more difficult tasks. The program, which began in 1976, has 130 male and female campers per year and nineteen staff.

Changes to the physical plant: Several changes can be made to the physical layout of school to prevent violence. For example, limiting access to school grounds, limiting places for loitering, patrolling bathrooms, placing lockers where supervision is possible, and installing parabolic/convex mirrors in stairwells or video surveillance equipment are all ways of improving school safety and reducing violence in schools.

**Chicago Area Project:** The project was initiated by the Institute for Juvenile Research and the Behavioral Research Fund in 1929. It was one of the most widely known examples of a coordinated ecological program aimed at the reduction of juvenile delinquency. Clifford R. Shaw was the founder and director of the project, which consisted of a series of studies from 1929 to 1933 as well as a classic experiment in delinquency prevention at the local level that lasted until 1962. The studies conducted by Shaw and McKay (1972) concentrated on two areas: (1) the epidemiology of delinquency in different areas of Chicago and (2) the acquisition of delinquent beliefs and behavior from delinquent subcultures. Shaw and McKay found that a disproportionately large number of juvenile delinquents came from certain areas of Chicago. The high rate sectors were termed *delinquency* areas.

**Child and Adolescent Functional Assessment Scale (CAFAS):** A standardized multidimensional assessment tool that is used to measure the extent to which the mental health/substance use disorders of youths age 7 to 17 impair functioning. It is completed by the clinician and requires specialized training. A major benefit of the CAFAS in helping practitioners determine a youth's overall level of functioning is that it covers eight areas: school/work, home, community, behavior toward others, moods/emotions, self-harmful behavior, substance use, and thinking. The adolescent's level of functioning in each of these eight domains is scored as severe (score of 30), moderate (20), mild (10), or minimal (0).

**Childsavers:** This refers to an organized movement in the United States during the early 1800s whereby middle- and upper-class women volunteers provided food, shelter, and educational and religious instruction to wayward and poor children.

**Christ's Hospital:** This institution opened in London, England, in 1552, to house orphaned, destitute, and delinquent children. Early institutions served as a catchall for all "needy" children, with no distinctions for background or behavior.

**Cognitive behavioral approaches:** Can include social skills training, parenting skills training, anger management, problem solving skills, and behavioral contracting. The "skill-streaming" component teaches a progression of very specific pro-social skills through performance feedback, role-playing, and modeling. The anger control element helps youth learn what triggers their anger and how to modify and control it. Problem-solving components teach strategies for identifying problems, alternative actions, and pros and cons of actions. Parenting skills training helps guardians learn to develop behavior modification plans, utilize various reinforcement schedules, and problem solving as creative discipline for youth. These components have been found to be effective with children and youth, as well as families dealing with mental illness and offending behavior.

**Cognitive-based interventions:** Interventions including conflict resolution, peer mediation, social skills, and anger management programs.

**Cognitive-behavioral focus:** If behavior change is to be "portable," that is carry past the detention center program, residents need to make fundamental changes in how they see the world, themselves, and their response to situations around them. The cognitive focus shows residents how their thinking (their beliefs and attitudes) affects their behavior. The goal is to help residents change their thinking, and thus their behavior.

**Cognitive-Behavioral Therapy (CBT):** An approach that employs progressive relaxation, cognitive reframing, and communication skills. The approach presents clients with options that draw on these different interventions and then encourages them to correct distorted thinking and develop individualized anger control plans using as many of the techniques as possible.

**Comorbid psychiatric disorders:** When a juvenile has two or more separate and distinct psychiatric problems at the same time. This situation poses significant theoretical, conceptual, diagnostic, and treatment planning difficulties. Comorbid conditions spawn confusion and questions with regard to the course of the disorders. For example, are observed symptoms part of one disorder or two? How does one disorder affect the occurrence or onset of another disorder? Did the disorders begin at the same time, or should one be considered primary? Treatment issues are challenging as well. For instance, should both disorders be treated simultaneously or should one disorder be treated first? If so, which one and with which types of interventions? In addition, how can disorders that seem to be polar opposites occur in an individual at the same time? Depression and Conduct disorder are disorders that have very different symptomatology, yet they occur together frequently and warrant concern.

**Comprehensive interventions:** Comprehensive interventions have been found to be the most effective programs in that they address multiple dimensions of the child (cognitive, behavioral, social, emotional, physical, spiritual) at multiple levels (family, peer group, school, community).

**Conduct Disorder (CD):** Youth with CD persistently violate norms or rules and disregard the rights of others. They may be aggressive toward animals and people, and destroy property. These juveniles also have deficits in social skills and problem-solving skills and they tend to see others' interactions with them as hostile. They are also impulsive and tend to lack empathy.

**Conduct Disorder Diagnosis:** The overriding feature of CD is a persistent pattern of behavior in which the rights of others and age-appropriate social norms are violated. Exhibiting conduct such as aggressive behavior toward others, using a weapon, fire setting, cruelty to animals or persons, vandalism, lying, truancy, running away, and theft. The *DSM-IV-TR* allows for coding a client with one of two subtypes of CD: childhood-onset type (at least one criterion characteristic occurs prior to age 10) and adolescent-onset type (absence of any criteria prior to age 10). While an adolescent may be considered a "juvenile delinquent" after only one delinquent act, to warrant a diagnosis of CD, that same adolescent must be engaged in a pattern of behavior over an extended period of time (at least 6 months) that consistently violates the rights of others and societal norms.

**Conflict resolution and mediation:** An approach emphasizing communication, anger-management, and perspective-taking skills, usually taught as a curriculum unit with a prescribed number of lessons. While some programs employ peer-mediators, increasingly school district-wide approaches that teach conflict resolution and mediation skills to all students are being utilized.

Coordinating council movement: The movement was considered a significant step in the treatment and prevention of juvenile delinquency. Its roots can be traced to the founding of several national organizations in the early 1900s: the National Probation Association in 1907, the Family Welfare Association in 1911, the Big Brother and Big Sister Federation in 1917, and the Child Welfare League of America in 1920. The major focus of these organizations was on improvement of standards of community service and development of national policies. The success of these councils was based on their ability to enlist the cooperation and coordinated efforts of community facilities. Councils that functioned most effectively not only stimulated and utilized the skills of local residents but also had access to a planning board or a broader coordinated community organization that supplied personnel, funds, and planners. Social historians have noted that the coordinating council movement played an active role in delinquency prevention efforts during the 1930s. Over 250 coordinating councils were operating in 163 cities and towns in twenty states during 1935 and 1936.

Corvallis House: Located in Salem, Oregon, Corvallis House is a community-based group home program that incorporates wilderness trips (e.g., snow camping, skiing, rock climbing, mountaineering) as an important component of its overall treatment approach. But unlike many other wilderness models, its program is not based totally on outdoor adventures. It offers a comprehensive program providing not only wilderness trips but also academic education, work-study, drug and alcohol treatment, and independent living programs.

Crack baby: An infant born to a mother who used crack cocaine during pregnancy.

Crack cocaine: A freebase cocaine product produced through a process of mixing cocaine salt with baking soda and water. The solution is then "cooked" or heated until a brittle form of cocaine forms. This product is then broken into small, smokeable pieces of crack referred to as "rock".

Creative arts education: A component to provide youth with alternative forms of expression to help build self-esteem. Various fine arts are taught, such as drama, art, dance, and music. Fine arts instruction emphasizes cultural diversity and ethnic sensitivity.

Delinquency offenses: Illegal acts that are considered crimes whether committed by an adult or a juvenile (e.g., aggravated assault, arson, burglary, drug-related offenses, theft, rape).

Dependency cases: A documented pattern of child neglect, physical abuse, and/or sexual abuse and identification of a minor needing foster care or other residential placement outside the home.

Depression: A disturbance of mood marked by inability to enjoy activities and relationships, feelings of hopelessness and worthlessness, problems sleeping and eating, and thoughts of suicide.

Detention education: A number of detention education program operators believe that effective education must be more than rote academic maintenance and that detention education should respond to the juvenile's needs. Presented with students at multiple levels and with multiple needs, a quality detention education curriculum should provide a continuum of academic services ranging from special education to GED preparation to post-secondary options. The detention education curriculum should teach and reinforce pro-social behaviors that translate into success for the student at home, at school, in the community, or in a future placement. Youth in juvenile detention facilities need instruction in communication, problem solving, decision-making, interpersonal relationships, values, critical thinking, and healthy life-style choices.

Diagnosis: A discrete process of determining through observation, examination, and analysis the nature of a client's illness or functional problems.

*Diagnostic and Statistical Manual of Mental Disorders, Fourth Edition, Text Revision (DSM-IV-TR)*: The latest edition of the official manual of mental disorders used in the United States and many other countries, published by the American Psychiatric Association. It provides a listing of all the officially recognized mental disorders and their code numbers, as well as the diagnostic criteria used in identifying each disorder. The codes and terms are a subset of the mental disorders listed in the *International Classification of Diseases, Ninth Revision, Clinical Modification (ICD-9-CM)*.

Diagnostic criteria: Detailed descriptions, called diagnostic criteria, are provided in *DSM-IV-TR* for each of the specific mental disorders. These specify the rules for inclusion and exclusion symptoms and other features when making each diagnosis.

Dialectical Behavioral Therapy (DBT): A gender-specific treatment model that focuses on emotional regulation. The use of DBT with severely disturbed female juvenile offenders found that it was effective in reducing certain behavior problems (e.g., aggression, parasuicidal behavior) with the population.

Direct calendaring: A "one family-one judge" approach that allows the judge to remain with the case for all stages of case processing. Direct calendaring is believed to result in courts making more consistent decision-making because judges will be more familiar with the complexities of the family situation, what the family needs, and the expectations for the family. Direct calendaring is also thought to make the family less likely to feel that a stranger who is not familiar with their situation is making life-altering decisions on their behalf. This is in contrast to master calendaring.

Discrimination: Discrimination refers to being treated differently based on a group status rather than one's behavior or qualifications. Discrimination due to race or ethnicity occurs when one group is treated differently than another group based wholly or in part on their race or ethnicity. *See disparity and over-representation for additional information.*

Dismissed cases: Cases that are dismissed (including those warned, counseled, and released) with no further disposition anticipated.

Disparity: Disparity refers to different groups having different probabilities for a particular outcome due to their group status. *See over-representation and discrimination for additional information.*

Dispositions: Categorized as the most severe action taken or treatment plan decided upon or initiated in a particular case. Disposition cases include: waived, placement, probation or dismissed.

Disruptive behavior disorders: ADHD and CD are termed *disruptive behavior disorders.* Thirty-fifty percent of youth diagnosed with ADHD also receive a diagnosis of CD and approximately 28% of detained youth have a diagnosis of ADHD. Youth, diagnosed with ADHD and CD who have deficits in social skills, problem-solving skills, and increased impulsivity are prone to have problems with law-abiding behavior. Faced with daily temptations to break the law, these youth are unable to control their initial impulses or think clearly about the pros and cons and future consequences of their behavior. They are also more likely to surround themselves with negative peers and have difficulty refraining from peer pressure. Both disorders place youth at risk for school failure, school suspensions, and school violence.

**Drug abuse:** Any use of drugs that creates legal, social, emotional, family or social harm as the direct result of behaviors of the individual taking the illegal drug.

**Drug trafficking:** Drug trafficking means doing or being concerned in any of the following, whether in the State or elsewhere, that is: (a) producing or supplying a controlled drug where the production or supply contravenes any regulations made under section 5 of the Misuse of Drugs Act, 1977, and is in force at the material time (whether before or after the commencement of the relevant provision of this Act) or a corresponding law, (b) transporting or storing a controlled drug where possession of the drug contravenes section 3 of that Act or a corresponding law, (c) importing or exporting a controlled drug where the importation or exportation contravenes any such regulations as mentioned in paragraph (a) of this definition or a corresponding law.

**Drug urinalysis:** Urinalysis by definition refers only to the chemical analysis of urine. However, analysis per se is defined as identification or separation of ingredients of a substance. Hence urinalysis can take on a broader meaning. In practice, routine urinalysis refers to (1) macroscopic analysis, which includes assessment of physical characteristics and (2) chemical analysis or microscopic analysis for formed elements.

**Early childhood education:** High-quality early childhood education can provide a measure of school violence prevention. Several early comprehensive intervention programs have had favorable impacts on the prevention of delinquency and violence.

**Emotional discharge:** Can be conceptualized as a three-phase process: facilitating the feeling; encouraging its recognition, acknowledgment, and expression; and validating its expression. Therapists must be specifically trained in techniques to encourage emotional discharge.

**Empathy training:** Empathy training is designed to help an individual to feel a sense of connection with others. The juvenile delinquent is encouraged to see the victim as a human being, as someone's son or daughter, or mother or father. Several approaches to teach victim empathy currently exist.

**Empathy:** Enables a person to feel what another is feeling and to understand what another individual is feeling and why she or he is feeling that way.

**Evidence-Based Practice (EBP):** An approach to practice that requires the examination of research findings from systematic clinical research (e.g., randomized controlled clinical research) in making decisions about the care of a specific population with a specific problem. The process of critically identifying and employing treatment or practice approaches that have the strongest basis of empirical support for attaining desired outcomes. An evidence-based practice is considered any practice that has been established as effective through scientific research according to a set of explicit criteria. The term *evidence-based* *practice* is also used to describe a way of practicing in which the practitioner critically uses best evidence, expertise, and values to make practice decisions that matter to individual service recipients and patients about their care. Evidence-based practice is the use of interventions that are based on rigorous research methods. Evidence-based practice includes the integration of different studies and establishing the combined probative value. An example of an EBP approach to supporting and serving families and children would be based on the likelihood that certain types of supports and services can be shown to be more effective than other interventions.

**Families and Schools Together (FAST) program:** Applies community organizing principles, group work practices, and child and family therapy strategies in multifamily groups to enhance protective factors for children, to reduce delinquency, drug abuse, and school failure. The criteria for inclusion are based on identified family risk factors, and the program seeks to provide services to families before delinquent behaviors are manifest.

**Family systems theory:** Family systems theory is the foundation of the majority of family treatment programs. This theory states that the family is the major socializing agent that influences and helps shape the child's attitude, values, behavior, and personality. Basic principles include: the family is seen as an organized whole, behaviors should be seen as actions and reactions rather than one-way communication, families resist change unless it meets their needs, well-functioning family systems are less resistant to change and are more willing to adapt, and family systems are comprised of subsystems such as the parent subsystem or the parent-child subsystem. Lastly, family systems theories identify boundaries between individuals and subsystems and interaction across these boundaries occurs based on rules and consistent behaviors.

**Family-focused interventions:** Programs that focus on the family as a whole, rather than only on the child or only on the parent. Comprehensive treatments that address the needs of the child, parent, and family have been found to be the most effective for youth with antisocial behaviors.

**Fetal alcohol spectrum disorder:** Often referred to as Fetal Alcohol Syndrome (FAS) or Fetal Alcohol Effects (FAE) and other Alcohol-Related Birth Defects (ARBDs). A pattern of mental and physical problems that may occur in some children whose mothers drank alcohol during pregnancy. While the baby is developing in the mother, alcohol the mother drinks is passed to the developing child. Drinking during any stage of pregnancy may cause FAS or FAE.

**Florida Environmental Institute:** Also referred to as the Last Chance Ranch, this program seems to have rehabilitated some of the most serious felony juvenile offenders in Florida. The youths committed to this small therapeutic facility learn to clean and maintain wetlands and swamps in the Everglades, dig up tree stumps and clear land, cut grass, weed, and grow corn, peas, and cucumbers on the ranch grounds, and raise cattle, pigs, and horses. These adjudicated juvenile offenders also have the responsibility of repairing and renovating ranch buildings, and in some cases building new buildings. The centerpiece of this program is a strict behavior management protocol. The youths are assessed five times each day on seven areas of behavior including appearance, attitude, punctuality, participation, enthusiasm, and manners.

Forestry camps: The early camps that were operating between 1933 and 1943 for juvenile delinquents were generally modeled after the Civilian Conservation Corps camps. The goal of those camps was to provide a treatment program that included conservation of natural resources in addition to employment and vocational training. These camps were utilized because they were an open setting with no gates, bars, guns, or isolation facilities. Two basic types of camps developed in the late 1940s and early 1950s: senior forestry camps and junior probation camps. A senior forestry camp was for youths between the ages of sixteen and eighteen. Emphasis was on work such as nursery, reforestation, various maintenance and construction activities, brush clearance, and fire suppression. During World War II, the forestry camps added to their program training in the fundamentals of military life and drill (provided by the army). A number of boys who received this training went directly from the camp into military service.

Formal assessment: Before a youth is placed within the juvenile justice system, a formal assessment should be conducted that includes a thorough history of the youth's development from birth to their current age, the family, psychological, social, and academic history. Details regarding child abuse, alcohol and drug problems, lethality, family violence, traumas, and previous mental health issues are crucial. A formal assessment by the school for learning disabilities that may have previously gone unnoticed is also a must. The offending behavior must be explicitly identified in order to assess the severity and chronicity of the offenses.

Freebase: A substance as separated or freed from its base (salt). The separated form of the substance is thus called *free base*. Prior to the processing of crack cocaine freebasing was a process of smoking cocaine.

Functional Family Therapy (FFT): An integrative approach that relies on systems, behavioral, and cognitive views of functioning. Clinical problems are conceptualized in terms of the function that they serve for the family system and for the individual client. Research underlying FFT has found that families with delinquents have higher rates of defensiveness, blaming, and lower rates of mutual support. Treatment is grounded in learning theory. FFT has clinically significant and lasting effects on recidivism.

Functional Family Training (FFT): Functional family therapy (FFT) has been found to be an effective practice in the mental health arena with families and troubled youth. It has also been found to reduce recidivism in youth involved in corrections, substance abuse, and with very serious juvenile offenders. Additionally, FFT has also been found effective with diverse youth in various geographic areas. Trained therapists utilizing FFT work to modify the family's functioning and therefore the youth's symptoms that are thought to be a symptom of problematic family functioning. The emphasis for change and treatment is on the family as opposed to singling out or blaming the youth for all of the problems of the family.

Gang: A juvenile gang is tied together by common interests, has an identified leader, and, generally, acts as a group to achieve illegal, immoral, or harmful objectives.

Gang suppression unit: A specialized unit that is located within some police departments whose purpose in to intervene to prevent gang violence and other gang activities.

**Gender-specific treatment:** Treatment designed specifically for one gender.

**Gulf Coast YouthBuild Program-Texas:** Teaches the youths how to lay a foundation, frame a house, put up sheet rock, and construct the roof of houses, as well as the building of tool sheds, outdoor shelters, and picnic areas in state parks. Average length of stay is 6 to 9 months.

**Heroin:** A substance produced via chemical processing of morphine. The result is a drug more potent than morphine and is now demonstrating a resurgence of abuse and addiction across the United States within urban areas.

**Homeward Bound:** A rigorous wilderness education program for boys developed by Alan A. Collette. Participants are oriented to survival skills, and then they embark on a particular wilderness experience involving such activities as rock climbing, rappelling, canoeing, camping, cross-country skiing, and pullboating. The program also provides individual and group counseling; psychological, educational, and vocational testing; and tutoring. A ten-day trip across the Appalachian Trail, often through snow four feet deep, is an example of one excursion in which the youths participate. The culmination of the program is a three-day solo experience in the wilderness with only rudimentary supplies.

**House of Refuge:** Opened in New York on January 21, 1825, it was the first prison for juveniles that was completely separate from an adult prison. Similar juvenile institutions opened in 1826 and 1828 in Boston and Philadelphia, respectively. Between 1845 and 1854, several other large cities established houses of refuge for juvenile offenders. These first houses of refuge were built in order to counteract the poverty, vice, and neglectful families that were breeding grounds for delinquency. The houses of refuge were supposed to provide a home for unruly and troubled children, where they would be reformed, educated, and disciplined. Children were put in such places for protection from the temptations of immoral, unfit, and neglectful families and vice-ridden disorganized communities. In addition, juveniles in cities with Houses of Refuge would not have to be incarcerated in adult jails and prisons. As a result, young juvenile offenders would not be corrupted by repeat adult offenders. Houses of refuge were built as secure facilities. Some were surrounded by brick walls, and their interiors were designed to confine inmates securely while instilling order, respect for authority, and strict and steady discipline.

**Intoxication:** A transient state of physical or psychological disruption secondary to the ingestion of mood-altering substance that impacts functioning of the central nervous system (e.g., alcohol).

**Intramuscularly:** Administered within the substance of a muscle, frequently associated with administration of pain medications and steroids, at times referenced to on the street as "skin popping".

**Intranasal:** Within the nose, this term is associated most frequently with taking cocaine by sniffing the drug through a straw into the nose, where the drug is absorbed through the mucous membrane of the nasal cavity.

Intravenous: Administered within a vein or veins, frequently associated with the administration of cocaine and heroin directly into a vein. This type of use increases the risk of blood-born disease such as HIV and Hepatitis. Referred to on the streets as *mainlining*.

Jack and Ruth Eckerd Foundation Therapeutic Wilderness Program: Through the Eckerd Foundation, Jack Eckerd has established a number of nonprofit therapeutic and educational camping programs to treat troubled and delinquent youths. At the Eckerd camps the emphasis is on helping children develop improved ways of dealing with their emotions and teaching them realistic methods for solving problems. As of June 2003 there were 39 Eckerd Youth Alternative Programs that have provided services to over 50,000 troubled youths over the past 35 years.

Judicial waivers: Judicial waivers are one of the most common mechanisms to transfer a juvenile case to adult court. Judicial waivers can occur three ways: at the *discretion of the judge*, on a *presumptive basis* with the waiver assumed unless it is determined otherwise, and on a *mandatory basis* when certain criteria have been met. See *statutory exclusion* for a contrasting approach.

Juvenile Addiction Receiving Facilities (JARFs): Youths in need of alcohol/other drug detoxification, stabilization, assessment, and referral assistance are brought to these facilities by various referral agencies (e.g., schools), and JAC processed youth in need of immediate alcohol/other drug services are brought to these facilities for care.

Juvenile aftercare plan: Upon release from a state training school, also known as a juvenile correctional institution, the juvenile may be ordered to a period of intensive aftercare or parole. During this period the juvenile may be monitored or under the supervision of the juvenile court or the corrections department. Aftercare programs should include a continuum of services and scheduled activities, such as after-school recreational and creative arts programs, alternative dispute resolution programs, mentoring and tutoring programs, career development and vocational training programs, religious group meetings family counseling, volunteer work with the homeless and disabled, and neighborhood crime prevention projects.

Juvenile assessment center (JAC): The first juvenile assessment center was established in Hillsborough County (Tampa), Florida, in 1993. Most JACs share the following four characteristics: *single point of entry*: a 24-hour centralized point of intake and assessment for juveniles who have come or are likely to come into contact with the juvenile justice system; *immediate and comprehensive assessments*: service providers associated with the JAC make an initial broad-based and, if necessary, a later, in-depth assessment of youths' circumstances and treatment needs; *management information systems*: needed to manage and monitor youth, helping ensure the provision of appropriate treatment services, and to avoid duplication of services; and *integrated case management services*: JAC staff use information obtained from the assessment process and the MIS to develop recommendations to improve access to services, complete follow-ups of referred youths, and to periodically reassess youth placed in various services.

Juvenile court: The first juvenile court was established in Cook County, Illinois, in 1899, and was viewed by the vast majority of social reformers as a milestone in the developmental process of American justice. The purpose and function of the court was to have been rehabilitation rather than punishment. During the first quarter of the twentieth century, both the general public and public officials warmly and enthusiastically hailed the juvenile court movement as a panacea for the misbehavior, troubles, and social ills of children and youth. In recent years, judges and their chief probation officers have advocated for and developed restitution programs in the form of monetary and community work service assignments in order to hold juveniles accountable for their offenses. Juvenile offenders in property-related crimes are the most likely candidates for these restitution programs. In addition, during the current decade the threshold of public tolerance for violent juvenile offenders has decreased considerably. The result has been harsher handling by prosecutors and judges for violent and chronic juvenile offenders. To increase violent juveniles' accountability for their offenses, the strategy used with increasing frequency is the meting out of harsher and more severe penalties

**Juvenile delinquency:** Juvenile delinquency is a violation of state or federal law or municipal ordinance by a minor, which, if committed by an adult, would constitute a crime such as burglary, robbery, simple assault, and aggravated assault.

**Juvenile delinquent:** A minor who commits one of many diverse forms of antisocial behavior. In general, most state criminal codes define juvenile delinquency as behavior that is in violation of the criminal code, and is committed by a youth who has not reached adult age. This includes those juveniles who have been arrested or contacted by the police, even though many of these individuals are merely reprimanded or sent home when their parents pick them up.

**Juvenile detention:** The temporary and safe custody of juveniles who are accused of conduct subject to the jurisdiction of the court who require a restricted environment for their own or the community's protection while pending legal action. Juvenile detention provides a wide range of helpful services that support the juvenile's physical, emotional, and social development. Helpful services minimally include education, visitation, communication, counseling, continuous supervision, medical and health care services, nutrition, recreation, and reading. Juvenile detention includes or provides for a system of clinical observation and assessment that complements the helpful services and reports findings.

**Juvenile Detention Alternatives Initiative (JDAI):** The Annie E. Casey Foundation established the Juvenile Detention Alternatives Initiative (JDAI) in 1992 to demonstrate that jurisdictions could establish more effective and efficient systems to accomplish the purposes of juvenile detention. In the largest detention reform effort to date, JDAI sought to reduce the inappropriate detention of youth in selected metropolitan jurisdictions around the country. JDAI had four basic objectives: (1) to eliminate the inappropriate or unnecessary use of secure detention; (2) to minimize failures to appear and the incidence of delinquent behavior; (3) to redirect public finances from building new facility capacity to responsible alternative strategies; and (4) to improve conditions in secure detention facilities.

**Juvenile diversion:** Any process that is used by components of the criminal justice system (police, prosecution, courts, corrections) whereby youths avoid formal juvenile court processing and adjudication. *Diversion* refers to the channeling of cases to nonjudicial community agencies or facilities, in instances where these cases would ordinarily have received an adjudicatory (or fact-finding) hearing by a court. The major goal of the first juvenile courts, established at the turn of the twentieth century, was to provide an alternative to, and thereby divert youths from, the criminal court. The juvenile court was created to avoid the unfair and inhumane treatment to which juveniles were subjected when processed through the criminal court and incarcerated with adult felons. Diversion has also existed for a long time in the form of informal station adjustments and discretionary handling by police officers when they have given youths a warning and sent them back home. However, the development of formal programs for the purpose of diverting juveniles from adjudication in the juvenile justice system did not begin until the late 1960s. The main objectives of juvenile diversion are to: (1) avoid labeling; (2) reduce unnecessary detention and incarceration; (3) reduce repeat offenses; (4) provide counseling and other services in the community; and (5) lower justice system costs.

Juvenile intake unit: A department, either located within or attached to the court, or outside the court that decides whether or not to dismiss a case due to a lack of sufficient legal cause or to resolve the matter through a formal petition or informally through referral to a social service or family counseling agency, substance abuse treatment program, or restitution. When the intake department makes a decision that a case needs to be formally processed within the juvenile court, a petition is then filed and the case is then placed on the juvenile court's calendar (or docket) for an adjudicatory hearing and judicial disposition. For example, in 1999, 57% (575 of out of every 1,000 cases) based on all juvenile delinquency cases, which were disposed of by the juvenile courts, were handled formally while 43% (425 of every 1,000 cases) were handled informally.

Juvenile Justice and Delinquency Act of 1973: In 1980 President Carter signed the reauthorization of the Juvenile Justice and Delinquency Prevention Act into law. This revised act contained an historic amendment mandating the removal of juveniles from adult jails. Only those juveniles who are tried as adults for criminal felonies are allowed to be detained or incarcerated in adult jails. OJJDP focused attention on rural jails that were often the only place police could detain juveniles.

Juvenile Justice and Delinquency Prevention Act of 1974: This legislation strongly discouraged the holding of status offenders in secure juvenile correctional facilities, either for detention or placement. This important legislation and policy mandate are called *deinstitutionalization of status offenders*.

Juvenile justice processing: The nine steps include the following: initial contact by law enforcement agencies; law enforcement informal handling, diversion, arrest, and/or referral to the juvenile court; court intake via the juvenile probation intake unit or the prosecutor's office; preadjudication juvenile detention; prosecutors file a delinquency petition in juvenile court or waive to adult criminal court; investigation or predisposition report prepared by a probation officer; juvenile court judges adjudicatory decision and sanctions; participation and completion of mandated juvenile offender treatment program; juvenile aftercare plan.

**Juvenile Offender Reentry (JOR):** Reentry is the return of the offender from a placement outside of the home community back to the home community. For the juvenile justice community, reentry expands the concept of reintegration. An overwhelming majority of youth released from juvenile facilities return home. Detention must address the physical and emotional component of reentry since both are important to the crafting of a successful outcome. A systematic involvement of community-based programs throughout incarceration enhances the likelihood of successful community reintegration.

**Juvenile probation:** Professional probation officers provide juvenile offenders with supportive services and referrals that, depending upon the youth's individual needs, might include individual counseling, group counseling, referral to community mental health centers for outpatient treatment or inpatient psychiatric services, appropriate referrals to addiction treatment programs, family counseling, vocational training, assistance in finding employment, enrolling in alternative education programs, or preparing for the high school equivalency examination.

**Juvenile status offender:** A juvenile who engages in deviant acts or misbehavior that, if engaged in by an adult, would not be considered crimes (e.g., truancy, incorrigibility, and running away from home). For status offenders, many states have separate legislation that views these juveniles as individuals "in need of supervision." An array of crisis intervention services, runaway shelters, youth service bureaus, addiction treatment programs, day treatment programs, and family counseling programs have been developed to serve these youths.

**Labeling approach:** The labeling approach is not so much concerned with why juveniles commit delinquent acts as with what happens to such individuals when they are officially processed and labeled by the juvenile court. Labeling focuses on societal reactions, the individual's response to those reactions, consequences of the labeling for an individual, and why and how certain behaviors come to be defined as deviant. According to the labeling perspective, there is no significant difference between the social-psychological characteristics of those youths labeled delinquent and those who engage in delinquency offenses but never get caught. Sociologists and social psychologists who have advanced the labeling explanation for delinquency have tended to focus on the negative consequences of being labeled.

**Labeling perspective:** Juveniles and adults who commit minor offenses become habitual offenders because they are singled out from their peers and differentially treated.

**Law Enforcement Assistance Act in 1965 (FL. 89–197) and the Omnibus Crime Control and Safe Streets Act of 1968 (P.L. 90–351):** Together, these two laws provided money and the administrative apparatus for providing new grants to state and local agencies for law enforcement and related programs.

**Learning disability:** Includes specific learning disabilities, mental retardation, emotional disturbance, and health impaired (ADHD, epilepsy etc.). Children who qualify for this category are eligible for special education services in the least restrictive environment possible. Most schools provide special education services and classes within their school building; however, some schools utilize alternative schools for children who have a disability but who are also exhibiting disruptive or offending behaviors. Juveniles exhibiting severe behaviors are often removed completely from the school system and placed in the juvenile justice system.

Longitudinal Data: Involves the collection of data at different agreed upon points in time such as 1 month, 3 months, 6 months, and 12 months post-treatment completion. In the context of social interventions for families and children, a database that tracks the experience of families and children from their initial involvement with the formal service system through their continued involvement with that system, and that provides a valid and reliable basis for describing and assessing the experiences of families and children served by that system over time.

Mandated reporter: Professionals who are required by law to report child abuse. Typically, mandated reporters include teachers, social workers, probation officers, health professionals, day care providers, or anyone who has a professional capacity working with children as determined by law.

Master calendaring: Master calendaring refers to different judges being assigned to different stages of a child's case. See *direct calendaring* for a contrasting approach.

MAYSI-2: The Massachusetts Youth Screening Instrument (MAYSI-2) was designed specifically for evaluating psychological distress of youth entering the juvenile justice system. It does not focus on psychological diagnoses, but rather on situational and characterological distress in youth who are in the juvenile justice system. The instrument has seven subscales including: alcohol and drug use, angry-irritable, depressed-anxious, somatic complaints, suicidal ideation, thought disturbance, and traumatic experiences. Scores above the cutoff warrant mental health referrals. The easy-to-score instrument has been proven reliable and valid with youth in the juvenile justice system and with only 52-items, can be completed in 10 minutes.

Methamphetamine: A variety of illegal amphetamines used for its stimulant action, this drug can be taken by snorting or injecting.

Methylenedioxymethamphetamine (MDMA): Ecstasy is a form of drug frequently referred to as a designer drug. This drug combines hallucinogenic and amphetamine compounds in a designer drug format and has harmful effects including delusions, drug-induced psychosis, sleep disturbances, com, and fatalities upon overdose or in combination with alcohol.

Midcity project: Developed in 1954 in one of Boston's lower-class districts, this social action demonstration project utilizing a "total community" philosophy focused on improving three of the societal units that seemed to be an important influence in the genesis and perpetuation of delinquency: the gang, the community, and the family. The project's primary emphasis was its work with gangs. Professional social workers known as "detached street workers" reached out to approximately four hundred youths who were members of twenty-one gangs. The staff met with the groups three to four times a week, visiting with the gang members for five to six hours at a time. Contact was maintained for a period ranging from ten to thirty-four months.

Mobilization for youth (MFY): In response to the alarmingly high incidence of juvenile delinquency and gang welfare on the Lower East Side, Helen Hall (director of the Henry Street Settlement House) and sociologist Richard Cloward (of Columbia University's School of Social Work) developed the plan for *Mobilization for Youth*, with Cloward becoming its first director. The program sought to reduce delinquency by orienting the youths toward social change; it emphasized education, work, and social organization, including the use of social casework. MFY sought to convince youths that there were viable, law-abiding ways to participate in community life. An important aspect of the program was related to job training and placement.

Mood disorders: Mood disorders include depressive disorders as well as bipolar disorder. Depression is characterized by depressed or irritable mood, diminished interest in activities, difficulties with concentration, and fatigue. Manic episodes are characterized by grandiosity, talkativeness, distractibility, and decreased need for sleep. Youth suffering from bipolar disorder that includes cycles of depression, as well as mania, may exhibit delinquent and risk-taking behaviors during the manic phase. During this phase, youth often feel invincible and cannot comprehend future consequences of their behavior.

Moral education: A set of procedures designed to raise the young person's level of fairness, justice, and concern with the needs and rights of others.

Multisystemic therapy (MST): A family- and community-based treatment approach that is theoretically grounded in a social-ecological framework and family systems. A basic foundation of MST is the belief that a juvenile's acting out or antisocial behavior is best addressed by interfacing with multiple systems, including the adolescent's family, peers, school, teachers, neighbors, and others. Thus, the MST practitioner interfaces not just with the adolescent, but also with various individuals and settings that influence the adolescent's life. Services are delivered in the client's natural environment, such as the client's home or a neighborhood center. MST is an intensive multi-modal family-based treatment approach focusing on the juvenile, their family, peers, school, and community networks. MST aims to improve parental discipline practices and family relations, decrease the youth's contact with deviant peers, improve the youth's academic performance, and develop support systems to maintain the changes. The approach uses intensive case management and a team of other professionals to target multiple problems. The team is available to the family on a 24-hours-per-day-seven-days-per-week basis and utilizes various therapies in addition to multiple concrete services to meet the needs of the youth and family. The main goal is to divert the youth from juvenile justice and mental health residential placements, and help the youth and family progress toward their life goals.

Needs assessment: A formal process that identifies needs as gaps in results between "What Is" and "What Should Be," prioritizes those gaps on the basis of the costs and benefits of closing versus ignoring those needs, and selects the needs to be reduced or eliminated. Needs assessments serve to identify gaps between current and desired results that occur both within an organization (at the Micro level of results), as well as outside (at the Macro and Mega levels of results) in order to provide useful information for decision-making.

Nonpetitioned cases: Informally handled cases in which duly authorized court personnel screen for adjustment prior to the filing of a formal petition. Such personnel include judges, referees, probation officers, other officers of the court and/or an agency statutorily designated to conduct petition screening for the juvenile court.

Office of Juvenile Justice and Delinquency Prevention (OJJDP): Created in 1974 within LEAA to coordinate efforts to control delinquency (P.L. 93—415). For the fiscal years 1975 through 1977, 89,125 JJDP formula grants to state and local agencies were approved. Since LEAA became defunct in 1981, OJJDP is now part of the Office of Justice Programs of the U.S. Department of Justice.

Opportunity Theory: Asserts that there is a major disparity between the aspirations of lower-class youth and the legitimate opportunities available to them. Lower-class youths internalize a set of conventional values and goals. Despite very limited access to legitimate avenues for achieving these goals, they are unable to lower their aspirations. Blaming others rather than themselves for their limited access to the opportunity structure, many of these alienated youths join delinquent subcultures.

Oppositional Defiant Disorder: Defined by a pattern of negativity, noncompliant defiance to authority figures (e.g., parents, teachers, and other adults), and temperamental outbursts that impair a child's ability to function effectively in home, school, and peer environments. This maladaptive pattern of behavior must have endured for six months or longer for the diagnosis to be made accurately. The DSM-IV TR (APA, 2000) is careful to note that these behaviors must occur more often than in peers of comparable age and developmental level.

Outcome: Outcomes are measurable changes in daily practice.

Outcome Measures: Outcome measures help staff make specific decisions about program change. Outcomes that are closely linked to day-to-day management can be used routinely to monitor strengths, weaknesses, or trouble spots. (This requires ongoing assessments of the conditions of confinement.) Outcome measures provide assurance to administration, staff, and the public that the total program functions with reasonable effectiveness. For detailed information on Outcome Measures, see A. R. Roberts and K. Yeager (Eds.) (2004), *Evidence-Based Practice Manual: Research and Outcome Measures in Health and Human Services*, New York: Oxford University Press.

Outward Bound: A program designed to train merchant seamen to succeed in accomplishing rigorous physical challenges as well as to develop group pride and a shared trust as the group worked together to achieve strenuous goals.

Outcome evaluation: A determination of the extent to which the intervention produced the intended short-term or long-term goals. Usually, outcome evaluations involve comparisons with a pre-intervention state and/or with comparable, untreated (control) groups. In most cases, an outcome evaluation is not very useful unless preceded by a process evaluation, which helps interpret the results. Evaluations focus on what happens to clients as a result of the program and the program's level of success. Outcome evaluations study goals such as changes in knowledge, attitude, behavior, or improvements in client conditions. A study conducted to determine the impact of the program on the intended target(s), is sometimes called impact evaluation.

**Over-representation:** Over-representation refers to a larger number of youth of a particular racial or ethnic group being represented in the juvenile justice system than would be expected based on their proportion in the general population. See *disparity* and *discrimination* for additional information.

**Parens patriae:** A principle enabling the court to act in lieu of the parents who were found to be unwilling or unable to give their child appropriate guidance. This paved the way for the juvenile court in the United States to assume jurisdiction for dependent and neglected children. The principle evolved from a 1772 English court case, *Eyre v. Shaftsbury*. There has been some confusion between the terms *parens patriae* and *in loco parentis*. The former refers to the responsibility of government to serve the welfare of the child, not (as the latter might suggest) to replace the parents. The doctrine of *parens patriae* was used in order to free the juvenile court judge to accept social and psychological evaluations and provide informal proceedings, thus departing from due process of law. It also justified the court's right to save children who had committed noncriminal offenses, such as disobeying parents, truancy, and associating with immoral and criminal persons.

**Parent management training (PMT):** A summary term that describes a therapeutic strategy in which parents are trained to use skills for managing their child's problem behavior, such as effective command-giving, setting up reinforcement systems, and using punishment, including taking away privileges and assigning extra chores. While PMT programs may differ in focus and therapeutic strategies used, they all share the common goal of enhancing parental control over children's behavior.

**Peace Builders:** A schoolwide violence prevention program that incorporates strategies to change the school environment by promoting positive behavior and enhancing social competence based on the following five principles: (1) Praise people, (2) avoid put-downs, (3) seek wise people as advisers and friends, (4) notice and correct any hurts you cause, and (5) right wrongs. Rather than being curriculum-based, Peace Builders promotes itself as being a "lifestyle." Much of the program material is expected to be infused into the current academic curriculum.

**Performance-based standard (PbS):** Stresses the objectification of outcomes (the use of objective and empirical measures), the verification of outcomes (measurable changes in daily practice), and dynamic or continually improving criteria for acceptability. PbS starts with a definition of the desired outcome. Once the desired outcome is defined, the PbS process moves to the development of policy and procedure that support the production and verification of the desired outcome. For juvenile justice facility administrators, it allows the construction of new and unique visions for their facilities. PbS remains a very popular concept that an increasing number of juvenile detention administrators view as an effective strategy to improve conditions of confinement.

**Persistently Dangerous School and Unsafe School Option:** Part of the No Child Left Behind Act of 2001 (U.S. PL 107–110, Title IX, sec. 9532), it emphasizes physical acts of violence. The option states: The federal No Child Left Behind Act of 2001, at Title IX, Section 9532, entitled "Unsafe School Choice Option," requires each state receiving funds under the Act to establish and implement a statewide policy requiring that a student attending a persistently dangerous public elementary school or secondary school, as determined by the state in consultation with a representative sample of local educational agencies, or who becomes a victim of a violent criminal offense, as determined by State law, while in or on the grounds of a public elementary school or secondary school that the student attends, be allowed to attend a safe public elementary school or secondary school within the local educational agency, including a public charter school (The No Child Left Behind Act of 2001). Thus, the onus is on school administrators to demonstrate that they are providing safe environments in which students can learn, or those students can take their business elsewhere.

**Petitioned cases:** Formally handled cases that appear on the official court calendar in response to the filing of a petition or other legal instrument requesting the court to adjudicate the youth a delinquent-status offender or dependent child- or to waive the youth to criminal court for processing as an adult.

**Placement cases:** Cases in which youth are placed out of the home in a residential facility housing delinquents or status offenders or are otherwise removed from their home.

**Positive peer communities:** This treatment milieu is very important in the rehabilitation process for young killers, who typically reflect the negative thoughts and behaviors of similarly situated peers. Accordingly, they are more likely to change their thoughts and their behaviors in the desired prosocial direction if they are part of a positive peer environment. A positive peer culture can foster healthy role models and moral leadership and encourage tolerance and respect for others. Empathy training, as well as cognitive behavioral restructuring, prosocial skills training, and anger management is optimally implemented in a positive peer culture.

**Posttraumatic stress disorder (PTSD):** PTSD is usually caused by an overwhelming or traumatic event outside the range of ordinary human experience. After the event, individuals suffer from intrusive recollections, avoidant/numbing symptoms, flashbacks, nightmares, and hyperarousal for at least one month.

**Prepare curriculum:** Includes components that provide social skills training (skillstreaming), anger control training, moral reasoning training, problem-solving training, empathy training, situational perception training, cooperation training, recruiting supportive models, and understanding and using group process modules. The first three modules serve as the core for the program. Youth are taught appropriate social skills through a social skills training program. Through a role-playing and performance-feedback process the skills are mastered. They are taught to control their anger by identifying their personal physiological and psychological triggers and developing new ways to respond to those triggers. The moral reasoning element is taught by introducing a series of moral dilemmas in group sessions, with youth discussing possible responses to the dilemmas.

**Preventive approaches:** The teaching of skills and ways to alter the school environment that will decrease the likelihood of violent events occurring. Preventive approaches offer much more promise as a strategy of reducing school violence. These approaches can be as simple as installing metal detectors or involve more complicated interventions such as social skills training, conflict resolution training, and organizational changes. Preventive approaches are based on the belief that there are identifiable risk factors associated with violence. Interventions that address these risk factors are likely to reduce violence. Many components of school violence prevention models can serve as points of departure for post-occurrence interventions with the perpetrators.

**Primary deviance:** Acts of deviance caused by a combination of etiological factors.

**Principles of effectiveness:** As of July 1, 1998, all public schools receiving funds through the Safe and Drug-Free Schools and Communities Act (SDFSCA) are required to assure that they are meeting the *Principles of Effectiveness* developed to ensure that schools implement science-based drug and violence-prevention programs. These principles mandate that schools will: (1) base their drug and violence prevention programs on needs assessment data, (2) develop measurable program goals and objectives, (3) implement programs with research evidence of effectiveness, and (4) periodically evaluate its programs relative to their goals and objectives.

**Probation:** A legal status created by order of the sentencing court as an alternative to incarceration. The term *probation* is derived from *probare*, meaning, "to prove," that is, it allows the juvenile offender the opportunity to prove himself.

**Probation camps:** Started during the 1950s in California, probation camps evolved into an integral part of the probation process. A youth was sent to the camp by the juvenile court and assigned to a probation officer. The relationship between youth and probation officer continued during the stay in the camp and then for approximately six months after the juvenile returned to his own home.

**Probation cases:** Cases in which youth are placed on informal/voluntary or formal court-ordered probation or supervision.

**Problem-Solving Skills Training (PSST):** A cognitively based intervention that has been used to treat aggressive and antisocial youth. The problem-solving process involves helping clients learn how to produce a variety of potentially effective responses when faced with problem situations. Regardless of the specific problem-solving model used, the primary focus is on addressing the thought process to help adolescents address deficiencies and distortions in their approach to interpersonal situations.

**Prosocial skills training:** A curriculum has been developed that teaches youths how to solve problems, manage feelings, and relate in interpersonal situations. Skill alternatives taught to deal with aggression, for example, include asking permission, sharing something, helping others, negotiating, using self-control, standing up for one's rights, responding to teasing, avoiding trouble with others, and staying out of fights.

**Psychiatric hospitalization:** Adolescents are more likely to be hospitalized if they appear psychotic, remain homicidal, or need intensive psychopharmacological management. Inpatient treatment can be particularly helpful in stabilizing the youth, redirecting his suicidal, self-destructive, or homicidal impulses, and reducing his internal conflict. It can also provide an optimal setting for evaluating the youth, assessing his potential for continued violent behavior, and understanding the family system of which he is a member. Unlike the homicidal child who is typically viewed as psychologically disturbed, an adolescent killer is generally regarded as antisocial and is likely to be institutionalized in a facility for juvenile delinquents or adult criminals.

**Psychopharmacology:** The management of psychiatric illness using medication such as antidepressants, antipsychotics, anti-anxiety medications, and more.

**Psychotherapy:** Those practice theories and models used by psychologists and social workers that put particular stress on the inner life of the client, both as a way of understanding the client's strengths and limitations and, more important, to seek to effect changes that will enable a client to function in a more satisfying, growth-enhancing manner.

**Psychodynamic therapy:** Based on Sigmund Freud's concept, psychoanalysis or psychodynamic therapy is a treatment of mental or emotional disorder or of related bodily ills by focusing on early childhood problems and fixations during the first six years of life. These development stages or fixations are known as the oral, anal, and the genital stages.

**Psychotropic drugs:** Drugs that alter central nervous system functioning.

**Qualitative research:** A branch of research that is viewed as naturalistic and encompasses a range of methods that, broadly defined, describes and provides insights into naturally occurring phenomena and everyday experiences, and the meanings associated with those phenomena and experiences.

**Quantitative research:** A type of research that tests specific hypotheses concerning pre-determined variables. It gathers information in numeric form and produces findings by statistical procedures or other means of quantification. It aims to answer questions such as whether or how much. Examples include whether the number of juvenile auto thieves are higher among different immigrant populations or what proportion of violent juvenile offenders in the U.S. have mental disorders such as anti-social or borderline personality disorders.

**Quasi-experimental designs:** Experimental designs in which people are not randomly assigned to different forms of the program. Quasi-experimental designs can compare different forms of the program that naturally occur or can use procedures such as matching or waiting lists to form quasi-control or comparison groups.

**Randomized control trial:** An outcome study or treatment effectiveness measures using an experimental design. Such designs usually involve pre- and post-assessments of client-system functioning and random assignment of clients to treatment and to alternative conditions such as no-treatment, standard care, or placebo treatment.

**Rapid assessment instruments (RAI):** RAIs provide a brief standardized format for gathering information about clients. These instruments are scales, checklists, and questionnaires that are relatively brief, often less than 50 items, and easy to score and interpret. RAIs have established psychometrics and, thus, reliably and validly ascertain traits of an individual in terms of its frequency, intensity, or duration. Such instruments are useful for determining the nature and/or extent of symptoms and behavior patterns, assessing the presence of psychiatric disorders, or monitoring client progress and evaluating treatment effectiveness.

**Reactive approaches:** An approach to school violence that relies on tough disciplinary action and punishment. The recent public frenzy over school violence has influenced the type of approach that is taken toward school violence. Many concerned parents, educators, and politicians advocate "get tough" and "zero tolerance" policies for youth responsible for school violence. Catch phrases like "get tough" and "zero tolerance" translate into *reactive* and punitive disciplinary actions.

**Recidivism:** Recurrence of criminal delinquent behavior in an offender. Recidivism rate refers to the general frequency of reoffense or re-adjudication in a particular group of offenders after a specified follow-up period.

**Reformatory movement:** The underlying philosophy behind the reformatory movement, which flourished during the late 1800s, was that proper training in a residential environment could offset the early experiences of poverty, poor family life, and corruption. A key feature was separating youthful offenders from older, chronic offenders and providing more individualized education in reading, arithmetic, and vocational trades. The goal was to prepare the youth for the future by removing him from his adverse living conditions. The philosophy and goals of reformatories emphasized the values of sobriety, thrift, industry, prudence, and ambition. Juveniles were to receive only an elementary education so that they could direct the majority of their time and energy to industrial trades and agricultural training.

**Reintegrative shaming:** A process for controlling crime in some societies in which citizens and victims are actively involved in an effort to make offenders aware of the harm caused by their behavior to the collective and to affirm community values. In these "low crime" societies, sanctioning is a community function in which a denunciation process is generally followed by a process of reparation to victims and the community, reintegration, conciliation, and forgiveness.

**Relational aggression:** Behaviors that harm others through damage (or threat of damage) to relationships or feelings of acceptance, friendship, or group inclusion. Examples of these types of behaviors include gossiping, spreading rumors, or ignoring someone with the intent to exclude them from a social group. The majority of research on relational aggression focuses on peer-to-peer interactions in the school setting. Recent research has suggested a link between prior victimization and relational aggression in the treatment setting.

**Restitution:** Restitution is sometimes incorporated as part of a post-adjudication court order. It often takes one of three forms: *monetary restitution* or paying back the victim for losses or damage suffered; *community service* in which juveniles are ordered to perform a given number of work hours at a private nonprofit or governmental agency; or *direct services to victims*, victim-offender reconciliation programs (VORPs), in which trained staff bring the victim, if willing, together with the offender. *See also* Victim-offender mediation.

**Restorative justice:** Emphasizes three goals: (1) identifying the obligation created by the juvenile's offense and ensuring that he/she is held responsible for it (accountability), (2) returning the offender to the community competent to interact in a successful prosocial manner (competence), and (3) ensuring that the community is not further injured by the juvenile's future delinquent behavior (public safety). Restorative justice is based on the assumption that none of the essential functions of the justice system—rehabilitation, community protection, sanctioning, and victim restoration—can be effectively accomplished without the joint involvement of victims, offenders, and the community. It is based on the belief and value statement that justice is best served when victims, offenders, and the community receive balanced attention and gain tangible benefits from their interactions with the juvenile justice system. Restorative justice also speaks directly to the need for societies to make allowances for offender repentance or forgiveness and to make possible and encourage offender reintegration following appropriate sanctioning.

**Restorative sanctioning:** Imposed by the court in the form of restitution, community service, fines, or direct payment as compensation for property damage or whatever will equitably compensate the victim in lieu of severe criminal penalties.

**Retributive justice:** Gives priority to punishment through incarceration as the primary means of sanctioning offenders for violations against the state.

**Risk factors for delinquency and mental health problems:** Individual risk factors include: substance abuse, mental health problems, poor social problem-solving skills, learning disabilities, and cognitive impairments. Family risk factors include poor parental supervision, poverty, paternal criminality, family history of psychiatric disorder intense marital conflict and dysfunction, ineffective discipline practices, and exposure to domestic violence. School risk factors include truancy, poor academic achievement, and untreated learning disabilities. Peer risk factors include association with delinquent peers and anger membership. Community risk factors include exposure to violence and drug dealing. These risk factors can assist personnel in understanding the severity and potential severity of problems the youth may have. For instance, a youth who has only two risk factors for mental illness will have less of a chance for developing these problems than one who has seven risk factors. The age of the youth in combination with the known risk factors should shed light on where the youth should be placed and treated.

**Runaway Youth Act:** Title III of the U.S. Juvenile Justice and Delinquency Prevention Act of 1974, this legislation provided another major boost to the development of social services for diverted youths, particularly status offenders (such as runaways). With the Act, millions of dollars in federal funds were allocated for the establishment of runaway shelters, youth telephone hotline services, and crisis counseling services. Federal funds were used to develop runaway programs across the country. They provide emergency services such as food, shelter, as well as counseling services in a safe and wholesome environment, which is separate from law enforcement and juvenile justice systems. Sixty-six grants were awarded in 1975 during the first funding cycle to support programs in thirty-two states, Puerto Rico, Guam, and the District of Columbia.

**School violence:** Commonly thought to encompass an array of behaviors ranging from verbal taunts to bombing persons in a school building. These behaviors have in common that they are overt, aggressive acts that result in physical or psychological pain, injury, or death. For instance, violence includes behaviors that aggress against property as well as persons. Thus, school vandalism can be seen as a form of school violence. Most of the literature relating to this issue limits the scope of the concern to behaviors evidenced on the grounds of the school itself. Physical acts of violence are much easier for school officials to document; they demand attention by virtue of their visibility and tendency to provoke outrage. Nonphysical acts of violence involving feelings of intimidation or fear are difficult to document and less likely to be reported.

**Secondary deviance:** The development of deviant self-concepts, deviant careers, and deviant acts as a result of the sanctions applied to, and stigmatization of, the individual through agents of social control.

**Second-generation social decision-making strategies:** The family of programs referred to as second generation social decision making, social problem solving, and interpersonal cognitive problem solving are implemented by teachers and parents. Their principles become part of school and home routines. Thus, teachers and parents are instructed to use social decision making and problem solving in a wide variety of situations; most critically, by so doing, they find themselves in new, positive, relationships with their children, relationships that serve to bolster children's mental health and prepare them for social and academic success.

**Self-assessment process:** This self-correcting and self-evaluating element requires a dynamic approach to setting standards, including benchmarks, criteria, and so on. Data-driven systems cannot be static. Standards must have sufficient flexibility to reflect changes in the empirical evidence that informs their definitions of acceptability. For PbS, the self-evaluating process permits regular adjustments of internally generated benchmarks.

**Single intake facilities:** These facilities involve representatives from a range of community agencies, including law enforcement, juvenile justice, and human service agencies, who are co-located at the facility. Successfully operating single intake facilities help overcome major workload and juvenile justice "systemic" problems.

**Skillstreaming:** An intervention in which a fifty-skill curriculum of prosocial behaviors is systematically taught to chronically aggressive adolescents and younger children. The skills that students learn from these procedures fall into one of six families that compose the entire curriculum and include beginning social skills, advanced social skills, skills for dealing with feelings, alternatives to aggression, skills for dealing with stress, and planning skills.

**Social skills:** Social skills can be defined as a complex set of skills that facilitate the successful interactions between peers, parents, teachers, and other adults. The "social" refers to interactions between people; the "skills" refers to making appropriate discriminations—that is, deciding what would be the most effective response and using the verbal and nonverbal behaviors that facilitate interaction.

**Society for the Reformation of Juvenile Delinquents:** Until 1923, known as the Society for the Prevention of Pauperism, they reported on the horrendous conditions at Bellevue Prison. They focused on the plight of young children confined there with adult offenders. This report and the subsequent study by the Society pointed to the correlation between crime and delinquency, and poverty and parental neglect.

**Stationhouse adjustments:** Informal decisions made by police officers regarding juveniles brought to the police station—adjustments frequently result in a reprimand or stern lecture from the arresting officer, followed by release to the custody of one or both parents.

**Status offenses:** Deviant acts or misbehavior committed by a juvenile that, if engaged in by an adult, would not be considered crimes (e.g., truancy, incorrigibility, curfew violations, and running away from home). *See also* Juvenile status offenders.

**Statutory exclusion:** One of the ways that a juvenile case can be transferred to adult court. Statutory exclusion is also known as *legislative exclusion* and refers to cases that are defined in state law as automatically being referred to adult criminal court. *See* Judicial waivers for a contrasting approach.

**Teen Courts:** These Courts are also referred to as Youth Courts and provide a method for diverting juveniles from the formal justice system.

**Therapeutic jurisprudence:** Therapeutic jurisprudence is a legal reform theory that considers the law as a therapeutic agent, without displacing due process. It considers how legal rules, legal actors, and legal procedures act as social forces that can impact legal outcomes, including the emotional and psychological well being of the parties involved.

**Timeline follow-back procedure:** This procedure is a structured interview technique that samples a specific period of time. A monthly calendar and memory anchor points are used to help substance abusers reconstruct daily use during the past month. Whereas adult studies have found that direct self-report measures have high levels of sensitivity in detecting substance use problems and compare favorably to biomedical measures (blood and urine tests), the timeline follow-back may offer the most sensitive assessment for adolescent substance abusers.

**Training school:** A state-operated large institution for long-term incarceration of juvenile delinquents.

**Transfer:** The process of certifying and waiving a juvenile into the adult Criminal Court. This can only be done through a legislative judicial waiver.

**Uniform Crime Reports:** Refers to the annual Federal Bureau of Investigation (FBI) statistical report of all arrests taking place annually in the United States, based on police department reporting.

**Urban Youth Service Corps:** A program that hired several hundred unemployed neighborhood youths to work in a variety of activities, including conservation. The Youth Service Corps focused on fostering the types of attitudes and behaviors (e.g., following orders, reporting to work on time) necessary to succeed in the world of work and on strengthening the participants' job skills. A Youth Jobs Center was created to locate permanent jobs for those who successfully completed the training program.

**Victimization surveys:** Victimization studies have been completed in a large number of cities throughout the United States. These studies have been conducted as joint efforts by the U.S. Bureau of Justice Statistics and the Bureau of the Census. The most well-known victimization survey is the National Crime Victimization Survey (NCVS), a massive, annual, house-to-house survey of a random sample of 60,000 households and 136,000 individuals. The NCVS provides annual estimates of the total number of crimes committed by both adult and juvenile offenders. The six types of crime measured are rape, robbery, assault, household burglary, personal and household larceny, and motor vehicle theft. Based on the survey data, it has been estimated that 40 million serious crimes occur each year in the United States.

**Victim-offender mediation (VOM):** A process that provides interested victims (primarily those of property crimes and minor assaults) the opportunity to meet their offenders in a safe and structured setting. The goal is to hold offenders directly accountable while providing important support and assistance to victims. With the assistance of trained mediators, the victims are able to let the offenders know how the crime affected them, receive answers to their questions, and be directly involved in developing a restitution plan that holds the offenders financially accountable for the losses they caused. *See also* Balanced approach; Restitution; and Restorative justice.

**Victims of property related crimes:** Persons whose material, cash, jewelry, or property is damaged or stolen as a result of theft, burglary, malicious mischief, arson, or vandalism.

**Victims of violent crimes:** Persons who are victimized by rape, robbery, aggravated assault, and homicide.

**Violent Crime Control Act of 1994:** It is the largest crime bill in the history of the country and provides for 100,000 new police officers, $9.7 billion in funding for prisons, and $6.1 billion in funding for prevention programs that were designed with significant input from experienced police officers. The Act also significantly expands the government's ability to deal with problems caused by criminal aliens. The Crime Bill provides $2.6 billion in additional funding for the FBI, DEA, INS, United States Attorneys, and other Justice Department components, as well as the Federal courts and the Treasury Department.

**VisionQuest (VQ):** An outdoor adventure program operated by a for-profit organization based in Tucson, Arizona. VisionQuest began in 1973, headed by Robert Burton, a controversial figure who has generated high praise as well as considerable criticism for his unorthodox treatment methods. VisionQuest operates several types of programs: group homes, wilderness camps, residential programs, HomeQuest (a home-based family counseling program), OceanQuest, and the Wagon Train.

**Wagon Train:** VisionQuest's Wagon Train program, which travels fifteen to twenty miles per day, have transported youths thousands of miles across the country in much the same way the early settlers explored the new frontier more than one hundred years ago. The adolescents must all work together to keep the wagon train on its scheduled course. Staff and youths live and work side by side in a family atmosphere. Each "family" has responsibility for its own wagon, horses, mules, and equipment. The ratio of staff to youths approaches one to one.

**Waived cases:** Cases that are waived or transferred to a criminal court as the result of a waiver or transfer hearing.

Wardship: A child becomes a ward of the court because the child's parents or guardians are deemed unfit by the court due to gross physical abuse or neglect. One major and unintended consequence of wardship or adjudication to a correctional institution is stigma. Stigma results in the juvenile being handicapped by the corrupting influences of the institution heightening police surveillance, neighborhood isolation, lowered receptivity, and tolerance by school officials, and rejections of youth by prospective employers. Thus, juvenile court wards often become stigmatized and labeled by probation officers, judges, and police as the type of youth destined for failure. In addition, data indicate that the more a youth is engulfed in the juvenile justice system, the greater are the chances of future arrests for serious delinquency acts.

Wickersham Commission: In 1931, the commission studied and wrote a report stating that 54.8 percent of the prisoner population at that time was under the age of twenty-one when committed. They recommended that all youths should be in separate juvenile and youthful offender facilities, away from the corrupting influence of repeat adult offenders.

Wilderness probation program: These programs provide group meetings for the juveniles twice a month; group sessions for parents twice a month; a wilderness excursion one weekend per month; and a twelve-day "primitive expedition" in the summer.

Wilderness programs: Provide adjudicated and troubled youths with a rigorous physical and emotional challenge unlike anything they have ever known. In small, closely supervised groups, the juvenile offenders learn to follow instructions and to work cooperatively with other youths to accomplish a series of difficult physical challenges, thereby enhancing their own self-esteem. Most programs also strive to strengthen the youths' academic skills by incorporating aspects of learning directly related to outdoor living (e.g., map reading and compass skills). Present-day wilderness programs for juvenile offenders evolved from two separate directions: forestry camps for youthful offenders and the Outward Bound model created in Wales during World War II. *See also* Associated Marine Institutes, Camp Woodson; Eckerd Foundation Wilderness Adventure Programs; VisionQuest.

Wine, Enoch: Credited with being one of the nineteenth century's foremost American authorities on reformatories for children. In 1872 he became the first president of the International Penal Congress. Wines expressed great faith in the rehabilitative power of reformatory institutions.

Wraparound programs: Wraparound programs provide an array of formal and informal services to youth and their families while maintaining youth in their community. These programs are effective for low-risk or first-time offenders, since community safety must always be assured. The Wraparound programs focus on the youth and family's strengths and build on the natural supports that exist within the family. They expect family involvement in the treatment and utilize individualized service plans.

Youth service bureaus: A type of community-based juvenile diversion program that has a full array of after school and evening programs that are structured such as field trips to museums, ping pong tournaments, billiards, volleyball, basketball, chess and chess tournaments, and so on. During the 1970s, major federal funding for Youth Service Bureaus was provided through the Law Enforcement Assistance Administration (LEAA). The modern-day version of a coordinating council is a community-based youth service bureau (YSB). Developed to provide and coordinate programs and services for both delinquent and nondelinquent youths, these youth service bureaus have five basic goals: divert juveniles from the juvenile justice system; fill gaps in service by advocating for and developing services for youths and their families; provide case coordination and program coordinating; provide modification of systems of youth services; and involve youth in the decision-making process.

**Youth shelter:** A short-term residential facility to house status offenders and younger juvenile delinquents who can benefit from being detained and cared for in a social services-oriented setting.

# Name Index

# Subject Index